391.42 K96f   FV
KUNZLE
FASHION AND FETISHISM : A
SOCIAL HISTORY OF THE CORSET,
TIGHT-LACING...   27.50

FASHION
and
FETISHISM

LE DERNIER CHATEAU FORT   1885)

Un distingué savant, l'éminent docteur Maréchal, vient de partir en guerre contre cet ennemi du genre humain qui s'appelle le corset, et qui reste, dans notre société moderne assoiffée d'hygiène, comme un dernier rempart de pierre que ni le temps, ni les efforts des hommes n'ont pu jeter bas. Nous devons saluer comme un héros l'éminent praticien qui engage une lutte inégale avec un adversaire...

... Qui a résisté victorieusement aux ordonnances des Rois...

... Qui s'est moqué des décrets des Empereurs...

... Qui s'est ri des excommunications des papes
et des anathèmes des évêques...

... Qui a haussé les épaules aux exhortations des orateurs
sacrés...

... Qui a méconnu les conseils des médecins...

... et les avis éclairés des savants et des philosophes...

... Qui n'a même pas voulu entendre la voix des peintres
et des poètes...

VIVRE
PRISONNIERS
OU
MOURIR!

... Et, à l'annonce de la nouvelle croisade,
la garnison jure de mourir plutôt que d'être libre!

FASHION
and
FETISHISM

A Social History of the Corset, Tight-Lacing and Other Forms of Body-Sculpture in the West

DAVID KUNZLE

ROWMAN AND LITTLEFIELD
Totowa • New Jersey

First published in the United States of America in 1982 by
Rowman and Littlefield, 81 Adams Drive, Totowa, New Jersey, 07512

Distributed in the U.K. and Commonwealth by
George Prior Associated Publishers Ltd.
High Holbourn House
53/54 High Holbourn
Lower Ground Floor
London WC1 V 6RL, England

Library of Congress Cataloging in Publication Data

Kunzle, David.
    Fashion and fetishism.

    Bibliography: p.
    Includes index.
    1. Corsets—History.   2. Foundation garments—
History.   I. Title.
GT2075.K86   391'.42   80-14872
ISBN 0-8476-6276-4

Printed in the United States of America

Hoffart will Zwang haben
Pride must have constraint
　　　　　　　—Proverb

Contents

List of Illustrations and Captions

Preface

"Fashion" (the culturally dominant mode of dress) and "fetishism" (an individual or group redirection of the sexual instinct onto an aspect of dress) collide and merge in the unique phenomenon of tight-lacing. Unique, because the corset, the instrument of tight-lacing, has accumulated over the centuries far greater moral abuse than any other article of clothing; because it represents the primary equivalent in the civilized West of the "primitive" body-sculptural devices of non-European peoples; and because its sexual motivation has always been uppermost. The evidence (long-suppressed) is overwhelming that the corset gave in the past as it still does, vestigially, in the present not merely physical support, but positive physical and erotic pleasure. This is not an easy notion to defend nowadays, when the associations of this particular article of clothing are probably more negative than any other in the historic wardrobe, and the "corset" stands before the public eye as a sinister looking orthopedic machine, associated with disease, physical degeneration, and sagging or bloating flesh.

Research for this book was started many years ago in an atmosphere of intellectual taboo attached to approaching a sexually oriented problem in a "non-scientific" (i.e. non-sexological, non-psychoanalytical) way. There existed no model of "scientific objectivity" for the analysis of a practice always regarded as irrational, not to say foolish and vicious, the rationale of whose sexual motivation was ignored or evaded by costume historians. As I wrote and rewrote the book in more recent years I became gradually aware of another, more troublesome kind of subjective limitation: I was a man, writing in an age of feminist revival, about an aspect of female behavior regarded still—and afresh—as one of the more obvious and crude symptoms of the historic oppression of women.

Public hostility to tight-lacing derives, as I shall prove, primarily from a very vocal conservative male tradition which has severely limited our understanding of this ambivalent practice. This traditional hostile view, which has been recently refurbished by certain feminist writers,[1] assumes the corset to have had a wholly repressive function; my "heresy" is to show that it also had an expressive and dissident function tending to a kind of female sexual self-assertion, even emancipation. The tight-lacers were sufficiently abused in their own time; historic as well as moral justice requires that the critical imbalance be corrected, and that their practice be honored according to their own criteria.

The historic issue has been clouded by widespread resentment against present-day manipulation by sexist advertising and the fashion media. Corsetry in the past played a very different role from the "body-manipulative devices" (girdles, slimming cures, etc.) of the present. The "bondage" which still holds women in thrall today is that of fashion consumerism; the "bondage" of tight-lacing was an expression not of conformity with fashion, which never condoned it, but against conformity with the "fashionable" (i.e. culturally dominant) role of the socio-sexually passive, maternal woman. Nor can the vestigial survival of tight-lacing fetishism today be viewed merely as an attempt to repolarize stereotypical male-female relations threatened by feminism, if only because there are so many instances of the fetishism being shared by heterosexual partners, and indulged by men on their own (as was also the case historically).

The publication of a chapter of this book (the fifth, here condensed) as an article in an art-historical anthology entitled *Women as Sex Object* provoked a feminist reviewer to an indictment of it (the article) as a "provocative instance of misogyny."[2] A man enters such a realm at his peril. Yet the true misogynists were those (chiefly males) most vociferous in their vilification of tight-lacing and tight-lacers, not those who defended it, and them. The tight-lacers were abused out of fear of women, and of female sexuality. The abuse was part of the Victorian repression of sexuality, and particularly female sexuality, which was regarded as subversive of the social order. Tight-lacers were, like witches and prostitutes of old, social and sexual scapegoats.

And yet the corset is *also* undeniably a symptom and symbol of female oppression. The manner in which this symbol of oppression became an agency of protest is the topic of this book. As Marx said, in effect, in his famous passage about religion being the opiate of the people, self-imposed (masochistic) suffering is both expression of and protest against the suffering caused by external oppression. The process is fraught with contradictions and ambivalence. While I do not pretend to have resolved this ambivalence or explained all the contradictions, I have tried to present the material fully and in such a way that the readers, whatever their sex-political persuasion, whether they are feminists or not, can form their own judgment. I have tried above all to dispel certain mythological clouds from the historical scene, particularly the claim that tight-lacing was universally fashionable and universally harmful. The tenacity of this myth is extraordinary, as is the hyperbolic, almost hysterical embellishment it receives in even the most recent and scholarly of texts. Thus the Hallers in *The Physician and Sexuality in Victorian America* (1974), despite all their research based on primary sources, present tight-lacing in a completely false light, as "inexorably compelling to the majority of middle-class women . . . clothed in respectability (!) and self-righteousness . . . (they) created a chasm between themselves and the working classes. . . Suffering in the close air of their own social ionosphere, they walked around breathless and half-swooning. They fainted by the score in crowded drawing rooms and gallant males rushed to their rescue with trusty pocketknives which they used with almost surgical precision to cut corset strings as the quickest remedy for collapsed lungs."[3] Social historians have tended to treat tight-lacing as one of the quintessential Victorian social horrors, the forcing of young females into narrow corsets being regarded as morally and hygienically on a par with the forcing of small boys into narrow chimneys.

Fashion is not a culturally isolated phenomenon. The aspect of it chosen here, more than any other, impinges upon a daunting array of "separate" disciplines: medical history, anthropology, sexology, psychology, costume history and theory. To students in the above disciplines, the present work, written by a specialist of none of them, will hopefully prove of some use. I believe that my topic represents a curious conjunction of issues in a variety of specializations, perhaps the most obviously relevant of which, the social history of medicine, is also that in which I am most conscious of deficiency. The recent agitation around abortion, which has now become a major socio-political issue of our age, has caused me, after the book was largely written, to assign much greater importance and credibility to it as a conscious or semi-conscious motive for tight-lacing, than I originally conceived; indeed, my instinct at the outset was to regard medical accusations of women using corsets as abortifacients, as a typical male-hysterical exaggeration. I have now changed my mind, and made some small, late adaptations to the text accordingly; but I would have preferred the book as a whole to have incorporated much more of the context of abortion history, such as James Mohr's *Abortion in America,* which appeared too late for inclusion, and the equivalent of which for England I have been unable to find.

As a fashion, as a social phenomenon, tight-lacing is dead, surviving now only in the lives and imaginations of a few individuals. This book is a late obituary notice of a phenomenon which once lived in a very special sense, for it was literally embodied in the living. As the practice of tight-lacing diminished, so did available firsthand living sources, which has meant that I have depended more than I would have wished upon literary evidence. Certain links with the past, certain unique repositories of information disappeared even as I was engaged over the last years in the final version of this book.

The topic is a charged one. Even specialized costume libraries look askance at "fashion-fetishist" material.[4] Very recently a gentleman of great distinction in British public life, and possessed of a unique experience of tight-lacing, died in his late eighties. I was fortunate to be able to interview him once briefly, but neither I nor other interested persons were able to prevent the willful and total destruction, by his family, of the unique documentation (incriminating evidence of a private vice) he had amassed. The circumstance is not exceptional. Certain social taboos have hindered my search, and I have been able to contact all too few elderly persons with personal reminiscences to offer. Those reminiscences, which have as a rule been oral, have constituted a precious form of verification for the kind of material which, in published form, tends to be dismissed as literary fantasy.

My "field-work" amongst that small, dispersed but interlocked group of dedicated fetishists has not been conducted according to scientific principles. Professional sexology, which fears no intrusion upon psychic privacy, may fill the gap eventually. To generalize about certain fetishisms and their incidence in contemporary mores on the basis of information drawn from a statistical sample of about twenty or thirty persons is hazardous. I have had extensive and repeated conversations, I have not conducted interviews. The major issue that personal contact has settled is the question of whether tight-lacing taken in its extreme, Victorian sense, has survived. It has. And although I have been able to meet only a handful of men and women who are tight-laced in a certain permanence, "as a way of life," there are many others of all ages who have, from time to time, more or less systematically, indulged in the practice and still do so. Their experience, verified at first hand, tends to establish a continuity of the fetishist syndrome since Victorian times, even (or especially) in its more bizarre, manic or extreme elements. None of the contemporary fetishists I have met are psychoanalytically oriented (none, as far as I know, have even been analyzed), but in assessing the psychological mechanism of body-sculpture today, I have nonetheless relied on their feelings, experiences and judgments rather than upon such limited medical data as is available. In the past this data was based exclusively upon pathological case histories and was forensic and

psychiatric in intent. Now that non-psychiatric, non-repressive research is being oriented towards the patterns of deviant or variant
sexual behavior, we should gain a clearer view of the sexual psychology of non-pathological fetishism, which I take to be the commoner
form.

Fetishism has long lain under a moral pall. Struggling from under
it, the fetishists developed a literary style which is not, on the face of
it, very attractive or elevating. It is low-key, cautious, defensive, and
compulsive. Fetishism has rarely reached truly poetic or imaginative
heights, possibly because of the very psychological limits which it
imposes on itself.[5]

Anti-fetishist writing (most of it medical) is not attractive either:
petulant, humorless and intolerant, it is remarkable chiefly for its
extravagance and sheer bulk. The most strident reformers were men
of narrow mind. I have tried to respect the individualistic and
obsessive character of both fetishist and anti-fetishist writing by
preserving contexts and citations intact and entire. I have given a
layman's rein to the physicians' obsession with a phenomenon described all too often in a welter of medical terminology which mingles
observed data with hyperbolic guesswork, and science with hysteria
and superstition. The critics claimed that tight-lacing induced
hysteria. It did: not in the tight-lacers, but in the critics.

Our historical picture of the tight-lacing fetish is impaired by
several factors. The primary source material used here has been
medical[6] and confessional writing, which tends to strong partiality
one way or the other. Lack of familiarity with the fields has allowed
me to make only chance and sporadic use of potentially more impartial secondary sources, the memoirs, biographies, autobiographies,
etc., of the extensive period under review.

My concurrent research into the history of the 19th century comic
strip has allowed me to comb systematically the innumerable caricature magazines of seven countries and five languages, which have
yielded a rich harvest. In the world of fashion generally, and in
tight-lacing particularly, caricaturists were confronted with actualiza-
tion, in real life and on real bodies, of formal exaggerations and
distortions which in the realm of graphics were their own special
domain. Fetishist fact and fantasy vied with the cartoonists' own
imaginative flights and propelled them, as it were in competition, to
even more frenzied conceptions, as the illustrations in this book
testify.

Individually, the 19th century fetishists remain anonymous. The
essential biographical data to construct the individual fetishist psychology is largely lacking (with the possible exception of the Empress

Elizabeth of Austria, cf. Appendix). Even in our own day certain public figures known for their openly fetishistic tastes have been protected by their biographers.[8]

The appendix here includes various forms of documentation, notably such "hard statistics" on the incidence of tight-lacing as I have been able to uncover, and some autobiographical accounts which I have been able to elicit, and for whose authenticity I can vouch. For reasons of space I have had to keep the latter brief and relatively few in number. The autobiography of the best-known tight-lacing fetishist of our own era, that of Will and Ethel Granger (cf. p. 336) I have now deposited in some public libraries[9], together with that of "Eric and Mollie", another long, circumstantial and truthful account.

There is surely more fetishist correspondence to be discovered beyond those magazines I have been able to identify, which do however present an almost continuous genealogy from the 1860s down to *London Life* (1923–41) and beyond. The latter is a well-nigh inexhaustible as well as highly exhausting source, an initially impenetrable jungle of exotic undergrowth, with which I have had to limit myself for reasons of space to a description of basic character, rather than content.

In my concern to mitigate the litter of footnote numbers in my perhaps over-documented text, and prevent them from rising into three digits in any one chapter, I have occasionally grouped several references together under one number at the end of a paragraph, with a code-word to designate the particular citation. For the same reason I have occasionally given the page reference to an author not footnoted, in the bibliography.

I would like to acknowledge first and foremost, a tremendous debt to Hillel Schwartz, a researcher into dress-fastenings as well as many other matters of historic moment, who went through my entire typescript with a fine-tooth comb, suggested many improvements affecting phrasing and structure, and offered many new directions and connections only a few of which, alas, I have been able to point up, even minimally.

Special thanks for so many inspirational conversations go to Kurt Ingerl, sculptor, Pope of Constructivism, Vice-President of the Vienna Künstlerhaus, and corset-fetishist.

I am indebted for help of various kinds to: Jean Adhémar, Leslie Agnew, the late Howard Brown M.D. of New York, Mike and Connie Butler, Basil Costin, Cornelia Christensen and Paul Gebhard of the Kinsey Institute, Geoffrey Dunne, the Comte Roland de la Ertée, Ethel and (the late) Will Granger, Harry Philip Edwards, who sent many bibliographical references, Deirdre Le Faye, Arthur Gardner,

Anne Hollander (who provided moral and practical support at critical junctures), Deborah Klimburg-Salter, Barbara Laslett, the late Sir Basil Liddell-Hart, Roland Loomis, Barbara Loebel, Peter Martin, Hyatt Mayor, Diana Medeq, Graham Munton and Maureen Bell, publisher James Mitchell (for initial faith and impetus), Ynez O'Neill, R. W. Robertson-Glasgow, Maggie Starr (who typed indefatigably), A. Vigner, Frau Wagner of Berlin, and Sandra Agalidi, who provided proofing, indexing and other help.

My thanks also go to necessarily unnamed feminists with whom I shared my ideas, for their sympathetic and intelligent response.

Notes

1. E.g. Helene Roberts. Cf my "Response" ibid.

2. The review by Lisa Vogler appeared in *Feminist Studies,* vol. 2, no. 1, 1974.

3. Haller p. 151.

4. Institutional prejudice may be illustrated with an anecdote from costume authority James Laver's autobiography (*Museum Piece,* pp. 242–3). A lady came to Laver, then (around 1930) Keeper of the Department of Prints and Drawings of the Victoria and Albert Museum, to propose the sale of her "psychologist" husband's collection of "fetishist material, admirably arranged and classified. All the pictures were of excessive tight-lacing and excessively high heels." Laver proposed a paltry ten pounds, advising her to find a private collector with more to offer. Which she did. Comments Laver: "A curious moral problem arises. I had helped (sic) a poor widow, deprived the Museum of an interesting collection of material, and promoted somebody's private vice" (sic). The incident prompted a Great Thought, which has borne fruit in the chapter "Frou Frou and Fetishism" in his latest book *(Modesty in Dress):* "I was visited that night by a Great Thought . . . Fashion is the comparative of which Fetishism is the superlative." Thus, a Superlative Vice provoked a Great Thought.

5. An exception is the demonic possession conjured up by Oskar Panizza's short story "Der Korsetten-Fritz." The (perhaps deliberate) banality or matter-of-factness of Pauline Réage's best-selling *Story of O* does not, in my view, rise very much above the average level of fetishist correspondence.

6. Bibliographically I have drawn heavily upon the *Index to the Library of the U.S. Surgeon General's Office,* which is however demonstrably incomplete. That the corset should be deemed worthy of a separate classification in a catalogue published under the auspices of the U.S. Army may be explained by the fact that William Alexander Hammond (1828–1900) was Surgeon General from 1862 to 1864 when the Library was first formed. This controversial but distinguished specialist in nervous and mental diseases sponsored George Scott's Electric Corset (advertisement of 1883 reproduced in Rudofsky, 1971, p. 119).

7. Nora Waugh's *Corsets and Crinolines* proved an invaluable initial resource in this area.

8. E.g. Marjorie Worthington in her recent biography of the popular anthropologist William Seabrook. Gerald Hamilton in his autobiography *Mr. Norris and I,* discusses his resemblance to the fetishist hero created by Christopher Isherwood in *Mr. Norris Changes Trains,* without even mentioning the fetishism.

9. British Library, New York Public Library, Victoria and Albert Museum Library, and Library of Congress.

Introduction

Special Historic and Psychological Role of Tight-Lacing

F*ashion* is the culturally dominant mode of dress expressing, as a rule, the dominance of a social class. But fashion can also express, in ways that we do not yet fully comprehend, the finer nuances of shifting relationships between the sexes, as well as between segments of dominant, rival, or upwardly mobile classes.

Fetishism may be defined as the individual displacement of private erotic feeling onto a non-genital part of the body, or onto a particular article of clothing by association with a part of the body, or onto an article of clothing in conjunction with its effect on the body. As such it serves to express a special socio-sexual attitude or relationship within the normal functioning of fashion as outlined above; put simply, it may be an attention-getting device used by a socially repressed or aspirant individual or minority. When the fetishism is publicly manifested, it may cause a social reaction. If it is manifested by people in sufficient numbers, or of sufficient social standing, it can acquire a certain limited or temporary status as custom or fashion. In the 18th–19th century such "fetishistic fashion" tended to come under sharp social censure, and there is a very real sense in which fashion and fetishism must always be regarded as potentially antagonistic, even or especially when the fetishism is an exaggeration of what is fashionably acceptable (the tight-laced as opposed to the moderately slim look).

Never, not even during the 1870s, arguably the most fetishistic decade in the history of Western costume, can one speak of fashion and fetishism as one. When fashion (group cultural expression) and fetishism (individual sexual expression) are perfectly harmonized, we may speak of a "cultural" or "national" fetish. Such a term is, I believe, properly applicable only to non-Western, non-individualistic cultures such as China where foot-binding was a universally accepted and, for much of its history, relatively uncontested component of social and sexual life.

The capitalist West has been under constant and often acute ten-

1

sion between assertions of individualism and the demands of con-
formism. The "kaleidoscope of fashion" represents one of the most
spectacular arenas of this struggle. The fashion established by the
élite has, in the modern age, permitted a high degree of variation
according to individual taste, as well as the particular needs of
essentially labile economic, professional and other social groups.
Fashion at court or among ruling aristocratic circles may, for obvious
reasons, be characterized by extreme luxury of economic display; but
it also permitted a luxury of sexual display (in décolletage, for
instance) prohibited to a lower social group which saw both economic
advantage and cultural identity in the exercise of sexual self-restraint
(puritanism). The immoral luxury (economic *and* sexual) of the aristocracy has been a topos of middle-class morality ever since the
emergence of the commercial middle classes as a social force (for our
purposes, with the "birth" of tight-lacing, in the mid-14th century).
Those individual members of a lower but ascendant social order who
engaged in erotic display were condemned, both from within their
own class and from above it, for exploiting their sexuality in order to
win attentions beyond those warranted by their social status. As we
shall see, legal restrictions were sometimes imposed to prevent this
("sumptuary laws"). All this is true of the dress of both sexes, but
more so of women's than men's. Women used their sexuality, and
sexualized forms of dress, as women always have, to rise out of a
socio-sexually subject position. And they got morally scapegoated for
their pains.

Our assumption here is that female sexuality is a very special,
socially manipulable and psychologically separable force. As such, it
has been severely repressed by male authority. The history of tight-
lacing is part of the history of the struggle for sexual self-expression,
male and female. This may not be immediately apparent because the
corset hitherto has not been regarded in a light essentially different
from other accessories of clothing, and its extreme use, in tight-
lacing, has not been recognized as essentially different from the
"small waist of fashion," and as involving forces and motivations
essentially different from those which underlie other extreme or
eccentric sartorial formations. Whatever the erotic intention concealed in other articles or styles of dress, that inherent in tight-lacing
remains unique and overt, and thus subject to a unique and overt
level of moral repression.

The crusade against tight-lacing and other erotic forms of dress is
part of the crusade against sexuality, which is as old as Christianity.
The socio-sexual symbolism of tight-lacing and its ritual components
reveal its essentially ambivalent purpose—to enforce the sexual taboo

by objectively oppressing the body, and simultaneously to break that taboo by subjectively enhancing the body.

Apart from its overt sexualization, its sheer longevity sets tight-lacing apart from other fashions and tends to elevate it from a mere (changeable) style in dress to the status of a continuing social practice. Its capacity for survival which so astonished the 19th century observers represents an element of continuity in the perpetual flux of taste. Tight-lacing is not worn, cast on or off like, say, an outrageous hat, but practiced as a continuous ritual. It tends to permanence, when fashion generally thrives on change.

The taste for novelty for its own sake, the commercial pressures towards constant change in style, and the small, year-to-year political and economic "accidents" to which clothing styles tend to make symbolic reference, are all factors which may determine the flow of fashion in general, but appear to have had relatively little influence upon the evolution of tight-lacing. Here the causes are more radical, striking deep into the roots of our sexual culture, which changes but slowly.

Anthropologists use the term "body-sculpture" to cover various forms of mutilation, compression, distortion, piercing, scarification and relief tattooing of the flesh, customs which have been termed "the most enduring as well as the most intimate of the cosmetic arts . . . the permanent reminders of a new and irreversible identity."[1] Body-sculpture in the West, limited as it is in scope, shares some of this purpose, and partakes, all along the range from strictly private to fully public, of some of the symbolic and ritual function normally associated with primitive custom.

The arts of costume work by optical illusion. A small (clothed) waist can also be a matter of illusion. Historians, like fashion advertisers, accept that the waist can be small without being compressed, and that it can *appear* tight without actually being so. They tend to describe it as becoming objectively smaller and tighter, larger and looser, without stating whether this is a physical reality, a visual illusion, or a combination of both. The obsession of our era with statistical data has infected historians who invoke some mythical standard of maximum waist size (17, 18, 19 etc. inches) which qualifies as the "fashionable" degree of constriction.

The manner in which a skirt, a sleeve, a hat grows or shrinks over the years can be objectively measured by means of surviving costumes and (to a degree) pictures. But what is meant by a "small" waist? Small in comparison to the skirt or sleeve, smaller than the "natural" waist, or simply smaller than that of the preceding fashion? We are concerned here not with the degree to which fashion may be perceived, as the popularisers put it, to "decree a small waist," but with deliberate acts of constriction, the making of "conspicuous waist" (to pun on Veblen) as a social provocation, and for private gratification. The only workable definition of tight-lacing as opposed to "normal" lacing, is as the *conscious and visible* process of artificial constriction of the waist, whereby the very artifice becomes an attraction (or repellent).

In the 19th century comparisons were always being drawn between European tight-lacing and Chinese foot-binding.[2] Horrible as the latter seemed, the comparison was usually to its advantage, such was the hyperbolic revulsion provoked by the habit of a small European minority. The differences between the truly cultural fashion of the Chinese and the controversial minority fashion-fetish of the West are revealing. Today, foot-binding is morally doubly repugnant to us, because it was inflicted universally on small children of all but the poorest classes, and only female children. Tight-lacing was never universal, although corsetting in one form or another was usual. Corsets were, as a general rule, imposed on children only in a relatively mild form and for a limited historical period (17th to 18th centuries), when even small children were dressed like adults. They functioned to protect the body, rather than restrict it, to keep it growing straight rather than confine it in the middle. In the 19th century, when specific costumes were devised for children, corsets were not applied at all until puberty.

The chronological coincidence in the life-span of tight-lacing and foot-binding is close; at the beginning less so, but at the end quite remarkably and not fortuitously so. The Chinese custom arose probably in the 12th century A.D., the European one in the 14th. The fact that both customs expired simultaneously during the early years of this century is not a matter of chance, for there was a direct interaction in the campaigns against the two kinds of deformation.

Chinese foot-binding gives us an important analogical context which the body-sculpture of primitive peoples cannot provide, not only for Western waist-constriction, but also for the immediate anatomical counterpart of the Chinese custom and the second major fetish of Western fashion, constrictive footwear. This has been an essential concomitant of tight-lacing over the more important half of the latter's history. We who still take a degree of impracticality in footwear for granted may regard as far-fetched the Victorians' comparison between the (to us) mild constriction of Western fashion and the severe deformation of the Chinese. But the constriction of fashionable footwear in the 18th–19th centuries was viewed by contemporaries as very severe indeed; the "average" high heel of fashion was considered by some as positively crippling to the internal organs as well as the feet. Yet this historic heel was lower, broader and altogether more stable than that of the mid-20th century. The "stiletto" fashion shoe of our own age would have staggered the Victorian imagination as much as Victorian tight-lacing does ours, and it is evident that vis-à-vis Victorian footwear, postwar styles have grown more, not less "Chinese"—this at the very time, ironically, when foot-binding disappeared completely from China, and the People's Republic gained a reputation for a looseness, not to say bagginess designed to convey practicality and classless uniformity— anti-fashion.

Tight-lacing and high heels appear, for a good two centuries, as a kind of inseparable Siamese twins, sustained by the same historical, psychological and perhaps complementary physiological cir- cumstances, and following each other into the same decline. But the high heel, the dramatically sculptured foot revived concretely in the mid-20th century, whereas tight-lacing returned only vestigially at that time. The meteoric career of the stiletto heel (returning, perhaps, in 1979?) is a phenomenon in itself, which is here no more than sketched.

This brings us to our second major "fashionable fetish". The shoe and boot clearly sculpt in a sense very different from, and less permanent than the corset. The traditional compression of the toes, rendering them pointed in their alignment where nature made from broad and square, is very real, and certainly significant; but even more significant (and more akin to the Chinese custom) is the way the high heel has radically modified the range of action in the foot, and thereby the stance and walk of the wearer. This heel has altered not so much a form as a relationship of forms in movement, transforming body posture and body-action; it is kinetic sculpture (as indeed is tight-lacing, with its variety of kinetic side-effects).

After the essentially female corset and high heel, the third most prominent target under intermittent attack was primarily a male fashion. Constrictive neckwear, like shoe and corset, compresses a vulnerable and sensitive part of the body; like the high heel, it rigidly restricts movement over adjacent areas. A fourth potentially constric- tive article of dress, the glove, was the object of relatively slight and rare criticism, presumably because although it can readily incapacitate for basic manual tasks, it cannot subject the hand to the basic visual transformations of which footwear and corset are capable; the reign of the tight glove was relatively short, and its explicit enemies few and faint.

The long, exquisitely manicured fingernail is another fetish which, although technically body-sculptural (in a sense similar to that in which coiffure "sculpts" head-hair), we cannot deal with here. In its extremest form, it became an important male cultural fetish in China, and its significance has definitely increased in the West, as the fashion for gloves (with which it is largely incompatible) has declined. Fingernails of "excessive" length (i.e. beyond the one quarter inch overhang recommended by today's fashion magazines) fascinate fetishists for the total transformation they can achieve over the simplest, most commonplace manual operations, imposing upon them a great range of restrictions and controls, turning the automatic and unthinking gesture into the contrived and self-conscious, or impossible. Excessive fingernails are seen not as a mere ornament of the hand like bulging rings, but as a means of inflecting its very expression, and (by those who also share the tight-lacing fetish) as in some way analogous to the restrictions and controls which the corset imposes over the body as a whole, so that the manner in which long fingernails can enhance the language of manual gesture, is sensed as comparable to that in which tight-lacing enhances body-gesture. The fingernail and hand fetishes, with their particular socio-sexual symbolism, are surely worthy of separate study.[3]

We now turn to a fetishism in many ways inseparable and yet also distinct from that for small waists. Breast fetishism has become a major cultural phenomenon of the postwar era, and has aroused much comment. The post-war admiration for largeness of bust has, arguably, replaced that for smallness of waist and extremities per se; and the big bust was until very recently regarded (as it still is in some sectors) as a virtue in itself, irrespective of other proportions. Artificial means of bust enlargement are now of two kinds: the real and chemical (silicone injections, etc.) and the apparent and engineered (uplift brassière), a function assumed by the corset in the past. Surgical breast-reduction is also on the increase.

Tight-lacing has traditionally pre-supposed a degree of breast sculpture. Mammary tissue, even more than that of the waist, is a malleable substance, which responds to pressures both subtle and extreme. Normally, the breast has been both raised and reshaped (the upper half being made to rise and swell by pushing from below). Breast flattening, obviously the "pure" form of reductive breast sculpture, is always associated in the popular imagination with the waistless, corsetless twenties, but it is also characteristic, to a degree, of the 16th–17th century, when the whole thorax was sometimes rigidly encased.

Breast reshaping and exposure attracted a censure which, in the violence of its tone and the sexual disgust which it discloses, can only be compared with that engendered by tight-lacing in the 19th century. Any form of décolletage was already offensive; to use artificial means to thrust the breasts even more prominently into view, was doubly damnable.

We may at this point mention some of the commoner contemporary fetishes which are discernibly linked with developments in fashion but which will not otherwise concern us. Lingerie fetishism has been with us since the late 19th century and is, like the voyeurism upon which it thrives, relatively uncontroversial, customarily acceptable and commercially profitable. When corset fetishism survives as an aspect of lingerie fetishism, it does so independently of and ancillary to its sculptural function. Lingerie is essentially body-extensive and body-additive, when it is not merely a means of simultaneously concealing and revealing. It is decorative and passive, or externally active, rather than sculptural and internally active; psychologically it is also different in that it lends itself to object-fetishism, that is, to detachment from the human body.

Since around 1960 there has thrived a fetish for total envelopment of the naked body in a "second skin" of rubber and leather, analogous to that of the diver's wetsuit, but generally of a much finer gauge material. These pass commercially as slimming garments, and being occlusive, cause sudden loss of body-moisture which many people find erotic. Insofar as they are designed to exert a light, even pressure over the whole body, they may be defined as sculptural. In terms of contour the change caused by a rubber suit is minimal, that of a smoothing out or unifying, although the visual transformation can be complete, like that of a dancer's all-black leotard. Rubber or leather suit fetishism is often combined with truly constrictive fetishes (bondage, corsetry), when of course the body-contour *is* radically altered. The paramount psychological factor in rubber-suit fetishism is, however, that of a physical sensation of change in shape via a rise in body-temperature, local cutaneous sensations, and small, local muscular restraints; these may combine to create the sense of having acquired a second skin which is so overwhelming as to provide the experience of a total change of identity. In one important respect rubber-suit fetishism is diametrically opposed to truly sculptural fetishism: in its "pure" form it provides a total and relatively benign enclosure, which is very far from the object of the latter.[4]

Rubber and leather, like velvet and fur, are basically fetishes of material or texture, which induce or enhance certain tactile or cutaneous sensations. Rubber and leather fetishisms are often combined with body sculpture fetishism. A leather corset, with its soft, shiny surface of black skin stretched taut over the hard boning, is held by many fetishists to be the superior kind. Having been made in recent years supple and workable like a textile, and retaining its strength at the same time, leather is able to supplant older corsetry materials like coutil. Bondage devices in leather unite pleasures on two levels, the associative atavistic one of the animal skin, and the immediate sculptural one.

Leather is considered a "masculine" fetish, and is certainly characteristic, perhaps the commonest form, of homosexual fetishism. Silk and satin are considered "feminine" fetishes, and it is noteworthy that for a long time the only clinical studies of female fetishism concerned satin and silk kleptomaniacs.

Sculptural tattooing or scarification, that is the creation of relief patterns over the skin, is not as far as I know practiced in the West. Surface tattooing has been common since the 19th century, and has in recent years spread from its traditional locus, the military and seafaring men, to civilians and women. The principal connection between the tattooing and sculptural fetishes lies in the fact that both involve a degree of discomfort or pain in the initiation, and both involve, to very different degrees, the concept of irreversibility and permanence.

Temporary relief-tattoo or scarification effects, as a by-product of tight-lacing, are prized by some who admire the visual impression and tactile invitation of the striation and criss-cross pressure-marks left by the boning and laces of a corset after its removal. Such pressure-marks apparently increase epidermal sensitivity for erotic purposes, as do tattooing and scarification.[5]

Piercing is the only real mutilation common in the West. Technically although very mildly sculptural, it has been customarily confined in a non-sculptural and virtually invisible way to the ear-lobe. Fetishists, however, including many who also tight-lace, pierce elsewhere (ear-rim, nostrils, nipples, navel, male and female genitals etc.) and sometimes enlarge the holes, like primitive peoples. While piercing has lost much of its ancient magical and status-conferring purpose in the West, its psychological significance may be on the increase today, as ear-lobe piercing among girls becomes a commonplace minor puberty or sexual initiation ritual (it is primarily Latin societies that pierce a girl's ears in infancy), and acceptable among heterosexual as well as homosexual men, especially in the U.S. (usually one ear only is pierced); while the pierced, and bestudded or beringed nostril, once seen in the West only on East Indian ladies, is adopted increasingly by young Western women, and even on occasion, by men (again chiefly in the U.S.). Fetishists pioneered multiple piercing along the ear rim, and fashion, seeing its commercial opportunity, now encourages more than one hole in each ear-lobe. As a matter of fashion the ear has been pierced not because it was considered beautiful but because it was the safest way of permanently affixing jewelry. The connection with tight-lacing may appear remote to the laity, but is very real to fetishist initiates, some of whom practice both fetishes with equal intensity. Piercing has, however, never been the subject of public controversy, and is mentioned in the present work only in passing.

The resistance to the concept of mutilation in the West is so great that it is never for a moment considered even as an adjunct to traditional forms of body-sculpture. The relevant mutilations would be, admittedly, very severe indeed: the surgical removal of a lower rib to facilitate extreme tight-lacing, and the amputation of toes to enable smaller, tighter shoes to be worn. While rumors and allegations used to circulate in public papers that certain women in the late Victorian and Edwardian ages had willingly subjected themselves to such operations, and while the belief that they did so has survived today, I have never found confirmation of them; and it is surely significant that the fetishists seldom, if ever, fantasize about them.[6]

A peculiar form of "zöo-fetishism", that relating to the horse, belongs here for its evident relationship to human fetishism. The horse and its trappings in the 19th century were eminently a matter of fashion. Styles changed and were highly connotive of social status and artistic taste. The automobile has, of course, today superseded the horse (and carriage) as the basic fashionable sex-power symbol: in its styling—its shape as a whole,[7] embellishments, and interior design—the way it is advertised, and the way it is driven. The horse, like the car, served as a vehicle of transportation and (sexual) "transport", but being a living thing, was a more natural and responsive embodiment of fantasy and symbology. We shall be dealing with some symbolic correspondences between human body-sculpture and equine disciplines. The connection survives most starkly today, when few people ride, in the sado-masochistic games where the human mount substitutes for the horse.

Fetishism and Metaphor:
Fetishistic Discipline and Christian Asceticism

Sculptural fetishism is essentially concerned with an idea rather than an object. Tight-lacing fetishism is not the same as corset fetishism. It is tight-lacing, rather than the corset as such, that enjoys a rich range of metaphorical and symbolic associations. Beyond the object lies the activity, with all its associated ideas and emotions, which transcend the merely sexual.

The historical origins of fetishist psychology are not to be limited to the sexual domain in any narrow sense. The idea of an object being endowed with powers properly attributable only to a person (or to nature) is rooted in the most ancient magical thinking. In medieval Europe a literary tradition developed, in conjunction with the cult of religious relics, which elevated this kind of magical process by investing an object associated with the beloved with her amorous power. An article of clothing is treated as sacred because it has touched a body which is ultimately untouchable; it incorporates and reconciles the paradox of desire to possess that which is essentially unattainable. In possessing the glove or handkerchief, the lover in a symbolic sense possesses the beloved whom he cannot possess in reality. This mode of thinking survives in literature through the baroque age down to our own day.

The "fetish-object" in the tradition of courtly love is a surrogate and decreases in value as the loved one is present or appears more attainable. Similarly, the true tight-lacing fetishist does not wish to possess (or masturbate with) the corset in itself, but to apply it possessively upon the beloved, so that it, his desire and her body become one. The male fetishist corsetting the female symbolically enacts possession of her, even as she, physically possessed only (or initially) by the corset, is preserved from real violation. The fetish-object serves both as a symbol of union and as symbolic obstacle. It separates the lovers, and yet incorporates emotions of conquest and surrender, resistance and yielding. To the female, it is the armor of virtue (like the chastity-belt, but avoiding or denying its technical function), to the male it is a symbol of his dominance and desire.

Another aspect of the metaphoric fusion of object and person can be derived from Christianity. It is from within the Christian tradition which had absorbed and revived primitive belief in sympathetic magic in the form of the doctrine of transsubstantiation, that fetishism as a form of sexual transsubstantiation emerges.

The word "fetish" derives from the Portuguese *feitiço* meaning fated, charmed, bewitched, and entered the English language with reference to primitive belief in magic. Our own sexual form of fetishism retains primitive associations of erotic, magical and religious power, through which a semblance of supernatural control is achieved, and states of transcendence and ecstasy may be entered. The fetishist act becomes a means of acceding to grace and power, and of uniting the participants in a religious-erotic ritual, which (unlike Christian sacramental ritual) is based upon a real and visible physical transformation—real and visible, but also comparable to the internal physical transformation experienced by Christian and other mystics. The sexual motive of this transformation is effectively purified through elevation to the moral realm.

Spirituality and asceticism have often been represented by thin and emaciated bodies; north European late Gothic art (14th-16th century) especially has used extreme narrowness of waist to convey the purity of spirit and suffering in figures of Christ and the saints, while on contemporaneous clothed figures of courtiers, the wasp waist expressed aristocratic elegance. In anatomically detailed German statuary of the Reformation era the extreme contraction of the lower ribs and the sucking in of the belly appear as the primary physiological indicators, after the expression of the face, of sacrificial agony.

Modern fetishist-masochist practices may be regarded as a late flowering of monastic penitential disciplines. Once suffered in Christian humility and penance where the sexuality was only latent, corporal disciplines were turned by women into an expression of sexual pride, and were condemned as such by the clerical and medical descendants of the ascetics who had invented them. Most clerics and physicians saw only the sexual exhibitionism, not the penitential or self-disciplinary component of masochistic fashion. Alone, in the 16th century, Montaigne honored both.

In the late 17th century, when (as Molière's *Tartuffe* reminds us) physically painful forms of penitence were losing their spiritual sanction, the Viennese Augustinian monk and Imperial preacher Abraham à Sancta Clara tried to reconcile the paradox of physical asceticism and sexual display, by reminding his flock that not only the seeking of pleasure, but also the self-infliction of pain could minister to pride and the devil. In a sermon all the more impressive for its breathless, dialectal, spontaneous style (very close, one imagines, to its original pulpit delivery), the preacher tells how he chanced upon a corset lying on a table, and asked a chambermaid what it was. "A corset (Mieder)? Almighty God! But it is so tight that a marten (Mader=Marder) could not slip into it; it is rightly called Mieder, for it is no small torture (Marter). Oh, if only the body could speak, how it would moan, that it must live all the time in such agony, and suffer more than a Carthusian monk, who always wears a rough hair-shirt." Sancta Clara goes on, ingenuously, to ask the chambermaid why the corset is cut so low at the top, and wonder "that the tender skin does not complain at suffering such cold in winter." He then passes, with a powerful oath, to fashionable footwear, which causes the toes to be squeezed together "like herrings in a box" and "like the damned in hell." "Ach, such suffering, such suffering? And suffering only for the sake of the devil . . . so little suffering for God . . . but for hell the proud suffer gladly."

The 19th century set the paradox of masochism aside altogether, until the very end, when psychology and physiology began very hesitantly to throw light upon it. A cartoonist as early as 1878 shows the witty doctor feeling obliged morally to condone the excessively tight cuirasse style, "for in so narrow a space no mortal body can exist, only the soul has room." But the dress-reformer takes refuge in the "typically female spirit of contradiction" as she invents a pseudo-historical origin for an object which can have no historical, that is rational origin: women in the "Dark Ages" obstinately "refusing to yield under pressure of a barbarous punishment (that of the thoracic vice, allegedly inflicted by the husband for adultery) and in a spirit of contradiction turning their prison into an attractive article of fashion."[9] In 1910, the pioneer sexologist Havelock Ellis struck half the truth when he said that "the corset arose to gratify an ideal of asceticism rather than sexual allurement."[10] Ellis should have written "as well as" for "rather than"; the concomitance of the asceticism or pain and the sexual allurement is accurately sensed by the popular versifier, who projects the amorous pain back onto himself, the lover: "How dex't'rously she'll waste the lace / And lace the pretty waist . . . Till the whole effect is stunning and immaculately chaste . . . The sterner sex they torture, caring nothing how it hurts."[11] In an Austrian poem of 1890, the pain of a girl's love is equated with the pain of the corset, with the heart bursting like and with the tight-laced body; and when the lover becomes bride, at last, she summons the "ironclad corset, as befits the chaste woman . . . pull and heave on the laces, that the bridally enhanced body be truly *ethereal*" (my stress).[12]

Religious reformers warned that corporal disciplines by their very severity could minister to personal pride and dangerous forms of ecstasy. It is surely no accident that fetishistic disciplines were domesticated and moralized primarily in a Protestant country. For Protestantism discouraged the showier forms of religious self-denial, and refused women the right to set themselves apart in nunneries in order to practice them. Penitential pain and discipline were transferred to everyday life and ordinary things: education, household, work, and even dress. The overt antagonism between the religious-ascetic and the erotic is a psychological contradiction which mystics and fetishists in their very different ways attempt to reconcile.

The German reformer Troll-Borostnani in 1897 spoke, as much in amazement as anger, of the "fanaticism" and "intoxication" of woman's "lust for self-torment", expressed in clothing whose constriction induced states of consciousness she likened to those of flagellants and Asiatic dervishes. There is a sense here that tight-lacing sought to circumvent specifically modern and European strictures against "irrational" and "immoral" forms of mysticism.

Social and Sexual Symbolism

SEXOLOGY AND REPRESSION OF FETISHISM

Psychoanalysis originated at a time when sexual repression had reached an intolerable level, and new avenues of sexual expression were forged, one of which took the form of fetishism. Scientific recognition of the sexual origins of certain forms of aberrant behavior did not, however, induce sympathy, nor did research into sexual deviance increase tolerance; indeed, the very opposite happened.

Medical science has rendered most forms of fetishism pathological, or potentially so. Medical science, as well as the law, has focused on the pathological and criminological manifestations of fetishism, and has also impaired social tolerance of private and harmless fetishist behavior. Study of fetishism, like that of other forms of social deviance, was motivated by the desire to repress or erase it, which has put fetishists on the defensive.

Systematic collection of data relating to pathological fetishism started in the "fashionably fetishistic" 1870s-80s, and was united in Krafft-Ebing's *Psychopathia Sexualis*, of 1886.[13] Case material was overwhelmingly criminological, with heavy emphasis on sado-masochistic foot and shoe fetishism and the kleptomaniac collector syndrome. Apart from footwear, criminal fetishists were involved with gloves, handkerchiefs and hair-despoliation.[14] In Germany, the censor banned innocent, strictly non-pornographic books catering to fetishism, such as the short story collections of Delorme and Dolorosa, which contain sentimental, poetic and moral (not to say didactic and therapeutic) tales showing how erotic feeling is, and should be, transferred from the fetish-object to the person.

Judges have enacted the repressive and ignorant theory that it is "fear of punishment that keeps many criminal fetishists from capitulating to their impulses,"[15] and that jail is the proper place for men who like to sit in shoe shops watching women try on shoes. This attitude has even infected the otherwise intelligent costume-theorist: "a perverted interest in women's underwear recently (1957) resulted in the murders of several women by a mentally defective sex criminal."[16] Aversion therapy represents the ultimate cruelty in contemporary treatment of fetishists.[17] If in the 1970s a California boy can be jailed for twelve years as a dangerous sex-criminal for privately masturbating[18] one cannot doubt that harmless fetishists are even today rotting away with their fantasies in jail.

In these circumstances, it is understandable that fetishists have been reluctant to submit to therapy. At a time when tight-lacing was still a common recent practice, it was stated that corset fetishism was "rare,"[19] and very few cases appear in the psychoanalytic literature of the period[20] down to and including the compilation by Wilhelm Stekel (1924), who obviously was only interested in the most pathological forms of fetishism. Given the manner in which Stekel plunges the whole phenomenon of sexual symbolism in relation to clothing into a miasma of psychosis, it is not surprising that costume theorists, who are concerned with the "cultural norm," were wary of applying psychoanalytic method, phallic symbolism, etc., to their material.[21] The reduction by psychoanalysis of human personality to intrapsychic traits, and its elimination of the social factor, has rendered it useless, if not actually harmful, when dealing with fetishism.

SEXUALIZATION OF FORM AND ACTION: SHOE, CORSET, COLLAR; HORSE

"I have gloved my language as you gloved my hands because they were vulgar . . . my feet are encased in boots made by the shoemakers of the Parisian Cinderellas; my torso has been inured to the torture of the corset, and my waist has become so slender, that if I lost my belt, I could just about replace it with my bracelet!" Thus was the simple 19th century country girl transformed into a Parisian mistress.[22]

In the taste for small extremities and a small middle, sexual and hierarchical or social principles are mutually supportive. Feet, hands, neck and torso, when used for laboring tasks, grow thick and muscular. The physically idle upper classes can afford to keep them small and confined, preserving them as symbols of sexual refinement and social leisure. It was Thorstein Veblen, in his famous *Theory of the Leisure Class* (1899) who first enunciated the theory that women tight-laced in order to show distance from labor, and dedication to conspicuous leisure. This idea was taken up by Flügel as the "hierarchical principle." We shall see, however, how it must be adapted to include lower or lower-middle class women, probably the tight-lacing majority, who sought to acquire the physical insignia of leisured status which they lacked in reality. The hierarchical principle governs not only predilection for smallness of foot, but also the desire literally and symbolically to lift it out of the mud, via high heels raising the woman visually above the common herd and at the same time suggesting that walking is a special and difficult, rather than commonplace activity for her.

Let us start by considering the foot and shoe, which have been imbued by the most ancient folklore with a broad symbolic range and powerful magical properties. A rich proverb lore relates the shoe with female sexuality,[23] the fitting of foot into shoe with sexual union and (in the Cinderella myths, for instance—treated below) the small female foot with aristocracy, purity and virtue.

Uniquely sensitive to touch, despite the fact that they have constantly to bear the full weight of the body, often played with and cosseted in infancy, and phallic in shape the feet have become, quite understandably, a very particular erotic center, and sexual symbol. The foot is moreover a special mark of human superiority to the animal. As Rossi puts it: "What we refer to as "the figure" or the voluptuous architecture of the body, owes much of its sensuous character to the foot, which was responsible for the upright posture and gait that altered the entire anatomy. The unusual structure of the human foot which made the upright posture possible, also made possible frontal human copulation, a coital position unique in all nature."[24]

East and West, the foot has traditionally played an essential role in erotic preliminaries, and is sometimes used in the sexual act itself. The use of the foot as a phallic stimulant, and in some sense as a phallic substitute as well, was customary in China, and is by no means uncommon in the West. The Chinese believed, in addition, that compression of her foot by the male hand was erotically stimulating to the female; binding increased its responsiveness and sensitivity. (This may also have been experienced as true of the bound Western torso). Permanent compression of the foot was also believed by the Chinese to induce a kind of walk which enlarged the hips, which in turn increased the capacity and constrictive power of the vagina. A similar idea presented itself on a less conscious level also to the Western imagination, for which the restriction of high heels and tight shoes (as also waist compression) was a means of enlarging the thighs, and enhancing the hips and hip action, as we shall see. The expressed Chinese ideal of a foot small enough to fit inside a man's mouth probably reflects an oral-genital fantasy (or: replicates an oral-genital act), which in the West takes the milder form of a foot small enough to fit into the hand, and fit to be raised to the lips for a kiss; or else, in the ceremonially sanctioned form of the shoe serving as champagne glass. In the Western tradition a woman's foot, believed to be proportionately smaller than man's, is viewed as ideally to be encompassed in the grasp of a male hand, and thus lends itself to possession symbolism.[25] (Similarly, the phrase "handspan waist" connotes manual possessibility, cf. Plate 66).

Apart from the compression of the whole foot in a boot too small for it, there are two other major ways in which the foot has been sculpted: the forcible raising of the instep arch, and the formation of a slender pointed shape at the toes. All three methods are of course interdependent.

The raising and arching of the instep is achieved in the West principally by means of a high heel and is sometimes reinforced by means of arched inner soles; a boot shorter than the foot can also serve this purpose. An extreme instep arch was procured in China by permanently binding the toes towards the heel; this radically shortened and reduced the foot in size. The raised wedge beneath the heel (equivalent of the Western high heel) also contributed illusionistically. The high heel and/or arched insole shortens the foot, in reality[26] and optically; and, by a visual incorporation of the permanently stretched ankle, lends it a kind of phallic extension, which is also present in the artificial heel. The narrow, finely arched foot was supposedly aristocratic and high on the evolutionary scale, whereas the lower classes and races, as well as many quadrupeds, supposedly had flatter and broader feet. Paradoxically, today we see such a foot, although historically imbued with hierarchical symbolism, as functional, in that the high arch is generally regarded as functionally advantageous for quick movement.

Freud did not identify the high shoe heel specifically as a phallic symbol,[27] but it is generally accepted as such by the laity today. The peculiar visual emphasis on the high shoe heel in post-war advertising, coupled with the tendency in fashion at certain periods (notably the 1870s and even more in the 1950s) to equate sheer height with chic (in fetishism, height equals difficulty equals chic) is strongly suggestive of phallic-erectile symbolism. Slenderness of heel, which has often accompanied height as an absolute aesthetic criterion, has weapon-related sado-masochistic associations heightened by sharpness of toe ("stiletto" heel).

Now to our third factor in foot-sculpture. Unlike Chinese footwear, the precise shape and length of the shoe-toe in Western fashion has undergone innumerable variations, as have those of the high heel. The pointed-toe effect, recurrently fashionable for women and sometimes shared by men as well, has been obtained in two ways. It is formed illusionistically by lengthening the shoe beyond the natural toes, and it has compressed the toes, eliminating the space between them.

The propensity of Western man and woman to force their feet into a pointed shape has recently been rhetorically dramatized by the architectural and costume theorist Bernard Rudofsky, who has no explanation for it but castigates it, Rousseau-like, as a sign of civilized depravity. Yet, the hierarchical symbolism is fairly clear. As observed above, the big, splayed-toe foot has been generally regarded as "low;" anthropology has associated it with the Negro race; the hierarchical principle with the working-class. Fashionable footwear has sought for centuries to produce "bilateral symmetry", i.e., a foot longer and pointed in the middle, a shape lambasted by 19th century reformers who cited the projecting big toe (not possessed by apes) "as a mark of elevation in the scale of organized beings."[28] It was confusing, not to say embarrassing, that artists, following the ancient Greek canon, should show a preference for ideal figures with a second toe longer than the first, thus tending to justify the "perverted aesthetic" of fashion.[29]

In the post-war era, the donning of the first "fashion shoe" has become a rite of passage. Insofar as infants' and schoolgirls' footwear is made with ample breadth, the narrowing of the toe, like the raising of the heel, become symbols of sexual maturation. The distinction moreover between adults' "sensible" or walking shoes, flat-heeled and broad-toed like children's wear, and the fashion shoe confirmed the latter in its aesthetic and ceremonial, as opposed to practical role.

Extreme height and slenderness of heel, accompanied by an acutely pointed toe, serve to increase the wearer's sadomasochistic appeal, endowing her with predatory feet much as long, pointed fingernails give her clawed hands. The phrase "erect ankle", moreover (as also "erect torso"), appears to hold a special significance for fetishists. Extremists, not content with exaggerating the heel height to the point that the instep stands vertical, or even arches backwards into the shoe-vamp, have raised the foot on tip-toe in a shoe blocked in the manner of a ballet-slipper, but retaining an enormous foot-length heel. The "tip-toe" boot, often rising to the crotch, represents a "classic" if extreme form of fetish footwear, one which in the fetishist mind reduces the whole leg to a huge hyper-erect, hyper-constricted or engorged "phallic" unit.

In ballet, the tip-toe stance has semi-contradictory associations with the ethereal, spiritual, air-borne. The rising popularity of classical ballet and other forms of tip-toe dance in the 19th century represents a major public, artistically more-or-less sublimated manifestation of foot and leg fetishism. Some have seen an erectile phallic symbolism in the high-flailing leg of the can-can dance, also a product of the 19th century. The ballet-girl was the erotic priestess, a Terpsichorean hetaira, while the high heel gave to the woman of fashion the erotic lift of the dancer.

Just as certain parts of the body lend themselves by virtue of their shape, size, etc., to sexualization, so certain movements of the body can suggest sexual action. Body-sculpture is designed to enhance and sexualize the movements of everyday life, as much as it is designed to enhance and sexualize the shape of the human form itself. Ultimately the two factors are inseparable. In the non-Western world, costume is movement, dance, theatre and sexual ritual. In the West, its role in the social rituals involving body-movement (including most obviously social dance)—in "body-language" as the current term goes, deserves further study.[30] Costume historians have tended to view dress as a static agglomerate, outside its social-kinetic context.

Footwear alters not only the appearance of the foot, but also the action of the body as a whole. Significantly, the ordinary act of walking has become imbued with sexual connotations, which are reinforced by language, in equally ordinary words such as "to come" and "to go." The more technical words such as "coition" (from Latin *coire*, to go together), "congress", and "intercourse", also mean sexual walk.

The intensity and ingenuity with which the West reinforces this association is unique. While the bound foot of China, and the ankle-chains and high pattens of the Middle-East suggest immobility and captivity, the Western shoe inhibits movement in order to increase it, at least in appearance. Standing in her high-heeled shoes, woman presents herself already half-walking, ready to go, ready for action. By reducing the length of the step, the high heel fosters the illusion of speed. It can even appear to increase step-capacity, lending some women the air of giants in seven-league boots. While there are women who walk more securely in high heels than their sisters in low or no heels, and there are those whose locomotion in high heels is an aggressive appropriation of space and time (which is why such heels are no enemy to feminism), the contrary and complementary associations are with precariousness and imbalance, the appeal for a supporting arm, the promise of imminent fall, surrender. High-heeled woman thus becomes, for man, a tantalizing object of the chase, an incarnation of the restlessness of his own spirit and the socio-sexual contradictions with which it is fraught. The higher and more unstable-looking the heel, the more clearly these contradictions are expressed, and the more clearly is the duality exposed between woman immobilized, viewed as a passive sex-object, and woman elusive, (literally) *impeding* sexual fulfillment.

Since with the high and slender heel, the points of support for the foot are drastically reduced (especially when the heel is also pitched forward), the ankle is obliged to undertake all sorts of compensatory actions, so that it, the instep and even the whole leg adopt a "wobbling" or "quivering", "tottering" or "teetering" action. Each word has its own associations, negative and positive. The lateral quiver of the ankle each time the foot hits the ground as the woman approaches the man, may be unconsciously interpreted by him, if he is at all susceptible, as sexual invitation.

The woman, moreover, experiences narcissistically a muscular provocation within herself, for the redistribution of muscular effort over the whole of her body serves to increase her sense of the body kinetic.

As described to me by an habitual wearer of extreme stiletto heels, whose work in an office required constant movement: "I feel I am in a constant state of tension; simply standing, I am on the go; turning round, bending to file a paper, is a balancing act; I am at rest only when I sit, which is never for long. I wear these heels because they make me feel in constant contact with my body." Which distracted her, no doubt, from the mental boredom of her work.

Physicians assumed in the 19th century, as they still do, that this muscular adaptation would produce long-term adverse muscular and even organic changes in the body, but the physiology of these changes has been little studied.[31] Objectively, a rather radical change in posture is involved, the exact character of which is problematical, and seems to vary according to the cultural epoch, as well as with the individual. Opponents of high heels have stressed the ungainly thrusting forward of the chin by the inexperienced high-heel wearer, supposedly as a counter-weight. But the thrusting chin may be as much a psychological as a physical reaction, deriving from the fear of falling backwards and the instinctive search for some forward point of support. Little Chinese girls, learning to walk again after their feet were first bound, were explicitly warned against the bad habit of poking out their chin. In the 1870s, Western critics complained that high heels caused a pitching forward from the waist ("Grecian Bend" Plate 54); in the 1950s, on the other hand, such heels were accused of causing a slouched back and excessive bending at the knees. The defense has always claimed that they produced an upright carriage and out-thrust chest. Clearly, there are many variables at play, the relative influence of which will depend upon the individual type of body, gait, and psychology.

The way in which women walk has always varied from culture to culture, as has the socio-sexual symbolism. The Western high-heeled walk involves a quickening of leg and hip action which the Easterner would find unfeminine. The Chinese ideal gait was evidently a quiet, liquid waddle or shuffle, which binding, even more than the raised heel, was designed to induce. The walk of the Renaissance Venetian lady of fashion on her zoccoli was sometimes actually supported by servants on either side, and described as "majestically deliberating of every step." The nobility in some primitive cultures so shackle their feet with metal rings (connotive of wealth) that, on the ceremonial occasions when they wear them, they can barely move at all.

The hierarchical symbolism here is simple enough. In the West it operates in a contradictory manner. As exaggerated by the fetishist, footwear takes on powerful sadomasochistic associations, defining woman as submissive-aggressive, both predator and prey. To extrapolate from the fetishist literature: the modern Amazon shoots arrows into the ground with her feet, and strikes two-fold pleasure-pain, imagined or real, into the fantasy of the male: that of her own fight against peculiar self-imposed shackles, and that of his own physical subjection, his body trodden (dented, even pierced) by the goddess before whom he secretly wishes to abase himself. A tight-lacer who works as a primary school teacher told me that one of her pupils, an 11 year-old, confessed to her his fantasy that he was a carpet over which she walked with her five-inch stiletto heels.[32]

We have started with the symbolism of the high heel because, as a "fashion-fetish", it is still very much with us and appears less fraught with historical problems. Tight-lacing, however, historically the primary "fashion-fetish" of the West, is imbued with the more potent hierarchical and sexual associations.[33]

The most immediate visual effect of waist-compression is to enhance the secondary female characteristics of comparative breadth of bust and hips, and at the same time increase the comparative slenderness of waist, with its evident connotations of youthfulness, and physical leisure. The corset has also traditionally served to suggest firmness of the torso, and to raise the breasts, two other features associated with youth.[34] Cultivation of the appearance and symbols of youth, which may be a characteristic of dynamic Western civilizations, has climaxed over the present century, degenerating now into a pre-mammary, pre-pubescent ideal (Twiggy, etc.) which has paradoxically inhibited the return of the corset.

Waist or torso compression and breast-sculpture have been historically inseparable. The "uplift" obtained by modern brassière engineering was earlier achieved by the corset, the top of which pushed against the lower part of the breasts. Even the older and less well-endowed woman could thus produce an interesting and essentially juvenile swelling over the upper half of the breasts, thus reversing the concave-convex shape which becomes more marked and pendulous with age. Thus are intimated the perfect hemispheres beloved of the poets and artists. Round and succulent-looking, these carnal apples (to use an age-old metaphor) are temptingly hidden and offered by the daughter of Eve, whose arms clasped over her bosom imitate or enhance the pressure of the stays (as in the Rubens portrait, Plate 10).

At certain periods of history, which are hard to delimit with precision, but which reach intermittently from the 16th through the 18th centuries, thoracic constriction was accompanied not by the raising, but the actual compression of the breasts as a whole. Such breast-flattening served to emphasize breadth of hips, and suggest procreative power rather than sexual pleasure. Inconspicuous and flattened breasts have, however, never established themselves for long in the Western tradition, as they have in Asia.

The consciously modulated and aggressive forms of breast-sculpture which emerged in the post World War II era seem to correspond to a peculiarly Western sexual anxiety which has taken positively phallic forms.[35] Manipulation of the breast by (male) fashion-designers has recently been castigated with feminist fervor: "(the female breasts) are a millstone around a woman's neck . . . they are not parts of a person but lures slung around her neck, to be kneaded and twisted like magic putty, or mumbled and mouthed like lolly-ices . . . Recent emphasis on the nipple, which was absent from the breast of popular pornography, is in women's favor, for the nipple is expressive and responsive."[36] The recent emergence into fashion of the natural nipple, the contour of which may be clearly delineated beneath an extra-light brassière (or, if the owner goes bra-less, under a clinging fabric), is indeed new, although the peaked bras of the '50s may have been unconsciously intended to stylize erection of the nipple. These, like the male codpiece of the 16th century, served the illusion of a body in a permanent state of sexual excitation.

The constant reshaping, resizing and relocating of the bust by fashion in the course of this century may reflect the acute social instability of the era and embody very variable socio-sexual associations, examination of which would, however, take us too far from the subject at hand.

The nurturance or fertility symbolism of the full, round breast is obvious and needs no further elucidation; the hierarchical symbolism is principally that of the sexual toy. The symbolism of the slender waist in itself, that is apart from its role in throwing breasts into higher relief, has many dimensions. Sylph-like delicacy of body, fragility of waist have exercised an almost archetypal attraction for man, for whom it connoted both vulnerability and elusiveness. It is both foil and invocation to his superior socio-sexual power. The slender waist suggests the romantic and ethereal, the pure and virginal, all qualities which appeal to man's erotic imagination. The anti-maternalism (or -paternalism) it also embodies, insofar as it denies, defies or even reverses the idea of pregnancy, is another matter, with far-reaching (and scandalous) social implications. As with high heels, the corset may create a dynamic between restriction and movement. Compression in a relatively non-sexual area—the waist—induces movement in other, primarily sexual ones—bust and hips. The complementary character of high heels and tight-lacing, confirmed time and again in fetishism and in the history of costume, has its basis as far as body-dynamics are concerned in the fact (axiomatic with fetishists) that both enhance hip action, and that both mutually reinforce or complement each other in procuring "erect" posture.

The correct posture of a lady since the 18th century has been erect; as with footwear, the "erect" connotes social dignity and superiority. It distinguishes man from the animal: "The erect human posture is an erogenous feature of its own . . . The entire problem of posture is an deep-seated sexual significance."[37] It was the lower classes who went around with bowed backs, "bad posture," because of the work they did and because they knew no better.[38] Erect also means taller; posture can literally increase height, as can waist compression which forces the lower ribs upwards and the pelvis downwards, stretching the spine ever so slightly and making it more comfortable to stand as tall as possible.

Erect posture, correct gait involved a degree of immobility in the upper half of the body. It is assumed today that in long, wide skirts which concealed her hips and legs woman "floated" or progressed as if on wheels. While it is easy to understand how the stiff, tight-laced corset induced an erect posture, it is not clear that it would necessarily induce a floating walk. Indeed, the very opposite may be the case. The dress-reformers' charge that tight-lacing induced a poor imitation of the correct walk, that is, a stiff "parlor-tongue" gait, whether generally justified or not, may be based on the observation of a reaction *against* its movement-enhancing properties. It is self-evident that small movements about the pelvic girdle and ribcage will appear magnified if the area between is restricted. Additional movement may also be induced by certain compensatory actions, especially when walking, as a more or less unconscious, quasi-physiological response to intense local pressure, which may be relieved by changing the relative positions of pelvis and ribs. The tight-lacer may also seek to compensate for the relative immobility of the torso by exploiting the relative flexibility of hips and shoulders.

The swaying hips and flaunting bust can easily become overtly provocative. What is socially permissible in our own times, legitimized by the sex-goddesses of screen and stage, was, however, taboo to the Victorian lady, who, if she dared to tight-lace, may have felt (unconsciously) obliged to fight any body-expansive tendency induced by her corset which might over-determine and betray a purpose hidden, as often as not, even to herself: that of sexual seduction.

In the late Victorian and Edwardian periods, on two distinct occasions, fashion discovered a further means of enhancing body-contour and movement, which, although not strictly sculptural, modified body-action in the most drastic way: binding of the legs by means of knee-tight skirts. The open-legged position has always been regarded as potentially indecent (one has only to think of the resistance to the idea of woman riding astride, and the fear of accidental breaking of the hymen in this position) and was totally prohibited to respectable women. It was even found suspect in its modified form of the crossed or slung leg and acted, in art, as a metaphor for sexual intercourse.[39] The close-pressed thighs and hobbled gait characteristic of fashion in the 1870s and 1910s are arguably connotive of chastity in an ambivalent, perverse, but by now not unfamiliar way. The tight skirt may be regarded as an even more provocative kind of hobbling than the high heel, especially in the 1870s, when tight-lacing was carried to new extremes, hips, thighs and buttocks were anatomically moulded, and locomotion depended upon vigorous agitation of the pelvic girdle. We have here a mutually reinforcing yet inherently contradictory cause-and-effect cycle: hips and breast swelling and agitated, legs tied together—thus sexual invitation and sexual denial simultaneously, the ultimate in provocation.

Tight-lacing also heightens sexuality by quickening the action of the lungs. It suppresses breathing over the belly and forces it upwards, momentarily and eventually permanently enlarging the thoracic cage.[40] Many women experience inhibition of breathing, on a swing or by other means, as erotic, "breath-taking." Sexual experience is "like when a swing goes too high. You feel you're cut in two, you swoop down, and you scream 'Ha!'" (This from Colette, who goes on to relate the mysticism of breathlessness, of "losing all sense of existence, dying" to Polaire, the most famous tight-lacer of the age, whom she sets up as the young girl's ideal.) Elimination of abdominal in favor of pectoral breathing creates, moreover, movement about the breasts, which may be imagined constantly palpitating with desire. This sexualized change in breathing, this "subclavicular enticement" and "unnatural agitation" agitated fearful males.[41]

The spasms to which the body is subject during orgasm involve, of course, an often violent quickening of breathing, sensations of breathlessness, heaving of the chest, and contraction of the belly, all of which may be erotically enhanced by manual pressure at the waist, and artificially induced by means of a corset. Similarly, the climactic response of spasmic twitching of the feet, stretching of the instep and curling up of the toes, is mimicked by the action and position of the feet in high heels.

Although the neck has never been and can never be distorted to the same degree as the waist,[42] it is nevertheless an area in which the slighest external restriction can have a quite radical effect on freedom of movement about the head and shoulders, as also upon facility in breathing. The male neck has been more or less continuously subject to various, and often exaggerated forms of protection and restriction. Just as the corset protects a vulnerable area in the female, so the collar protects an area in the male vulnerable to an enemy weapon or disease. It was an ancient belief that diseases and evil spirits entered the body through the throat, and any knot about the throat originally had a magical apotropaic function, like the knot in a girdle which protects the vulnerable belly. The precise manner in which the neck is bound has been invested with an extremely intricate and potent social symbolism. This has long been recognized and analyzed; in the Romantic era, the contrasting moral, psychological, social and political implications of the dandy's tight stock and cravat, as opposed to the Byronic open collar, or, in the Decadent era, those of the immense masher collar as opposed to the aesthete's effeminate décolletage, became a matter of semi-humorous, semi-serious excogitation. The cultural abyss separating the 17th century English puritan and Spanish nobleman can be measured by comparing the simple neckcloth of the one with the extravagant ruff of the other.

Even today the collar and tie are among the most readily identifiable and widely ramified social symbols. The form of the tie-knot—loose, tight, single or double ("Windsor knot"), large or small, rectangular or triangular—is taken as indicative of personality-type. Our language uses this symbolism as a means of stratification both moral ("stiff-necked" and "collet-monté" have associations similar to "strait-laced") and social ("blue-collar," "white-collar" workers). In that high neckware tends also to elevate the head and contributes to an upright bearing, it connotes superior social and moral rank: "being above it all." "Elevation" of the head may be taken so far as to suggest its separation from the body. Cartoons imagine the masher actually severed by his collar at the neck, as they also imagine women severed by the corset at the waist (Plate 49–51).

We are still apt to determine the political or social conservatism of an individual or professional group by the stiffness, tightness or height of the collar. The military, usually the most conservative of all social classes, have traditionally worn constrictive neckware, and still do.[43] The conservative, catholicizing English High Churchman wears a high collar, the more liberal lower-class Low Churchman a low one; the London city banker, symbol of conservative stability, still wears the kind of tight, stiff (detachable) collar abandoned by most office workers nowadays. It is a decisive step indeed when such a group is permitted to leave their ties off and their shirt-collars open. The gesture of loosening one's neckware is symbolic of one's need for physical and moral relaxation. The woman who unties the man's tie (another phallic symbol) may be making a sexual invitation.[44]

Like collar, like man. "What were collars like during the Great Revolution? Male, gigantic, rigid, inexorable like the characters. How could they be floppy at a time when one was more likely to carry one's head to the scaffold, then to rest it on the two voluptuous pillows of opulent breast? Nowadays, collars are narrow and mean like the men."[45]

The underlying sexual symbolism of the stiff collar is assumed by Flügel in his chapter on the psychology of protective clothing, where stiffness and tightness are "liable to be overdetermined," and the stiff collar is identified as a primary symbol of duty as well as of phallic erection.[46] The two symbolisms are only superficially contradictory, for they represent, in combination, either the concept of sex-as-duty, or else the duty of sexual (or moral) restraint.

Sexual or moral restraint is traditionally the male responsibility, since women were considered prey to their instincts, and the stiff collar is primarily male, as the corset is primarily female; but in both cases only primarily. Flügel does not account for women sharing the ruff in the 17th century, or the masher collar in that critical period 1880–1910. Worn by women, such a collar becomes patently ambivalent, or bisexual because it is a male symbol used to hide (and draw attention to) a feminine center of erotic interest. In puritanical times and societies the female neck tends to be concealed; it is also concealed, and can even be constricted, like man's, when the female identifies herself with the male world, denying herself that erotic sign language provided by free play of the head, neck and shoulders.

Those men (dandies and mashers in England, the military everywhere, but not guerillas or bandits), who wore excessively tight, stiff or high collars, were accused of feminine narcissism. Their feminine readiness to "suffer in order to be beautiful", their desire to enhance their physical self-awareness through constriction (applied often enough also to the waist by means of feminine corsets) was deemed contemptible and subversive, like the complementary transvestite tendency of women. The entire fashion-fetishist syndrome takes on a peculiar aspect in the late 19th century when transvestite tendencies became overt, and in a curious reversal, the moderate male collar retained its conservative, military, moral-duty symbolism, while in an exaggerated form it became a symbol of perverse, narcissistic sexuality.

In adopting the masher collar, women were transferring to the neck a form of constriction to which they had already been conditioned at the waist and feet, and which was generally lessening in those areas. The aggressively "emancipated", i.e., masculinized woman tended to wear a low, unconstrictive male collar and soft shirt-fronts, while it was the feminine woman of fashion who went for the masher collar and stiff shirt-front. The woman of fashion managed to have her cake and eat it by wearing the male collar by day, out of doors and for sport (i.e., in the masculine domain), and retaining in the evening feminine symbols of small waist, décolletage, etc. The idea of symbolic male wear being used simply to enhance femininity is of course a basic tenet of contemporary fashion, and is strikingly exemplified in the uniform of the Playboy Club bunny, who wears a small, but stiff collar and cuffs on her bare neck and arms, in perverse contrast to the rest of her corset-cum-swimsuit of a costume. Here the idea of sexual service is allied to the older moral duty symbolism (the bunnies are theoretically inaccessible), which is strikingly exemplified in nurses' uniforms. These might incorporate, as a matter of individual choice, the tallest of masher collars at the time when such collars and the profession of nursing were both new, and fashionable while even today, in Britain, a stiff, if low and unrestrictive collar is often prescribed by regulation.

Male neck constriction took distinct forms at different periods in the 19th century. The masher collar which reached its height (literally) in the 1890s, unlike the stock worn by dandies and the military in the 1820s, was not necessarily tight; indeed, its very height and stiffness precluded inward pressure on the throat. Its purpose was to elevate and restrict the movement of the head, and to press upon the flesh immediately above the collarbone and under the jaw, areas which some individuals find erogenous.[47] Women adopted this kind of collar, which was of course detachable, for wear with the male shirt and "tailor-made" coat, but transferred it in principle also to day-dress of all kinds, which was given a high, lightly boned neck of the same material as the dress. Unlike the rigidly starched masher collar, but like the dandy's military stock, this followed the exact contours of the neck and allowed for "feminine" movements of the head. Being more flexible, the lacy dress collar could rise even higher at certain points than the masher collar, following the line of the jaw in a curve and peaking towards the ear-lobe, another area of particular erotic sensitivity.

With the military and economic advantage conferred by the domestication of the horse, riding became endowed with a magical power symbolism. This lent itself readily to sexual analogues, as we know from ancient witch-lore. Woman on horseback has availed herself of a unique forum for the public display of private sexual emotion, and her performance has been perceived as both physically and metaphysically analogous to her sexuality. The horse appeals to human sexual polyvalence, allowing man or woman to act out a whole range of roles and modes. Riding is high sexual theatre. To the rider, the mount is both sexual partner and sexual self, and the spectator can project himself or herself into either role alternately or simultaneously. As D. H. Lawrence perceived, the horse represents an ambi-sexual life force which one tries to release and control.

The sporting equestrienne of the 19th century acquired the perilous status of a woman asserting her independent sexual identity. Thus her right to ride and her manner of riding became surrounded with an aura of controversy which represented a subliminal response, by critics of stridently opposing views, to the sexually symbolic component in an activity which also offered a real degree of physical freedom. Independently of man, she sought a corporal bond, a physical harmony with a large and powerful beast, apparently tamed, but always potentially dangerous. She could also give vent to sexual frustration, fantasies of dominance, and her need to punish or exact revenge.

Certain minutiae relating to equine discipline were given such inordinate stress by fetishists (and some reformers as well), that they compel far-reaching speculation as to their possible symbolic range. The two major areas of controversy affected the spurring of the ridden horse, and the bitting and reining of the driven horse, both of which are also rife with linguistic metaphor and emblematic meaning, standing iconographically for energy, continence and discipline.

While the very act of sitting upon the horse represents an erotic interlocking of form, the act of spurring, reserved for the climactic effort of spurt or jump represents an actual insertion. The best type of spur for whatever occasion was a matter for endless discussion in the fetishist correspondence, as was the technique of its application, the two aspects being wholly interdependent.

Argument over optimum length of spur-point and the insistence by some on unfashionable extremes, may have a phallic significance; some of the fascination of the idea that if it enters cleanly at right angles to the horse's flesh and at the psychologically correct moment, even the longest spur-point could be thrust in to the very hilt without hurting the horse too much, may derive from a coital analogue. Taken as a whole, argument over spur shape and length is reminiscent, and at certain periods runs parallel to, argument over the proper shape and height of shoe-heels. Both are symbol-laden and sexually charged. The idea of adding a spur to the high-heeled shoe or boot was first conceived by the fetishist in Victorian times, before it passed, as a gimmick, into modern fashion-design. The phrase "spur-like sharpness of heel (or toe)" is a commonplace of fetishist literature, which also appears occasionally in high fashion magazines.

Extravagant spurring necessitated special forms of control over the horse's head, which was subjected to the severe so-called curb-bit. Its excessive use by women was sternly denounced by equestrian experts, despite the fact that the arched neck which it induced was traditionally regarded as the quintessence of smartness. (In old portraits of race-horses the neck is often shown in an extreme arch, which was considered a mark of breeding.)

On the driven horse, a principal mark of breeding and "smart" action was the position of the head in relation to the shoulders. In order to teach a horse to hold his head "proudly aloft", as the phrase went, he was subjected to a rein permanently fixed to his tail or the carriage harness, known as the bearing-rein. This forced the head backwards and upwards and could be adjusted to the shortness or tightness desired by the driver. The extremists raised the horse's head to a degree which was supposedly impressive but which surely decreased his pulling power. The curbing-in as well as the bearing-up, the arched and compressed neck as well as the outstretched and elevated head, became in the fetishist literature sexually charged, symbolic elements, analogized with the "curbing" of the girl's head in a backboard and collar, and the "reining in" of her waist in a corset in order to teach her erect posture. The term "erect" in respect to the smart horse's head[48] occurs with extraordinary frequency; it is hard to ignore the possibility of phallic erection symbolism.

In the principle of applying severe external pressures in order simultaneously to constrict and enhance movement or posture, the equine and human figure training fetishes obviously operate in an analogous way; and their essential reciprocity was recognized by those riders who preferred to be tight-laced in order the better to enjoy the results of their spurring. The restriction imposed on their own body seemed to magnify their sensation of the horse's movement beneath. They were also extremely conscious of the manner in which the horse provided, vis-à-vis the onlooker, a pedestal for their carefully sculptured forms.

The Corset as Ritual

PARTICULAR SYMBOLIC COMPONENTS

The corset sexualizes the body in form and action; in so doing it becomes itself sexualized, in its material components and the associations they arouse, and in the manner in which the garment as a whole is put on or off.

"Tight" and "stiff" are words and concepts to which fetishists attribute quasi-magical powers, and which embody ancient hierarchical associations with control, duty, morality, rank, etc.[49] In French, the same word is used for "tight" and "right" (correct).[50] Fetishists extrapolate from the material stiffness and tightness of the fetish object a moral posture of stiff determination and tight control vis-à-vis the object, themselves, and others. This is forcefully expressed by Emile Zola, whose work generally is imbued with a dense interlock of sexual symbolism, and who in *Le Ventre de Paris* particularly renders eloquent what the fetishists express in cruder forms.[51]

In the corset, degrees of tightness and stiffness are precisely manipulable, and adaptable to the needs of the occasion. The corset entered the course of existence on many levels, marking the "rites of passage" from childhood to adult world, and enhancing the significant daily rhythm of life. The difference between the light, loose morning corset, and its tighter, stiff evening counterpart, of which the French in the 19th century were particularly conscious, expressed the changing rhythm of woman's social role, the alternation, for instance, between the relative safety of the daytime, and sexual exposure in the evening. At social evenings, bodily provocation becomes socially sanctioned, but demands a corresponding control. The extra tight-laced corset is a means of exercising that control while enhancing the provocation. Even as she induces sexual temptation, woman is seemingly armored against it.

The corset as a protective device embodies masculine associations; morally in danger of man, it is as if woman puts on the man over her vulnerable womanhood, which is, however, preserved—indeed exaggerated—beneath. This very act of hardening and stiffening herself, which is on one level defensive, becomes a militant form of transference to herself of masculine eroticism. The hard armor she dons seems to protect physically the vital organs located in the thorax and abdomen, but insofar as it stops short of the sexual nodes, i.e., nipples and genitals, it also serves to expose her sexual vulnerability, and enhance the softness of her (exposed) breast and mobile thighs. The bawdy toast "To both ends of the busk" referred to the two points of sexual interest which seemed all the more vulnerable, the heavier the armor in between. The waist-compressive corset has always stopped short of the pubic area; only around 1900 did the girdle begin to cover this part and furnish an actual obstacle, like the legendary chastity belt, to penetration.

The primary stiffening agency of the corset was in earlier centuries concentrated in the busk. This was a wide, heavy, inflexible, detachable strip of wood or other materials, inserted down the front of the bodice, sometimes inches in breadth and of variable length. Made by specialist craftsmen, phallic in shape, often finely engraved with amorous verses[52] and devices, and sometimes even concealing a dagger, the erotic symbolism of the busk is beyond dispute. It played in 17th century France a public ritual role: women might withdraw it and use it with coquettish reproach upon male knuckles;[53] sailors on long voyages habitually carved it from whalebone in order to give it to their sweethearts on their return, and as late as the early 20th century it was the custom for a Sicilian bridegroom to present a hand carved busk to his bride as a token of his commitment.

The erotic symbolism of the front busk diminished when it became non-detachable, narrower, and was joined by other busk-like stiffeners around the rest of the corset, and eventually (and slowly, from about 1840) split in two. The tight-lacing enthusiasts who found the split busk "improper" long after it had proved his practicality, sensed that the splitting tended to negate the traditional phallic symbolism. The bifid, front-fastening steel busk, which saved one the very considerable trouble of removing the lace completely from the corset and then reinserting it at each wearing, diminished an erotic ritual elaborated in the 18th century, in which a maid, or better, a lover was the active participant. It was this ritual and the absolute necessity of outside help in the lacing (the hierarchical principle) that opponents of the split busk wished to preserve, as well as the prolonged pleasure of passing the lace-end through the lace-holes (cf. Plate 25).[54] With the front fastening corset, the time and effort formerly spent putting in the laces could be spent on the actual tightening of the laces, which introduced a new dynamic, one correlated moreover with the distribution of the stiffening over the corset as a whole, which in itself permitted tighter lacing.

When lacing became tight-lacing, and fell into general disrepute, one of the means of degrading it socially was to suggest that it necessitated the muscle-power of the male lower servants, from valet and groom down to kitchen- and stable-boy.[55] To admit a low-class male servant, rather than a lover, to the intimacy of a sacred ritual, was to vulgarize it, and arouse the suspicion that a footman permitted such physical exertions on his mistress' behalf, might be allowed to develop them to an even more intimate stage. This suspicion is confirmed by the simultaneous emergence of another theme in French cartoons of the 1880s, showing ladies permitting just this, the footman being more potent and attractive than the husband.

The pressure of the corset symbolized, replicated, and gave permanence to that of the lover's clasp. Initiation into the corset prefigured sexual initiation. At puberty, "on those occasions when she was allowed to wear her first tiny pair of corsets she was exalted to an almost celestial pitch of silent ecstasy. The clasp of the miniature stays around her small body was like the embrace of a little lover." Another popular novelist uses the term "snuggle" (schmiegen) to describe the manner in which the pubescent body should respond to the first corset. The nuptial corset (white satin, firmly boned) was "a silken vice whose gentle pressure reminds the bride of her groom whose arm clasped her waist so tightly during the waltz of only yesterday." The equation is confirmed by a number of cartoons of the late 19th century: the tight-lacer justifies herself to her lover, who has his arms around her waist, on the grounds that he would be the first to complain if she didn't enjoy being squeezed; she adapts the size of her waist to the length of her fiancé's arm ("the shortest you ever saw"); she coyly admits to her prospect that she is merely anticipating, by artificial means, the advent of the real thing; and the very wasp-waisted lady is supposed, by the naive Irishman, to have "a bear of a husband t'git hugged the shape o'that."[56]

THE PROCESS—LACING AND UNLACING

The lacing and unlacing of the corset were rituals which retained ancient levels of symbolism and the magical associations of the concepts of "binding" and "loosing". In folk language, to be delivered of a child or to be deflowered, was to be "unbound"; to unbind was to release special forms of energy. The untying of the nuptial girdle has represented since ancient times and in many different cultures a significant act. In Circassia the husband literally severed the bark-corset with a slash of his dagger; and in France the husband lingered delightedly, or fumbled confusedly, with the knot and lacing of his bride's corset.

The state of being tightly corsetted is a form of erotic tension and constitutes ipso facto a demand for erotic release, which may be deliberately controlled, prolonged, and postponed. To the male the corset represents an intricate erotic obstacle, the deft removal of which permitted the development of all kinds of erotic foreplay, and betokened amorous expertise.[57] To the woman, unlacing meant (promise of) sexual release. The French punned on "se délasser" (to relax) and "se délacer" (to unlace oneself). By the end of the 19th century, when the corset was no longer taken for granted, a woman would, according to joke-lore, complain to her lover or prospect, that her corset hurt her in order to invite him to undress her. Dressing again afterwards she would also, in her hurry (and guilt), leave the corset behind, or in a cab—primary evidence for her sexual indulgence.

The erotic value of the lacing-in process, as performed by the lover, may also be fixed on a scale according to the degree of his fetishistic commitment. The lacing-in (afterwards) may merely represent the privilege of one who has enjoyed the sexual favors of a woman; but it may also suggest the imposition of a kind of chastity belt, over which only the lover has control; and, to the true fetishist, in addition to the above, it re-enacts and perpetuates, in an extended visual concretization, the violence of his desire to (re-) possess, and the (imagined) desire of the woman to be (re-) possessed.[58]

The very acts of lacing and unlacing—the threading and unthreading, the pulling in and out at various points in different degrees and in a certain sequence, the reducing, closing and leaving of gaps—are elaborately ritualized in fetishist scenarios. It is as if the connoisseur of tight-lacing, by regulating through the laces the location, extent and timing of pressure upon his partner's body, were mimicking the connoisseur of the art of love, who measures his prowess in comparable terms. The obsessive quality of fetishist discussion of lacing techniques, as that of spurring techniques, may be regarded as a sublimated response to the anxiety surrounding the performance of the sexual act, open discussion of which is, of course, taboo.

PUBERTY INITIATION—NUPTIAL INITIATION

Culturally, the process of lacing and unlacing may be regarded as no more than one aspect of the erotic ritual of dressing and undressing. The fetishist, however, exaggerating it, desired that the whole process of corsetting become a prolonged initiation, and a long-term moral, physical and sexual discipline to be taught and learned, to be passed from mother to daughter, encouraged among siblings, practiced competitively in the adolescent peer-group and in private schools. Corsetting, as such, was always a part of the social ritual of dress; in its exaggerated, fetishist form, it became virtually a rite of passage in itself.

There were two major rites of passage in a woman's life: puberty and marriage. The corset played a role in both, the significance of that role varying in particular cases. With the fetishist, the puberty corset may represent initiation into serious "figure-training", that is, a form of social and sexual training, and the nuptial corset a kind of social and sexual consummation. After which, in the mind of the French matrimonial cynic, it was cast off: the rigors of the nuptial corset were left behind, to express the greater moral freedom (including adultery) enjoyed by the married woman.[59] (Cf. "My first corset", appendix p. 305)

The ritual role of the corset and tight-lacing fully flowered in the 19th century. From the 17th and partly through the 18th century, corsetting began even earlier in life than foot-binding in China. As soon as it had learned to walk, the infant (male and female) passed from the confinement of swaddling clothes directly into that of a stiffened bodice designed to help it grow straight and protect it from bruises and accidents. With little boys, the hard bodice was abandoned as soon as he became active; with girls, it was preserved, and followed the development of her form, curving when she did.

In urban families both infant swaddling and childhood stays had fallen into disuse by the later 18th century, and were never revived. The renewed adult tight corsetting of the 19th century therefore represented not the mere continuation of childhood custom, but a new experience, one to be actively enjoyed, or at least consciously tolerated, unless rejected altogether. The first adult corset obviously meant more to the pubescent girl who had never worn any kind of stays than to one who had. The mass of evidence from the 19th century, both pro- and anti-corset, indicates that girls were allowed to develop quite freely until around thirteen years and more (in France, a year or two younger).[60] The English in particular seem conscious of the impropriety of imposing what they sense as an essentially sexual device upon childhood, the supposed innocence of which they sought to prolong. The fetishist observed this convention also, and introduced the adult corset, and the idea of tight-lacing, at around fourteen or fifteen years. By around sixteen years, at her "coming-out" (the basic social puberty ritual) most girls had assumed the sartorial signs of passage into womanhood: long skirts, hair tied up, high heels, and a corset to announce and protect the new mammary bud. In the conventional family this last was done discreetly, the corset serving more as protection than as a means of display. In fetishist families, on the other hand, the corset served to define the wearer as having reached the age of sexual aggression; and it was hoped that by the time a girl "came out", she had herself taken charge of her figure training, and was lacing voluntarily.

In their letters to the magazines, the younger fetishists tended to play down the role of adult example and persuasion, stressing the spontaneity and voluntary character of their beginning to tight-lace, and pursuing the practice in friendly rivalry with their peers. The existence of voluntary lacing of this kind is confirmed, apart from the autobiographical testimony, by sources as far apart in their interests as the corsetière and the abolitionist, as well as in the popular novel.[61]

The fourteen to sixteen age bracket was also that chosen by fetishist disciplinarians, who chiefly but by no means exclusively announce themselves as male, to bring the "neglected" figures of their charges up to par. Some writers dramatize rebellion, resistance and successful repression through the corset; how far these actually took place is another matter, for the more colored and sadistic stories along these lines may be fabrications. It is, however, rare for the tight-lacing initiate to claim that the process was a comfort and joy from begin-, ning to end; indeed, by stressing initial resistance and discomfort, some sought the doubly honored status of convert and martyr.

The parental disciplinarian, one of the least attractive Victorian types, and one which fetishism could only exacerbate, saw tight-lacing as a means of enforcing filial obedience in a special, sexually significant way, and fostering those cardinal "natural" virtues of Victorian woman: submissiveness, self-denial, endurance, willing-ness to suffer on behalf of men. These qualities are, however, not among those stressed by the practitioners themselves, who preferred to enlarge upon active participation, rather than the passive submis-sion.

The recent development of sartorial puberty rites as an expression not of integration into, but separation from adult values (girls don-ning shabby clothes, boys growing long hair, may be cited as exam-ples from the last decade) raises the question as to whether 19th century tight-lacing by young girls may not also be considered a form of protest—not necessarily against parents, as such, but against the maternal stereotype normally incarnated in the mother—a thesis which we will be able to confirm.

In "nuptial initiation" tight-lacing was begun only at marriage, usually by the desire of the husband. The psychological and physical difficulties of "training" a fully grown figure from scratch were sensed to be considerable, but also to represent a unique challenge to the viability of the pair-bond. As in the puberty ritual, women writing of their achievements in this respect tended to stress the voluntary character of their decision, which was encouraged but not imposed by the husband. Tight-lacing was viewed as a permanent bond between husband and wife, as a guarantee of fidelity, and as a means of prolonging sexual interest at a time when it tended to wear thin through habit and age.

THE "EXTENDED FAMILY"; TRANSMISSION OF THE FETISH

The rituals of tight-lacing from the later Victorian age onwards, made for a special kind of "extended family" unit, including maids, governesses, cousins, friends, dressmakers, corsetières, and even (very occasionally) physicians. The sympathetic maid was considered the sine quâ non of any figure-training program, and the correspon-dence shows mistresses and maids vying with each other on equal terms. The tight-laced maid was also viewed (by the employer) as a social status symbol, not unlike the bound-foot servant in China. (For a vivid example of a governess chosen, in the first instance, on account of her figure, and helping infuse her charges with the fetish, cf appendix p. 327. The extended family unit pattern was imitated in certain small boarding schools where the children of tight-lacers gathered. The example was set by headmistress, teachers, and sometimes servants as well.

The "extended tight-lacing family" is however not well documented; evidence for even the above generalizations is fragmentary and muddied, especially in the post-Victorian fetishist correspondence, by much fantasy. It does seem however that the sense of a special identity developed in such a family increased as the opposition to tight-lacing intensified, as the limited fashionable sanction for it declined, and as the extended family in itself shrank in size. Today, when there are for the middle classes no more lady's maids and governesses, and fewer children, and those few grow up relatively free of direct parental constraints, the "extended fetishist family", if it is to be achieved at all, has to be created from among like-minded friends, who, even in these days of personal advertisement bulletins and sexual minority cults, are by no means easy to find, and when found, often turn out to live at insuperable geographical distances.

Furthermore, as we have seen, psychiatric attitudes have communicated to fetishists, whether analysands or not, a profound sense of their deviance, and taught them to hide themselves and their "perversions". The fetishist pair often find themselves in a bizarre isolation which can appear self-imposed, a predicament tenderly evoked by John Osborne in his play *Under Plain Cover* (1962).

Fetishism is no longer deliberately passed on from parent to child; and fetishists I have questioned as to the origin of their fetish can rarely trace it back to early childhood (I stress this as a caution against the rigid application to fetishism of Freud's theory of infant imprinting).[62] An instance of the manner in which the tight-lacing fetish was passed from generation to generation within the same family, in the present century, is transcribed in the appendix p. 329; it is extraordinary for its date, but may offer a model of an earlier pattern. Another example illustrates the manner in which parental example and conditioning managed to cut across the social grain. An informant born around 1905 told me that the conditioning she received from her mother to tight corsetting was for many years, in spite of fashion (the "waistless twenties"), entirely successful, up to the point when she discovered that boy-friends tended to reject her on discovering her "inner secret"; her relief was correspondingly great when she finally found one (her present husband) who was actually attracted to, and encouraged her "peculiar" habit, which developed into a major bond between them.

The Freudian conclusion, based upon the study of male autoerotic
practices, that fetishism was basically a form of psychic masturbation,
and that it generally led to homosexuality,[63] takes an impossibly
narrow view of the phenomenon, and is demonstrably false. Tight-
lacing, like all forms of fetishism, certainly exists as an auto-erotic and
homosexual practice, but there is ample evidence to regard it, within
the norms of fetishism, as normatively heterosexual, that is, as a
means of emotional and sexual exchange between partners of the
opposite sex.

Nor is it true that female fetishism is virtually non-existent, as
modern sexology (Kinsey, etc.) maintains. (Male) sexology has
clouded and narrowed the whole arena of female sexuality, perpetuating the Victorian view of it as naturally passive, or non-
existent, and when existent, "abnormal" and subversive.[64] The
capacity of modern woman for an active, rather than passive form of
fetishism[65] is confirmed by practicing fetishist pairs personally known
to me, amongst whom the female often assumes an active and
sometimes leading role (even, on occasion, against a husband's initial
resistance-Plate 87). Research is now showing woman's sexual response
to be intenser, broader and more subtle than was hitherto recognized.
The Victorian woman may also prove to have been altogether less
passive, sexually and otherwise, than has been supposed, which
should help dispel doubts cast on the Victorian fetishist correspondence as representing authentic female experience, as opposed to
male fantasy.[66]

Heterosexual fetishism is a dialectical affair, which may transcend
sexual roles and lead to a special kind of equality between the
partners. At its worst, fetishism can frustrate and paralyze sexual
relationships altogether; at its best, it can deepen mutual understanding and the emotional bond. The fetishist relationship acts out,
ritualizes and even publicizes repressed sexual feeling. The male who
initiates or encourages the fetish does not necessarily see himself as
unilaterally imposing it, but nevertheless often assumes responsibility for the difficulties it may cause, and compensates with increased
attentions. Sometimes the desire to compensate and share is the
motive for the imposition upon himself of the same discipline, despite
the considerable social prohibition attached to transvestism and masculine masochism. (There are, in the light of my personal contacts,
few men who have not at some time or another experimented upon
themselves; several husbands are to my knowledge as permanently if
not as drastically corsetted as their wives). Switching of roles is

another aspect of the partners' equal sharing of the sexual experience. The pair-bond induced by fetishism has a strength equivalent to that of the psycho-physiological sensations it arouses, and to the difficulty of confronting the sexual guilt it embodies. Like other, more overtly sado-masochistic scenarios, the tight-lacing ritual, if properly shared, openly confronts, parodies and sometimes reverses the convention of "sexual conquest:" both partners partake of both victory and surrender, which at a certain point may be said to merge. This should not be taken to exclude the fact that with tight-lacing and other fetishisms, as with sado-masochistic scenarios generally, a sex-role polarization may take place: with the male sadistically acting out guilt over his real (social) weakness, and the female acting out her fear of power.

Reporting that psychoanalytic rarity, a case of auto-generated female fetishism (specifically, tight-lacing), Reik comments that pure masochism is rare among women because the "male urge for (self) torture is titanic; women are more inclined to endurance."[67] (The "endurance" necessitated by tight-lacing appears explicitly in a popular magazine of 1872 as one of a series of "Virtues (not Cardinal)."[68] Endurance is precisely the quality required for body-sculpture, because the tight-lacer's ultimate objective is to extend the erotic experience in time. Unlike "pure" sado-masochists, sculptural fetishists aim less for the momentary violent ecstasy than to prolong a state of just-bearable tension. The fetishist ritual can extend into the everyday, eroticizing the common experience of domestic existence, as well as that of the social occasion. The latter furnishes an opportunity for the indulgence of peculiar narcissistic and voyeuristic instincts, such as is denied to most sado-masochistic scenarios, which cannot be publicly exposed.

No scientific studies are known to me on the physiology of fetish-induced pleasure-pain. Speculation upon the physiological basis for the gratification offered by tight corsets has tended to be wild, and biased by a puritan prejudice which has linked it to masturbation.[69] A physician whom I questioned closely on the subject, who was himself an inveterate tight-lacer, had no explanation at all (the fact that he enjoyed it was what mattered to him).

Touting the postwar return of the belt, a fashion magazine purrs, "Today every smart little waist knows the tugging, hugging security of it . . ."[70] But there are no rules visual or otherwise to tell the individual just how much tugging and hugging will make him or her feel secure but not uncomfortable. The transition from "close-fitting" to "too tight" can be a fine one.

One definition of fetishistic tight-lacing, as opposed to the simple feeling of support offered by the conventional corset or belt, is that moment when the corset "takes over"—the body, or the willpower—the moment of "surrender." As they become conditioned to the corset, the muscles stop resisting and let the corset do the work for them. According to this category of experience, the corset replaces the muscles; but according to another it transmits muscular activity, almost as if the boning itself were acting as a physiological conductor. A local pressure (as of the partner's fingers) is immediately transmitted over adjacent areas. Any movement in the hips passes at once to the breast and vice-versa. At the same time, if compression at the waist is such as to induce a numbness, the sensations are (as one informant put it) transmitted like sparks of energy or pain leaping across a dead point. The feeling of coming in two can, in extreme cases, apparently be very real, and in a most mysterious way can render the most intense pressure pleasurable. "Floating" is a key concept of tight-lacing fetishism, as of fashion corset advertising. But in fetishism, the experience is necessarily more intense. "As my body goes dead, marvelous things happen to my head"—this from a young woman with prior experience in psychedelic drugs, the sensations of which she regarded as comparable. "It is as if my body were perceived at a distance": this is a sentiment common to mystical experience. A feeling of total helplessness giving paradoxically the sensation of total freedom, and a numbness leading to the feeling that the body is extended in space, are among other experiences cited by tight-lacing fetishists (as by certain bondage addicts).

Intense pressure can also have the very opposite effect of numbness, inducing sensations of extreme heat. Very sudden and localized contraction at the waist can provoke a sensation "like a red-hot searing band of steel" (this or similar phrases appear in the literature, as well as on the lips of contemporary informants). One of the more evident major physiological factors in compression or air-tight enclosure, is that of generating heat, as anyone knows who has suffered from a tight collar on a hot day, or running for a bus. (How the masher bore his high collar in a typically humid August midday of New York defies the imagination.) Since sexual activity also induces a marked rise in body-temperature (especially over the thorax and neck) the "sense of security and support" enjoyed by corset-wearers may well have a basis in sexual physiology, as may another effect of abdominal compression, the rise in blood-pressure and the stimulation of blood flow to the heart.[71]

The removal of the corset after extreme compression can also lead to sensations enjoyed for their own sakes, ranging from that of simple relief, to that of a tingling stimulation which may persist for some time. Psychologically, the feeling has been described by contemporary practitioners as one of purification.

Tight-lacers attempt to measure precisely the pain threshhold. They seek out and push back that razor-thin line where pain no longer incorporates pleasure, analyzing their sensations fraction of an inch by fraction of an inch, marvelling at the radical and not always logically sequent changes wrought by the very gradual tightening.

The dependency which tight-lacing may quickly induce is both psychological and physical. One young woman described her feelings when she wanted to be tighter than the corset could make her as "really hurting" and "being out of touch with my body."

Once the threshhold of pain has been passed, it is experienced as pure pain, a condition the fetishist (as opposed to the masochist) does not seek. Different states appear with different people at the point of extremis: pain, giddiness, nausea, fainting and even hallucination. If the fainting-point is cherished by certain fetishists, it is more as a fantasy and as an important element of the mythology, than as a reality. ("Fainting would be lovely. Alas, I just feel sick"). The fantasy represents the moment of fainting as the reconciliation of opposing sensations: that of falling softly asleep and that of violent sexual extinction. "As the lacing proceeded, it seemed as if the walls of the room were slowly closing in on me, pressing tighter and tighter—on and on. Suddenly a delicious warmness welled up in the pit of my stomach and gradually spread over me. I'm not breathing properly, I must take more oxygen. I felt calmer. Suddenly a whirlpool rushed upon me, and I thought 'All I have to do is let it come to me, accept it.' Then a velvety curtain drifted over my consciousness . . . I will learn to do this if it kills me. But it won't, of course."[72] Tight-lacers discuss extinction, and the severing of the body and life-line like Leopold von Sacher-Masoch and his mistress discussed beheading: "It was agreed by both parties that nothing could be more agreeable to both parties, if it were not for the inconvenient after-effects."[73]

Death fantasies may not be typical, but they cannot be excluded from tight-lacing psychology. It is doubtful that tight-lacers flirt with death in reality, as do some bondage, "hanging", and "total enclosure" addicts; with the latter group, the risk lies with sudden quasi-accidental and irreversible suspension of breathing (especially through neck-constriction), which even the severest contraction at the waist is less likely to provoke. The possibility cannot, however, be discounted that some women in the past did indeed, as the press loved to report "die of tight-lacing"—that is, unconsciously but fatally exacerbate by means of corsets whatever disease they were suffering from, psychologically or physically. But most such reports must be treated with a pinch of salt; the newspaper headline "Death by Tight-lacing" is so much more obviously dramatic than "Death from

an Abscess in the Stomach, etc.,'' and represented a temptation to
any physician or coroner not adverse to publicity, the sensational
verdict, and the dramatization of female folly.

"Suicide'' by tight-lacing was a favorite topos of the Victorian press
at a time when the idea of women aspiring to extreme physical
sensations and mystical experiences was inadmissible. Access to
mystical experience of any kind, such as is sought by an increasing
number of young people of both sexes in our own age, was largely
closed to Victorian women. Tight-lacing extremism may be viewed as
an attempt to open up a prohibited area of sensation, despite the fact
that the sensations themselves are not or barely described at that
time.

Tight-lacing and Female Emancipation

FEMINISM

Writers on fashion and social history have singled out the corset as
the emblem of patriarchal Victorian tyranny, and the supposedly
widespread fashion of tight-lacing as the surest indication of woman's sexual enslavement. Women's magazines and the media generally continue to conjure up the horrors of that ancient instrument of
torture, in order the better to tout the wonderful "freedoms'' of
modern fashion—(of material, cut, choice, etc.) The constant harping
on this word is not without its political implications, rather as if those
"freedoms'' represented typical democratic rights under capitalism,
the enjoyment of which woman (like man) ignores at her peril.

The freedom-mongering of so much fashion copy plays a construct
of the present against a myth of the past, and does so with a
commercial motive which is obvious and an ideological purpose
which may be less so. Those who summon up the demons of
oppressive fashion in the past align themselves with reformist men
who were very far from being motivated by libertarian, feminist or
progressive sympathies.

The most strident enemies of the corset, from Rousseau and Napoleon to Renoir, as we shall see, were often autocratic males with a low
opinion of the female sex and an attachment to the concept of the
"natural woman'', that is, one dedicated to home and children. Many
of the most vocal (male) critics flaunted their misogyny. At the same
time, there were prominent 19th century feminists who were critical
of current fashion in general, and its dependence upon the corset in
particular, as obstacles to the emancipation of their sex. As Susan
Anthony put it, "I can see no business avocation in which woman in

her present dress *can possibly* earn *equal wages* with man."[74] In the early years of the movement, in the U.S. in mid-century, several feminists adopted the Bloomer costume, and many later ones favored dress-reform, themselves wore one or another of the new garments, and encouraged others to do so. But it is significant that no important feminist, to my knowledge, singled out the corset and the tight-lacers for sustained attack, like the (chiefly male) physicians, or regarded the dress reform question as paramount. This question, while often present, was simply allowed to peter out as the feminist movement concerned itself increasingly with the larger social, economic and political issues. There was a well-grounded fear that radical dress reform, apart from being too vulnerable a target of derision,[75] distracted attention from the larger issue, and encouraged audiences at Women's Rights conventions to look at what the speakers were wearing, rather than listen to what they were saying. As the movement matured in the course of the 19th century, there were few feminists who would have agreed with the German writer who opined that "the highest and most important mark of women's progress . . . the Woman Question (*Frauenfrage*) is (in effect) the Corset Question (*Korsettfrage*)."[76] And dress-reformer-historian Mary Tillotson's effort (1885) to increase comprehension by "rationalizing" the customary spelling of the English language seemed as doomed as her simultaneous effort to achieve female emancipation through the "rationalization" of fashionable clothing.

Significant differences of attitude within the movement can be determined by comparing that of a male sympathetic to the Women's Rights movement, and that of a famous woman feminist, in the exchange of letters between Gerrit Smith and his cousin Elizabeth Cady Stanton in 1855.[77] Smith upbraids the "woman's rights women" for wearing dress that both makes and marks their impotence, and expresses amazement that the relationship between female dress and female oppression is not more apparent, as it is with Chinese foot-binding, which marks the degradation of Chinese women. But Stanton, without wishing to defend "crippling" dress and, significantly, avoiding all reference to corsets, implicitly defends fashion insofar as it represents an *individually chosen* style which may easily be changed at will. She then redirects attention to those things that are hard to change such as institutions, which can only be changed by revolution. Look at the freedom of Negro dress, she exclaims, yet *he* is still totally a slave.

Stanton goes further, defending a degree of impracticality in dress, especially among working-class women, which may help sustain the vestiges of gallantry still left among working-class men. She ends, with a fine sense of paradox, begging that women's dress be seen as an inhibition not of demands for freedom, but rather of oppressive and degrading forms of labor, and that rather than submit to the threat of such labor or an increase in it, women should "add at least two yards to every skirt they wear. . ." The famous feminist, in other words, is invoking on behalf of the lower classes just that hierarchical principle on which lower-class tight-lacers acted instinctively: the right to the insignia of leisure.

The correlation between tight-lacing and female servitude breaks down on the most basic historical level: those periods when the corset was abandoned altogether, around the French Revolution and after the First World War, are not recognizably those of female emancipation; rather, the very opposite. The period when tight-lacing reached its peak, the 1870s and 1880s, was one in which the feminist movement was truly launched and highly productive. The last third or quarter of the 19th century was moreover a time of considerable liberalization in attitudes toward sex (as to social reform generally), after the high period of repression in the early and mid-Victorian era, as is revealed in various aspects of custom and culture, in art and literature, in the growth of sport for both sexes, the use of birth-control, etc. Increasing sexual explicitness at this time (down to and perhaps not excluding pornography) contributed to rather than hindered the emancipation of woman. The perception (and self-perception) of woman as a sexual object, which has degenerated so horribly in the commercial media of our own age, represented a necessary, pioneering and even courageous effort to come to grips with instinctual, life-enhancing components of human nature, which the previous age sought to suppress. To pursue the question of the role of the late 19th century "sexual revolution" (a term with a definition then very different from our own) as a factor of social liberation of both man and woman, would take us too far; but it does provide the context within which the problem of sartorial sexualization through tight-lacing, high heels, etc., should be viewed. It is my thesis that, insofar as this kind of sexualization contributed to the breakdown of the repressive stereotype of woman as a passive, exclusively home and children oriented and indeed essentially sexless creature, it should be regarded as progressive.[78]

In the late 1860s there appeared in England the first great literary manifestoes of feminism (by John Stuart Mill and Josephine Butler), and the publication in a popular woman's journal of the first literary "manifesto" of fetishism. Reactionary male voices were raised to condemn both, in the same magazines, in the same breath. The "fetishistic" decade of the 1870s was also that in which higher education was opened to women. The emancipated so-called "Girl of the Period" was accused of going in for Women's Rights and outrageous fashions, including an 18 inch waist. Excess in corsetry, sport and booklearning was bracketed as equally unhygienic. (One day) "it will be a crime for a young wife voluntarily to ill-treat her person, either by excessive study, or excessive attention to sports, by tight-lacing. . . ."[79] The artificially cultivated figure and artificially cultivated mind both led to feminine neurasthenia.

Women who publicly proclaimed, in word and deed, that they tight-laced to please men were not affirming their subservience to the male so much as asserting their right to appeal to his—and their own—libido. In so doing, they drew upon themselves accusations of infantilism, barbarism, sexual depravity, masturbation, drug addiction, atheism, and most frequently of all, contempt for the sacred duties of the mother.

SURPLUS OF SINGLE WOMEN, MATERNITY CRISIS

Some hard demographic and economic factors underlay the movement for female emancipation. From mid-century onwards Victorians became more and more worried over the statistically proven surplus of single women,[80] which in 1875 was used as an explanation for the unparalleled (fetishistic) flamboyance of the reigning fashion: "The reasons for the present extraordinary luxury of dress is that the surplus millions of women are husband-hunting and resort to extra attractions to that end."[81]

At the same time the great period of "mid-Victorian prosperity" was sensed to have reached an end, money became tight (especially after the Depression of the 70s), men became even more reluctant to marry, and families began to shrink in size. Progressive reduction in infant mortality had contributed to the increased family, which was now felt as an intolerable economic burden. In the second half of the 19th century abortions among middle-class married women increased; infanticide and baby-farming were also becoming alarmingly common. Married women were accused of provoking abortions by means of unusual sporting exertions during the first months of pregnancy.[82] In 1868 the conservative *Saturday Review* (also a vocal enemy of the tight-lacers) was wont to moan that "society has put maternity out of fashion," and eight years later actually was accusing women of refusing to submit to their husbands' sexual demands for fear of pregnancy. *The Englishwoman's Domestic Magazine* (standard-bearer of fetishism) dared to print an article in 1877 entitled "Have we too many children?" That same year the subject of birth-control gained wide publicity, in the wake of the sensational prosecution of Charles Bradlaugh and Annie Besant for publishing a pamphlet containing advice on the practice.

As families shrank, women and men became (in the words of John Stuart Mill) "for the first time in history, really each other's companions, . . . with woman no longer either a plaything or an upper servant."[83] Children ceased to be "fashionable," to the point that the new woman, according to a cartoon of 1899, warns her husband that if he wants any children at all, he had better take a mistress.[84]

The desire to practice birth-control has been linked by a distinguished modern costume historian to the increasing and fetishistic luxury of underwear during this period;[85] the connection would warrant exploration. A French magazine of 1888 darkly hints that "birth-control" resulting from sexual perversion and impotence, both associated with a taste for the newly fashionable black corsetry, is causing depopulation on a national scale[86] (the great fear of the French, after their defeat in the Franco-Prussian war, vis-à-vis unified and populous Germany).

The "cuirasse style" of the 1870s, with its tightly swathed hips following the age of the crinoline, may be viewed as little less than the overt denial of that maternity which, as we have seen, had "gone out of fashion". The anal emphasis of the bustle in the 1880s and in the popular graphics of the period might reflect an increase in anal intercourse, if such could be proven; it stands, at the very least, as another "anti-maternal" effect concentrating the "maternal" fullness of the crinoline at the back, and enhancing the smooth compressed belly at the front.

Tight-lacing in its heyday, and especially during the "cuirasse" period, may thus be interpreted as an unconscious (and perhaps conscious) protest against the total absorption of woman into a life of constant child-bearing and rearing, and the limitation of her sexuality to exclusively procreative ends.[87] Increased competition for a husband contributed to a heightened sexual consciousness, which left woman reluctant to enter passively into that traditional maternal role already undermined by economic conditions. The families of tight-lacers seem to have been small. Physicians accused women of using tight-lacing as a deliberate abortion device; it is probable that tight-lacers tended to use the contraceptive techniques developed during the last two decades of the century. Emile Zola in his later years defines the tight-lacer as a vain, frivolous and sexually depraved woman who wishes to avoid the basic social responsibility of bearing and raising children. But earlier, the same writer had shown, with compassion, how the corset was used by unmarried, lower-class girls to conceal pregnancy and, wilfully or not, to provoke an abortion or still-birth. In *Gone With the Wind* the heroine who, in her sexual pride, finds that maternity has added inches to her tight-laced slenderness, refuses to have any more children. Scarlett may well incarnate her creator's memory of a truly cultural propensity. Most telling of all is the example of the Empress Elizabeth of Austria, a tight-lacer in her youth and always obsessed with her own slenderness, who risked severe political and social censure for her refusal, after the age of 31, to attempt to give the Empire a second son—and left the Empire eventually without any direct heir at all.

In sum: the young girl of the late Victorian era tight-laced in protest against the stereotyped social role awaiting her, and in hopes of attracting a man for whom companionship and erotic pleasures weighed more than parenthood and family.

AN "OPPRESSED MINORITY"

Never "fashionable" in the sense of being generally acceptable to the wealthier classes, tight-lacing stands out as a minority cult which tended to cut across lower and middle class-boundaries. From mid-19th century, corsets were mass-produced, and cheap. By the later 19th century cheap mass-produced corsets were specifically advertised as suitable for tight-lacing. The incidence of the practice among workers, servants, shop assistants, courtesans, and lower-middle-class women generally was sufficiently marked, especially towards the end of the century, for reformers to be able to stigmatize it as "the very badge of vulgarity." "Common women may be instantly recognized by the long, indented dress-waist heavily outlining the hips . . . (which is) vulgar and tasteless". Its major concentration was probably among the lower-middle classes, and that otherwise "respectable", middle-middle class, such as composed the readership of the philo-fetishist *Englishwoman's Domestic Magazine,* although we also find occasional complaints that the bad example was set by the "so-called leaders of fashion" (none of whom is, however, identified or identifiable by name).[88]

The tight-lacer stood in a very difficult position within a society generally and vocally hostile to the practice. Whatever her class or motives, whether she acted out of a calculated or instinctive exhibitionism, whether she was moved by a conscious or unconscious spirit of defiance, the tight-lacer cannot have persisted for long in the practice without being confronted with the tremendous moral stigma attached to it. This was especially true in the 1880s and 90s, when lines were more clearly demarcated, the reformers became more strident and the fetishists more audacious. In closing ranks against the enemy, they developed the identity and something of the psychology of an oppressed minority.

The accusation of tight-lacing was a serious one. It cannot have been easy for any girl or young woman, whatever her compensations in the form of male admiration, to cope with being officially branded as a depraved, criminal being, as a potential infanticide and willful destroyer of posterity. It is thus not surprising that few tight-lacers could admit publicly to the practice, although they might confess to it privately and to the sympathetic magazine readership. Rather, they would claim that their slenderness was inherited, was natural, had nothing to do with corsets which hung loose about them, etc. Depending upon the degree to which their figure gave credence to the charge, the onus was upon them to prove that the practice was not detrimental to their health, by engaging in sport, leading an active life, and generally maintaining an appearance of good health.

SPORT AND HEALTH

The improvement in health which medical science had offered to the Victorian middle-classes was offset, as they saw it, by the sedentary and self-indulgent nature of their life. Consequently they prized the recreative value of sport very highly indeed. Sport had been designed for men, but gradually and against continuous opposition, women won the right to join them. Walking and riding in mid-century, skating and croquet in the 60s, archery and tennis in the 70s, rowing and gymnastics in the 80s, bicycling and golf at century's end: woman became progressively more free in the use of her body.

Each sport seems to have had its effect upon fashion. Cross-country hikes were facilitated by crinoline, as was croquet, insofar as legs were thereby freed of clinging petticoats; tennis encouraged the reduction of the skirt both in width and length; gymnastics aided the adoption (in the gymnasium) of breeches which, with the advent of bicycling, became more or less acceptable public wear.

With her admission to each new type of sport, woman passed a milestone in the emancipation of her sex. But, in spite of such apparent "advances" in her costume mentioned above, she did not achieve a simple and linear, progressive emancipation from the physical restrictions of fashion. Each "advance" was ambiguous, and contained a regressive element. Exaggerated breadth of skirt accompanied the new "freedom" of the crinoline, and subsequently, exaggerated narrowness of the skirt at the knees seemed to more than offset the advantage of a raised hemline. Why did women emancipated enough to engage in sport not adopt "emancipated" reform costume? And why does the heyday of tight-lacing fall into the very period (1870s and 80s) when women established themselves in sports which the practice would appear to inhibit?

The preservation of "impractical" fashions on the playing-fields had to do with the requirement that sport, as long as it was promoted as a social activity between the sexes (as tennis pre-eminently was), become yet another opportunity for exhibitionism and sexual competition. The tight-lacer, whose figure was cultivated to those ends, found sport a good pretext for displaying it in motion and to aesthetic advantage.

It is a curious fact accepted by fashion chronicle, cartoon, and fetishist correspondence alike that many tight-lacers took more than the usual amount of exercise, were of superior physical agility, and enjoyed exceptionally good health. Pupils of the boarding schools where tight-lacing was common stressed that long open air walks were an essential part of the curriculum, and that such schools were in consequence remarkably free of illness. There may, of course, be a physiological basis for the urge to take regular physical exercise on the part of those who imposed extreme constraints upon their cardio-vascular system (the need to keep the blood circulating, relieve pressure on the heart and lungs, etc.).

Another benefit claimed by and on behalf of tight-lacers was that their addiction inhibited over-indulgence in eating and drinking. Males sang the praises of severe self-corsetting as a cure for personal corpulence and chronic indigestion, and female tight-lacers valued the "overwhelmingly" hygienic side-effect of inducing sparse diet.

Another unexpected by-product of tight-lacing which is to the modern mind distinctly progressive and rational is the tendency to wear less clothing altogether. The average Victorian woman wore layer upon layer of underclothing, which added (in contemporary estimates) an average of fourteen to sixteen thicknesses of material, or an extra two to three inches at the waist. The average woman's winter street costume weighed 37 pounds.[89]

Anxious to minimize anything which threatened to enlarge the "sacred circumference", tight-lacers had every incentive to lighten and reduce their clothing all round, the younger ones typically wearing above the hips no more than the sheerest silk combination, corset, and outer dress. They discarded all other undergarments to a degree which contemporaries found perfectly astonishing, and threatening at once to their health and morality.

This is yet another unexpected and paradoxical example (which could be multiplied with regard to other objects of fetish interest, such as sandals), of how the fetishist, wearing less in order to reveal more, may be regarded in a progressive light.

THE CORSET AS A POLITICAL SYMBOL

One of the most curious and tenacious embellishments of corset history is the legend of Catherine de' Medici, 16th century Queen and

Queen Mother of France, having tyrannically imposed exceptionally severe corsets (according to the English, with a "standard" 13 inch waist) upon her hapless female subjects. We treat in the appendix (p. 320) the origin, accretion and proliferation of this legend, which is entirely lacking in historical foundation, but which fits in here insofar as it raises to an historical (or pseudo-historical) and political level, the tradition which sees the corset as a means of social oppression, and tight-lacing as a manifestation of female enslavement.

It was French liberal-romantic historians who created the distorted picture of Catherine as a luxury-loving tyrant. In the embellishment of legend that makes her also an enforcer of tight-lacing, the view of the corset as agent of social and physical oppression merged with the need to turn certain political leaders into tyrant-figures. This bizarre fusion was facilitated by the literary use of lacing as a metaphor for many kinds of pressure, political, financial, administrative, religious, geographic, etc. (cf. figs. 26 and 27).[90] The tyranny and depravity of Catherine's regime was further indicated by the transvestite tendencies of her son, King Henri III (whom she supposedly dominated, and who, according to Bernard de Palissy, did wear a busk), and his effeminate male favorites, the *mignons*. Such depraved habits were contrasted with the manly tastes, betokening wise rule, of his successor Henri IV. According to the distinguished art and social historian Henri Bouchot, France had been virile at the time of Rabelais and François I, but after the death of his short-lived successor Henri II and with the dominance over her sons of his wife Catherine, began the political and moral degeneration of the race which was hastened by savage corsetting.[91]

The polemic against the political and sartorial culture of the past common to many liberal cultural histories of the ancien regime, was clearly colored by antipathy to political regimes and fashions of the writer's own age which he perceived as analogous. At the same time, the corset acquired a broader and more favorable, or at any rate, mixed political role as a symbol of female militance, resistance to clerical oppression, and combativeness in the war of the sexes.[92] The new cuirasse style in fashion summoned up medieval associations, the age of heroism, heavy armor, and Jeanne d'Arc.[93] The cuirasse corset became a diffuse and bizarre nexus of patriotic, militarist and even martyrological sentiment, which was united in the immensely popular person of Jeanne d'Arc, then being promoted for canonization, and represented in many armor-breasted effigies throughout France. Since everyone knew that her patriotic sacrifice had involved the donning of armor, it was sometimes humorously (and at least once seriously) suggested that she was the inventor of the supposedly very French "corset-cuirasse." The discovery of old, supposedly medieval iron stays gave weight to the supposition.[94] A famous French corset manufacturer (Plument) advertised the "corset-cuirasse Jeanne d'Arc." The descendants of Jeanne's English enemies frivolously slandered her by claiming she died as a martyr not to the salvation of France, but to the tyranny of fashion—a victim of tight-lacing.[95]

The cuirasse fashion, like the Joan of Arc revival, followed closely upon the catastrophic defeat of France by Prussia in 1871. French caricature shows Frenchman and Frenchwoman, cuirassiers and cuirassières, both donning armor in the spirit of revenge; or else, the women putting on the armor the cavalry was leaving off. The Germans on their side, for whom the whole dress reform movement acquired a decidedly nationalist tinge ("Reformtracht" was often identified with a "Nationaltracht" based upon early 16th century German fashion), accused the French fashion tyrants of having invented the corset in order to impose it on other nations, and summoned German patriots to throw off the cultural yoke symbolized by the Korsett just as they had thrown off the political yoke of the Korse (Corsican, Napoleon).[96] They also identified, not inaccurately, tight-lacing fetishism as a (primarily) English perversion.[97] The term "tight-lacing" has no exact equivalent in any other language.[98]

The yoke of the corset was indeed cast off—by government fiat. The corset, used so often as symbol of political repression, was declared illegal in those countries of Eastern Europe regarded as the most socially retarded and politically repressive, and where women had the fewest rights: Russia, Bulgaria, and Rumania, all of which banned corsets in girls' schools. In Prussia, the female factory workers of Spandau were forbidden to wear the corset at work because it alledgedly made them sleepy and slothful. These are hardly the actions of governments bent upon the emancipation of women, but rather of those which identified the corset as an individualizing, sexualizing and work-distracting factor incompatible with the social subjection of women, especially in the lower classes, upon whom economic productivity depended. The propensity of working-class girls in Germany to tight-lace was even adduced as a defense for their being paid less than men for the same job: being relatively incapacitated physically, they *must* be less productive economically.[99]

The sense that the corset represented a quintessentially female weapon with quintessentially female and subversive associations lent it symbolic currency at times of political emancipation movements. The recognition that to attack the corset was to attack woman, and that in order to attack woman one could use the corset as her symbol, carried as its corollary the idea that woman, under attack, should rise in solidarity to defend that symbol. This is, in effect, what happened

in the English magazine correspondence of the 1860s. But twenty
years earlier, in the pre-revolutionary year 1847, at a time when the
rising tide of socialism was joined by the first voices for female
emancipation, the foremost satirical magazine of Germany imagined
a "Corset Revolution."[100] Under this heading, filling the first three
pages of an eight page weekly issue decorated with some rousing
vignettes (a woman publicly haranguing her sisters, another in-
timidating her husband, a third engaging in heroic tight-lacing), there
appeared a series of mock newspaper reports, which may be summarized as follows:

At Hüpfenheim during an official ball given by the mayor, the
virtuous but excessively tight-laced Fräulein Rosamunde Yberg suddenly exploded after the fifth allemande, with a detonation that broke
all the windows in the town, and with such violence that her limbs
were hurled around the ballroom, killing two students including one
who was beheaded by the flying busk.

The mayor thereupon ordered all corsets confiscated and destroyed, personally conducting a house-to-house search to this end.
An auto-de-fé was prepared in the marketplace to burn all the lethal
instruments, and the flames were already leaping merrily when a
variously armed mob of women and girls stormed the poorly defended town hall, wreaked havoc upon documents and windows,
threatened to burn the building to the ground, and stoned the mayor.
The women recovered a major part of the corsets, and carried them
around in triumphal procession. The civic guard was prevented from
intervening by their wives, according to first reports forcibly so, but
according to later ones, owing to the sabotage they suffered by the
wives' cutting of their suspenders.

The revolt is now spreading as the girls from the surrounding
countryside join it and stream to the town. It is—incredibly—the
sister of the original victim who is leader of the insurrection, which
demands Freedom for Woman. It is reported that women have laced
men to death, and the soldiers of the line sent to restore order have
gone over to the side of the rebels.

The next day all is back to normal, women have resumed their
usual occupations, the only exceptional symptoms observable being
that the women are very tight-laced and the food is oversalted. The
revolt was fomented by discussion of the question of the emancipation of women, broached by certain "ladies perverted by the literature." But these fanatics got no support because the majority of the
rebels feared that something bad lay behind the foreign word "emancipation."

An Act for the Abolition of the Corset is now before the sanitary
authorities. One Barthel Kroglinger, a domestic servant with the

Yberg family, has been arrested and charged with complicity in the plot, and for having been the wilful accessory to homicidal lacing.

This fantasy embodies a classic revolutionary process, and a classic tactical recipe for stemming it. The initial martyrdom by tight-lacing is due to an explosion, which dramatizes at once the evidence for social suffering, and the need to arm the people; it is also reminiscent of a home-made bomb killing its maker during manufacture. Also killing others, it becomes a lethal threat to society at large. It is seen as a provocation, like a small demonstration or strike, the potential violence of which the authorities, or the press, choose to blow up out of all proportion. (The parodistic report and counter-report format, which my summary rather ignores for brevity's sake, devised by a satirical journal writing from a moderate or liberal viewpoint, mocks the interest of the press, whatever its political position, in exaggerating, polarizing and politicizing trivial incidents.)

The subsequent repressive measures and forcible disarmament undertaken by the mayor, which are deemed justified by the initial provocation, are met dialectically by a wide-based, armed popular insurrection, which is accompanied by an effort to undermine the militia and regular soldiery, some of whom fraternize (so to speak) and appear to secede, and the formulation of "extreme" and revolutionary demands (Freedom for Woman).

Suddenly all returns to normal, and but for some minor residual acts of defiance, the revolt fizzles out, because it is proven to be lacking in a real popular base, and only the work of a few, foreign fanatics. To cap it, and prevent a resurgence, the authorities prepare to declare illegal the very means of the provocation (i.e. the corset, representing the right to protest, or bear arms) which sparked the revolt. Finally, the government makes selective, exemplary arrests.

The enactment around 1900 of laws to abolish the corset among the lower classes, like the medieval sumptuary laws which we shall cite, represented an effort at social control of a type whose anachronism was offset by the fact that the object of the legislation was fast losing fashionable sanction among the middle and upper classes, and thereby its status symbolism. But even at this time one of France's leading cartoonists could view it as the last bastion of female resistance to male authority of all kinds, defying Law, Religion, Medicine, Philosophy, Aesthetics and Reason, culminating in the most telling image of the paradox of corset-as-prison-as-protest (frontispiece).

The image of the power-hungry, calculating, manipulative, upwardly mobile woman is omnipresent—one is tempted to say absolutely dominant—in French caricature magazines of the last third of the 19th century. She appears typically in the form of the cocotte or courtesan, and is typically represented in her boudoir, talking to her keeper or husband-figure, lover, maid or female friend. Graphically the contrast between the woman and the man she confronts is striking: she is all shape and flexibility, he is shapeless and rigid. She is, typically, in a state of semi-dress or undress, usually in a corset, often in the process of getting in or out of it. It is thus armored that she exercises her control over men and society, proving time and again her superior guile and moral (or immoral) strength in the matter of economic advantage. Her corset is both the symbol of her potential or theoretical availability, and of her self-control, which renders her ultimately invulnerable, always victorious, in the war of the sexes.

Notes

1. Cole, p. 17.

2. Havelock Ellis, who should have known better, called the "foot-bandage" of the Chinese *strictly* (his stress) comparable to the "waist-bandage" of the West (1910, III, p. 22).

3. Especially since the excessively, inconveniently and "dangerously" long nail, frequently on a single thumb, but also on several and even all the fingers, is becoming increasingly common among women, and is also appearing among men. The readiest explanation is that of protest against the drudgery of so many female occupations requiring some manual and little mental skill, such as typing.

4. Cf Maurice North for a malignant view of this relatively benign form of fetishism.

5. Cf Rachewiltz p. 129. There may be a connection with algolagnia. Cf. "Her belt had left a red mark around her waist; she looked as if she had been flagellated" (Montherlant, p. 29). Isak Dinesen saw the marks in a more poetic light: ". . . with her waist still delicately marked by the stays, as with a girdle of rose-petals" (p. 13). Erotic massage is suggested by Harsanyi (p. 226): "in the evening as she undressed . . . she rubbed the reddish weals on her skin just as cosily as her mother."

6. The fantasy lives more in the minds of the reformers than in those of the fetishists. Cf Germaine Greer, a scholarly if hardly impartial source, who believes that removal of the lower rib was *customary* (!) among tight-lacers (*Female Eunuch*, p. 34–35).

Nor can one credit the word of the podiatrist, who writes with prurient glee of the "sex-scars and pleasure wounds" resulting from the "not uncommon" incidence of women having "their little toe amputated to be able to get the foot into a smaller shoe" (Rossi p. 181).

7. The evident relationship between the styling of clothes and that of the automobile has led the business expert into the curious suggestion that the automobile, too, has been "tight-laced." In his *Waste-Makers* (1960, p. 87) Vance Packard reports this analogy between waist-making in fashion and cars: "Fins began jutting up as stylists sought to push mid-sections lower and lower . . . The analogy between this squashing effect and tight-lacing of the waist and expansion of the skirt in the crinoline era [or more relevantly, of course, the 1950s], is almost irresistible. The tail fin is a last resort of over-extension, an outcropping that quite seriously serves much the same purpose as the bustle or train."

It would seem that industrial designers have succeeded in infiltrating erotic wasp-waists elsewhere. Raymond Loewy, creator of the Coca Cola bottle, described it as "the bottle with the hour-glass figure."

8. L. Bechstein in *Fliegende Blätter*, v. 69 (1878), p. 15.

9. Butin, 1900, p. 23, citing the *Lancet*.

10. I, p. 171. The fetishist confessions seldom stress asceticism in any orthodox

religious sense. The following is an exception: "My aunt herself insisted on lacing her, and as my sister occasionally appeared uncomfortable, my aunt, who was a Puseyite (the High Church movement which revived ancient doctrines of penitence) would say in a severe tone of religious admonition: 'My dear child, if your corset hurts you at all, suffer it for the love of God' " (Seeker).

11. "The Girls" by H.A.B., *Judge*, 5 Dec. 1885, p. 10.

12. "Brauttoilette" in *Wiener Caricaturen*, 22 March, 1890, p. 3 and ibid 1 March, 1890, p. 5.

13. It was translated (over considerable opposition) into English in 1892. The various enlarged editions absorbed specialist studies such as that by Binet, first in the field with a monograph in 1888.

14. Officialdom regarded hair-despoliation as among the most contemptible of crimes, at once petty larceny and petty bodily aggression. Epidemics of this around 1890 may have been responsible for some extraordinary severe sentences imposed at the time for even innocuous manifestations of the fetish. Although hair-fetishism is of no direct concern to us, we may pause to contemplate the degree of moral vindictiveness shown by the law. The French police doctor Paul Garnier in his monograph of 1896 tells the story of a seventeen-year-old boy watching a show in the Tuileries gardens, and pressing up to a girl whose hair he silently, amorously rolled between his fingers, so softly that she did not even notice. Suddenly two plainclothes policemen sprang upon him. One seized with his hand the boy's erect penis through his trousers, and cried, "At last we've got you . . . after all the time we've been watching you!" Garnier impassively adds that for this harmless act the boy was sentenced to three months in jail (p. 70; Krafft-Ebing, case no. 101).

15. Stekel II p. 350.

16. Langner p. 178.

17. "Aversion therapy" is sometimes euphemistically called "negative conditioning." To summarize the procedure of D. F. Clark, 1963: The patient, who suffered from the compulsion to wear a woman's girdle during the day, was given a subcutaneous apomorphine injection. He was then allowed to put on his beloved female underwear, and a soliloquy on the delights of his fetish was played back to him, at ever increasing volume as the nausea progressed. He was told to look at pictures of corsetted women while he vomited; it was even arranged that he vomit on his favorite photograph. The treatment consisted of sixteen half-hour sessions, after which the patient was declared "cured." Vernon Grant in 1953 records a case of a man who was arrested and jailed merely for following high-heeled girls in the street; his photograph was even published in the newspapers.

18. The respectable *San Francisco Chronicle* publicized the case of "Carl," a young man incarcerated in Vacaville prison for 12 years, on the charge of masturbation ("lewd and lascivious conduct"). He had been observed through the keyhole of his bedroom by his landlady who called the police (*Los Angeles Free Press* 6 April, 1972).

19. Naecke 1910, p. 168, and Veriphantor p. 26.

20. The major contribution is that of Karl Abraham who in 1912 treated a case of tight corset and high-heel fetishism in a youth. His interpretation of the sado-masochistic mechanism has a chillingly authoritarian ring.

21. The psychoanalytic method entered costume theory through Flügel, whose pioneering *Psychology of Clothes* (1930) with its brilliant synthesis of sexual, sociological and economic determinants, has had a profound effect on two leading costume historians of our own day, C. W. Cunnington and James Laver, and has yet to be superseded. Flügel's particular contribution is to have first isolated the sexually symbolic components of various aspects of dress, and then to have determined their social symbolism. Sexual and hierarchical principles are thus perceived as mutually supportive, and it is the interplay of these principles which is illuminated by the study of sculptural fashions.

In the 60s a number of popular paperbacks on fetishism appeared, by Carlson Wade, Hugh Jones and, notably, Dr. Harvey Leathem, which contain some very arresting but entirely unverifiable case-material, especially as regards the operation of fetishist clubs.

22. Henry Murger 1852, p. 146.

23. Cf Rossi, who however overemphasizes the sexual to the virtual exclusion of all other factors in the folklore of foot and shoe.

24. Rossi, p. 5.

25. Apart from the hierarchical symbolism of the small foot, we may consider a symbolic parallelism with a small clitoris (promising compression of the penis): "She had a temptingly small foot, giving tokens of the excellent smallness of the delicious slit" (*The Pearl*, 1879, quoted by Pearsall, p. 71).

26. Voiart in 1822 (p. 286) believed that a well-arched instep on a shoe (heel-less at that time) could reduce a 6 or 7 inch foot to 5 inch length.

27. Despite the Master's silence on the subject, Stekel stressed the role of the heel (notably when broken or wobbling) in castration anxiety. A present-day psychoanalytic popularizer (Edmund Bergler, *Fashion and the Unconscious*) has linked the idea of compression with castration. Believing fashion to be the creation of homosexuals (whose "cure" was his specialty), he argues that women's constrictive clothing is a projection of the male homosexual castration complex.

28. Flower, p. 345. In the statistical sample collected by the podiatrist Lelièvre (p. 104), 49% were found to have this kind of foot ("Egyptian foot") and 22% had the second toe longer ("Greek foot"). 21% had the big and second toes equal in length. A statistical survey from another source (cited ibid.) revealed 73% Egyptian and 6% Greek. The Greek (i.e., "fashionable") foot is apparently that of the minority.

The pioneer of evolutionary anthropology, Petrus Camper, also the author of the first critical monograph on fashionable footwear (1791), observed that the high-heeled shoe worn by humans suggested "equinism" and thus another evolutionary stage.

29. "Bilateral symmetry" in footwear also possessed an advantage which had little to do with aesthetics, and much to do with economics: one shoe-maker's last and one pattern were sufficient, so long as no distinction was made between right and left shoe, for both pointed in the center at the same place. Deep into the 19th century cheaper shoes knew not their left from their right, and while the more expensive made-to-measure shoe (like all modern footwear) did observe the distinction, one cannot discount the influence of an older commercial consideration upon the perpetuation of aesthetic preference for the pointed effect. In 1822 a Philadelphia shoe manufacturer introduced lefts and rights but received no public response whatever. They were ridiculed as "crooked shoes" (Rossi p. 170).

30. It is a major lacuna that Ray L. Birdwhistell, the pioneer of the new science of Kinesics, makes no reference whatsoever to the role of costume in determining modes of body-communication.

31. Lewin, p. 92, accepting the empirical evidence that many women find walking actually more comfortable on high than low heels, notes that the strain on the Achilles tendon is transmitted to the hamstring muscles, knee, thigh, hip and back. Rossi, p. 165–66, illustrates and describes how the angle of the pelvic bone doubles when a woman is wearing three inch heels, compared with no heels, as does the "mobility of the buttocks".

Most podiatric writers are hostile to fashionable shoes, without explaining how high heels damage the foot, except to exacerbate hammer toe (hallux valgus) which is blamed in the first instance upon pointed toes. The standard manual of Lelièvre (p. 104) describes with distaste the typical high-heeled walk, and its dire physiological consequences in a manner which testifies more to theory than observation. Of the dozen or so extreme heel addicts personally known to me, none shows any deformity or damage to the foot whatsoever. One must assume, of course, that like dancers who subject their feet to the greatest strains of all, they had strong feet and well-balanced bodies to begin with.

32. It is curious that so sensitive and psychoanalytically oriented a writer as Willett Cunnington should reduce the function of the modern high heel and the tottering gait to an attempt on the part of emancipated woman to raise herself to the height of man. "The outcome (of such heels) seems to be that the foot—like the hand—is no longer a weapon of sexual attraction" (*Why Women*, p. 158).

33. The hierarchical and sexual are vividly fused by a major erotic novelist of the 18th

century, Restif de la Bretonne, in a passage from his autobiography (p. 211). He imagines his own genteel amorous attentions as having lent his lowly sexual partner the required slenderness, noting that the waist of the scullery-maid Jeanneton "which was usually thicker below than above, had grown more slender while I was taking my pleasure." Subsequently, in order to celebrate her seduction by a gentleman, which marks her initiation into the fashionable world, Jeanneton begins to wear fashionable stays.

34. Lacing as a permanent ritual for the preservation of youth and aesthetic/social surplus value are exquisitely conjured up in the first chapter of Victoria Sackville-West's *The Edwardians* where the tiny-waisted Duchess' toilette is observed by her 17 and 19 year-old children, and causes the boy Sebastian to become ashamed of his virginity.

35. Without entering into psychoanalytic considerations of breast-as-phallus, we may be observe that popular imagery of all kinds—advertising, cartoons, pin-ups—tend to fantasize on the phallic aggressive potential of the outsize female breast.

36. Greer, *The Female Eunuch*, p. 34.

37. Rossi, p. 63, and citing podiatrist J.R.D. Rice.

38. Cf Pestalozzi's model school: "While standing, sitting, writing and working, they (the poor, peasant children) were always taught to keep the body as erect as a candle" (*Leonard and Gertrude*, p. 154) and "uprightness of bearing is the outward sign of inner dignity; it distinguishes man from the beast. This belief, says Pestalozzi, is generally accepted, at least in the upper classes" (Silber, 1973, p. 185).

39. "Crossing one's legs looks disgusting, and is not permissible even en famille" (*Right Behaviour in All Situations*, 1883, quoted by Norgaard, p. 8). For masturbation in this position, cf below p. 171.

For the case of a shoe-fetishist sexually aroused by the motion of a slung leg swinging free from the knee, cf. Grant. For the slung leg in art used as a metaphor for sexual intercourse, cf. Steinberg.

40. Jacob Bronowski's film "Drive for Power" in his *Ascent of Man* series shows a charming French 18th century automaton of a fashionably dressed lady incorporating a special mechanism to make her breast heave.

41. Colette, *The Gentle Libertine*, p. 202. Cf the same writer's "The Photographer's Missus", a short story which throws curious light on the connection between breathlessness, tight-lacing, and fear of suffocation. "Unnatural agitation": Godman p. 189.

42. The only people who radically distort the neck are the Padouang, or giraffe-necked of Burma who extend it (on women only) by means of gradually added brass rings, up to 8 inches in height (Pl. 76).

43. The fainting of at least one high-collared guardsman during the Trooping of the Color in London has become a matter of tradition, which probably evolved in response to press criticism of Guards Regiments as idle, soft-living, and unnecessarily expensive luxuries. The fainting bridegroom is naturally considered more newsworthy than the fainting bride; one instance of the former was explicitly blamed (by the rector performing the service) on "his beastly tight regimental collar" (London *Sketch* for 16 Sep., 1957).

To the allied political leaders assembled at Naples in August, 1944, the tight collar of Marshal Tito, like his self-assumed military title, seemed a symbol of military-political arrogance. Churchill wrote "he wore a superb blue and gold uniform, very tight at the neck and remarkably ill-suited to the heat then raging." In the evening, for dinner "he was still encased in his gold-braided strait-jacket" (quoted in *Historia* magazine (Paris) No. 88, p. 2440.

The high collar of Hitler's finance minister Hjalmar Schacht seemed to symbolize the economic repression of a fascist regime, just as that of President Hoover "looking over the top of a high protective collar" (i.e. tariff bill of 1930) did the economic measures of a bourgeois-democratic regime (Blaisdell no. 70). The same idea was revived by Interlandi showing President Gerald Ford ("Gerald Hoover") in an enormous "conservative collar" such as he did not, of course, wear in reality (Los Angeles *Times* 19 Aug. 1976)

44. As the man plying the corset-lace pre-enacted his sexual service to the woman, so she tying his cravat symbolized her sexual service to him. Cf the Grévin cartoon where the mistress coos, "Come on now, be good, yes, sir . . . be good . . . otherwise you will tie your own cravat." Her posture, holding the cravat *ever* so tenderly, and even more that of the lover sitting with a ravished expression and his hands in his crotch, leave no doubt as to the sexual allusion (*Petit Journal pour Rire,* N.S. 21, 1869).

45. *La Vie Parisienne,* 1869, p. 119.

46. Flügel, p. 76.

47. This sensation is induced, occasionally to lethal degrees, by practitioners of masochistic strangulation, the most celebrated historic case of which was the "suicide" of the last Prince de Condé in 1830. An extreme case of voyeuristic collar-fetishism is described by a patient of Stekel (I, p. 289f): "To scratch these starched linens was pure delight. When shown by a handsome little friend the chafed spot in the neck caused by a tight collar, I experienced a sudden and overpowering sexual irritation, and ever since I have been spellbound as by a hellish influence . . . if the collar stood high, I would become dizzy with excitement . . . if I saw a woman in the street who wore a high collar, I would follow her until I would see her either adjust it with her hand or make some movement of her head which indicated that the collar was chafing her . . . in that instant I would feel as if struck by lightning." (The patient found a cooperative girl for whom he bought a collar). "I got her to go through the almost endlessly repeated movements of loosening with her finger the collar which I had purposely tied tightly about her neck until I noticed that she had chafed her skin. My joy and gloating were nothing short of the delight of a sadist. Every time her hand went to her collar, I suffered a pleasant jolt in the pit of my stomach."

48. And occasionally the tail also, which at certain periods was, as a matter of fashion, docked (i.e., cut short) and nicked (i.e., cut at the muscles which enabled it to hang down, so that it had always to stand upright). Nicking is now illegal.

49. In the stiffened bodice of 16th century court fashion, hierarchical symbolism was predominant, and perhaps overtly so (the Spanish nobility from whom the stiff style emanated to other European aristocracies, were notoriously "stiff" in manner and morals). This stiffness was gradually absorbed into folk-costume, preserving through the 19th century, among the wealthier peasantry, the status symbolism which the corset lost in the urban centers. The evolution of the bodice or Mieder (a word also used for the urban corset) in the folk-costume of a Swiss canton has been thus described: "The bodice was stiffened as hard as a board with cane or whalebone and widened in the back (beyond the armpits). The once comfortable and flexible bodice (of the pre-19th century period) with the elegant, narrow back was stiffened into a velvet-covered, armour-plated breast-piece" ("Zur Geschichte der Unterwaldner Tracht," in *Heimatleben* nr. 73, p. 73). The stiffness of the front bodice served in many forms of peasant costume as a frame and backing for the display of jewelry and ornament, which were, of course, the principal symbols of rank.

50. "Une toilette sévère, mais excessivement *juste*" (*Charivari,* 22 Oct. 1882. Pun intended, and word stressed in original).

51. La Belle Lisa, the heroine of *Le Ventre de Paris* (1873), is successful because her expansive animal-sexual nature, epitomized in her profession (pork-butcher) and the animals she sacrifices as the beautiful, voluptuous High Priestess of the bourgeois religion of Food, is kept tightly under control by her very personal, calculated, and socially pragmatic sense of self-discipline. She is also tight in money matters. All this comes together in her habitual costume, which contains two basic "fetishistic" elements symbolizing hygiene and control: great expanses of stiff white linen (huge apron, deep cuffs, tight collar), and a tight-laced corset under a tautly stretched bodice, which is referred to on repeated occasions in the course of the novel.

Her performance cutting meat is a ritual of power and seduction, during which muscular control is transferred to her corset. Here she is, closely watched by a delighted admirer: "Raising the cleaver with her solid, naked wrist, she struck three times, sharply. With each blow, the back of her black merinos dress rose markedly, while the whalebones of her corset stood out against the taut material of the bodice."

The beautiful butcher has a professional and sexual rival in the fishmonger, la Belle

Normande, who is also voluptuous, but in a softer, more flowing, looser way. Uncorsetted herself, she accuses Lisa of being "armoured" (blindée) and as tightly tied-in (ficelée) as one of her own pork sausages. Lisa's response to this rivalry, whenever it enters a new phase of publicity in Les Halles, is to tighten her corset further. She is indeed well-armoured, socially; and although successful to the very end, we understand that she is too hard, too clean, too cool in her icy-smooth corsage, and that her self-discipline is, at bottom, socially and economically self-interested and morally deficient (pp. 637, 666, 675, 736, 756 and 874).

From the many references to tight-lacing scattered through Zola's novels one might form a comprehensive tight-lacer personality stereotype. The excessively cool self-control and calculation projected by the heroine of *Le Ventre de Paris* has its counterpart in Clotilde Duveyrier, a subsidiary character in *Pot-Bouille* (1882). She is described as beautiful and possessed of "the quiet obstinacy of a woman cloistered within her (social) duties . . . Her breast and waist squeezed (sanglées) in a corset cuirassed in whalebones, she treated him (Octave Mouret, the hero) with a cool amiability." Like her rigorous piano practice, which is a social not artistic pursuit, her tight-lacing daily and from the moment she rose in the morning (the custom in France being to remain un- or mildly corsetted until leaving the house) is an index of her complete personal and social self-discipline, amid women letting themselves go and getting into trouble (pp. 238 and 367).

52. The male identification with the busk is enunciated in such verses as "I have of my lady the grace to rest at length upon her breast, whence I hear the sighs of a lover who would replace me", or "Every young lover kisses me with much tenderness. I serve to entertain and my normal place is on my mistress' heart", or, best of all: "How I (lover) envy his (busk's) happiness, stretched out softly upon this ivory-white breast. Let us please share this glory—you shall be there by day, I by night" (cited by Libron, p. 31).

53. "For the most divine beauty often jests with her busk". Cf. also La Fontaine's line indicating that an indiscretion on the part of the male might be playfully reproved by the lady's rapping him over the knuckles with her busk: ". . . Sottise / Qui me fera donner du busc sur les doigts" (cited by Libron, p. 28). Madame de Sevigné would withdraw it, when feeling tired and rheumatic, and put it between "flesh and chemise" as a stimulus, sitting meanwhile bolt upright on the edge of her chair (Cabanès p. 507).

54. This gave rise to obscene puns as in the cartoon of the frustrated (or elderly) lover complaining that he cannot find the hole; similarly, he cannot force his (foot) into the too-tight (boot) (Fuchs, III, Erg. figs 226 and 230).

55. The whole household hierarchy, down to the pet dog, is involved in the immense tug-of-war depicted by Montaut (repr. Kunzle, "Corset as Erotic Alchemy," pp. 154–5).
A misogynistic story by Alphonse Karr about the stupidity of women who ruin their social life by wearing too-tight shoes, refers, contemptuously, to the type who not only tolerates the "brodequin torture" but even uses her coachman, of all people, to lace her in ("Des souliers trop larges" from *De Loin et de Près*, reprinted in *Charivari*, 8 Aug. 1862).

56. Little Lover: Norris, *Blix* p. 5. Snuggle: Harsanyi p. 216. Silken vice: Witkowski, p. 293. Enjoys being squeezed: *Ally Sloper's Half Holiday*, 12 Jan. 1895, p. 13. Short arm: *Judge*, 6 April, 1889, p. 442 and *Pick-Me-Up*, 23 Nov. 1889, p. 113. Awaiting real thing: *World's Comic*, 20 July, 1892, p. 19. Irishman: *Judge*, 28 Dec. 1889, p. 190.

57. On the nuptial night: "trembling, joyful, your husband unlaces you with an ill-assured and clumsy hand, and you mischievously laugh at him, happily noting that his confusion is caused by the sight of your beauty. You are content to feel your omnipotence: you take good care not to help him undo the knots or to find his way about the lace-holes; on the contrary, you enjoy the feel of his groping fingers, which tickle you deliciously . . ." (*Vie Parisienne*, 1884, p. 271). Balzac's Valérie Marneffe coquettishly mocks her lover, Count Steinbock, for his slowness and clumsiness in lacing her up; and it is at this critical moment, as if caught in the very act of love, that they are suprised by the rival, Baron Montes, who thereupon decides to murder Valérie (*La Cousine Bette*, p. 494).

A mid-century cartoon by Gavarni is based upon a transference of the idea that a man has to know how to "open" a woman sexually: the mistress mockingly asks her lover, who is engaged in unlacing her corset: "Tell me, my little friend, do you like oysters?" "Yes, but I prefer women." "Do you know how to open them?" "!!!" In another Gavarni lithograph, the husband discovers in the evening that the lacing knot is not the same one as he made in the morning, and begins to doubt his wife's fidelity (*Charivari*, 18 Sep. 1840). The same motif was used by Reznicek in 1908, and elsewhere.

The most potent example of unlacing as symbolic of deflowering is in Balzac's *La Vieille Fille*, 1836, pp. 301–4. The rich old maid, Mademoiselle Cormon, tight-laces herself in order to impress a gentleman she hopes to marry, and faints when she hears he is already married. Her corset is cut, and she is revived by Du Bousquier, a suitor she had just refused but whom she thereupon feels obliged to marry, in view of the fact that she had "been seen by a man for the first time, her belt (of virtue) shattered, her lace broken, her treasures (earlier described, when the lace was cut, as "gushing forth like a flood of the Loire") violently cast out of their casket." It is evident that it is not merely the fact of being seen in her undress, semi-naked, which makes her feel deflowered; but also that the "chastity belt" she put on as a symbol of her desire to marry, and of her new sexual vulnerability, had been violently forced by an accident, which she interprets as supernatural sign.

Finally, we may cite a censor's response to the eroticism of unlacing. This passage from Flaubert's *Madame Bovary* (1857) undressing before her lover: "ripping apart the thin cord of her stays, which hissed around her hips like an adder gliding . . ." (cf. fig. facing p. 1) was singled out by the Public Prosecutor in the trial for obscenity to which that novel was subjected, as an "admirable description from the point of view of the talent employed, but an execrable one from the point of view of morality" (cf. Hemmings, p. 60).

58. Woman to lover: "Pull me really tight—you, at least! When my maid or husband do it, the corset never seems to hold" (*L'Image Pour Rire* No. 16, 23 July, 1892).

59. Young lady to maid: "Lace me as tight as possible!" Maid: "But Gnädiges Fräulein will be unable to breathe!" "No matter! once he has married me, I will be able to breathe freely enough" (Köystrand cartoon in *Wiener Caricaturen* 13 May, 1893, p. 1).

60. One should not be misled by the evidence of the trade journals and magazine advertisements, which never gave up on a potential children's market. As late as mid-20th century French trade journals were recommending the corsetting of pre-puberty girls ("fillettes"), presumably as a matter of psychological conditioning in the manner of the American "training bra"; but I have found no evidence that corsets were worn by this age-group.

61. A young girl's first lover's kiss and declaration is immediately consecrated by her first corset, which she embraces as the next most important ceremony after her first communion. She eagerly "cheats" to get the tape to measure small, and smaller still, over her bare skin, as she thinks "That is the finger of God, to a bride belongs a corset. At last I must be treated as an adult . . . this great, great wonderful love has really arrived at just the right time" (Harsanyi pp. 216 and 226).

62. A distant antecedent of this theory may be found in Erasmus Darwin, grand-father of the more famous Charles, who in the following passage glowingly evokes Hogarth's Line of Beauty (cf. p. 197) which the artist demonstrated (as Darwin well knew) upon the varying forms of the corset: "Beauty derives from the child's original association of pleasure with his mother's breast, which the infant embraces with its hands, presses with its lips, and watches with its eyes . . . And hence at our maturer years, when any object of vision is presented to us, which by its waving or spiral lines bears any similitude to the form of the female bosom . . . we feel a general glow of delight, which seems to influence all our senses (*Zoonomia*, 1794, I, 145–46).

Infant imprinting was little understood by the Victorians, for whom the transmission of physical traits was considered the primary factor. It was commonly assumed by the reformers that the offspring of a tight-lacer, whether she continued to tight-lace through pregnancy or not, would either become deformed in the womb or else, if apparently well-formed at birth, would inherit the mother's supposed constitutional debility (cf. Carter 1846). Such defects would automatically be passed on to the next generation. Unable to accuse mothers outright of tight-lacing their small daughters, the later ("Darwinian") reformers accused men of seeking out wasp-waisted brides, and begetting children with poor constitutions and unnaturally slender waists, which would be further weakened when the pairing cycle was repeated. An intuition that non-physical factors were also at play was thus vaguely expressed: "The hereditary tendency to commit these deforming acts is hereditarily received" (Richardson, p. 473; cf. Diffloth, p. 55).

63. Stekel I, p. 350.

64. The major sexological expert of the later Victorian age, William Acton, denied that women had any sexual feelings at all; even the pioneering Krafft-Ebing stated that in the normal, well-bred woman, sexual desire was small (cf. Marcus, and Comfort).

65. Fantasies of highly active as well as passive roles in sado-masochistic scenarios are transcribed in Nancy Friday's anthology of female sexual fantasies, including ritual piercing and *Story of O*-type situations. "It seems that the more liberated I become (I'm really digging Women's Lib. now) the more I fantasize about the spanking and bondage" (p. 155).

66. Cf Doris Langley Moore, p. 17.

67. Pp. 63 and 218. The fetish derived from a childhood experience of having to wear an orthopedic cast, combined with memories of wrestling bouts with a brother.

68. *Judy*, 24 Jan. 1872, p. 128.

69. Cf below p. 170f. Flügel (p. 100) observes merely that a "tight belt produces sensations somewhat similar to those that accompany contraction of the abdominal muscles." Willett Cunnington, a qualified medical practitioner as well as costume historian, does no more than extrapolate from fetishist confessions in the following terms: "the pressure on the pelvic organs provoked 'very agreeable sensations' of an erotic nature . . ." (*Why Women*, p. 162).

70. *Harper's Bazaar*, March 1946, p. 150.

71. For the 19th century experiment confirming this effect, cf. p. 176.

72. *Fantasia* No. 9.

73. Cleugh, p. 35. The concept is not entirely foreign to fashion advertising copy: "Your waist is a strap, a strop . . . a neat trick, dividing you like a lady sawed in half." Taken aback, perhaps, by the implication of the image, the writer hastily adds: "and pulling you together too (*Harper's Bazaar*, March, 1946, p. 150).

74. Riegel, p. 391.

75. Haller, p. 146 f.

76. Wettstein-Adelt, p. 14.

77. Kraditor, pp. 125–131.

78. For Haller, who equates tight-lacing with female weakness, it is female prudery which is "progressive," a refusal of sexual status and therefore a mark of independence.

79. Ellen Key, p. 84. The author does not mention tight-lacing or any other aspect of dress, except in this passing allusion, significant just because it is a passing allusion, and picks up what was evidently a common association of three very different kinds of supposed physical self-abuse.

80. In 1851 in England, out of 100 women over 20 years old, 57 were married, 12 widowed, and 30 were spinsters (Roberts in Vicinas p. 57. The proportion for Germany in 1901 was the same: 29% women never marry, cf. Heszky). Expressed in absolute figures, in 1851 there were 2,765,000 single women aged fifteen and over; twenty years later the figure had increased by 16.8% to 3,222,700 (Banks p. 27). Continuous male emigration exacerbated the problem.

The female surplus became the occasion of callous jokes about tight-lacing; according to the "Philosophic Observer," shocking as the practice was, it was socially beneficial because it killed off undesirable females and helped correct the imbalance of the sexes (*Funny Folks*, 17 Dec. 1881, p. 397).

81. Cited by Cunnington, *English Women's Clothing*, p. 275.

82. Banks, p. 86. Mohr points out (p. 20f.) that, nowhere illegal in the U.S. until 1820, abortion was progressively illegalized thereafter. Britain passed the first laws in 1803.

83. From an address to Parliament 1867, quoted by Banks, p. 73.

84. Lethève, p. 139.

85. Cunnington, *Underclothes*, p. 16.

86. *La Vie Parisienne*, 1888 pp. 88–89: "So you certainly need these black corsets, you modern lovers, young men who are old and old men trying to become young! So you need to see white skin emerging from a black sheath, because white skin in itself hardly arouses you any longer? You prefer this black underwear in the hope that it will revive your languishing desires . . ." Ladies are warned to stay clear of *soupirants* who dream aloud of such eccentric underwear, and to return to the white corset which reveals unhesitatingly the quality (i.e., virility) of the man privileged to behold it. (An added advantage of the white corset is that its immaculate freshness reassures the lover that it is uncontaminated by rival lips and fingers).

87. Cf. Stekel II, p. 17 f. for a case-history which connects tight-lacing and fear of pregnancy.

88. On the upward and downward mobility, and status symbol-seeking of the lower middle classes, see the recent collection edited by Crossick. In 1889 an editorial in the *Rational Dress Society's Gazette* (January, No. 4) urged ladies to refuse to employ wasp-waisted servants. "Badge of vulgarity": Haweis, *Dress, Health*, p. 138. Indented dress-waist: cited in Vanier, p. 26.

89. Haller p. 31. We have little difficulty in seeing the Victorians as morbidly over-protective of their bodies. For the psycho-physiological relationship between sensitivity to cold and the need for love, cf. Flügel, p. 188 f. Flügel, who sees the matter as one of crucial social and psychological significance, points out that compared with the late Victorian age, when they wore far more clothing than men, women of the 1920s wore far less—as they still do in many quarters.

90. Cf. Schiller: "Shall I force my body into stays, and constrict my will-power within the bonds of law?" (*Die Räuber*, 1782, I. 2.) The metaphor has survived the object on which it is based; cf. the book title *Le Corset de fer du fascisme* (by E-Paul Graber, 1935), or the recent elaboration, on a very self-consciously humorous scale, by a (London) *Daily Telegraph* article (29 Oct. 1976), à propos of the Bank of England's financial "corset" designed to stiffen sterling. Cartoons are rich in corset metaphors, reducing major public issues to levels both familiar and farcical: under the title "Administrative Pressure" the Prefect hauls in his portly wife, in preparation for an official ball (Draner in *La Caricature*, 17 May, 1883, p. 1). Men at a capstan lacing machine haul in a distressed fat lady, over the ironic caption "Blind and Struwe strain every muscle to give the Grandduchy of Baden more air" (by J. Schweller, 1844, Ingerl archive No. 113). The Jesuit tries to add an excessively tight-waisted skirt marked "Concordat for the Power of the Church" to the cloak of the Austrian constitution worn by Austria, who says "It's not worth the effort, my friend, I grew out of that long ago" (*Kikeriki*, 4 Aug. 1872). Similarly, and more cogently, the Jesuit oppresses Austria by tight-lacing her (*Der junge Kikeriki*, 6 March 1887). The Law and the Military tug on the laces of Die Deutsche Presse (cover of *Sud-Deutscher Postillion* nr. 4, 1895).

In a metaphor for the city wall as corset, the minister Dunajewski is invited, by a new law, to use the knife on the excessively tight laces binding the city of Vienna (*Kikeriki*, 30 March, 1884, p. 8). A French version of this idea shows the city of Paris as a young lady in the streets begging a passing military officer to be so kind as to loosen her corset (Stop in *Charivari*, 26 July, 1890, p. 139).

91. p. 125 (cf. pp. 5 and 273).

92. Fanton in 1879 called the cuirasse corset the battledress of the prostitute at war with Man, Morality and Society. The idea is reversed by the anti-clerical *Kikeriki* (Aug. 4, 1872) in a cartoon showing women wearing corset-armor to protect them when they enter the confessional. A "fashion-study" of corset-as-armor is captioned "Little State-of-Siege dress with cuirasse body" (*Der Floh*, 28 July, 1878). "Armor for the summer campaign" shows the Venus de Milo corsetted and off to the spa to conquer man and her tendency to obesity (*Wiener Caricaturen*, 1 May, 1892).

93. The "early medieval" origin of the corset may be traced back to the neo-classical period, when it was alleged that the "hardened vest" (i.e. cotte hardie) was adopted by women in order to repel the Gothic invader, and that "from Charlemagne to Elizabeth,

ladies were like a fortress, with impregnable bulwarks of whalebone, wood and steel" (citation from 1811 in Laver, *Clothes,* p. 19). The idea was often taken up later: "The old defences having proved insufficient by virtue of the progress in offensive weaponry, the opulent cities had the ingenious idea of turning the defences into the ornament of what they had to contain" ("Traité de la Fortification," *Paris s'amuse,* 1882, p. 305, with drawing of elegantly corsetted lady).

94. "Jeanne d'Arc wore a very curious corset-cuirasse, the masterpiece of a master-armourer of Paris. In the Cluny Museum one may see a corset entirely composed of iron blades . . . (which) dates from the 14th century" (Ivière, 1876) Cf. p. 146 below.

95. Cartoon by Alfred Chasemore in *Judy,* 10 Aug. 1887; the same idea in *Ally Sloper's Half Holiday,* 24 Dec. 1887.

96. "Woman! You vie with the men in your hatred of the Corsican. Hate also the Corset and free your body! Every pressure is a bond and chain, every foreign custom a disgrace. So cast your corsets, German woman, after the Corsican!" These lines, first publicized in the late 19th century, were attributed to the patriotic poet of the earlier Franco-German conflict, Justinus Kerner. In another German source the invention of the corset was blamed upon the English, particularly Queen Elizabeth who "compelled her ladies-in-waiting to imitate her" (Neustätter, p. 13)

Other historical curiosa relating to the alleged invention of the corset, which may reflect some confused political prejudice, are in the *Encyclopedia Americana* (ed. F.C. Beach, 1903–6), for which the corset is a German medieval invention, introduced into France at the time of the French Revolution, and in the *New International Encyclopedia,* 2nd ed. 1923, with roughly the same information. The dunce's cap must go to the English popular weeklies of the mid 20th century, who commonly held Queen Victoria personally responsible for the spread of tight-lacing, perhaps because of her reputation for being morally "strait-laced" in character. One's imagination boggles at the thought of that prim and dumpy little monarch indulging in or condoning the most scandalous fashion of the age.

97. *John Bull beim Erziehen.* This collection of letters translated from the *Family Doctor* some time during the Boer War, testified, according to the Preface, to the British national character of "egoism, imperiousness and rapacity." The hypocrisy is blatant, since the translation obviously caters to Germans with exactly the same fetishes in exactly the same way.

98. The nearest French equivalent is "les corsets serrés" (tight corsets) which describes the particular object in a particular state, not a human physical condition and process. The phrases "se serrer" (tighten or squeeze oneself) and "se sangler" (literally to strap oneself) are by no means exclusive to the operation of the corset, although the addition of the phrase "à outrance, à étouffer", etc., usually connotes it, or a belt. The Germans say "das enge Schnüren" and "das Engschüren" (cf. Rosy, p. 75), but the latter, which appears to represent the verbal form exactly equivalent to "tight-lacing" does not seem to be in common use (it is not in Grimm's *Dictionary*).

By the late 17th century the English had coined the term "strait (or streit) laced", and by the late 18th century "tight laced". Around mid-nineteenth century tight lacing became tight-lacing and tightly laced became tight-laced. With the acquisition of the hyphen, an adverbial phrase defining a special condition became a noun defining a commonplace concept.

99. Wettstein-Adelt, p. 14f.

100. *Fliegende Blätter,* 5 (1847), nr. 115, pp. 145–47.

CHAPTER ONE

From Ancient Crete to Neoclassicism

The Ancient and Medieval World: The Minoan Belt; Greco-Roman Naturalism; Medieval Prudery

T he earliest "civilized" and for a long time thereafter the only Western culture to practice body-sculpture was the Minoan, which flourished on the island of Crete c.2000–c.1400 B.C., as the most advanced civilization in the Mediterranean. To historians of costume, the Minoan combination of face-painting, breast-exposure and waist tightening represents the earliest and until the later Middle Ages the only truly erotic form of dress. The Cretan woman's very modern "charm, chic and sexual allure" has fostered among archeologists a very positive, perhaps idealistic view of Cretan society, as dedicated to the finer pursuits of peace, commerce, domesticity, sexuality, sport and art. The Cretan was Homo Ludens. For Jacquetta Hawkes, in a chapter entitled, "The Grace of Life," Minoan female costume epitomizes cultural grace expressed in the anatomical stylization, the sense of movement and muscular play in representation of the human figure; in the sexual symbolism of religious ritual; and in the harmonious fusion in female dress of the various roles of priestess, mother, actress and sportswoman. "(Cretan dress) suggests a frank encouragement of sexuality such as would be appropriate to the high status of women in Minoan society, to their uninhibited liveliness in public and the freedom with which they mingled with men." For the bull sports in which they performed together with men, Cretan women wore masculine attire, loincloth and codpiece (Plate 1). While the dress of the two sexes was normally contrasted, there was also a tendency to ritual transvestism.[1]

This "emancipated woman" was also the distant and isolated ancestor of the modern tight-lacer. Most archeologists accept that the slender waist of the Cretan was no mere artistic convention, but a reality motivated by the desire to emphasize a peculiar ethnic characteristic,[2] and obtained by means of an ever-present tight, thick rolled belt. Sir Arthur Evans, the principal excavator of Knossos, born in 1851, remains the only as well as the first writer to have dealt with this aspect of Minoan culture in any depth. He traces the wasp waist back to M.M. I (or the last century of the third millennium B.C.) It survived continuously and revived during M.M. III (17th century B.C. onwards).[3] In his Victorian puritanism, Evans stressed that it was cultivated as a sign of strength and endurance, rather than for sexual or aesthetic reasons, which he does not mention. From minute measurement of surviving figures of children and adults, he deduced that "while children of both sexes were of very tender years (i.e., between about five and ten) metal belts were riveted around them, to which their growing bodies adapted themselves and which remained a permanency for the greater part of their life." Writing for an audience conditioned to believe tight-lacing to be highly injurious (and describing the Minoan belt to be "merely another form of tight-lacing") Evans defended the custom thus: "Considering the vital ducts and vessels thus constricted, this might have been thought an impossible interference with Nature. Expert medical and physiological opinion tells us that this result could be achieved without patent injury to the health of the subject."[4] (Evans' experts must have been carefully selected). More recently, a medical rationalization has been offered for the retention by the male bull-leapers of the combined belt and codpiece: "It is possible that the thick padded codpiece was necessary as a kind of primitive truss, for violent effort with an artificially constricted waist is very productive of rupture."[5]

The belt was probably composed of metal with a roll of padding in some soft material to prevent chafing. Apart from this belt and the all-metal codpiece borrowed from the men by the female acrobats, women (priestesses and acrobats) wore a steel-ribbed bodice which Evans has no hesitation in calling stays or corset, and which he supposes to have been a necessary artificial support for the very fully developed breasts (although in fact, it stops short of them).

Evidence is poor for any continued use of the belt after the destruction of Minoan civilization. One might speculate that the Minoan ideal of artificially enhanced slenderness found its way along the trade route to the Black Sea, and took root at some undetermined time in Circassia, where it developed into the very constrictive bark or leather corset described in 19th century travel books.

Minoan slenderness may, however, have passed with other aspects of that civilization onto the Greek mainland via the Mycenaean culture (cylinder seals from which show figures with a prominent belt around a very thin waist) and survived, according to the stylized figures painted on Greek vases, perhaps as late as the seventh century B.C. There is, however, no evidence, visual or literary, that the Greeks trained the waist in any form of hard belt. The Homeric epithet "bathyzonos" (if it means deep- rather than low-girded) suggests admiration for a slender, full-breasted but probably unconstricted figure. The ideal of the (naturally) slender waist subsequently diminished, however, as Greece approached the classical age of the 6th and 5th centuries B.C. Since the Renaissance, classical Greco-Roman dress, which lightly veiled the human form and preserved the natural contour, has been held to epitomize a style both ideal and natural. Although it included the use of breast-bandages to support and/or confine the breasts, it never tried to throw out the bust or confine the waist which remained, to judge from the sculpture, comparatively wide. In a passage invariably cited by historians as proof of the antiquity of the corset, the Roman dramatist Terence refers to the regrettable fashion for binding the breasts of the more solidly built girls and starving them in order to make them look slender.[6] Galen, the Greek physician of the first century A.D. complains that girls were too tightly swaddled in infancy, and in adolescence were subjected to tight bandages about the breast (*tainiai* in Greek, *fasciae* in Latin) in order to increase the size of the hips; the result was various deformities of the back.[7] The references to breast-binding in ancient literature are fairly numerous,[8] but in the absence of visual documents to indicate that it was constrictive of normal figures, one may conclude that it was used either like the modern brassière as a means of light support, or in order to reduce abnormal figures. Breast-binding in ancient times does not appear to have been either widespread, persistent or extreme; it was corrective rather than erotic. "Erotic" in the sense the term characterizes clothing of the Christian era, is not applicable to that of Greco-Roman times.

A repressed form of Eros entered the costume of the West when the early Fathers of the Church identified sexual desire as the root of all evil and ordered that its source and object—woman—be concealed as far as possible from view. With the body completely covered from head to foot, small wonder that certain occasionally glimpsed parts of the body—the elegant foot, the bare shoulder, the luxuriant tress or painted eye—acquired their peculiar sexual appeal. To use Lord Clark's now famous distinction, the Greeks created nudity, and the

Christians nakedness—that is, an undressed state laden with forbidden sexual desire and sexual guilt.

Medieval costume concealed, but did not modify the contour of the body. Body modification was introduced at the time of the Renaissance, paradoxically when ancient ideals of naturalism were revived. While art became overtly classical in its reference, costume became no less overtly anti-classical. The art of sculpture imitated classical form in the spirit of ideal naturalism, while the art of costume began to decorate and sculpt the human body with complex artifice. Revived ancient ideals of the "natural life" did not affect bodily hygiene; indeed, there may have been a regression in this respect. Sixteenth century man indulged probably in less sport and less bathing, and certainly in more clothing than fourteenth century man. Renaissance costume managed, progressively, both to constrict and expose the body. Décolletage, the concomitant of waist-compression, has been called "as much a sign of the first dawn of the Renaissance as the novels of Boccaccio."[9]

But the classicizing or neo-ancient nude of art has also responded directly, minutely and literally, as Anne Hollander has shown, to the pressures of fashion. The countless paintings of the nude from the 15th through the 19th century are witness to the anti-classical impulse to modify the body-contour and express fashionable, clothing-induced postural variations within classical poses. The nude as much as the naked body has born the mark of the corset.

Late Middle Ages and Early Renaissance: Décolletage and Tight Clothing; Illegal and Immoral Fashions; the Poetic Taste for Slender Form

Through the early Middle Ages and down to the 13th century, costume in Western Europe tended to be loose, uniform, and stylistically static. During the 13th century women's dress became more smooth-fitting, and in the course of the following century, the clothing of both sexes began to arouse hostile comment for its capriciousness and tightness. Its sexually provocative character was recognized in pulpit and lawcourt. The increase in clerical denunciation and civic legislation is most marked in Germany during the latter half of the 14th century, and reflects a change in costume and attitudes to costume connected with the Black Death of 1348–9.[10] In the words of the Limburg Chronicle, "Within a year after the dying, the flagellation pilgrimages, and the killing of the Jews, the world began to live again and to be happy, and men made new costumes . . . Men started to acquire new gay clothes, which were so tight and short that it was impossible to walk in them, and women wore deeply cut out necklines ('wide hauptfinster'), so that one could see almost half their breasts." The Italian chronicler Matteo Villani paints a dramatic picture of the desperate gaiety of survivors of the Black Death "mouldering in ease, dissolutely abandoned to the sins of gluttony, gambling, and unbridled lechery, inventing strange and unaccustomed fashions and indecent manners in their garments . . ."[11] The increasingly realistic painting in Europe around 1400 with its emphasis on elegant posture and dress ("International Gothic Style"), confirms the fact that costume had become truly figure-defining (Plates 2 and 3).

It was décolletage which aroused the most bitter clerical wrath, and a number of sumptuary laws. The permissible amount varied considerably according to time and locality, and city ordinances were often so vaguely worded as to be unenforceable. Speyer (1356) and Zürich (pre-1371) for instance, simply insist that the shoulders be covered. In the Latin countries, clerics objected to visibility, in one instance of "the throat and neck", in another to the "mamillae", i.e., breasts or nipples "which seemed about to burst out of their cleavage."[12]

Breast-exposure was not simply a matter of the low-cut dress, however, for it was enhanced by means of two subterfuges: first, slashing of the material to allow forbidden glimpses of flesh, and second and more important, artificial uplift of and compression below the bust. On the first count, the popular late 15th century moralist Geiler von Kaiserberg objected to the "pleated shirts, and slashed bodices . . . so far open at the front, that one . . . can see into the bosom and . . . the nipples."[13] These were particularly evident to the preacher from his raised vantage-point in the pulpit, whence he threatened to spit into the naked bosom of a lady seated below: "Women come into the church not in order to repent, but in order the better to display (like butchers) their carnal wares." Complaints of the breast being exposed "down to the belly" (pectus discopertum usque ad ventrem) may be exaggerated. Painting meanwhile, from mid 14th century, contributed to the new visibility of the breast by introducing the iconographic type of the Madonna del Latte, exposing one breast to give suck to the infant Jesus.

Artificial compression as a major instrument of décolletage, while not as frequently attacked as the décolletage itself, was singled out early on by the same Matteo Villani quoted above: "Who would doubt that humanity was slipping towards perdition when women appeared in public wearing artificial hair and low-necked blouses and with their breasts laced so high that a candlestick could actually be

placed upon them?" The comprehensive and explicit statute of
Speyer 1356 outlawed in particular décolletage and tightly laced
clothes "which force apart or bind the body or breasts by compression"
(die ir lip oder ir brüste mit enggenisse entzwingen order binden). In
France, Christine de Pisan demanded that women be not "excessively
tight in their dress" (en son habit et habillement non trop estrainte).[14]
The famous early 15th century Bohemian reformer John Huss saw the
outthrust breasts as diabolical horns: "One can openly see the shining
skin over the almost half naked breast, in the temples of the Lord,
before priests and clergy, as well as in the market place. In the home
moreover, one can see the part of the breasts that was previously
covered artificially enlarged and so thrust out, that they look almost
like twin horns on the chest."[15]

On one occasion, at least, such excesses received their just reward.
Friar Filippo da Siena, in one of his sermon-novelle written around
1397 (most of which are actually about the evils of face-painting),
recounts how a mother sends a daughter to her wedding dinner in an
excessively tight gown. Halfway through, right at the table before all
the guests, the miserable bride expires, suffocated.[16]

Clerical censure of male fashion during this period also centered
upon the tight and the short. The tunics sported by young bloods
tended to be cut so short as to expose the crotch of the hose, which
was, in addition, laced with gaudily colored laces like the shirt. The
genital bulge thus emphasized reached a kind of apotheosis in the
mid 16th century in the form of the codpiece, which simulated a
permanent erection highly visible in the portraiture of the period.
(Oddly enough, the codpiece seems to have escaped clerical wrath,
more exercized in mid-16th century Germany by "Pluderhose," the
enormous slashed breeches pioneered by the mercenary soldier.)

Sumptuary laws were designed generally to regulate and restrict
conspicuous material consumption in order to preserve the calibra-
tion of the social hierarchy. They were intended to prevent elements
with more money and ambition than present social rank, from acquiring upper-class status symbols. Most sumptuary laws, especially
in the 16th and 17th century, tried to restrict the use of excessively
voluminous and precious *materials* of dress; the minority of laws,
which seem to be concentrated in the earlier period, were directed
against sexually provocative *styles*. The difference of emphasis may be
partly due to the growing recognition that it was easier to legislate the
length of a train or sleeve, measurable in absolute terms, than the
depth or tightness of a bodice, measurable only in relative terms.
Décolletage also suffered from the disadvantage, from the cleric's
point of view, that it could not be literally consigned to the fire
(although it was consigned, from the pulpit, to the "fire" of cancer),

like the false hair, high headdresses (hennins), long-piked footwear (poulaines, Schnabelschuhe)—the staples of the public bonfires of female vanities, of which Savonarola's are only the most famous. The corset, once it had emerged as a distinct garment, was indeed to be occasionally thrown to the fire, but only privately by an irate father, or in a comic strip satirizing religious hypocrisy, or in a (fake) newspaper report.[17]

The ideal of the slender female figure antedated its artificial modification by a century or more. The ladies condemned for their vanity by the clerics were incited thereto by the poets, who as early as the 13th and even 12th century enthuse over the slender figure and small waist, enhanced with the aid of a bodice or "bliaud," as it was called in French, fastened with lacing. They are described in the *Lai de Lanval* as "laciées mult estreitement / De deux bliauts de purpre bis," which in English versions reads: "Ther kerteles were of rede sandel; / I lascid small, joliff and well," or else "The lady was in a purple pall, / With gentill bodye and middle small." Another source, believed to date to c.1200, notes approvingly "Middle she hath mensk (very) small."[18]

During the latter half of the 14th century, when fashion turned definitively towards a body-moulding line, poetic praise of slender waists multiplies. A Frenchman observed that the slitting and side-lacing of the bodices, which facilitated the closer fit, was introduced into France by the camp-followers of the English army and was a fashion appropriate only to "evil women."[19] It may indeed have originated at the English court, for the Carpenter's Wife in Chaucer was endowed with a "body gentil and small as a weasel;" that "body" here means waist is indicated by the further description of the lady as "long as a maste and upright as a bolt." And in Chaucer's contemporary John Gower we read, "He seeth hir shape forthwith, all / Hir bodye round, hir middle small."

In the later 15th century we find, for the first time, fashionable compression described as physically painful to the wearer, as well as morally painful to the moral beholder. "By a detestable vanity, eminent women now have their dresses cut so low in the bust and so open over the shoulders, that one can almost see their breasts and the whole of their shoulders, and deep down into their back; and so tight in the bodice (si estroites par le faux du corps), that they can barely breathe and often suffer great pain to make their bodies pretty and slender."[20] By such means their middles became, in the Scottish poet Dunbar's phrase, "as small as wands." The propensity to make them so at the expense of a present or future pregnancy is, for the first time in what was to become, through the centuries, a familiar medical dirge, indicated by Sir John Paston. In 1472 he tried to compliment the Duchess of Norfolk on her "long and large sides," and wide, unconfined body which promised a "fair child, not laced and braced in to his pain, but with plenty of room to kick around in, and to exit from." (These remarks were not at all appreciated by the portly Duchess, and caused some bad feeling.)[21]

Later Renaissance: Busk and Farthingale; Tight-Lacing in France, etc; Décolletage

It is unlikely that artificial stiffening of the bodice was widely used before about 1500. The French term "corset" i.e., small "corps" (body) or "cotte", which becomes common at this time, simply refers to the outer bodice or tunic worn by both men and women.[22] Around 1500 female costume underwent an important structural change in response to the new Italian Renaissance aesthetic of broader, squarer lines. Medieval dress on the whole presented a continuous, flowing vertical line. This was broken when in the early 16th century the bodice became separated from the skirt, both acquiring a stiff and angular contour. As the skirt became fuller, the bodice grew longer, straighter, and more rigidly tight.

A new sartorial architecture of polarization, division and contradiction was established, which was to prevail for four centuries. Arguably, it corresponded to the new capitalist ethic, simultaneously expressing power through bulk, and self-restraint through tightness. Over the upper half of the body, the bodice, fitted to the real torso through the new technology of tightening and stiffening, and in art cinched by the painter through the new textural realism of pictorial smoothness and tightness, conveyed self-control, sexual and social self-discipline; over the lower half of the body the heavy, expansive and luxurious skirt conveyed economic power and the accumulation of individual wealth, which the simultaneous look of self-discipline sought to justify. The contradiction between the top and bottom half of the clothed exterior was joined by another, equally fundamental: the body-shape of the more or less classically inspired nude was radically different from that of the fashionably clothed figure, a contradiction which artists continued to manipulate up to the 20th century (Plates 4, 5 and 11).

It can be no historical accident that the great bulk and stiffness of costume, both male and female, in the 16th and 17th centuries, coincides with the global expansion of European economic and military empire. And fashion corresponds, in some sense, to the new technologies which underlay this expansion. The steel armor which was becoming useless on the battlefield was preserved in the tournament lists and festival processions, where it took on highly elaborate forms and often (especially in Germany) with an extreme disproportion between the huge, bulging chest and the sharply incurved waist, as if to assert its primarily aesthetic function. Civilian costume also acquired a highly protective, decorated, padded and armored look; it expressed the lust of European upper-class society for military conquest and material wealth.

At first the bodice was probably stiffened by means of paste on linen or cardboard; then, a strip of really solid material was inserted down the front. This was known as a coche, or more commonly, as a busc (or buste, from the Italian busto, meaning breast), made of wood, horn, whalebone, ivory, or metal. It was tapered in shape, often very finely decorated and tied to the bodice (now called basquine, or vasquine) by a lace, which gallants also wore around the arm or in the hatband as a sign of their lady's favour. Some of the erotic associations which had accrued to the unstiffened bodice and its lacing[23] thus passed to the busc and its lace. Simultaneously, whalebone or wooden hoops were placed beneath the skirt, called vertugalles (farthingale, from the Spanish *verdugo*, or sapling). This device was current in Spain already by the later 15th century, and passed, together with the busk, via Italy into France, probably first with the arrival at the French court of Catherine de' Medici as bride of Henri II (1533).[24] The new highly artificial silhouette was accompanied by a raising and flattening of the bustline, which caused Rabelais' sensualist Panurge (1532) to lament that it was no longer possible for a man to put his hands down between a dressed lady's breasts. Whatever their degree of exposure, which was very variable, the breasts tended to be flattened as never before by the busk, and the thorax smoothed into a cone, appropriately to the reputation for rigidity, pride and moral discipline of the new world power, Spain (Plate 6).

Originating, then, in Spain and Italy, busk and hoop skirt encountered outspoken opposition when they were imported into France, especially in the 1560s. The clerical *Blason des Basquines et Vertugalles* inveighs against "lascivious mundanities," insists on mortification rather than indulgence of the body (without perceiving how fashion managed both at once) and demands that women "reject those great farthingales / Which cause scabs and blisters / Leave those ugly *basquines* which make you ugly as apes / Dress like decent women, without wearing those infamous busks." The busk was now commonplace and prominent enough to have "taken over" the wearer linguistically, for the same source condemns men who dilate on "pleasure / of being able to hold at leisure / So pretty an embusked woman (cette busquée si mignonne)." The backward projecting skirt was also viewed as offering a saddle for the devil to ride. These articles became the object of sumptuary laws under Charles IX and Henri III, despite the fact that the latter king, an occasional transvestite, himself wore the female basquine and busk to enhance his slender figure.

By the last third of the century the French had acquired an international reputation for exaggerating the effects of busk and hoop. A proverb of the time described a handsome woman as "English to the neck, French to the waist, Dutch below, and Spanish at the legs and feet."[25] By lengthening busk and bodice, the French made it possible to tighten more at the waist. Jerome Lippomano, the Venetian ambassador at the French court in 1577, remarked that "French women have extremely narrow waists. They like to swell out their gowns from the waist downwards by whalebones, stuffs and vertugadine . . . Over the chemise they wear a bodice . . . that they call 'corps piqué', which makes their shape more delicate and slender. It is fastened behind which helps to show off the form of the bust."[26] (Lippomano goes on to remark on the freedom of manner and authority enjoyed by French women, their relative lack of religion and their ability to stay out for hours at a time without their husbands asking where they have been.)

There is other evidence during the last third of the 16th century for tight-lacing in France. The famous surgeon and anatomist Ambroise Paré cites, among the causes of abortion, the "powerful compression exercised by busks, which compress the belly;" and among the causes of spinal deviation, the habit of excessive "tightening of the *corps* of girls in their youth. As witness to which, one sees that among a thousand village girls, not one is hunchbacked; because they never wore too tight and constricted a *corps*. Which mothers and nurses should take as an example." This emphatic paragraph, added in the 1579 edition, and much embellished in the English translation of 1634,[27] reinforces other evidence that tight-lacing increased in the 1570s. Paré(?) also cites two fatalities: a lady of the court who fell into a marasmus (began wasting away) following repeated vomiting of her food, due to the pressure on the stomach of a whaleboned "corps" which bore so heavily on the false ribs, that he found them, on opening the body, "overlapping each other;" and he went so far as to attribute to the constriction of her clothing alone, the sudden death of a young bride recently arrived in Paris, in the middle of the nuptial ceremony.

Taking as his pretext the replacement by the Italianate word "buste" of the more French-looking "busque," the noted linguist and scholar Henri Estienne, in a dictionary-cum-social critique of 1578, upbraids the tight-lacers, whom he divides into two categories, the married and the unmarried. The latter "without thinking it does any harm have themselves tightened and constricted in their dress, so that they suffer great discomfort, in order to show what a pretty waist they have, 'pretty' meaning here, of course, small. But would you believe that pregnant women go in for this as well? To such an extent that they deform the children they carry? Wearing a busk which contributes to this evil?"[28] Estienne anticipates the reader's reaction to this novel information as one of horror mingled with astonishment and even incredulity, which indicates that the habit was not that widespread, or "fashionable" in the proper sense of the term. He then deals with the husband's attitude. In the course of several paragraphs it emerges, most significantly, that the woman who tightens herself does so *in spite of* her husband, daring to assert thereby that it is not *his* taste that she is consulting: she is the type of woman who has been married less for her dowry than for her beauty, which she wishes to preserve above and beyond her obligation to beget children. She is, evidently, already that sexually conscious, lower-class, upwardly mobile type characteristic of the heyday of tight-lacing.

This was not Estienne's first treatment of a topic which was evidently of some importance to him. In an earlier miscellany of essays on the peculiarities of human behaviour, he concludes his chapter on the various forms of homicide and murder with the class of women who murder their children. The practice, admitted to be both common and ancient, is that of both the unmarried, who fear discovery of their loss of virginity and honour, and the married who fear to "shorten the term of their youth." A subgroup of infanticides spanning both groups is that of the tight-lacers (those whom Estienne has "heard speak of" and "even knows personally") who had no compunction in wearing "busks at the expense of the fruit in their womb" and at the risk of "losing what should be as dear to them as life itself."[29]

The attitude of the best known French social critic of the age, Michel de Montaigne, is significantly different. The passage where he summons up the effects of tight-lacing soon entered the English language in this highly colored form, and was used, misleadingly, as an early example of the horror which the "fashion" should inspire in the intelligent mind:

To become slender in the waste, and to have a straight spagnolised (i.e., Spanish) body, what pinching, what girdling, what cingling, will they not endure; yea, sometimes with iron-plates, with whale-bones and other such trash, that their very skin and quick flesh is eaten and consumed to the bones; whereby they sometimes work their own death.[30]

Although much quoted, this passage is never given in the context, which is actually one of puzzled admiration. Midway in a long chapter of the First Book, Montaigne approaches the problem of physical pain and the way in which it changes in meaning according to the attitude we take to it, and the circumstances in which we undergo it. He cites many examples of stoic suffering and pain subdued through fortitude, such as Scaevola deliberately burning his arm before Porsenna, the prisoner scoffing at the cruelty of his torturers, or the patient continuing to read a book while the surgeon operates upon him.

Now for the ladies! Who has not heard tell of the lady in Paris who, solely to acquire a fresher complexion and a new skin, had herself flayed? Some have had live and sound teeth drawn, to have them arranged in better order, or to render their voice softer and richer. How many examples we may see in this sex of contempt of pain! What are they not capable of, what do they fear, as long as they have any hope of improving their beauty? ''Root out the tell-tale grey hairs from their place;/Remove the skin to renovate the face'' (Tibullus). I have known them to swallow sand and ashes, and set about purposely to to ruin their digestion in order to acquire a pale complexion.

A modern translation then continues, more concisely and faithfully to the original: ''For a slender figure *à l'Espagnole* what tortures will they not endure, their ribs forcibly strapped and laced into large splints, which enter the living flesh, nay, sometimes even cause death.'' Montaigne follows this up with another example of female fortitude: a girl from Picardy, whom the author himself saw ''as witness to the vehemencie of her promises, and also her constancie, with the bodkin she wore in her haire, give herself four or five thrusts in her arme, which made her skin to crack and gush out bloud.'' Only Montaigne at this time, so tolerant, humane, respectful of women, and sensitive to the power of paradox, could recognize in the deformity of fashion not the immoral offense against God, nature, and motherhood, but the heroic spirit of the martyr.

The essayist's sense of paradox extends to that other bugbear of the reformers, the hoop, the veiled sexual purpose of which he recognizes with a tolerant smile: ''And what is the purpose of those great bastions with which our ladies have recently begun to fortify their flanks, but to allure our appetite and to attract us to them by placing us at a distance?''[31]

From France the tight waist spread to other parts of Europe. The author of an early comparative fashion book, Cesare Vecellio, hailing from Venice where women had to be fat, is sensitive to the degree of slenderness to be found in women elsewhere. He tells us that although (unlike the French) Neapolitan women avoided décolletage, they wore tight, front-fastening bodices, and an underskirt called "faldea" or "verducato" "which is very tight at the waist and falls in a wide rigid bell-shape." In France it is the noblewomen of Orléans who were reputed to wear their clothes tightest about the waist and hips, setting off their slenderness by means of copper hoops in the sleeves. The girls of Brabant and Antwerp wore very tight bodices and extreme décolletage below the ruff; and the noble Augsburgerin encased herself in a bodice which "compresses her sides so much that she appears to be extremely narrow in the waist."[32] The propensity of the women of Augsburg to tight-lace and to show off fine sloping shoulders is confirmed elsewhere.[33]

The hoop had settled in England by about 1550, but the bodice was at this date still stiffened and the waist contracted by means other than the busk, such as wire and paste:

> Her middle braced in,
>   as small as a wand;
> And some by wastes of wire
>   at the paste wife's hand.

This is, according to the archdeacon of Hereford, eminently "whorish", and is accompanied by the usual devices:

> Her face fair painted
>   to make it shine bright.
> And her bosom all bare,
>   and most whorelike dight

as well as hoop skirts and a "bum like a barrel".[34]

But by the end of the century the busk had become commonplace in England,[35] as it was in France, to judge from the way it spurred the imagination of Stephen Gosson, a parson of Essex, to some verses prurient in the truest sense of the word. Gosson enlarges upon the dangers and purposes of the busk which he experiences, like no other article of fashion, as a perverse sexual instrument. It is a piece of armor in form and material, yet one obviously designed to invite rather than repel attack, pointing to the dark (and weak) spot at which lusty hunters are to shoot. It is used, moreover, deliberately to repress (abort) the unwelcome fruits of the attack. The amazonian armour of these wicked women serves to kill their own infants, rather than repel male sexual importunity. The verses are worth quoting in their full metaphorical development:

The bawdy busk that keeps down flat
  the bed wherein the babe should breed,
What doth it else but point at that
  which faire would have somewhat to feed;
    Where belly want might shadow vale
    The busk sets belly all to sale.

Were busks to them as stakes to gaps
  to bar the beasts from breaking in;
Or were they shields to bear off flaps (blows)
  when friend or foe would fray begin,
    Who would the buskers fort assail?
    Against their sconce (shield) who could prevaile?

But seeing such as whom they arm
  of all the rest do soonest yield,
And that by shot they take most harm,
  when lustie gamesters (hunters) come in field,
    I guess busks are but signs to tell
    Where launderers (whores) for the camp do dwell.

These privie coats, by art made strong
  with bones, with paste, with such like ware
Whereby their back and sides grow long,
  and now they harnessed gallants are;
    Were they for use against the foe,
    Our dames for Amazons might go.

But seeing they do only stay
  the course that nature doth intend,
And mothers often by them slay
  their daughters young and work their end,
    What are they else but armours stout
    Wherein like giants Jove they flout.

Mere whalebone moreover was not always considered stiff enough, and horn (including ivory) was sometimes preferred. Unfortunately, very few early "whalebone bodies" of the 16th–17th century have come down to us, and the earliest surviving stays are reckoned to be some all-iron ones, preserved in the Wallace Collection, Victoria and Albert Museum and (formerly) in the Carnavalet and Cluny Museums in Paris (Pl. 7).[36] The best modern authorities on the corset consider them to be orthopedic instruments, designed for difficult or deformed figures.[37] This cannot be excluded. At the same time they are often beautifully wrought and very elegant in shape, sloping inward at the waist, and with a V-shaped dip at the front just like the dress-stomacher of the period, which could have no rational orthopedic purpose.[38] Most open very simply by means of hinges, and some have lace-holes like conventional stays. They were presumably well-padded when worn. The paucity of literary evidence[39] indicates they were not common attire, but they might logically be regarded as a quasi-fetishist exaggeration of the fashionable desire for rigidity.

It is also just possible that individual women of this time discovered in the iron corset a means of Christian penance, analogous to the hair shirt worn by some pious men; and that it was adopted by some of those worldly ladies who, entering convents for reasons of personal convenience and a necessity other than religious, found that it satisfied masochistic urges at the same time as it jibed with other elements of fashionable attire they were permitted to preserve (such as décolletage, not at all an uncommon sight in convents).[40]

The total, geometric rigidity which iron stays provided was certainly not out of keeping with the "mannerist" aesthetic of the late 16th century which, as we know from innumerable portraits (especially in northern Europe), favored the long and perfectly smooth conical torso. In England, at any rate, iconographic convention must have exaggerated the real-life contour, for Elizabethan and Jacobean literary satire, in its incomparable richness and breadth, could hardly have failed to follow the lead given by Montaigne (well known in England and translated by 1603), and to target tight-lacing, had it been at all prevalent. Philip Stubbes, for instance, in his horrific inventory of the Elizabethan wardrobe, rails gleefully against the exaggerations and stiffness of farthingale, headdress and ruff, but does not mention excessive tightness or stiffness of the stomacher or bodice. Queen Elizabeth's calculated sartorial ostentation may have incited her wealthier subjects to indulge in such vanities as Stubbes described, but there is scant literary evidence for any attempt they may have made to emulate, through artificial means, her natural thinness.

References to stays and busks of the Elizabethan or Jacobean periods do not suggest that they were used to tighten the waist excessively, as in France. In Shakespeare's plays, on the three occasions when a woman demands to have her laces cut, she does so from the excessive motion of the heart, rather than the excessive tightness of the stays in themselves; in other words, the stays only *become* too tight when the overstressed heart wants to break them.[41] The chief purpose of the busk was to thrust out the breasts, as we may guess from its inclusion in the array of artifices employed by the once-modest Ginetta, now become fickle and arrogant:

And being now in much request, and waxing proud of favour,
By artificial pride she changed her natural behavior:

Her face was masked, her locks were curled, her body pent with buske,
And (which was needless, she more sweet) her rayment scented Muske.[42]

In England, where Puritanism clashed with the sartorial pretensions of social ambition, satire on dress attained the status of a literary
subgenre. Although "breast embusking" is only a starting point, we
must quote here a passage imbued with a misogynistic sadism which
is comparable in its "medieval" way to all those much less poetically
inspired threats of natural vengeance for the abuse of corsets—cancer
of the breast, consumption, pneumonia, severed liver, lapsed womb,
and death—delivered by physicians of the later Age of Science:

Their breasts they embusk up on high, and their round roseate buds
immodestly lay forth to show at their hands their mind in the swellings and
plumpings out of their apparel . . . As many jags, blisters and scars shall
toads, cankers and serpents make upon your pure skins in the grave, as you
now have cuts, jags or raisings, upon your garments. In the marrow of your
bones snakes shall breed. Your morn-like crystal countenances shall be
netted over and (masquer-like) caul-visarded with crawling venomous
worms. Your orient teeth toads shall steal into the heads for pearl; of the jelly
of your decayed eyes shall they engender them young. In the hollow caves
their transplendent juice so pollutionately employed, shelly snails shall keep
house . . . Satan, take her to thee, with black boiling pitch rough-cast over
her counterfeit red and white . . . with glowing hot irons, singe and suck up
that adulterised sinful beauty, wherewith she hath branded herself so infelic-
ity . . . For thy carcanets of pearl, shalt thou have carcanets of spiders . . . For
thy flaring flounced periwigs low dangled down with love-locks, shalt thou
have thy head side-dangled down with more snakes than ever it had hairs.
Satan, take her to thee, with black boiling pitch rough cast over her counterfeit red and white . . . with glowing hot iron, singe and suck up that
adulterized sinful beauty.[43]

Tight-lacing declined around 1600, to judge from the paucity of
literary reference I have been able to find for most of the 17th
century.[44] A few medical voices were raised, but in Latin only, in the
early years of the century, and the following may be cited by way of
exception. Charles Edouard, physician to Louis XIII, delivered this
verse report on the autopsy of the Duchess de Mercoeur, whose
flippancy does not add to its credibility as evidence for tight-lacing:
"And the sides of the thorax had caved in such / That they pressed on
the lungs just a little too much."[45]

There are, no doubt, other sources to be uncovered, and in obscure
places. We find, for instance, in the writings of a very minor French
satirist, a rather complete profile of the sartorially provocative type:
the "petite bourgeoise" or "bourgeoise débauchée" of the Sieur de
Sigogne (1610), who represents a commonplace butt in the epoch of

the rising merchant class. She is the vain, idle, luxury-loving middle-class woman whose new-found wealth permits her to ape the aristocracy. In some raunchy verses, Sigogne lists all the extravagancies and eccentricities of fashion in which she indulges. There is an initial emphasis on tight shoes, the small foot being an indicator, as the proverb has it, of a large "thing" (labia?). Particularly curious, in the light of the 19th century development of the fetishist constellation, is the fact that, a lover of riding, she is "prompt with the spur."

Her "short legs, long sides"[46] suggest she makes herself the waist of the mannerist age, and her "arched back and iron stays" (corps de fer) may cautiously be assumed to indicate some excess in corsetry. She is, finally, as demanding sexually as she is exhibitionistic: as pitiless towards and wasteful of the 'sausage' (andouille, penis) as a young lawyer of his client's money.

In the baroque age the more typical abuse of the corset was probably by the older, rather than younger woman. Thus Madame de Gondran, once beautiful, much admired and courted in her youth, married now to a loutish husband and still eccentric and flirtatious; but grown fat, to remedy which she "tightened to such an extent . . . that she hurt herself badly, giving herself a wound in her side."[47] Her chronicler is reminded at this point, not of further instances of such an event, which is probably exceptional and unrelated to fashion, but of another kind of fashionable martyrdom: certain "ladies-in-waiting of the Queen, who, in order to appear prettily shod, wrapped their feet so tightly in their hair-fillets, that they fainted of the pain in the Queen's apartments." It seems doubtful, however, that such a degree of foot compression was a common or long-lived practice.[48]

After around 1600 the farthingale and hip-padding ("bum-rolls") continued to draw the heaviest fire, as the torso itself shortened and broadened. Very few portraits from the period ca. 1610–60 show particular slenderness of figure, compared with those from the adjacent periods. The round breadth of baroque, Rubensian form superseded the stiff attenuations of the mannerist age. At most, the bust was sculpted; some French verses of 1618 and 1642 complain at the forcible binding of the breasts in order to swell them out upwards, a procedure which was so damaging that the "marks remain for four days."[49] Breasts were not infrequently exposed, at this time, down to and including the nipple.

There is one often cited but isolated passage which suggests, deceptively in my view, that tight-lacing was typical of mid-17th century England. It is probably inspired by Montaigne and Paré:

Another foolish affection there is in young Virgins, though grown big enough to be wiser, but that they are led blindfold by custom to a fashion pernitious beyond imagination; who thinking a Slender-Waste a great beauty, strive all that they possibly can by streight-lacing themselves, to attain unto a wand-like smalnesse of Waste, never thinking themselves fine enough untill they can span their Waste. By which deadly artifice they reduce their Breasts into such streights, that they soon purchase a stinking breath; and while they ignorantly affect an august or narrow Breast, and to that end by strong compulsion shut up their Wastes in a Whale-bone prison or little-ease, they open a door to Consumptions, and a withering rottennesse.

This is taken from the impressively titled treatise of the physician John Bulwer (1650): *Anthropometamorphosis: Man Transform'd; or the Artificial Changeling. Historically presented, in the mad cruel gallantry, foolish bravery, ridiculous beauty, filthy finenesse, and loathesome lovelinesse of most nations, fashioning and altering their bodies from the mould intended by nature. With a vindication of the regular beauty and honesty of nature . . .* This encyclopedic tome gathers, magpie fashion, all published opinion about the references to "corporal fashion" around the globe and throughout history. It treats fact and fancy alike, and natural deformities such as misbirths and accidental physical deviations under the same head as deliberate body-modification. Bulwer expatiates upon the customs of primitive and non-European peoples, but has surprisingly little to say upon European or specifically English custom, despite the fact that his moral leit-motif is that customs in so-called civilized countries are as barbarous as those of people called barbarians. His chief bugbear among European customs, which he places in the chapter headed "Cephalique Fashion-mongers", is the propensity (traceable back to ancient Greece) among midwives and nurses to use headbands, fillets, and massage on babies in order to give them a nicely rounded head. Bulwer is concerned, too, with the effects of the swaddling of babies, which is treated in the same chapter as tight-lacing (Scene XX): "Dangerous Fashions and desperate Affectations about the Breast and Waste." This chapter, which one would expect to be extensive, were the fashion for tight-lacing and breast-sculpture at all prevalent at this time, is in fact one of the shortest, shorter even than the equivalent chapter on "Pap-Fashions," which deals with breast-stretching among primitives. Bulwer repeats Paré's English translator on the subject of mothers "plucking and drawing the bones of their daughters awry," and Montaigne (whom he uses chiefly for generalities), on the subject of "whalebone prisons," as cited.

He does not appear able to draw upon his own clinical experience as a physician, but does add the original observation that tight-lacers tend to become asthmatic, and in order to breathe more easily "they are forced to hold up their heads, whence also they seem to have great throats."

Someone may have pointed out to Bulwer the inadequacy of his treatment of contemporary European female fashion, for in a second edition (1654, with the emasculated title *A View of the People of the Whole World*), the author added an appendix bringing a conventional array of accusations against hoops, chopines, and bare breasts. The latter had not figured at all in the first edition, were no longer at all customary and are here summarily dismissed as immodest and conducive to the loss of the use of the hands, when the nerves leading to those extremities become refrigerated.[50]

The Civil War and the advent of the Puritans to power certainly inhibited luxury in the dress of both sexes. Bulwer's motive in writing his book seems to have been as much to incorporate recent increases in knowledge of the customs of primitive peoples, as an animus against current fashions in his own land. It is his analogy between the two, and his attempted demonstration that Christians treat God's own image as barbarously as savages do their own bodies, if not worse, which commands our attention, in view of the 19th century reformers' sense that tight-lacing represents a barbaric historical regression to the infancy of the human race. Bulwer, not quite incidentally, is impressed by the belief, to which he alludes in his Introduction and which was apparently not that rare two full centuries before Darwin, that man was "an artificial creature who was at first but a kind of Ape or Baboon, who through his industry (by degrees) in time had improved his Figure and his Reason up to the perfection of man."

Décolletage revived dramatically during the last quarter of the 17th century, as may be judged from the numerous portraits of the period in which the ladies' breasts are bared to the nipple. This was one of the many fashions imported into the court of Charles II from Versailles, where it was encouraged by Louis XIV. Its adoption by the bourgeoisie and in the cloisters was lashed by the French, German and English preachers in tracts of exceptional venom. The great weapon was cancer. The link between breast-exposure and breast-cancer had been forged earlier in the century, by a Flemish cleric called Jean Polman, in a very nasty pamphlet entitled *Cancer or the Female Breast-Covering*. With the aid of repeated puns on the word for cancer (chancre) and the cut-out of the dress-neck (échancrure), he equates the horrible gradual metastasis of cancer of the flesh with the progressive inroads over the body of the cancer of fashionable nudity. It is significant, however, that although his purpose was to damn the "nudity of the breasts and nipples" he never once at this date (1635) mentions their being thrust out by binding, which is stressed by the best-known clerical mammaphobe of the 1680s, Jacques Boileau. This French abbé specialized in what he termed "difficult" subjects like a history of flagellation, which he wrote, allegedly for fear of censorship, in Latin. *De L'Abus des Nudités de la Gorge*, however, was published in French, first (for safety) in Brussels in 1675 but subsequently in Paris, 1677 and 1680. An English version came out in 1677–78. Boileau aphorises the attitude of an entire corpus of mammaphobic literature: "The sight of a fine breast is no less dangerous than the sight of the basilisk" and "the demon uses the windows of our body in order to introduce death together with sin into our soul." In the same spirit, in Germany, the breasts become "Bellows of Lecherous Desire" (title of a work by Ernst Gottlieb). An anonymous German pamphlet of 1686 bears the motto "Young ladies with their naked busts, a tinder to all evil lusts" (Des Frauenzimmers blosse Brüste/Ein Zünder aller bösen Lüste), later improved under the title; *"The naked bust/framed and trussed/for evil lust" (Die Blosse Brüste/Ein Gross Gerüste/Viel Böser Lüste).*[51] The wearing of necklaces adorned with crucifixes is described as "hanging Christ anew between two thieves". The essentially gradual and agonizing progress of breast cancer, as the natural punishment God inflicts upon the décolletée woman, is described with sadistic precision. The mammaphobes cite legendary examples of voluntary breast-mutilation in order to ward off rapists, and praise those pious ladies like the Abbess Aldegund and St. Ediltrud, who thanked God for sending them cancer and tumors of the breast and neck as a punishment for the lechery of their youth. Women who expose their breasts on earth will have them eternally tortured in hell, says the Parisian Pierre Juvernay in 1637, with a relish, and praises the saint who refused out of modesty to let the doctor treat her cancerous breasts.

In his wandering diatribe Boileau perceives, dimly, the paradox of masochism: Women willingly endure the present physical pain of breast binding and exposure to the cold but choose to ignore, as Boileau reminds them, the future and eternal physical agonies of cancer and hellfire. The Devil's martyrs do his own work for him: "Are they not to be blamed, for putting themselves upon the wrack and torture, only because they would appear to be dressed up in the mode, and to give some Charm and Grace to their breasts, because they would have them seen? To how many infirmities and distempers do they not expose themselves in their overlacing their gown-bodies, and so thrusting up their breasts, on purpose that they might shew them half-naked? How cold soever the weather be, and sharp the air, yet they endure it without complaining, provided it does not alter or prejudice the beauty to their necks, or bring about them fluxes and rheums, which are the ordinary effects of their going naked; they support with a resolute courage and constancy the rigour and severity of all seasons, to have the pleasure of being seen, and the hopes of being able to please."

Boileau concludes in amazement at the perversity of those who are "content to endure those wracks and tortures to damn themselves, (yet) will not be persuaded to suffer the least thing in the World for their own Salvation."

There were also native English mammaphobic tracts of comparable venom, such as the anonymous one entitled *England's Vanity or the Voice of God,* but the more typical forms of criticism as we approach the age of Addison and Steele are lighter in tone. The following passage tells us that tight-lacing was beginning to return in 1694 as a concomitant of décolletage (Boileau had spoken of lacing the breasts out rather than the waist in), but the initial tone of moral stricture is now a mere mask. The action of the stays upon the breasts, contestants locked in a kind of amorous struggle, is described with a wit and positive affection hitherto entirely lacking:

They then begin to commit their Body to a close imprisonment, and pinch it in so narrow a compass, that the best part of its plumpness is forced to rise toward the Neck, to emancipate itself from such hard captivity; and being proud of her liberty, appears with a kind of pleasant briskness, which becomes her infinitely. As for her fair breasts, they are half imprisoned, and half free; and do their utmost endeavour to procure their absolute liberty, by shoving back that which veils the one half; but they are too weak to effect it, and whilst they strive to free themselves they cast over a veil, which perfectly hides them. The desire they have to be expos'd to view, makes them beat it back continually, and not being able to remove that small obstacle, they look quite thro' it.[52]

Around 1710 there revived an ideal target for the wit of the new satirical journalists. The Cause of the Hoop was debated by *Tatler,* *Spectator* and *Guardian* with the highest mock solemnity. Physical inconvenience, the danger of the wearer falling "like an over-turned bell without a clapper," and passers-by getting their shins barked— these were the obvious complaints; but the sexual implications of the garment did not pass unnoticed. The wearers defended hoops on the grounds that they were comfortable because cool, and virtuous because they kept men at bay (like the old farthingale). These appealing lines of defense were subjected to a gentle Shandean tongue-in-cheek mockery: ". . . it is well known that we have not had a more moderate summer these many Years, so that it is certain the Heat they complain of cannot be in the Weather . . . a female who is thus invested in such a variety of Outworks and Lines of Circumvallation is sufficiently secured against the approaches of an ill-bred fellow."

But is this her true intention? Elsewhere we are reminded that "many ladies, who wear hoops of the greatest circumference are not of the most impregnable virtue," and use them, moreover, in order to give "the Feet a Freedom of Motion, shew the beauty of the Leg and Foot which play beneath it, and gain admirers when the face was too homely to attract the heart of any beholder."[53] The 19th century crinoline will have a similar erotic function.

18th Century:
Medical Opposition to Tight-Lacing and Other Forms of Constriction

As the hoop finally began to wane around mid-century, torso-molding as opposed to merely breast-enhancing stays began to move, as never before, into critical focus, to be castigated with a passion both moralistic and medical.

This article of dress had itself undergone a profound change. The 17th century "busc" was in a real sense an accessory, removable at will; the busk, and other means of stiffening the bodice were relatively clumsy and could not be tailored to the individual shape of the wearer. From around 1650, stays as a separate garment in the 18th and 19th century sense began to develop. They descended lower over the hips, at which point side-tabs were often added. Whalebone in flexible strips was now definitely the favored material, superseding the unyielding blades of iron or wood. It was cut narrower than before (down to one-eighth inch) and placed at subtle angles, instead of straight up and down. In the words of a modern historian, "The whalebone was inserted straight at the under arm, but fanned out to follow the side front and side back seams. This arrangement gave a more rounded shape and consequently a more slender appearance to the body, which from the wide oval neckline seemed to taper down to nothing. The center front seam was often curved and the busc followed this shaping."[54] By mid-18th century, the art of boning to shape the stays reached its acme, with the innumerable whalebone strips of varying width and cut placed on the basis of their relative flexibility and strength, and carried in all directions, on curved diagonals and even transversely across the bust and shoulder blades. These stays laced either at the back or at the front, or both. The front lacing was often made into a feature of the dress, especially when the gown opened in front as in the loose "robe battante."

Fashion has of course always been closely linked historically with current styles in the dance. The shape of the new stays of the rococo age, tightly moulding and lengthening the torso but cut away over the hips at the side, determined in part (or was in part determined by) the character of the dance, which in the early 18th century became very sophisticated technically and very important socially. "In dancing (the dancer) could not be expected to have very much forward or backward flexion in ribs or waistline, but she could execute subtle and expressive épaulement—twisting and tilting the upper torso on the spinal axis . . . From the restrictions imposed by the structure of corsets a manner of holding and using the upper torso, arms and head evolved, and affected conventions around the stylistic execution of step and patterns of movement."[55] Outside the ballroom, stays were the central means of encouraging a very erect, very carefully balanced, "kinesiologically very efficient" posture which distributed the great weight of the clothing precisely around a central axis, in order to reduce stress resulting from curvature in the alignment of body-parts.

The beautiful and intricately made new stays were not without their admirer, as we shall see, but Hogarth's was a minority opinion drowned out by the rising chorus of physicians and *philosophes*, who saw in them a threat to the natural development of the human body, and a symptom of a corrupt civilization. Since stays had become an important commodity, and their manufacture affected entrenched economic interests (including the entire whaling industry),[56] such opposition acquired a widely controversial character.

The cue was given by the major philosophic forerunner of 18th century Enlightenment, John Locke, in his book on Education (1693). Locke, concerned with the clothing of children rather than that of adults, pleads for freedom from physical compulsion, which is a harbinger of the mental and psychological compulsion thoughtlessly inflicted on the child as he grows older:

> Let nature have scope to fashion the body as she thinks best. She works of herself a great deal better and exacter than we can direct her. And if women were themselves to frame the bodies of their children in their wombs, as they often endeavour to mend their shapes when they are out, we should as certainly have no perfect children born, as we have few well-shaped, that are strait-laced, or much tampered with . . . I have seen so many instances of children receiving great harm from strait-lacing, that I cannot but conclude, there are other creatures, as well as monkeys, who, little wiser than they, destroy their young ones by senseless fondness, and too much embracing.

Locke concludes, in the next paragraph, which is concerned with Chinese foot-binding as the barbaric counterpart of Western "strait-lacing": "Narrow breasts, short and stinking breath, ill lungs and crookedness, are the natural and almost constant effects of hard bodice, and clothes that pinch . . ."[57]

In his attack on the confinement of young bodies Locke is embattled, like so many physicians, against part of that extensive repertory of female folk-traditions and folk-remedies, which medical science was trying to extirpate. He is joined by William Congreve who, in the *Way of the World*, a serio-comic play about the relations of men and women in marriage, shows prospective spouses sparring and bargaining with each other for power and influence. They draw up a marriage contract in which the husband tries to extract, against some resistance, a guarantee that his wife will not, when pregnant (a prospect she does not, or pretends not to, relish), engage in "strait lacing",[58] or when the child is born, "squeezing (him) for a shape, till you mould my boy's head like a sugar-loaf." Once again, tight-lacing is presented as a symptom of un- (or anti-) maternalism. Here Congreve uses the adult practice as an extension of the commonplace binding, swaddling and head-moulding in infant heads, which Locke also opposed, and which was, unlike tight-lacing, soon to die out in England among the urban classes altogether. 18th century physicians on both sides of the Channel tend however to bracket the two types of practice, ignoring the essential difference of their purpose.

The copious literature on these subjects, much of which is in Latin and buried in the broader medical treatises, remains to be sifted. The crescendo of opposition to stays can be judged from the bibliography given in Soemmerring (1788) of "some writers on the danger of stays," which lists seven articles or references from the period 1602-1670, all in Latin, and most of them published in Germany; from 1670-1762, however, there are twenty-seven books, articles and references, many of which are in the German language, and a few in French and Dutch. From 1762 to 1788, there are over sixty items, of which two are in English; one was published in Siena and one in St. Petersburg.

But for much of the 18th century the campaign reached only a limited audience, professional colleagues and those able to read Latin. Of the early treatises, the one most frequently quoted by later writers was composed by a Saxon physician and royal councillor called Plattner (later to be vouchsafed the title "the immortal"), entitled *De Thoracibus* (On Bodices), and published at Leipzig in 1735. Plattner favors the moderate use of flexible stays for growing children and women against an existing medical opinion disapproving of them in all forms and in any circumstances. His moderate attitude was soon to be superseded by extremer opinion, backed by a full panoply of "scientific" data. In 1741 Dr. Jean-Baptiste Winslow read a paper in French, the first such presentation in the vernacular, before the Parisian Academy of Sciences, in which he described the damage the ribs, forced inwards by stays, caused to the intestines, liver, kidney, lungs, and heart. He is particularly concerned with the weakening of the pectoral muscles through the compression immediately beneath the arms and the action of the shoulder-straps, which combine to thrust out the chest and flatten the back.

Winslow found (or set) himself in opposition to Andry, the senior Dean of the Faculty of Medicine in Paris and the most famous orthopedist of the age, whose *Orthopédie* of the same year became the standard text for the laity of 18th century Europe. The posture we admire so often in 18th century pictures is deplored in 1770 by Bonnaud, a Rousseau-ist critic, who lays the blame on Andry: "Imbued with the vulgar prejudice, the author advises one to push in (enfoncer) their stomach, to pull back the top of the shoulders, flatten the shoulder-blades and back, so as to free the front of the chest, and give them thereby a fine figure." In fact, Andry merely stresses the importance of holding the head high, of having the "corps piqué" (stitched, not necessarily boned bodice) constantly renewed at each stage of growth, and always leaving a "two-finger" gap at the top of the chest; but it is significant that the later 18th century saw the thrust-out chest and hyper-erect posture as the product of a "vulgar prejudice", into whose general popularity (i.e., among the middle classes) Rousseau was the first to make serious inroads.

There are no portraits and genre pictures of young girls where this posture is more pronounced than those of Chardin, painter of middle-class life. Could it be that the posture of young girls, like their prowess in the dance of which it is of course the basis, became of paramount importance in mid-century because desirable men were assumed to marry increasingly for personal inclination, out of a sexual attraction, than for the traditional social and economic reasons? This was the time when the dubiously born Poisson girl could be groomed to become Marquise de Pompadour and first lady of the realm. The "vulgar prejudice" of hyper-erect posture (as of tight-lacing) revealed the lower-class person's ambition to marry above her station.

Criticism of stays first reached the lay intelligentsia in Germany, where an encyclopedia (Zedler's of 1743, the first encyclopedia in the modern sense) carried a lengthy article under "Schnürbrust". Stays, put on both sexes when the infants are barely out of their swaddling clothes, are blamed for bad digestion, blood and menstruation, miscarriages, hernias and general debility. At twelve years the young girl's body begins to be "gedrechselt" (turned as on a lathe) from morning till night, the mother insists the girl wants to be slimmer than all the others, the tailor can never make, or the maid lace, the stays tight enough, "so that you can almost span her." The French laity got the message in the more famous French *Encyclopédie* (s.v.

Corps, 1753), which more-or-less reproduces the views of Winslow. But infant swaddling was still the primary concern of the French physicians at this time. Buffon, for instance, after dealing with the dangers of this practice, compares it briefly, in passing, with the putting of stays on young girls.[59]

The first real popular monograph in the vernacular, by a physician of Breslau called Gottlieb Oelssner, is as a whole as prolix as its title: *Philosophical-Moral-Medical Considerations on the several harmful forcible means devised in the interests of pride and beauty by young and adult people of both sexes. Together with the harmful misuses of stays and busks by young ladies. Philanthropically drafted during evening leisure hours by G.O.* (1754). This work takes as its motto "Pride must have constraint" ("Hoffahrt will Zwang haben"), and deals exhaustively and exhaustingly with the variety of external pressures clothes exert upon the body. Oelssner is fairly cursory with the other traditional abuses, to which he adds bizarre medical embellishments. Décolletage causes toothache, amnesia and the mumps, as well as colds. Amongst the secondary external pressures of male clothing are the tearing back of the hair into a pigtail, which causes colds on the neck, headaches and heart throb (hard, tight hats have similar effects); shirt-sleeve fastenings which strangle the wrists until the hands grow blue; constrictive breeches, stockings, and belts; but, above all it is the throat (chapter 8) which is martyred by neckclothes so tight "that the eyes start out of the head." Younger men especially claim that they feel unsupported without this "ghastly custom". This "lacing in" (Zusammenschnürung—the word used for stays) of the neck has terrible results, impeding the respiration, causing roaring in the ears, and stupidity of the face. (Winslow had noted the existence of this fashion amongst the Scandinavian military; it was to survive in European armies for over a century—cf. below).

The effects of female stays occupy nearly half Oelssner's book and are divided into twelve hyperbolically furious chapters. Describing himself as a "moderate", that is, one who is not opposed to orthopedic, preventive and protective corsetry, Oelssner blames on tightly laced stays all sorts of respiratory and digestive diseases, consumption, convulsions, and, of course, cancer of the breast (by virtue of the upward pressure). "The creeping murderer", "the torture stick" (Qualholtz, i.e., busk) causes premature birth, weak babies, Caesarians, abortion, and sterility. Feminine efforts to appear "straight, thin, delicate, pretty and slender" are alas, approved by men, and, worse, children "subject themselves willingly to their torture, and become as used to it as their daily bread, without which they cannot live."

Oelssner's work also incorporates the first sustained attack on footwear,[60] the dangers of which had been dealt with briefly by Winslow. The pointed, high-heeled shoe causes crippled, turned-in toes and gout. A woman putting her feet into fashionable shoes is like a camel trying to pass through the eye of a needle; once on, they are so tight that the sweat of fear breaks out to fainting point. The quarter-of-an-ell high, inward-curving stilt-like heel (which the Germans called Holtzer or Klotzer) causes such difficulty in walking, that it is a wonder the wearers do not fall over more often, and break a limb or even their neck.

Published hard on the heels of the angry Oelssner, the *Satyrical Treatise on the Diseases of Women caused by their Apparel and Clothing* by the Royal Prussian Physician in Sagan, Dr. Christian Reinhard (1757), is less harsh. Reinhard adopts a bantering, at times sympathetic tone. Instead of bludgeoning his fair readers, he tries to cajole them, assuring them of his friendship and respect for their cunning. He even throws in some recipes for relatively innocuous cosmetic treatments. Even so, his warnings are quite horrific. The work is again terribly prolix, filling two books to a total of 326 large octavo pages. With a bureaucratic thoroughness so characteristic of German didactic literature, Reinhard passes methodically through the human body, from top to bottom, part by part. In the following summary of this work (like Oelssner's, now exceedingly rare), we shall note only what appears new.

Anticipating the satire of twenty years later, when coiffures were (literally) at their height, Reinhard conjures up sweat-pores clogged with grease and powder and the scalp a breeding-ground for lice, further wounded by our scratching. He accuses the principal red face-paint, cinnabar, of causing cancer of the mouth, rotting of the gums, loosening of the teeth, stinking breath, and dripping eyes. White paints containing litharge of silver, acetous sugar of lead, essence of ox-gall, or tincture of benzoin, will eventually turn the skin yellow and brown. And there are those (as Montaigne had observed) who eat ashes, chalk, plaster, and even raw buckwheat, in order to whiten the skin—"what lasciviousness!" cries the author in amazement. Women even court death itself, by the ingestion of raw alum, arsenic, and coffee. Those who pluck their forehead suffer more than all the grades of torture, and suffer gladly as well. Ear-piercing (nonsensically supposed, says Oelssner, to prevent the vapors) is also a painful procedure, as is the wearing of heavy ear-pendants, which is "born with truly Christian patience."

On the subject of décolletage, the author loses altogether any bonhomie left to him. Décolletage is (in the hardy metaphor already familiar to us) a sexually-motivated "meat-stall display" ("Eröffnung der Fleischbank"). It is from the butchers that women have learned the art of stuffing out their roasting joints (Nierenbraten), and thrusting them towards the avid customer's eye, so that they look as if they were about to jump off their chests in lust. Like the hibernating bear, they live off their own flesh. Reaching at last the medical perils of breast exposure, the author rather loses the poetic impetus he had derived from its sexual motivation. And it is this which clearly emerges from his astonished exclamation on the compression of women's clothing generally: "And don't women have themselves pressed and laced into their clothing to such a degree, as to make the soul in their body cry out like an oyster? And why do they do such violence to their body? Perhaps out of sensuousness (Wollust)?! Ha! that's a fine sensuousness, and quite a new-fangled pleasure! Yet it is perhaps after this torture that the pleasure shall arise and grow a thousand times stronger than the discomfort caused by the previous rigorous constraint, to which she has subjected herself on account of the future pleasure." Presumably the "thousand times stronger future pleasure" is that experienced after the lady has removed her stays and enters the embrace of a lover, which the stays entice and anticipate.

Reinhard is evidently under contradictory pressures to condemn female vanity outright, and to deal sympathetically with the idea of female sexuality, which clothing enhances, as an independent entity. Entering the old debate whether sexual sensation was markedly inferior in women than in men, as Hippocratic medical tradition maintained, Reinhard boldly asserts a position which has been confirmed, experimentally, only in very recent times, that, far from being inferior, the female orgasm was in fact both longer and more intense than the male. The bizarre proofs he adduces need not concern us; the claim in itself, and any discussion of female sexuality in a book intended for susceptible young girls, is scandalous, as is the following titillating (and otherwise there as here irrelevant) anecdote: A girl claimed to be pregnant by a certain rich gentleman who denied ever having slept with her. In the courts, the girl stated that he must be lying, for how else could she know that he had a wart on his penis? He did, and she won her case. But it was she who had lied, having deduced the existence of a wart on his penis from the wart he had on his nose: "Noscitur ex labiis quantum sit virginis antrum / Noscitur ex naso quanta sit hasta viri" (One can judge from the mouth the size of a girl's labia, and from the nose the size of a man's member). 20th century fashion has made much of the former equivalence; popular art, custom and humor have had much fun with the latter.

The corset trade was not slow in springing to its own defense. The earliest surviving pro-corset tract was written by a Master-Tailor for women, and corsetier to many members of the royal family, the Sieur

Doffémont. Originally a mere twelve-page advertising pamphlet when it was first printed in 1754, in a second edition of four years later it swelled to twice the size and was reprinted in this form three times, the last in 1775. It enjoyed Approval and Patent from the Royal Academy of Surgery, members of which cooperated in its formulation and were vouchsafed the dedication. It was also approved by the Faculty of Medicine and at Court.

While they are unnecessary in the country, "Corps de Santé" by Doffémont are held to be indispensable in cities where children breathe thick air and live too close to each other. Stays and bandages, adapted to increasing stature, preserve the "soft wax" of the infant body, until the bones are perfectly solidified. This applies to males as well as females, and stays should not be removed from boys as soon as they are put into trousers. They should retain them even in puberty, as might many adult sportsmen and desk workers. (There is no evidence that men commonly wore any form of stays at this time.) The important thing (and here speaks the businessman as much as the pediatrician) is that all stays shall be renewed each year, as the child grows. They should also be worn at night, for what gardener ever went around removing supports from young trees[61] at night-time? (Once again, there is no evidence for the prevalence of night-stays).

Doffémont evades the awkward question of adult dependency, and the propensity of young ladies to tighten excessively at the waist. He was concerned with the young, and the norm, which was threatened by the abolitionists and Rousseau-ists. There were enemies also in another, opposing quarter: among the engineers eager to apply massive steel machinery to any orthopedic problem. The same Academy of Sciences to which Winslow presented his papers against stays, etc., had approved (in 1733) "a machine for keeping the feet turned out, and another to keep the head up."[62]

Doffémont stresses the fact that his articles (including corrective foot and leg braces) contain no ironware ("ferraille" is the pejorative he employs), but only the best flexible whalebone. He also recommends his whalebone collars to support the heads of those inclined to droop to the front or side. Writing three years earlier, the artist William Hogarth laments the fact that "steel collars and other iron machines" were in common use to correct this problem, so that Doffémont's whalebone support may appear a sensible compromise. Hogarth himself (a keen student of the theory of both costume and deportment) recommends a third solution, milder yet: a ribbon fastened to the hair and back of the coat which does not touch the throat at all.[63] In the Quack Doctor scene of his *Marriage-A-La-Mode* (1745), Hogarth painted ludicrous homage to the French genius for orthopedic machinery: a vast, complex, and diabolical all-steel apparatus, which looks something like a printing press but which is (according to the French inscription) approved by the Royal Academy of Science as a means to correct uneven shoulders. This sinister-looking object is presided over by a most malevolent-looking medical operator.

A compromise defense is presented by a German tailor of Lyons called Reisser (1770), who readily accuses his colleagues of creating terrible machines which worsen rather than cure any incipient deformity; at the same time, Reisser is opposed to the new "Corps à la Grecque", a super-light affair which he claims gives a round back and protuberant belly. He does not share the admiration of the Rousseau-ists for the uncorseted peasant girl, whom he finds has a bad posture. Amongst the various technical hints for the proper construction and application of stays are the very two which are seized upon and reversed by the tight-lacing enthusiasts a century later: the eyelets should, says Reisser, be closer at the top and bottom than at the middle, and the lacing should proceed from top to bottom, rather than from bottom to top. This reduces the risk of tightening excessively at the waist.

Amongst the defenses originating from the trade we should include the finely engraved illustrations of corset-construction contained in the *Enciclopédie,* which obviously derive from the workshop of the *tailleur de corps.* They are the first of their kind, and affirm the idea of stays, like the other objects in the technical illustrations, as evidence of technological and therefore social progress, contradicting thereby the very text of the anti-corset article accompanying them. These early revelations of "trade-secrets" must have caused great resentment generally among staymakers in an increasingly competitive area of manufacture. The first technical manual fully to unveil the secrets of corset construction was published under the auspices of the Academy of Sciences, by Fr.-A. de Garsault in 1769, under the title *L'Art du Tailleur de corps de femmes et d'enfants.* It contains detailed instructions how to make the different types of stays required by different circumstances—stays for riding, for pregnancy, for boys, for girls, and the redoubtable "Corps de Cour", reserved for court functions.

Enmity to the corset crystallized in the popular arena a little later in France than in Germany, but it did so in an uncompromising form and a highly controversial, not to say scandalous, context: in Jean Jacques Rousseau's *Emile ou L'Education,* which was banned on publication (1762). It had a tremendous cumulative effect; no work did more, during the latter part of the century, to bring to the attention of mothers and educators the dangers of unnatural dress. For Rousseau loose baby clothing, like fresh air and cold baths, is an aspect of that negative education which should govern the first years of the child's life when a parent can only aspire to avoid corrupting him and interfering with nature. In a stirring passage, Rousseau conjures up the sight of the child in the home of the wet nurse. While the parents are bent on frivolous amusement, their baby is swaddled and ligatured, choking, screaming, and purple-faced in his crucified position on the wall, where he hangs from a nail. (He is still to be found there in the late 19th century).[64] The peasant foster-mother meanwhile goes unconcernedly about her household duties.

"All that constricts nature is in bad taste; that is true of the decoration of the body as of the mind." Having been preserved from swaddling in his babyhood, Emile will of course be preserved from stays in infancy. But with Sophie, his female counterpart, for whom stays would normally become a permanent feature of childhood and adolescence, special aesthetic as well as moral arguments are necessary. Rousseau's starting point is that of the neo-classicist Winckelmann: the superiority of Greek costume—here adduced for the first time in such a context—over that of modern "Gothic" (loosely, the term meant anything un-Greek, or tasteless):

Of all these Gothic fetters, of this multitude of ligatures, . . . they (the Greeks) had not one. Their women knew not the use of whalebone stays, by which ours deform rather than enhance the figure. I cannot imagine but that this abuse, pushed in England to an inconceivable degree,[65] will not eventually cause the race to degenerate, and it is not pleasant to see a woman cut in two, like a wasp; that shocks the sight and does violence to the imagination. Slenderness of waist has, like all the rest, its proportion, its just measure, beyond which it is certainly a defect; this defect would even be striking on the naked body; so why should it be a beauty on the clothed one?[66]

Rousseau's strictures, which became the shibboleth of the 19th century reformers, appeared unassailable as long as "Nature" was understood as imbued with a kind of absolute, religious virtue. But the famous attack on female stays must be viewed in the context of the philosopher's attitude to women generally, which, as feminists are reminding us, was not at all progressive, however progressive his educational theory (conceived primarily for boys) may appear. Rousseau recognized that stays on a woman sexualized the body, a function antithetical to an educational system designed to develop moral sensibility at the expense of sexual maturation, which he regarded as a dangerous time, especially in girls who tended to stimulate it in boys. Woman was naturally inferior and subject to man; her physical beauty was threatening to his moral fiber, and any attempts to enhance it were to be viewed as corrupt and corrupting. The puritanism of Rousseau's attitude to sexual and aesthetic (and artistic) matters was to pass into the mainstream of 19th century dress reform.

In 1770 Rousseau's position found medical support in the first popular monographic polemic in French opposed to all stays: Bonnaud's *Degradation of mankind through the use of stays, a work which proves that to put man to torture from the very first moments of his existence, on the pretext of forming him, is to act contrary to the laws of nature, to increase depopulation, and so to speak bastardize him* . . . This work (which no 20th century writer has seen, and which must now be extraordinarily rare), was expressly conceived as a handy, portable (a mere 219 octavo pages) popularization for the laity. The topic of the title, however, is partly a mere pretext for the display of anatomical and physiological terminology and processes, constituting a comprehensive kind of medical manual by one probably not licensed to practice. Tumors, abscesses, squirrusses and cancers abound, as well as apoplexy, epilepsy and the vapors.

The most interesting and most virulent pages are the dozen or so devoted to abortion. The corset can have been invented only to depopulate the earth. It is used recklessly by married women, so many of whom seem to be incapable of taking the slightest precaution against (Bonnaud charitably supposes) accidental abortion; and it is used deliberately by unmarried women who succeed better with it than all other remedies. A German colleague (Kositski) stated outright that tight-lacing during pregnancy was used more effectively than any other abortifacient—and demanded police intervention. Abortion, still-births and feeble infants were the plague of the cities; whereas for the country the astonishing statistic invented by Bonnaud is "hardly one (stillbirth) in 10,000." The lucky peasants are so healthy as not to be at all inconvenienced by pregnancy, and are happily able(!) to continue working up to the last moment, whereas urban ladies are afflicted with every ailment for the whole period.

Aborting at whatever stage of the pregnancy, even down to the last minute, dangers to lactation through flattening or even inversion of the nipples, and the problem of latency (even if a woman stops tight-lacing at marriage, diseases implanted will pursue her to the grave) are the gynecological stock-in-trade of the rising tide of anti-corset literature in France and especially Germany over the last quarter of the century. Nor did the doctors rely on women reading their tracts; one told his patient directly and "constantly" (during delivery?!) that her sufferings were due to previous tight-lacing.

We may single out passages which give a class orientation, notably Kositski in 1788 who notes that it is the middle classes who are hardest to dissuade from tight-lacing, as opposed to those unambitious classes below (he apparently had no contact with the upper classes). Another, anonymous German writer of the same year locates the propensity with German girls of the "classes and grades" below the upper classes they seek to imitate, and particularly blames ignorant, low-class French governesses who supervise their education. In Holland, apparently, there were even working-class women ("femmes du peuple") who followed a "fashion" which was quite widespread there, according to other sources; these women considered it shameful to appear in a city street without an extremely stiff (and probably crudely made) corset.[67]

In Denmark, too, the lower classes (daughters of "common citizens") tended to wear very rigid cheaply made breast- and nipple-flattening stays. This was observed by Dr. Tode, a Royal Physician and Professor of the University of Copenhagen, the only professional of his generation who (describing himself as a "moderate" but unashamed to reveal his erotic mammaphilia) not only opposes the abandonment of the corset and adoption of the lighter English version, but praises well-made stays which confine only below the breasts. He suggests the wealthier classes instruct the poorer ones how to make them themselves.

Two years after Bonnaud, in Dr. Alphonse Leroy's *Women's and Children's Clothing* (half of which, or nearly two hundred pages, is devoted to stays) we find a physician who claims to have actually dissected the corpses of tight-laced women of the working class, and is thus able to report at first hand the deformed ribs, displaced viscera, and diminished stomach, etc. Leroy also cites two cases from the other end of the social scale, of the Comtesse de ***, who suffered from a descent of the false rib into the lesser pelvis, and that of the late Queen (Marie Leczinska, 1703–68), whose autopsy revealed a concave rib cage and an indented liver (and yet the numerous portraits of her, by artists whose instinct was to slenderize the sitter, show her to have been at all times comparatively wide of girth). There is little reason to believe these latter two, if correctly reported by Leroy (at second hand) to be victims of tight-lacing, especially in the case of an otherwise blameless Queen of France. Leroy's level of hyperbole and exaggeration is extreme even by the standards of writing in which such traits are endemic: he claims that 90 percent of all cancer cases are due to corsets, and that "a plague which ravages Asia and Africa destroys less than this barbarous instrument."

English stays were, according to Leroy, more sensible than the French kind, because they did not compress the upper part of the thorax up to armpits, preventing free movement of the arms. The English had abandoned the "épaulette" (part of the stays reaching up to the armpits and fitted with shoulder straps) and had whiter arms for this reason.

Leroy's gloomy conclusion is that (despite Rousseau) fashion is getting worse, not better, for in earlier times stays were only applied in puberty (here Leroy errs), a time when the bones are more resistant and when "even in the most horrible of tortures, the executioner does not always succeed in breaking the ribs."

Leroy also enlarges upon abuses which had hitherto passed relatively unscathed: tight garters and neckwear.[68] The French are particularly addicted to the tight garter as a means of improving the appearance of the leg by causing the calf to swell, a practice which, according to a leading authority on the heart, Jean-Baptiste de Sénac, has caused a "multitude of soldiers," to die of hydropsy and oedema of the legs. It was in an attempt to throw off the tyranny which the garter exercised over Prussian youth that King Frederick William II in the summer of 1797 showed himself in trousers. That the cult of the tight garter is of some antiquity is suggested by the scene in *Twelfth Night* in which Malvolio, to impress Olivia, appears before her in yellow stockings and "cross-gartered"—a fashion to which she is known to have an implacable aversion. "I could be sad," says Malvolio, "this does make some obstructions in the blood, this cross-gartering; but what of that."[69]

The French are also subject to apoplexy more than other nations, because of their excessively tight neckwear.[70] It is the French military command under the Duc de Choiseul during the Seven Years War which is most forcefully blamed by an English writer for the introduction of tight neckwear, a fact Leroy omits to mention, presumably for fear of offending the military and the Duke himself:

> The stock (introduced into the French army under the Duc de Choiseul) has ever since formed a part of the military costume. Invention has been racked to diversify it as much as possible; and as appearance alone was consulted, each change has rendered it more injurious; (already stiffened by parchment and cardboard) it has been transformed into a collar as hard as iron by the insertion of a slip of wood, which acting on the larynx and compressing every part of the neck, caused the eyes almost to start from the spheres, and gave the wearer a supernatural appearance often producing vertigo and faintings, or at least bleeding at the nose. It rarely happened that a field-day passed over without surgical aid being required by one or more soldiers, whose illness was only produced by an over-tightened stock. As the same kind of stock was used for the necks of all sizes, whether long or short, thin or thick, it rendered the wearer, in many cases, almost immoveable; he was scarcely able to obey the order 'right face—left face' and was entirely prohibited from stooping.[71]

As with the tight garters, the tight stock was supposedly designed to hide the famished condition of the soldiers, to bring a "healthy flush" to their faces and induce an appearance of glowing health—as is stressed by later, socially conscious writers.[72] The practice also infected the German army at the end of the century, as we know from the educator Vieth, who in his *Encyclopedia of Sport* (1795) gives the medical data: "The blood of the arteries is driven into the extremities with greater force than that which it afterwards returns in the veins to the heart. Through pressure on the bloodvessels at the throat, the blood is driven through the arteries, but cannot force its way back, which results in an accumulation of blood in the head, with all the disadvantageous consequences."[73]

These extraordinary descriptions of the devastation caused by military neckwear, like those of the internal havoc caused by tight-lacing, should be taken with a grain of salt. In the case of the former, there may be a heavy political bias behind them. It is hard to credit that commanders would permit or encourage such evident debilitation among common soldiers who had to do most of the fighting, or that compression of the throat could hide their famished condition (although famished they may often have been). The peacetime physical restriction of the dandy officer-class was, as we shall see, another matter. The political bias is very obvious indeed in the Napoleonic era, when the English saw the French military stock as a typically French slavery symbol, such as appears so often in English caricature. Thus Napoleonic "volunteers" are depicted on the way to the conquest of England, chained together from the iron collar clasping the rigid leather stock which they still retain, bedraggled and totally unmilitary-looking as they otherwise are.[74]

It is evident that during the 1770s and 1780s a polarization took place, comparable to that which occurred a century later. An increasing number of progressive families tried to observe the system of "natural education" of Jean Jacques Rousseau, leaving their children unswaddled and uncorseted: "it must be allowed indeed that the female *infant* now enjoys more liberty of tender limb and body than formerly."[75] And to the voices of the philosophy, pedagogy, and medicine was joined that of art: the prestigious art-historian and theorist Winckelmann, in his *Thoughts on the Imitation of the Greeks* (1755), was convinced that the alleged habitual nudity of the Greeks had formed in them a superior taste, as well as superior bodies, and that by dint of tight binding of neck, waist, and thigh mankind had succeeded in producing a mentally and physically degenerate race. The contrast between fashionable distortion and ancient natural perfection became a commonplace, and the Parisienne, groaning in her whalebone mould, was from here on to stand in perpetual confrontation with the Medicean Venus.[76]

Ancient sculpture revealed the "divine proportions" of a race of heroes, built in the image of their gods. In a typical Enlightenment

identification of the unaesthetic with the immoral, a highly popular
didactic poem thus condemns any alteration of the "divine image":

> Heaven! that the human mind,
> Warped by imagination, should believe,
> Or e'en suggest it possible, the form,
> Whose archetype the Deity himself
> Created in His Image, could be changed
> From its divine proportion, and receive
> From alteration, comeliness and grace!
> That round the zone which awkwardly reduced
> E'en to an insect ligament the waist,
> The blooming loves should sport, enticing charms,
> And young attractions![77]

The dangers of corsetry were even expounded in art-schools. The
foremost art theorist in England, the famous portrait painter, President of the Royal Academy and disciple of Winckelmann, Sir Joshua
Reynolds, warned Academy students against the "operations (of
fashion which are) painful or destructive of health, such as some of
the practices at Otaheite, and the strait-lacing of the English ladies; of
the last which practices, how destructive it must be to health and long
life, the Professor of Anatomy took an opportunity for proving a few
days since in this academy."[78] Sir Joshua himself set the example by
costuming his portraits, or encouraging his sitters to come dressed
either in classical drapery or in a loose-flowing style with neo-classical
associations. The better English portrait painting of the '70s and '80s
would lead one to assume that tight-lacing in that country had been
banished forever—among the élite. The aristocracy probably were
among the first to classicize their dress; but lower on the social scale
tight-lacing seems to have intensified.

By the 1760s ladies commonly appeared *en déshabille*, in loose
high-waisted gowns without their petticoats and stays, or wearing
only a very light "corset" as the French termed it, rather than the rigid
"corps". The new informality allowed occasional relief from courtly
pomp and artifice, and a switching of roles: "Now plain as a Quaker,
now all a puff;/Now a shape in neat stays, now a slattern in jumps,/
Now high in French heels, now low in your pumps;/Now monstrous
in hoop, now trapish and walking/With your petticoats clung to your
heels, like a maulkin . . ."[79] The aristocracy were tiring of the rigors of
the old courtly etiquette: "We are beginning to retreat from the barbarous custom of imprisoning children in 'corps' loaded with
whalebones . . . women have reserved them for special occasions.
Those light and flexible 'corsets', which taste and reason substitute
for the old kind, still yield to the latter under court dress, and with

persons delighting in the so-called grace of a stiff, pinched waist."[80]

For the increasing number of girls whose figures had not been trained since infancy in the traditional way, the initiation into full or court stays ("grand corps") was a drastic ritual. Madame de Genlis, the famous writer of children's stories, who grew up wild, uneducated and often dressed as a boy, remembers the occasion with a certain martyrological relish:

> Mesdames de Puisieux and d'Etrée really persecuted me the next day, that of my presentation . . . they wanted me to wear my 'grand corps' for dinner, in order to accustom me to it, as they said: these 'grand corps' left the shoulders uncovered, cut into the arms and were horribly tight; to show off my waist, moreover, they had me laced excessively small . . . the whole dinner passed in discussions on my toilette. I ate nothing at all, because I was so constricted that I could barely breathe.

She appears to have forgotten any discomfort in the excitement of the presentation itself, which went off very well, with the King (Louis XV) paying her much attention. Retrospectively, her feelings about the fashion were ambivalent; writing in an age of monarchical reaction, Madame de Genlis actually defended the stays of the ancien régime, considering the enlargement of the bust and the throwing back of the shoulders not only an aesthetic, but also a physiological advantage: "since they are no longer worn, chest diseases are infinitely more common among women."[81]

The elaborate transformation wrought for a upward-bound young woman's first appearance at court is recounted in popular fiction as well, with the relish of exaggeration and an ironic complaisance: "Poor Winifred . . . broke two laces in endeavouring to draw my new French stays close. You know I am naturally small at bottom. But now you might literally span me. You never saw such a doll. Then, they (the stays) are so intolerably wide across the breast, that my arms are absolutely sore with them; and my sides so pinched!—But it is the *ton*; and pride feels no pain . . . to be admired is sufficient balsam."[82]

The tendency, suggested by the above citation, for stays to compress the waist rather than the torso as a whole, is confirmed by a diarist with reference to her sixteen-year-old sister's coming out, in 1780. "The perfection of figure according to the *then* fashion was the smallest of circumference into which your unfortunate waist could be compressed, and many a poor girl hurt her health very materially by trying to rival the reigning beauty of the day, the Duchess of Rutland, who was said to squeeze herself to the size of an orange and a half."[83]

The voluntarism which appears from such citations from women writers contrasts with evidence from male bourgeois critics grinding their axe against the aristocracy, and blaming the "fashionable" sufferings of a helpless bourgeois bride, on the depraved taste of an aristocratic suitor.[84] If we are right in our theory that tight-lacing was the practice of the arriviste rather than the arrivée, we may attach particular significance to the fact that the undisputed leader of fashion in France at this time, the future Queen Marie-Antoinette gained a reputation for casting off the corset altogether. Such behavior would be consonant with her much publicized ventures into the "natural life" à la Rousseau (such as playing milkmaid) but her mother the Empress Maria Theresa, at one in this with her daughter's closest advisers, saw it as expressive of her childish, self-indulgent and pleasure-seeking character. Marie Antoinette's habit of appearing in public uncorsetted occasioned a flurry of diplomatic correspondence between Vienna and Paris, the upshot of which was the ambassador's cry of victory: "Madame la Dauphine is again wearing her whalebone corset."[85] Marie-Antoinette's own motivation, quite apart from the drift towards staylessness on the part of the upper classes, may well have been to show off her regal shoulders, of which she was very proud.

By 1785 the compression by stays is stated to have been brought to a "stupendous magnitude," especially by "the young charmer of fifteen, eager to expose her beauties, and catch the allured eye" with the "spinal tenuity" of the adolescent combined with the "mammillary exuberance" of the mature woman. Unlike most critics, at this time or later, the writer here makes the significant admission that "there is an air of gaiety, and a resemblance of health, that the sex are able to assume under all the oppression of dress and ornament, and even when they are ready to faint away with the uneasiness they endure." He senses moreover that the inhibition of normal breathing was no mere unfortuante side-effect, but the result of a deliberate design to make "ladies heave as it were a sigh at every inspiration."[86]

In one country, what had by now become the common opinion of enlightened men was enacted into law. Governments in the more advanced European countries had by and large given up attempting to regulate the private lives of citizens by means of sumptuary laws. Imperial Austria, however, promulgated an anti-corset edict which was obviously aimed at every urban family, although enforceable only in the public schools. Its author was none other than the Emperor Joseph II of Austria-Hungary himself, whose mania for regulating the minutest details of life in his realm was combined with a sweeping and progressive vision of reform. On the one hand he introduced in the 1780s universal compulsory education, and on the other hand and at the same time he prohibited peasants from baking gingerbread cake "because it was bad for the stomach," determined whether a zebra should be bought for the zoo, and forbade girls from wearing corsets in the public schools, especially in those where they had to sit in the same room as boys.[87] Clearly, Joseph II saw stays as an instrument of seduction and a threat to maternity, rather than like his mother Maria Theresa who saw them as a form of discipline, the inculcation of which was always his guiding educational and political principle. (He also probably saw the corset as typically French, and was strengthened no doubt in his hostility by the anti-French policy he developed in opposition to that of his mother).

The text of this first and only comprehensive law to abolish corset-wearing is worth citing in full:

Whereas the dangerous consequences arising from the use of stays, are universally acknowledged to impair the health, and impede the growth of the fair sex; when, on the contrary, the suppression of that part of their dress cannot but be effectual in strengthening their constitution, and above all in rendering them more fruitful in the marriage state: we hereby strictly enjoin that in all orphan-houses, nunneries, and other places set apart for the public education of young girls, no stays of any kind whatever shall be made use of or encouraged from henceforth and from this instant; and it is hereby further hinted to all masters and mistresses of academies and boarding-schools, that any girl wearing stays should not be received or countenanced in any such schools. We hereby also will and command, that it be enjoined to the College of Physicians, that a dissertation adapted to everyone's capacity be forthwith composed, shewing how materially the growth of children of the female sex is injured by the use of stays, for the better information of parents and school-masters who wish to procure a handsome shape to their children or pupils, as also those who are not rich enough to alter the stays in proportion to the growth of such children, or having the means neglected to do it. The above dissertation shall be distributed gratis, and dispersed among the public; the more so, as whole nations unacquainted with the use of stays, bring up a race of children remarkable for the healthiest constitutions.[88]

This law was generally admitted (outside Austria, at any rate) to have been well-intentioned but ineffectual, despite the pleas of the Viennese police doctor Frank that the police actively enforce it.[89] Austrian women and the Austrian military were, in the 19th century, regarded as pre-eminent in artificial slenderness of form; and the English tight-lacing enthusiast, in particular, cites the Viennese as the master figure-trainers.

The Emperor's appeal to the Imperial College of Physicians for a propaganda "dissertation" was answered by physicians all over Germany, to judge from the sudden rash of tracts published during the years 1785–8. The best known was the monograph of Dr. Soem-merring (remembered primarily as the inventor of a new system of telegraphy), which was presented in response to a competition launched around 1788 by Salzmann's progressive Educational Institute in Schnepfenthal. Soemmerring's work was several times reprinted and enlarged in the succeeding years, and became for the 19th century the standard monograph. It is more collected and less emotional in tone than preceding writing on the subject. The author confirms that tight-lacing among women is still extreme, and laments that it has spread to young males. During the decade 1760–70, according to Soemmerring, it was the custom in Berlin and elsewhere in Germany, and still was to an extreme degree in Holland, to select the best-looking boys in the family for corsetting. Soemmerring claims that all men who were "severely and consistently" corsetted in their childhood are now developing hunched backs or high shoulders; girls, being more supple in the spine, can sometimes withstand the treatment better.

But the carnage amongst the female internal organs remains horrific. Most methodical of them all, Soemmerring's Cohors Morborum breaks down as follows: thirteen diseases of the head, twenty-three of the upper body, fifty-one of the lower body, and twelve maladies of a general character such as epilepsy, melancholy and atrophy. In a work of a mere eighty-four pages, the author has room only to expatiate upon the particular dangers to pregnancy, birth and parturition, to which young girls seemed scandalously indifferent. He confirms the incidence of voluntary tight-lacing by teenage girls, who commonly faint away when their stays are *removed*. There is more hearsay than observation in Soemmerring; empirical observation did not always match the medical dogma. The author tacitly admits as much when he speaks of a girl who attracted his attention through her excessively tight-laced waist and who was "otherwise very beautifully formed" and not demonstrably unhealthy.

It is Soemmerring who gives us the first statistics on comparative waist measurements. Whereas the Greek Venus measures twice as much around the waist as around the head, two young girls of the doctor's acquaintance (one of whom is described as "prettily formed") were found to measure considerably *less* around the waist than around the forehead: the first had a 22 Zoll forehead and 14 Zoll waist; the second an 18 Zoll forehead, 15 Zoll waist, and 30 Zoll bust. An illustration (which was to be reprinted ad nauseam throughout the 19th century—Plate 28) comparing the torso of the Medici Venus with the deformed one of fashion, takes as its guideline this degree of compression, which "even defenders of stays found not at all too slender, too thin, or, as the expression goes, too wasp-like."

By the time Soemmerring wrote his book, the campaign against a fashion in dress had already become something of a fashion in medical writing. In this context, another noted physician turned to relatively virgin polemical territory. Petrus Camper, a Dutch friend of Soemmerring, was the first to publish a monograph on high-heeled shoes, a modest little book which became very successful.[90] Camper was an orthopedist famous in his time, Professor of Anatomy in Amsterdam, and is now recognized as an early theorist of evolution. After some humorous apology for dealing with so trivial a subject, and ironic observations to the effect that anatomical expertise was customarily devoted to the shoeing of horses rather than humans, Camper asserts that improper footwear has always preoccupied him and that the present monograph merely develops certain complaints he had already delivered in his *Dissertation on the Physical Education of Children* (1777).

Camper starts with the geometry of the foot and locomotion, observing that the high heel causes women to walk like most quadrupeds, that is on the toes, and necessitates adaptation of the entire frame to a marked shift in the center of gravity. High heels have many of the same effects as stays, such as distortion of the spinal column and the hindering of pregnancy, and have necessitated many painful surgical interventions at the moment of delivery. A peculiar danger is that of breaking the rotule of the knee. Habitual high-heel wearers (including quite young girls) found it positively painful to walk in low shoes or barefoot (as Winslow had already observed). Although the aristocracy was to blame for leading this fashion, the growing counter-tendency within this class to allow children to run around barefoot in the home was highly commendable.

As with tight-lacing, high-heel wearing reached a peak during the decade Camper was writing, and was as firmly entrenched by a generations-long tradition. King Louis XIV, who was small of stature, had set the example among male courtiers of wearing elevated heels, usually in a contrasting red color ("les talons rouges" was a popular designation of the aristocrat until the Revolution). The King's brother Monsieur, who was bisexual with transvestite tendencies, wore heels so high that he tended to trip over them while dancing. Ladies heels rose correspondingly, and continued to rise in the 18th century while the male heel descended. In the course of the new century, a cultural kind of foot-fetishism manifested itself in various media: rococo painting, new styles in stage and social dancing, and the popular novel (especially those of Restif de la Bretonne) threw particular erotic emphasis on the finely arched foot and the delicately curved, high heel. The Censor of Great Britain made the appropriate response, by objecting to provocative window-displays featuring "fine wrought ladies' shoes and slippers on public view at a (certain) great shoemaker's shop . . . which create irregular thoughts and desires in the youth of this realm . . . The said shopkeeper is required to take them in and be prepared particularly to answer to the slippers with green lace and blue heels."

The "French heel" became a byword of dangerous elegance: "Mount on French heels when you go to a ball/Tis the fashion to totter and show you can fall."[91] From surviving shoes, it would appear that the four inch heel was standard for much of the century; during the 1770s, however, it rose to as much as six inches.[92]

The continental reformist tradition passed into England in summary form via Walter Vaughan's *Essay Philosophical and Medical concerning modern clothing* (1792). His omission of high heels as a major cause of concern is the surest sign that by the last decade of the century, the extremer heel heights had abated. This Englishman, a physician of Rochester, is less choleric, more detached, more truly "philosophical" in tone than his continental colleagues. He is inclined to blame unhealthy clothing less upon individual vanity and folly, than upon civilization as a whole; precociously, he holds the belief that man walks erect not by nature but by art, and that he would do better, in some respects, to go on all fours. His list of fashionable evils is in no sense new and still fairly horrific, but the relative sobriety of his tone may reflect an actual diminution of their incidence.

Neo-Classical Period: Breast Exposure; Thin Clothing

As the combined effect of revolutionary ideas and the neo-classical aesthetic helped sweep away the artificial modes of the Ancien Régime, dress reformers turned their attention again more exclusively to the breasts, décolletage, cancer and pneumonia. As the stays diminished and relaxed their grasp upon the waist, they were used a fortiori to press up and throw out the bared breasts. A novelty designed for this purpose, called a karako, a shorter, lighter but very closely boned outer corset enabling the wearer to dispense with the inner one, was considered as damaging as the old stays. Carl Creve, a friend of Soemmerring and surgeon in Mainz, complains in a monograph of 1794 that breasts are being pushed so high that one can scarcely see the lady's face (cf. Plate 24). This, together with the voluminous padding, causes overheating and inadequate ventilation, which in turn, causes cancer. It is perhaps on the basis of some personal clinical observation in the convents of Mainz, a city-state which had recently secularized in the wake of the French Revolution and expelled the Catholic archbishop, that Creve is able to claim that cancer of the breast is very common amongst nuns, because they bind and otherwise mortify that part of the body.

PLATE 1

PLATE 2

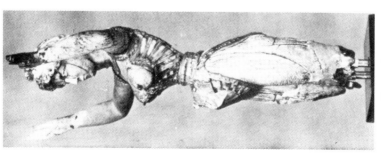

PLATE 3

PLATE 5

PLATE 4

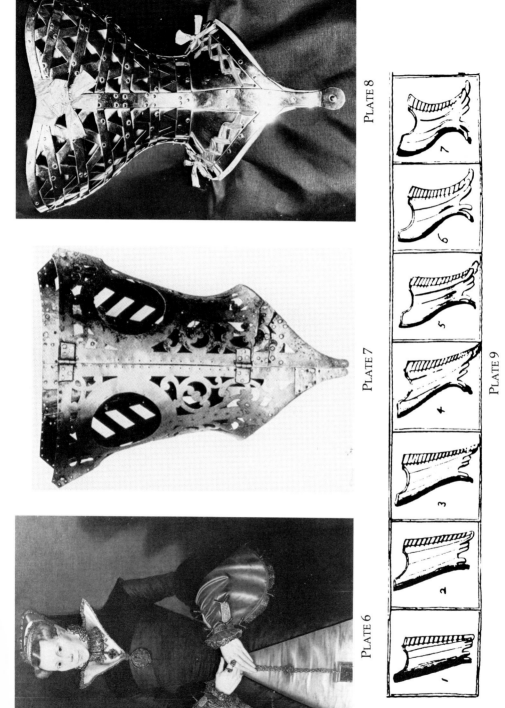

PLATE 6

PLATE 7

PLATE 8

PLATE 9

PLATE 10

PLATE 11

PLATE 12

PLATE 13

PLATE 14

PLATE 15

A LITTLE TIGHTER.

PLATE 17

PLATE 16

PLATE 18

PLATE 19

PLATE 20

Au bout de cinq ans Tadet meurt un Samedi matin, pour avoir trop serré sa crinoline imperméable.

87

PLATE 21

The Dandies Coat of Arms

PLATE 22

PLATE 24

PATENT-BOLSTERS.— _Le moyen d'étre en bonpoint._

Designed by an Amateur　_Progress of the Toilet._— THE STAYS.— _Plate 1._— ...

London Publish'd February 26 1810. by H Humphrey 27 S.t James's Street.

PLATE 23

PLATE 25

THE EFFECTS OF TIGHT LACING ON THE OLD 'LADY
OF THREADNEEDLE STREET.

PLATE 26

Difficile à faire paraître svelte

PLATE 27

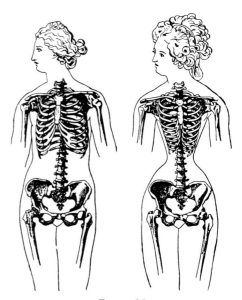

PLATE 28

PLATE 29

PLATE 30

PLATE 31

PLATE 32

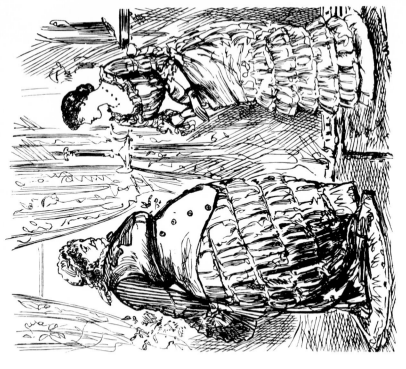

A DISQUISITION ON WAISTS.

"MY *DEAR* SOPHY, YOU ARE KILLING YOURSELF BY *INCHES!*"
"MY *DEAR* AUNT LOO, *YOU* ARE KILLING YOURSELF BY *YARDS!*"

PLATE 34

MR. PUNCH'S DESIGNS AFTER NATURE.

MIGHT NOT WASP-WAISTED YOUNG LADIES ADOPT THIS COSTUME WITH ADVANTAGE?

PLATE 33

MR. PUNCH'S DRESS DESIGNS (AFTER NATURE).

Costume du Soir—Robe en Homard.

[*A Suggestion for Tight Dresses.*

Plate 35

Plate 36

Plate 37

THE WAIST OF FASHION.

Plate 38

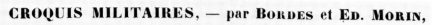

CROQUIS MILITAIRES, — par BORDES et ED. MORIN,

Gravé par POTHEY.

— Cré nom ! tu m'étrangles...
— Va toujours, mon vieux, tu seras ficelé pour la revue du colonel...

PLATE 39

MADAME DOWDING,

8 & 10, CHARING CROSS ROAD (Opposite the National Gallery, Trafalgar Square),

Ladies' Tailor, Corsetiere, and Court Dressmaker.

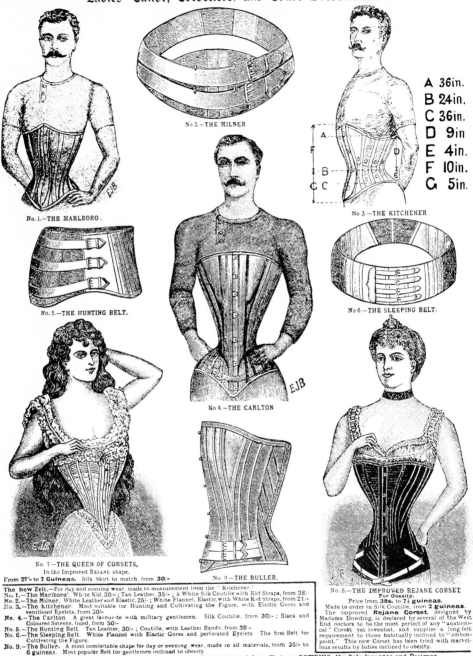

A 36in.
B 24in.
C 36in.
D 9in.
E 4in.
F 10in.
G 5in.

No 2.—THE MILNER

No 1.—THE MARLBORO.

No 3.—THE KITCHENER

No. 5.—THE HUNTING BELT.

No 6.—THE SLEEPING BELT.

No 4.—THE CARLTON

No 9.—THE BULLER.

No. 7.—THE QUEEN OF CORSETS,
In the Improved REJANE shape.
From 27/- to 7 Guineas. Silk Skirt to match, from 30/-

No. 8.—THE IMPROVED REJANE CORSET
For Obesity.
Price from 38s. to 7½ guineas.
Made to order in Silk Coutille, from 2 guineas.
The improved Rejane Corset, designed by Madame Dowding, is declared by several of the West End doctors to be the most perfect of any "anatomical" Corset yet invented, and supplies a long-felt requirement to those habitually inclined to "embonpoint." This new Corset has been tried with marvellous results by ladies inclined to obesity.

The New Zelt.—For day and evening wear, made to measurement from the "Kitchener"
No. 1.—The Marlboro. White Kid, 30/-; Tan Leather, 35/-; & White Silk Coutille with Kid Straps, from 38/-
No. 2.—The Milner. White Leather and Elastic, 25/-; White Flannel, Elastic, with White Kid Straps, from 21/-
No. 3.—The Kitchener. Most suitable for Hunting and Cultivating the Figure, with Elastic Gores and ventilated Eyelets, from 30/-
No. 4.—The Carlton. A great favourite with military gentlemen. Silk Coutille, from 30/-; Black and Coloured Sateens, lined, from 50/-
No. 5.—The Hunting Belt. Tan Leather, 30/-; Coutille, with Leather Bands, from 30/-
No. 6.—The Sleeping Belt. White Flannel with Elastic Gores and perforated Eyelets. The first Belt for Cultivating the Figure.
No. 9.—The Buller. A most comfortable shape for day or evening wear, made in all materials, from 35/- to 6 guineas. Most popular Belt for gentlemen inclined to obesity.

All these Belts are absolutely Hygienic, and can only be procured from Madame DOWDING, the Sole Inventor and Designer.

No orders can be executed under seven days' notice. The demand for these Corsets is daily increasing, and is, indeed, a great satisfaction to the Inventor.
MADAME DOWDING begs to thank the numerous West End Tailors for their kind recommendations. All Communications STRICTLY PRIVATE in Belt Dept.

PLATE 40

Under the Rousseauist Enlightenment the female breast had moved into a new cultural prominence. In life, as in art,[93] breasts became visible as a symbol of Motherhood, Fertility, and Nature. And not just visible: the breast must be active, productive. Having discovered from Rousseau the virtues of suckling their own children, some audacious women began to do so in public and in a manner condemned as a provocation, sheer lechery. The sexual satisfaction derived from suckling was singled out by an anonymous German physician, who damns mothers for their lecherous thoughts as they suckle, and hopes their milk will become sour and their breasts deformed.[94]

By 1804–5 the critics were speaking of the tight-lacing of "former times", and were chiefly exercised by exposure to cold—not only through décolletage, as before, but also through the new mode for thin dress materials. With the Revolutionary, Greco-Roman style, the pendulum had swung to the opposite extreme: the hoop skirt and multitudinous petticoats had been banished in favor of the thinnest muslin dresses, worn over the scantiest underclothing, and sometimes dampened to adhere more sculpturally to the body. Exposed breasts, scanty and dampened clothing, and sudden transitions from an overheated ballroom into a cold night, were alleged not only to jeopardize lactation but even cause death. In 1804 a French physician gives a list of some celebrities who thus sacrificed their lives to fashion: the nineteen-year-old Mme. Charles de Noailles suddenly died on leaving the ballroom; the seventeen-year-old Russian Princess Tufaikin died of "an epidemic of French fashion at St. Petersburg"; and in the Cimetière des Quatre-Sections in the Rue Vaugirard one could see a tombstone dated December 22, 1802, with the inscription "Louise Le Febvre, agée de 23 ans, Victime de la Mode Meutrière . . . Rose, elle a vécu ce que vivent les roses" (victim of murderous fashion, rose, she lived as roses live).[95]

Notes

1. Hawkes, pp. 110–113.
2. According to Pendlebury (p. 117) it may still be observed among the modern inhabitants of the island.
3. According to Schachermeyr (p. 123) however, the waist in the early Minoan period was "natural", was later compressed by the women, and then taken over by the men.
4. III, p. 446 ff. and IV, pp. 31–32.
5. Pendlebury, p. 117.
6. *Eunuch,* Act II, scene iv (161 B.C.): "vincto pectore ut graciles sint".
7. Passage translated in full by Bouvier 1853 p. 360
8. Compilation in Bouvier, 1853.
9. Laver, *Modesty,* p. 29.
10. Eisenbart, p. 94.

11. Cited by Ziegler, p. 279. The emergence at this time of the "modern" style of dress clearly warrants special study. "I would argue that male (and possibly female) clothing was more tight-fitting in the 15th century for technological reasons (appearance of buttons, popularity of knitting, weaving on bias for tighter-fitting hose), meteorological reasons (beginning of Little Ice Age in northern Europe, c. 1300/50–18th century), and by way of changes in military clothing toward form-fitting armor which is still flexible" (communication from Hillel Schwartz).

12. Friar Galvani de la Flamma, and Jean de Mussi (1388), respectively, cited by Bouvier, 1853, p. 363.

13. Eisenbart, p. 94.

14. *Trésor de la Cité des Dames* (1400) cited by Paul Lacroix p. 134.

15. Wachtel, p. 227. Huss saw horns everywhere—in the hair, beard, headdress (hennin), sleeves, skirts, etc. The horns were those of the Apocalyptic Beast (passage cited by Wendel, p. 27). Cf. also Lydgate's *Ditty of Women's Horns* (quoted by Rhead, p. 38f.) which says that horns were given to beasts for defense, "a thing contrary to femininity". Horns have, of course, often served as phallic symbols. The phallic symbolism of breasts is widely accepted and manifested today.

16. Third Novella, p. lxx. The resurrection of Friar Filippo's hitherto unpublished sermons in 1862 may have to do with the resumption in that decade of face-painting by ladies of fashion.

17. Irate father: Livermore, p. 122 (about 1834); comic strip by Wilhelm Busch, *Fromme Helene*, 1872, II, p. 281; newspaper report: a revivalist called J.F. Fraser, from a community of Free Methodists, arranged a bonfire on which he urged women to throw their corsets until "nothing remained in the blaze but a mass of twisted steels." The scene was described in full in the *Scientific American* of 19 Dec. 1891, p. 185, c. 1, with reference to the New York *World* of recent date; but a correspondent to *Scientific American* of 10 Oct. following, stated that the *World* report was a fabrication from beginning to end.

18. These and the following quotations passed into the corset literature (Lord, p. 45, and Libron, p. 2) via Strutt (1796–9), together with the suggestion, based upon his misinterpretation (p. 38) of an 11th century ms. illustration of the devil supposedly wearing front-laced "stays", that tight-lacing dated back to the 11th century.

19. Chevalier de Latour-Landry (1371), p. 30. In his popular treatise on female education, Latour-Landry writes entirely in the clerical spirit, citing horrific examples of the punishment for face-painting and plucking, and describing how a devil thrust a burning needle into a woman's brain through each pore whence she had plucked a hair, and another devil came and enflamed her face with boiling pitch, oil, earth, grease and lead (LII, p. 67 and LIII, p. 69).

20. Pierre des Gros, *Jardin des Nobles*, c. 1470. Original text in Paulin Paris p. 156.

21. *Paston Letters*, 1472, p. 216, Letter 106 (citation modernized).

22. Cf. Kay Staniland, pp. 10–13.

23. Cf. poets Olivier de la Marche and Clément Marot, quoted in Léoty, p. 27.

24. For Catherine's reputation in the 19th century as "inventor" of the tight-laced corset, cf. above p. 48 and Appendix p. 320.

25. Cf. Fairholt, *Satirical Songs* p. 139, where a version includes the male: "The thrifty Frenchman wears small waist . . ."

26. Tommaseo, p. 557.

27. *Oeuvres* v. 2, pp. 611 and 624. The embellishment in the English 1634 translation (pp. 875–6) is worth citing: "In the meanwhile, that I may not omit the occasion of crookedness, that happens seldom to country people, but is much incident to the inhabitants of great towns and cities, which is by reason of the straitness and narrowness of the garments that are worn only by them, which is occasioned by the folly of mothers, who while they covet to have their young daughters' bodies so small in the middle as may be possible, pluke and draw out their bones awry and make them crooked."

Our text following, which cites two fatalities, derives from the learned and usually reliable Bouvier, 1853, pp. 366–367, who is evidently paraphrasing Paré, in passages I have been unable to find in Paré's *Works*. The 19th century physician's sense that Paré might be exaggerating ("he went so far as to attribute . . .") is emphasized by him in a later article (1877 p. 755), when he tends to discredit both stories. Subsequent medical references to Paré derive, it seems, from Bouvier.

28. *Deux Dialogues* t. I pp. 209–10, somewhat condensed.

29. *Apologie pour Hérodote*, p. 393.

30. John Florio translation, 1603, which embroiders considerably on the original: "Pour faire un corps bien espagnolé, quelle géhenne (torture) les femmes ne souffrent-elles, guindées et sanglées à tout de grosses coches sur les costes jusques à la chair vifve. Oui, quelque fois à en mourir." The word "coche", fancifully enlarged by Florio as "yronplates, whalebones and other such trash" and commonly supposed to refer to strips of wood used to stiffen the bodice, more probably means gashes or notches (entailles) made in the flesh.

Florio's baroque embroidery of Montaigne surprises us less than that of Paul Lacroix, the premier antiquarian bibliophile of the mid-19th century, who gives this paraphrase of the passage (1852, v. 5, p. 121): "they (women) were so compressed between the wooden strips (coches) since childhood, that the flesh of their breast became as hard and insensitive as the horn or callous which forms on the hands of workers; so that they accustom themselves to this torturous garment only at the price of long suffering . . ." Montaigne, of course, says nothing of childhood training or callouses. Lacroix evidently picked up his gloss from the Pierre Coste edition of the *Essais*, first published in 1724.

Our modern translation is from the 1946 Oxford edition translated by E. J. Trechmann, I, p. 53–54.

31. Chapter XV of the Second Book, "That our desires are augmented by difficulty."

32. *Habiti Antichi at Moderni* (Venice, 1590). His predecessor Ferdinando Bertelli, also a Venetian, included in his costume book of 1563 woodcuts showing the Frenchwoman as much more slender waisted and bare-breasted than any other national.

33. By Hoechstetterus, cited by Bulwer, pp. 339–340.

34. Robert Crowley, 1550, p. 45.

35. In Cotgrave's *Dictionary of French and English* (1611) the principal entry for this word is under *Buc,* with references to alternative spellings Busq and Buste, and English equivalent "a Buske."

36. Other examples are in the collections of Mr. Anthony Pont; the Musée Le Secq des Tournelles, in Rouen (reproduced Libron, p. 21); and Moyse's Hall Museum, Bury St. Edmunds. The latter, which lacks provision for breasts, might be a piece of male armor but for the lace-holes at the back (or possibly front—from a photograph it is hard to tell which way round it was worn).

I am informed by the two Parisian museums cited that the iron stays reproduced in the literature as located there, are not (now) in their possession.

37. Libron, p. 21, Waugh, Figs. 4 and 5, and Cunnington (*Underclothes*, p. 48), who adds with mysterious sagacity, "when are they not—as is commonly the case—fanciful 'reproductions'." Does he mean they are forgeries? Or fetishistic reconstructions?

38. This dip is missing from the orthopedic "iron breastplate" described and illustrated in Paré (1634 edition, p. 876), following the passage cited above, condemning fashionable stays which *cause* deformity.

39. Libron (pp. 18 and 22) unearthed two references, both more ambiguous than he is prepared to admit: Marguerite de Valois, when she became very stout added, "du fer-blanc aux deux côtés de son corps pour élargir la carrure," a phrase which from the context surely means she employed metal (hoops) to conceal the extent of her girth; and the Bourgeoise Débauchée of Sigogne (cf. below). Waugh follows Léoty in considering the iron stays to date from the early 16th century. Léoty apparently took over a misinterpretation by Bouvier (*Bulletin Academie Nationale Médecine* 1853 p. 365) of a passage in Vecellio's *Habiti Antichi e Moderni* (1590, p. 76), describing a Venetian costume of about one hundred years earlier, which was prohibited, and whose "iron blades" (lame di ferro) "to make the waist *larger*" (my stress) must refer to an early form of farthingale, not a form of bodice-stiffening.

Peter Rondeau's French-German Dictionary of 1739 has, under "corps de fer" (the only entry for corps meaning corset) the specification that it is designed "with small iron plates for badly grown (i.e. deformed) girls (Schnürbrust, mit kleinen eisernen blechen, für übel gewachsenes Frauenzimmer)." The modifier "small" would suggest that the plates were inserts into a corset composed of another material, rather than those of all-iron framework.

40. This is pure speculation, which might conceivably be corroborated from the "secret" histories of monastic customs, along the lines of the following story, dating from a much later period: During the disorders of the French Commune (1871), the National Guard occupied the Convent of the White Nuns in the Rue de Picpus, Paris. They discovered various horrors such as huts occupied by some old idiot women who were enclosed in a tiny cage, and in an isolated building "mattresses furnished with straps and buckles, also two iron corsets, an iron skullcap, and a species of rack turned with cogwheels evidently intended for bending back the body with force. The Superior explained that these were orthopedic instruments—a superficial falsehood." There was a Jesuit establishment next door, communicating with the convent by a private, hidden door (London *Times* for May 10, 1871, p. 12 c., picked up by *Days Doings* for May 13, pp. 246a, 258a and 267a.)

41. "O, cut my lace, lest my heart, cracking it, Break too" (*Winter's Tale* III, 2, 174). "O cut my lace in sunder, that my pent heart May have some scope to beat, or else I swoon" (*Richard III*, IV, 1, 34). Cleopatra: "Cut my lace, Charmian, come; But let it be: —I am quickly ill, and well, So Anthony loves" (*Anthony and Cleopatra* I, 3, 71).

42. William Warner, 1586, p. 175.

43. Thomas Nashe, 1593, II, pp. 137–8.

44. It is conspicuous by its absence from various French manuals on dress and hygiene, notably Pierre Jacquelot, *L'Art de vivre longuement* (Lyon, 1630); Sieur Domergue, *Moyens Faciles pour conserver la Santé* (Paris, 1687), and M. de Comiers, *La Médecine Universelle* (Paris and Brussels, 1688). The decline may have set in as early as 1613, the date of a *Discours nouveau sur la Mode:* "Les busques ne sont plus comme jadis aimez" (Lacroix, 1852, vol. 3, p. 356).

45. Cabanès, 1902, p. 506.

46. "cuisses", but here referring surely to the thorax (*Oeuvres*, pp. 252–263).

47. Tallemant des Réaux, vol. 4, p. 389.

48. It seems to have been known in Spain, where an extreme code of prudery surrounded female feet. 19th century testimony may reflect an older custom: "In Spain the art is practiced with astonishing success in causing beautifully small feet. I have known ladies there, who were past twenty years of age, to sleep every night with bandages on their feet and ankles drawn as tight as they could be, and not stop the circulation" (Montez, p. 64).

49. Quoted by Libron, p. 26.

50. Pp. 327–344 and 545. For complete breast-exposure in England, cf. Stone, pp. 520–21, with references from 1608, 1616 and 1620.

51. Cf. *Curiosa Theologica*.

52. John Dunton, *Ladies Dictionary*, 1694, quoted by Waugh, p. 50.

53. This letter is quoted in full, together with many others on the subject, by Waugh, pp. 54 and 60, from *London Magazine*, 1741.

54. Waugh, p. 37.

55. McCormick, pp. 66–67.

56. The demand for whalebone in hoop skirts and stays was such that in June 1722, the Dutch government authorized a loan of 600,000 florins to support the East Frisian Whaling Company (Libron, p. 42). From the 16th to the 19th century whale fishery was closely tied to the demands of the corset and the movements of fashion. "The vanity of women has contributed not a little to the chase and destruction of this now rare and interesting animal" (Waugh, p. 167).

57. *Thoughts Concerning Education*, p. 22. From an earlier date (1665) there is evidence—isolated, but evidence nevertheless—that very small children were treated even worse than Locke describes. Thus George Evelyn telling the diarist John how his two-year-old daughter died: "She was never sick; all her complaint was difficulty of

breathing . . . I had the advice of a very able physician Dr. Hailey . . . let her blood four ounces and gave her other things inwardly . . . His judgment was that her iron (sic) bodice was her pain, and had hindered the lungs to grow, and truly the surgeon that surclothed her body found her breast bone pressed very deeply inwardly, and he said two of her ribs were broken, and the straightness of the bodice upon the vitals occasioned this difficulty of breathing and her death. . . Both the Doctor and Surgeon did conclude that going into the bodice so young, before her lungs had their growth, and the depression of those parts hastened her death" (Wiscock p. 55).

58. *Way of the World*, 1700, Act IV. The term "streight-lac'd" occurs (first)? in a bawdy catch called "Tom the Taylor" (to music by Henry Purcell, who died in 1695). Here the lady's waist measurement (calculable at 21 inches), reduced as it is by tight-lacing to meet the tailor's inadequacy of craftsmanship, becomes a cover for his phallic shortcomings (omitting the repetitions): "Tom, making a Mantua (coat, dress) for a Lass of Pleasure/Pull'd out his long and lawful measure;/But quickly found, tho' woundily (excessively) streight lac'd,/Nine inches would not half surround her wast;/Three inches more, at length brisk Tom advances,/Yet all too short to reach her swinging hances (haunches)."

59. *Histoire Naturelle Générale et Particulière*, II, p. 457.

60. Of the ten German sumptuary laws found by Eisenbart dating from the second half of the 17th century, several are directed against the high heel, which does not, however, seem to have aroused the attention of the preachers.

61. Sometimes called by French gardeners "corset-tuteurs".

62. Davies, p. 63, n. 56.

63. *Analysis*, plate 11, fig. 121; cf. the text, p. 154: "The awe most children are in before strangers, till they come to a certain age, is the cause of their dropping and drawing their chins down into their breasts, and looking under the foreheads, as if conscious of this weakness, or of something wrong about them. To prevent this awkward shyness, parents and tutors are continually teasing them to hold up their heads, which if they get them to do it is with difficulty, and of course in so constrain'd a manner that it gives the children pain, so that they naturally take all opportunities of easing themselves by holding down their heads . . . (which) is apt to make them bend too much in the back; when this happens to be the case, they then have recourse to steel collars, and other iron-machines; all which shacklings are repugnant to nature and may make the body grow crooked."

64. Cf. caricatures by Daumier in 1843 (Delteil 1006) and Meggendorfer in the later 19th century.

65. Testimony to an international reputation, for Rousseau had not yet visited England. In the *Nouvelle Héloïse* (Pléiade ed., II, p. 265), he assumed that Parisian women, not being naturally possessed of a slender waist, try to disguise it by tight-lacing. When the naturally slender Englishwoman tight-laces, the results would presumably be all the more startling. Ironically, Rousseau also recognized that the English were ahead of the French in the abolition of baby-swaddling, "almost obsolete" in England by 1762 (Stone, p. 424). This apparent contradiction deserves attention.

66. *Oeuvres Complètes*, II, 1892, p. 338. This is the earliest comparison I have found of the tight-laced woman to a wasp.

67. Bonnaud pp. xvi (on Andry), pp. 164–179 (on abortion. Cf. Franckenau 1722 p. 217 for earlier bibliography on the corset as abortifacient). Kositski pp. 99–102. "Lower classes and grades": in Soemmerring 1788 p. 134; "French governesses": ibid p. 184. Holland: Bonnaud p. 13 (citing Formey's Notes on *Emile*), and Soemmerring, 1793 ed., who says that the Dutch actually lace tighter than any other people; presumably he got this information from Camper; it is contradicted in the *European Magazine* for July 1785 pp. 23–27.

68. Plague: p. 198. Comtesse: p. 228. Epaulette: p. 239. Executioner: p. 254. Garters and neckwear p. 169 f.

69. King Frederick: Hauff, 1840, p. 13; *Twelfth Night* III, 4, 22.

70. According to Rougemont, p. 10, the French were also reputed to tie up their queues so tight that the skin on the back of their heads became wrinkled. This peculiar

habit was satirized by George Cruikshank in an amusing caricature about a recruit who complains to his drill-instructor that he cannot move his eyes, as ordered, because his pig-tail has been tied back too tight (*Scraps and Sketches*, Part 4, 1832 pl. 6).

71. Leblanc, 1829, p. 19.

72. Cooley, pp. 169–70.

73. P. 82, n. 18. According to Vieth, tight trousers or breeches were to be blamed for the premature development of the sexual drive. Today, by contrast, tightness in the crotch of male jeans, and the heat it generates, has been associated with sterility.

74. B.M. Sat. 10117 (year 1803), repr. in Gillray, *Works*, No. 278.

75. *European Magazine* for July, 1785, p. 24.

76. Mercier, p. 674.

77. Downman, pp. 102–03. The passage does not appear in the first two editions, (1774–78) and was introduced in the 3rd (Edinburgh 1790) after tight-lacing increased.

78. *Discourses on Art* (1776), p. 122.

79. *London Magazine*, April 1762, p. 205. A "malkin" is a slut.

80. Roland de la Platière in the *Encyclopédie Méthodique* 1784, quoted in Libron p. 58.

81. *Mémoires* pp. 240–1, and *Dictionnaire* p. 272. A comparable retrospective upon such an initiation is that of the 71 year-old Johanna Schopenhauer, mother of the famous philosopher, recalling in 1837 her extraordinary transformation as a sixteen year-old in "wasp-like" stays of a "thickness sufficient to turn a musket-ball," but without mentioning any discomfort at all.

82. Cavendish, I, 1779, p. 69.

83. Frampton, p. 3. If the Duchess of Rutland did indeed tight-lace, she would represent an illustrious exception to the rule that the practice was confined to lower-class women. But I have found no other evidence that she did, and some that she did not. First, we should note that the phrase "who was said to" indicates that Frampton had not actually seen her, but was repeating hearsay, possibly put about by adherents of the Duchess of Devonshire, with whom Rutland was in friendly rivalry, as the other reigning beauty of the day. The Duchess of Devonshire's good-natured ridicule of tight-lacing, in the passage cited from her novel *The Sylph*, may have been directed against a habit imputed to her rival or her adherents.

The aristocratic lineage of Mary Isabella, Duchess of Rutland, is impeccable. She was a daughter of the 4th Duke of Beaufort, and married the Duke of Rutland in 1775, giving him six children in quick succession before he died of drink and other sensual excesses at the age of 33 (she lived to be 75). Several of these children were born in or near the year Frampton refers to (1780); it is very unlikely that she was able to tight-lace to any degree at this time. The most detailed description of her, moreover, says only that she was "slender but no means thin" (Wraxall pp. 36–37). The dozen or so known portraits of her (including several by Reynolds) show her in classicizing or loose costume; one by J. Downman of 1781 shows her to be slight-breasted, with a narrow thorax, but not at all wasp-waisted (*Connoisseur*, July 1931 p. 11).

The curious phrase "an orange and a half" may have some currency in this connection, to judge by its appearance in a news report of 1788, beginning "As a warning to young ladies who wear small stays, and lace them into an orange and a half . . ." and following with an account of a young lady, "blessed with every pleasing feature and accomplishment," who fainted in company, and was discovered by the physician to be "exhausted by pain and want of nourishment" through tight-lacing (Gillham, p. 29 v.). The patient confessed to having taken no food for three days—a circumstance rare among accounts of illness or death from tight-lacing, which reminds one of the psychosomatic disease known today as anorexia nevrosa.

84. Cf. a passage in *Sophiens Reise von Memel nach Sachsen* (1778), Bd. VI, p. 11, quoted in Charlotte Steinbrucker, *Chodowiecki's Briefwechsel*, p. 213, No. 299.

85. Castelot, pp. 49 and 60.

86. "On the bad effects of some of the present modes of female dress," *European Magazine*, July 1785, pp. 23–27. The same year, a French medical journal reported the death of a "plump, healthy lady" of a hydropsy occasioned by tight-lacing (cited in *Observations* 1785).

87. Padover pp. 188 and 199.

88. This translation of the edict appeared in the *European Magazine,* July 1785 p. 24.

89. According to Fournier, p. 119, the Emperor went so far as to oblige female prisoners condemned to hard labor and specifically prostitutes, to wear stays and paniers, in a vain effort to discredit these articles of fashion.

90. Following the original French language edition (La Haye 1781), German editions appeared in Vienna (1782) and Berlin (1783); there is an Italian edition of 1787, and there are English versions as late as 1861 and 1871.

91. Wilcox, pp. 122–123. "Fall" like a fallen woman? The French coined the term "penchant vicieux" for the inclined heel of this period, when it was revived a century later (*Charivari,* 19 Dec. 1879).

92. Brooke, p. 74. Her fig. 35a is drawn after an original with a six inch heel, "said to be a man's shoe"; her fig. 35b, also with a six inch heel, is presumably a woman's.

93. Cf. Rosenblum, pp. 43–64.

94. *Vernünftige und bewährte Mittel . . .* 1795, p. 72.

95. Marie de Saint-Ursin, p. 54.

The Artificiall Changling.

339 Small Wastes pernitiously affected.

selves to attaine unto a wand-like smalnesse of waste , never thinking them-selves fine e-nough untill they can span their Waste.

By which deadly Artifice they re-duce their Breasts into such streights, that they soone purchase a stinking breath; and while they ignorant-ly affect an angust or narrow Breast, and to that end by strong compulsion shut up their Wasts in a Whale-bone prison, or little-ease; they open a doore to Consumpti-ons, and a withering rottennesse : Hence such are justly derided by Terence;

CHAPTER TWO:

Revival of Tight-Lacing (c. 1810–1860); Popularization of the Reform Campaign

Corset Revival

The interval of "revolutionary" and neo-classical liberty from stays was brief.[1] The French Revolution soon became Empire, Neo-classicism Romanticism. By 1805, the year of Napoleon's coronation as Emperor, even as physicians were celebrating the demise of stays, these began to revive, less tight at the waist but longer than ever, binding down the hips as well as the torso. French caricatures appeared under such titles as "Marvellous Effects of Lacing" (1807) and the "Fury of Corsets" (1809), which shows everyone, the young and old, rich and poor, lacing each other up.[2] By 1810 journalists in France and England were vying with each other in picturing the horrors of the corset revival. In England, caricaturists seized on the sheer length of the new stays and of the solider-than-ever busk, shown reaching from chin to mid-thigh. "Tired of being at ease, and ambitious of the sufferings and martyrdom of their grandmothers, our young ladies fearlessly advance to the torture of steel and whalebone. . ." The French saw the situation as actually worse than under the *ancien régime*: "They not only tight-lace, encase themselves in whalebone busks as in days gone by, but the corsets are now longer and stronger than ever. The corset of today not only confines the stomach, waist and shoulders but encircles and restricts the bust in such a way that a lady so encased cannot move at all . . . They cannot laugh, eat, bend or turn around. They can hardly breathe. The least sigh must break the lace and cause disaster to their toilette."

A German physician in charge of public health describes the busk as attaining up to four fingers, even a hand in breadth, as rigid as the spoke of a wheel, often poking indelicately out above the breasts and reaching down as far as and even beyond the genital region, so that the wearer could barely sit, even to defecate.[3] The Germans were reproached by a French authority with flattening the breasts so that they "resembled a repulsive cellular mass."[4]

A new device intended to define—and separate—the breasts as never before, caused the horrified outcry: "The ill-named . . . 'divorce' . . . consists of a piece of steel or iron, of a triangular form, gently curved on each side. This formidable breast-plate (for the attraction of love's arrows, not to repel them!) is covered with soft materials; and thus bedded, placed in the centre of the chest to divide the breasts. . ." This, in conjunction with the stays, has "effected a hideous metamorphose (which) forces the figure of the wearer into whatever form the artist pleases. . . In consequence we see, in eight women out of ten *(sic)*, the hips squeezed into a circumference little more than the waist; and the bosom shoved up to the chin, making a sort of fleshy shelf, disgusting to the beholders, and certainly most incommodious to the bearer" (Plate 24).[5]

From the above citations it appears that critics are transferring to one of the most bizarre aspects of fashion, their sense of the power of material metamorphosis under the new industrial iron and steel technology, which the caricaturists show used as an aid to the actual lacing process ("winch theme", Plate 18). The forcible extrusion of the breasts by the new corset plays upon the ongoing or revived Rousseauist "fashion" for lactating motherhood reflected in the art of the period. But the nurturance symbolism of breast extrusion was almost immediately contradicted by the renewed anti-procreation symbolism of the thoracic binding below; and it was the latter which was noted by the new political fathers, whose "daughters'" toilette seemed a matter of national importance. The Emperor Napoleon, under whom, ironically, the neo-classical so-called Empire style, actually the creation of the Revolution, began to wane, took a view characteristically both imperious and imperial, describing the corset as an "assassin of the human race . . . which maltreats their progeniture, presages frivolous taste and imminent decadence." Napoleon, who himself contributed more than any other man of his age to the killing of Frenchmen, might, in the year of the invasion of Russia, indeed worry about depopulation. His successors, Louis XVIII and Charles X, followed the tradition of royal utterances on the subject, the latter complaining that whereas formerly one could see plenty of Dianas, Venuses, and Niobes in France, now there were only wasps.[6]

In England the corset revival was less dramatic only because the neo-classical style had never been fully accepted. Sometimes it is hard to tell whether a satirical allusion is in response to the old critical tradition, or to a fashion revival, as in a children's book of 1815, with its medieval procession of victims of fashion: men who gamble and duel to death, women who die of too little clothing and faint from lacing too tight.[7] The latter have joined the ranks of the former, as basic moral and social types whose existence is threatening to society as a whole.

The Dandy:
Stays and Cravats; Military Lacing

The men were also taking to corsets at this time, and to an unprecedented degree. The evidence for male corsetry in earlier ages is both sparse and unreliable; male corsetting as the fashion of a highly conspicuous minority becomes a subject of ridicule only in the second decade of the 19th century, the age of the dandy.

Transvestite fashion is often regarded as an indicator of social anxiety and pressure for a redefinition of sex-roles. This, if true of our own day and the late 19th century, should also be true of the early 19th century. Female fashion was transformed by neo-classicism, and male fashion moved toward what costume historians have called "the Great Masculine Renunciation", that is, the age when the peacock finery of earlier centuries was rejected as both feminine (therefore degenerate) and undemocratic. The English country gentleman was the original model for that plainness and practicality, sobriety and uniformity which is still the hallmark of masculine clothing today. Tending at once to the non-hierarchical (democratic) and non-decorative (practical and asexual), such a style suited the needs of a society based, supposedly, upon work and merit rather than birth. The reaction was led by an influential, aristocratic (or would-be aristocratic) minority of English dandies who exaggerated precision of details and cut, and evolved a "philosophy" of the toilette. Clothing became for them a special form of narcissism, with anti-bourgeois, anti-democratic and anti-classical (Romantic) associations. Dandy fashion conveyed a sexual narcissism which the more sober-minded men denied themselves, and which was calculated to appeal to "the ladies." At a time when there was increasing pressure on the upper and middle classes to appear economically productive, the dandy asserted his right to be (merely) self-productive. He affected an air of physical indolence, but perfected a toilette which required infinite patience with small detail, and imposed a special kind of physical discipline.

An important sub-species of dandy formed within the military. The corsetting and other special, self-conscious sartorial effects cultivated by both the military and the civilian dandy may derive from the social insecurity they shared, and their common desire for upward social mobility. Military corsetting in the 19th cenutry is a chapter unto itself, presented here only in fragments. The growth of huge standing armies during the Napoleonic age, and the subsequent development of a large, underemployed, socially restive, peace-time officer class, is the background to the emergence of the tight-laced military dandy. It is however far from clear that corsetry is more typical of off-duty rather than combat uniform; in either sphere it presumably retained some of the duty symbolism of body-armour whose practicality had declined over the centuries. The socially (if not militarily) aggressive dandy was also thus protected, and the bodily constriction he suffered may have acted as a kind of surrogate for the physical hardship of combat which the wearer (whether a professional or civilian) hoped to evoke symbolically while he was spared it in reality.

Dandy tight-lacing preceded its resumption as a female fashion. To Hazlitt it seemed that men had taken to stays just at the time women left them off.[8] This appearance was due to the fact that the high "neo-classical" waist survived in women's dress, especially in France, but also in England. According to the popular annual series of etchings by George Cruikshank, now the premier caricaturist of the age, called *Monstrosities of Fashion*, the women of 1819 are absurdly high- rather than narrow-waisted, while it is the men, the dandies, who have taken to tight-lacing in earnest. As early as 1792 we read that (in England) "a certain class of finical gentlemen have begun to wear them (stays);" but they did not become common for men until after around 1815, presumably in connection with a large-scale demobilization among military officers, and the struggle for admission of middle-class elements into fashionable Regency society.[9] Numerous literary references to dandy lacing and caricatures by Cruikshank etc. from the years 1818–19 indicate that it was precisely as this time that a new species of dandy arose, composed of low-class imitators who exaggerated and feminized the discreet and masculine Brummellian style. (Brummell himself left England for good in 1816.) Too poor to impress otherwise, they flaunted a pinched waist and swaddled throat, which were satirized (Plate 22) as comic substitutes for the armorial bearings they lacked in reality. The low-class midshipman, contemptuously identified as "Jack Greathead the cheesemonger's son," applies the windlass to his staylace, summoning four sailors to "pull-away! Heave away! Pull away, hearties!" much to the disgust of the old veteran.[10] Thus did the military exquisite prepare himself for his appearance in the ballroom or opera-box, where according to other Cruikshank caricatures, he was apt to faint away like a maiden and require the frightened solicitude of his friends who exhort each other to cut the stay-lace and apply smelling salts. Stays were the mark of the effeminate sensualist; the Prince of Dandies, the Prince-Regent George (IV), was accused of over-indulgence in stays, food and mistresses. Political enemies fastened gleefully upon such proofs of his depravity; as a boy Charles Dickens was warned about "the existence of terrible banditti called *the radicals*, whose principles were that the Prince Regent wore stays."[11]

An early example of military stay wearing was given by the Russians. When the French Imperial Guard invited their defeated Russian counterparts to dinner on the occasion of the meeting between Alexander and Napoleon in 1812, the French were appalled at the Russians' gluttonous behavior and the way they unbuttoned their excessively tight uniforms at table to disgorge a quantity of chest padding.[12] An (allied) English officer on the other hand found the Russians very fine looking "in scarlet jackets fitting like stays and, as usual, the waist drawn in to the capacity of a decent grasp." At the occupation of Paris in 1815 it was noted how the corps of General Woronzoff and that of the Grand Duke Constantine seemed to vie with each other in the matter of tight waists. A French caricature of the following year shows dark-skinned, barbaric-looking servants barbarically hauling on a blond young Russian officer, whose eyes are popping out of his head.[13]

In the early 19th century the cadet colleges of Moscow and St. Petersburg may have gone in for systematic corset training,[14] similar in character to that which, according to the fetishist correspondence, was practiced a generation later in select Austrian (but not necessarily military) boys' schools. Western physicians working in or visiting Russian and Polish military hospitals were struck by the incidence of heart diseases, which they attributed to stay-wearing.[15]

An English source claimed that tight-lacing by Austrian and Russian officers was not just a matter of individual choice or vanity, but allegedly enforced as a kind of military discipline; "hideous and unnatural" as it made them appear to the English, they were "compelled" to reduce their waists to a certain size.[16] French caricatures of the Crimean War show Russian officers, and even the young Russian Emperor himself, as possessed of very female wasp-waists.[17] The custom filtered down to the Austrian and Italo-Austrian common soldier in the form of an excessively tight uniform belt (eventually replaced by braces) which supposedly caused a high incidence of kidney complaints.

It is hard to establish the precise lines of fluctuation in 19th century military corsetry. The dandy may have declined as a topic of caricature and as a social phenomenon, but officers certainly continued to corset, although perhaps less visibly. An English manual of 1830 takes it for granted that stays are worn by cavalry officers: "The coat, padded well in every direction, sits perfect, while it is rendered small at the waist by the use of stays—or a belt, as the former term should never be uttered in ears polite."[18] Male civilian stay-wearing probably declined in the 1840s, in England at any rate, although to judge from the novels of M.M. Noah, it survived in the U.S. Noah describes two sixteen-year-old boys, for whose appallingly effeminate appearance the parents are blamed: "dressed in the extreme of fashion, blue coats of superfine cloth buttoned tight over a pair of corsets, so that not a wrinkle was seen . . . Wide pantaloons, short boots, gold seals and chains, and white cravat round their throat tight to suffocation;" and in a later passage: "A young gentleman stood before me, in an attitude inexpressibly inelegant, though it may have been fashionable—petticoat pantaloons, varnished boots, flashy silk vest, waist compressed by corsets to the shape of a wasp's, and a cravat which nearly choked him."[19]

Discounting Russia, for which further research would be required, military tight-lacing probably survived best in Austria and France. A French source blames the "stupefyingly ridiculous" practice of tight-lacing for the high incidence among the military of gastroenteritis, pulmonary consumption, and inflammation of the brain. The military corset was the "Sebastopol [then resisting protracted siege from Anglo-French forces] of the empire of the absurd."[20] The English surgeon Bernard Roth, who lived in a French garrison town around 1865, marvelled at the officers' wasp-waists, marked by "very tight leather belts quite deforming their bodies." He came to the conclusion that "the notorious physical inferiority of the French as compared with the German officers during the Franco-Prussian War may have been due in part to this foolish custom." The "Germans" referred to by Roth were presumably the Prussians, who formed the backbone and officer élite of the German army, rather than the (Frenchified) Bavarians, shown by the caricaturist Wilhelm Busch tightly imprisoned in their "courage" tunics, mockingly so-called because the wearers "look forward to bullets as the only means of ventilating, and therefore rush fearlessly into danger."[21]

The French literally dramatized the habit: in *Enfants de Troupe*, a comedy of 1840, the curtain rises to disclose a dressmaker secretly lacing in Captain Sévelas, who demands that he be drawn tighter still, until the sixth lace breaks.[22] *La Vie Parisienne*, the magazine of fashion, approved of the French military wasp-waist, in contrast to the shapeless dowdiness of the Prussian, but the French humour magazine caricatures the officer suddenly overcome by malaise: "It can't be that I've eaten or drunk too much, on the contrary . . . it's not because of my belt either, . . . no, it must be that wretch of a lascar (servant) who's laced my corset too tight"[23] (cf. Plate 39).

Baudelaire, whose aesthetic philosophy was inclined towards "Art" over "Nature", enthused over the exquisite staff-officer drawn by Constantin Guys, "tight-waisted, swaying his shoulders and leaning unabashed over the lady's arm-chair, and with a back view which makes one think of the slenderest and most elegant insects." It is from Baudelaire also that we learn of the propensity of Greek soldiers to make a wasp-waist above the spreading skirts of their national uniform, a fashion adopted by King Otto "as a token of his subtle Hellenic patriotism."[24]

After the stays, the most important aspect of dandy toilette was the cravat. For novelists such as Dickens and Balzac, and artists like Daumier and Gavarni, the cravat was one of the most "physiologi-cally" expressive elements in the social mask. It was also cultivated in reality as a "label of identity" by notables such as Gladstone in England, and the publisher Pierre Véron in France.

The status of the perfectly tied cravat as the hallmark of genteel elegance, as "the last key-stone of Fashion's arch", had been estab-lished by Beau Brummell. He despised stays and, as a dandy in the higher, philosophical-literary sense, that is, one for whom "exquisite propriety" (the phrase is Byron's) extended to the whole social being, Brummell demanded that the neckcloth, like all behavior, avoid exaggeration and ostentation; its perfection was a matter of absolute cleanliness and fit. To the Brummellian dandy, there was no elegance without ease; he despised the absurd affectations of the "ultra-fashionable . . . collared like the leader of a four-horse team, and pinched in the middle like an hour-glass [elsewhere the author compares him to an earwig], with a neck as long as a goose, and a cravat as ample as a tablecloth."[25]

In the 1820s there appeared several little manuals on the art of tying the cravat, in French, Italian, German and English, designed, no doubt, for an upwardly mobile middle class. There were twenty to thirty different types of cravat-tie, one for every occasion and for every character. The base for the cravat was a leather stiffener modelled on the old military stock so much cursed in its time, as we have seen, by the physicians, but now very carefully formed so as to follow the contours of the neck from collarbone to jawbone, and "beaten into shape upon a proper block so that it became of so unyielding a nature that no force of neck can bend it."[26] The milder form of stock was composed of some dress material stiffened with whalebone thinned at the edges and bordered with white leather, to prevent the bones from sticking into the chin. The neckcloth which went over this shape should be starched to the consistency of fine writing paper. Stiffness and tightness of neckwear varied according to the occasion; the Eastern tie, which "shows not the slightest crease and is starched as rigid as possible" contrasts with the Ball-room tie, which was "easy and graceful"; and exerts only a "gentle pressure" on the throat. Outright discomfort was accepted as inherent to styles such as the Cravate Collier de Cheval (the horse-collar cravat), which was much admired by women although the editor considered it vulgar. "Human life is often compared to a painful journey; and it is probably on the same philosophical principle that the Cravate Collier de Cheval was considered a proper costume for man, who often drags on his weary way, loaded with evils more insupportable than the heaviest burthens."[27] The reader is at the same time assured that stocks have very much improved since the days when they were the torment of the common soldier.

Most manuals contain a cursory warning against wearing the cravat too tight. The popular medical writer who claimed it causes "blotches and eruptions in the face, head-ache, apoplexies and sudden deaths" was presumably exaggerating. And yet elsewhere we are told, humorously, that a "lad who goes into the world" is expected to "have his neck tied up . . . almost as tight as some lads who go out of it" (i.e. hanged). Dickens compared it to the Gordian knot, "when the difficulty of getting one on, was only equalled by the apparent impossibility of ever getting it off again."[28] English caricature, despite its love of the grotesque and macabre, does not represent the cravat as actually lethal, although the typical English military "snob" seemed to the French to be living in a perpetual agony of self-strangulation. An American satirical fairy-tale called "The Demon Tie" tells how a vain youth sells his soul to the devil in exchange for help in tying the perfect tie. He is the sensation of the ball on this account, but at the height of his success, demon hands reach out and pull his tie so tight that he strangles to death.[29] At the end of *Monsieur Crépin,* the comic strip-picture novel by the Genevese Rodolphe Töpffer, the vain pedant Monsieur Fadet accidentally asphyxiates himself with his waterproof crinoline cravat, of which he was the proud inventor (Pl. 21). Elsewhere Töpffer cites the cravat explicitly as a symbol of an unnatural social constraint.[30]

For the Spanish dandy, who stood in a class of his own, neckwear was redolent with a symbolism peculiar to that people. The Spanish, who bore the reputation of being so morally stiffnecked, continued to make stiff neckwear a point of national honor long after it was abandoned, in the course of the 17th century, by the rest of Europe. Under Philip IV the plain, single-layered, plate-like "golilla" replaced the large frilled ruff. It was a symbol of gentility and gravity. Its inconvenience and discomfort were borne with pride by the Spanish laborer, who liked to think of himself as an hidalgo fallen on hard times. "A cart driver exercised as much caution as the grandee lest his golilla break, and a farmer preferred to have just a handful of onions that he had cultivated and gathered with his golilla about his neck rather than to have thousands of bushels of wheat if having them meant going without his beloved cardboard collar. It was generally believed that one degraded the golilla by following a manual occupation." Gradually displaced by the French cravat in the course of the 18th century, especially amongst the educated classes, the golilla was dead by the time of the French Revolution. By then, however, the Spanish dandy or "petimetre" was wearing a huge cravat (called corbata or pañuelo) "so tightly fastened about the neck that it made the eyes to bulge and the face as purple as a lily." Goya, obsessed as he was with bondage and imprisonment, shows woman fastened into the grotesque prison of her husband's jealousy, a chastity-belt in the form of a padlocked suit of armor reaching from her knees to her shoulders, and the dandy as a prisoner bound at neck and waist in the iron shackles of his vanity (Plate 20).[31]

The self-oppression of the dandy, as well as the whole dandy phenomenon, is surely a symptom of social pressures from below. We have further evidence that the species of tight-laced and tight-cravatted dandy, like the tight-laced female, came from a lower, but upwardly mobile social class. The cheap satirical illustrated pamphlets of the period, surely aimed at the young of this class, stress the low-class origin, poverty, pathos and folly of those trying to keep up appearances beyond their station. The poor dandy has to wash his own linen and darn his own socks. His physical incapacitation in the ballroom—unable to eat or dance or pick up a lady's handkerchief—clearly connotes his social incapacitation. A special kind of humiliation awaits him when he rides into the country: he is thrown off his horse and has to be unlaced in a peasant's cottage, to the great hilarity of the local rustics.[32]

Romantic Wasp-Waist; Technical Improvements

By around 1825 the transition in women's dress from the classical to the Romantic or neo-Gothic age was complete, and the whole costume seemed to deny the (very brief and incomplete) revolutionary freedom of yore. Romanticism incorporated a revival of the forms and ideals of the rococo and ancien régime. Monarchist reaction created a climate of nostalgia for the "four inch heels and good solid stays"[33] of the Louis XVI period. After the moral rigors and formal austerity of the neo-classicists à la David, people became susceptible, once again, to the siren call of the Boucher nymph. The major Romantic writer Alfred de Vigny conjures up such a figure, in a self-consciously and quasi-parodistically voluptuous description calculated to titillate the senses, corrupt the moral fibre and prey upon the romantic weaknesses of the poet. She is Mademoiselle de Coulanges, mistress of Louis XV, a creation existing only in art (and the sexual imagination), a dream both vapid and seductive. In the lengthy tabulation of her physical charms, a kind of romantic irony tries to recapture the magic of artificial rococo shapes and colors, while dispensing with the artifices themselves: "her lips were rosy without coral, her neck was white with blue shadows, without white paint or blue shadows; her wasp-waist could have been encircled by the hand of a twelve-year-old girl, and her steel-ribbed corset was scarcely tightened, since there was room for the stem of a large bouquet, which stood perfectly upright."[34]

The paradox of the tiniest imaginable waist, surrounded by the most solid corset which does not even press upon it, is designed to gloss over the contradiction between the charm of art (or sex) and that of nature. The Romantics, no more than the Neo-classicists, wish to dwell unduly upon this contradiction, as Baudelaire (and Montaut) were to do. But it obtruded more and more as fashion became more artificial and responded to technological inventions. Skirts broadened and were even sometimes stiffened, hoop-like, with whalebone, as was the gigot and balloon sleeve which lent balletic wings to the new sylph-like figure. Bust and hips were padded, and tight-lacing was renewed in earnest with the aid of certain technical innovations: the metal eyelet, invented in 1828, and the split busk, fastened with catches ("busc mécanique à verrous") and patented in 1829 although not in current usage until mid-century. Between the years 1828 and 1848 no less than sixty-six patents were registered in Paris, most of them affecting these two features.[35] Tighter lacing was certainly good for business, since corsets thus treated wore out much faster, and a broad increase in demand for luxury or semi-luxury goods gave an impetus to mass-manufacture. Various systems for easier or instantaneous lacing and unlacing were devised, to permit a lady to get out of her corset unaided, but until the split busk was generally adopted and combined "à la paresseuse", one had to follow the eighteenth century method of removing the lace completely from the corset and threading it back every time the corset was put off or on—a time-consuming operation which normally required the assistance of a maid or a gentleman admirer (cf. Plates 12 and 14).

There was evidently already a demand, which increased as the century progressed, on the part of women without personal maids (according to Mme S. of Lyon, the majority), for a garment they could get in and out of on their own. It is curious to reflect that some early socialist communities of the 1830s in France, moved in the opposite direction, devising a uniform for both sexes which buttoned all the way down the back, so as to *prevent* one from getting in and out of it on one's own, and thus to further people's sense of their interdependence. The democratization of the fashion corset depended to a great extent on its technical evolution towards ease of solo manipulation, while its two basic factors (split busk and waist loops) facilitated tighter lacing. Democratization and tight-lacing are therefore connected on the strictly technical level. The invention of the sewing-machine in mid-century was of course a major technological factor in the cheapening and democratization of the corset, as of well-fitting clothes for the lower classes generally.

Lacing "à la paresseuse" (lazy-style), introduced in 1843, meant that the "endless" lace could be left in the corset, to be loosened and tightened from the waist by means of a dual loop. This not only simplified getting in and out of a front-opening corset, but also, as the term implies, permitted a lady to relax an inch or so of pressure at the waist by simply (and secretly) untying the knot, letting the lace slip a little, and retying it. At the same time, the new system encouraged the potential tight-lacer to experiment with degrees of pressure which s/he could precisely control.

The Opposition Popularized

The chorus of opposition amongst physicians and educators, to which was added the voice of journalists and fashion writers, begins to swell during the later twenties and early thirties. It seems to ebb away somewhat during the early forties,[36] to pick up again momentarily around 1848, and to ebb once more after 1857, when the crinoline came in. During the '30s a sustained effort was made to reach the people at large, especially women. The articles printed in the medical journals, and distributed also as separate offprints, are sometimes couched in a chatty style designed to appeal to a wider, lay audience.[37] It is not only books on dress, hygiene and health which carry warnings against excessive corsetry, but also popular dictionaries, encyclopedias, and the new general-audience magazines of useful and entertaining knowledge, whose readership included the educated woman.[38] From the realm of physicians and educators in the eighteenth century, the subject became a matter of general interest to a lay intelligentsia eager for lessons combining anatomy, morality and aesthetics. The *Magasin Pittoresque* warns against the "Danger of Tight-laced Corsets" between articles on the religion of the Gauls and the Raphael cartoons, so that the eyes of readers interested in the Gauls or Raphael willy-nilly fall upon the topic of tight-lacing. The famous naturalist, such as Georges Cuvier, became the source of anecdotes which were to be repeated continuously down the century,[39] and the anthropologist, such as Professor Serres of the Museum of Natural History in Paris, included the topic in his lecture courses.[40] Popular journal articles were often illustrated with simple anatomical diagrams outlining the thoracic cage and showing the position of the inner organs, and contrasting the shape of a healthy liver with that of the tight-lacers.[41] One can imagine the effect of such illustrations, and of the sensational descriptions of internal organic havoc, upon young girls, all the Miss Podsnaps whose formal education was carefully designed to avoid "indecent" subjects like anatomy and physiology. One innocent person even told a doctor who warned her against tight-lacing on account of the liver, etc., that she had supposed only the poor had livers (presumably because alcoholism, with malnutrition the chief enemy of the liver, was an affliction of the lower classes). The popular family journals invariably had a medical column written by a professional which included the hygiene of dress, but which seldom entered into clinical detail unless corsetry were at issue. This topic was, oddly, a catalyst for basic information (or misinformation) in a century when, as late as 1882, "it is considered improper, indecent (for ladies) to know anything of the structure and functions of the human body."[42]

It was a bold innovation, and one redolent of the sensationalism accruing to the topic, when Madame Caplin mounted her "Anatomical and Physiological Gallery" containing various "specimens" and "models" in her shop at 58 Berners Street, London, with lectures on Wednesdays. It could be visited only by invitation and only by ladies, who were assured that "nothing is admitted that can offend the most sensitive, nothing omitted that is necessary to be seen by the class of visitors who patronize the establishment." Madame Caplin had a dual vested interest: she was a corsetière, but was married to a physician specializing in spinal diseases.

"The considerable number of people doing the stays movement" was ridiculed by Thomas Jefferson Hogg, who was so affected by his visit to a lecture-demonstration on tight-lacing that he felt compelled to insert a lengthy account of it, with total disregard for its relevance not to speak of chronology, into his 1855 *Life of Percy Bysshe Shelley*. The lecture he attended was delivered by a "first-rate, scientific Blue" to a group of philanthropic ladies; he was the only male present. The Lecturer stood behind a "large table with a green cloth (upon which) were plaster-casts, drawings and engravings, and a rabbit with its chest cut open, so that the lungs appeared." She spoke with "professorial solemnity" on the "upper works" of woman, and deduced the "whole economy of respiration" from the rabbit, explaining how inconvenienced the rabbit would be by stays. "The peroration was exceedingly impressive and authoritative" and "as if from revelation." She was, however, afterwards thrown into confusion by Hogg's pointing out that her subject was not a doe-rabbit, but a buck-rabbit, which had never been intended by Providence to wear stays.[43]

HORROR STORIES; TIGHT-LACING AMONG THE WORKING CLASSES

Hospital and coroners' reports of death caused by tight-lacing were eagerly taken up by the daily press—and not necessarily with undue exaggeration and embellishment, for the reports themselves were ghoulish and garish enough. For obvious reasons, there was a reluctance to release proper names and personal information which could lead to an actual identification of the martyr, whose family would naturally do the utmost to avoid publicity; and if a private physician did diagnose tight-lacing as the cause of death, he would naturally be urged by friends and relatives of the deceased to keep quiet about it. If a girl known for her slenderness of waist died unexpectedly, the family would be well-advised to have any autopsy undertaken in secret, and avoid the scandal occasioned by the tragedy of the young Parisian Madame Virginie de C. According to a newspaper report of 1859, two days after a ball at which she had shone with particular brilliance and at which her figure was the envy of all, she was found dead. Her family decided on an autopsy to explain the tragedy. "The findings were shattering: the liver bored through by three ribs!!! Thus one dies at 23 years! Not of typhus, not in childbed, but of the corset!"[44] In a case publicized (exceptionally—the victim was working class) with considerable biographical detail,[45] the jury might return a verdict of "Died by the Visitation of God" but the physician performing the autopsy was in no doubt as to the real cause: "The victim was Miss Elizabeth Allen, aged 22, a pupil of Madame Devey . . . a fashionable milliner, one of the finest young women he (the doctor) ever saw . . . He hears she was subject to fits. He had no doubt the stooping posture and tight-laced stays had brought upon congestion of the vessels of the head, which, no doubt, was the cause of her death." Her waist measurement (very rarely given in such cases) was 23 inches, on a person described as "full of body" (the only other recorded measurement from this period is 17 inches[46]).

Consumption, the fashionable disease of the Romantic age, was considered by many as largely due to corset-wearing, on account of the higher incidence of the disease amongst women. The Registrar General's Reports explained the discrepancy between male and female death rates from consumption or phthisis as due to the "Chinese Deformity" of small waists, "natural only to wasps and other insects."[47] Consumptives were believed to live in a constant state of sexual excitement, and their pitiful compulsion to copulate often led to death. Hypersexuality or nymphomania was also held to *cause* consumption. The vaginas of consumptives became sewers, and the combination of corsetry and venereal disease gave them cancer of the breast.[48] Autopsy reports cited consumption, dropsy and abscessed livers as among the worst immediate results of tight-lacing, but physicians reserved their heaviest cannons for diseases of the uterus and the other female organs affecting pregnancy and parturition. If, compared with those we have encountered earlier, the accusations tend to become less erratic and more scientific as the century progresses, they do so with a more strictly gynecological orientation. The corset is recognized and condemned as a means used by women to manipulate their own sexuality, and to engage in certain pernicious socio-sexual practices. The charge that women use tight-lacing as a means of abortion, either deliberately or (as it was supposed) accidentally through vanity, became more and more common.[49] A certain young actress died from having continued to lace through her seventh or eighth month of pregnancy.[50]

The most popular work on health and physiology of its day[51] observed that "women of fashion and the countless flocks of their imitators, *down to the lowest rank of life,* have gradually come to regard a narrow or spider-waist as an ornament worthy of attainment at any cost . . ." (my stress). By mid-century *ladies* were denying that tight-lacing was practiced by any but the lower classes.[52]

Since it was easier to obtain permission to open bodies of the poor, we have plentiful information on the propensity of the lower and working classes to tight-lace, as revealed in post-mortems from prisons, workhouses and lunatic asylums. The Report of the Glasgow Lunatic Asylum 1838–39 cited "a female pauper, aged fifty-two, who died of dropsy of the chest, connected with a singular displacement of the liver, lungs and heart, in consequence of the very injurious practice of tight-lacing, to which she had been addicted, with maniacal obstinacy, from early life." Post-mortems from the Salpêtrière Hospital revealed much deformation at the base of the thorax. Young dressmakers in London were noted, by the Children's Employment Commission of 1864, to wear their stays "too tight and too long waisted for persons who have to sit and stoop." Other, individual examples of fatalities or near-fatalities among the working classes attributed to tight-lacing, include a 21-year-old prostitute, who died in a police station of syphilis, consumption and corsets; a servant-girl who collapsed carrying a pail of water and whose life was saved in the nick of time by a doctor passing by; a chambermaid who died of fearful stomach cramps and was found to have her stomach almost cut in two, leaving a canal only as narrow as a raven's feather; and a villager who suddenly fell dead while dancing at a wedding.[53] In cases such as these, of course, we may assume today what contemporaries tended to ignore, the fact that the tight-lacing may well have exacerbated what it was intended to hide: physical debilitation through the malnutrition endemic among the poor. This decreased as a major factor as the century progressed, and the "epidemic" of tight-lacing asserted to exist among the working (urban, and including servant) classes, or among rustic communities, later in the century, probably had more to do with social aspiration or psychological stress, than with the pangs of poverty and malnutrition.

Domestic servants, who had close and constant contact with the superior classes among whom they lived, were often accused of dressing and generally taking on airs above their station (especially by *Punch*, who called it "servant galism"). They were of course also often very badly treated and if not literally starved for food, deprived in many other ways, including basic physical comforts such as heating. This emerges from a case-history which the local newspaper (of a middle and lower class area of London) and then the *Lancet* dramatized at some length. The legal verdict that the death occurred "from congestion of the lungs and brain due to tight-lacing" was followed by the moral verdict, which condemned the "silly and wicked vanity" of the victim's "severe and systematic (self) torture." But certain other non-medical circumstances, mentioned in the reports only in passing, are striking, and shocking: the victim (Jemima Hall of Islington) was "fearfully emaciated" and "indifferently nourished" (anorexic?), and the doctor's first diagnosis was that she was suffering from "the intense cold acting on a weak heart." She had complained of a "severe headache and an intense feeling of cold" in the afternoon after returning from an errand, and was allowed to take to her room, which was unheated. She was left unattended the whole of the "intensely cold" evening and night. Her inert body was discovered, still fully dressed as on the previous day, when she failed to show up for work in the morning. The callousness of the mistress seems, to us, criminal, as also the negligence of the doctor in not having her immediately removed to hospital, treated, and kept under observation (at his first 7:30 a.m. visit, he merely cut off her corset and prescribed some stimulants, returned at 10:00 a.m. to find the patient "powerfully convulsed (clonic)", and without apparently doing anything about it, returned again at 2:00 p.m. to find her dead). The mistress could (or would) provide no history of the case, except that she had remonstrated repeatedly with the girl, who was of "prepossessing appearance" although of "little pectoral or mammal development", for her "persistent folly" in lacing so tightly. The tight-lacing here was surely part of the psychosomatology of oppressive social conditions.

One turns with relief from such tales of horror and tragedy to a situation which would strike anyone but the physician reporting it as comic: Dr. Godman was staying at a boarding house, the daughter of whose landlady, "a tall, good-looking woman", was after considerable effort unable to perform so simple an operation as to place the kettle on the fire; the reason being that she had her "long busk on" (as she put it) and her lacing was in a hard knot, which prevented her from stooping. The same writer was much struck by a girl sweeping the gutters of Seventh Street (New York), attired in gorgeous ballon sleeves and laced to the "fashionable" degree; he also noted the inquest report on a black servant who died while standing at the ironing board, as a result of her corset.[54]

FOWLER AND PIERQUIN

Occasionally an individual would take direct action against the fashion. Thus the General, arriving from the French army in Africa for his son's wedding (arranged during his absence) refused to accept the tight-laced daughter-in-law proposed to him, although she was the daughter of the Duchesse de xxx: "I will marry my son to one who can perpetuate our noble race, not one whose ribs have been crushed by a corset." The campaign of a certain Dr. Alibert was aided by a coincidental (and somewhat incredible) real-life enactment of his theory. At a party attended by various famous beauties, he thus upbraided some young men present: "You provoke them to suicide by complimenting them on the slenderness of their waist . . . Perhaps at this very moment one of these élégantes—who will not have eaten, the better to please you—is going to faint . . ." At that moment, two women fell gasping to the floor; Alibert rushed to them, cut their laces, and made the young men he had been addressing promise never again to compliment a lady on her fine waist.[55]

Many reformers were convinced that such severe derangements of the internal organs must necessarily be accompanied by fearful psychological and sexual disorders. "Her corporeal powers at an early period begin to evince decay—her intellectual faculties to manifest imbecility—her mind becomes irascible and her temper fretful and peevish;" the face acquired "deep and indelible lines of peevishness, etc."[56] The mere desire to tight-lace is, to some, the sign of pathological vanity. The critics must have sensed that this vanity was based upon the principle of sex-attraction, but I have found only one author of the period who openly recognized that a tight corset produced in the wearer sexual feelings, which were to be considered ipso facto pathological, independently of the effect upon a male admirer. This brave soul is Orson Squire Fowler (1809–1887), editor of the *American Phrenological Journal,* a man of "immense reputation" and "inordinate conceit," and writer of a mass of "semi-scientific and pseudo-philosophical works".[57] In 1844 he published in its 40th (!) edition a book, which also circulated internationally, entitled *Amativeness: or the Evils and remedies of excessive and perverted sexuality.*

Fowler's premise was shared by some very eminent Victorians: sex leads to insanity. The evils of sex were particularly manifest in the tight-lacing mania, as demonstrated in another highly successful pamphlet by Fowler called *Intemperance and Tight-Lacing. Founded on the laws of life as developed by Phrenology and Physiology* (1844). The motto to this astonishing work, which went through many subsequent editions (an eleventh appeared in London, 1890), is "Total abstinence (from alcohol) or no husbands, natural waists or no wives." The same phrase became the slogan of the Anti-Lacing Societies which Fowler claims were formed as a result of the "brief but pungent remarks" on the subject in his work on Matrimony. After some grandiose "phrenological" generalizations ("All aged and gifted people have large chests; all grandmothers have large waists"), and after depicting the pathetic, consumptive appearance of tight-lacers, Fowler comes to the point (p. 35):

My conscience contrains me reluctantly to allude here to one other evil connected with tight-lacing . . . I do so although I know it will injure . . . the popularity and sale of this work(!) Compression produces inflammation . . . retains the blood in the bowels and neighbouring organs and thereby inflames all the organs of the abdomen, which thereby excites amative desires . . . It is high time that virtuous woman should blush for very shame to be seen laced tight, just as she should blush to be caught indulging impure desires. Many physiologists know this fact but do not mention it. This explains the fact that tight-lacers so easily get in love. The fact is indisputable, and the reason obvious.

Tight-lacing disorders the nervous system, and this inflames the base of the brain, which necessarily excites the organs of Amativeness, situated at the lowest point in the base of the brain.

The city dandy is blamed for the perpetuation of the habit because he encourages this amativeness and "adhesiveness." Fowler ends in a thunderous tirade against "these infanticides, with their corsets actually on, (who) are admitted into the sanctuary of the most High God, and even to the communion-table of the saints! . . . I really do not see how it is possible for tight-lacers ever to enter the kingdom of heaven . . ."

Fowler's flowery rhetoric, and his open coupling of tight-lacing with sexual desire, was evidently pitched at a popular, lower-class audience, which he found not only in the U.S. but also in England, where the lower classes were less puritanical than the middle classes. His perception (garbled as it was) of the physiological connection was a generation ahead of its time. Sexual physiology was an undeveloped field, within which it was possible to argue almost anything without fear of contradiction.

Fowler was quoted extensively by Mrs. Angeline Merrit in a book called *Dress Reform practically and physiologically considered*, which is chiefly about tight-lacing, and like Fowler's, sees the practice as on a par with and as an adjunct to alcoholism and atheism. On the subject of corsets used to provoke abortions, her always tortured prose goes into paroxysms. It was apparently her dreadful experience to have to take Holy Communion kneeling next to, contaminated by foeticidal tight-lacers, upon whom she calls down God's "infinite disgust and loathing." The term "infanticide" is too mild for her: "God of Heaven! . . . When the world give it the tame appellation of infanticide, instead of the scathing, withering rebuke and unfeigned contempt which it so richly and unsparingly deserves, will high heaven account her guiltless?" Mrs. Merrit's Christian outrage is fueled by a perception in sexual physiology which goes a step beyond Fowler, for she sees the tight corset as serving to "crowd the abdominal viscera down into immediate contact and collison with the sexual organs of the pelvic cavity, creating unnatural excitement and diseases in both . . . to the morbid excitement of the nervous energy, and the effeminacy of the physical system."[58]

At this same time (1840s) a French physician, amateur orientalist, linguist and writer on madness called Pierquin de Gembloux, turned Fowler's thesis upside-down: tight-lacing acts as a commendable restraint upon the passions. To "repress excessive development of the internal and external pectoral muscles is incontestably to moderate the activity of the sympathetic organs." The physical and moral passions act principally through the lungs, and it is in the breast that love resides. "The larger and more active the lungs, the more fire there is in the breast, and the more dangerous this 'devouring hearth' becomes to morality and virtue." It must therefore be protected, confined and fortified, especially during the morally vulnerable period of adolescence and youth. The oblique positioning of women's ribs and their mobility invite compression, which also helps to support the breasts, and is altogether "therapeutic, preparatory,

accessory and operatory, and moreover hygienic; the tissue is benefi-
cially condensed, and a rarefaction sets in which increases the consistency of certain cellular, muscular and cutaneous tissue." The pressure of the corset is thus one of neutralization and counterbalance.
Pierquin delights in the perversity and extremism of a position which
holds that the very tightest of stays, even their *abuse* ("même l'abus
de cette partie de la cosmétique") is harmless. Beneficial side-effects
of tight-lacing include an increase in body-warmth, which aids the
delicacy and beauty of the voice, as any visitor to the Opéra or
Bouffes will attest; and a hastening of the digestive process. In sum,
the beauty, modesty and chastity of women, the very superiority of
Western civilization, is due to corsets; non-corsetted peoples are
hideously deformed, polygamous, demoralized and underpopulated.

If we can hold on, among this welter of hyperbolic, nonsensical and
topsy-turvy sounding argumentation, to Pierquin's point of departure, that tight-lacing acts as a *restraint* upon emotion, we can recog-
nise that it was shared, with widely differing moral inflections, by
other writers: by the abolitionist Réveillé Parise, for whom the
restraint was the anguish of repressed feeling ("passion rentrée",
"coeur serré"), by the novelists Dickens and Zola, for whom it was
emotionally anaesthetizing, in differing ways, as we shall see, and by
the fetishists themselves.[59]

Fictional Stereotypes in Charles Dickens and Charles Reade

The frequency of the reference to tight-lacing in the novels of Charles
Dickens is the surest guide to the prominence of the issue in the
minds of the early and mid-Victorians; just as the prominence of foot
and hair fetishism in these novels testifies to their role as typical
displacements of Victorian sexuality. Dickens was as enamoured of
the beauty of tiny feet and luxurious hair as he was repulsed by the
associations of the wasp-waist.

Dickens followed the convention which held tight-lacers to be
ruining not only their health, but also their character. The novelist
was concerned less with what happened to their inner organs, than
with the way in which moral tightness and stiffness signified in their
physical appearance could be represented antithetically to his ideal of
soft, yielding feminity. "Beside her sat her spinster daughters, three
in number, and of gentlemanly deportment, who had so mortified
themselves with tight stays, that their tempers were reduced to
something less than their waists, and sharp lacing was expressed in
their very noses." The daughter of an ambitious industrialist is

described as a "premature little woman of thirteen years old, who had already arrived at such a pitch of whalebone and education that she had nothing girlish about her."[60] (The pejorative pairing of tight-lacing with education is prophetic). In a later novel, Dickens responds to renewed popular interest in the topic, with his own version of the personality profile of the tight-lacer. When Mrs. Snagsby first appears she is the "short shrewd niece, something too violently compressed about the waist, with a sharp nose like a sharp autumn evening, inclining to be frosty towards the end. (Rumor had) that the mother of this niece did, in her daughter's childhood, moved by too jealous a solicitude that her figure should approach perfection, lace her up every morning with her maternal foot against the bedpost for a stronger hold and purchase . . ." (These rumors did not deter her suitor, who married her) ". . . and the niece still cherishes her figure—which, however tastes may differ, is unquestionably so far precious, that there is mighty little of it." Mrs. Snagsby also took vinegar and lemon-juice, which acids had mounted to her nose and temper. She is tight emotionally and behaviorally, as well as physically: "tightly she shakes her head, and tightly she smiles."[61] She is sexually jealous, scheming and manipulative, and to cap it all, financially tight as well, being endowed with a fierce business instinct. All these moral qualities, bad enough in a man, are absolutely detestable in a woman, and combine into the perfect antithesis of Dickens' feminine ideal: generous, soft, flowing, innocent (in matters sexual as well as financial), and childish.

Perhaps the most highly elaborated fictional stereotype of the tight-lacer is to be found in Charles Reade's *A Simpleton*.[62] This novel raises a monument to selfless scientific and humanitarian dedication jeopardized by a vain, foolish, and disobedient wife. With consummate scientific insight, the hero Dr. Staines recognizes his adored fiancée's propensity to spit blood as the product of a secret tight-lacing. Despite her promises to reform, soon after marriage "the simpleton" relapses into her old vice, along with others typically feminine and particularly calculated to ruin her husband's precarious career. Severely berated, Rosa falls in abject repentance at his feet and bids him kill her. He magnanimously pardons her with the words, "All you ladies are monomaniacs, one might as well talk to a gorilla . . . A tiny waist (is) as hideous as a Chinese foot, and to the eye of science, far more disgusting." The fault of Rosa, child of a weak father, is her refusal to submit to authority, of which her tight-lacing is a major symptom, an authority doubly binding on her for it is both biological and scientific and vested in a husband who has also to act as a father.

Reade is playing upon a popular social stereotype of the foolish young woman, in which her tight-lacing is a significant emblem of folly. But Rosa is weak and demands domination by her husband, unlike Dickens' Mrs. Snagsby, who is strong and dominates her husband. Thus the English literary stereotype of the tight-lacer incorporates both weakness on the one hand, and strength on the other (in combination, they constitute the essential ambivalence we described at the outset) as reprehensible traits. Dickens' transference of the physical self-repression of the strong woman to moral repression of herself and others, is paralleled in Zola, for whose tight-laced heroine Lisa, however (as we have seen above), the positive term "disciplined" is more appropriate. The much less manichaeistically inclined Zola recognizes Lisa's degree of physical and moral self-discipline as a less than admirable, but nevertheless socially sanctioned trait, one essential to economic survival. It is an instrument, moreover, not only of female social but also sexual power, both of which were much more threatening to Dickens than to Zola.

Notes

1. The change in fashion, and the consequent inflection of medical attitudes, can be traced in the succeeding editions of Dr. William Buchan's *Domestic Medicine*, the most popular do-it-yourself medical manual of the age (it was translated into seven different European languages and went through 21 English language editions between 1769 and 1813), and the same author's also very popular *Advice to Mothers*, with which *Domestic Medicine* was often combined. The 1772 edition of *Domestic Medicine* (Philadelphia, p. 12) is chiefly concerned with the stays as the "bane of children". The revised 1798 edition (New York, 1812, p. 40) notes that the "madness in favour of stays seems, however, to be somewhat abated." The 1803 and subsequent editions add a cautionary footnote (p. 13) "I am sorry to understand that there are still mothers mad enough to lace their daughters very tight." The 1807 (Charleston) edition of *Advice to Mothers* has a long passage (pp. 24–5) describing the *former* system of tight clothing (my stress), which can only be designed to counter a threatened revival: "It is not many years since the sugar-loaf shape (of an infant's head) was universally admired, (as was) the small waist, though contrary to nature . . . Husbands often used to make it their boast, that when they married their wives, they could span them around the middle." Buchan is increasingly concerned at this time with foeticide. Citing the author of a poem called *Paedotrophia*: "Remember not to gird too tight/ Your swelling waist, though pleasing to the sight;/ Nor, for a shape, within the straiten'd womb,/ Like Gallic mothers, the poor child entomb." In the 1812, New York edition of *Advice to Mothers* (p. 47), he adds in a dramatized and surely exaggerated form, the "once familiar spectacle" which "we no longer see" but which he evidently feared might revive, "of a mother laying her daughter upon a carpet, then putting her foot upon the girl's back, and breaking half a dozen laces in tightening her stays, to give her a slender waist." The description of the danger to pregnancy, the reference to the "damnable" practice of abortion and a lengthy passage (p. 24) on the permanent marks left by tight-lacing on the foetus are also written in "dread" of a return of the fashion. The "want of nipples" (presumably, meaning their flattening or introversion) was, according to Buchan, transmissible to the next generation "since even today it is common among girls who never wore stays, inherited from mothers who did" (p. 10).
2. Reproduced in Libron.
3. Schneider, 1824, p. 345. The English caricature showing excessive length of busk is by Gillray (1810), *Works* no. 570.

4. Fournier, 1813, p. 117 f.

5. This and the above passages from journals ot 1810–11 are extracted from the extensive citations in Waugh, pp. 98–100. Manufacturers advertised exaggerated effects, offering corsets with the "top part proportioned as to admit of enormous growth . . . the bottom part (i.e. waist and hips) proportionably small" (1789, Gillham no. 28).

6. Larousse, s.v. corset (Napoleon, 1812, to Dr. Corvisart, Louis XVIII to Madame du Cayla), and Mitton, p. 54 f.

7. Mant, p. 99.

8. *The Plain Speaker*, 1826 (cited in Waugh, p. 133).

9. Cruikshank *Monstrosity* of 1819: B.M. Sat. 13445. "Finical gentlemen": Vaughan, p. 69. cf. *Hermit in London* I p. 123; cf. ibid I, ix, II, p. 200, III p. 51 and p. 79, IV lxix passim and p. 134.

10. March 6, 1819, "Lacing in Style" (B.M. Sat. 13440). A month earlier Cruikshank had published "The Cholic" (B.M. Sat. 13438) one of a series of illustrations of the sensations of disease, in which demons are shown tugging on ropes wound tightly about the slender waist of an elderly woman, who screams in pain. The metaphor seems to be influenced by tight-lacing caricature.

11. Forster, I, p. 12.

12. Castelot, *Napoléon*, p. 205.

13. B.N., Tf. 60, p. 90, *Caricatures Historiques sur les Anglais*. This album also contains a caricature on English (dandy) tight-lacing of 1820 (?), showing an older man being mechanically hauled in from an English patented winch (p. 61). The preceding album (Tf. 59, *Caricatures Historiques, Costume*, p. 40) has a Naudet print of 1822 showing "Monsieur Belle-Taille ou l'Adonis du Jour" pulled in by a Negro servant and a tailor, hair, hips, breasts and shoulders popping out of him like a female caricature. A third print by Philipon (Tf. 61, *Caricatures sur les Modes*, p. 12), shows a black servant lacing a (military?) gentleman, who is painting his face.

14. A. Williams in a letter to the *Family Doctor* for 9 Sept. 1893.

15. Godman, 1829.

16. *Habits of Good Society*, p. 145. The reason given by Leouzon le Duc was not only aesthetic but also to hide real physical weakness (*La Russsie Contemporaine*, Paris 1853 p. 378).

17. E.g., Daumier's "St. Serge . . ." in *Charivari*, 29 Oct., 1855, Delteil 2554 ff.

18. A Cavalry Officer, *Whole Art of Dress*, p. 83.

19. "The Refectory," p. 95–96.

20. DuBois, p. 19, and Charles D. (same author?) p. 3.

21. *Werke*, I, p. 102.

22. By Bayard and Bieville, presented at the Gymnase (Witkowski, p. 296 f.)

23. Randon in *Petit Journal pour Rire*, No. 525, circa 1868.

24. *Painter of Modern Life*, p. 25.

25. Fashion's arch: Henry Luttrell, 1820, cited by Laver, *Clothes*, pp. 90–92. Brummell: "The stay is a part of modern dress that I have an invincible aversion to" (*Male and Female Costume*, 1822, p. 283). Many of the most distinguished later dandies, such as Count d'Orsay, Bulwer Lytton, and Disraeli, wore stays, which were not, however, demonstrably wasp-waisted. Cleanliness and fit: cf. Moers, p. 35. Cravat as tablecloth: *The Hermit in London*, 1813 (quoted by Cunnington, *Underclothes*, p. 106).

26. A Cavalry Officer, 1830, p. 19. Cf. Saint-Hilaire, 1827, and *Cravatiana*, 1823.

27. Leblanc, p. 19.

28. "Blotches": Buchan, *Domestic Medicine*, and *Advice to Mothers*, 1807 p. 47; "Into and out of this world": Brown, 1818, p. 23; Dickens, *Sketches by Boz*, 1836, "Seven Dials."

29. Demon Tie: *The Lantern*, 1852, p. 131; Military snob: Captain Slasher, a British hero of the Napoleonic Wars, visiting Boulogne, "seated himself at the breakfast-table, with a surly scowl on his salmon-colored bloodshot face, strangling in a tight, cross-barred cravat; his linen and appointments so perfectly stiff and spotless that everyone at once recognized him as a dear countryman." Everytime he cried out "O!" meaning water (the only French he had), he was thought to be in a death agony of strangulation (Thackeray, *Book of Snobs*).

30. *Réflexions*, p. 20.
31. Golilla: Cardinal Alberoni, quoted by Kany, p. 175. Cravat: Kany, p. 179. Goya drawing of woman: Domingo, p. 114.
32. *The Dandies' Ball*, 1819, and *The Dandies' Perambulations*, n.d.
33. Madame de Genlis (attr.), 1825, cited in Wachtel, p. 232.
34. *Stello*, 1832, p. 15.
35. Libron, pp. 88 and 149, and Vanier, p. 56. Cf. Thiel, p. 527 for a device patented in Vienna 1833, an instant release mechanism for ladies feeling suddenly ill. 1828, the date Dandé registered his patent for metal eyelets, is generally accepted as that of their introduction into corsetry; they are, however, already recommended in Mme. Celnart's *Manuel* of 1827 (p. 207) and were presumably in common use by 1828, for a letter of that year from a tradesman complains that his daughters were reducing themselves to ant-like proportions in stays "bound with iron in the holes . . . to bear the tremendous tugging" (cited in Cunnington, *Feminine*, p. 59). Madame Celnart also describes how lacing should be done—upwards and ending top right as in the eighteenth century. There is no question at this date of tightening by means of a loop at the waist.
36. "The art of suicide by the corset is not as widespread as is generally believed. Some women have even abandoned it altogether by necessity or caprice" (Réveillé Parise, 1841, p. 788). "Tight-lacing has decreased of late" (*Habits of Good Society*, 1859, p. 172); cf. Cunnington, *English Women*, p. 131. The theme is conspicuous by its absence from Cham's caricatures of *Deux Vieilles Filles à Marier* (a series of 1840), in which various artifices are used by a mother to improve her elderly daughter's appearance, from the same artist's *Les Tortures de la Mode* (ca. 1856), and from Gustave Doré's "Il faut souffrir pour être . . . laid" (*Petit Journal pour Rire*, 1856, No. 16, pp. 5–7).
37. Réveillé Parise is a case in point.
38. E.g., *Magasin Pittoresque*, a pioneering general interest, illustrated magazine, in the year 1833, p. 99. The really cheap press also took over the responsibility. *Cleave's Penny Gazette of Variety*, on the front page for Saturday, 25 August, 1838, carried an article addressed "To the Young Women of England, On the Evils of Tight-lacing," which derived from similar ones published in the *Penny Magazine*, 23 Feb. 1833, pp. 77, and in Barlow's *Cyclopedia of Practical Medicine*, and ran parallel to another similar article in the *Magazine of Domestic Economy*, of the "current month." These articles contained the illustrations from Soemmerring mentioned above. *Cleave's* refers to the "numerous and painful evidence of its (tight-lacing's) continued prevalence." Cf another cheap popularization of the period, the *Penny Encyclopedia*, 1837, s.v. corset.
39. Cuvier accompanied a tight-laced lady to a greenhouse where he showed her a blooming flower. Gazing upon her constricted form and pale face, he said, "Madame, previously you resembled this flower, tomorrow this flower will resemble you." They returned the next day to find the flower withering away, in explanation of which the naturalist pointed to the string which he had previously tied tightly about the stem (Debay, 1857, p. 173 f.; Larousse, and *The Girl's Own Paper*, 1892, p. 587).
40. Debay, p. 165 and Roux 1855.
41. E.g. *Die Gartenlaube* (Leipzig) 1855, pp. 213–5. Sagarra, p. 19, assumes that this kind of article was a circulation-building device.
42. Barnett, p. 68.
43. II, pp. 18–19. To justify the anecdote, Hogg adds that the lecturer had expected Shelley, "who would certainly have decided the momentous question" but who failed to show up. It is unlikely that Shelley had anything to do with the matter, since at the time (ca. 1818) such lectures were unknown, or rare.
44. Quoted by Wachtel, p. 269.
45. *Times* for 12 August, 1844, quoted by Bagshawe.
46. Nottingham, 1841, p. 110.
47. *Second Annual Report* (1840), p. 73, and *Nineteenth Annual Report* (1858), p. 194, quoted (dates misquoted) by Combe, 1860, p. 177. The statistics given for the year 1838 do not, however, indicate a very large differential: 3.8 male deaths per thousand, compared with 4.1 female died per thousand. According to the American Tilt (1853, pp. 195–9), for the age-span fifteen to thirty years, which corresponds to the peak period of tight-lacing, the female mortality rate was 13% higher than that of the male;

altogether, 8% more females died of consumption than males. Not, surely, statistics which convince one either of the lethality or the universality of tight lacing.

48. Hardy, 1824.

49. A treasure-trove of such case-histories is a source which is not demonstrably medical but nonetheless obsessional (Dubois, 1857): Two wasp-waisted sisters married, one died as she miscarried of her first child, and the other shortly after the first delivery, both of acute peritonitis. The mother died of grief (p. 10). Another tight-lacer, married to a friend of the author, suffered two still-births, and then produced one hunchback, who died at the age of three. He was immediately followed into the grave by the mother, still furiously tight-lacing despite the counsel of friends, doctors, etc. The husband died of grief (p. 14). The author also saw a beautiful but deformed eleven-year-old boy, whose mother had died of tight-lacing. He soon followed her to the grave (p. 30). A very pretty wasp-waisted shop attendant died in "atrocious suffering;" the father almost died of grief, the mother went mad (p. 8).

50. Layet, 1827, p. 36. Dubois asserts (p. 2), surely hyperbolically, that many women continue to tight-lace up to the very moment of giving birth.

51. Combe, pp. 173–5.

52. Merritt, p. 165.

53. Salpêtrière: Dubois. Dressmakers 1864: Pike, p. 180. Prostitute: Espagne, p. 310. Water-carrying servant-girl: Schneider, p. 347. Dancing villager: *Die Gesunde Frau*, 15 Feb. 1900, p. 20 (cf Ivière, p. 6). For the fatality of a farmer's daughter, see Childs, p. 38, and Duffin, p. 24, both from the same *Times* report of 1834. Jemima Hall: *Lancet* 18 Feb. 1871, p. 256, and *Islington Gazette* 27 Dec., 1870. My thanks to Peter Martin for the latter reference (cf. Martin pp. 16–20). Ironically, the *Lancet* for 17 April, 1869, p. 554 had occasion to pour scorn on an advertisement "from a leading London paper," addressed to "Staymaker's assistants, dressmakers, and ladies' maids" committed to tight-lacing, for "an important position in the country." It is not clear whether the advertiser had in mind a maid, wife or mistress. Gillham no. 28 contains an advertisement of c. 1800 for "good home-made stays for Servants and Working Women at one guinea."

54. Godman, pp. 191–4.

55. Both stories in Debay, 1857 p. 165 f.

56. Carter, 1846 p. 409, and citation in *Aunt Fanny's Album* p. 17.

57. *Dictionary of American Biography*, 1930 pp. 515–16.

58. Pp. 50, 138, and 157.

59. Réveillé Parise, p. 789. Pierquin's book is as rare as it is curious and, published in Bourges, may have passed quite unnoticed. The only copy known to me is the U.S. National Library of Medicine.

60. *Martin Chuzzlewit*, pp. 42 and 102.

61. *Bleak House*, pp. 90 and 252. The allusions to a "frosty" and "acidic" nose, if connoting redness, pick up the reformers' stereotype in which tight-lacing caused redness of the extremities and nose, the red nose being the awful stigma of the alcoholic. There may also be the verbal connection between tight (laced) and tight (drunk).

62. pp. 180–81. I owe this reference to a draft of Helene Roberts' article.

CHAPTER THREE

The Campaign of the Humorists (Punch, etc.) 1846–1900

Punch and Tight-Lacing

P unch, born in 1841 and still staggering along, has come to be regarded as the perfect mirror of Victorian bourgeois mores. After its early radical fling, eschewing all extravagance and the grosser forms of satire, it became an accurate barometer of the conservative male upper-middle class view of women's role in society, one of its staple themes. *Punch* was, first of all, a respectable family journal, especially during the period with which we are principally concerned (1860–90). Any kind of joke about sex, adultery or immorality such as formed a constant of the French caricature journals was taboo. But Mr. Punch (as he called himself, and as we may call him—all *Punch* articles are anonymous) kept a hawk-like, moralistic eye on developments in women's fashion. It was an essentially Olympian male eye, for the female staff member, the Mrs. Judy promised by the founder Mark Lemon was never found. Other magazines such as *Fun* and *Judy*, lower-class imitators of *Punch*, aiming at women and less sophisticated males, stand less on their dignity, but even they never approach the imaginative ribaldry and erotic abandon of the French.

Tight-lacing was a continuous thorn in Mr. Punch's side. Other fashions came and went, but tight-lacing obstinately resisted the scourge of satire. *Punch* satire in this area is more verbal than graphic, for two reasons: first, *Punch* cartoonists (from the 1860s) were not caricaturists but illustrators for whom the outré, the grotesque, and all forms of graphic exaggeration were tainted with vulgarity; second, the same moral convention which inhibited the English novelist from describing underwear, forbade the artist in "respectable" magazines to draw a woman in any state of undress. The principal society artist, George Du Maurier, made it a rule that in scenes mocking female vanity set in the dressing room or at the modiste's, the lady appear fully dressed; if the maid still has a lace in her hand, it is that of the dress bodice, not the stays. The corset is never shown on the body; it would be suggestive of nakedness, as would that fetching description in an anthropological journal of natives with tattoo marks resembling "fine lace and a tight-fitting suit of clothes"—the drawing for which limits itself to a view of the Materfamilias, seated in the drawing room, reading the relevant extract aloud to a delighted younger set.[1] How *La Vie Parisienne* revelled in such opportunities!

In 1846 Mr. Punch delivered his first "Lecture on Tight Lacing", illustrated by his premier artist, John Leech. The vain and ignorant women who cared not one whit about the internal havoc they cause themselves, should at least worry about the deleterious externally visible effects. Tight stays cause mental decay which shows in "deep and indelible lines of peevishness, fretfulness and ill-temper," and (horrors!) symptoms of the vulgar, drinking classes: red noses and enlarged hands and feet. The complexion, so sacred to the Victorian eye, was a particular victim: "on the spot where the rose and the ruby had shed their lustre, they pour bile and sprinkle ash. They do still more; they dapple the cheeks with unsightly blotches, convert its fine cuticle into a motley scurf, blear the eyes, discolour the teeth and destroy them by caries, and (worst of all) tip the nose with cranberry red."[2] All knew the dread associations of the red nose, with old age, drunkenness and disease: "The circulating fluid, from a disagreeable law of nature, is forced up into the head. The colour of the fluid is rosy, as you know." (The delicate euphemisms are a heavy sarcasm). "The delicate health attendant on tight-lacing forbids it (the blood) to adorn the cheek, and accordingly it is transferred to the nose; which its tint does not adorn by any means . . ." The Lecture closes on the metaphorical associations of the hour-glass shape with the Sands of Time, or Life and Death itself, which became almost a cliché of the humorous journal.

Mr. Punch takes every opportunity to castigate tight-lacing, even in passing in the course of some "charivariety" (short polemical piece on any odd subject). For example, an objection to the new habit of putting small boys into colorful leggings rather than proper trousers is prefaced with scant relevance by this lament, which we cite for the novelty of its humorous tone: "How many a blue-eyed, pink-faced, rosy-lipped, dark-haired houri has fallen victim to the restrictive policy of the staylace, which in her days of gushing womanhood has been employed to check the exuberance into which she would otherwise have gushed, and caused her to waste away in a slenderness of waste, until life has proved indeed a mere span."[3]

The puns, the euphemistic, pseudo-poetic style as well as the new emphasis on the complexion, are all masks for very real sexual fear. The satirists of the early and mid-Victorian period were, in their puritanism, unable to face the sexualization of tight-lacing implicit in much criticism of previous periods. So much so, that they turned that criticism upside down. The corset was now paradoxically viewed as an instrument of puritanical repression, the stigma of celibacy, which not only confined woman physically, but also shrivelled her up emotionally, causing the "panting dove" to become "pent up and pinched up with whalebone." The stereotype of the tight-lacer is no longer that of the woman bent on exaggerating her natural charms, but that of the woman with no natural charms to exaggerate. Tight-lacing was seen as morally repressive by those who were doing the repressing of it (and sex generally). The physically tight-laced are represented as morally strait-laced and embittered (like Dickens' Mrs. Snagsby), whereas in fact it is their opponents who are often, demonstrably, the strait-laced ones. Unable wholly to deny the function of tight-lacing as sexual provocation, *Punch* brands it as that of the desperate spinster who is so lacking in the normal attractions that she will resort to any extremity in order to catch the bachelor eye.

The crinoline had the effect of diminishing tight-lacing, making the waist look small by simple contrast. It also deflected the attention of the fashion satirists, who in *Punch* alone produced during the years 1856–59 alone about two hundred cartoons and comments on this garment. But tight-lacing was not to be squeezed out altogether: The skeletal shape of the crinoline inspired some verses on the Memento Mori pattern, reminding ladies that "There's a skeleton within thee—/Then this gift, for all its lightness,/Warn thee will, arrayed in brightness,/Not to lace with too much tightness,/That thy waist may be a wonder,/Not to squeeze it half asunder,/Crushing so the bones thereunder!" In 1862, over the (false) rumour that crinoline was going out, Mr. Punch resumed the anti-tight-lacing campaign. The pretext was the exhibition of the Empress of Austria's "Grecian girdle" in the Greek Court of the International Exhibition. After a show of pretence that the Empress's waist is a natural deformity for which she is not to be held responsible, *Punch* launches into a tirade of exceptional virulence, which ends upon the characteristic threat that "the smaller (a lady) contrives to make her waist, the smaller will be her chances of getting married."[4]

The news from Paris that the scandalous Comtesse de Castiglione, a famed beauty and an intimate of the Emperor Napoleon III, had cast aside stays altogether (not for reasons of hygiene, but in order to enhance her décolletage), and that fashionable Paris at large had adopted the unconstricting *ceinture suisse,* provided yet another occasion for an attack on tight-lacing. *Punch* compared the two major excesses of fashion, crinoline and tight-lacing in favour of the former: "An absurdly-widened skirt is not so dreadful a disfigurement as a pinched-in narrowed waist. Crinoline is a nuisance, but at least there is no crime in it. Now, tight-lacing is a sin, for it is virtual slow suicide; and if they did their duty, parsons ought to preach against it." Mr. Punch's anger was probably fuelled by the burgeoning correspondence in the fashionable *Queen,* where an enterprising editor, Samuel Beeton (cf. Chapter Six), was printing the first letters defending the practice. Without publicising the journal by name, Mr. Punch held up to ridicule the self-imposed martyrdom and exhibitionism of its correspondents: " *'Mais n'importe'* [never mind my bent spine, reddened nose, headache, fainting fits, etc.], gasps the victim, 'I am in the fashion. My waist is smaller than Miss CRUSHRIBBE'S and hers is only sixteen inches in circumference. Yes, it *would* be five and twenty, if Nature had her way; *mais la Mode change tout cela,* distortion is the fashion.' But the Venus de' Medici—'O, don't talk to me of Venuses! You say her great thick clumsy waist is twenty-seven inches round, and yet those stupid artists speak of her as 'perfectly proportioned!' Now *I* stand five feet three upon my military heels, and measure fifteen inches and three quarters round my waist, and you *don't* mean to compare *my* figure with the Venus's!! Besides, Sir, Gentlemen—I don't mean nasty smoky slovenly-dressing artists— admire a slender figure, and think it most becoming. And as I'm dying to get mar—I mean, to please the gentlemen, why you see of course I *must* lace in my waist a bit, though it makes me feel quite faint at times and sadly pant for breath, especially when waltzing!" Mr. Punch would convince his readers that tight-lacers don't get married, and if perchance they do find a gentleman foolish enough to take them, that they will cause him endless torment through heavy medical bills and the waspish temperament which always goes with a wasp-waist. He closes in pleonastic desperation "there is not a man among us—not being a born fool—that does not hate, detest, abominate, and occasionally swear at the sinful suicidal fashion of tight-lacing, which is every whit as frightful a personal disfigurement as the squeezed skulls of the Flat-Heads, or the crushed feet of the Chinese."[5] Strange language from a journal which prided itself on the lightness of its wit.

The revival, five years later, of pro-tight-lacing correspondence in the popular and lower-middle-class *Englishwoman's Domestic Magazine*, once more galvanized Mr. Punch's pen. This time the sheer volume and longevity of the correspondence, and its notoriety among the press at large obliged *Punch* to take it more seriously. A piece headed "A Plea for Tight-Lacing" is the first of about a dozen articles and drawings on the subject published 1869–70. It now reveals the peccant source by name, and quotes extensively from the most improbable-sounding of the letters—from a woman who claimed to have reduced from 23 to 14 inches within a week. Mr. Punch tried to discredit the correspondence as a whole by treating it as the work of some fellow satirist, closing thus: "It is gratifying to find *The English-woman's Domestic Magazine* instructing its readers by satire. They must be very intelligent, let us hope that none of them are so much the reverse as to take the irony of a wise and clever man for the credible communications of a vain, silly and disgusting woman." In the last phrase, the mask of humor drops, and the scorn poured upon "inferior female grammar" and "admirable vulgar colloquialisms," shows that Mr. Punch is snobbishly (and misogynistically) trying to discredit the tight-lacers as ill-educated, lower-class women.[6] Many, of course, in fact were, but the choice of the tactic as indeed *Punch*'s preoccupation with practice generally, shows how high its incidence was among the middle classes in the broader sense.

The tone of heavy irony is sustained in an attack published the following year, which (I suspect) unconsciously takes as its point of departure the unspeakable revelation made by male correspondents to the *Englishwoman's Domestic Magazine*, that men, too, were capable of tight-lacing—and boasting of it. Under the heading "Elasticity of Young Ladies" Mr. Punch pretends to believe, with heavy sarcasm, that since the sexes are so differently constituted, it is physically possible for ladies to tight-lace and not suffer for it. Men, of course, would be afflicted with all the ailments ascribed by physicians to the practice, whereas "the plastic nature of woman's organisation, in substance resembling caoutchouc (rubber) enables her to lace almost as tight as she pleases with impunity."[7]

As the pro-tight-lacing letters continued to pour into the *EDM*, *Punch* took to inventing letters of its own, printed without comment, and reporting at some length fictitious meetings of tight-lacers. These letters are designed to ridicule the very idea of women (feminists, etc.) formally gathering, like men, for purposes of rational debate, or, more to the point here, engaging in some kind of conspiracy. In their parodistic disguise they steamroll two cornerstones of the defense: first, that tight-lacing is a purely personal matter, and is not to be dismissed as mere response to the "dictates of fashion"; and second, that practiced *with discretion*, it need not cause damage to the health. *Punch's* tight-lacers meet together in order to boast crassly of their enslavement to fashion, and their miserable health.

Mr. Punch not only truly believed in the authenticity of the *EDM* correspondence but also in its corollary, the fact that tight-lacing was generally on the increase. With another jibe at the *EDM*, he pretends to chide the *Morning Post* "which we used to call our fashionable contemporary," for reporting a verdict of death by tight-lacing on a nursemaid who collapsed while out with a perambulator. Surely the *Morning Post* was not so naive as to imagine that such a report would deter young ladies from following a fashion which—*Punch* despairingly recognized—had revived with a vengeance, and was not to be stemmed, given the number of "fatuous" and "fat-headed" young women who cared not one whit about the threat of "fatty degeneration of the heart" (which the tight-lacing had in this case lethally accelerated).[8]

Pretty Feet and Ugly Heels; Chignon; "Girl of the Period"

In the year 1869, the heyday of the fetishist correspondence in the *Englishwoman's Domestic Magazine*, *Punch* fashion satire climaxed in a hyperbolic onslaught on tight-lacing set within an ever-expanding campaign against other, newer fashionable evils, notably high heels, the chignon, face-painting and décolletage. These were attributes of the "fast young lady" of fashion, or "Girl of the Period."[9] She represented in every respect an insult to nature. "Would you then know my Celia's charms?/. . . By lacing tight deforms her waist/. . . Her hair is only half her own/. . . Her cheeks a dab of rouge reveal/. . . Her boots three inches high of heel . . . her talk is slang/. . . in dancing she can twist and twirl/. . . As deftly as a ballet-girl./Yet never has learned with grace to walk/But struts with an audacious stalk/. . . loves shopping, bonnets and bazaars;/Can skate, ride, row, and smoke cigars:/Reads trashy novels by the score. . ."[10] Thus the frivolous stereotype of the emancipated girl.

Hitherto Mr. Punch had looked favorably, not to say gleefully, upon the development and increasing visibility of ladies footwear. In a crinoline the wearer had only to sit, bend forward, climb stairs or a hillside, to reveal not only her ankle but several inches above it. At the seaside and in the country the crinoline was often abandoned, so that the wind swept a virtually unpetticoated skirt against the legs, in an effect so appealing that even sober-minded Mr. Punch risked an occasional cartoon on the subject. The new game of croquet, in conjunction with the crinoline, helped catalyze a cultural form of foot-fetishism in the '60s, to which the new, higher-heeled boots contributed. Ladies cheated by moving the ball with their foot under the skirts short enough for them to be caught at it; gentlemen knelt at their feet to adjust touching (technically called "kissing") balls. The cartoons about and allusions to the privilege of tiny feet, and the affliction of large feet (typical of the elderly spinster) are legion in Victorian art and literature. To the opportunities of the croquet field may be added the even better avenues for foot-hand contact offered by another new sport, skating. Du Maurier evokes the torments of the lover obliged to permit the vulgar, mercenary hand of the rink-attendant to fit the skate to the beloved's boot, or the consummate gaffe of Mr. Green, who on being requested to put Miss Gladys' lawn tennis shoes in his pocket, replies, "I'm afraid my pockets are hardly big enough; but I shall be delighted to carry them for you."[11]

Tiny, more visible and almost-touchable feet were one thing; the high heel, with the increased stature and more sexual-aggressive gait it induced, was another. Mr. Punch, who had never commented on footwear styles as such, decided that the rising heel (accelerating, it seems, rather suddenly in 1868) made a pretty foot into the quintessence of ugliness, a "poisoned hook" to catch the unwary male. By another, even more telling "medieval" analogy, the heel became the cloven hoof of the devil or witch, one of *Punch*'s favorite metaphors. The cane (a male symbol), introduced for fashionable ladies' walking in 1868, became the maleficent gnarled stick of the wicked fairy (when not recognized as a practical necessity to prevent the tottering bearer from falling over[12] (cf. Plates 55 and 56). Punch feared but did not openly confront the other primary purpose of the high heel: that is, to endow woman with a physical and thereby moral superiority, as did an Italian cartoon-fantasy: woman on stilts 20 foot high, enabling her to converse with the denizens of heaven and as she does so, cock a snook at her husband below, screaming to have a button sewn on his pants.[12]

The new heel engendered a pitched-forward walk known as the "Grecian Bend" after the attitude of some figures painted on Attic Greek vases (Plate 54). By this time the post-crinoline train had been abolished and skirts further shortened, so that the foot was fully visible when walking. The continuing campaign of the 1870's terminated, typically, on a note of bitter hopelessness which like many of the anti-tight-lacing diatribes in *Punch,* has little to do with satire: "So let them (feet and toes) be deformed and crumpled up by these instruments of torture, and grow misshapen and distorted like the feet of the Chinese. Deformity becomes a proof of fashionable breeding, and it is better to be hideous than not dress *à la mode.*" *Punch* saw female addiction to such absurdities as the final proof that women were incapable of higher thought, and affected such sneering headings as "*The Higher Education of Women*—Learning to walk in French boots with six-inch heels" (similarly, a discussion of newly founded Girton College is derisively entitled "The Chignon at Cambridge"). Du Maurier was wont to prophecy that feet would soon be worn bare as a form of retribution against those addicted to high heels and narrow boots, who would no longer be able to appear in public; and he summoned up the ghosts of sandal-shod grandmothers (i.e. from the neo-classical period c. 1800) to vindicate the honour of the British tootsicum. By the 1890s, the high heels and tight shoes were no longer an issue, having been superseded by *Punch's* fear of heavy, masculine, sporting footwear: "Great them with derisive hoots-/ Clumsy, huge! For feet so tiny!/Oh, those Boots!"[13]

The chignon was in the 19th century still most decidedly a luxury article, and therefore carried a particularly heavy hierarchical charge.[14] It reached its greatest fashionable excess during the years 1869–74. It was bracketed with tight-lacing as a form of suicide, on the basis of the remarkable statistic that brain-fever had increased 73 percent since its introduction, with the colossal pressure it allegedly exerted on the skull, calculated in a chignon 18 inches high at forty pounds per square inch. It was even supposed to cause spinal meningitis.[15]

The free interplay of twisted braids characteristic of the chignon gave a young artist new to *Punch*, Linley Sambourne, an opportunity to display his virtuosity in graphic transformations. The chignon became (among a host of other more or less sinister—and sexual—beasts) a gigantic spider, a serpent, an octopus, a hedgehog, and a porcupine. With the bizarre, clinging modes of the seventies, Sambourne let the transformation envelop the body as a whole, which was turned very prettily into fuchsia, butterfly, fish, porcupine, beetle—and, inevitably, hourglass, dumbbell and wasp (Plate 33). The rigid cuirasse fashion invited adaptation to the hard shell of the lobster (Plate 34), as also to the medieval armour appropriate to ladies admitted to the knighthood. For roller-skating, woman was mechanised and rivetted all over, for tennis wrapped most fetchingly in netting.[16] An ancient emblemology here, delivered with fresh, quasi-erotic, grace.

With Sambourne, *Punch's* attitude to the extravagances of fashion shows signs of softening. His tranformations, which dispense with the text otherwise de rigueur, express a certain complaisance with the eroticism and theatricality of fashion which is almost French in flavor and unique in *Punch* illustration at this time.

Cuirasse, Tied-Back and Jersey Styles; Tennis; Masculinization

After 1870 *Punch* makes no more frontal attacks on tight-lacing. Greater enemies had arisen, first in the "aesthetic," then (worse) the "rational" styles of dress. A ballad parodying Rossetti imagines "Kent-born Helen, England's pride," weary of the neo-Greek, Pre-raphaelite, "aesthetic" mode, and hankering passionately after the latest development in corsétry, the heavy cuirasse corset (Plate 37). Helen kills herself by tight-lacing, but her martyrdom is the product of a misplaced idealism, not just a foolish vanity. This is indeed an important shift. Nostalgically *Punch* contemplates the supercession by Aesthetic Beauty of the fashionable ideal against which he had once railed. Flowing tresses, sylph-like undulations, boneless grace were perhaps, after all, preferable to frizzed flamboyant hair, cavernous cheeks, spare frame and a generally morbid demeanour. *Punch* comes to terms at last with the "willow-waisted Grace," and the "witchery" of the "tasteful cincture of the trim-laced zone."[17]

Punch's change of mind is all the more remarkable in that tight-lacing not only actually increased during the 1870s and 80s, but also became more anatomically exposed through the tightening of dress at the hips. We deal below with *La Vie Parisienne's* paroxysms of delight over the cuirasse style: the reaction in German humorous journals was as intense, in its own graphically tepid way. Louis Bechstein in the *Fliegende Blätter* 1877–83, executed a continuous series of cartoons on the subject. The lady rash enough to take a decent meal in her new sheath is unable to extricate herself from it, and must be rushed to Carlsbad for a slimming cure. No one dares tell a girl funny stories any more, lest she burst her dress in laughter. She has to be carried into a train by the guard. Arriving at the customs she passes without inspection, since she cannot be smuggling anything under her skin. Unable to walk, she has to be propelled along by means of roller-skates, or a sail. These and other such cartoons are interspersed with more Bechstein drawings relating specifically to the waistline: a fat rustic couple wonder at a youthful wasp-waisted city girl. "Look, Nanni, she could never get a dumpling down her, she has to live off macaroni."[18] By 1883 the tight-lacer reached a macabre humorous apotheosis in a comic strip (Plates 50 and 51).

The realisation that the new tight fashion of the '70s coincided with the economic recession of the same decade, after the boom of the '50s and '60s (reflected in the buoyant crinoline?) underlies the cartoon in which the husband warns his wife that owing to the cost of living, she must restrict herself in her toilette. She replies that she is already so restricted that she can barely walk. In a similar joke, "Times are tight, and I must dress accordingly."[19]

Du Maurier, meanwhile, showed tolerance and amusement. In a famous cartoon a lady at a ball declines an invitation to sit down "because my dressmaker says I mustn't". To overcome which problem Du Maurier philanthropically invented a new form of chair, based on the principle of the shooting-stick with a sloping seat. The beauteous Mrs. Vavasour Belsize and her lovely sisters arrive at Mrs. Brabazon de Vere Tomkynne's reception in dresses so tight that they cannot mount the stairs at the top of which their hostess awaits them. Cissy drops her parasol during her country walk, and neither she nor Fanny can stoop to pick it up. This is not out of flirtatiousness, for there is, alas, no gentlemen around for miles and miles. Once down, the roller-skater could not rise again; for bowling, a girl could not even stoop. The swaddling was likened to that of an Egyptian mummy, and most cogent perhaps of all, women were imagined to be poured, hot, into the mould of their corset-dress, and left to cool; to get out again, they have to be melted down. The fashion was dangerous in a new sense: "The explosions of gas, nitroglycerine, dynamite, gun-cotton—all these aren't enough, now women are about to explode at any moment!"[20]

Supreme paradox: The tight skirt coincided with the rising popularity of tennis which became the fashionable game of the 1870s as croquet had been that of the 1860s. Tight skirt and tennis were not considered incompatible. The game was, presumably, played less athletically than today; but Du Maurier also shows just how strenuous the action could be, even by our standards. And he sets up as rivals in beauty to the finest French actresses you can name, four young English tennis-players, dressed in the height of the cuirasse style and tightly tied-back skirts.[21]

The tightness at the hips introduced with the cuirasse style was soon matched, in the 1880s, by a corresponding tightness at the bust achieved by the jersey, which stretched to a perfect fit. The fisherman's jersey was introduced into fashion in the summer of 1879 and named after the actress Lily Langtry (known as "Jersey Lily" after her place of origin). "Then she wore a jersey fitting/Like an eel-skin all complete,/With a skirt so tight that sitting/Was an agonising feat."[22] Its tightness enhanced the action of the corset pushing it up from below. The surging breasts over the wasp-waist, hailed with delight by the French, satirised by the Germans, and of necessity ignored by the prudish English cartoonist, gave what was generally known as the "pouter-pigeon" effect (cf. plate 36). The moulded line was reminiscent of nudity—or, at least, of underwear, as witness that serving-maid who, seeing her mistress leave the house in her jersey, cried out "What, mum? Do yees go right out in the street in yer figger?" By August 1880 *Punch* was already trying (vainly) to discredit the fashion for jerseys over exaggerated wasp-waists by showing 'Andsome 'Arriet the 'Ousemaid wearing one over her squat, cotton-reel figure[23] (fig. p. 158).

The jersey seemed the ideal garment for tennis and boating. The *Punch* imitator *Fun* was very much taken with the way the jersey seemed to encourage tennis-players to show off the effects of tight-lacing: "Surfeited with tennis pleasure,/Sitting/Screwed within the smallest measure/Fitting;/Hoping soon to be released,/Hoping!/ From that garment so uncreased,/Sloping/O'er each curve, so weary, her see,/Keeping/Watch for friend to peel her jersey!/Weeping." A vignette and verse similar in spirit, published six weeks later, shows the tight-lacer in action under the heading "Tennis Agony": "Jersey-clad perchance to show her muscle,/Try to run in pads, tie-back and bustle,/She serves eight faults and sorrows she is wrong,/ Strains her corset when she tries to volley;/Her twelve inch waist is bound by leather thong . . ./She thinks it 'nice' to 'suffer and be strong'/To call her awful sufferings—jolly!" An old lady spectator marvels at the girls' ability to play for hours on end, when they claim to be tried after half an hour of needlework.[24]

The new-found physical energy of sporting women was also putting men to shame. Miss Lorne Tennys justly reproaches her partner with losing the game for her. Languid aesthetic, already "decadent" youths lounge in deck-chairs, watching the girls play, and declining to join in because the sport has become "so effeminate." There is even a dark hint of sexual impotence, for with his "aesthetic droop" and "feline grace," modern youth is able to indulge in only the most torpid forms of courtship, out of which his beloved would shake him by chasing after him and boxing his ears for him—were she not momentarily prevented by tight sleeves and high heels.[25] These are the precursors of that staple of '90s cartooning: Puny Male versus Tall Amazon, he absurdly repudiating the possibility of equality between the sexes on the grounds that man is physically so much the stronger, or pathetically lamenting that he cannot even reach her waist, let alone clasp it.[26]

The campaign against tight-lacing, abandoned or softened in *Punch*, survives with ever-decreasing seriousness in the lower-class magazines during the 80s, in cartoons and vignettes prompted, more often than not, by some newspaper report of a fatality. Peculiar efforts were made to lend an air of originality to what was generally felt to be an outworn issue. In a series "Historical Errors Corrected", it is claimed that Joan of Arc was not burned at the stake. "It is not generally known that she was excessively vain and was very particular as to the fit of her armor, and actually died a victim of tight-lacing." The accompanying vignette shows her in an iron corset and greaved bustle standing before a mirror.[27]

Around 1879–80 the Du Maurier woman, without losing her statuesque quality, became visibly more slender in the waist. Tight-lacing became a perfectly pardonable foible. If an elegant lady should engage, even over the objections of her dressmaker, to get into a dress 19 instead of her usual 21 inches around the waist, in order to outshine a rival, this is merely another manifestation of the society lady's perfectly rational, proper, and diverting preoccupation with social climbing, Du Maurier's staple theme.

More significant still of the change of attitude, the innocent Miss Lightfoot finds her fashionable addiction actually winning her an entirely unhoped-for and ideal husband. To her mother's horror, she has declined an invitation to dance from a Modest Youth, with the candid and spontaneous confession that her shoes and corset ("waistband" is the euphemism she uses) are so tight, that she cannot move. This touches the Modest Youth (who turns out to be an Earl of Richard the First's creation, six foot eight in his pumps, with eight hundred thousand a year) so deeply that he proposes on the spot.[28]

As the subject of benign and casual cartoons tight-lacing loses much of its moral opprobrium, in the humorous press at any rate. We may speak here of a popular attitude, shared even by *Punch*, which could no longer take the medical orthodoxy seriously. *Punch's* indulgent attitude was facilitated by the new enemy on the horizon, the "masculine" styles of dress for women which supervened around 1880. *Punch* equated "masculine" with Emanicpation. Increasingly reactionary in its politics, *Punch* bitterly opposed Women's Rights in any shape or form, especially since the movement was penetrating so deeply into the upper middle classes, which constituted the backbone of the *Punch* readership.

Mr. Punch regarded the "theft" of his clothing by woman as symbolic of her ambition to enter and subvert his world. The women themselves were, by and large, not conscious of so profound a purpose, and many used masculine effects as a means of setting off their femininity, rather than in order to assert their independence, although the former motivation does not exclude the latter.

It is characteristic, in this regard, that while they adopted one article of male fashion (the loose jacket) for its practicality, they also took another (the high stiff collar) which seemed highly unpractical, especially for outdoor activity, where it was chiefly worn. Practicality, with hygiene the shibboleths of the dress reformers and Rational Dress Society, was only one consideration, and the garment which was touted by the Society as the most rational advance of all, the

Divided Skirt (very wide trousers) failed to achieve general acceptance not so much because trousers were excessively male and
"emancipated," but because the divided skirt possessed insufficient
practical advantage to outweigh its entire lack of aesthetic-erotic
appeal (later, successful versions of the trouser idea, notably the
bicyclist's calf-revealing bloomers, combined both erotic and practical
advantage).

The loose coat (known as "sack"), borrowed from the men, could be
used to conceal a woman's desire to go uncorsetted altogether. On
the other hand, another much satirized novelty of the early 1890s, the
large gigot or balloon sleeves, which were feared to presage colossal
muscular development of arms and shoulders, also served to enhance
feminine smallness of waist.

The masculinisation of female fashion, far from leading to the
complete defeminisation feared by Mr. Punch, permitted woman
greater freedom of choice, enabling her to appear more "masculine"
at one time and more feminine at another, to put a loose coat on and
cast a corset off, according to her mood and the occasion. Having at
her disposal both masculine and feminine elements, she could combine them in a manner which expressed her socio-sexual personality
with greater precision and flexibility than hitherto. This represented
to *Punch* an expansion of her social role, and thus a threat to male
supremacy. The transvestite confusion of the age is summed up in a
Du Maurier cartoon entitled "The Sterner Sex" and showing a young
woman wearing her brother's shirt, tie, coat and hat, and taxed by her
girl-friend with making herself "look like a young man, you know,
and that's so effeminate!"[29]

Male Corsets and Collars

The incidence of military stay-wearing, after its heyday in the second
and third decades of the century (cf. above p. 114) is not well established. English graphic satire, whether out of patriotism or because
the habit was simply not visible, seldom alludes to it. I have found
nothing in English humor magazines like the grand chromolitho-
graphic double-spread of an American comic journal lambasting the
addiction of a notoriously effeminate regiment to seven-button
gloves, perfume, wigs and "breast-plate" corsets.[30] Transvestite tendencies from the late 1880s may have brought military corsetting
more into the open,[31] as it did that of the civilian, contrasted in one
cartoon with the loose jacketed woman (Plate 63). Around 1900 *Punch*
took up leads from fetishist correspondence that male tight-lacing
had become a serious matter. According to *Punch,* male corsetry was a
natural reaction to the fact that women had stolen all men's clothes:

"So in revenge, to make things square, / Their corsets we have taken!"[32] By 1904 male corsetting was taken so much for granted, that un-corsetting was news: the (female) reform campaign had infected the officers of the Guards, who thereby rendered themselves less likely to faint away in the ballroom.

We have adduced above evidence for the Prussian officer as natural-waisted compared with his French, Austrian or Russian counterpart. I have found nothing to contradict this up to and through the Franco-Prussian war period, but by the late 1880s there are numerous German and Austrian cartoons on the corsetted Prussian. In two (ironically) Austrian cartoons the Prussian officer, with his "quite pyramidal waist" already sufficiently on display, resents a new ordinance obliging him, if present at a ball, to dance; and he complains (also in Prussian Junker dialect) at the stupidity of journalists, who report that his ancestors had a waist three centimeters thinner than his own. "Ridiculous, more slender waist than mine unthinkable. Otherwise, torso would completely lose contact with hips" (which is exactly what another cartoon shows happening, as a lieutenant ill-advisedly stoops to pick up a lady's handkerchief). Officers swore by their waist "Auf Taille" as one might by any sacred object; both the wasp-waisted uniform and the oath were appropriated by natives in German West Africa. There is also some punning on "schnüren" as slang for to cheat: returning from leave, the officer complains he has been "fearfully laced/cheated" (schrecklich jeschnürt).[33]

The military were the last bastion of the corset. Asked by society ladies his opinion of the anti-corset movement, the young officer replies, "Ladies of course I prefer without corsets! But it remains an indispensible fixture (Möbel) for lieutenants!" An anecdote was told of Professor Ranke lecturing at the University of Münich on the difference between the waist in man and monkey, and permitting himself a mild joke about the propensity of ladies and German officers to tight-lace. A student in the auditorium, Prince George of Bavaria, was offended, and the professor was obliged to tender a public apology: "I had no intention of offending any corset-wearing German officer."[34]

The principal object of satire and the much more generalized instrument of restriction in male dress was the collar. The tight leather stock, self-imposed by the officer-class in the early part of the century, was the British common soldier's torment at the time of the Crimean War (as it had been a century before on the Continent). It came under fierce attack in a full-page drawing at a time when *Punch* was still radical in politics and grotesque in graphic style (Pl. 41). It was also satirically suggested that military surgeons be provided with smelling salts to revive the soldiers, who were fainting away by the dozens on the battlefield and being captured by the Russians. In France it was hyperbolically but seriously averred that "entire regiments" had been carried off by cerebral affection due to uniform collars".[35]

In England the abuse of tight collars was apparently not eradicated, for in 1869 we find *Punch* noting under the heading "Why strangle your soldiers?" a physician's opinion that aortic aneurism in the army could be diminished by making the tunic fit more loosely about the neck and upper chest. Three years later progress was being made, to judge by the military order that "in the future, clothing for recruits be fitted as loosely as possible, to enable them, as they increase in size from good diet and healthy exercise, to undergo their drill without impeding the free use of their lungs and the action of the heart."[36]

At the time of the Crimean War, in an obviously connected development, the civilian shirt collar surpassed itself in height, pattern and colour, although not, apparently, tightness. The rising expanse of collar favored by the "swells" was likened to the epidemic which was in reality decimating the Western armies in the Crimea—the cholera ("Collar-ah"). One might catch the disease not only on visual contact, but even by reading accounts of it. Its symptoms were an "eruption of a whitish hue (we have seen it in cases of two days standing take on a dubious yellowish tint) then spreading over the cheeks and back part of the head, giving the poor victim it seizes a most frightful aspect."[37] The collar might engulf the head of the wearer altogether; or be furnished with a padlock under the chin. On the continent the pointed, projecting kind of collar was known as a "Vatermörder" (parricide), on the basis of a famous anecdote about a student returning home, embracing his father and cutting his throat with his collar-point.

In 1856, when there was an epidemic of strangling in London, *Punch* invented the anti-garotte collar, studded with steel spikes. "Anti-garotte" spikes would not have been necessary thirty years later, for at that time the linen was being starched almost as rigid as steel, and instead of bypassing the jawbone, formed a close cylinder about the throat. It was to the satirical poet *literally* the armor of European imperialism against the African spear or Afghan sword, which were dashed in vain against it. Together with stick, monocle, long coat and spats, it was the uniform of the "masher" or (in the U.S.) "dude," who succeeded the swell, "a large class of very young, very soulless, very snobbish and altogether very stupid and would-be smart specimens of manhood." *Punch* cited a proposition of the (mock) Masherium Club, to the effect that "all the tables be made very high so that they shall not cut their throats with their collars more than is absolutely necessary." The collar acted as a physical support, like a corset, in conjunction with the stick which the masher propped against his mouth. "When they weren't leaning on them (collar and stick), or sitting down, or propped up against something, they'd tumble down and shatter all to bits;" the masher collar was deemed an object as difficult to live up to, as it was to live above. It was a symbol of aristocratic duty at a time of diminishing respect for such duty: "Bai Jove! Miss Mayne, I assure you that our awistocwacy may bweak, but it will nevah bend!" Miss Mayne (U.S.): "If all your aristocrats wear collars like yours, I don't wonder at them not being able to bend!"[38]

The masher collar was the male epitome of clothing which physically restricts as it symbolically protects. One was supported by, and subjected to one's collar. It was hard, like armor, elevated, like social duty, and impractical, like other symbols of the leisured class. It imposed "aristocratic" self-restraint, but was viewed by its critics as a symptom of narcissistic weakness, and as a substitute for rather than a symbol of willpower. The basic physiognomic indicator of mental weakness or lack of willpower was lack of chin ("weak chin"), another mark of the masher; the iron collar substituted for the iron jaw.

The masher collar was worn by an aristocratic sector which social change had put on the defensive, and which needed to find cultural forms to assert itself. But, like the dandy cravat, it was also affected by an upwardly mobile of pseudo-fashionable sub-aristocratic class, who found models in the smart New York clubs, and even Royalty.

A parody of First Aid advice suggests that in case of strangulation symptoms, the first check should be whether the victim is a member of the Knickerbocker, an élite New York club, in which case his collar should be removed. "This will undoubtedly destroy all his self-respect but will save his life."[39] The masher collar is one of the few fetishistic fashions which received a royal imprimatur, although not an altogether unambiguous one: that of Prince Albert Victor, the weak-minded and sexually bizarre heir of the Prince of Wales, who was known as Prince Collars and Cuffs for the particular attention he paid to those articles which he wore as deep and shiny as possible, even or especially when he visited India.[40] In Germany another kind of contradiction emerges. The high collar was not considered incompatible with the back-to-nature and gymnastics movement; in German gymnastic magazines one frequently finds a photograph of the Kunstturner in action on the apparatus, wearing a "near-naked" costume many contemporaries found quite scandalous, next to another picture of him posing in street wear including the highest of masher collars. A basic everyday body-restriction was complemented by conscious displays of free physical movement and the near-naked human body: both, from opposite poles, served narcissistic physical and body-kinetic needs.

In Germany restrictive neckwear preserved a very pronounced moral-duty symbolism, by virtue of its exaggeration by the notoriously stiff-necked Prussian officer (Plate 42). It even survived the First World War, among military and civilians alike. Its longevity generally, throughout the West and for military and civilian wear, was aided by the fact that it enjoyed bi-sexual associations, being quickly incorporated into women's fashion as part of the masculinization process. The femininity of the dress of the British aesthete such as Oscar Wilde, or his French equivalent, the much caricatured "gommeux," was marked by its very low and loose neckline; but the widespread adoption of the masher collar by women gave a point to the accusation of effeminacy against the masher, lacking in similar accusations against his predecessor, the dandy, whose tight stock and cravat were not worn by women. The contradiction here is extraordinary: this plain, virtually cravatless male collar, hallmark of a costume totally lacking in femininity or sexual-decorative appeal, this "super-masculine" object worn also (especially after c. 1900) by ordinary masculine (non-masher) men, this strictly abstract gell of moral duty, was taken over by woman, unchanged. Within the realm of dress, it was one of her most potent appropriations in the masculine domain.

Ladies Collar

Ladies first used the high stiff male collar on their riding habits. This was one of the two features of English riding costume to be adopted by the continental equestrienne, before entering fashion generally. The other was the culotte, or tight-fitting breeches in silk or chamois-leather, the object of an ecstatic cult in *La Vie Parisienne* but beyond the scope of this study. The stand-up collar soon passed into everyday dress. In its half-way stage, from the 1870s through early 1880s, the day-dress collar consisted of a lower half composed of the same material as the bodice, on a starched linen or buckram base which rose above the lower band by an inch or so. Around 1882, this part freed itself of the day-dress collar altogether, in imitation of the men. In the evening also the throat tended to be covered, above copious décolletage, by means of a velvet jewelled dog-collar and (c. 1880) a ruff. During the 1880s the stiff, detached collar rose progressively in height, and maintained itself at between two and four inches, depending on the taste and neck of the wearer, until well past the turn of the century.

Tightness of fit was essential, but manufacturers came up with various devices to mitigate discomfort, such as the moveable stud on an Indiarubber stem (1889), which permitted the collar to move a little with the movement of the head. Commonly worn heights around 1900 may be judged from the fact that the Vorwerk collar company sold stiffening in widths up to four inches; collar-heights advertised by American mail-order houses rose to three inches (there were also pretty little caskets to keep collar-and-cuff sets in). German magazines advertised "absolutely unbendable" aluminum plated watchspring steel collar supports up to three inches in height, in the same material that was used for belts. The starching of the linen did not in itself provide sufficient stiffness, although it was upon the perfectly smooth and white immaculately laundered effect that the status symbolism depended. The English did not take to the celluloid collar invented by the Americans, which saved the trouble of starching and allowed for easy washing, but which, being cheaper to maintain, diminished the status-value.

To colonials, the collar meant more than social status, it was a symbol of civilisation itself. It was an Englishwoman in India who, despairing at the limpness of her collars in that hot climate, hit upon the notion of keeping them erect with circles of metal cut from food cans.[41] Joseph Conrad, exploring darkest Africa, met an accountant residing there who astonished him by the splendor of his high starched collar and deep cuffs: "In the great demoralization of the land he kept up his appearance. His starched collars and got-up shirt fronts were achievements of character"—the maintenance of which he had painstakingly taught to a native woman. It was the accomplishment of his dreadful existence there.[42]

The French saw England as the land of sartorial exaggeration and eccentricity. They blamed the English for exporting the masher collar for female wear across the channel, to the culture which invented the term "décolletage" (a word which, like chic, coquette and retroussé, has no equivalent in English). At the same time, English women's exaggerations in décolletage, and the adoption of total nudity on the beach astonished and delighted French artists (notably Renoir). Total nudity may not have been common, but the English custom of segregated bathing (observed by males at a distance through binoculars) permitted very brief costumes: the French illustrator Mars in Margate notes the ogling of extreme revelations of leg and shoulder, and the exaggerated contours of wasp-waist and padded bust enhanced by the jersey material clinging directly to the corset, which Frenchwomen tended to discard altogether for bathing.[43] The French perceived English girls as very contradictory, sexually free and puritanical at the same time, relishing both nudity and constriction in their dress.

Not content with wearing the masher collar for sport, she also adopted the rigidly starched shirt front, the very symbol of male ceremonial wear, to "relax" upon the river: "she at the tiller in serge jacket open onto a blue or pink striped shirt, whose starched front bulges awkwardly over the breast; the neck imprisoned in the ugly "carcan" of a stiff collar . . . slender waist, flat hips . . . he seems to find her charming thus, in athletic attire." A *Vie Parisienne* centerspread on Brighton fashions shows everyone in "masculine attire: black, barely any bright colours, all with a crick neck, compressed and patented for ladies and gentlemen. Impossible to turn the head, but why bother, the England, he always go straight ahead (Le Angleterre, il allait toujours droit au but)." The French magazine also feared that the English collar gave young women premature wrinkles on the neck, and whenever the occasion arose, applauded the disappearance (in summer) of the "hausse-col" (gorget) and "col carcan" (iron collar). In the summer of 1897, which also witnessed an alarming diminution of evening décolletage, women of fashion, alas, "find that it is not yet hot enough to renounce in daytime the high, imprisoning collar; there must be a scarcity of pretty necks! One would prefer to see only mediocre necks and be reassured at least that the unfortunate creatures are able to breathe, and are not suffering torture. With the young girls, this is becoming a madness; their collars measure up to 8 cm. (3¼ inches) in height." A woman is practically prevented from turning her head to chat to someone at a neighbouring restaurant table or drawing-room chair. One American writer, however, sees a positive, if unintended orthopedic side-effect to the collar: it forces a woman to sit upright, preventing round shoulders and lounging postures.[44]

There were unfortunate aesthetic after-effects; even a liberal application of powder on the evening décolletage could not always hide the heavy red line ("high-water mark") left by the day collar around the throat under chin and ears. Constant tight enclosure allegedly threatened young women with prematurely withered necks as well as those ailments traditionally associated with the military stock (impeded circulation of the blood, constant headaches, etc.).[45] The male was threatened with worse: with his head held perpetually by his collar at a strained angle, he had to breathe through the mouth instead of the nose, and "mouth-breathing has caused the angle of the jaw to become permanently rounded; the chin is protruded; the chest is underdeveloped, and the high collar serves to perpetuate the deformity . . . giving a stupid and listless effect." The only fatality I have found reported is that of a servant-girl in Birmingham, who died of an epileptoid fit caused by asphyxia brought on by a tight collar in combination with a tight belt worn under her stays.[46]

The leading ladies' magazine, the *Queen,* was at first opposed to the stiff collar for women, noting that when a *Times* writer vituperated against the collar "worn by our brainless youth, rasping the chin and throat, rendering the wearer grotesquely uncomfortable and incapable of any other movement of the head than that of rotation of the neck on a vertical axis," he ignored the fact that "precisely similar collars are worn by women." The complaint is however exceptional; the English reformer was, by and large, more concerned with the dire effects of uncovering the female throat (and inviting lumbago, pneumonia, etc.), than with any minor disadvantage accruing to the manner of its covering.[47]

As the decade progressed, the high masculine collar for ladies made its way virtually unopposed in England. From 1889 the *Queen* insisted repeatedly that for outdoor and sporting dress, and with mannish shirts, even if they were soft-fronted, the collar must always be "very high and stiff and straight." With boating dress (and women often took the oar) this style was de rigueur and also for a certain kind of riding dress: the "ultra-masculine style, with everything as stiff, hard and neat as possible." The hard, masculine look of outdoor dress was enhanced by a variety of wide and heavy fancy leather and steel belts, sometimes accompanied by braces.

There was no activity in which the high collar can have proved more inconvenient than that of golf, one of the new sports conquered by women in the 1890s, and one which demands freedom of movement about neck and waist. Yet is is an account by a woman who became a champion golfer, famous enough to publish her golfing memoirs, which confirms our thesis that some sportswomen (like some fetishists) exaggerated fashionable restrictions as if they were part and parcel of the athletic feat in itself: "How on earth we bore the stiff collar is another mystery. I can remember, and myself wore, all the grades of collar—first the plain stand-up, then this was superseded by the double collar, highly glazed, and as deep as it was possible to wear it (we used literally to peep over these), and sometimes one got a raw sore all round the neck on the left side after playing golf in one of these monstrosities . . . Then in the old days every self-respecting woman of girl had to have a waist, and the more wasp-like it was the more it was admired. This was a terrible drawback at golf or tennis, but for a time it had to be endured . . . the girl of the present-day has no conception of the handicap it was."[48] The author leaves unexplained just why she allowed fashion to impose such a handicap on her game, when the game obviously meant so much more to her than fashion, and when fashion in fact, far from "imposing" a single, impractical style for sporting activity, was also evolving towards physical freedom and comfort.

From *Punch*, which was but one angry voice in a much larger campaign against tight-lacing, we have been led into consideration of collars, which aroused amusement rather than ire, and occupied cartoons and the miscellaneous news item and brief comment sections of the popular press, rather than the whole articles, pamphlets and books directed against the abuse of corsets. Compared with corsets, collars seemed a trivial matter; even their theft by women was not regarded as of much social consequence, or in itself as a particularly significant symptom of the otherwise disquieting process of female masculinization. The transvestite or bisexual character of the collar may have served to confuse sexual feeling, without catalyzing it like the corset.

Notes

1. Undress scene, e.g. 19 Sep. 1885, p. 138, or 10 March, 1888, p. 11. Tattoo: 9 Nov. 1878, p. 210.
2. *Punch*, 1846, II, p. 238, and Southgate.
3. 1849, I, p. 71.
4. "The Skeleton of Crinoline", 15 Nov. 1856, p. 193.
5. "Fashionable Suicide", 19 Sep. 1863, p. 122.
6. "A Plea for Tight-Lacing," 8 Feb. 1868, p. 64.
7. 18 Sep. 1869, p. 113.
8. "A Wanton Warning to Vanity", 2 Oct. 1869, p. 126.
9. This term gave the title to a sprightly, irreverent and short-lived magazine of 1869–70. It specialized in graphics of sexy, fancy fashions à la *Vie Parisienne*, using the characteristically English pretext of sporting exertions to show undress styles and erotic postures, and the characteristically English tactic of pretending to chastise the feminine frivolities and audacities (including tight-lacing) it obviously enjoys. *Girl of the Period* called itself the "Sister's University", to which all " 'the girls' might contribute their startling outpourings . . . (and) the gorgeous unfoldings of their private opinions." It adopted certain overtly feminist positions, such as the right of (middle-class) women to work, and alternatives to marriage: "Marriage is *not* the sole, or even the chief end of woman".
10. "Lines by a Lover", Dec. 14, 1872; Adburgham, p. 103.
11. Windswept legs: 17 Sep. 1859, p. 116 and 30 Oct. 1869, p. 166. Feet: 4 Oct. 1856, p. 134; 1 July 1865, p. 261, and citation in Adburgham, p. 84. Skate: 26 Jan, 1867, p. 34 (cf. 8 Jan. 1876, p. 288). Green's gaffe: 18 July 1885, p. 30.
12. *London Society*, 1869, 16, p. 42, and *Pasquino*, 17 April 1870, p. 125.
13. "Chinese" feet: 10 May 1873, p. 191. Higher Education: Adburgham, p. 97. Chignon at Cambridge: 14 Jan. 1871, p. 12. Du Maurier on feet: 19 March 1870, p. 110 and 28 June 1879, p. 294. "Those Boots": 19 Aug. 1893, p. 77.
14. In Zola's *Pot-Bouille* (1882, p. 295) the 95 franc article bought by Berthe precipitates a crisis in her deteriorating relationships with both husband and lover.
15. Safford-Blake in Woolson, 1874, p. 25; *Judy*, 11 Jan. 1870.
16. Knighthood: 19 Jan. 1878, p. 14. Roller-skating: 16 Oct. 1875, p. 156. Tennis: 13 Sep. 1879, p. 118.

17. "The Two Ideals," 13 Sep. 1879, p. 120; "The Modern Ars Amandi," 22 Dec. 1883, p. 300.

18. Vol. 66, p. 13. Vol. 68, p. 140. Vol. 68, p. 206. Vol. 73, p. 95. Vol. 74, p. 87. Vol. 78, p. 72. Vol. 70, p. 21. cf. also Vol. 75, p. 62 for the amazement aroused in the naive by the new wasp waist.

19. *Wild Oats*, 28 June, 1876, p. 5. The implications of the equation between economic "tightness" and sartorial tightness are far-reaching, and have exercised many costume historians, with little conclusive result.

20. Dressmaker forbids sitting: 26 Feb. 1876, p. 68, repr. Adburgham, p. 110. Shooting-stick: 22 May 1875, p. 218. Roller-skater, bowler: *Judy* 15 Oct. 1879, 13 Oct. 1880, etc. Egyptian mummy: *Fliegende Blätter* v. 66, no. 44. Mould: *Illustrated Bits* 17 Aug. 1878. Explosions: *Pasquino* (Turin) 25 Dec. 1881 p. 411

21. Strenuous action: *Punch*, 1881, repr. Adburgham, p. 133; Four Beauties: 18 Oct. 1879, p. 174. Cf. 19 July 1879, p. 23, for the opposite effect, the "classicizing" of female anatomy through addiction to sport.

22. Quoted by Adburgham, p. 134.

23. Figger: Steele, 1892, p. 72. 'Andsome 'Arriet: 6 Dec. 1879, p. 254 and 28 Aug. 1880, p. 86.

24. Weeping tennis player: *Fun* 16 June 1880 p. 243. Twelve inch waist (recklessly reduced by exigencies of scansion, for want of a monosyllabic figure in the 'teens?): 28 July 1880, p. 37. Needlework: 14 Sep. 1881 p. 114

25. *Fun* 6 July 1881 and 24 Nov. 1880 p. 205

26. *Punch* 12 Aug. 1893 p. 66

27. Fatality reports: *Judy*, 7 Jan. 1885 and 29 June 1887. Joan of Arc: *Judy*, 10 Aug. 1887.

28. 19 instead of 21 inches: *Punch*, 28 July, p. 30. Modest Youth's proposal: Nov. 10, 1883, p. 218. Cf. yet another benign Du Maurier cartoon, entitled "A Modern Waist", where at a garden party Jones offers some tea and strawberries to Miss Vane, observing to himself in amazed admiration "By Jove! She takes 'em—she's going to swallow 'em! But where she'll put 'em—goodness knows!" (10 Aug. 1889, p. 71). Or, on a lower social level: Mistress: "I'm afraid you will have to look for a new place before the first of the month, Bridget." Bridget: "What fur, ma'am?" Mistress: "Mr. Smith objects to so much waste in the kitchen." Bridget (who is rather fat): "Lor', ma'am, if that's all, I'll lace mesilf widin an inch of me loife" (*Illustrated Chips*, 1 Nov. 1890).

29. 26 Sep. 1891, p. 147.

30. *Puck*, 18 Dec. 1879, pp. 614–5.

31. *Funny Folks* for Feb. 16, 1889, picked up from the *World* an article heading or advertisement: "A Waist of Discipline. Madame Sykes is now making special pairs of stays for officers in the Guards," and placed it over a drawing of a guardsman who has fainted during a review. In true Cruikshankian dandy style, Colonel Swanbill (trade-name of a corset) cries "Pway don't bleed him, give him fwesh air, a little more awomatic vinegar, and *cut his staylaces!*" Madame Sykes' claim to diminish male waists harmlessly was also the topic of lengthy comment in *Truth*, 5 Feb. 1885, p. 223.

32. Quoted by Adburgham p. 203. The issue was picked up by the German dress reform magazine, "Männer in Korsett", *Die Gesunde Frau* March 1889, p. 32, noting that the annual turnover in men's corsets had reached "one million", and that an Indian army officer had had a garment made in richly decorated pink and Nile green silk.

33. Pyramidal Prussian: *Der Floh*, 10 Jan. 1892. Ancestors thinner: ibid 3 Sep. 1892. Bisected officer: *Münchener Humoristische Blätter* 1892 p. 6. Negroes: *Humoristische Blätter* 31 Aug. 1884. Cf also *Lustige Blätter* 28 Feb. 1889 and *Ulk* 1 March 1888 p. 6.

34. Indispensable fixture: *Lustige Blätter*, Berlin, 1903, repr. Wendel, fig. 311. Ranke: O'Followell, 1905, p. 203.

35. "Our Soldiers in the Stocks", *Diogenes*, 1854, p. 258. Dubois p. 19 n. 1.

36. *Punch*, 15 May 1869, p. 203, and "Tight Lads", 15 June 1872, p. 250.

37. *Diogenes*, 1853, II, pp. 139 and 220, and *Punch*, 1854, I, p. 97, "The Collar Mania".

38. Anti-garotte collar: *Punch*, 27 Sep. 1856, p. 128; Afghan sword: "A mighty throw; or saved by his Collar," *Judge* 7 July 1894, p. 74; and *Punch*, Christmas no. 1893. Masherium Club: 1883, cited by Adburgham, p. 143f. "Difficult to live above" : *Judy*, 3 Jan. and 7 Feb. 1883. "Nevah bend!" *Fun*, 17 Sep. 1884.

39. *Life,* 1883, Vol. II, p. 245.

40. *Funny Folks,* 29 March 1890.

41. Pearse, 1882, p. 33.

42. *Heart of Darkness,* 1899.

43. For Gavarni on English décolletage, see Lemoisne II, p. 14. For Mars in Margate: *Journal Amusant,* 1 Oct. 1887. For strictures on the nudity of emancipated girls, see *Saturday Review, Modern Women* p. 334

44. "In her collar she is already cut enough as she sits as straight as she can. Fashion is good because it prevents the round shoulders that Fathers and Mothers rail against. Fashion steps in . . . and without any moralizing fixes us all with backs as upright as ram-rods. Give her the credit of doing a good thing occasionally even if she does not intend it" (*Judge,* 10 Apr. 1886, p. 7). *Vie Parisienne* citations: 1890, p. 389; 1883, p. 555; 1887, p. 449; 1897, p. 402.

45. Kuhnow, 1893, Watt, 1902, p. 19, Muthesius, 1903, p. 36, and Arringer, 1906, p. 43. The most commonly identified symptom of a red, swollen face was the least of it. Professor Forster, Director of the University Ophthalmic Clinic in Breslau, observed 300 cases of short-sightedness in children, which he blamed on tight collars (Ecob, p. 75; cf. *Scraps,* 11 May 1889, citing the *Daily Telegraph*). This was held to explain why mashers and the military also affected eyeglasses.

46. Cantlie, p. 129; cf. Webb, 1912, p. 204. Fatality: *Lancet* 3 Aug. 1889 p. 231.

47. Cf. Pearse, p. 33; *Queen,* 1883, I, p. 495.

48. Stringer, p. 28.

SIC TRANSIT !

ALAS, FOR THE PRETTY JERSEY COSTUME ! 'ANDSOME 'ARRIET, THE 'OUSEMAID, HAS GOT IT AT LAST, AND IT FITS HER JUST AS WELL AS HER MISSUS.

CHAPTER FOUR

The Final Phase (1860–1900):
Extremists, Moderates, Swan-song

The End of Civilization

T he campaign against tight-lacing, by 1860 already a century
old, now enters its final but most acutely sensitive phase, in a
climate of mounting tension caused by the gains of feminism
in so many domains of life, and a concern for reform in all
areas of social and physical hygiene. The crescendo of anti-corset
writing and activity over the last third of the century is marked by an
escalation of repetitious and often hysterical and apocalyptic over-
statement on the one hand, and an attempt at scientific objectivity on
the other. The myriad books on dress, hygiene and health published
during this period seem to have regarded some critical reference to
tight-lacing as de rigueur, and many discourse on the subject at
length. The time-worn accusations were served up again and again
without so much as a pretence at a new sauce. The physicians,
assuming the responsibilities of a "new priesthood" (as a lay reformer
called them)[1] were more prolific than ever. They wrote regular
columns in the ladies, family and general interest journals, and
published their opinions and findings in professional magazines
which were insatiable on this topic (they seem to have regarded one
article per year as a minimum),[2] and which were assiduously quarried
by the press at large. In addition there were the privately printed
articles, and above all the lectures delivered to the increasingly
numerous ladies and other clubs · whose activities, even when
undocumented, must be considered highly influential.[3] Even men's
clubs devoted to the combatting of tight-lacing were announced.[4]

159

Embittered by their apparent failure, some reformers became savagely pessimistic. For them, the habit of tight-lacing lay beyond the reach of reason, for women were creatures devoid of brainpower. The editor of the august *Lancet*, premier medical journal of the age and primary mouthpiece of misogynistic attitudes, waxed satirical on the subject. He invited the "fashion-loving women of England" to try the experiment of compressing the heads of their infants, in the manner of some Indian tribes, "albeit there can be no need to adopt artificial measures for the repression of feminine brains." After briefly lambasting pointed toes on shoes, a noted chemist wearily continues "it may be expected I speak of high heels . . . in so doing, I should be assuming that ladies are rational beings . . . endowed with intelligence . . . I am subject to no such delusion." Is it even worth combatting tight-lacing, whose practitioners "are beyond the reach of reason?" Cynically, the writer adds, "besides this, the suicide they perpetrate is beneficial to society; it promotes the 'survival of the fittest'."[5]

Capitalist and social Darwinist theory merged in the proposition that the purpose of economic competition was to weed out the weaker or least adapted members, in order to strengthen the society or race as a whole. The proposition was applied to tight-lacers to explain how and why, lacking the normal mental and physical attributes of marriageability and having to compete in a society where the supply of women exceeded the demand, they resorted to an extreme and dangerous tactic. While some critics were crass enough to hope that the tactic would result in the tight-lacers weeding themselves out through suicide, and thus solve the problem once and for all, others feared that the outcome would be the progressive debilitation of the race through the ever-increasing fragility and wasp-waistedness of the women.

A German critic who wanted the corset abolished by law, conjured up a nightmarish folk tale in which a tyrant-king used constrictive clothing to punish rebellious female subjects. When they continued to rebel he imposed truly torturous tight-lacing, which the women eagerly accepted, and used as a form of sexual competition, so that they gradually declined physically and mentally, and were capable of producing only physically and mentally degenerate children. The women at the same time became increasingly hysterical, neurotic and (significantly) adulterous.[6]

"Survival of the fittest" became something of a slogan among the more vindictive who despaired of any change in fashion, and sought consolation in the hope that tight-lacing would kill off all the foolish girls and leave only the wise ones to grow into women, and that nature would soon put an end to that "pretty imbecility which she (the tight-lacer) calls her life." "Imbecility" and "insanity" are terms which became increasingly part of a polemical vocabulary directed against non-conformist women generally, as well as against tight-lacers; such a term is justified, in connection with the latter, by the similarity of the corset to a straitjacket: both "article(s) of garmenture only worn by violently insane females."[7]

Editorializing à propos a letter to the *Times* in which a tight-lacer had dared to defend herself, the *Lancet* callously hoped that "like the occasional accident to a railway director, her actual death by suffocation might even do more good than her theories will do harm."[8] *The Times* had magnanimously offered a tight-lacer sufficient rope to hang herself; signing herself "Not a Girl of the Period," and noting that the corset was to be found "by no means among our sex alone," she amiably renounced the title of martyr, since tight-lacing was "not only harmless but often beneficial to health, and extremely pleasant." The threat of a real controversy with letters pro and con was quickly nipped in the bud by a brutal editorial which likened tight-lacing to "not very dissimilar" Chinese footbinding and set the matter to rest with a lapidary "Tight-lacing creates more domestic unhappiness than any other circumstance in life."[9]

Tight-lacing was viewed as both cause and symptom of an irreversible racial degeneration. Writings appeared under such portentous titles as "The Great Evil of the Age," "The Curse of Corsets," "Corsets and the future of Women," and "Civilisation in relation to the abdominal viscera." Utterances became apocalyptic: "tight-lacing has done more within the last century than war, pestilence and famine towards the physical deterioration of civilized man." Or: "The Salvation of the race depends upon the abolition of the corset."[10] As late as 1909, Marcel Prévost was lending the weight of his reputation as a leading novelist and Academician to the claim that alcohol and the corset are "the two worst plagues that ravage civilization, one masculine, the other feminine."[11] Even more than alcohol, the corset was the Vice of Vices: "No tongue can tell, no finite mind can conceive the misery it has produced, nor the number of deaths directly or indirectly of young women, bearing mothers, weakly infants it has occasioned; besides millions on millions it has caused to drag out a short but wretched existence." Tight-lacing was a form of class-suicide, which left the advantage with the enemy: "If this murderous practice continued another generation, it will bury all the middle classes of women and children, and leave propagation to the coarse-grained but healthy, lower classes."[12] The word came down from the International Medical Congress convening in Rome, 1894: if Darwin's theory was correct, we would all become before long physically helpless, sterile, wasp-waisted creatures, and lapse into a barbarism worse than that of the most primitive tribes, none of whose body-deformations was as pernicious as ours.[13]

The statistics produced to buttress these dire prophecies were truly staggering. Female mortality rose in relation to male mortality in exact proportion to corset compression.[14] Fifty percent of German women over sixteen years of age suffered from tight-lace liver.[15] Eighty percent of the German female population, and ninety percent of German women over the age of thirty, were ill owing to corsets.

Perhaps the most bizarre onslaught of all was the article in the popular American magazine *Nineteenth Century* (1904) by Arabella Kenealy. This was inspired by the results of some experiments on monkeys who were subjected to severe abdominal restrictions in simulation of tight-lacing,[16] and died within a few months of various diseases. In her attempt to "exorcise an evil about which too much cannot be written" Dr. Kenealy sees tight-lacing as both cause and symptom of the inherited degeneracy of the Anglo-Saxon race, a degeneracy being actively furthered by poor nutrition and over-education. Body and brain, moreover, are mutually robbing one another; "men and women are top-heavy with mentality, because the brain has robbed the body; men and women are overweighted with animality (i.e. sexuality) because the body has robbed the brain." Corsets have contributed simultaneously to physical and mental debilitation. But to throw off stays in order to free the body for exercise and sport would be to jump from the frying-pan into the fire, for although woman today may be more athletic she is not really any fitter. Muscular capacity is also a symptom of degeneracy, represent-ing in a grown woman an arrested state of physical immaturity. The proper physical exercises for women, as propounded by Kenealy in a later book called *Feminism and Sex-Extinction*, is not sport but the commonplace household chore, like bending for long hours over the stove, the exemption from which provided by the new labor-saving devices has contributed to the tight-lacer's neurasthenic debilita-tion.[17] The conclusion of the article, and the reactionary farrago it contains, is that woman today is peevish, immature and degenerate, although possibly muscular, all because of the Curse of Corsets.

It is significant that the magazine which published this had a clearly conservative political line.[18] The anti-feminist bias which lumps to-gether with tight-lacing major aspirations of feminism such as free-dom from household drudgery, education, sport and sexual ex-pression, appears also in a famous French painter noted for the beauty, sensousness and "naturalness" of his image of woman: Pierre-Auguste Renoir. His ideal woman was one who scrubbed floors (the only proper exercise for her sex), remained illiterate, and was passive to the point of slavery (he uses this very word); and she did not wear corsets. On the same page in his son's biography which sets out this ideal, Renoir père excoriates at some length the practice of tight-lacing, which was not the only fashionable vice which "terrified" him: "Certain fashions terrified my father. We know his fear of corsets and high heels. His descriptions were so dramatic that for a long time I believed girls perched on high heels could walk only at the price of terrible pain. 'A dropped womb is inevitable' he told me, forgetting my age. I was six years old and this idea of the womb tumbling down gave me nightmares." The son also stresses at several points his father's great prudery, his fear, "almost to panic" of letting people see his feelings, thus testifying to his general emotional and perhaps sexual repression.[19]

To these examples from England, the United States and France, let us finally add a highly disdainful one from Austria which also forges, quite unequivocally, the link between fear of tight-lacing and fear of the educated woman. Satiric proposals for New Courses at the Highest College for Girls (Höchste Töchterschule) include Theory of the Last Word; Spasmic Exercises, with cramp- and fainting calisthenics; Xanthippothanatology, or the art of nagging husbands and sons-in-law sick; and finally, Lacing Technique (Schnürotechnik) with directions for the production of ethereal waists, and special seminars in the theory of extra-high-heeled gait (Doppelstöckelschrittlehre). The same source at an earlier date proposed to the deliberations of the Women's Congress in Paris, educational programs on botany, i.e. study of flowers "he loves me, he loves me not"-style; Women's Crafts, i.e. how to tie his cravat for him; Natural Science, i.e., making babies; and Sculpture (Plastik), i.e. tight-lacing. The use of the corset as the feminine folly-emblem par excellence to ridicule women's aspirations in the male domain, has today reached the acme of crassness: The *Los Angeles Times* for 20 May 1975 "celebrated" the conquest of Everest by the first all-woman team, with an Interlandi cartoon showing that rugged mountain peak clad (literally) in an elegant cuirasse-corset.

Abortion; Lung-Capacity; "The vice to which we never confess"; Masturbation

The more scientific literature emphasized three areas of the body as peculiarly vulnerable to tight-lacing: uterus, liver, and lungs. The uterus, having a primary sexual and reproductive function, was treated with the least objectivity; the lungs, being of measurable capacity, with the most. The uterus was still regarded as a mysterious, sacred and inviolable zone, difficult and dangerous to investigate, susceptible to damage through any kind of shock to or strain on the body, through (normal) sex, sport, or otherwise. If even high heels could cause its displacement one need hardly enlarge upon the danger to which the uterus was subjected by a tightly laced corset.

Depopulation statistics for New England as a direct result of tight-lacing were offered by Dr. John Ellis (who also wrote extensively against free love, alcohol, and socialism): whereas seventy years ago New England families averaged four and five children, now they averaged only one or two; and that whereas in mid-century most American mothers could nurse their own children, now only about half could. As late as 1911 sterility was being seriously imputed to corsets. To blame tight-lacers for the declining birth-rate was an easy way to avoid confronting the real cause: the increasing use of contraceptives, abortion, and other birth-reducing techniques. There is a certain ironic logic to the appearance of an advertisement for Towle's Pennyroyal and Steel Pills to "correct all irregularities and relieve the distressing symptoms so prevalent with the sex" immediately below a long statistical letter on the incidence of tight-lacing.[20]

Reports of women using corsets to conceal pregnancies and/or abort multiply during the later part of the century. A frightful, improbable but impeccably authenticated instance is described by a woman doctor in Paris 1898, where a twenty-two-year old servant girl managed to pass through the full term of her pregnancy without her employers noticing it. She was rushed, ostensibly suffering from a sudden illness, to hospital where before she could reach a bed, the corset broke, her belly swelled "and she had hardly taken a few steps before the baby fell on the floor; the woman died of peritonitis on the seventh day."[23] It is a scene out of Zola.

Towards the end of the century there was widespread anxiety in France that the country was depopulating and weakening vis-à-vis the prolific, enemy Germans, because of the increased use of contraceptives, sexual perversions, etc. Tight-lacing as a form of more-or-less deliberate foeticide is a practice excoriated (along with all other forms of birth-control) in Emile Zola's *Fécondité* (1899), one of the sillier of his later, didactic works. In this novel-cum-tract in praise of large families, the worldly Madame Séguin continues to tight-lace ("se serrer à étouffer") in order to prevent her pregnancy from interfering with her fashionable life; the child is born sickly. The fashionable vice is accompanied by that of satisfying "exasperated sexuality" and "perverted needs" without the risk of procreation. According to the same novel factory girls also tight-lace, even up to the sixth month of pregnancy, in order not to lose their jobs, and plan to visit a midwife specializing in the delivery of stillborn babies. And there is the sinister Madame Broquette, a tight-lacer herself, who runs an infamous "bureau de nourrices" ministering to those unnatural women who refuse to suckle for fear of losing their figures.

Zola took a more sympathetic view of the practice in an earlier and much better novel, *Au Bonheur des Dames*, where one of the shop assistants, a class whose suffering and exploitation is à major theme of the work, gets pregnant and tight-laces to conceal it for fear of losing her job. Another *vendeuse*, who had just been fired for this reason and had resorted to this tactic, was dying after giving birth to a still-born baby. (The propensity of shop-assistants to tight-lace in order to attract customers and increase sales is well-attested; an extreme instance involved a "demonstrator," whose prior habit was encouraged by the management, who attracted crowds, and whose health broke down completely after a month).[24]

It was by the binding back of the swelling belly and courting abortions that one could recognize the prostitute, said the German philosopher F. T. Vischer, angrily terming the cuirasse style which imitated the effect "the fashion of whores" (Hurenmode). A number of jokes at century's end about courtesans or prostitutes defending the tight corset as an essential equipment of their profession seems to refer not only to its sexualizing, but also to its abortist function ("ridiculous to abolish the corset! Anyone attempting that, I would sue for restraint of trade.")[25]

"Tight-lace liver" was a concept in itself (the Germans had a single word for it: *Schnürleber*). If a woman died in mysterious circumstances, and was slender of form, the physician performing the autopsy looked for malformations of the liver as a sign that she had been guilty of tight-lacing. During the years 1895–1910 the Pathological Institute in Erlangen kept statistics on the incidence of "tight-lace liver," which seems to have been the specialty of one of the professors of surgery there; the incidence, as given, is rather too high to be credible.[26]

It is only with regard to the action of the corset upon the respiratory apparatus that original experimental research was done. The capacity of the lungs ("vital capacity") was used by life insurance companies as the simplest and most accurate way of measuring a person's health. Scientific discussion of the subject was, however, complicated by the ancient and ongoing medical dispute over whether the reason that women breathed higher up (thoracically, pectorally, costally) than men, who breathed abdominally, was because of corset-training, or because of a nature-given difference in anatomical structure. Those opposed to corsets naturally assumed the higher locus of breathing to be the product of lifelong conditioning, and blamed on corsets the alleged inferiority of vital capacity in women, as compared to men. The tight-lacers themselves claimed for their higher breathing certain physiological advantages, based on the fact that since their corsets enlarged and thrust out the upper part of their chest, their lung capacity was actually increased.

Medical researchers demonstrated the alleged reduction in vital capacity suffered by tight-lacers in neat comparative tabulations of the results of experiments conducted with the aid of specially made pneumographs or spirometers. The average loss of lung power caused by corsets laced with "average" tightness was agreed to be about one fifth, although one distinguished surgeon (Browne) put it as high as one third.[27] Experiments upon American Indian girls indicated that the purer their blood, the more abdominal their breathing.[28]

One team of doctors undertook the trickier task of measuring the external pressure exerted by the corset. The results were published in an article "heretical" in that it tended to corroborate the medically taboo experiences of the tight-lacers themselves. The writer concluded that there existed no direct correlation between the reduction of the circumference of the waist and the pressure exerted upon it, nor between the latter and the diminution of the vital capacity. He found, moreover, considerable variations in the strength of the abdominal wall and the readiness with which the internal organs yielded.[29]

Medical research on tight-lacing was hindered, above all, by the impossibility of getting its practitioners to submit to examination. Many physicians and dress-reformers were puzzled and exasperated by women's refusal ever to admit that they tight-laced. Those who came under suspicion commonly protested that they wore their corsets "positively loose" or "hanging about them" and would push a hand down between busk and skin to prove it. *Family Doctor* reporter Hygeia was invited to do this by a girl with a 14-inch waist. Says one reformer: "Tight-lacing resembles Envy amongst the Passions: the Vice to which we never confess;" and another: "There is a curious consensus of opinion on the subject of tight-lacing. No-one questions that the custom exists; no-one personally admits to it." A French physician expressed this reluctance in the most forceful terms: "she will never admit to it, however great her suffering; no, the young Spartan who allowed his entrails to be devoured by a fox [which he had stolen and hidden beneath his shirt] showed no greater constancy; it is like a point of honor upon which one must never yield."

In fact, as we shall see, many tight-lacers were confessing openly but anonymously to their "vice" in the safety of the pages of a popular family journal; but the reformers were too entrenched in their prejudice to give credence to a lively magazine conversation in favor of the practice, over the stubborn silence of the consulting-room. An author cited above and writing under the title *Common Sense Clothing*, lacks the common sense (and sense of humor) to recognize that the "otherwise sensible woman" who gravely assured her that "nature had reduced her waist to 17 inches" was simply putting her on.[30]

Doctors apparently believed that women were capable of tight-lacing without being aware of it. The true fetishists generally avoided medical visits. Many claimed never or seldom to need medical attention; those who did (for whatever reason) visit a doctor, would exchange their tight corset for a loose one beforehand and hope that, if they were required to undress, they would not be betrayed by any abdominal markings.[31] The fear of admitting to the great crime is best illustrated by the story recounted by Dr. Taliaferro, called to a Negro woman who was "threatened with a miscarriage." He examined her, and told her he suspected that she was not even pregnant. The woman's companion finally got her to confess the true story: she had dressed to go out one Sunday, laced unusually tightly, and after walking for half a mile was seized with sudden uterine pains which compelled her to return home. The doctor considered that she was lucky to have escaped with her life.[32]

Women resorted to subterfuge because doctors at this time could not be relied on to show any understanding for the psychology of disease, self-inflicted or not. Medical students in the pre-Freudian age received no kind of psychological or psychiatric training. John Stuart Mill found it necessary to remind physicians that their lack of psychological training rendered them unfit to pronounce upon the allegedly "irrational" mentality of women.[33] Themselves as inhibited in sexual matters as their patients (if not more so), and using their ignorance to bolster their social prejudice, physicians regarded the female psycho-sexual mechanism as taboo and women apparently intent upon gradual and sometimes not-so-gradual suicide, as simply vicious and/or crazy. It is a revealing fact that none of the numerous reports on "death by tight-lacing" ever refers to the victim's psychological background. The most glaring case in point is that of an eighteen-year-old Lyonnese working-girl who was (rara avis) a self-confessed tight-lacer and had been for several years, despite the "suffocation, giddiness and anguish" she experienced thereby, and despite the fact that the pain subsided whenever she removed her corset (which she sometimes retained even at night). The doctor reporting the case was more concerned with the minuter measurements of her lower ribs than the social or psychological conditions oppressing the poor girl.[34]

Victorian prudery was respected in the consulting room. A female patient would rarely be asked to undress; the physician simply asked her to indicate the location of her pain on a diagram. The difficulties of diagnosis without stripping the patient were keenly felt by Dr. Wilberforce Smith, who was wont to divide his casesheet into two columns headed "Observed" and "Reported." "In the case of women who had 'reported' faulty state of health, the armour-casing in which they were clad had long furnished a serious hindrance to the routine acquirement of 'observed' facts." It is as if women felt the need to protect themselves against a kind of medical rape. Eventually, after many years, Dr. Smith came to insist upon an examination "without stays," and to develop an anatomy and pathology of corset-wearing, which, however, remained limited. "I have little experience in the extreme vagaries of tight corsetting. Women who practice it do not, as a rule, present themselves for medical inspection, or, if they come at all, the make-up is so elaborate that investigation is practically impossible." He detected some tight-lacers by the three or five inch band of purplish discoloration at the waist which was "especially distinct in the young, in whom the compressing process is actively progressing, and who have not yet acquired permanent constriction." Wilberforce Smith was exceptional among his profession, for few doctors opposed to tight-lacing were prepared to admit their lack of opportunity to observe its effects in real life (as opposed to post-mortem), and to recognize that "some old ladies of hardy constitution show a degree of permanent constriction suggesting that any modern change in the degree of compression is happily not for the worse." Dr. Smith closes on a note of "wonder and awe" as he contemplates the "tolerance of Nature," and the "marvels of a human body against which society and fashion are allowed to sin without (Nature) bringing heavier penalties upon it."

The physicians' claim to knowledge of the adverse physical effects of tight-lacing was as great as their ignorance of its psycho-sexual motivation. Having, as males, railed for so long against the practice, they were largely unable or unwilling to see or admit the extent to which they, as a sex, were to be held responsible for and accomplice to it. While the more simple-minded majority of critics blamed tight-lacing upon the vanity and irrationality characteristic of the female sex, a minor strand of argument developed towards the end of the century around the complicity of men, the question whether they really admired the practice, and whether this admiration had a sexual basis. Some explicitly denied the latter possibility,[35] but Mary Tillotson, taking up where her fellow American Orson Fowler had left off a generation before, and blaming both sexes simultaneously, inveighed against the vicious way in which women exploited male depravity. *Household Words*, a journal founded by Charles Dickens and edited by his son, in a characteristically English way ignored the sexual issue, preferring to assume naively that men could be shocked out of their admiration of the "insensate custom" merely by being apprised of its present and later consequences, and the "misery, pain and torture" it causes. "Was such knowledge theirs, they would have turned from the object of their whilom admiration, possibly with pity, probably with disgust . . ."[36] The word "disgust," which is repeated further on, conceals the sexual fear.

By century's end, in the United States where sexual matters were more freely discussed in the press than in England, the sexual basis for tight-lacing and male responsibility were confronted simultaneously in the editorial of a medical journal which establishes, belatedly, a perspective so conspicuously lacking hitherto:

The hand of Science falls with a dull, uncarnal, thud upon the constricted waist of woman. It tells why she constricts, and that the purpose from the beginning was an unholy one . . . The simple physiological act of respiration was perverted by the tightened girdle until the act became one of subclavicular enticement. In fine, squeezing the waist brought into lustful prominence the capacity of women for easy reproduction and subsequent plentiful lactation . . . Still the waist was tightened and the double ovoid continued to glide before the ardent gaze of man. The fact, then, is that women have tightened their girdles not because they wanted to do it, but because men approved of them and desired them the more for it. Why should women, then, be blamed? The practice is admitted unsound by all authorities from Hippocrates to Dio Lewis, but men have insisted upon it.

Let the sanitarist and the artist direct their attention, then, to man, the brute; not to woman, his victim. When this carnal but necessary factor in society and dress reform is cured of his evil ways, women will dress as they ought, but not before."[37]

The fact that tight-lacing exercised sexual appeal and was cultivated to this end is the catalyst of the polemic against the practice, and becomes more explicitly so at the turn of the century. The citation above is exceptional among medical sources for its good-humored acceptance of what was more likely to arouse anger. The characteristic reaction was that which saw tight clothing generally as a "moral loss not simply because it cripples the working power of the brain, but because it makes the mind ever-conscious of the body by reason of its uncomfortableness . . ." Stricture produces physical discomforts and disease "which chain the animality (i.e. sexuality) when unfettered, it should be unfolding in spiritual strength and glory." This from a woman who speaks of the "atheism of women's dress", the study of which is "a pitiful comment on human progress, hardly less sickening then the study of . . . wars and rapine."[38] The use of the word "atheism" shows that the author's critical standpoint is that of orthodox Christianity.

The sexual physiology of tight-lacing as understood in late 19th century America may be read in one of the best selling manuals of the age, Dr. J. H. Kellogg's *Plain Facts for Old and Young* (also called *Plain Facts about Sexual Life,* new editions almost annually from 1877 to 1894), which is typically obsessional and terroristic in character, and full of prurient, biblical rhapsodies on the Filth of Sex. Tight-lacing has a physiologically verifiable sexual purpose: "The circulation of the blood toward the heart is obstructed. The venous blood is crowded back into the delicate organs of generation. Congestion ensues, and, with it, through reflex action, the unnatural excitement of the animal propensities . . ." Later, after warning once more against "barbarous" tight-lacing as destructive of sexual health, Kellogg passes to the necessity of monitoring the slightest minutiae of a young girl's menstruation, as well as her social activities, down to preventing "improper liberties" which a young man might take by applying any "significant pressure" of his hand on hers. And thence, the sinfulness of conjugal onanism.[39] Such was the contribution to our sexual health, of the man whose well-known contribution to our dietary health, the pre-prepared breakfast cereal, afflicts us still.

The heyday of tight-lacing falls into a period of fierce and open repression of strictly private sexual activity. In America, for instance, Anthony Comstock's Society for the Suppression of Vice achieved 700 arrests 1873–82. Sex manuals, such as J. L. Milton's *Spermattorrhoea* (12 editions up to 1882), recommended instruments of torture to inhibit masturbation, blistering the penis, and cauterising the clitoris (the latter also approved by Krafft-Ebing). Lord Acton recommended that *all* adults should sleep with their hands tied ("a common practice"). Women who masturbated were "castrated" by means of circumcision, clitoridectomy, and oophorectomy; such surgery was recommended for sexual discipline and all kinds of psychological disorders generally, was much "in fashion" 1880–1910; it is superseded nowadays by mastectomy, ovarectomy, and hysterectomy.

The charge that females used the corset for forbidden autoerotic purposes had been largely unspoken since the late 18th century. The neurologist S. A. Tissot, whose voluminous writing against onanism (as masturbation was then called) was known throughout Europe, referred in his *Manual on Nerves and their Diseases* (1781) to the "pernicious habit of excessively compressing young girls (which) does as much damage as all other errors of upbringing," producing "extremely violent activity in the nervous system which develops particularly towards the fourteenth and fifteenth year." It is evident that he means the activation of sexual feelings, but he does not undertake further explanation. But the Schnepfenthal Institute prize essays of 1788 by Soemmerring etc. give a specific account of how young girls used their corset to masturbate with, in a passage which warrants translation in full:

But I must leave it to doctors and moralists for further consideration, whether girls from a young age do not find something pleasurable in leaning with the front (lower) point of the corset and the busk inserted therein, against the corner of a chair, a table etc., resting or even rubbing there, and whether they do not provoke thereby innocently and unperceived sensations of which we will quite simply say nothing, after this hint. Adults of course oppose such bad habits as soon as they notice them, but are not children also left alone and to themselves? Does the world not know of sins, horrible ones, sins creeping like a plague in the dark, whose beginning lay always in unsought for, innocent sensations? But a blush upon it! Let a hint suffice!

It was the Germans in some early 20th century manuals on female health and hygiene directed at young mothers who made the most decisive identification of the physiological effects of tight corsets as akin to those of masturbation.[40] The most extensive elaboration of this connection is that of an expert in skin and venereal disease, Dr. Friedrich Siebert in his *Book for Parents*. As polite as possible and with a studied show of embarrassment, he deals with the dread problem of masturbation. Posing as a moderate (presumably against the physically torturous anti-masturbation devices in vogue earlier) he recommends constant surveillance of small children, especially when dropping off to sleep, and cognizance of the "astonishing and frightening variety of methods and occasions for masturbation" open to the adolescent. Among these are too tight trousers and underpants on boys, and corsets on girls, the effects of which are minutely described.[41] Both sexes should be prevented from folding their hands together under the table. Girls should be prohibited from sitting cross-legged or walking so as to rub their thighs against each other, and watched while sitting on piano stools or at sewing-machines, lest they use these for "impure purposes". Siebert recommends searching underwear for stains, catching the "sinner" if possible in flagrante delicto, forcing confessions, beatings, and punishing through shameful visits to the doctor.

Such medical terrorism had not abated twenty years later, when we find a post-Freudian monument to the new permissiveness in the public discussion of sex, the *Dictionary of Sexual Science* edited by Max Marcuse, citing Siebert with approval and insisting on the bad effects of corsets on sex life, because of their tendency to "provoke the sexual organs". Such warnings were, alas, as ineffective then [1926] as earlier. Siebert is also cited in a political polemic of 1924 entitled *Women's Emancipation and its Erotic Basis* by Dr. E.F.W. Eberhard. Examples of women confessing sexual feelings when they tight-lace (derived from the English fetishist correspondence) are used to prove how women as a sex are sunk in "perverse lusts" and "degeneracy". Vaunting his detestation of "political women" Eberhard blames moral degeneration and criminality in Germany on the Woman's Movement.[42]

Women's demands for political, economic and educational rights were accompanied by demands for sexual rights, greater "sexual freedom." We have now thrown light from different quarters on the seeming paradox that tight-lacing was viewed and criticized as an assertion of sexual freedom; that it was also, semi-consciously, experienced and intended as such, we shall show in a later chapter. It is already evident that the woman who asserted her sexuality through tight-lacing was bracketed with the woman who asserted her sex through demands for social rights; both were the target of puritanical conservatives suspicious of woman as a sex, and fearful of her sexuality.

Organized Dress Reform

The first formally organized dress reform societies appeared in the United States, in the aftermath of the Anti-Slavery movement which did so much to inspire subsequent feminism in that country. Elizabeth Phelps in a book of 1873 demanded total liberation for her sex from the bondage of society and fashion, and summoned womankind to throw off her shackles as the Negro had his. This same year the first Dress Reform Society was founded in Boston by a group of laywomen and women doctors headed by Abba Gould Woolson. An anthology of 1874, edited by the latter, makes the first practical proposals for alternative dress, examples of which were placed on view in permanent exhibition rooms, together with facilities for ordering from manufacturers working to the reformers' specifications. The "New Dispensation" in dress hoped to protect the vital organs from compression and cold; attain uniformity of body-temperature, divided at present between frigid (shoulder and upper chest), temperate (thorax) and torrid (waist and hip) zones; reduce the total weight and bulk of clothing; and suspend it from the shoulders rather than the hips. Problems of compression, temperature, weight and bulk would all be solved by altering the system of suspension.

Suspension was a critical matter. Recognizing that there was no way of eliminating pressure at the waist as long as the hips were the sole point of support, and that an accumulation of up to sixteen thicknesses of material at the waist[43] invited its compression in order to restore it optically to its natural size, Mrs. Woolson demonstrated that all clothing may be conveniently, decently and pleasingly suspended from the shoulders. (The poor aesthetic result may be judged from the accompanying illustrations).

A woolen combination (union) suit was recommended as the basic undergarment, and although the skirt was considered "uncomfortable, unhealthy, unsafe and unmanageable" the reformers here were prudent enough to content themselves with shortening it, rather than dividing it. The "Divided Skirt" espoused by Lady Harberton, the leading English dress reformer, was to be the rock upon which the movement shattered in her country.

American dress reform theory was brought to England via editions of American works pirated by the publishers Ward, Lock and Tyler, who also, ironically (or, conveniently), produced the fetishist books of the period. Organizationally, the dress reform movement in England, which has at last been given the history it deserves,[44] starts with the foundation of the Rational Dress Society in 1881, also a climactic year in the campaign against tight-lacing.[45] Through the Society the reform campaign found a focus, a real if limited (and generally upper-class) social context, and new, more positive directions. Less obsessed with the corset in isolation, the Society came up with concrete proposals for alternative attire, which would make the corset unnecessary and generally answer the demands for hygiene in a (hopefully) aesthetic manner. The huge International Health Exhibition of 1884 included an important section on hygienic dress organized by the Society which, next to the Food Section, attracted the most attention of all. But if one is to measure the impact of the reform movement in terms of the longevity or distribution of its journals, its success was slight: the *Rational Dress Society's Gazette* lasted only six issues, which are very hard to find, 1888–89, and its successor *Aglaia*, the Journal of the Healthy and Artistic Dress Union, managed only three issues, 1893–94, which are rarer still. Neither of these journals nor any literature known to me associated directly with the Women's Movement confronts the sexual purpose of corsets. Although continuously debated in artistic circles, neither the corset question in particular, nor the dress reform question in general seems to have generated much heat in primary feminist quarters.

Moderates and "Counter-Opponents"

Against the excesses of medical and dress-reform rhetoric there emerged a non-fetishist middle-ground sympathetic to the corset and even "moderate" tight-lacing. In 1853 a physician with no known connection with the trade or other vested interest, ridiculed the wild effusions of traditional anti-corset writing. Sauveur-Henri-Victor

Bouvier was a distinguished French orthopedist and founder of one of the first specialist orthopedic hospitals in 1840. In the course of a long report (first published in the *Academy Bulletin*) on a new seamless "plastic" corset which had been sent for examination to the National Academy of Medicine by the Minister of the Interior, Agriculture and Commerce, he gives us the first comprehensive history of the corset, indicating that whatever faults it may possess today are infinitely less than those of earlier times. As a demonstration of his familiarity with and contempt for the anti-corset literature, old and new, he lists in one comically endless sentence a number of the major diseases traditionally blamed on that article, and pours scorn on the compulsion for "mindless repetition of hypotheses as facts."[46]

Bouvier denies categorically that corsets cause either spinal curvature ("In 380 cases not one is due to corsets") or consumption, any statistical rise in the female mortality rate being due to other causes.[47] The famous orthopedist then asserts that contrary to received opinion,[48] woman is not naturally endowed with a conical (base below) thoracic cage, but a barrel-shaped one which tapers inwards towards the waist. Bouvier concludes that corsets have always been worn and will always be worn, because apart from the support and comfort they afford to the body, they express in the proper aesthetic fashion the differing sexual and social roles of man and woman.

Bouvier maintained for over a quarter of a century in France his notoriety as a major, if lonely, medical defender of the fashion corset. In a medical dictionary of 1877, far from joining his colleagues' lamentation over the new, controversial, heavy cuirasse-corset which encouraged tight-lacing, he actively recommended it to any grown woman. One cannot resist speculating on the professional reputation[49] of a physician prepared publicly and laconically to condone the behaviour of three women under his constant observation, who *"concealed"* (my stress) their pregnancy with "infinite art and the aid of a "grand corset" and an extremely tight abdominal belt ("très fortement serré"); we are blithely assured that no serious accident took place, and that the deliveries were normal. In sum, tight-lacing and pregnancy were not at all incompatible.

Bouvier's position found scattered support among writers on hygiene and even in a popular encyclopedia such as Zell's, which indicted not tight-lacing but the "indiscriminate warfare carried on by medical men and public writers . . . (which) is marked by as much cant as ignorance." Even the prestigious Larousse *Grand Dictionnaire du 19e Siècle* failed conspicuously to condemn the contemporary corset, while its rival, the *Grande Encyclopédie* made up for the omission by substituting a long, hostile passage on Hygiene for the usual one on History.

The more reasonable English reformer like Dr. Treves was embarrassed by the "reckless exaggeration," "sweeping assertions," and "explosive and hysterical vigour" of many reformers. Other English writers declared the subject banal and passé. By the early 1880s, we sense an impatience with an issue which one could neither ignore nor engage without seeming to side with all those intolerant reformer windbags. As early as 1867 the *Lancet* admitted that attacking tight-lacing was "like slaying the slain"; although thirteen years later the same journal in a fresh misogynistic spasm judged "unmerciful criticism" to be as necessary as ever.[50]

Meanwhile, the fetishist defence had made itself heard. Sensational, alarmingly candid and often seemingly incredible, publicly either discredited or ignored, it served to polarise and exacerbate but also to broaden the range of opinion. There emerged a "counter-opposition" in which one may detect a sympathy with the much-beleaguered tight-lacer. Thus Mrs. Douglass, who considers tight-lacing a crime, expresses humanitarian concern for the criminal—not because of the physical martyrdom she inflicts on herself, but because of the moral martyrdom inflicted on her by the reformers: "The woman who reforms suffers from an excess of fervour, and the sanitary enthusiast is a little apt to forget that the tight-lacer, with all her sins, is still a woman and a sister. She has received so much vituperation already that I shall not add to it here . . . Indeed . . . I have it not in my heart to denounce (her). She is a criminal, but she wears her vice becomingly. To the artistic eye her curves are, of course, abrupt, but her tout ensemble is charming . . . Plain in her neatness (like Pyrrha), she attracts by her triumphant trimness, her perfection of detail. The tight-lacer is a person who respects herself, and is careful in all departments." Praise indeed!

An upper-class ladies' magazine like *The Queen* printed pretentious medical diatribes on the "Evils of Tight-Lacing" but by 1882 was itself ridiculing the absurd Dr. Benjamin Richardson with his 78 ills of the corset (summarised in Disease, Deformity and Dissolution), and his claim that the dramatic recent decrease in the size of ladies' hats being sold indicated that hereditary mental degeneration had set in. Ambivalence, even a secret admiration are confessed in *The Queen* feature-writer's enthusiastic description of "a very pretty girl I saw lately playing lawn-tennis, whose face and appearance I much admired when I could take my attention from the surprising smallness of her waist; she looked as if she might break in two. While this may be born with impunity a few times . . . ."[51]

In 1888 there were two dramatic defections from British medical orthodoxy in the persons of two Cambridge men, C.S. Roy, Professor of Pathology and his assistant, University Administrator John George

Adami. The 26 year-old Adami was probably the leading spirit behind the enquiry credited to them jointly; he was later to become a Vice-Chancellor of the University of Liverpool, a most distinguished pathologist, and a controversial Darwinian. In a paper read before the British Association called "The Physiological Bearing of Waistbelts and Stays,"[52] Roy and Adami reported on the results of cardiometric experiments which measured the flow of blood pumped out by the heart. "In one experiment, compression of the abdomen increased the quantity of blood thrown out by the heart, to the extent of 29.6 per cent during the period of compression. In some of our other experiments even a larger increase was obtained. Further, the increased outflow from the heart, which is in this way produced, is not limited to the few seconds after the first application of the pressure, but persists concurrently with the pressure." It was concluded (quite contrary to Dr. Kellogg, for instance, as cited above, p. 170) that abdominal pressure "diminishes the quantity of blood which is stored in the abdominal veins and venous capillaries, and places it more at the disposal of the organism as a whole . . . Pressure on the abdomen, or constriction at the waist, which comes to the same thing, increases the amount of blood placed at the disposal of the brain, skin, etc . . . and the organism as a whole." Since physical activity demanded an increase in blood supply, preferably without a marked increase in pulse rate, abdominal constriction could be deemed an aid to such activity. This fact would explain why active males in all periods of history and all over the world, from the Bedouin horseman to the British navvy, wear and have worn broad, tight, leather belts. Although they avoid the term "tight-lacing" and make every effort to distinguish between the physiology and pathology of stay-wearing, Roy and Adami boldly assert that "extreme pressure, harmful as it must be, is not equally so at all time," affecting the body according to the state of digestion, degree and type of activity, etc.; and that "extreme pressure" did not necessarily interfere with the nutrition of the abdominal organs.

Denied access to the medical press, Roy and Adami published their heresy in a political weekly, the *National Review,* adding a note which testifies to the controversial and prejudicial reception of the original oral delivery, and the various "erroneous reports as to its contents"

The British Association meeting was fully reported in the recently launched *Rational Dress Society's Gazette:* "Many people considered the paper as only a piece of humour on the writers' part; but two doctors present . . . denounced the paper as most dangerous." The chairman of the session invited comments from the floor, in response to which (after a rather stunned silence) Mrs. Stopes made a short statement in opposition. "Miss Lydia Becker next arose, and spoke amusingly, though rather disconnectedly, in support of stays and tight-lacing, though she brought no physiological reason in support of her arguments." There was some more discussion, which was broken off (it being Friday evening) and resumed the following Tuesday at the Anthropological Section. Dr. Garson spoke on lung capacity; General Pitt-Rivers, the distinguished President of the Anthropological Institute and Chairman of the Section, vowed never to admire a small-waisted woman again. Discussion ended on a note of alarm sounded by Mrs. Stopes who stated tight-lacing to be on the increase, with the average waist size having decreased by two whole inches during the last twenty-five years. This information she had obtained from London corsetières (presumably via the *Family Doctor*—cf. below. The tight-lacers themselves, from their redoubt in the *Family Doctor* correspondence columns, must have been as delighted with the Roy-Adami heresy as the medical orthodoxy was horrified.)

The Roy-Adami paper was accepted by one major feminist, at least. It emboldened Lydia Becker, botanist, friend of Charles Darwin, leading Women's Rights advocate, and editor of *Women's Suffrage Journal*, to publish in the *Sanitary Record* an article which blamed the reformers for oppressing the female lungs by making women carry the whole weight of their clothes upon their shoulders, rather than the hips which being wide in women are natural bearers of such a burden. The reformers would do better, says Miss Becker, to direct their fire at the layers of excessively long skirts, rather than corsets, which when moderately laced, are beneficial.

Miss Becker was countered in the same journal by Dr. Wilberforce Smith (cf. above) but supported by Dr. Howard Haughton, the first Briton to bring the fetishistic viewpoint to the pages of a scientific journal.[53] Dr. Haughton expressed open admiration not just for tight-lacing, but particularly for the character of the tight-lacer. No wonder, he says, citing Dr. Wilberforce Smith, that "tight-lacers seldom present themselves for medical examination" when they are under constant "intemperate" attack from the profession. According to medical theory tight-lacers should be more ill than others, but the reverse seemed to be true. "It is not my purpose to endeavour to account, at present, for the extraordinary immunity from illness (of tight-lacers). But of the fact there can be no doubt whatever; and I will venture to hint at one possible cause." The cause, in a word, is avoidance of overeating, a vice about which the Victorian middle classes felt very self-consciously guilty. (Doctors actually encouraged pregnant women to eat heavily.) "Upon this rock the tight-lacer never is wrecked, for the obvious reason that the slightest indiscretion in eating brings certain and immediate punishment." This observation was confirmed in the fetishist magazine correspondence, with which

Dr. Haughton was obviously familiar. This "desirable" side-effect was conjured up rhetorically in a current squib: "Grace before Meat, as the young lady remarked when she laced herself so tight she couldn't swallow."[54] Haughton's classification of degrees of tight-lacing is clearly fetishist in character, ranging from "comfortably tight" (a 3-6 inches reduction) to "outrageously tight" (over 10 inch reduction), a degree which, "one need scarcely say, no novice in the art can safely attempt, and which would require very special circumstances to justify . . ."

Moderates and counter-opponents such as Roy-Adami and Becker occupy a narrow bridge between the reformist and fetishist positions. One wonders whether either of the parties was familiar with the fetishist correspondence flourishing at the time in the *Family Doctor.* It is possible that the Roy-Adami research was prompted by this correspondence in the first place. If Dr. Haughton, whose familiarity with it is evident, fails to mention the journal by name, it is surely because it was professionally a pariah, and because he did not wish to associate himself directly with testimony part of which, at least, must have struck many contemporaries as incredible, fictitious, absurd and disgusting.

The New Anti-Classical Aesthetic

Important changes in aesthetic philosophy during the second half of the 19th century, the advent of such artistic and literary movements as Realism, Impressionism, Naturalism and Symbolism, undermined the neo-classical ideal of the dress-reformers, who, taking their cue from academic artists, persisted in regarding the Venus de Milo as Perfect Beauty and Perfect Nature, and fashionable dress as aesthetically unworthy. An illustration to the fetishist pamphlet *Figure Training,* which satirically dressed the ancient marble in contemporary dress (see Plate 53), presupposes a theory of the artistic avant-garde, according to which each age establishes its own aesthetic criteria and adapts them to the social reality of the moment. There could therefore be no absolute mathematical systems of proportion, such as had governed the anatomical ideal of artists since Vitruvius and continued to dominate academic thinking in the 19th century.

It was the perception of the poet and art-critic Baudelaire that every age set its own standards in dress which were designed to satisfy that age and that age alone. In the passage on fashion-plates which he inserted into his *Painters of Modern Life*[55] he proposed a "rational and historic theory of beauty, as opposed to the theory of the unique and absolute beauty." All fashions are charming, even the grotesque. The ideal, always the aim of art, must be redefined according to the needs of each age. "Fashion should therefore be regarded as a symptom of the taste for the ideal . . . as a sublime deformation of nature, or rather, as a permanent successive attempt at reforming nature." Exotic accoutrements, the bizarre artifices of dress—face-paint, chignon, corset (as we shall see)—all appealed to Baudelaire as part of the strange and sometimes sinister eroticism exuded by contemporary woman, who was the bearer of the unique cultural and historical physiognomy of the age.

A neo-classicist, on the other hand, such as the artist John Leighton, inveighed simultaneously against tight-lacing and three centuries of costume history, which he saw as marked chiefly by "an egregious absurdity of conception and figure," and "depravity of taste and purpose."[56]

The latter phrase combines aesthetic and moral (sexual) judgment. Artists and art theorists saw epitomized in the exaggerated curve created by tight-lacing, the "coarseness," "vulgarity" and "violence" of so much contemporary fashion, which they did not regard as a fit subject for the paintbrush.[57] The fetishists, for their part, justified their aesthetic in the anti-classical and popular painter William Hogarth. With phrases such as "the curved line of the swelling wave and sinking hollow," they at once described the visual transformation wrought by tight-lacing and the 18th century artist's famous "Line of Beauty" which he had demonstrated theoretically upon the fashionable stays of the period. Thomson's, the manufacturers of tight-lacing corsets, advertised them (from the 1860s) as constructed on strictly 18th century, Hogarthian principles, without a single straight bone in the the whole garment.

Conscious deviations from ideal and classical form have often been felt to have an inherent erotic potential. They represent "life" rather than "art." Anne Hollander has shown that in painting since the Renaissance, idealized figures in the most classical poses wearing apparently classical dress or shown altogether nude, bear the particular pressures of the clothes they have taken off. Goya's two famous reclining *Majas* testify directly to this and with exceptional erotic effect: "One of the most telling features of the nude *maja's* body is that it seems to show the effects of corseting without the corset—which, on the other hand, is very definitely present in the dressed version. The high, widely separated breasts and rigid spine of the recumbent nude lady are as erotic as her pubic fuzz or sexy smile. Her breasts indeed defy the law of gravity . . . It is the emphatic effect of her absent modish costume that makes her a deliberately sexual image."[58]

The system of classical proportion was experienced as a tyranny by many 19th century artists of differing tendencies. To show a female

nude with an unclassical slenderness of waist was the clearest statement of defiance of that tyranny, and classicist critics were quick to
accuse artists who did so of using corrupt, tight-laced models. But the
wasp-waisted nude could be used for very different purposes: to
underline the boneless elasticity of rhythm in a romantic lithograph
by Devéria, or to emphasize the massive, nature-rooted haunches in a
realistic painting by Courbet ("La Source"). It is also significant that
among the élite painters of his age, Eduard Manet, who made the
most radical break from the classicizing academic tradition, has left us
the most acutely tight-laced portrait of the woman of fashion (the
exquisite, doll-like Madame Michel Lévy, 1881); while his much more
academic contemporary James Tissot preserved a degree of classical
form beneath the complex accoutrements of fashionable clothing
which he detailed with much greater precision than Manet. It is not
necessary to assume that Manet had any sympathy for tight-lacing in
itself, for him to have welcomed a portrait commission which allowed
him to create one of the most startlingly anti-classical contours in the
history of 19th century art.

Manet may have been struck by the fact that fashion, like art, works
by certain optical illusions. In the case of tight-lacing the "secret" of
this illusion was well-known to fetishists, although rarely commented
on by others: the compression at the waist not only reduced the total
circumference but also and perhaps more important, changed its
shape from oval to round, so that in front or back view it appeared
even smaller than it actually was. Museum costume display invariably exploits this illusion, making Victorian dresses not particularly
narrow in the waist, appear so. The term "illusion waist" was
sometimes used at the time as a more flattering alternative to "wasp
waist", especially in reference to Americans.

Classical art-theory held that quite apart from the disproportions of
fashionable dress, few women in their natural state measured up to
the ideal proportions prescribed by art. It was not only prudery which
inhibited art academies from using nude females for life-drawing
classes, but also the lingering belief that the female presented an
inferior model of proportion, compared with the male. There even
emerged, in Germany, the extraordinary theory that tight-lacing was
designed (unconsciously) to correct a supposed aesthetic error of
nature, which had denied women the ideal proportions in the Golden
Mean vouchsafed to males. Woman had therefore to disguise the
relative shortness of her legs by means of an optical lengthening of
her waist and a lowering of her center of gravity to the level of
man's.[59]

The sociological implications of the new sartorial aesthetic of the
'70s, the "violent" or dynamic effect of the cuirasse style which

contrasts so sharply with the visually static effect of fashion in the preceding decades, has been recently noted by a costume historian who is very far from accepting our view of tight-lacing as a "progressive" phenomenon: "From the point of view of composition women could be thought of as having stepped out of the encircling bird-cage (crinoline) to assume a forward-looking attitude well-suited to their sociological and educational aspirations, the insipid charm of earlier colour-schemes was replaced by effects which if not actually violent were certainly aggressive." The idea of woman, seen in profile and (despite her tightly swathed legs) *forward* movement, as the aesthetic embodiment of the new dynamic age, was observed at the time by Charles Blanc, the distinguished art-critic and founder-editor of *La Gazette des Beaux-Arts,* and developed visually by the avant-garde painters. Blanc closes his book on *Art and Ornament in Dress* with an apologia for the aggressive style of fashionable women, "walking on high heels which throw them forwards, hastening their steps, cleaving the air, and hurrying through life as though to swallow up space, which in turn swallows them up." It is an image from an Impressionist picture; and the condemnation of this same fashion as a "kaleidoscope" and "meaningless dazzle of broken effects" is reminiscent of the public's experience of Impressionist painting style.[60]

Footwear; Cinderella

After Camper in the late 18th century, there is no major criticism of women's footwear until Hermann Meyer's monograph in 1857,[61] from which time the campaign intensified, especially with the advent of the high heel in the late '60s. Before this period, criticism was levelled as much at the tight, pointed shoes worn by men. David Copperfield's martyrdom (i.e. that of the youthful dandy Dickens himself) in his new too-small shoes when he goes to visit Dora, is well-known, and finds a parallel in cartoons by Daumier etc. of the same period.[62]

As with the anti-corset campaign, the sweeping statement abounds: "There is no such thing as a well-formed foot in the fashionable world." Europeans were little better than the Chinese, and maybe worse since the Chinese did not confine the feet of men. The high heel, no less than footbinding, reduced the foot to hoof-like proportions and a bunch of crumpled deformity. The "innumerable malformations and deformations of the foot" such as corns, bunions, chilblains, ingrowing toenails, hammer toes, diseased and enlarged joints which might lead to fatal abscesses these are merely the obvious dangers to a part of the body most immediately affected, for improper footwear could also cause displacement of the abdominal organs, uterus and spine. There were cases where contraction of the leg muscles was such that their surgical separation became necessary. An instance of amputation, suffered, it would seem, gladly by the martyr, is cited by Dr. Treves with heavy irony: "A week ago I had to amputate a toe from the foot of a young girl who came to my outpatient room at the London Hospital completely lamed by so-called fashionable boots. She was pleased at the prospect of the operation because it would allow her to wear a still smaller shoe. Ladies who must wear fashionable boots should, as a preliminary measure, have three middle toes amputated—the operation would add to their comfort and would render their gait not one whit more awkward than it is at present . . ."[63]

Treves also comments on the artificial flexible steel insole arch designed to raise the instep, which, in conjunction with the high heel, adds even further to the difficulty of walking (which, however, "like other acrobatic feats, becomes less irksome through practice"). The artificial arch was objected to in many quarters ("there is nothing so ridiculous as the 'graceful high step' even in Sterne's catalogue of Roman shoes") despite the fact that it enhanced what was widely supposed to be a preeminently aristocratic and European racial characteristic, the "lowest type of foot", that of the Negro, allegedly having little or no instep.[64] "Aristocratic" shoes with tight uppers, pointed toes, high heels and raised arches were also worn, in the familiar phenomenon, by the lower classes, who are specifically blamed for perpetuating and exaggerating the fashion.[65]

The bulk of European folk and fairy tales have come down to us in their 19th century form, and bear the flavor of the age of their transcription. The popularity of the Cinderella story undoubtedly has much to do with 19th century foot fetishism and warnings against fashionable foot-compression. It is, significantly, in the north European versions of the Cinderella story that the Ugly Sisters suffer agony and even mutilation in order to fit their feet into Cinderella's slipper. In versions from India, on the other hand, where women did not confine their feet in any way, there is no question of squeezing and mutilation on the part of the false claimants. Those European versions, favored today, in which the Ugly Sisters merely squeeze their feet are mild compared with the horrific and fantastic sufferings traditional elsewhere. In a Danish version the mother takes an axe and a huge pair of scissors, admonishing the groaning daughter with the adage of fashion: "You must suffer if you want to be beautiful" and "better to lose a toe than a Queen's throne." An Ugly Sister from Russia whose feet are virtually chopped off altogether is consoled with the thought that when she is a princess she will not need to walk. In Russian and Finnish versions, which tend to be the most gruesome of all, the stepmother/ogress does a complete remodeling job: she files down the foot and fingers as well, and even hammers the head into a new shape, in order to make shoe, glove and hat fit.[66]

The versions preferred today, which eliminate the actual mutilation and refer only to squeezing of the foot, lose an ancient and once significant ritual element and a dramatic moment.[67] The Prince drives off with his false bride and only discovers his mistake when he observes the blood oozing out of her shoes, and is tipped off by a raven who croaks (in a Scottish Ashpitel tale):

> Haggit (i.e. hacked) heels and hewed toes
> Behind the young prince rides;
> But pretty foot and bonnie foot
> Behind the caldron hides.

Unlike the shoe, the corset does not figure prominently in the European folk-tale and folk-lore. Tight-lacing of the Ugly Sisters was assumed by some dress-reformers to have been an essential part of their preparations for the ball,[68] and the motif survives in modern comic pantomime versions; but it does not occur in any of the 345 variants of the Cinderella story collected by Marian Cox. The corset is stated by a German folklore dictionary to be "almost unknown" presumably because this essentially urban garment did not enter the costume of rustic communities until relatively late, i.e., 18th–19th century. Tight-lacing does, however, occasionally figure as a motif in the folk-tale, notably Snow White, where it is presumably a late accretion to ancient formula. In Scandinavia, the witch (or wicked stepmother) makes various attempts to kill a beautiful girl (or step-daughter), in the course of which she sells her a corset and laces it on her so tightly that she faints (sometimes the lace is also poisoned, the lacing motif here being rather unrealistically superimposed on the older poisoning one). In Grimm, she is revived by the dwarfs; in the Scandinavian version, her brothers presume her dead, carry her to the grave, but stumble so that the girl is jolted, the staylace breaks, and she revives.[69]

The End of Tight-Lacing as a Custom

As tight-lacing among a minority peaked in intensity, the corset began to be left off altogether or exchanged for a much lighter garment, and its tightness generally relaxed, with the introduction in the 1880s of looser alternative styles of clothing, "aesthetic," reform, masculine, sporting. By 1900 tight-lacing had too few adherents to be a popular issue, and the controversy had exhausted itself. The market was flooded with "reform," "rational" and "hygienic" garments, many of which were new only in name, but which were intended to obviate the medical strictures of old.

The decisive innovation, which both hastened the demise of tight-lacing and rescued the corset from the threat of abolition, was that of the famous French couturier Jean Worth, who in 1888 introduced the "straight-front" corset (corset droit) as opposed to the old arched one (corset cambré). The straight-front corset used a straight busk, which tended to incline inwards over the belly, was cut lower at the bust and descended further on the hips. It took the pelvic girdle as its point of anchorage, and was proclaimed as the solution to the perennial problem of direct pressure on the abdominal organs. It reduced indentation at the waist, and was favored with looser fitting dresses, blouses and jackets. It helped create the typically Edwardian elongated S curve profile, with the bust pitched forward and the hips flowing backward. With the right figure and posture a woman could achieve this effect without wearing a corset at all, and although few dared appear in public completely uncorsetted, many began to receive at home in a tea-gown without any foundation. A compromise much favored for sporting activities was the very brief, lightly boned Swiss belt.

The pre-eminence of the straight-front corset was uncontested by 1901, especially in France, where it was celebrated by the launching of *Les Dessous Elégants*, the first trade journal anywhere to be devoted exclusively to underwear.[70] The purpose of the magazine was twofold: first, to combat the abolitionists, who hover as a sinister threat in the background of an interminable series of articles on corset hygiene by Dr. O'Followell. Second, the magazine protected the made-to-measure trade against the twenty to thirty Parisian wholesale manufacturers, who sold through the Grands Magasins. *Les Dessous Elégants*, in which the accent is very much on the second word, is the apotheosis of the corset, once a strictly functional object designed to create a silhouette, now an object of luxury in its own right, vying with the petticoat in elegance, variety and decorative refinement. Like the petticoat, the corset was meant to be savored by male eyes, and in its rapturous evocations of these articles, *Les Dessous Elégants* sometimes reads like *La Vie Parisienne* in its fetishistic heyday.

The corset trade was too important an economic factor (especially in terms of the export trade) for any French politician seriously to consider legislation against it. A prohibition introduced by the Ministry of Education in 1895 and a special tax proposed in 1894 failed completely, and ten years later certain West European educationists and dress reformers were still looking enviously to remote "un-civilized" autocracies like Russia, Rumania (both had enacted laws in 1899), and Bulgaria, where schoolgirls were not admitted to classes without having first deposited their corsets in the entrance-hall. But many German girls remained adamant, refusing to uncorset even for gymnastics. Physical education experts in Germany where gymnastics flourished, despaired over the apparently irreconcilable demands of modesty and aesthetics against practicality in girls' gymnastic costume. But in some parts of Germany legislation was passed and enforced.[71]

Reformers in England and France had often talked about legislation but seldom got so far as concrete proposals. An exception was Dr. Philippe Maréchal, who lectured tirelessly all over Europe with an extremely punitive and impracticable program of legislation: 1. All persons under thirty years of age were to be prohibited from wearing any kind of corset, on pain of one to three months imprisonment, increased to twelve months if the wearer were found to be pregnant. If she were a minor, the parents would be condemned to a fine of 100 to 1,000 francs. 2. Persons over thirty years of age would be permitted to wear corsets, except during pregnancy. 3. The most rigorous control would be imposed upon the sale of corsets (akin to that already existing with regard to dangerous drugs), and vendors would be obliged to enter the age of each purchaser in a book.[72]

The demise of the corset was gradual and undramatic. It became progressively lighter, and looser; and it was progressively abandoned by the younger generation. In 1911, when Paul Poiret, with his loose, free-flowing Ballets Russes style, claimed to have dealt the corset its "death-blow," it was already moribund. The true death-blow was delivered by the First World War.[73]

There is little evidence of continued activity on the part of dress-reform organizations in either France or England. In Germany, on the other hand, where the need appeared to be less (the Berlinerin was reported as early as 1905 to have largely abandoned the corset), the journal of the Deutscher Verband fur Neue Frauenkleidung und Frauenkultur,[74] which had absorbed the various reform organizations active in the last years of the 19th century, and another leading dress-reform journal, *Die Gesunde Frau,* continued to press for abolition. The reform movement in Germany was ill-served by the Lex Heinze, a broadly repressive law affecting public morality, which was hotly debated in the Reichstag with particular reference to corsets as such and the way they encouraged décolletage.[75] The law was supported by a deputy named Roeren who angrily brandished in the chamber a poster depicting a woman in tight-laced corset and very low neckline.

In the later 19th century, denunciation of "indecent" corset advertisements on hoardings and in newspapers (as, earlier, corsetted dummies in shop windows) became increasingly common in Europe.

The corset controversy even split the German Imperial household where the Kaiser, backed by the Crown Princess and his sister the Crown Princess Sophie of Greece, forbade it at court, while the Empress, herself very stiffly corsetted and backed by two other sisters of the Kaiser, forbade ladies at court to appear without one. Other examples of royal concern may be cited, such as that of the Queen of Portugal, who passed x-ray photographs of victims of tight-lacing around the ladies of her court, and the Italian Queen Helen and Dowager Queen Marguerite, who also voiced disapproval of the practice.[76] Three of the daughters of Queen Victoria, Princess Victoria, the Duchess of Fife and Princess Maud (later Queen of Norway) appear, from photographs, as very small waisted, as does Princess (later Queen) Mary—perhaps in reaction to the enormous girth of Queen Victoria herself. Fetishists have fancied these as primary English royal examples of tight-lacing; the effect is more likely due to a natural slenderness aided by diet, no more than fashionable corsetting, and of course the inevitable retouching of the photographs.

Swansong of Tight-Lacing: The Stage

Dying as a custom, tight-lacing was found to be good publicity value by certain actresses, and was heavily exploited on their behalf by the press.

Lesser actresses in the 19th century, like some in our own times, found tight-lacing an effective means of arresting public attention. One can moreover readily understand how the corset might serve, in the manner we have frequently observed, to conceal, with or without deliberate intention to abort, a pregnancy which in this particular profession would certainly threaten the retention of a role, if not a whole career.[77] The propensity of serious singers to tight-lace, difficult to credit under any circumstances, may be traced back as far as the mid-18th century[78] and a mid-19th century source testifies that it was a "common and painful experience to witness the difficulties and immense efforts required of those unfortunate singers in order to produce their voice, when a roulade obliges them to hunch their shoulders, arch their back, and hollow their breast in order to make a bit of space under their corset, and in order to lend breadth to their voice: but this deprives it of its charm and paralyzes their talent."[79] Around 1873 there performed in Boston a "celebrated Prima Donna with a waist thinner than her stalwart male supporter's arm."[80] Opera stars lent their name to fashion corsets: thus we have the incongruous-sounding Patti-Nicolini corset, which was also endorsed by Ellen Terry and other luminaries of the stage.

Dancers usually wore light waist cinches (often with rubber inserts) which caused that sudden indentation in the middle so clearly illustrated in the paintings of Degas. One very distinguished ballerina, Virginia Zucchi (Princess Vasetchkoff) used to wear such a corset outside her rather short-skirted costume, an undress effect which, in conjunction with the emotional realism of her dramatic style, earned her the sobriquet of the "Emile Zola of the dance."[81] No example of a named dancer who tight-laced has come to my attention, but at least one instance is recorded of an unnamed dancer who, on post-mortem examination, was found to have a 16-inch waist, ribs overlapped several inches, and the abdominal organs pressed almost into the pelvis. The fatality of a Berlin actress/dancer aroused comment in England as well as on the continent.[82]

Aesthetic effect was only one of the reasons that dancers wore corsets. An elderly lady teaching classical dance in Toronto, Canada, told me that at the school in Russia where she had been trained during the early years of this century, the girls were required to wear, for partnering classes, a particularly tight corset under their practice costume. Three reasons were given: first, that it helped pull up the body and flatten the stomach to the point that, ideally, a girl could "feel her spine at the front"; second, it enabled the partner to grip better when lifting; and third, it prevented him from feeling her naked flesh, which would have been improper.

Despite the example of Sarah Bernhardt and Eleanore Duse, outspoken opponents of the corset who did much to restore classical proportions to stage costume, complaints multiplied at century's end that, with their breathing radically impeded by corsets, actresses were unable to come up with the breadth of gesture and flexibility of thoracic and abdominal movement necessary to express deep emotions.[83]

The view that the corset was to blame was vigorously contested by Corah Brown Potter, a distinguished actress born in 1859. "I here take up the cudgels in favour of binding," she announced bluntly in her *Secrets of Beauty*. "I have always laced tightly—the parts I have played necessitated it—and I have found it also helped in creating volume (and projection) of the voice. [Without it] I would never have been able to stand the strain of exhausting seasons . . . Binding . . . is healthy; besides creating a curve conforming with the Line of Beauty." In the course of an extensive medical justification of all this, she cites experiments made on rabbits, who by means of abdominal supports learned to stand upright for prolonged periods of time.[84]

Germaine Gallois was another important actress who regarded

severe corsetting as a basic element of theatrical discipline, and an aesthetic necessity. She did not accept seated roles on stage, preferring to remain upright, including the intervals, from 8:30 p.m. to midnight. "An inflexible bastioned beauty . . . sheathed in a corset which began under the armpits and ended near the knees, fitted with two flat steel springs in the back, two others down the thighs, in the crotch a 'tirette' (I am giving you the current term), supporting a structure the lacing of which, moreover, required a staylace six metres long . . ."[85] Colette, sensitive to the byzantine splendors of the acresses of the demi-monde as well as the appeal of tight-lacing (in which she, with her husband Willy, encouraged Polaire), begins her *Apprenticeships* with vivid recollections of her "protector," the famous courtesan Caroline Otéro, whom she describes as a "motionless icon" of the music-halls, in her "gala corset" and "huge bejewelled breastplate." But the illusion was maintained off-stage as well, as we know from the youthful Jean Cocteau, entranced by the perverse fascination of heavily armored "ladies of easy virtue", the undressing of whom he imagined to be of a magnitude akin to that of moving house, and of a violence associated with some scandalous scene of murder. Thus La Otéro and la Cavalieri lunching at Armenonville: "It was no small affair. Armour, escutcheons, carcans (chokers), corsets, whalebones, braids, épaulières, greaves, thigh-pieces, gauntlets, corselets, pearl baldricks, feather bucklers, satin, velvet and bejewelled halters, coats of mail—these knights-at-arms bristling with tulle, rays of light and eyelashes, these sacred scarabs armed with asparagus holders, these Samurais of sable and ermine, these cuirassiers of pleasure who were harnessed and caparisoned early in the morning by robust soubrettes, seemed incapable, as they sat stiffly opposite their hosts, of extracting anything from an oyster beyond the pearl."[86]

In the United States at the end of the century the corsets of the stars became a major subject of newspaper gossip. Lilian Russell possessed one worth $3,900 which it took her an hour to get into. Pressed by an interviewer to admit that her corsets were designed to keep at bay a thickening waistline, she skillfully deflected the conversation onto her daughter, at fourteen years now just arrived at the dignity of her first corset, "an epoch in her life which has convulsed the prima donna's household with the most intense excitement." In 1899 the journalists were discussing the New Shape (complete with diagrams), the result, one was assured, purely of gymnastic exercises, which had reduced her bust from 42 to 38 and her waist from 27 to 22 inches. The photographers reduced the latter even further by some heavy and obvious painting out, as was the custom. There were few actresses who did not have their waists painted out in photographs, like

"Gibson Girl" Camille Clifford, whose corsetted slenderness was not considered equal to the drawings of Charles Dana Gibson. Even Anna Held had this done, although she displayed a real enough wasp-waist on stage. Her gymnastic exercises served "to neutralize the effects of a corset which I never remove before going to bed." Held died in 1918 aged forty-five of "anemia, over-work and excessive discipline." She was even rumored to have had one rib surgically removed, and to have actually died of tight-lacing: "Doctors said she had almost literally squeezed herself to death."[87]

The most famous wasp-waist of the era, that of Polaire, became a major publicity gimmick (it is discussed more fully in the appendix p. 325), but represented in the immediate pre-War years a completely isolated phenomenon, a peculiar emblem of a calculated barbarism which was quickly forgotten afterwards, except by fetishists. It was even omitted from Polaire's autobiography of 1939. Although much sensationalized at the time by the press, Polaire's waist was no longer controversial, but part of a stage persona exempt from traditional medical strictures and contrived for theatrical effect. As the corset lost its controversial aura, it acquired a facile erotic appeal exploitable by other media, particularly music-hall, strip-tease cabaret, picture postcards and stereoscopic photographs. The co-optation of fetishist feeling has proceeded ever since this time, reviving into fashion, as we shall see, with the "waspie" of the mid-20th century.

Notes

1. Cobbe, 1878, p. 292, accusing them quite unjustly of being "feeble and cautious" vis-à-vis tight-lacing.

2. West, 1892, p. 220. The *Lancet* maintained this average over a period of twenty-five years (1867–92).

3. They were certainly numerous and prominent enough to provoke a cartoon which tried to show the effect of such a club meeting to be counterproductive to the cause of dress reform. The throng of ladies are depicted doting upon a dummy in the very tight-laced dress they are being warned against (*Funny Folks*, 18 March 1882). A cartoon with the same intent has a living male in the role of the tight-laced dummy (*Funny Folks*, 15 March 1890).

   The lecture on tight-lacing did not have to be announced as such to be remembered as such: The German gentleman who lectured in Blackpool on "Tempers and how to control them" was reported only for his demonstration on corsets (*Family Doctor* 3 Sep. 1887, p. 7).

4. The *World* announced the Society for Protecting the Natural Form of Woman, consisting of gentlemen whose object is to "oppose any fashion which may injure or disfigure the beautiful form of woman" (*Funny Folks*, 15 April 1882). The Society, which may well have been a hoax in the first place, was not taken seriously by the two papers which carried the item.

5. *Lancet* 10 Jan., 1880, and Matthieu Williams (chemist) pp. 119 and 143.

6. Wettstein-Adelt, 1893, p. 1 f.

7. Imbecility: Phelps, p. 66, and *Girl's Own Paper*, 1886, p. 494. Straitjacket: *Puck*, 8 Oct. 1879, p. 488.

8. 18 Sep. 1869, p. 426.

9. 4 Sep. p. 8b; "Not a Girl of the Period," 2 Sep. p. 4c; cf. letters 3 Sep. p. 9e and 6 Sep. p. 9d.

10. Great Evil: Ellis. Curse: Kenealy. Future of Women: Schweninger. War, pestilence, famine: Treves, 1886, p. 72. Salvation of race: B. O. Flower, "Fashion's Slaves," *Arena* 1891, p. 413.

11. Article in *Le Figaro*, 1909, reviewed in the New York *Review of Reviews* for May, 1909, pp. 621–22.

12. Stockham, 1883, p. 110.

13. Cannaday, 1894.

14. Wilberforce Smith, 1888, p. 323.

15. Kratschmer, 1894, p. 409, on the basis of a Dissertation by Leue published at Kiel in 1891.

16. Animal experiments simulating tight-lacing (the animals are not specified, but they died) were performed in New York prior to 1874 (Safford-Blake in Woolson, p. 19). The *Lancet* (22 March 1890, p. 662) reported on the outcry raised by animal lovers against the experimental tight-lacing of some female monkeys, which was alleged to be cruel (although choloroform was used) and unnecessary, because the effects of tight-lacing among humans were already well-known.

17. Haller, p. 34.

18. The political bias of *Nineteenth Century* may be judged from the racism of an article called "The Black Peril in South Africa" and the clericalism of an article called "Anti-clericalism in France and England," both published the same month as "The Curse of Corsets."

The Kenealy article was favorably reviewed, especially as regards its extremer conclusions, in *L'Illustration*, March 5, 1904, p. 158.

19. Renoir, pp. 88, 89, 227, 288 and 323.

20. Sterility: Baus 1911, p. 72. Towle ad: *Family Doctor*, 3 Sep. 1887, p. 7.

21. Scharlach in *Der Floh*, 31 Dec. 1890. Gratz in *Der Floh*, 28 July 1878.

22. Hastings in Woolson, p. 75.

23. Tylicka, pp. 63–4.

24. McMurtrie, p. 173.

25. Köystrand, "Unsere Mieder Enquête," *Wiener Caricaturen*, 11 Nov. 1894.

26. See Gänssbauer, p. 9 f. The fair-minded reformer Dr. Treves testifies to the existence of "tight-lace liver" in uncorsetted women; citing the case of one with a "broad peasant waist," who on post-mortem examination proved to have a liver cut in two, and held together only by a calloused bit of tissue (1886, p. 72).

27. Cf. Farrar, 1880, Treves, 1882, p. 19, Smith, 1888, and Sargent, 1889; bibliographical summary in Havelock Ellis, *Man and Woman* (1904 ed.), pp. 228–244. The most comprehensive early experiments were those of Garson in 1888, who found the average vital capacity in women aged 20–30 years of average height 62.9 inches to be 40 ccs. and in men of the same age, average height 68.7 inches, 63 ccs. Younger women tended to have less lung power than older women because they were more tightly laced. At this time, the Russian Dr. Boris I. Kianovsky published the results of similar experiments (with bibliography) in *Vratch* Nos. 20 and 21, 1888, p. 385, as reported in the *British Medical Journal* for June 4, 1889, pp. 791–792.

The theory that the thoracic breathing of women was due to stay-wearing was first advanced by Winslow in 1741, but never generally accepted. The belief that women breathe *naturally* higher up in the body than men goes back (at least) to the early 18th century when Boerhaave observed the phenomenon in male and female infants. He was followed by the illustrious Albrecht von Haller, and, in the period we are dealing with, the distinguished biologist Thomas Huxley, who was certainly not gullible (cf. Cunnington, *19th Century*, p. 369). Havelock Ellis dismissed the belief (*Man and Woman*, p. 278), while conceding to the Roy-Adami theory (cf. below) that corset-like pressure upon the abdominal viscera could help stimulate the circulation of the blood and promote mechanical mixture of air in the lungs. Cf. also *Punch,* 8 Jan. 1898, p. 1, Webb, 1907, p. 240, and Laver, *Modesty,* p. 117.

28. *Century Magazine* for August, 1893, reported by Crutchfield, 1897.

29. Dickinson, 1887. A one to one-and-a half inch reduction in the waist of one woman caused more total pressure (73½ lbs.) than a reduction of 5 inches in another woman (65 lbs). The average pressure over the sixth and seventh ribs after deep inspiration was found to be 1.625 pounds per square inch. This figure may be compared with that given by Taliaferro in 1873, who concluded that the total pressure exerted by a "moderately laced corset" averaged out at roughly the individual's body-weight. Cf. also the carefully controlled experiments of Thiersch in 1900, who concluded that the "typical" corset exerts constant pressure of one and a half to two kilograms on the waist.

30. Hygeia: *Family Doctor,* 22 May 1886. Envy: Cobbe 1878, p. 284. Spartan: Réveillé Parise, p. 788. *Common-Sense Clothing:* Barnett, p. 65.

31. This was the experience of a German doctor as reported by Heszky, p. 103. Audry in 1900 noticed "exuberant scars" at the waist of a "beautiful young girl" as the only palpable evidence of tight-lacing.

32. Taliaferro, p. 693.

33. *Subjection of Women,* p. 42.

34. Chapotot, 1891, p. 80 ff.

35. It would be "unworthy" to suppose that men admired small waists as a sexual characteristic, for which there was no evidence ("The Philosophy of Tight-Lacing," *Saturday Review,* September, 1887, p. 816). According to Shoemaker, 1890 (pp. 156 and 259) "the wasp-waist elicits not only disgust at the vulgarity of it, but abolishes sexual attraction" and suggests "sexual deficiency."

36. "What a Tiny Waist!" *Household Words,* 31 May, 1881 p. 76.

37. "The etiology of the tight waist," *Medical Record,* 23 March 1895, p. 370.

38. Ecob, pp. 236 and 231; cf. *Arena,* 1891, vol. 3, p. 419.

39. Pp. 188 and 432. Cf. the same author's *Ladies Guide,* pp. 144–156 (on masturbation), pp. 249–262 (on tight-lacing), and pp. 351–369 (on abortion).

40. E.g. Dr. Anna Fischer-Duckelmann, in a work which had been printed in 600,000 copies by 1908 (pp. 147–8) and Dr. Hermann Paull (1908, pp. 43–56, and 103), both of whom reproduce the well-worn Soemmerring diagram, inveigh against tight-lacing, and cite masturbation as the first of the sexual perversions. Fischer also reproduces pictures of various painful anti-masturbation devices.

A non-repressive source citing the case of a well-developed, healthy, vigorous and athletic" woman using tight-lacing as a form of masturbation, is Havelock Ellis, *Studies,* 1926 ed., p. 300.

41. They are of two kinds: direct and indirect. Directly, the corset "contracts the abdominal organs from above and provokes a engorgement of the blood in the abdomen, which for its part brings the oblique stomach muscles into a voluptuous position" (wollüstige Stellung). Indirectly, "these muscles, in women, serve the purpose of pressing the abdominal organs downwards during sexual intercourse, thereby bringing the uterus towards the male member. The corset brings these muscles into a similar position, and this seems to be associated in many females with pleasant sexual feelings. The firm place which our corset has in fashion, and also with demi-mondaines, is due in no small part to this effect" (p. 93).

An English authority, after linking masturbation in boys to tight trousers, continues: "Close-fitting stays are said to have the same effect on girls . . . (who) acquire the auto-erotic habit through irritations which occur in the vulva and clitoris. The early wearing of stays is said to cause precocious sexuality. When it is known that a degenerate cult of tight corset wearers exists in England with a journal devoted to their craze, the relation between tight-lacing and sex hyperaesthesia (heightened feeling) seems to be well-established" (Gallichen, pp. 111 and 132. I am indebted to Dr. Michael Clarke for this reference).

42. Marcuse, pp. 384–5, article by O. F. Scheuer. Eberhard, p. 314.

43. Composed of single or double (i.e. folded) layers of drawers, underskirts, balmoral, dress-skirt, overskirt, dress waist and belt (p. 190). Phelps (p. 70) put the

number of thicknesses at between fourteen and eighteen. The figures given by other writers average at about sixteen.

44. By Stella Mary Newton.

45. I have counted at least eighteen books and articles published during the years 1880–82 alone. The high density period continued through the early '90s. At the Pathological Institute at Kiel there must have been a senior professor (probably called Heller) obsessed with the dangers of tight-lacing, to judge by the existence of no less than eight dissertations on various aspects of the subject submitted during the period 1884–94 (bibliography in Hackmann, 1894).

46. Pp. 373–4.

47. This claim is supported by an English colleague, Walshe, at exactly this date in an article with figures showing that female mortality from phthisis (consumption) compared to male mortality from the same disease, is actually greater among rural populations which do not tight-lace, than in the metropolis where tight-lacing is common.

48. E.g. Woolson, p. 190ff., who asserts that the lower ribs are invariably wider than the upper ones. Bouvier's claim is based on a statistical sampling of 150 persons of both sexes and all social classes.

49. For attacks on Bouvier by his colleagues in the Academy of Medicine, cf. Fanton, 1879/80.

50. Treves, *Influence of Clothing,* p. 72. *Lancet,* 6 July 1867 and 28 May 1881. In a 25 June 1887 editorial, the *Lancet* enjoined the use of a "forcible language" as violent as the "embrace of the most fashionable strait corset."

51. "Evils": Arthur Edis in *The Queen,* 1880, I, p. 22, Richardson: 1882, II, p. 303; Tennis-player: 1879, II, p. 391.

52. Meeting of The Physiological Department of the Biological Section (D), at Bath September 7th, 1888, reported in *Rational Dress Society's Gazette* no. 3, 1888.

53. He is possibly identical with the "Medicus" who had defended tight-lacers writing to *The Englishwoman's Domestic Magazine;* he is surely identical to the Dr. Haughton who took the same position in the *Family Doctor,* then the major forum of fetishism.

54. Cited by Adburgham, p. 110.

55. *Oeuvres Complètes,* tom. 3, p. 52.

56. Limner, 1870, p. 13.

57. Cf., apart from Leighton, the painters Mrs. Haweis and George Frederic Watts. The role of English artists in the dress-reform movement has yet to be clarified. In 1883 Edward Armitage R.A. lectured at the Royal Academy on dress reform. In 1894 Hamo Thornycroft R.A., G. F. Watts R.A. and the famous surgeon Sir Spencer Wells banded together as Vice Presidents of the Healthy and Artistic Dress Union.

58. Hollander, p. 91.

59. Cf. Fritsch, *Gestalt,* 1899, p. 93f.

60. Encircling bird-cage: Newton, p. 274. Blanc, p. 274. Kaleidoscope: Phelps, p. 11.

61. This went through English editions in 1860, 1861 and 1863; bibliography of early works in Günther, 1863.

62. Daumier in *Le Charivari,* 24 Jan. 1840: "That'll teach me to try to make my feet look small". Cf. also a cartoon by H. Emy in *Le Petit Journal pour Rire* for 6 Sept. 1850: "Les Bottes Neuves, ou la prison de Saint-Crépin." The literary and iconographic allusions to the topic are legion.

63. No well-formed foot! *Harper's Bazaar,* 22 Feb. 1868, p. 258. Innumerable malformations: *Household Words,* 30 April 1881, "What a pretty foot." Fatal abscesses: *Lancet,* quoted in *Queen,* 1884, I, p. 6. Abdominal displacement: Barnett, p. 74. Surgical separation: Woolson, p. 75. Treves: *Dress of the Period,* p. 26.

64. "What a Pretty Foot!" *Household Words,* 30 April 1881, and *Lancet,* quoted in *Queen,* 1884, I, p. 6.

64. Saint Crispin, 1868, and Shoemaker, p. 259.

65. *The Queen,* 1884, I, p. 652.

66. Danish version: Cox, pp. 284–7. Russian version: Cox p. 379.

67. Cox, pp. 127–144.

68. "More than a dozen laces were broken on her sisters" (Woolson, p. 246).

69. *Folklore Fellows Communications,* Helsinki, vol. 90, no. 453; cf. Stith Thompson, *Motif Index* K. 953.1.

70. Discounting the short-lived *Les Dessous Féminins,* started in 1896 by the Baronne Jehanne d'Argissonne, and surviving only in fragments in the Bibliothèque Nationale. The editor piously proclaimed her policy of excluding advertisements for "the deformers of the finer half of humanity," but in practice was wedded to the old-fashioned "corsets cambrés" of Mélanie de Gruyter. Her descendant, also called Mélanie de Gruyter, was still making tight-lacing corsets for fetishists in the 1950s.

71. Cf *Deutsche Turnzeitung* 1900, p. 286, and Meinert. Ministerial edicts prohibiting the wearing of corsets and high-heeled shoes in gymnastic classes were promulgated in Prussia 1894, 1905 and 1908; in Saxony, 1900 and 1907, and in Baden, 1908. In Belgium, by 1909, the Ministry of Public Instruction forbade corsets in all girls' schools (*Photobits,* 11 Dec. 1909). The attempts of Dr. Robert Sangiovanni (*Abolition of the Corset,* 1910) to persuade the U.S. Secretary of State and the Mayor of the City of New York to legislate against the corset, seem to have fallen on deaf ears.

72. *Les Dessous Elégants,* 1901, p. 42, with the caustic comment: "Of all the labours of Doctor Maréchal, this legislative delivery may be considered the crowning of his work."

73. The role here of economic factors is undeterminable. According to a member of the U.S. War Industries Board, women's sacrifices of stays during the War released 28,000 tons of steel—enough to build two battleships (Cortes, p. 266).

74. The journal of this Association was edited by the leading German feminists, Clara Sander and Elsa Wirminghaus; cf. Anthony, Ch. III.

75. *Die Gesunde Frau,* 1 April 1900, p. 56.

76. Bray, pp. 219–220, and Webb, p. 240f.

77. Layet, p. 26, with reference to a young actress who died after tight-lacing into the seventh or eighth month of pregnancy.

78. As a boy the antiquarian Strutt (p. 175) saw on stage an opera singer "laced to such an excessive degree of smallness, that it was painfull to look at her; for, the lower part of her figure appeared like the monstrous appendage of a wasp's belly, united to the body by a slender ligament."

79. Petit, p. 10.

80. Safford-Blake in Woolson, p. 10.

81. F. Giarelli in *La Scena Illustrata,* 15 March 1888.

82. Overlapped ribs: Charlotte West, p. 220. Berlin lady: *Bombe* 11 May 1890 and *Lancet* 14 June 1890, p. 1316.

83. Steele, 1892.

84. pp. 232–240.

85. Colette, *Apprenticeships,* p. 10.

86. Cocteau, pp. 63–64.

87. *Life* Magazine, 19 Nov. 1951, pp. 116–117. This legend is very pervasive, but has absolutely no demonstrable basis in fact.

CHAPTER FIVE

The Corset as Erotic Alchemy: Graphic Transformations in the 18th and 19th Centuries[1]

T he erotic function of the corset is illuminated in certain popular currents of 18th-19th century graphic art and illustration, notably in France where erotic art flourished with the greatest freedom and sophistication. French graphic artists found in the corset not just a convenient foil for nakedness or one aspect of undress among many, but a very special and expressive instrument in the social and erotic ritual. The French created a new genre in art: the "toilette galante," which, in turn, generated what amounts to a sub-genre, the "essai du corset" (fitting the corset). This went through several transformations, from the documentary to the satirical, the idealizing to the degrading, the poetic to the grotesque.

Rococo: Essai du Corset

During the renaissance and baroque periods it was a common device of the erotic to show a half-draped and undressed female in certain mythological and biblical scenes. The stories of Diana, Susanna, and Bathsheba, who were spied upon in their bath by lustful males, were an opportunity to present the power of female nakedness in a moral context. The components of such themes included a male voyeur, a naked or almost naked heroine and a clothed attendant, all placed in an outdoor setting (landscape or patio) with classical associations.

In the age of the rococo, the eroticism of nudity is supplemented by that of the toilette—the everyday process of dressing and undressing. The bibli-classical heroine is replaced by the woman of fashion, who is moved indoors to take her bath, and invites the (male) viewer to contemplate the preliminaries to her graceful and complaisant surrender.

The 18th century artist no longer viewed clothing as a covering for a body of ideal, classical proportions; he acknowledged the fact that contemporary fashion, to the realistic representation of which he was committed, also served to mould and recreate the body along lines which were anti-classical, and potentially erotic. In the early rococo or transitional phase a twin code of feminine proportions prevailed, according to whether the figure was clothed or not. Watteau was capable of painting a relatively abundant classical nude, but preferred the clothed ladies of his fêtes galantes with their fashionable, unclassical slenderness. His principal pupil, Jean-Baptiste Pater, combined the two ideals in a single painting (Plate 11) in such a way as to suggest a reversal of the hierarchical symbolism usually attached to slender form. But if here the maid is so much more slender than her mistress, it is only because the former is dressed, while the latter is naked.

Such a picture represents a transition between the traditional outdoor bathing scene and the indoor dressing scene, or toilette galante. The male, very subordinate as he is, is still cast by Pater in the traditional role of lecherous spy. In the toilette galante of the later rococo, the male role changes into one expressive of respectful admiration (Plate 12). He becomes the *assistant:* a spectator "assisting" in the French sense, first psychologically, then physically. The actual physical assistance required by a lady in her toilette provided a natural and realistic framework into which erotic desire could be projected. Thus we find the lover appearing in the guise of a *tailleur,* and then maid.

This merger of roles may be traced back to another iconographic tradition—that of costume illustration and representation of trades and professions, popular genres which contributed, like the high art genre of the historical bathing scene, to the formation of the toilette galante. The tailleur de corps, or staymaker, in an engraving by Arnoult of 1697, stands formally, at a proper distance from his client, passing the stays over her arm. But his dress marks this craftsman who "knows how to conceal the faults of nature, and how to keep the secrets of an amorous adventure," as a gentleman, ennobled as it were by the delicacy and intimacy of his craft. The strong hint of his amorous role is to be more fully developed later, and eventually to cause him to merge with the *galant* himself.[2]

By the age of the rococo, in an engraving by Cochin, the gentleman-staymaker has become more familiar as he presses closer to his client, burying his knee into her skirt, and taking the measure of the busk with his upper hand actually touching her naked breast, while the maid (in the earlier print, concerned only with some drapery), watches attentively, perhaps approvingly. The verse confirms the increase in erotic charge, expressing a lover's identification with the tailor, and his readiness to suffer in silence, could he but entertain the hope "of taking her measure as I crave." There can be no doubt about the sexual connotation—a "tailor's yard" was a common phrase for the male member.

By about 1760 the staymaker has abandoned all pretence at professional decorum. Dispensing with the outward symbols of his trade, the *tailleur*, identifiable as such only from the print-title, stands behind the lady in her stays, his hand and gaze hovering hungrily over her breasts. Then the gallant comes to "assist" at the operation, thus merging Essai du Corset with Toilette Galante (Plate 12). It is important to understand that this situation corresponds to actual upper-class social custom. The final stages of an 18th century lady's morning toilette, known as the lever or levée, was considered an appropriate moment for entertaining friends; to be admitted to one was a sign of intimacy. In the Baudouin picture the tension of the maid pulling on the staylace is paralleled, on the other side, by that of the gallant, who elegantly expresses through the forward pitch of his body and the commonplace symbols of rose and sword, the ardor of his desire.

Baudouin, heir to the clientèle for erotica formed by his famous father-in-law François Boucher, also made a more intimate portrait of the corsetted female form, viewed as it were in an oval mirror. The dove flaps his wings as he gazes at the well-exposed breasts and the invitation to the gallant viewer is one of open enticement, as the caption indicates.

The delicate eroticism with which Baudouin suffused the theme of the Essai du Corset, and which was also characteristic of the Toilette Galante and cognates like the Coucher de la Mariée, later turned to the risqué, satirical, grotesque and even semi-pornographic. In a design of about 1780 (Plate 13) the staymaker helps fit the stays not merely by lacing them, but by firmly settling them in place, one hand clasping the lady's waist, the other fingering the breasts, which are bared to inches below the nipple. He conveys more than professional concern, and the older man seated right (and well below the line of the lady's dreamy gaze), may reveal some sad sense of this.[3]

In a print of 1796 illustrating—ironically—the *Confessions* of that arch-enemy of the corset, Jean-Jacques Rousseau, the Essai du Corset is rendered in a vulgar and lascivious manner reminiscent of English caricature of the period. The "gallant" is a grinning abbé who tugs mightily at the laces, his skirts hitched up to reveal a nicely muscled calf.[4]

Line of Beauty: Hogarth

The heir to rococo art in England was William Hogarth, whose oeuvre provides a unique corpus of information on the minutiae of contemporary dress. Hogarth was a keen student of both costume and posture, in theory and in their practical application to problems of pictorial representation of daily life. He was the first art-theorist to set the quirks of fashion sympathetically within the context of a general aesthetic theory, viewing the traditional butts of fashion moralists, such as hoops, as the embodiment of the aesthetic principle of quantity, and stays, in their differing shapes, as a demonstration of formal variety.

All this appears in his famous and controversial treatise, *The Analysis of Beauty* (1753). The quintessence of elegance was to be found in what its inventor called the Line of Beauty. This term (exploited, as we have seen, in puffs and advertisements for certain tight-lacing corsets over a century later) describes a "perfectly beautiful", sinuous, swelling and tapering curve, of a type favoured by French rococo artists for elegant composition and individual posture. It has come to be regarded, by art historians, as quintessential rococo. According to Hogarth, this line, which may be found on objects both natural and artificial, does not necessarily derive from nature, but may be imposed upon nature when otherwise lacking. Thus, Hogarth finds it not in the natural female anatomy, but in a series of disembodied stays (Plate 9), his description of which reads both as praise of the staymaker's skill and as a bizarre tribute to the superiority of art over nature. The special value placed by Hogarth on the aesthetic and symbolism of stays may be judged from the beautiful "still-life" inserts in major works such as *Rake's Progress* III and *Marriage A-la-mode* V. In the former they are placed center foreground, in deliberate counterpoint to the lovely, abundant and natural forms of their owner, an acrobatic performer called Posture Nan; in the latter, their abandonment symbolizes sexual dishonour. In the *Harlot's Progress,* the change in the shape of the stays worn by Moll Hackabout between the first and second scenes embodies the all-important shift in her status from simple country girl to sophisticated courtesan, and her corresponding moral decline.[5]

"A still more perfect idea," writes Hogarth in the *Analysis,* "of the effects of the precise waving-line, and of those lines that deviate from it, may be conceived by the row of stays (Plate 9) where number 4 is composed of precise waving-lines, and is therefore the best-shaped stay. Every whalebone of a good stay must be made to bend in this manner: for the whole stay, when put close together behind, is truly a shell of well-varied contents, and its surface, of course, a fine form." Hogarth is concerned here, as always, not just with a contour or silhouette, but with three-dimensional, spiralling movement: "so that if a line, or the lace were to be drawn, or brought from the top of the lacing of the stay behind, round the body, and down to the bottom peak of the stomacher; it would form such a perfect, precise, serpentine line, as has been shown round the cone" (illustrated elsewhere in the diagram). There was, apparently, no comparable Line of Beauty to be found in the male form, naked or clothed; and it is Hogarth's altogether remarkable, not to say heretical conclusion that the existence of this line in female stays "proves how much the form of a woman's body surpasses in beauty that of man."[6]

This thesis is enacted in a painted sketch in which Hogarth juxtaposes the comic, awkward angular and plebeian posture of the male staymaker with the dignified, graceful and fluid and aristocratic lines of the client he is fitting: Toilette Comique, rather than Toilette Galante.[7]

Hogarth's selection of the perfect shape of stay may conceal a subtle polemic against a mid-century trend in fashion towards a straighter and flatter torso, a shape protested also by his friend the novelist Henry Fielding, who enthuses over his heroine Fanny as "not one of those slender young women who seem rather intended to hang up in the hall of an anatomist . . . (but) so plump that she seemed to be bursting through her tight stays, especially in that part which confined her swelling breasts."[8] Another friend of Hogarth, with advance knowledge of his *Analysis,* enters this more specific protest: "But the worst reason for coming to London that I ever heard in my life, was given me last night at a visit by a young lady of the most graceful figure I ever beheld; it was 'To have her shape altered to the modern fashion.' That is to say, to have her breasts compressed by a flat, strait line, which is to extend crosswise from shoulder to shoulder, and also to descend, still in a strait line, in such a manner, that you shall not be able to pronounce what it is that prevents the usual tapering of the waist." The writer goes on to cite "the nicest observer of our times (Hogarth), who is now publishing a most rational Analysis of Beauty and has chosen for the principal illustration of it, a pair of stays, such as would fit the shape described by the judicious poet, and has also shown by drawings of other stays, that every minute deviation from the first pattern is a diminution of beauty, and every grosser alteration a deformity."[9]

The "judicious poet" referred to here was Matthew Prior, the relevant passage from whose *Henry and Emma* (1708) is quoted verbatim; it had been used already in a letter from one Clarinda to the *Guardian* in 1713. Probably concocted by the editor Joseph Addison himself, the letter with its commentary fills the whole of an issue (for 18 June), recounting the moral sufferings of a fair and eligible young lady of fifteen, whose beauty excited the envy of all her female acquaintances. Their envy singled out, among her many attractions, her slender shape "fine by degrees and beautifully less", which they publicly accused her of owing (now quoting Congreve) to the blacksmiths,

> The Mulcibers who in the *minories* sweat,
> And massive bars on stubborn anvils beat;
> Deform'd themselves, yet forge those stays of steel
> Which arm Aurelia with a shape to kill.

Already very famous in the 18th century and, like Hogarth's diagrams of stays, much cited by fetishists in the 19th century, Prior's original verses are worth repeating:

> No longer shall the bodice, aptly lac'd
> From thy full bosom to thy slender waist,
> That air of harmony and shape express,
> Fine by degrees, and beautifully less . . .
> An horseman's coat shall hide
> Thy taper shape and comeliness of side.

The key epithet "taper," also used to characterize Hogarth's Line of Beauty, appears in a similar context in John Gay's *Toilette* (1716): "I own her taper form is made to please/Yet if you saw her unconfined by stays!" and again in the same author's *Araminta* (1713): "The rich stays her taper shape confine."

Prior's phrase "fine [often corrupted to small] by degrees and beautifully less" attained the status of a locus classicus. The Regency satirist who wrote "What straps, ropes, steel the aching ribs compress, to make the dandy beautifully less"[10] relied on the reader's recognition of the allusion to a famous formulation of ideal femininity.

It was the very triviality of stays which appealed to Hogarth, bent on discrediting classical theories of decorum, the classical emphasis of the general over the particular and the common assumption that classical costume was aesthetically superior to the "mean" lines of contemporary fashion. A taste for the particular and trivial was shared by Laurence Sterne, who in *Tristram Shandy* raised a great literary monument to the power of trivial circumstance to shape human experience. In a witty and well-veiled allusion to the work of an artist he much admired, Sterne turns Hogarth's extraction of ideal shape from a diversity of stays, into a great metaphor for moral and aesthetic transformation through the shape of circumstance: "Need I tell you, Sir, that the circumstances with which everything in this world is begirt give everything in this world its size and shape! and by tightening it, or relaxing it, this way or that, make the thing to be, what it is—great,—little,—good—bad—indifferent or not indifferent—just as the case happens?"[11]

Toilette Grotesque: English Caricature

Four English tight-lacing caricatures have survived from the year 1777, the moment when, as we noted, fashion tended to polarize. This was the moment when England was entering upon its "Golden Age of Caricature," that of Gillray and Rowlandson, who in the company of many other artists helped to turn dignified French galanterie to farce, the erotic to the satiric, the ideal to the grotesque.

In one caricature the young girl of the French Essai du Corset has become an old hag, clinging to a four-poster as she is tugged in by an equally old and ugly maid. Another shows a cobbler taking a leather strap to a vain and extravagant wife, one lacing deserving another. "But ah! when set aloft her cap / Her bodice while she's bracing, / Jobson comes in and with his strap / Gives her a good tight lacing (beating)". A third satire shows a smithy, in which blacksmiths are hammering out (fanciful) all steel stays. Only the fourth satire, by Hogarth's principal follower John Collet, shows a young and pretty woman being laced in;[12] this was well enough known to be adapted, sixteen years later, by James Gillray (Plate 16). At this time tight-lacing had declined under the influence of neo-classicism, but the revolutionary political situation offered a metaphor, based upon a pun and Collet's original title. The cartoon satirizes Tom Paine, radical author of the *Rights of Man*, who had once exercised the profession of staymaker, now shown subjecting the fair body politic of Britannia to "fashionable," revolutionary constraints. The metaphor was to have a rich future (cf. p. 60 n.90).

In 1781 Elizabeth Farren, a popular actress who was evidently very tight-laced for her role in a play called *The Fair Circassian*,[13] became the occasion of a caricature which is the earliest illustration of the fantasy which has haunted 20th century fetishists (and some modern cartoonists): the complete separation of the body in the middle, as the extreme consequence of the tight-lacing mania.

The most famous as well as the most cruel tight-lacing caricature is Thomas Rowlandson's "A Little Tighter" (Plate 17), a satire not so much on tight-lacing as such (which was by now out of fashion), as

THE BLACK CHOKER.

Dedicated to the Powers that Be.

Private Jones "HERE, 'I' BILL !! C-C-C-CATCH HOLD O' MY MUSKET! MY HEAD'S C-C-C-COMING OFF!"

PLATE 41

PLATE 42

A WAIST OF (WOODEN) MATERIAL.

PLATE 43

EST MODUS IN REBUS.

PLATE 44

PLATE 45

PLATE 46

PLATE 47

PEOPLE WHO *WILL* HAVE THEIR OWN WAY.

THE GIRL WHO WANTED A SMALL WAIST.

PLATE 48

PLATE 49

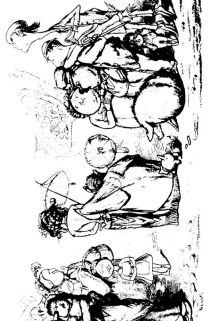

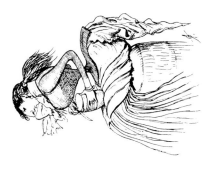

PLATE 50

PLATE 51

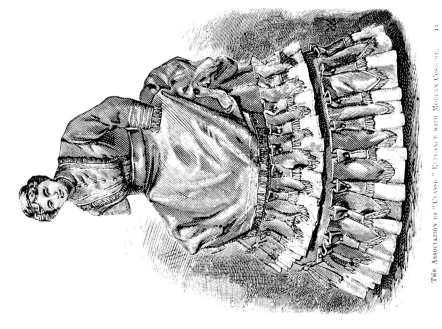

PLATE 52

HISTORY REPEATS ITSELF

(From a *very* Ancient Vase in the Possession of *Mr. Punch*.)

PLATE 54

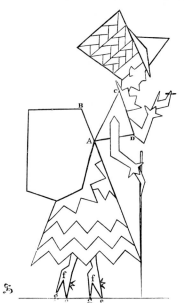

MR. PUNCH'S LATEST ADDITION TO THE LAST BOOK OF EUCLID.

Prove the angles A B C D and the angles *e g f* are absurd.

PLATE 55

La façon de marcher avec les nouveaux talons de bottines.

PLATE 56

PLATE 57

PLATE 58

PLATE 59

PLATE 60

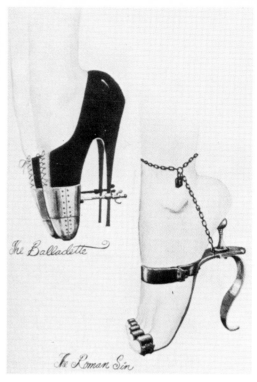

PLATE 61

THE PROBABLE EFFECT OF THE CHECK REIN ACCORDING TO THE LAW OF EVOLUTION.

PLATE 62

PLATE 63

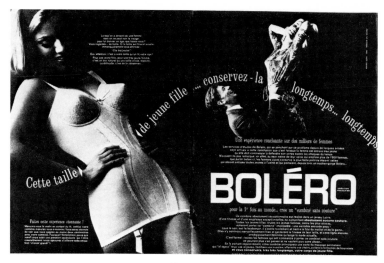

PLATE 64

THE HUMAN SPANNER, OR, HOW HE PROVED SHE
HAD A THIRTEEN-INCH WAIST.

PLATE 65

PLATE 66

PLATE 67

PLATE 68

PLATE 69

PLATE 70

PLATE 71

PLATE 72

Uncultur und Uebercultur in der Mode.

Mittelafrika.

Mitteleuropa.

PLATE 73

PLATE 74

PLATE 75

PLATE 76

PLATE 77

BEARING-REIN.
" *Fair for the Horse, fair for the Man.*"
SWEET LITTLE DEVICE TO KEEP COACHMAN STRAIGHT ON THE BOX.
PLATE 78

PLATE 81

Pull Yourself Together, Darling, There Are Curves Ahead!

This season, it isn't what you have—it's where you have it! The hourglass silhouette is here and Warner's Cinch-Bra makes the most of it.

Skillful folds of nylon marquisette make the bra top a three-way blessing. Start with the half bra, turn a fold and you have a beguiling bodice line; turn both folds . . . voila . . . a three-quarter bra!

Then, that completely feminine allure, the cinch middle that makes your waist more dramatic, more appealing. A gentle persuasion that gives you a two- to three-inch intake on your waist! Dainty embroidered marquisette over shimmering satin—a challenge to the loveliest dressmaker.

It comes in sizes . . .

WARNER'S
Bras · Girdles · Corselets

PLATE 80

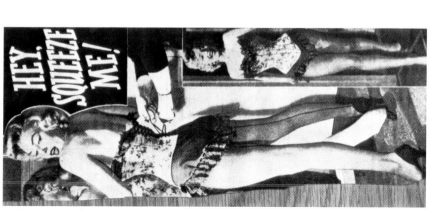

PLATE 79

PLATE 83

PLATE 82

PLATE 85

PLATE 84

PLATE 87

PLATE 86

on that constant butt of the caricaturists, the grotesque old coquette trying to recapture the charms of her youth.

Fashion caricature in revolutionary France, under the formal influence of the English, ridiculed the enemy for conservatism in dress as in politics (the English never adopted the full-blown neo-classical styles, and abandoned stays to a lesser extent than the French). With some knowledge, no doubt, of the Rowlandson or Gillray etchings or their analogues, a French cartoonist shows an elderly Milord hauling in his lady, dressed like himself in the style of fifteen years earlier (the stays are made to lace in front in order to reinforce the archaic effect). This is the earliest representation of a mechanical aid to lacing, which was to have a rich future in satire. By 1820, when tight-lacing was reviving on both sides of the channel, the "winch theme" (as we may term it) was used by William Heath in a caricature (Plate 18) which inspired several similar ones in England and on the Continent.[14]

The Progress of the Toilet, a (for Gillray) rather bland series probably executed after the designs of an amateur, is a stark reminder how quickly the busk returned, and in how formidable a degree, after the brief neo-classical interlude.[15] The word "progress" in the title of this three-plate set is ironic. It refers to the resemblance of actual under-wear (shift and stays) to outerwear, satirized as an immodest un- or under-dressed effect: the Empire style. The busk is the only solid part of the whole outfit.

The English tight-lacing caricatures, like so much caricature of the "Golden Age" generally, serve as a deflation of erotic charge. They use laughter to relieve sexual tension, as caricature tries to relieve social contradictions generally. The grotesque acts as a cover for anxiety and aggressive feeling around female sexuality. But grotesque erotic imagery of this kind, and bawdy caricature generally, also represented a *conscious* heightening, by aesthetic means, of erotic pleasure, in a way which was in the Victorian era to lose its sanction. As we have noted, it was virtually impossible for *Punch* to depict a corset on the body under any circumstances. In France, on the other hand, erotic imagery was never suppressed, and the need for violent graphic castigations in the Gillray-Rowlandson manner much less developed. French grotesque, as we shall see, is seldom as crude, although quite as aggressive in its more sophisticated way.

The Romantic Era: French Lithographs

As pre-eminence in caricature passed from the English to the French, the latter revived the old "winch theme" (e.g. Plate 19), and rendered it in new and even more fantastic variants, such as Le Poitevin's "diablerie" of a devil paring down the fashionable waist with a grinding-wheel.

But it was the sentimental lithograph rather than caricature which produced the most characteristic transformation of the Essai du Corset during the Romantic 1830s. Numa Bassaget, under the title "La Marchande du Corset", shows the corsetière (for by now women had taken over the trade) kneeling before her client in a humble veneration with which the (male) viewer is supposed to identify. The soft eroticism and the soft curve of the corset (now gusseted) are enhanced by the new soft medium of lithography.

Another, anonymous lithograph stands in the first instance (as the title indicates) as a straightforward advertisement for a newly patented system of instant unlacing, indispensible for those of fragile constitution; but setting, lighting and mood all indicate that the print was intended to have a broader aesthetic-erotic appeal. The lady's attitude with her back to the spectator may in this case be explained by the necessity of demonstrating how the lacing functions; but this rationale disappears as the erotic factor is strengthened. In a Vallou de Villeneuve lithograph the young lady appears to be struggling with the laces at the back, as if in mute appeal for our help. In Devéria the girl faces us, smiling in gentle invitation, holding the lace in her hand. In a Bassaget print she actually offers the lace to her beloved, who is seated opening his legs to receive her; the title "La Lune de Miel" (Honeymoon) leaves no doubt as to the symbolic significance of this nuptial delacing. Two themes distinct in the eighteenth century, the Coucher de la Mariée and the Essai du Corset are thus merged. Finally, we have another anonymous, but exquisite lithograph (Plate 14) in which the ardent lover is actually engaged in the unlacing, like a medieval knight transforming the servile task into a peculiar sexual privilege. It was with a single stroke of the dagger that the Circassian bridegroom slashed the corset of his bride; the French romantic lover is all tender, trembling fingers as he unweaves the chastity belt.

In all these prints there is no suggestion that the corset does anything but veil, protect and repeat the naturally wasp-waisted form beneath. The persistence of the neo-classical aesthetic, as well as considerations of propriety, prevented the artist from representing *naked* forms of a romantic slenderness which violated all the canons of antiquity. Being both clothed and unclothed, the corseted woman was placed ambiguously between two contradictory aesthetic realms: that of classical sculpture and that of the fashion-plate. But the romantic sense of irony welcomed this kind of ambiguity, and embraced the contradiction. The crass, moralistic juxtaposition of "natural" (classical) and artificial (modern) form, which first appeared in Soemmerring's, tract is wittily resolved by Octave Tassaert (Plate

15). The living goddess stands modestly with her back to us as she holds the tape to her breast, her arms in their puffed sleeves enhancing her romantically wasp-waisted and slope-shouldered contour. She hopes she will measure the same between the nipples (a critical dimension) as the marble goddess, whose thickness of waist is however no standard at all and is masked by the hands of the fully clothed woman. The dual code—fashionable and classical—is reconciled only in a momentary and fragmentary way. The artist, whom we may imagine concealed behind the canvas to the right, must choose between the two models: between his mistress and the Venus, between the living and the dead. The choice in favor of the former was not finally to be made and affirmed until the age of Baudelaire and Montaut.[16]

Realism: Daumier and Baudelaire

By mid-century the illusions of romanticism were giving way to attempts at penetration of unwelcome realities; artists sought the truth—that is, confronted their own disillusionment with the gaudy deceptions of fashion. The figure of woman bathing, for so long the pretext of erotic idealization, served to reveal a sense of the painful disparity between the perfect (corseted) social illusion, and the dowdy (uncorseted, bathing-suited) reality as shown in Daumier. The "natural undress" of the bathing-suit was perceived as a human and social degradant in its profoundest sense, which exposed (as Daumier shows in another lithograph) the ungainly waddle supposedly natural to the female of the species, held by the swimming instructor like a monkey on a chain.[17] There are many other cartoons by Daumier and his contemporaries which use the increasing popularity of swimming to debase the female form in its natural state.

In a more drastic spirit, a statuette by the caricatural sculptor Dantan shows the lady's crinoline cut away behind to reveal the sagging contours of her flesh.[18] The shocking revelation is akin to that of the old Vanitas transformation prints, in which one lifted the flap of a sumptuous skirt in order to disclose the skeleton beneath; the difference being that now the sight of degenerate human flesh is a sufficient reminder of human frailty and mortality, and that whereas the old transformation prints tended to pair woman with man, now it is woman who bears the brunt alone.

The skeleton of fashion summoned up the skeleton of Death, who by the immemorial tradition of the Danse Macabre, mocked Life as reality mocked illusion. "Danse Macabre" is the title of a sonnet by Baudelaire from the *Fleurs du Mal* (1857) in which he describes a sculpture by Ernest Christophe[19] showing a skeleton dressed up for a ball: "Did you ever see a more slender waist on the dance-floor? O spell of the void, crazily bedizened! Some will call you a caricature, those whose drunken love of the flesh hides from them the unspeakable elegance of the human scaffolding." The Danse Macabre of morbid, artificial beauty casts its spell on other Baudelaire poems as well. The bones of the human skeleton are to the sensuous flesh as those of the corset and crinoline are to the sensuous stuffs of outer dress; both stand as profound symbols, reaching beneath the surface of the externally visible to an unwelcome truth, generating fascination and disgust. Clothing punishes guilty flesh, and in so doing provides an erotic frisson. The armature of fashionable dress is a brutal prison imposed on the body ("le corset brutal emprisonnant tes flancs").[20] From the depths of a profound desperation, racked by a sexual disgust directed at women in general as well as at himself, Baudelaire uses the manner in which the busk bruises the soft breast to epitomize the contradictory nature of woman as a cultivated, perverse, sado-masochistic, lethal illusion: " . . . pétrissant ses seins sur le fer de son busc, / (elle) laissait couler ces mots tout imprégnés de musc . . ." (kneading her breasts on the steel of her busk, she let flow these words impregnated with musk.) The virtuose rhyming of "musk" with "busk" is entirely characteristic of the poet, who loved to juxtapose the sharp and painfully tactile sensation with the intangible aromatic. A final image in this poem ("The Metamorphoses of the Vampire", one of the so-called "damned pieces" which ran foul of the censorship) summons up woman as demon, who devours man and destroys his illusions, metamorphosing from a splendid, ecstatic, living ("blood-filled") dummy, into a heap of old bones; and from breasts like soft cushions into a "wine-skin with gluey sides, all full of pus."

La Vie Parisienne

Some of Baudelaire's sense of sexual disgust, and his extreme moral and aesthetic polarities pass, albeit in an attenuated and trivialized form, into *La Vie Parisienne*. Baudelaire, like many other distinguished art-critics and literary figures of the period, contributed to this magazine,[21] which claimed to take social frivolities with scientific seriousness, and is as typical of French bourgeois society, in its very different way, as *Punch* is of English. Through the collaboration of men concerned with fashion, caricature and the more elegant social phenomena, *La Vie Parisienne* approached the toilette of woman as both social behavior and art form, to be criticized, interpreted, and enlarged into a "social physiology" of the toilette in the manner of

Balzac. *La Vie Parisienne* attempted, if not a *comédie humaine*, at least a kind of *comédie socio-érotique féminine*, of a subtle kind calculated to attract a female readership as well. The pretty, fussy, powdery draughtsmanship of Henri de Montaut, the principal fashion illustrator in the 1870s and 1880s, was admirably suited to catch the character, at once evanescent, capricious and trivial, of fashion—of woman—of a hedonistic society conceived to be in perpetual transformation. The clothes (the corset) made the woman: "the toilette is the preface of woman, sometimes the whole book" (1886, p. 54). And woman made society what it was: a changeable, fascinating, and exotic one with multiple masks, which, in the case of corsetry (with which it developed an extraordinary, symbiotic relationship) could hide what *La Vie Parisienne* saw as an often very ugly reality.

The magazine made no secret of its economic ties to the fashion industry and particular manufacturers. Its great and long-lasting affection for corsetry was manifested in innumerable editorial-commercial puffs, or "réclames racontées" as they were sometimes called, scattered at regular intervals throughout the magazine. There seems to have been a special editorial relationship with the high-class corsetière Madame Billard,[22] who became a rich source of professional secrets, trade jargon and social gossip. No metaphor was too extravagant, no hyperbole too absurd, to express the majesty of her creations; constantly, relentlessly permutated in style and content, the little puffs present a kind of cosmic mosaic, in language remarkably similar to that of the more pretentious fashion journals of our own day. Trite, purple and humorous (when not just plain silly) the puffs conceal a true anxiety about the aesthetic shortcomings of the flesh unadorned; like the embroidery on a corset, the linguistic hyperbole is designed to hide its true function, which is to sublimate the (male) sexual disgust aroused by the ugliness of the naked body—and the underlying assumption is that most female bodies are in their natural state, imperfect. Thus the corset is elevated as Mystery and Philosophy (the Sphinx with unfathomable secrets), Religion (Thy Kingdom come, Thy Will be done . . .), Art (sonnet, syntax, and, of course, sculpture[23]), and landscape. Madame Billard, landscape artist, "by means of undulations of the ground relieves the monotony of a desert plain; by judicious smoothing out, she improves terrain compromised by exuberances too rich. To align the hilltops, fill in the valleys, separate the little knolls by creating gulleys, prevent landslides etc. . .—this is child's play to the skilled corsetière . . . Corset country! What a world in miniature, what an enchanted land to explore, offering what fabulous excursions!"

The criticisms of this landscape from the "so-called explorers, armchair Livingstones," that is, the dress-reformers, are brushed aside as so much fuss about a thing of the past. It is with a gruesome relish that Madame Billard's eulogist contemplates the supposed barbarities of an earlier age, the tortures, the *géhenne*, the *carcere duro*, all now swept away by the "Billard Revolution". "Examining the other day a corset of the old school, I trembled as if I were confronted with an ancient instrument of torture. The brutal busk must have caused an agony equal to that of the *question*, when the torturer cracked the bones and lacerated the flesh of the victim."[24]

In such fanciful dramatizations, the puffs were simply projecting into the past the accusations of the present. The last citation appeared at the very moment when, far from becoming lighter and gentler, the corset was developing into a new and more powerful style known as the "cuirasse." This was the basis of the fashion of the mid and late '70s, the "cuirasse style," so-called after the manner in which the dress-bodice itself was shaped, cut, moulded, boned and even laced, an exterior corset duplicating the interior one. Fashion underwent a dramatic anatomical erotization: the immense skirts of the previous era suddenly shrank tight, and were further tied back around the knees, so as to expose, for the first time in living memory (arguably, in Western history) the natural hip and thigh contour. The swelling of the hips was enhanced by even tighter lacing of the waist, rendered possible by fortification of corset construction and busk. The aggressive silhouette was rendered more shrill yet by the use of new artificial dyes and glaring color contrasts, with excessively complicated ornamentation and swathing. Increased evening décolletage completed the erotic impact, and women were declared to "have reached the minimum of dress and the maximum of brass. The female bosom is less the subject of a revelation than the feature of an exposition."[25] Never had fashion seemed so strident and perverse. Fashion illustrators with a taste for the risqué like those of *La Vie Parisienne* responded with amusement and enthusiasm, but most critics were less tolerant. The effect was condemned as a burlesque of nature, and at the same time, shamefully reminiscent of nudity. The cuirasse style was not a dress, but "a sheath, which in its indiscreet revealings were only fit for the jealous walls of a harem" and in the same breath, it was likened to a whalebone coffin.

In a witty, observant, but angry essay the German philosopher F. T. Vischer marvelled at the effrontery of countrywomen who wore such a "whorish fashion" (for German ladies had, alas, picked up this typical French depravity), revealing, when seated, shameful "indentations and shadow-lines in the groin on both sides, converging towards the crotch."

La Vie Parisienne, meanwhile, was ecstatic about all this "fortified nudity," and rhapsodized over the very contradictoriness of the cuirasse style. "The constriction and immobilisation is accompanied by expansion. Everything is forced upwards, so as to form, as it were, an avalanche over an abyss. The legs are tightly clasped full length, woman is impeded, fettered . . . her knees touch, visibly . . . she has to sit down sideways, in an uncomfortable but not ungracious attitude. Beneath this sheath, undulations must be slow and soft, almost imperceptible." Far from losing her capacity to breathe, women seemed to increase it, and visibly: "One can see the whole body breathing; previously the eyes judged the movements of the heart by the breasts alone," her shape rendered more evident by the abandonment of the chemise and the development of shaped undergarments. Immobilized, "woman is obliged to observe herself."[26]

Sculptured and armored: woman was both naked statue and medieval knight, a "cuirassière" in a "costume-machine all armor-plating and padding, which makes people look for her weak points." By late 1877, however, one critic in *La Vie Parisienne* was tired of seeing woman perpetually "under arms," and decided that the wasp-waist (the term had recently lost its pejorative associations) had been pushed to an "ugly and crazy" extreme. Montaut himself described many cuirasses as little better than orthopedic appliances, the busks and steels of which pressed disagreeably into even the best-gloved hand of the male dancing partner, and "ploughed up the flesh, sometimes even leaving bloody traces." Anecdotes of tight-lacing abuses abounded: there was the politician's wife who missed an important state occasion because she fainted away before even leaving her home; and there were the socialites who either altogether stopped visiting friends in apartments located on upper stories, or else "manage the first floor, groan at the second, emit their death-rattle at the third, and expire at the fourth."[27]

Even the corsetière puffs are wont to cheerfully accept that the fashionable silhouette is bought at the expense of great discomfort. It is difficult to believe that the following actually figures in an advertisement for corsetry: "despite the constraint of her whalebone prison, and her shoes which are a torture to her, woman is becoming ever more perfect. The dream of the young girls today is for a wasp-waist of the Louis-Philippe era; and to gain this there is no torment they will not endure. They don't give a fig for what the doctors say."[28]

Assuming an aesthetic rather than moral stance towards the corset, *La Vie Parisienne* altogether ignored the dress-reform movement, which was also much less active in France than in England. The only bad corsets are the ugly ones, such as those of the English. These constitute an insult to the true function of any aspect of the toilette, which is seduction. In the course of a special feature on the corset in

London, this is described as "astonishing, improbable, it explains all. It does not exist; it is a single piece of coarse padded canvas, without form, without purpose, without forethought, without malice. It is a child's undervest. It explains the entire philosophy of the English-woman's toilette."[29] This description, which may derive from an English reform corset on exhibition somewhere, corresponds precisely to the French stereotype of English puritanism, and as such offered nothing new. The English corset had already been damned among comparable aesthetic disasters from other parts of Europe in a "review" of the corset section in the 1867 Exhibition (Pl. 30 and 31). Its anti-erotic effect was similar to that of Theophile Gautier's typical English governess, "as stiff as a stake, red as a lobster, tied up in the longest of corsets, the mere sight of which was enough to put love to flight."[30]

A *Vie Parisienne* reader signing A. B. de C sprang instantly to the defense of the English corset and the English figure, on the basis of his experience with the huge English colony at Boulogne-sur-Mer—and in terms reminiscent of the *Englishwoman's Domestic Magazine* correspondence.[31] His long letter, appearing by special editorial privilege which did not normally extend to unsolicited correspondence, reiterated the English fetishist position in favor of tight-lacing as established in the *EDM*, down to the finer details of the "scientific" training methods.

The figure of the English girl came under renewed attack in the 1880s, when English "masculine" fashions were invading France. *La Vie Parisienne* and its artists denounced such styles as suited only to the thin, flat, wooden figures of the English, whose miraculously small waists (exceptionally low measurements were given) were to be regarded as an inherited ethnic defect.

Montaut's "Physiologies"

The full flavor of *La Vie Parisienne's* erotic ambivalence towards the corset, and woman, is conveyed in the centerspread illustrations of Henri de Montaut. The loosely arranged centerspread was a device new to journalism, and well adapted to express the multiplicity and variety of a social "physiology." Like the *Playboy* centerfold today, it was the "clou" of the magazine to which the readers turned first, which they often preserved and which, when the subject was a really popular one (i.e. erotic), was also available printed on art paper and boxed in sets (Plates 29 and 32).

During the early years the centerspreads concentrated upon the formal dress worn at the Opera, balls, dinners, concerts, the races, etc. During the 1870s the accent was upon social occasions for bizarre or fancy dress, at the beach and on the floor of public dance halls. Then Montaut penetrated the social facade more deeply, looking beyond the beau monde to the demi-monde, from the ballroom to the boudoir, from outer to underclothing. The 1890s brought drawings of nudity and near-nudity and with the diminution of fetishistic analysis of underwear, the psychology of fashion ceased to be a major concern.

Underwear reached its apotheosis in a special series called *Etudes sur la Toilette*, which was so successful that Montaut immediately followed it up with a New Series.[32] He was stimulated by two external factors. First, there was the relaxation of the censorship laws in July of 1881, which he seems to have anticipated. Second, the fashion industry was making its first serious efforts, in the wake of the cuirasse period, to design underwear which was not merely functional but artistic in its own right, with a luxurious display of new materials, trimming and colors. The sky-blue corset worn by Manet's *Nana* (1877) carried an electric erotic charge which ran through the scandal it occasioned, as did the scarlet corset discarded by Gervex's *Rolla* (1878), in a painting less famous today but also very scandalous in its time, and also exquisitely rendered.[33] Manet's *Nana* was, so to speak, advance publicity for his friend Zola's *Nana*; and she, the vampire-goddess whose beauty of form and sexual power was, as Zola stresses, a gift of nature needing no artificial enhancement from corsetry, was imagined by the caricaturists encased in a cuirasse corset, heavier and tighter even than Manet's (Plate 52). It was at a moment of great public sensitivity in this matter that Montaut elaborated his "physiology" of underwear, with a richness and on a scale unrivalled before or since. In his approach to the corset, which clearly exerted a unique fascination on him, he manages to express both sympathy and hostility, erotic attraction and erotic repulsion, and in so doing, builds a kind of aestheticist bridge between the moral polarities of reformers and fetishists.

It was the contradiction between the armored cuirasse style and the vulnerability of the female body exposed, in its relative nudity, on the beaches of Trouville,[34] which prompted Montaut in 1876 to reflect upon the discrepancy between the social illusion and physical reality. Subjecting themselves to drastic transformations, from fat to slender and from thin to gracefully rounded, Montaut's bathers embody the Before and After, Inside and Outside adumbrated by Daumier and others in mid-century, but now contrasted in a manner both exaggerated and precise.

Then, penetrating the boudoir to reveal the secrets of this alchemy, Montaut shows, in turn, the varieties of corset employed to achieve such transformations, by different types of woman with different types of body. From the gross matron winched in à l'anglaise, to the young girl's mail-box; from the prude's medieval armor to the corset permitting instant unlacing (for the adultress, no doubt)—these and others surround the heroic lady of fashion in her desperate tug-of-war between stubborn flesh and social ambition, enlisting her whole household and a garland of sweating putti.

So much for the rude mechanics of the transformation. In his next centerspread, Montaut treats the corset as a richly nuanced instrument of the social ritual. There is the little girl longing for the true corset which will consecrate her maidenhood; the Old Beau trying to stay young (like the rubber-corsetted Baron Houlot in Balzac's *La Cousine Bette*); the "respectable" lady anxious to avoid the impression that she is compressing herself; and the "excessively respectable" i.e., prudish lady who affects a plain corset furnished with an "enormous, long, high, hard, penetrating busk." (There must be an ironic play here on busk-as-penis). The bridal corset, "more comfortable in the taking off than the wearing" (a dark hint here that matrimony is a social constraint to be shed as soon as possible) contrasts with the outright provocative (courtesan) corset, which is extravagantly ornamented and bejeweled, and "gives off an odor of Spanish leather which intensifies as the body warms up." Enthroned above all stands the classically poised, unclassically shaped figure of the truly ideal woman who needs no corset—having been endowed (as it would appear) by nature with the hourglass perfection her sisters have forcibly to strive for.

In his fourth and final corset centerspread Montaut unfolds the full extent of the frightful disparity between Nature and Ideal, which Fashion may try to conceal, but which the aesthetic of Naturalism (Zola was now the literary rage) must relentlessly scrutinize. No longer can the loose bathing-suit veil the defects of nature, which, gross as they already are, become even more repulsive still under the extravagant machinery devised to counter them. Where in his earlier analyses Montaut had balanced the "good" with the "bad," now all five body types are highly imperfect, and require in varying combinations and degrees, addition, subtraction, multiplication, division. The cures are always worse than the disease, and fact is allowed to fade into sadistic, misogynistic fantasy. To paraphrase the pitiless characterization: "The bony bottle-rack whose only projecting parts are her shoulder-blades, which are so sharp that they chafe her when she sleeps on her back, wears the Corset Venus de Milo with perfumed rubber breasts supported by steel springs placed at the back of the waist. If a caressing arm touches her, she begins automatically to palpitate and continues to do so until the pressure ceases. The back and hip are also graciously rounded off in rubber, and provided with dimples where necessary. Even the gloves are padded." Montaut concludes with heavy sarcasm: "the whole is singularly ideal and provocative." Other women, with the converse problem, apply machinery of prodigious ingenuity and strength against the pendulous and the plump, against natural disasters such as "a stairway of double-chins under the arms, in which the back appears to have taken the wrong floor" (Plates 28 and 31).

La Vie Parisienne, founded ostensibly as a celebration of Woman as High Priestess of Society, has stripped her of her mysteries, in order to reveal the "real" woman as Nature supposedly made her, and in order to expose in detail the process—alternately charming and amusing, and ugly and threatening—by which she is transformed into a socially acceptable object. Montaut, like Baudelaire before him and like many other writers and artists of the later 19th century (Guy de Maupassant is another example)[35] projected the structural state of social disease onto the body of woman.

We have now arrived at a transitional or fusionary stage between the negative and positive perceptions of the corset, between the reformers' and the fetishists' view. The reformers' hostility to and fear of the sexual transformation wrought by tight-lacing is usually couched in medical rationalizations. The sexual fear is turned by the French caricature-cum-fashion magazine in an aesthetic guise, and acquires in the process nuance, ambivalence, and a rich spectrum of feeling where morality co-mingles with aesthetics. But the 19th century can never see the corset purely as art-object, as Hogarth did. Giving full rein to his ambivalence, Montaut celebrates the corset as an artistic and erotic object in its own right, while at the same time seeking to set up a demarcation between his pleasure in the artistic and erotic corset, which envelopes and enhances without repressing the body beautiful, and his disgust at the "orthopedic" corset which is used in a violent and extreme way to conceal natural defects. This line of demarcation is however, highly fluid, which is what makes much of the fascination of the *Physiologies.* The fetishists will also, from their very different starting point, seek to demarcate between "healthy" and "aesthetic" tight-lacing and that which is harmful and ugly. But it is, above all, their acceptance and celebration of the sexual feeling induced by tight-lacing *in the wearer,* which is beyond Montaut's conception, and which marks an entirely new departure.

Notes

1. A longer version of this chapter appeared as an article in the *Woman as Sex Object* anthology, where the engravings referred to (including all of Montaut's) are excellently reproduced. Many are also in Libron. Beatrice Farwell's "Courbet's Baigneuses. . ." in the same anthology pp. 65–79, also sheds light on the evolution of the toilette scene in France.

2. Staymakers in France had recently (c. 1675) split from the guild of tailors to which they had traditionally belonged, to constitute a new one, calling themselves "tailleurs de corps de femmes et enfants" (tailors of stays for women and children). Staymaking, like tailoring generally, remained a male preserve; the couturières or female dressmakers, permitted to form a separate guild in 1675, were expressly forbidden to do anything to stays but embroider them. The Parlement recommended their admission to the craft on the grounds that some ladies did not care to be dressed by men, which suggests that staymakers were feared to be in the habit of taking liberties while fitting them ("in consideration of the fact that it was only decent and proper to the modesty of women and girls to permit them to be dressed by persons of their own sex, should they so prefer"—Léoty pp. 47–8).

3. One wonders whether there is any significance to the fact that the cane which should belong to the elderly gallant has been placed on the side of the staymaker. However this may be, it is probable that the lute, a traditional symbol of amorous harmony and here placed face down, signifies the older man's inaptitude for love.

4. The Abbé is the Superior of the Seminary at Annecy, where Jean-Jacques received instruction. The print illustrates the passage: "He sometimes visited mother who welcomed him, caressed him, teased him even, and sometimes had herself laced by him, to which task he lent himself willingly. While he was engaged in it, she would run around the room from one end to the other, doing this and that. Tugged by the lace, M. le Supérieur followed grumbling, saying all the while: But Madam, do stand still. It made quite a picturesque scene" (*Oeuvres* pp. 179–180).

5. The change also corresponds to the difference between nos. 2 and 4 in the *Analysis* diagram. It is also noteworthy that Hogarth added a prominent pair of stays in the *Before* and *After* engravings of 1736, missing from the paintings of 1731/2. Hogarth's best 18th century commentator, George Christoph Lichtenberg, has many amusing things to say on the possible range of symbolism of the stays in *Marriage A-la-mode* V (the duel scene), which is littered among other objects with "whalebone harness for hand-to-hand and distant fighting" (p. 133).

6. Burke ed., p. 66.

7. Antal, *Hogarth*, pl. 80, discussed p. 113. Antal suggests that Hogarth derived his design from that of Cochin described. If so, the English artist may have intended a kind of parody of the French engraving, exaggerating the slenderness of the woman and the clumsiness of the staymaker.

8. *Joseph Andrews* 1742, ch. XII.

9. *The World* for 13 December 1753, no. 50, p. 301. According to Paulson, *Hogarth*, II pp. 497–8, the author is the poet-essayist Richard Owen Cambridge. Paulson adds the nice observation "Here Hogarth has himself become the staymaker."

10. Cited by La Santé, p. 9.

11. *Tristram Shandy* (1760), 1843 ed., p. 108.

12. B.M. Sats: Four-poster: no. 5452; cobbler: 5464: smithy: 5444, reproduced Waugh, fig. 32; Collet: print 4552, reproduced Waugh, fig. 29. A fifth caricature from this period (datable to the 1770s by the enormous headdress, Gillham No. 27) is entitled "Tight-Lacing, or hold fast behind" and shows a young woman holding on to a four-poster bed, while her gallant has his foot braced against her rump and hauls on the lace which he has wrapped round a bone for better grip.

13. B. M. Sat. 6359A. For the slenderness of the Circassian dancer, cf. p. 297.

14. Cf. an illustration of c. 1825 reproduced in *Ueber Land und Meer* 1912, Nr. 15 (a similar, slightly bowdlerized design in Gec, *Donna*, p. 24); a very crude woodcut probably of earlier date, showing a woman being strapped into stays by men armed

with pincers, reproduced by Saint-Laurent, p. 106; "The Effects of General Emancipation. Mrs. Kentelo's new machine for winding up the ladies," 1833, an American print which I have not seen, mentioned by Weitenkampf; and "Madame Dona Urraca. . . Barcelona, Lluch", a print showing a man hauling on a big woman's corset with the aid of huge pincers (B. N. Estampes, *Images Populaires*—Espagne, Li 58 España t. III, "A.11004").

15. Gillray, *Works*, 570–2.

16. According to Newton pl. 5, caption, she is a candidate for employment as a model in a dressmaker's salon. Other prints of the period include one by N. Maurin, "Le Lacet" in which the girl stands admiring herself in a mirror, holding up a loop of lace not unlike a Diana stretching her bow, the lace continuing down in an immense length to the floor, where a cat is playing with it as if it were a ball of wool. In others the invitation to the spectator to unlace is conveyed by the wearer crooking her thumb into the lacing at the back, and holding up the loop with the other hand (e.g. Devéria's "Le Coucher" and "Le Corset", and Weber's "La Toilette"; cf. repr. in Vanier, p. 57). At the coarsest level, we find the kneeling attitude of the groom before the altar paralleled to the similar position he adopts a few hours later, with a lascivious smile, to unlace his smirking bride. A good collection of such prints may be found in the Paris Musée des Arts Decoratifs; reproductions in Libron and Grand-Carteret.

17. Delteil 1633 and 1642.

18. Reproduced Grand-Carteret, *Moeurs*, p. 347, fig. 217. Dantan may have taken the idea from Hogarth, who in *Taste in High Life* (engraved 1746) depicts on a painting on the wall the Venus de' Medici attired in a hoop cut away at the back.

19. *Art in Paris*, p. 212–3, and pl. 62.

20. "A Une Malabaraise". The mid-century was a period when tight-lacing appears to have relaxed somewhat, but it is noteworthy that Baudelaire's own graphic visualizations of women, especially his own creole mistress ("quaerens quem devoret"— seeking whom she may devour) are often wasp-waisted (cf. Crépet).

21. In a characteristic apparent contradiction, both with his own position established earlier in the *Fleurs du Mal* and with *La Vie Parisienne* itself, Baudelaire published there an article on facial cosmetics (1864, p. 235). He defined the role of "maquillage" as that of ennobling woman; *La Vie Parisienne* called the recently introduced fashion of face-painting a "filthy barbarity".

22. She was apparently an exclusive property of *La Vie Parisienne*, which remained wedded to her and her alone until 1882. She was then supplanted by Corsets Léoty. Ernest Léoty, son of the founder, was the author of the first historical monograph in French on the corset, and the owner of a fine collection of period garments.

23. Madame Billard's sculpture is compared with that of the ancients (the Parthenon, Phidias) as well as the moderns (Clésinger, Pradier). The academic Pradier would not have been flattered to be held up as a model for a corsetière, as the following anecdote testifies:

Alphonse Karr was invited by the sculptor to view the most beautiful model he, Pradier, had ever met. Karr agreed she was quite perfect. Suddenly Pradier contracted his brow. "Oh you wretch etc. etc." he cried, swearing volubly. The girl tried weakly to defend herself, having immediately understood the reason for the sculptor's sudden anger: "no, no, I assure you, Monsieur Pradier, you are making a mistake . . ." "A mistake, a mistake? You must be more stupid than—all I have just said. Do you imagine I can't tell . . ." Karr was stunned, unable to grasp the cause of all this fury. Pradier finally explained: "What a shame that such beautiful bodies are given to such foolish hussies! Like giving the plumage of a swan to a donkey who would go and dirty and trample it in the mud! No way of preventing them from wearing that abominable apparatus they call a corset! They want to be slender, to be held in the ten fingers of their lovers! And in order to be more slender, they dishonour their hips, they ruin their breast, they atrophy their belly! All that for some rogue, some dance-hall creep!" Pradier was seized again by a violent anger. He threw the model her clothes. "Go and dress, I don't want to see you again, get out!" (Treich).

24. 1874, p. 102.

25. Cunnington, *Perfect Lady*, p. 41.

26. 1875, p. 152; 1877, pp. 96 and 333; Cunnington, *Englishwoman's Clothing*, pp. 275 and 289.

27. Cuirassière: 1874, p. 713. "Ugly and crazy: 1877, p. 333. "Bloody traces" 1877, p. 78. Anecdotes: 1879, pp. 150–52, and *Salon de la Mode* 1879, pp. 14–15.

28. 1884, pp. 85 and 113.

29. 1874, p. 477.

30. *Militona*, 1847, p. 64.

31. 1874, p. 507. The letter in translated by Vernon in the *EDM* for November 1874.

32. The First Series started in the issue for December 18, 1880 (p. 746), and continued through to June 11 the following year (pp. 38, 109, 196, 286, 316, and 344). The subjects are, in turn, the chemise; the corset; *pantalons*, stockings and shoes; *décolletages*; stockings; "Dessus and Dessous" (appearance contrasted with reality); and *postiches* (bustles and bust-improvers). Such was the demand for this collection that a special edition consisting of a hundred drawings was printed on de luxe paper and sold in a satiné box for five francs. By 1892 this was in its 19th edition. Famous (or notorious— there is a shocked description of a Montaut underwear centerspread by a contemporary publication of 1881, cited by Roberts-Jones, p. 73), Montaut launched his Nouvelle Série from October 22, 1881 onwards, but the series stalled twice, either because the artist found he was repeating himself, or because he ran afoul of the censorship. This had probably objected to the fellatio symbolism of his centerspread on "How they (the ladies) eat asparagus" (1879, p. 330) and, even when relaxed, probably continued to harass him. Significantly, the naked body proved inadequate material for a social "physiology": an attempt to launch in 1896 a series of *Nouvelles Etudes sur le Corps de la Femme*, foundered almost immediately.

Beautifully colored drawings for or after Montaut's underwear centerspreads are preserved in the Metropolitan Museum, New York.

Montaut was imitated in Austria: cf. Köystrand, "Die Kunst sich anzukleiden", in *Wiener Caricaturen*, 22 June 1884 and Roland, "Boudoir Geheimnisse", ibid. 20 May 1888, both series more or less concerned with the "social physiology" of the corset; and there is also an imitation by Draner, "La Question du Corset", in *Le Charivari* 8 March 1888.

33. *Nana*, refused at the Salon, was exhibited in a shop window to such controversial effect that the police had to intervene. Gervex's painting was also rejected from the Salon and partly, at least, because of the prominence of the corset and petticoats in the foreground. It, too, was exhibited elsewhere with great success, with the critics picking on the underwear as particularly outrageous (this information comes from a paper read by Holly Clayson before the College Art Association meeting in New York, 1978). For a fashion manual recommending corsets in any color except dull, cf. Aincourt, 1883, p. 29.

34. Where the scales fell from the eyes of Flaubert as well: "What a hideous picture! And the feet! Red, thin, with bunions, corns, deformed by the boot, long as radishes or broad as paddles" (cited by Mespoulet, p. 40 f.)

35. "Women and girls with overdeveloped breasts and hips, rouge-plastered complexions, charcoal-daubed eyes, blood-red lips, laced up, strangled, rigged out in outrageous dresses, trailed the crying bad taste of their toilettes over the fresh green sward . . . ("Paul's Mistress", vol. II, p. 258).

CHAPTER SIX

The Fetishist Correspondence of the Victorian Era

The Role of the Victorian Magazine and its Correspondence Columns

The fetishist correspondence had no apparent effect upon established opinion except to exacerbate it and render tight-lacers more visible and vulnerable. Relegated to that marketplace for the exchange of trivia, the correspondence columns of a handful of family magazines, it was either ignored or discredited. Although these magazines enjoyed a mass distribution, the "letters to the editor" format put the writers at a tremendous disadvantage compared with their opponents, as can be vouched today by anyone who has tried, with a letter, to counter an editorial or article in a contemporary mass-circulation newspaper. Always condemned to argue from square one, seldom allowed the space to fully develop an argument or enlarge upon an experience, lacking the skills or support of professional writers, the fetishist correspondents would have been the first to regret the repetitious and monotonous character of their endeavours.

Editorial restrictions on space were the least of the inhibitions placed upon the fetishists. To varying degrees, but increasingly so as the century progressed, the writers became conscious of the sexual component of their addiction, to confess which laid them open to the charge of immorality.

When a woman speaks briefly of the "pleasure" or "delight" she experiences when tight-laced, we should, given the moral temper of the age, be surprised less at the limitations of her analysis than at her daring to assert her right to any kind of physical self-gratification. She also asserts an individualistic right. It is noteworthy that the fetishists never seek any general social sanction for their taste, never once citing the desire to be in fashion as its raison d'être, although they invariably welcome evidence that it is shared by others, and never question the right to display it in public. Having come out openly in print to defend their fetishism, some tight-lacers may have found it easier to brave the hostility of the wider social circles in which they moved; but neither the social display nor the literary defense were easy to maintain in the face of opinion which might be tolerant towards private and secret eccentricities, but which was quick to condemn any conceivably immoral form of public ostentation, especially on the part of women. We must also remember that tight-lacing was not the preserve of a relatively immune aristocratic minority, but the practice of middle-to-lower class groups bound by a more rigid moral code and under greater pressure to conform.

The Victorian family magazine is the last place one would expect to find sexually revealing confessions. Yet the monolithic image one has of such magazines as bastions of "Victorian morality" in the usual sense is demonstrably false, especially as regards the character of the most successful of them, *The Englishwoman's Domestic Magazine*. The *EDM* is typical, in its way, of the extraordinary growth of magazine culture, which, in alliance with the serial novel, transformed the Victorian social and literary scene. Selling up to 50,000 or even 100,000 copies per issue, with perhaps five or ten times as many readers, family magazines and serial stories cut clear across class-boundaries and acted as a kind of social cement. Their success depended upon the extent to which editor or author correctly judged common needs in their mass-audience.

Samuel Beeton, editor of the *EDM* and pioneer of the controversial correspondence column, like the successful serial novel writer (Charles Dickens is the obvious example), knew the importance of cultivating the good will and adjusting to the taste of his readers. What Thackeray said of the serial is also true of the correspondence column, for both promoted "communion between writer and public . . . something continual, confidential, something like personal affection"[1]—and a special kind of personal affection, one may add, peculiar to the correspondence columns, one not only between (professional) writer and public, but between individual members of the public otherwise unknown to each other. It was, clearly, in response to what he saw as a legitimate and wide-spread readership pressure, that Beeton decided to open the correspondence columns of his magazines to the other side of a question upon which Science and Morality were unequivocal and immoveable. He did not do this lightly;

as an editor, he was conscious of a particular responsibility towards readers who, being predominantly young and female, were to be regarded as vulnerable and impressionable. But their sex, their youth, their very innocence spoke in their favor; and if their immaturity prevent them from engaging in any but the most elementary form of self-analysis, it also permitted them the naive confession of habits which, harmless seeming to them, were interpreted by their elders and betters (and the editors of more conservative magazines) as foolish, wicked or both.

Beeton admitted the fetishist correspondence not in order to allow a bizarre sexual minority to flaunt themselves, but in order to relieve the silence imposed by conservatives upon a youthful, female viewpoint which commanded the sympathy of perhaps a majority of his largely female readership. Politically, Beeton was a radical; he became, even if he was not yet, a "flaming radical." It is evident that he was temperamentally inclined towards the controversial and a kind of sensationalism not lacking in commercial advantage. Just as his serializations of "scandalous" writers like Poe and Hawthorne boosted the circulation of the *EDM*, so did the fetishist correspondence. The fact that the publication of such material aroused the ire of conservative elements notoriously prejudiced against young women, confirmed Beeton in his conviction that his magazine was, more than ever, a bastion of freedom of thought.

The correspondence in the *EDM*, edited jointly by a young man and a young woman (Beeton's wife), was sustained jointly by young men and women. The latter were uppermost, and they knew that just as it was women who inevitably suffered the brunt of the dress reform campaign, so it was women who had most to gain in mounting a defense against it. In a battle ranging male physicians against the young of the opposite sex, the latter raised their voice, if not in the language, nevertheless in the context of feminism. The *EDM* was, cautiously and moderately, committed to Female Emancipation; and it is not merely by chronological accident that the fetishist correspondence runs parallel to, and to a degree both morally and physically integrated with, sympathetic discussion of Women's Rights.

It is necessary to incorporate some of the history of the magazines, and the context in which the fetishist correspondence penetrated. From slow beginnings, and through the back door as it were, rapidly collecting adherents, it developed from a trickle into a flood which forced the gates of editorial resistance, and ended up transforming the magazine altogether. This is the pattern set in the *EDM*, and it is more or less repeated with more marked polarities, in the *Family Doctor*. Finally, in *London Life* of the 1920s and 1930s, the fetishist correspondents, within a few years of their first appearance, swamped the magazine, seized control altogether, and maintained it for many years. The magazines are characteristic of the ages which produced them: the *EDM* promoting the quieter domestic virtues, the *Family Doctor,* a generation later, more brash and vulgar, but still utilitarian; at the turn of the century a scattering of the new penny weeklies exploiting fetishistic, like other bizarre and scandalous social phenomena strictly for entertainment purposes. Finally, during the inter-war period, fetishism finds a permanent home in a magazine based on the now familiar escapist formula of film, fashion, sports and sex miscellany.

Over this long period, the character of the fetishist correspondence changes, according to the type of magazine, and the cultural temper of the age. The range of fetishes expands progressively, although tight-lacing remains dominant. Editorial tolerance increases, as does that of correspondents towards each other. Writers are more open about themselves, and more receptive to new ideas. Sexual inhibitions are shed, although never completely. The sense of the fetishist community grows more intense, especially in *London Life,* where the social isolation was surely felt most keenly of all.

The Queen

The first correspondence of an overtly fetishist character started in the principal English sporting magazine, *The Field.* This was aimed chiefly at men, although with its columns of miscellaneous "fashionable intelligence", it was also read by women. Soon after its founding in January 1853, *The Field* acquired correspondence upon a topic which was to have rich future in fetishist magazines down to our own day—the use and abuse of the spur by women riders,[2] a topic to be joined later by the high heel.

The first magazine to entertain tight-lacing correspondence was *The Queen, an Illustrated Journal and Review* which was born on 7 September, 1861, and appeared weekly at the price 6d.[3] It was announced as "the Ladies' equivalent of *The Field,*" but for the first six months showed little signs of "feminine" orientation, and contained no fashion news at all. Its immediate success, however, encouraged its enterprising proprietor, Samuel Beeton, to enlarge its scope. Assuming full editorial control, in conjunction with his wife Isabella, he engaged to produce the perfect *Ladies* journal, in which "the lords and masters (would) serve the ladies" by writing on feminine toilette and pastimes, in such a way as to retain masculine interest as well. To reassure the prudish Beeton placed the note "The *Queen* is edited by a lady" (presumably Isabella)[4] in capitals under the masthead. Apart from introducing regular features on dress, he pioneered another major change: the correspondence columns, for which he made the hyperbolic, tongue-in-cheek solicitation "a letter a day from each of the 20,000 readers of the *Queen* will be most heartily welcome."

The very first correspondence columns, headed "Confidences" so as to encourage intimate revelations, raised two potentially sensational subjects—dipsomania and tight-lacing. The former struck so raw a nerve that after a flurry of letters (mostly from victims, sympathizers and others who favored discussion of this supposedly "low-class" disease) Beeton had to order it closed, probably on outside pressure. Discussion of tight-lacing was initiated by Maria P. of Dublin (17 May 1862) who posed the ingenuous question, whether the redness and coldness of her small and well-shaped hands could possibly be caused by the tight-lacing to which she had been forcibly subjected at a fashionable Kensington School. To which came the expected, curt editorial response: of course. The letter failed in its purpose of initiating a general discussion, which did not develop until just over a year later.

Meanwhile, letters arrived on all sorts of topics relating to fashion, under the stimulus of provocative feature articles by Anson Hartley Turnour and Frank Buckland. The latter combined his interest in feminine toilette with his acknowledged expertise in natural history and anthropology. He reported with sad ambivalence on the "cruelty of fashion", which killed lovely monkeys to beautify fashionable furlovers; and praised with undisguised enthusiasm the effects of the "barbaric" ornaments—lip plugs, iron bracelets, etc., brought into England from Africa. Defender of the much-abused crinoline, devotee of feminine chaussure, Buckland's erotic sensibility towards fashion was evidently broad and frankly positive. But it did not extend to tight-lacing, to combat which he had a plaster cast of the Venus de Milo clothed in a corset and exhibited in the Natural History Museum.

Anson Turnour wrote with warmth upon the various accessories of dress, especially riding costume (helping thereby to revive the spurring controversy, dormant since it had been abandoned in *The Field*), boots and gloves. She seems to have been a woman in her mid-thirties or older who welcomed the new developments in fashion, especially the new footwear—the tall, lace-up Balmoral boot, whose taller heel she urged to further heights. Her rhapsodies over the sensations of tight, incapacitating gloves prompted letters from a glove addict calling herself Mary Blackbraid who played the piano in her gloves (a not uncommon habit among the English) and described "an ungloved hand popping out of a cuff as indecent as a naked foot." The Bracelets and Earrings section of the Great Exhibition prompted Miss Turnour to the "barbaric" suggestion that "the exquisite ear-pendants would unquestionably be seen to greater advantage did they hang in full front view over the upper lip . . . trembling, rising, falling . . ."[5] A premonition of *London Life* here.

All this might be forgiven as mere eccentricity; far more disturbing was Anson Turnour's permissive attitude to tight-lacing, the correspondence on which was catalyzed on a letter from Constance (appendix, p. 301). Under the capitalized heading THE CORSET—THE SLENDER WAIST, Constance addresses to the readers at large (not just the editor, as was the custom) a charged question, couched in the casual tone of one inquiring after developments in the proportions of bonnets or shawls, whether one was to believe the rumors about long, slender waists returning to fashion; whether the size of the writer's waist, 16½ inches, was to be considered small; and whether there were readers possessed of a smaller measurement. The grave doubts she cast upon the competence of the medical profession, and the case she cites of a friend recently died at the age of eighty-six, who had been laced "cruelly tight" (down to 15 inches) when young, leave one in no doubt as to her attitude. The next week a reader called Fanny, writing at even greater length, assured Constance that her waist measure was "quite satisfactory," inquiry among fashionable corset-makers revealing that "many brilliant persons" possessed a waist equally small, and a few even smaller. Fanny goes on to relate her initiation into "the art and mystery of tight-lacing". This remarkable letter, innocent of all suggestion that she had been coerced like Maria P. of Dublin, was printed in a column adjoining that of Fashionable Intelligence, i.e., information concerning the movements of aristocracy and royalty, domestic and foreign, so that one may assume it to have fallen willy-nilly under the eye of the many thousands of *Queen* readers, dozens of whom participated in the ensuing controversy (see appendix, p. 301).

Expressed doubts as to the authenticity and sincerity of the letters soon evaporated, and in order to allay suspicion that (male) editorial prejudice was "fixing" the correspondence, Beeton reminded readers that the Confidences column, like all those relating to feminine matters, was edited by a lady. A debate, in the true sense of the word, was now well under way, with the effusions of Constance and Fanny countered by various anti-corset parties, headed by Frank Buckland, and including a person calling herself Firefly, who also wrote on various other, less controversial topics. Firefly cited some instances of voluntary but lethal or near-lethal tight-lacing; her own flirtations were fortunately foiled by a watchful mother.[6]

The pro-corset party called upon an exceedingly prestigious example—that of the beautiful Empress Elizabeth of Austria, reputed to possess the smallest waist ever seen. Together with her portrait, her girdle had been on view at the Great Exhibition. A query as to the exact length of this girdle was answered by Miss Turnour, who, when she visited the Exhibition, had seen the exhibitor hold it up in his hand, "so beautiful, purple velvet stiff with rich gold thread, looking like a dog-collar when clasped." Miss Turnour was even allowed to make a "frantic and futile effort" to close it round her own slender waist, and was enabled to certify the measurement to be exactly 16 inches; and the Empress was tall, 5 foot 6 inches (cf. appendix, p. 323).

The unspoken inference was, of course, that the Empress indulged in tight-lacing, which thereby acquired a social cachet otherwise totally lacking. Another kind of cachet, of a pseudo-historical kind, was found in the person of Catherine de' Medici, alleged to have imposed a standard 13 inch waist on the ladies at her famous (or infamous) 16th century French court (for this legend, cf. appendix p. 320). She is introduced, amid other historical matter, by a lady from Edinburgh, who from internal evidence was probably a corsetière, and a proponent of early childhood training (which was definitely not customary) as a means of obviating the necessity of tight-lacing as such. She enlarged upon the details of her program in *The Corset Defended*, which she published under the pseudonym Madame La Santé. This 31 page pamphlet, now extremely rare, is pleasantly written, and reasoned in its bias in favor of "gradual and moderate" lacing.

The fetishist viewpoint seemed well-launched. Meanwhile, the *Queen* promoted not only riding, but also other sports such as croquet, archery, fencing, skating and swimming. It is on the subject of bathing and bathing-costume that the journal disputes with that grave arbiter of morality, the *Times*, which had inveighed against the "grossly indecent" British habit of swimming in the buff (or almost so) at seaside resorts. In Britain, unlike France, the sexes were for practical purposes segregated from each other, and took advantage of the fact; *Queen* readers rush to the defense of those mermaids who sport among the waves, seemingly oblivious to the male binoculars trained upon them (one young lady archly inquires where she may find "a more substantial covering than seaweed and flowing locks"). The pleasures of walking, too, gave a correspondent the chance to mock the prudery of his age, and at the same time vent his enthusiasm for fancy petticoats, scarlet stockings, and "Polish boots, seven inches high, front-laced", very effective against the mud and "very nice on a good le-, ankle I mean."[7]

The high density point of fetishism was reached during the early years of the *Queen*, while it was still owned and edited by the Beetons. After the death of his wife and co-editor in 1865, Samuel found himself obliged to sell the magazine. While the pro-spur faction survived the changeover for a couple of years, and another, bigger book favorable to tight-lacing (William Lord's) received an enthusiastic review, the fetishism disappeared from sight, discouraged by the new editor, and/or diverted to another of Beeton's journals. By late 1868 the *Queen* had taken to reprinting from the American *Harper's Bazaar* completely conventional reformist opinion.[8]

Samuel Beeton's "Literary Picnic": The Englishwoman's Domestic Magazine

In 1852, the twenty-one year old Samuel Orchart Beeton brought off a significant publishing coup: the English edition of Harriet Beecher Stowe's *Uncle Tom's Cabin*. From the small fortune this work brought him, Beeton launched the monthly *Englishwoman's Domestic Magazine*. This was always to be the publisher's favorite, and has been recognized as a pioneering effort to meet the special needs of girls and young women.[9] (Its counterpart was his equally pioneering and lively *Boy's Own Magazine*). The aim of *EDM* was "the improvement of the intellect, the cultivation of the morals, and the cherishing of the domestic virtues." Emphasis on the latter, the management of the home, rather than the usual (upper-class) gossip and frivolities, was indeed unusual at this time, and is eloquent of the morality of the new, lower-middle classes thrown up by an already heavily industrialized Britain, which were just beginning to acquire a distinctive culture. The better to capture a youthful, broadly lower-to-middle class audience (as opposed to the higher class readership of the *Queen*), every effort was made to avoid the priggish and pedantic, and to adopt a tone (as Beeton put it) "of morality free from severity, and to blend amusement with instruction."

The magazine enjoyed an immediate and phenomenal success. At the very low price of twopence, by 1856 the circulation stood at 37,000; by 1863 at 60,000—more than *Punch*, the *Times* or Dickens' monthly parts. Like the *Queen*, it was edited jointly by Samuel and his wife Isabella, who provided the domestic and cookery notes which were eventually to be gathered together into the famous *Book of Household Management*. Innovations included the insertion of paper patterns, which must have done much to encourage home dressmaking, and finely engraved, hand-colored fashion-plates, as well as good black and white engravings. The serialized fiction tended to be provocative, including Nathaniel Hawthorne's *Scarlet Letter*, and Edgar Allan Poe's *Manuscript Found in a Bottle*, the kind of literature few mid-Victorian editors would have considered suitable for adolescent girls.

A much expanded New Series, launched in 1860, included correspondence inserted on the back page in small, double column type, under the heading "The Englishwoman's Conversazione." Here Beeton ran up encapsulated responses to some of the literally hundreds of letters pouring in every month. He saw himself in the role of the popular schoolmaster, and often adopted the bantering tone of one returning holiday essays to his pupils.

But the literary contributions which the editors undertook to appraise and consider for inclusion in the magazine presented a real problem. The following is typical of how Beeton handled it:

Lines on 'Autumn' are not without merit; but poetical seasoning has been overdone; there are autumn leaves shed every year on our editorial head enough to bury us. 'This Day a Year Ago' might be pathetic if we knew what it meant: we do not. A young lady of sixteen sends us 'A Sunbeam', and begs us to be lenient. We will, by saying nothing; but, at the same time, requesting her not to do it again . . . 'Song of the Sea-Nymphs', who reside 'down among the coral rocks', and occupy themselves in singing a 'Tra, la, la, la,' has also been kindly sent to us; but we do not believe in them . . . In conclusion, we have a few lines under the title of 'The End of it', but we fear it is not.

Such a tactic might amuse for a while, but soon became, as Beeton surely realized, tedious and discouraging. Subscriber participation was better stimulated by inviting the submission, not of bad verse, of which women's magazines were already all too full, but of unusual real-life experiences. Taking his cue, perhaps, from the tight-lacing correspondence which had just burgeoned in the *Queen*, Beeton printed in the paragraph next to the "literary criticism" cited above, a long extract (he had never before quoted a correspondent verbatim) from "eight closely-written pages on a subject of very serious importance, that of having one's poor ribs tortured into a fashionable figure." Orthodoxically, Beeton thereupon inveighed against Dame Fashion, and not for the first time, for he had already had occasion to reprimand one Seraphine for suggesting that her ("natural") 15¾ inch waist was a thing of beauty in itself.[10] If, in the *Queen*, Beeton had not visibly obtruded with his personal opinion on this matter, in the *EDM*, with its younger readership, his or Isabella's personal and "parental" opposition was overt.

The first signs of a change in editorial attitude occurred at the end of 1866 when, in the course of a series of illustrated articles on the Human Form Divine, waists come under consideration. A brief statement on the dangers of tight-lacing is accompanied by this curious modifier: "There may be a few cases where a woman is born with a small waist, or has induced it by tight dress, and still her internal organs seem unharmed . . ." This concession was probably the result of pressures from tight-lacers who were besieging the editorial offices, and to whom he now decided to give full rein. There is evidence that other magazines, too, were feeling this pressure.[11]

Among Beeton's aims, in promising as he did at this time, a fetishist "literary picnic," was to pep up circulation. His circumstances—personal and financial—had recently undergone a dramatic reversal. The loss of his wife (noted above) at the age of twenty-eight after the birth of a son, was a crushing and totally unexpected blow. In May the following year (1866) he suffered financial disaster through the failure of the famous banking house of Overend, Gurney & Co. In considerable straits to avoid bankruptcy himself, Beeton was obliged to dispose of the *Queen* altogether, and sell the copyrights on all his publications to the publishers Ward, Lock and Tyler, whose salaried advisor he became, taking one-sixth of the profits. Isabella was replaced, both as mother to Samuel's children and as co-editor of the *EDM*, by a Mrs. Matilda Browne.

Although the *EDM* was now only one-sixth his property, Beeton continued to direct much of his energies towards it. In November 1866, he appealed to the readers for suggestions and criticisms. The response was such that the editor was emboldened to expand its format from a total of thirty to fifty-six pages, and triple the Conversazione section from one small-print double-column page to three, and subsequently, even four or more. The correspondence, now dominated by the subject of tight-lacing, changes in tone and function: the letters, invariably printed verbatim and without editorial intervention, are no longer content to ask questions, but also proffer advice, state convictions, correct misapprehensions. The readers become a source of authority, to which the editor bows. His opposition to tight-lacing becomes token, and finally vanishes altogether. The fashion editress Silkworm (presumably Mrs. Browne), was willing to commend Thomson's "glove-fitting corset" as ideal for tight-lacing.[12] So permissive was her attitude that she was happily suspected of being a tight-lacer herself by readers who wrote in to inquire (in vain) as to the precise measurement of her own waist.

The new style of correspondence was announced as "a literary picnic—there is sure to be somebody with pickles, and somebody with sparkling champagne, and a 'wee drop' of cognac." Heady fare indeed, especially for adolescents. Three Warmhearted Sisters express unmitigated delight: "Your magazine has reached perfection, the subjects promised for our benefit and pleasure are such as we shall heartily enjoy." The enjoyment was not restricted to those with a prior sympathy for the fetishism, for there is ample evidence that the "tight-lacing controversy" drew many outsiders into a topic which had suddenly revealed a new dimension.

The correspondence on tight-lacing was catalyzed by a long letter (*Edinburgh Lady*, March 1867) which pretends to lament enforced tight-lacing at school. The pretense was immediately exposed by Staylace, who recognized the writer as "an advocate of the system she at first sight appears to condemn." In reply (May 1867) the Young Lady Herself, the supposed victim, enlarged upon her experiences, drawing the lesson that gradual and voluntary tight-lacing produces better results than and is to be preferred over the sudden and involuntary kind. Despite her initial sufferings, she herself now enjoys good health as well as a fine figure.

Writers soon developed that constant characteristic of fetishist correspondence, of conversing in the proper sense of the word: agreeing, arguing, begging to differ, building a special sense of community. They politely express gratitude to each other, and to the editor, for having opened his columns to this "instructive and important" and "all-absorbing" discussion, for allowing them to close ranks against the enemy, and to "rally to the banner now unfurled."[13]

An editorial veto upon further correspondence in November 1867 was overridden by the readership, reinforced now by males who averred they had taken out independent subscriptions purely on account of the Conversazione. In May the following year tight-lacing achieved the status of a big, handsomely bound monograph called *The Corset and the Crinoline*, an anthology of the best letters compiled by William Barry Lord (a naturalist and writer on shellfish, silkworms and minerals), who provided some historical notes indicating that throughout the ages, the woman of fashion had known the delights of tight-lacing in one form or another. Other equally abortive attempts were made by the editor to close the correspondence, and another effort was made to divert it into book form. *Figure Training*, or *Art the Handmaid of Nature* is another anthology culled from the *EDM* (these initials are credited with the authorship); to judge by its rarity today, this tract-like production was much less in demand than Lord's book, and its major point of interest (and access), apart from some amusing illustrations, is the fact that it is cited no less than twelve times in the big *Oxford English Dictionary*.

The serious press which deigned to notice Lord's shamelessly biased monograph was loftily contemptuous. A satirical weekly described it as "224 pages of vapid letterpress on a most paltry, uninteresting and contemptible subject . . . we recommend perusal of this work to no-one." Two weekly "heavies," the *Saturday Review* and the

Spectator used Lord's book as confirmation of a thesis they had always upheld, that women were incapable of "higher work." Here was the ultimate proof that women were frivolous, superficial, irrational, sheep-like creatures. (The hostile reaction of another influential journal, *Punch*, has been noted above).

The *Spectator*, avoiding mention of the title, author or publisher of the book, and sincerely appalled by its "thoroughgoing defence of tight-lacing in its ancient and wicked sense," gives lengthy extracts from the correspondence, which it is convinced is genuine. It also stresses, most significantly, the lower-class origin of the correspondents, betrayed by the fact they "use 'ladies' and 'gentlemen' for 'men' and 'women' when they want to mark sex, not grade." The *Spectator* is sure that educated taste does not admire small waists.[14] This review follows an article on the Girl of the Period two months earlier, which had condemned the new breed of aggressive, impudent, fun- and luxury-oriented, undomestic and unmaternal young woman, who imitated the demi-mondaine in her dress.

The true motivation of the conservative press, and its ruthless antifeminism (exacerbated by the temporary, and certainly mistaken, admission into the Conversazione of correspondence in favor of flogging adolescent girls—"respectable" conservatives preferred the flogging to be moral rather than physical) was scathingly exposed by Beeton on several occasions in the magazine. He recognized these "middle-aged arbiters of public morality" as the "grand maligners of women," as the "arch woman-baiters of the age," guilty of propagating the vicious and degrading "Girl of the Period" stereotype and scapegoating women for all the social corruptions of the day. The *Saturday Review* wanted, above all, to *silence* women, have them "do nothing, say nothing, hear nothing, write nothing, but be content to bear all, repress your wishes, and suffer in silence your wrongs." Beeton's spirited counterattack also involved a defence of the absolute and total authenticity of the correspondence, which many *EDM* readers, as well as other editors, were disposed to doubt.[15] Not only Beeton, but the readers themselves found the hostility of the press heavies a useful form of publicity; one reader at least wrote in to say he/she had been unhappily "falling into corpulence and indigestion" when he/she was "happily directed" to the *EDM* by the "derisive notice in *Punch*," and started to tight-lace.

The fetishist correspondence flourished, occupying down to 1873/74 perhaps a third of the total space allotted to the Conversazione. Repetitious as it certainly became, it was felt by young girls to be inherently more entertaining than housekeeping budgets, recipes for removing grease-stains from silk, and new techniques for teaching Latin grammar, other topics which were raised, momentarily. In 1876–77, when Beeton's health declined and his supervision of the magazine presumably slackened, fetishistic debate petered out and what the new editor applauded as a more "manly" attitude prevailed. At the time of Beeton's death (6 June 1877) and down to the moment two years later when the magazine expired altogether (to be absorbed into the *Illustrated Household Journal*), the Conversazione reverted to the conventional melange of domestic and social tips.

Did the decline in fetishist participation contribute to the decline of the magazine? Or was it the other way around? There can be little doubt that a "silent majority" among the readership condoned and perhaps even enjoyed the fetishist correspondence, despite its extremist elements. As a bored provincial testifies, the magazine was on this account alone a breath of fresh air compared with the tepid contents of most ladies magazines. The fetishist correspondence was regarded as a special property of the *EDM*, upon which one (unnamed, provincial) newspaper contemplated poaching, by soliciting similar letters through the column of the Conversazione itself. Beeton himself counselled a reader of another young ladies journal which he published, the *Young Englishwoman*, to offer her 14 inch waist to the *EDM*. And tight-lacers who, unable to penetrate their local newspaper through its correspondence columns, resorted to advertisements, gave a credit-line to the "house-organ": "Sophie. The correspondence in the EDM re-opened this month. Is the waist-band beautifully less?" "17½ inches, thanks to the EDM—Sophie."[16]

The *EDM* was remarkable not only for its fetishist correspondence. Among the larger issues discussed contemporaneously in the main body of the magazine as well as in the Conversazione, were Women's Rights, Female Suffrage, and the Married Women's Property Bills, all of which were defended by women who, conscious of the pervasive anti-feminism of the press, protested against the "slavery of silence" that men would impose upon them. The radical audacity of some of these letters may be judged from one which, deploring the rigid sex-segregation of schools and academic curricula, characterized that Sacred Cow of the English educational system, the Public Schools, as productive of "arrogance, licentiousness and barbarity . . . where slaves aspire to escape from slavery by imitating, as fast as they grow old enough, their masters' vices."

While the fetishists do not express themselves directly on the wider issues facing society, their opponents do. The anti-feminism of the *EDM* critics, both within and outside the Conversazione, tended to put even the tight-lacers, the espousers of that peculiar form of fashionable female "bondage", in a defensive and if not feminist, at least anti-anti-feminist position.

This is not to say that all opponents of tight-lacing were necessarily anti-feminist, or that all physicians who wrote against it were motivated by misogyny. Some well-known proponents of Women's Rights, such as Frances Power Cobbe, stated, briefly, their opposition. But the evidence is strong enough to indicate that the major social thrust of the polemic against tight-lacing was repressive of women generally, just as it was repressive of sexuality. Fear of sex and the Sex are branches of the same tree. The fetishists themselves, without openly declaring a feminist position, do reveal a consciousness that they are speaking out as women on a subject which only women can really understand, and upon which men would have them remain silent altogether.

The *EDM* Conversazione seems on so many levels to undermine the traditional concept of woman as a passive, domestic, child-rearing creature. Those who sought to preserve this concept detected some sinister link between female fetishistic exhibitionism and female political and cultural ambition. Thus a reader, deploring women's preoccupation with their figures, in the same breath admonishes them to stick to the "solid virtues" of domesticity, and to cease craving erudition and political power.[17] Such an attitude brackets two kinds of quest: for narcissistic-sexual and social-political power, both being subversive of the sacred domestic and maternal role.

Male Corseting: English Mechanic *and* Knowledge

In the course of the *EDM* correspondence several males had confessed to the wearing of ladies' stays; a few had vouchsafed lengthy autobiographical accounts. Further confessions appeared in two magazines devoted exclusively to male scientific-hobbyist interests, the *English Mechanic* and *Knowledge*. Both were edited by Richard Procter, a respected name in scientific publishing, who saw his magazines essentially as forums for the exchange of ideas among readers.

In 1873 and again in 1876 the *English Mechanic* printed a total of about thirty letters on corset-wearing, after former *EDM* correspondent Experience testified at some length how tight-lacing had cured his chronic indigestion. The ensuing correspondence was in favor of tight corsets, but chiefly from the point of view of improved health (they were claimed to cure corpulence, indigestion, tiredness and many other occupational diseases of the sedentary life). The pleasant internal sensations occasioned by the corset were cited as an added bonus. Aesthetic effect never enters into the matter since no gentleman, at this time, wanted to exhibit such a sign of effeminacy in public. Tight-lacing acquires, for the males, much the dimension of an athletic or endurance test. There is a great deal of discussion, natural to all-male magazines of this kind, of technical minutiae relating to construction, flexibility, strength, manner of lacing, etc., and unfortunately to the point that the psychology of it all, which is usually more interesting, is submerged in the mechanics. There are stated to be at least forty corsetiers in London specializing in a male clientèle, but it is invariably the expertise of the amateur wearer, rather than the professional maker, which informs the discussion. The editor gave Dr. W. H. Stone, who was "frightened, astounded and nauseated" by the evidence that so many men wore stays, a regular medical column in order to combat the tendency.

In *Knowledge*, from mid-1882 through early 1883, a body of about fifty letters on corsets was admitted. Discussion was this time initiated by a reformer, à propos the causes of consumption. The disease was rare in Turkey, according to one writer, because the Turks smoked, according to another because they abstained from alcohol, and according to a third (reformer-in-chief Lady Harberton), because Turkish ladies did not tight-lace. The ensuing debate was joined by both men and women, some of the latter associated with the new Rational Dress Society. They were strong on lung-capacity statistics (the new shibboleth among reformers, as we have noted), and triumphant tales of conversion to total staylessness. Editor Procter was even himself tempted to try the "tight-lacing cure" for his own corpulence, which he did manage to reduce thereby, only to find himself for the next three months dependent upon "that beast of a busk". While he remained unconvinced, an American colleague, editor of *Scientific American,* was sufficiently impressed by the *Knowledge* correspondence to conclude that tight-lacing was, indeed, probably safer than most anti-fat nostrums.[18]

One can readily accept that waist-compression should reduce corpulence by reducing appetite and making overeating uncomfortable; this may have been an unadmitted motive among ladies as well. One might argue that today, corsetting would be less dangerous than the ministrations of diet-drug and cigarette industries who grow fat upon young peoples' desire to be thin.

The Family Doctor 1885–1893

In the *English Mechanic* and *Knowledge* the corset correspondence was no more than a temporary diversion. In the *Family Doctor,* on the other hand, it came to dominate the magazine even more fully than it had the *EDM*. The *Family Doctor, or People's Medical Advisor,* declared itself a "journal devoted to the cure of all diseases, the preservation of life, bodily development, the laws of life, etc."[19] As a very cheap (one penny) weekly, it was aimed at a wide family readership and the kind of mild hypochondria which was characteristic of the middle classes.

From the very first issue the editor established an unequivocal pose of hostility which he maintained through a continuing series of editorials and articles. For the latter he engaged well-known authorities such as Lennox-Browne (an oral surgeon, author and ex-*Knowledge* correspondent) and Dr. J.M.W. Kitchen, who confessed, most significantly, to "almost uncontrollable emotion" on the subject of that "imperceptible murderer," the corset.[20]

On 20 February 1886, the *Family Doctor,* hitherto perfectly bland in its cover illustrations, was adorned with a sensational engraving (Plate 38). During the following three months no less than six cover graphics appeared dramatizing the internal havoc caused by tight-lacing. Covers depicted "the Female Waist at different Periods;" various forms and degrees of décolletage, back and front; Tight Boots and Deformed Feet; and High Heels and Deformed Feet (China and England). These were followed, as if in emulation of *La Vie Parisienne* a few years before, with covers on Garters and Suspenders, and the Ear and its Ornament (including examples worn by the "fair barbarians"—all of which, no doubt, helped to attain the boasted "larger circulation than all the Medical Magazines combined".[21] Some of the cover illustrations published subsequently were more macabre than erotic: (unfashionable) deformities, rupture appliances, extraction of teeth.

Although the editor maintained his overtly critical stance, he was surely counting on the erotic appeal of pretty young girls in their underwear (some of which were stated, moreover, to be drawn after photographs), and their eye-catching effects on railway station bookstands. Better this than the tedious anatomical diagrams of indented livers, etc. The fetishist correspondence, thus incited, continued unabated for the next six or seven years,[22] forcing out subjects of "lesser" interest such as alcoholism, and receiving every few months visual focus in some appropriate cover illustration. Meanwhile, protests of editorial innocence in the actual fomentation of the fetishist position became increasingly threadbare. By 1889 (21 Dec.), in fact, a moderate philo-fetishist correspondent had been promoted (in the company of a moderate reformer) to the status of feature writer.

Conducted as it was with a certain ruthlessness, the fetishist correspondence must have come as a severe shock to many Victorian sensibilities, even in an age when certain taboos were, since the *EDM* era, at last being relaxed. The *Girls Own Annual* recoiled in horror and, taking good care not to mention the peccant weekly by name, described it as "very dreadful to read". As indeed it was: in the tradition of first or "ice-breaking" letters, a "Victim to Fashion" had written to express stark regrets over her adolescent initiation, although she had enjoyed it at the time; an immediate (male) response was to express shameless delight at the suffering she had inflicted upon herself.[23]

In their greater candor and self-confidence, as well as in their immense numerical superiority, the fetishists were able to put the ever-vocal opposition on the defensive. The better known reformers such as Sir Frederick Treves, Ada Ballin, and Lady Harberton preserved a certain decorum, but other opponents sneered rudely at the "hoaxing", "rubbish-peddling" and even "insanity" of the fetishists. Veracity was indeed a problem, not least among the tight-lacers themselves, who were palpably embarrassed by their extremist-fantasy wing. But it was the male corset and high heel addicts, and those who demanded the right to cross-dress in public, who garnered the worst insults. The choleric reactions of the opposition, compared with the tolerance of the fetishists, moved Dr. Edward Haughton to pay tribute to the extraordinary good humor with which tight-lacers (male and female) bore the "almost incoherent spitefulness and vindictiveness of their assailants . . . corset-wearing seems to have some connection with the virtues of patience, self-control and even good temper."[24]

The tight-lacers' brave and insistent contention that their addiction afforded them the greatest physical pleasure was used as the ultimate proof of their immorally sensualist nature. The accusation seemed to carry all the more weight in that now there was less question of parentally or school-imposed figure-training, than of the conscious self-gratification of sexually precocious adolescent girls, and the shameless perverted exhibitionism of male transvestites.

"Society" Papers 1893–1900, Madame Dowding

The fetish correspondence which began to peter out of the *Family Doctor* around 1893, filtered into certain popular miscellanies of social and theatrical gossip and scandal euphemized as "fashionable intelligence". Two such papers were the penny weeklies *Titbits* and *Modern Society*. These made no pretensions to moral improvement, like the previous journals we have been dealing with, and were representative of a peculiar form of gossip journalism which developed at the end of the century, designed to appeal (also) to the lower classes.[25]

In *Titbits* the fetishism was released, yet again, by a story of enforced tight-lacing at school, which came with some embellishments so bizarre and improbable that the editor waxed righteously indignant at the imposition on his credulity, and demanded from the writer immediate corroboration, or retraction. A lady reporter sent to interview her (she had since become a corsetière and proud of her figure), was satisfied as to the truth of the story, and convinced the editor accordingly. Meanwhile an alarming appeal for rescue from bondage had come in from a milliner's assistant; here, as in most of the correspondence at this period, fact seems to shade off imperceptibly into fantasy.[26]

A third magazine, called *Society*,[27] older and a cut above the two aforementioned, appealed to a wealthier class. Having introduced extensive correspondence columns around this time, *Society* took its cue, editorially, from the scandalous subjects raised therein. Tight-lacing and transvestism became a preoccupation second only to that of flogging and "massage establishments". The subject of male corsetry, which became particularly prominent around 1894, was stimulated by illustrated advertisements (the first of their kind), placed by a corsetier specializing in the male market: E. Everett of 85 Great Portland Street. The tight-lacing correspondence, which reached a climax in 1899, contains a disproportionate amount of experience recounted at second hand, and lacks both novelty and conviction.

The principal interest of *Society* lies in the light it throws on the activities of Madame Rachel Dowding, Ladies Tailor and Corsetière, and Court Dressmaker, of Faraday House, 8 and 10 Charing Cross Road (just opposite the National Gallery). She advertised heavily between 1898 and 1900 (Plate 40) and was warmly clasped to the editorial bosom. Her clientèle was very brilliant; according to her huge advertisements (which at a double full page, tended to eclipse those of all others) she corseted fifty of the top female stage and society personalities[28] and many members of the best London military clubs, some of whom laced down to 20-21 inches.

Her advertisements printed testimonials from avowed tight-lacers such as H. Maud Grover, a "Society Beauty" (i.e., courtesan) of 26 Blenheim Road, St. John's Wood, grateful for her 15-inch Dowding corsets "even more comfortable than the last, 16-inch pair". The opposition viewpoint (otherwise missing) was introduced by the manufacturers of the Elastic Claxton Classical corset, which was recommended to those "ladies who despise the absurd and injurious wasp-waist of the dressmakers . . ." Madame Dowding retorted with further testimonials, this time from eminent physicians among her clientèle, and with an audacious "morality" pitch: the recipient, no doubt, of much confidential information, she averred that wives would be wise to indulge their husband's predilection, if only to prevent infidelity (i.e. consorting with tightly-laced courtesans.)

It was due to Madame Dowding that the article on corsets in the *Every Woman's Encyclopedia* acquired a fetishist bias. The only illustration is a Dowding creation "suitable for a young girl"; and it is on Madame Dowding's authority that the article confirms the prevalence of all kinds of tight-lacing excesses: punishment corsets, night corsets, extreme reductions, etc.[29]

Society was one of the first magazines to engage in public debate on the merits of birth control. Much in this, as in other controversial topics was censored, and the editorial policy which regretfully pruned "indelicate detail" surely also inhibited the fetishists from fully unburdening themselves. The last correspondence and the last Dowding advertisement appeared on June 30, 1900; a new proprietor took over, changing editor and policy. Immediately, *Society* physically began to dwindle, and soon expired altogether.

The fetishist view on tight-lacing also reached, during the 1890s, two little shilling handbooks of outwardly respectable appearance, published by regular firms. One of these, entitled *How to train the figure and attain perfection of form* (1896) is perfectly schizophrenic: one-half conventionally reformist, the other half purely fetishist, down to an appendix of correspondence[30] testifying to the strenuous efforts made by "*many* women" to reduce to an "absurdly impossible" limit in the region of 10 and 12 inches.

The ambivalence of another handbook, edited by Isobel of the *Home Notes* series, is less extreme, although no less visible. Tight-lacing is a "positive crime", although it is practiced with pleasure and impunity by admired society leaders and tennis champions; the 18-inch waist is both an "ideal minimum" and "absurdly small." Isobel also offers recipes for breast enlargement and eye make-up, approves of high heels, and pretends to caution that one may "hesitate to follow the lead of several 'Society' leaders, who to ensure good figures, shapely feet and hands, compel their daughters even to sleep in tight-laced stays, boots and gloves."

I have been unable to bridge the gap in fetishist correspondence between 1900 and 1909. In the latter year, the respectable society magazine *The Tatler*, shortly after having published a full page photograph of the actress Polaire over the caption "The Smallest Waist in the World" and a request for readers to send in rival photographs of themselves, printed among titbits of information about tight-lacers past and present,[31] the earliest example known to me of a published photograph of a private individual tight-lacer. This was Miss M— of

Kensington, evidently a real person, unretouched except for the face which was completely whited out. The *Tatler's* lead was followed by *Photobits*, founded in 1898 and self-described as "Up to Date, Bright, Sketchy, Smart, Witty, Pictorial, Pithy, Original, Spicy"—the last epithet justified by the emphasis, novel for the period, on cheese-cake: photographs and drawings of can-can dancers, music hall actresses, bathers and girl bicyclists. Repeating the question "Who has the smallest waist in the world," *Photobits* also answered Polaire and requested readers to send in rival photographs "to be reproduced in these pages to the eternal glory of British girls."[32]

A staff-member calling himself Amorist cracked the fetishist whip, and was able to print several photographs of private individuals (including a Russian lady who claimed there was much tight-lacing in St. Petersburg), all with their faces blanked out or altered, but otherwise surely authentic. Complaining that he was "drenched with letters," and being unable to print any of them (he did however do so later), Amorist promised to keep them in a special correspondence basket, a little pink corset set up under a glass shade in his study. The Christmas number (11 Dec.) celebrated Polaire once more, and the following week there appeared the first example known to me of a fetishistic (avowed) fiction serial, called Pearl of Piccadilly. This tells how a Prince searches for the owner of a thirteen inch crimson corset he chances upon (the formula becomes stereotypical)—which turns out to belong to a gentleman. A later serial was called "Adventures of a Wasp Waist." In the New Year of 1910 *Photobits* began to build up a great suspense for a special "Tiny Waists" number, which was followed by Second and Third Tiny Waist numbers. The Second Tiny Waist number starts a serial imagining a Corset Club, and carries the proposal of a reader from Eastbourne called Pullet Tite to found a Minoan League (complete with Draft Constitution), to encourage male tight-lacing.[33] Meanwhile the magazine—photographs, draw-ings (Plate 65), cartoons, serials, letters, advertisements[34]—became thoroughly fetishized, running a broader and more bizarre spectrum of fetishes than any previous magazine, and in an editorially totally committed fashion—becoming thereby the true forerunner of *London Life*.

The fetishism tapers off in the Spring of 1912, and was not resur-rected despite more photographs of Polaire. An underlying anxiety is revealed in articles such as that entitled, with deliberate ambiguity, "The Vanishing? Waist", that tight-lacing even as it ensconced and cultified itself as never before in a popular magazine, was disappear-ing entirely from fashion. The only consolation was that the fashion heel was rising, and the fashion hemline with it.[35]

The Fetishist Experience:
"Tight-Lacing Schools"; Voluntary and Involuntary Lacing; Unaccountable and Delicious Sensations

In view of the fact that any opinion in favor of tight-lacing could be expected to elicit only sharp editorial reproof, one can understand the tactic adopted by the letter which triggered the *EDM* correspondence, pretending to condemn a practice which the writer really endorses. A story of enforced tight-lacing was the surest—if not the only—way of winning editorial sympathy. Enforced tight-lacing of young ladies certainly existed, as many fetishists regretfully admit, but its locus was the home rather than the school, where it could hardly have escaped for long the notice of a parent. As the headmistress of a large ladies' school in Edinburgh points out,[36] no mother would select a school with a reputation for figure-training unless she approved this part of the curriculum. The parent who did would normally rely on the girl's prior commitment, added to peer-group rivalry. The emphasis throughout the correspondence is upon voluntary participation as more effective, as well more humane than compulsion; upon the active, rather than the passive: "the young lady (in our school) though being tightened till she could scarcely breathe to speak, would urge the maid to pull the stays yet closer."[37]

Evidence for the existence of "figure-training schools" is sparse before the 1860s, when they appear to have increased in number. They were situated in Edinburgh, Kensington and certain fashionable resort towns, but more precise data is lacking.[38] It should be noted that the small boarding school was a preserve of the middle, rather than upper classes, who could afford to educate their daughters privately.

In 1887 Materfamilias, writing on behalf of her own and her friends' daughters, requested addresses of such schools, which she had hitherto been unable to trace; her impression was that they were rare and little known. Any names and addresses which may have resulted from this inquiry must have been communicated privately, for the editor would have done the schools in question a grave disservice in publicizing them at a time when private girls' schools were subject to investigation by official bodies and prying jouralists. They surely relied on the word getting around through the grapevine. An "upper-class French corsetière", interviewed for a *Family Doctor* cover-story, with a clientèle which included finishing schools, knew of "only three or four in which tight-lacing was anything like general, and only one where the ladies are actually encouraged in the practice, and that school lies out Brompton way." According to a letter very possibly from an alumna of this establishment, all were expected to tight-lace except "those who objected, or whose parents objected, or were delicate in health." Night-lacing was optional and some apparently preferred to sleep in corsets in order to save themselves the trouble of relacing in the morning, thus winning an extra half-hour in bed. The usual limit was 16 or 17 inches, measurements were recorded in a register like marks or grades for scholastic exercises, and further reductions were authorized only by way of exception. "Girls caught secretly tightening without permission of parent and/or principal beyond the limits laid down were punished by deprivation of their corsets for a week." All this is a far cry from the concept of the "punishment corset," which most fetishists abhorred, and does not seem to have existed in English schools, although it was apparently used in Scotland.[39]

It also appears that "tight-lacing crazes" were apt to infect pupils of ordinary schools where the principal was opposed to the practice; one such principal purified her establishment of toxic waist by obliging any pupil thus tainted to hide it under a loose dress, and refused to employ a small-waisted teacher.[40] A concentration of "figure-training schools" in Brighton presumably reflects the high incidence of girls' schools in that resort town. The French cartoonist Sahib repeatedly commented on the visibility of very wasp-waisted young girls on Brighton promenade. The *EDM* correspondence testifies to the reputation of certain Austrian schools for figure-training, but I have been unable to verify this from other sources.[41]

The *Family Doctor* correspondence refers to the number of schools in France, in and near Paris and on the Côte d'Azur, which is described as "the Paradise of small waists". It is not clear whether these schools were designed specially for the English, flocking in increasing numbers towards the end of the century to enjoy the climate of the Riviera. An English girl, writing from Roquebrune, offered to give addresses of several schools, including that of her own, which "although not positively what might be termed a tight-lacing one . . . (is) one where tight stays were the rule, not the exception. Girls were not forced to tight-lace unless their parents wished it . . . All extreme tight-lacers were required by the principal to loose their corsets once a week . . . and exercise regularly."[42]

The absolute authority accorded culturally to the Victorian pater-familias tended to sanction even the most peculiar forms of discipline. Among the fetishists the extreme disciplinarians are relatively few and chiefly male.[43] They are often men in charge of motherless daughters, who write in tones of military peremptoriness. The colonel returning from colonial service, shocked at the state of his daughter's figure despite his previous instructions to the school principal, demanded that "every means known to art be applied to produce the fashionable degree of attenuation." In this case we are assured that the neglected girl was anxious to submit, but there are evidently others for whom the concept of discipline connotes or demands resistance and punishment, and for whom the corset is "an instrument of correction" and of bondage. Most fetishists abhorred such misuse of their fetish, even (or especially) when it was proposed as a more humane and aesthetic alternative to whipping, and expressed disapproval of various other bondage devices which are now considered part of the stock-in-trade of sado-masochistic games (muffs, straps, steel belts and padlocks, then recommended as a means of preventing lace-cutting, but obviously appealing in themselves, and bearing a sinister and paradoxical similarity to anti-masturbation apparatus).

Such letters tend to be written coldly and flatly, deliberately stripped of all emotion. The male disciplinarians also disciplined their literary style, and to quite chilling effect:

It is satisfactory for those grown-up ladies who are halting between two decisions—to lace or not to lace—to know that by proper advice, assistance and treatment, their figures, however thick and unsightly, may be made to conform to the exigencies of the present fashion; but in order to effect his object thoroughly well, skill, experience and perseverance are necessary on the part of the operator, and obedience, submission, and endurance are demanded on the part of the patient.[44]

Expressed in such terms, the cooperation can hardly be described as one of equals, but other fetishists—a majority perhaps—depend on the active and voluntary participation of the initiand: "Never by authority, but always by encouragement," says Perserverance, insisting that the wearer should always have control over the lace, especially at night. "Encouragement . . . a little tact" are the words used by Nemo who relies on the "natural vanity" of the fifteen-year-old.[45] Given the climate of public hostility to the practice, stories of fathers or father-figures enforcing tight-lacing seem less credible than the contrary situation, fathers prohibiting it and corsets altogether. According to her autobiography, the very severe and authoritarian Calvinist father of Mary Livermore never allowed her to wear the fashionable costume, especially stays and low-necked dresses, which she coveted. When he discovered her wearing stays she had had made in secret, her father literally cut her out of them with his "huge sharp jack-knife" and cast the offending garment into the fire.

The best form of encouragement was the example of a member of the Victorian "extended family" which embraced mother, sisters, governess, personal maid, cousins and even school-friends. The Conversazione itself became a kind of extended family, and offered an "institutional" model which inspired one middle-aged lady to reduce her own waist from 37 to 24 inches (she kept a diary of her sensations during this feat, which she offered to the curious). Only then did she start training the figure of her fourteen-year-old. Several young ladies speak of their brother encouraging them to tight-lace; sometimes brother and sister(s) write collectively. One surmises that the brother may, on occasion, be a mask for a lover; one, described as "adored" and "insatiable", seems to have developed a more than fraternal passion for his "sister's" figure. "Brother" tenderly rewarded "sister" with dresses and riding-habits "which I'm afraid cost the waist another inch". Perseverance was always able to coax a new dress out of her husband by promising that it be made "small by degrees and beautifully less in the waist." She was a former lady's maid who tells how she, the servant, was perfected by the mistress, and how subsequently she "from pupil became teacher in the art, and educated the figure of an *ambitious* young lady"[46] (my stress; see appendix pp. 302–304).

It was the "crash lacing" on fully grown figures, rather than the early, gradual training, which generated the bulk of the correspondence. The most extreme and rapid reductions were achieved; Mignonette, who had been allowed through the absence of her parents in India to reach the "advanced" age of fourteen with a totally untrained figure, survived even the severest appliances and night-time corsetting "without inconvenience"; while for the young wife deciding, soon after marriage on discovering her husband's penchant, upon a drastic reduction (from 23 to 14 inches), the pain was at first "very great", before she began to enjoy the sensation. She closes on an elegiac note: "although I am now grown older and the fresh bloom of youth is gone from my cheek, still my figure remains the same, which is a charm age cannot rob me of."[47]

It was obviously safer for a wife to write in the spirit of obedience to the whim of a husband than for a young girl to boast of cultivating a tight-laced effect as a sexual attraction. But such boasting is not uncharacteristic, touched here with a charming ingenuousness: "With a close-fitting dress the bones of my (19 inch) corset, which I have made excessively stiff, display themselves so palpably as to convey the erroneous impression that I am a victim of tight-lacing, which I find a great attraction for all my male admirers." By the late 1880s it was not unusual for a wife to admit that she caught her husband with her waist, continues to tight-lace as the surest means of retaining his affection, and (unthinkable admission fifteen years earlier) that she enjoys her husband imitating her. An older couple, both in their fifties, who also share the fetish (he, corsetted at fourteen years in a "continental" school, still possessed of a 22-inch waist; she, two inches less), boast of their six healthy children, whom another writer rudely assumes must be congenital idiots.[48]

The self-analysis of the men who admire and encourage tight-lacing, although in no sense profound, is not devoid of important insight. Benedict (Oct. '67), who confesses himself "positively absurd" and "spell-bound" in his "excessive admiration", experienced a sense of *"obligation"* towards the tight-lacer, who achieved ends so enchanting that they happily dispelled consideration of means. The widower La Gêne (whose very pseudonym means discomfort), speaking of the "half-pleasure, half-pain" in which the niece he had personally trained professed to delight, was convinced that "half the charm of a small waist comes not in spite of but on account of its being tight-laced, and that the uneasiness caused by the excessive pressure of a perfect corset gives an additional grace to the walk and movements of a graceful girl" (appendix p. 304).

The frank admission that the discomfort or pain suffered by tight-lacers formed an integral part of the male pleasure is more typical of the *Family Doctor* than the *EDM*. In an extreme example, the writer who professed not to care "what agony a girl may be in, if her waist be small," had decided from experiments on her own person that such "agony" was always tolerable by virtue of its pleasure component. Such insights are comparatively rare, as is the overt admission of guilt feelings such as those of a correspondent who, having imbibed a taste for tight-lacing in the example of his mother, married without taking into account what he readily calls a "morbid taint". Observing one day her husband's fascination for a wasp-waisted stranger, the wife determined to start lacing, although she had passed thirty years of age. Now, fourteen years later, she measured 19 inches over her stays, and could lace in to 16; and she had never called a doctor all this time. The apparent success of the whole experience did not prevent the writer from unburdening himself of his moral dilemma: to a man, the immediate pleasures of a woman's tight-lacing are so great that they tend to override all other considerations, including those of the long term. "I am in this unfortunate position, that although I know it is not right, I am tempted to gratify my wish to see a small waist without counting the cost."[49]

The ladies who, in private conversation, admitted to Benedict that they deliberately tight-laced and experienced "pleasurable sensations" thereby, were soon committing themselves in writing to this effect. Laura vouchsafes that after a bout of further tightening, she "has never till now experienced (such) exquisite enjoyment". Others speak in terms of "the luxury of the delightful sensation" and the "delicious sensation of perfect-compression."

To the words "delicious" and "exquisite", the *Family Doctor* correspondence adds "exciting", "strange delight", and testimony that the feelings engendered by tight-lacing are somehow "unaccountable", beyond analysis. A Mother of Three Daughters expressed particular curiosity on this subject, and seems to have encouraged her children to articulate their feelings. "At fourteen, when first really tight-laced, my daughters used to describe the sensation as delicious, adding, 'I can't describe the sensation, however, mamma.' "[50]

For some, however, the sensations were unambiguously those of pain. A male, whose fetish grips him like an "incurable fever", flirts with the pain threshhold by lacing, from time to time, below his "normal" minimum of 17 inches "which makes me sick, and causes great pain." Beautiful Bride of Highgate tells how when she began to lace at fifteen, for months she suffered agony, with splitting headaches and indigestion. The next phase was the "sickening cut-in-two feeling; which gave way to a sort of general numbness, and after a year I grew to enjoy it, and can walk and dance with less fatigue when extra tight-laced."[51]

The dress-reformers claimed that tight-lacing caused digestive troubles; the tight-lacers claimed that it cured them. The ladies, while not admitting like the men that tight-lacing prevented them from overeating (considered the commonest cause of indigestion), found that eating less (and in one case, having been able to eliminate dinner altogether), their health had improved. For Irish Girl formal dinners offered a special opportunity to savor the pleasures of "proud contemplation of my comparatively broad expanse of shoulders and bust" at the same time as "the delicious feeling of tightness, compactness and smallness around the waist" which the process of eating and drinking, far from turning to discomfort, actually heightened. She also found that eating less, she improved the transparency of her skin (others testify to the latter side-effect, which was considered a great aesthetic advantage, and diametrically contradicted medical theory that tight-lacing caused red nose and hands).[52]

The *Family Doctor* correspondence throws increased emphasis upon the voluntary character of lacing among teenagers. A Mother of Four Daughters, having delayed serious corsetting until the age of fourteen, and having set the family standard at 16 inches, found that the eldest voluntarily reduced to 13 and the next eldest to 14. (These same daughters were also encouraged to wear very low necklines and very high heels at dances "because the men like it so"). An assistant to a corsetière testified that "at the ages of fourteen and fifteen upwards these girls seem positively to enjoy the sensation of tight-lacing. I have often seen young ladies of fifteen or sixteen drawn in by their own desire until they could hardly breathe." The writer adds sagaciously, "perhaps there are physiological reasons for this."[53]

A truly reckless exploit is recounted by a mother whose young daughter entered her room one morning, followed by her nurse muttering, "It's not of my doing, Miss Gracie would do it." The daughter cried out, "Mother, I've done it! I don't care now." She let the cloak which had been concealing her body fall, "and I saw . . . a form as if cut in two. Her waist seemed a mere pipe, and she told me it was only 11 inches. I was quite alarmed and ordered nurse to unlace her immediately." The feat had been provoked by a friend and rival appearing unexpectedly with a waist smaller than hers (14 inches); Gracie had practiced for half an hour a day for more than two weeks; "How she endured it I cannot conceive. I permitted her one visit to her rival thus laced, and forbade her ever to lace below 13 inches again."[54]

Other Fetishes: High Heel, Backboard, Collar, Stocks, Equine

HIGH HEELS AND SHORT SKIRTS

Our second major fashion-fetish, the high heel, is a matter of almost as continuous, if never so heated a discussion as tight-lacing. Although obviously closely related, running chronologically parallel and often combined in the same writer and same letter, the two fetishes do not attain that symbiosis which 20th century fetishism gives them. There is also a connection between the fetishisms of high heel wearing and spurring, discussion of the former following closely upon the latter, and sometimes merging with it. Despite obvious differences in function, the formal resemblance between the two kinds of foot attachment makes for some similarities in the discussion, with respect to length (in either case, directly proportionate to powers of stimulus), sharpness, mode of attachment to boot, and frequency and angle of application or wearing.

As with tight-lacing, high-heel wearing was claimed to be not only harmless, but positively beneficial to the health (alleviating backache and stooping, rendering walking less, not more tiring). And, as with tight-lacing, there were extremists. In the late 1860s correspondents set up a three-inch "standard" ("which looks very graceful when running") against the editorial (and orthodox) position that even a two-inch heel is an absurdity. By the 1880s, correspondents were claiming to feel comfortable in a 5 and 6-inch elevation; and men were increasingly demanding the right to appear in public in feminine footwear.

High heel fetishism flowed, in the '70s, into other forms of foot fetishism: bare feet and bare legs for younger children, and sandals for older ones—at least in summertime. (Sandals were also, ironically, favoured by some dress-reformers). The erotic appeal of bare feet is thinly disguised under rationalizations of health (cold developed from dampness accumulated in boots, which were the standard wear for children at all times).[55] The co-existence of high heel and sandal fetishism in the same pages, and even occasionally in the same person, may appear surprising in that the former seems designed to restrict, and the latter to liberate the foot; but they shared a common aim: to emphasize the instep arch which, all agreed, must also be freed from clumsy paraphernalia like rosettes, buckles and bows, with which fashion sought to afflict feminine chaussure. The sandal enthusiasts, women and men, warmed to the minutiae of the matter, debating the relative merits of elastic as opposed to ribbon ties, their width, color, number and placing, etc. And it is soon apparent that the purpose of sandals is not just to expose a prettily arched instep and a delicate turn of ankle, but the appealing fact of female calves as well. Sandals led to short skirts. The proponents of shorter skirts (including many mothers writing on behalf of their daughters) have wider aims in mind than one usually finds stated outright in fetishist correspondence at this time: the shorter skirts were for girls who had reached the age when they would normally come out (around sixteen), at a period when fashion dictated ankle-length skirts for twelve-year-olds. Children are turned into adults too quickly, was the feeling; let us use short skirts, says Minnie, to prolong precious childhood, with all the physical charms, moral innocence and psychological freedom associated with that happy state.

The shorter skirt was also an exercise in historical nostalgia, reviving a fashion of the early Victorian age, when (as Dickens shows so vividly)[56] sandal tying was a ritual comparable to that of less mentionable corset-lacing. With the frilly drawers which accompanied them, short skirts for adolescents were redolent of a more innocent and romantic age, that of the 1840s. The emphasis now, however, is aesthetic (erotic): Minnie enthuses over "brilliantly white stiffly starched fine linen trousers, rather narrow . . . (leading the eye down to) pretty feet in open work stockings and the daintiest little shoes of glittering patent leather, with narrow sandals."[57]

The question of trousers for ladies was engaged in the *EDM* a decade before it became a major controversy of fashion and the dress reform movement. Could it be that dress-reformer and fetishist might agree on the desirability of trousers? Hardly, for the garment's purpose and design could not be more different. Lady Harberton demanded the simplest kind of bifurcation purely for reasons of health and convenience. Minnie wanted for strictly "aesthetic" reasons to reveal the action of the feet and legs, with a form of underwear made visible.

The desire to put adolescents into clothing associated with children, and the corresponding impulse to see the clothing of children as erotic, attempts to resolve a well-known Victorian confusion around sexual maturation. The sexualized child enabled the Victorian adult to experience guilt-free sexual feeling; the infantilized adolescent (or adult) could have the same effect. Much of the argument around short skirts, drawers and sandals centers on this reciprocity.

These are not, however, sculptural fetishes, which work in a different way. Body-sculptural or postural devices, when applied to children, express the need for total control which lies at the heart of an educational ethic much older than the Victorian era. The 19th century was too conscious of the sexual function of the waist-compressive corset to apply it before adolescence, but there were other, analogous devices which had been applied, as an integral part of the educational system, within living memory—up to the 1840s.

BACKBOARD, COLLAR AND STOCKS

The *EDM* correspondence is scattered with references, growing eventually into lengthy letters, to shoulder-braces, backboards, collars and stocks. The relationship of these to tight-lacing is close enough and their function as postural-sculptural devices is real enough to justify at this point a chronological break and an excursus into the historic evidence for their use. At the time of the fetishist correspondence, shoulder (or chest-expanding) braces were commonly worn, with or without some form of stays, by the young as well as by older people of both sexes (as is still the case today). But these were mild devices compared with the devices of an earlier generation, notably the plank of wood, strapped or held by the elbows to the back, known as the backboard, an invention of 18th century dancing-masters. This was often used in conjunction with a collar, designed to keep the head up, and the stocks, designed to turn the feet out. All these devices fell into disuse during the early Victorian period, but backboards and collars could still be obtained from surgical instrument makers and staymakers.

In January 1872, a severe lady from Glasgow called Janet Macaulay wrote to recommend the backboard and hinged collar as a cure for stooping (proven good on her own daughters), and to wonder whether any elderly ladies might care to reminisce ("for curiosity's sake, not that I would advocate their use today") about any neck and spine-stretching machines to which they might have been subjected in their girlhood. While no such reminiscences were forthcoming, the Scottish lady's letter touched off an intermittent series of letters with an orthopedic tendency.

The later 18th and early 19th century invented a quantity of machines in which the strictly orthopedic purpose of straightening deviations of the spine mingled with aesthetic notions of the proper upright posture. A stooping back and drooping head were considered the very worst of childhood vices, a deformity to be corrected at all costs. The horror in which stooping was held may be judged from a passage in Dickens' *Pickwick Papers,* where the elderly Miss Rachael Wardle denigrates her two pretty nieces before her "beau," Mr. Tupman: "You were going to say that Isabella stoops—I know you were—you men are such observers. Well, so she does; it can't be denied; and certainly, if there is one thing more than another that makes a girl look ugly, it is stooping. I often tell her that when she gets a little older, she'll be quite frightful."[58]

Some fairly severe methods were used to correct or prevent stooping, and in some instances (such as those employing suspension) it is not clear whether one of the aims is not simply to render a short girl taller. After lambasting infant swaddling, stays, shoulder braces, backboards and "steel boddices" ("one of the most mischievous inventions of the stay-kind which ingenuity has yet devised . . . those made to lengthen and shorten (being) by far the most dangerous,") one physician turns to the neck-swing, which rocked the body out in a hanging position by means of a pulley and tackle: "Were this not so notoriously common in families and schools, it might be thought we were describing the torturing of the inquisition, rather than a method invented . . . for the improvement of the female figure, and as a remedy for deformities."[59] Sometimes weights were even attached to the feet.

Edward Burney's "Elegant Establishment for Young Ladies" shows suspension as the centerpiece of an elegant education; but, according to Pat Crown, the drawing is a highly wrought satire on a type of boarding school suspected by contemporaries of being little less than training grounds for courtesans, high-class brothels masquerading under the euphemism "Establishment" and "Academy." These schools blent the new so-called "callisthenic" exercises (including, here, dumbells as well as suspension), with conventional training in dance (including stocks and backboard) and the usual elegant artistic accomplishments.

Suspension served another purpose, which is almost a commonplace of 20th century fetishism, but may not have been customary at the time, the lacing bar: "A beam across the ceiling still bore, in my time, a large iron staple firmly fixed in the centre, from whence had dangled a hand-swing. On this swing my great aunts were wont to hang by the arms, to enable their maids to lace up their stays to greater advantage."[60]

Another physician came out vehemently against suspension, backboards and especially collars: "Of all the contrivances which have been invented to torture children and to produce or aggravate deformities, none can rank higher in mischievous severity than collars . . . so long a fashionable apparatus as to be considered by many as an indispensable part of a young lady's dress . . . instruments of this kind may be seen in abundance, at the shops of manufacturers of trusses . . . Sometimes a piece of sharp pointed steel is made use of, placed so immediately under the chin, that should the child attempt to bend its head or body in the least forwards, it must inevitably be wounded."[61]

A popular woman writer on the social role of her sex compares the modern schoolroom (of the 1830s) with the chambers of a "refined inquisition," with stocks for the fingers, and pulleys for the neck, and weights and engines of suspicious form and questionable purpose; in spite of all our vaunts of philanthropy, we might pass in future ages for the inventors of ingenious tortures."[62] "Stocks for the fingers" must have been designed to taper them, but I have been unable to discover information on this bizarre device.[63]

The use of the backboard in American schools is attested by a poem of Oliver Wendell Holmes,[64] in which the physical agony of female education is compounded with the moral agony of one who fails to achieve its purpose: marriage. The maiden aunt continued to "strain the aching clasp" around her virgin, tormented handspan waist, despite the fact that as a girl

> They braced my aunt against a board,
>   To make her straight and tall;
> They laced her up, they starved her down,
>   To make her light and small;
> They pinched her feet, they singed her hair,
> They screwed it up with pins;—
> O never mortal suffered more
>   In penance for her sins.

"Speak in French when you can't think of the English for a thing,—turn out your toes as you walk—and remember who you are," admonishes that stickler for etiquette, the Red Queen, as Alice sets off to become a Queen herself. It is unlikely that Alice's original or many of her contemporaries were being put in stocks at the time when *Through the Looking Glass* was published (1872).[65] *EDM* fetishists at this moment, in the anxiety they bring to the idea of a revival of the stocks, indicate how completely they had fallen into disuse. Admirer of Fair Sex wanted to improve the gait of young girls in his beloved sandals, short skirts and trousers. According to his description, stocks consisted of a wooden board supplied with grooves and V-shaped arms adjustable by means of pegs. The feet, placed in the grooves, could be turned out progressively, and to the desired extent (between 100 and 180 degrees).[66] Like the backboard, originally devised, in all probability, by dancing-masters in the 18th century, stocks came to be used also, with and without backboard, for sitting in during lessons.[67]

A surgeon writing in the 1840s says he does not know "whether that miserable invention, the stocks, is still in existence, but I well recollect the time when the poor girl had to stand (in them) for half an hour or an hour . . . a most unnecessary torture . . ."[68] The instrument was attacked in its heyday as well: "It seems that Nature is a delinquent worthy of the stocks; yet, strange to say, it is not nature, the supposed assaulter, but the young ladies, the assaulted, who actually suffer the disgrace of being set in the stocks."[69] But the girl herself might accept this, with other forms of spartan living, as a matter of course:

There was a private discipline of such undeviating strictness, carried with me by my excellent mother . . . It was the fashion then for children to wear iron collars round the neck, with backboards strapped over the shoulders. To one of these I was subjected from my sixth to my thirteenth year. I generally did all my lessons standing in stocks, with this same collar round my neck; it was put on in the morning, and seldom taken off till late in the evening; and it was Latin which I had to study! (. . . and before I was twelve I was obliged to translate fifty lines of Virgil every morning, standing in stocks, with my collar on.) At the same time I had the plainest possible food; dry bread and cold milk were my principal food, and I never sat on a chair in my mother's presence. And yet I was a very happy child, and when relieved from my collars I not unseldom manifested my delight by starting from our hall-door and taking a run for half a mile through the woods which adjoined our pleasure-grounds.[70]

EQUINE DISCIPLINES: SPUR, CURB AND BEARING-REIN

We have noted in the Introduction how the Victorians used the horse socially to express status and individually to release sexual frustration. Around mid-century a great increase in riding among middle-class women coincided with the first controversial correspondence on the subject. This was to prove very extensive indeed, and continue throughout the century in the company of other fetishistic correspondence. The fanaticism of these letters sometimes surpasses even that of the tight-lacers. The issues raised, which range from the use of spurs to that of the astride position for women, are a chapter in themselves, which we here can do no more than summarise. The controversy differs from those surrounding the human body-related fetishes in that the opposing sides tend to argue against each other more directly. This may be partly because both sides were able to write from first-hand experience, which was not—could not be—true of the tight-lacing controversy, which was conducted largely by men against women.

In the second half of the 19th century it was no longer possible to deny women altogether the right to ride. But the conservative male held out against ladies on the hunting-field, saw no reason for them to ride cross country, and generally resisted their infiltration of male sporting preserves. He condemned "sporting" and "showy" riding, and the female use of controls (especially spurs) which men took for granted, but which women had supposedly neither the strength nor the discretion to apply properly.

Those in favor of women's right to hunt and wear spurs argued from several standpoints—health, practicality (safety) and aesthetics. As physical exercise, they despised tame walking and trotting in the Park on a docile (i.e., old or lazy) "ladies horse." On the hunting field or riding hard in the park, a woman needed, as a matter of safety, the basic controls over a vigorous mount. A whip was unladylike, clumsy and inefficient; a spur was both more feminine (because easy to apply and hidden from view) and more efficient. Finally (and most significant) it was considered elegant in a feminine and sporting way for a woman's horse to show a degree of animation which challenged the rider's ability to control it. Just how much animation and how much control, achieved by what means, became the major points of discussion, once the conservatives had dropped out of the race.

Opinion ranged from the moderates, who countenanced the occasional and light use of the spur and mild bitting, to those who liked to have the horse curvet and prance through the alternate application of spur and curb-bit: "provoking the caper that she seemed to chide". The extremists were those of a sadistic temperament who confessed to enjoying the sensation of spurring for its own sake, indulged themselves ruthlessly, and used the simultaneous application of spur and curb-bit to "send thrills of exultation through my body."[71]

Women of this type tended to see themselves as circus performers or horse-breakers, and found that their performance in the park, where aristocrats mingled with courtesans, was an irresistible attraction for certain men.[72] There was copious analysis of the relative merits of the single point versus the rowel spur; the precise length of point desirable (some countenanced up to a full inch); how to prevent the spur from tangling with the habit; and from this, by an easy transition, to shorter skirts. Shorter skirts were recommended both for reasons of safety and convenience, and in order to reveal (when walking) the "pretty weaponry" on the heel and the chamois leather trousers worn beneath the habit. There was also much discussion of the comparative pleasures and uses of various spurring techniques, such as the continuous tickle as opposed to the occasional deep thrust.[73]

The press at large, meanwhile, took up another closely related aspect of equine discipline, which was also very controversial, although it did not relate in any overt way to female sex roles in particular. This was the bearing-rein, used on the fashionable carriage horse in order to force it to keep its head up, and encourage it to step high. The bearing-rein had been introduced during the dandy and Regency period,[74] but its use became wide-spread, acquired a severer form, and ran into vigorous opposition during the late '60s and '70s. It cannot be an entire coincidence that this was the very moment when the full flood of fetishist correspondence (including that on the spur, etc.) was unleashed in the *EDM*. It is, however, odd that the bearing-rein controversy was not incorporated there, so that (until pro-bearing-rein correspondence is found in some other magazine) we must judge the custom, so appealing to fetishists of a later age, from the statements of its opponents.

Various animal lovers wrote pamphlets against the excessive use of the bearing-rein, the best known being Edward Fordham Flower's *Bits and Bearing-reins*, 1875. The agitation eventually succeeded in limiting their use on draught horses of the vulgar, but not on the carriage horses of the fashionable. The R.S.P.C.A., itself an upper-class institution, pronounced itself powerless (was in fact, unwilling) to restrain an abuse so prevalent among the gentry. It was, moreover, the coachman who generally took the blame (Flower encouraged humanitarians to bring lawsuits against them), although *Black Beauty* (1878) indicts the owner (in Anna Sewell's story, a beautiful, cold, aristocratic lady, against her coachman's advice), who insists on having the horses very tightly "borne up". About the same time "fast" young girls themselves began to drive, fast and recklessly, and with the help of the fearful gag-rein.[75]

The bearing-rein was sometimes used with a particularly severe form of bit known as the gag-bit which, as Flower put it, turned the discomfort of the ordinary bearing-rein into a "regular instrument of torture", the pain of which was forcefully rendered in the illustrations to his book. The gag-rein, which for structural reasons could never be relaxed even when the horse was at a standstill, came in a variety of forms, which later fetishist correspondence delighted to enlarge upon. Wide-spread use of the severer forms of bearing-rein declined in the 1890s. Certain prolific writers in *London Life*, however, combining nostalgic evocation of the fashionable excesses of the past with an expert knowledge of the secret cruelties of contemporary circuses, rodeos and cinema studios, have left detailed descriptions of the construction and effect of such exotic horrors as the brigadoon gag-rein or double-pulley bearing-rein, which was used with sharp-knobbed pear-gags and very high ported bits (the port is the up-standing U-shaped bar which gave great leverage on the most tender part of the mouth). Such bits caused the horse to froth at the mouth, which was considered "smart" and "exciting".

The connection between human and equine body-sculpture is occasionally explicit (later, in the 20th century, it became systematized in bondage games and fantasies). It is present in the analogies of the critics, who invited long-haired gentlemen or ladies to "form a better notion of the delights and utilities of the bearing-rein" by imagining "their back hair tied down to the small of their waists"[76] (cf. Plate 78). An even apter anthropomorphic analogy was made by a writer in the RSPCA journal: "In contemplating the half-helpless, wooden-looking beasts, one cannot help being reminded of our soldiers not many years ago, when they were compelled to wear high leather stocks round their necks, so that it was impossible for them to look at their toes or perform any kind of severe exertion without tumbling down in a faint or a fit of apoplexy."[77]

The explicit connection between equine and human body disciplines is made by certain male EDM correspondents who wanted to see the "severity" of woman's riding reflected in her costume (high-heeled boots, spurred thigh-boots, long gloves, stiff corset "all as tight as buckle or lace can make them"). It is not until the *Family Doctor* correspondence, however, that we encounter the ladies' own experience of the horse's movement enhancing her sensation of self-compression. Once a Governess writes of the "delightful sensation of feeling the horse spring under you when tight-laced. For complete enjoyment, the corset cannot be too tight, nor the spur too sharp." Another averred that constant spurring allied with extra tight-lacing provided her with an "exquisite sensation of pleasurable excitement."[78]

Equine fetishism differs from the others we have considered in that it is predicated upon a continuous interaction—almost an interlocking—of two living beings. It constitutes a paradigm of control not just over oneself alone, but over another being. The paradigm is both social and sexual. On the social level, it almost parodies and literalizes the hierarchical relationship in our society, where power rests entirely in the hands of the one, while the other is left no power at all, except that of rebellion, which may be punished by a display of yet more power. Fetishism incorporates structurally a state of rebellion—the horse against the spur or bit, the tight-lacer against the corset. The moral task, so to speak, of sculptural fetishism, is keep rebellion and restraint, as two sides of the same coin, in equilibrium or in a maximum state of tension short of breaking point.

We have argued that the rebellion/restraint of tight-lacing is not merely a masochistic reflection of socio-sexual subjection of woman by man, but a submissive-aggressive protest against that role. The sexualized and narcissistic form of that protest, and its sexually symbolic embodiment of social and spiritual stress (or distress) was calculated to take to a higher stage the dialectic of rebellion and repression, in a manner characteristic of social movements generally: under attack, but for long isolated and voiceless, the tight-lacers solidarized, found through the "radical" popular press a community and a voice; then, encountering intensified hostility for having done so, they re-asserted themselves, in word and deed, even more strongly, and so on, until changing conditions rendered this form of the struggle obsolete.

Although obsolete as a controversial social issue, the tight-lacing fetish nevertheless survived. As we shall now see, it did so in the face of the loss of the limited, popular social sanction it had long enjoyed, by celebrating its enforced privatization, by gathering other, more culturally relevant fetishes around it, and by becoming part of a broadly based sexual minority cult or congeries of cults, in which form it is still with us.

Notes

1. Cited by Johnson, *Dickens,* p. 69.

2. The correspondence, composed of about fifty letters from a dozen or so different writers, both men and women, for and against, lasted a little over two years (November 1853 to 1856). It is tinged with a passion, and often a sado-masochistic pleasure, which leaves no doubt as to its erotic content. There was no comparable correspondence on any other single topic.

3. The name was granted by Royal Privilege, and the proofs were shown to Queen Victoria, at her request (Quentin Crewe, p. 254). Was she a regular reader?

4. According to Hyde (p. 121) the *Queen* was edited by Frederick Greenwood, and the fashion articles were written by Mrs. Beeton. Regular fashion commentary from 1863 appeared over the name of Eliane de Marsy.

5. 1862, p. 330.

6. 1863, II, pp. 88 and 99.

7. La Santé letter: 1864, I, 145, transcribed by Lord, pp. 165–68; *Times,* 8 August 1864,

p. 12c; Polish boots: *Queen* 1863, II, 376. Madame La Santé's booklet is referred to in *Judy* 2 June 1875, pp. 63–4 as talking about slender waists "with pious enthusiasm."

8. Lord review, 2 May 1868; *Harper's* reprints: 1868, II, pp. 121 and 343.

9. Hyde, p. 45.

10. May 1862. Of two other early attempts to initiate tight-lacing correspondence, in which the original letters are not cited, one (April 1864) testifies that men (a brother in emulation of his sister, the writer) have taken to the practice.

11. *EDM* 1866, p. 272. In October 1866, the editor of *The Young Ladies Journal* had to set a "misguided" reader to rights on this subject; two months later she was commiserating with Lacee on the cruelty of her mother, and urging her simply to cut the laces. She adds, "We have had several letters from young ladies at fashionable boarding schools making the same complaint as you." The similar warning of 1 October 1892 (p. 222) could no doubt be duplicated by many others, in this and other ladies' journals of the period.

12. "Tight-lacers can please themselves by purchasing (them) five or six inches too small, for they will not give under even *their* pulling" (April 1870). In October that year she stresses that Thomson's corsets are provided with "extra holes . . . at the waist for extra lacing," adding mischievously, "but as I highly disapprove of tight-lacing, I will not say how much the waist can be compressed at will." The Thomson "corset gant" was launched in Paris 1868, and introduced into England the following year.

13. For several years no topic rivals that of the fetishes. In the course of 1867 there appeared about fifty letters, all on tight-lacing. In 1868 the number arose to around sixty, again all on tight-lacing. Over seventy different names of authors appear, most of them sympathetic. Thenceforth tight-lacing is joined by other fetishes: spurs and high heels; sandals, trousers, and shorter skirts for young ladies; and (towards the end) other "figure-training" devices such as stocks. By rough count (a precise one is rendered impossible by the fact that much correspondence on unrelated subjects touches more or less in passing on the fetishes)—there appeared during the period 1869–75 about fifty letters, some quite long, signed by about forty different names, on each of the two major fetishes, tight-lacing and footwear; and about forty letters from about twenty-five different correspondents on the subject of spurs.

14. "Vapid letterpress": *Tomahawk*, v. 3, 4 July 1868, p. 8, *Saturday Review* 23 May 1868, pp. 695–6. *Spectator* 23 May 1868 pp. 610–12. Girl of the Period: ibid. 14 March 1868 pp. 339–40.

15. *EDM* editorials, March 1869 and May 1869, p. 276. "Happily directed to *EDM*": E.M., June 1872. Doubts as to the authenticity of the correspondence were expressed by journals as far apart as the frivolous *London Society*, in the course of an otherwise favorable review of *The Corset and the Crinoline* (October 1869, pp. 312–19), and the grave *Daily Telegraph*. In our own times, costume authority Doris Langley Moore (p. 17) has deemed the whole corpus the fabrication of male sado-masochistic fantasy.

16. Poaching: *EDM*, Nov. 1870. Sophie: *Scotsman*, 9 and 11 Jan. 1868.

17. M.G., July 1872.

18. "Causes and Remedies for Corpulence," 4 November 1882, p. 289.

19. May's *British Press Guide*.

20. 1885, pp. 306 and 339.

21. May's *British Press Guide*.

22. During the first six-month period, corsets elicited about 40 letters printed, that is, more than all the other letters printed on whatever subject put together. The level settled at around 20–30 letters per six-month period down to early 1888, when other fetishes, notably high heels, and then earrings, began to establish themselves, followed at some distance by gloves, spurs and tattooing. The earring fetish generated correspondence on nose-piercing which, in turn, generated a few letters on breast-piercing.

According to an interim "State of the Controversy" summary (6 July 1889), from a total of 165 letters on tight-lacing there expressed themselves in favor: 45 ladies and 49 gentlemen; against: 32 ladies and 25 gentlemen. 5 ladies and 9 gentlemen remained neutral. Of those writers claiming to have had full experience of tight-lacing, 45 ladies and 20 gentlemen reported favorably, whereas only 7 ladies and 1 gentleman were unfavorable. These results, says the compiler (reader from Leeds), conform almost exactly with corresponding findings he has culled from the "public papers, 1860–70".

23. The *Girls Own Annual* (28 July 1888, pp. 697–8) had good reason to fear the intrusion of fetishists, having on several occasions had to deter "naively" inquiring readers (e.g. 1888, pp. 288 and 697–8). "Victim to Fashion": *Family Doctor*, 27 March 1886. I do not wish to suggest that this letter is insincere; indeed, there is much about it (the clumsy dual opening address, the attachment of an "irrelevant" inquiry about tennis dress, etc.) which speaks in favor of its strict authenticity. "Shameless delight": Lover of Stays, 22 May 1886, p. 179.

24. 15 Dec. 1888.

25. It is almost impossible to establish continuity of themes in the two magazines cited, for both are composed of brief paragraphs, separated by lines, without headings, laid out at random in uniform columns rather like pages of unclassified advertising. An impression of the contents can, in practical terms, only be gained by random dipping, which does, however, offer a surprisingly modern sense for amusing trivia. *Titbits*, founded by George Newnes in 1881, represents a milestone in the history of cheap journalism (cf. V. Neuburg, p. 231).

26. *Titbits*, 1894, pp. 63, 121 and 139.

27. Dealt with again by a system of intuitive dipping. The magazine, which should not be confused with others of the same name, is in the British Library in a mutilated copy at pressmark Cup. a. 10. In Willings' *Press Guide*, it claimed "an immense circulation" among the "Upper, Leisured and Middle Classes."

28. Including Nellie Farren (friend of the Princess of Wales), Kate Cutler, Kitty Carson, Madame Patti (!), Countess di Rossetti, the Duchess of Seremoneda, Mrs. and Miss Egbert (wife and daughter of the Lord Chancellor to the King of Norway), Miss Ethel Mortlake, the artist, Mrs. Corah Brown Potter (cf. p. 187), Ada Reeve and Gipsy Lee. The latter, a well-known clairvoyant of Brighton and protégée of the Princess of Wales, is the subject of an anecdote concerning her desire to render herself fit for the best London Society. Her oracle, consulted as to whether and how she should set about tight-lacing, had revealed to her Madame Dowding, who was now helping her make the necessary reductions.

A collection of period corsets amassed by Madame Dowding passed into the possession of the Charnaux Corset Company, now Charnos Stockings.

29. (c. 1900), p. 1830: "The Art of Wearing the Corset", by Mary Howarth.

30. In the British Library copy of the booklet, razored out early in the century.

31. Catherine de' Medici, "whose 13 inch corsets have been preserved" *(sic)*, the Duchess of Rutland, the Empress Elizabeth and two identifiable (or almost identifiable) contemporary examples: "the beautiful daughter of a well-known Irish baronet creating wonderment at the Dublin Horse Show by her waist of such marvelous slenderness (it was never over 14 inches) that people gaped aghast," and the "famous" waitress of a Viennese cafe (Bertha Kratz is the name given, later in *Photobits*), who had recently married her 12 inch waist to a rich habitué (17 Feb. 1909; photograph of Polaire 30 Dec. 1908, p. 357; photo of Miss M-- of Kensington, 13 Jan. 1909).

32. 29 May 1909.

33. Christmas number: 11 Dec. 1909. "Tiny Waists" numbers: 22 Jan., 14 May 1910 and 25 Feb. 1911.

34. Lawrence Lenton, personally remembered by fetishists living today ("he looked like Boris Karloff, and his workshop like Fagin's kitchen"), and then of Coventry, makes his first appearance as a specialist corsetier; Weingarten's"W.B." corsets, a north London firm, announced a Great Corset Demonstration, to show a positively 5 inch reduction could be achieved.

35. Polaire: 17 Aug. 1912. "Vanishing? Waist": 29 Oct. 1910.

36. *EDM*, June 1867, Lord, p. 177.

37. May 1867. Unless specified, the reference is either to the *EDM* (when the date is in the '60s and '70s) or the *Family Doctor* (when the date is in the '80s or '90s).

38. Inveterate Tight-lacer (Sep. 1867) refers to her experiences at a figure-training school a generation previous to the time of writing. This is exceptional, and among the various figure-training devices used in the school attended by Frances Power Cobbe (born 1822), corsets are conspicuous by their absence. A lady writing to *Society* in 1899

(p. 1810) cites, with reference to the *EDM* correspondence, a Miss K's Academy for Young Ladies in Tunbridge Wells, which she attended 1864–6 (the name of the governess was Mademoiselle Beauvoir, and the standard was 18 inches).

39. Materfamilias: 10 Dec. 1887. *Family Doctor,* 2 Nov. 1889. The Brompton School may be that referred to by another corsetière (interviewed 5 March 1887) where there were thirty pupils, none of whom had a waist over 19 inches, and several of whom were down to 14. Alumna letter: 15 Sep. 1888. A school in Glasgow is cited 19 March 1887; for the Edinburgh schools cited in the *EDM* correspondence, cf. p.

40. 10 Nov. 1888.

41. An American physician (Safford Blake, in Woolson, pp. 15–17) tells of her amazement at discovering that the broad, natural-looking waist of the Viennese female laborer was not what it seemed. Noting that the women do a great deal of manual labor in Austria because the men were always off fighting, she commends the practicality of their short, little more than knee-length skirts. "You can see at a glance that the broad peasant waist has never been crowded into corsets . . . but a fearful accident occurred in Vienna, while I was in the hospitals: a brick block of houses fell, killing and mangling several women who were employed in building them. 'Now,' I thought, as I entered the pathological room where a post-mortem examination was to be held on them, 'I shall once, at least, have an opportunity of seeing the internal organs of women normally adjusted.' To my utter astonishment, it was quite the reverse . . . in one case, the liver had been completely cut in two, and was only held together by a calloused bit of tissue. Some ribs overlapped each other; one had been forced to pierce the liver, and almost without exception that organ was displaced below the ribs, instead of being in line with them. The spleen, in some cases was much enlarged; in others, it was atrophied, and adherent to the peritoneal covering . . . the womb . . . was in every instance more or less removed from a normal position."

If it was indeed a custom among Austrian working-class women to tight-lace, they did so presumably in imitation of the middle classes. I know of no Austrian literary evidence, English style, of a fetishist cult.

42. Paris schools: there was one in the Rue de Rivoli as an alumna testifies (S. Gurney, 24 Dec. 1887); and another in Fontainebleau (near Paris) where the principal was tight-laced, according to a convincing circumstantial account from Lucy Greenwood in *London Life,* 11 Oct. 1939. Roquebrune writer: 23 Feb. 1889.

43. "Fierce aunts" and step-mothers are cited, but never natural mothers. An ancient mythological structure may be at work here. It was, for instance, a step-mother and older (presumably step-) sisters who tried to impose tight-lacing on Lover of Freedom (Oct. 1871) when she was thirteen years old. But her father intervened, and helped preserve her natural figure by sending her to a school run by a surgeon's wife; but he failed to prevent his older (step-) daughters from continuing to tight-lace.

44. Colonel: Aug. 1868. Chilling style: Jan. 1872.

45. Nemo: Jan. 1871.

46. 37 to 24 inches: Jan. 1872. Perseverance: July 1870 and Aug. 1868 (Appendix).

47. Jan. 1868, Lord. p. 168.

48. Male admirers: March 1871. Husband imitating: 11 Feb. 1888. "Congenital idiots": 12 June 1886.

49. Agony: 15 May 1886. "Morbid Taint:" 15 Sep. 1888.

50. Benedict: Nov. 1867. Laura: June 1870. "Luxury" and "delicious sensation:" Oct. 1868 and June 1870. Mother of Three: 13 Oct. 1888.

51. "great pain": 14 Feb. 1888. Highgate Bride: 25 Dec. 1886.

52. 18 Aug. 1888.

53. Mother of Four: 10 July 1886. Assistant to corsetière: 18 Aug. 1888.

54. 13 Oct. 1888.

55. Nudipes, July 1870.

56. "There was such a lacing of stays, and tying of sandals, and dressing of hair, as can never take place with a proper degree of bustle out of a boarding school" (*Sketches by Boz,* 1836, "The Dancing Academy").

57. Minnie, May 1873, etc.

58. Vol. I, 1837, p. 41.

59. *The Art of Beauty,* 1825, p. 38.

60. Cobbe, *Life,* Vol. I, p. 13. Since the author was born in 1822, the passage presumably relates to the later 18th century.

61. Dods, *Pathological Observations,* pp. 135-143. Backboards and collars seem to have survived better in France, where fashion journals frequently gave patterns for semi-orthopedic apparatus. *La Mode Française* as late as 1884 (p. 390) recommends as a cure for slouching an instrument consisting of a steel brace, backboard, stiff collar 3-4 cm wide, with "a holly branch at the throat to give a sharp reminder."

62. Sandford, p. 182. A comparable panoply of schoolroom machinery in the 1830s is conjured up in the *Life* of Frances Power Cobbe: "Deportment was strictly attended to: tortures innumerable were invented to improve the figure—there were steel backboards covered with red morocco, strapped to the waist by a belt; steel collars, stocks for the fingers, pulleys for the neck, and weights for the head." Cf. also Braddon, *Asphodel,* I, p. 144: " 'Think how I have been ground and polished and governessed and preached at, and backboarded,' (she said), drawing up her slim figure straight as an arrow, 'and dumb-belled, and fifth positioned, for so many years of my life.' "

63. If we can trust Bulwer (2nd. ed., 1654 p. 287), the Portuguese in the 17th century resorted to such devices: "In Portugal little long hands are in fashion and accounted a great beauty in women; wherefore they use Art to have them so, wrapping the hands of their female children from their infancy in cloths, and binding them straight in with fillets, whereby they constrain them to grow narrow, and to run out in length. An ingenious gentleman, a merchant . . . assures me that gentlewomen and ladies of Lisbon have for the most part such small hands, and that this tradition of their artifice is there generally acknowledged. Spanish women are noted to have the least hands in the world." Extraordinarily tapered fingers are depicted in many idealized 16th and 17th century paintings. According to Lola Montez (1858, p. 61) Spanish ladies used "devices (which) are not only painful, but exceedingly ridiculous . . . Some of them . . . sleep every night with their hands held up to the bedposts by pulleys, hoping by that means to render them pale and delicate." Sleeping in pomaded gloves to render the hands soft, also mentioned by Montez, was not uncommon in Europe.

64. "My Aunt" (1831), in *Poems* 1836.

65. Carroll directly instructed Harry Furniss, illustrator of *Sylvie and Bruno* (1889) to make Sylvia "as naked as possible—bare legs and feet we must have, at any rate. I so entirely detest that monstrous fashion high heels (and in fact have planned an attack on it in this very book), that I cannot allow my sweet little heroine to be victimized by it" (cited by Pearsall p. 351).

66. Oct. 1873.

67. The dancing-master Mereau in 1760 (p. 127) condemns the zeal of some colleagues who relied excessively on the stocks. Vieth in 1795, p. 83f, sees no use for them at all, except in the case of deformities, noting (as would any dance teacher today) that it turns out the legs at the ankles, and not at the knees and hips, as dancing technique requires. There was a (different?) device called the "hip-turner" (tourne-hanche), which is condemned by Noverre, xii, p. 296.

68. South, p. 329.

69. *Art of Beauty,* p. 46, citing Bampfield.

70. Sherwood, p. 34. The passage refers to the 1780s. For backboard and stocks as normal lesson-time wear cf. Haldane, *Record,* p. 45, and Kilner, *The Holiday Present* 1803, a children's chap-book where taking the feet out of the stocks while left alone in the schoolroom is cited as a cardinal example of disobedience, and a chain of terrible accidents ensues from a girl's trying hurriedly to get back into them on hearing her mother approach. This is the kind of disobedience which, as another example shows, could result in the girl's being left a hunchback cripple for life.

71. *Field,* 1854, p. 318.

72. Showy riding was associated with the "grande cocotte". Cf. the popular rhyme (quoted by Pearsall, p. 247; cf. also Pike, pp. 52-3):

> The pretty little horse-breakers
> Are breaking hearts like fun

For in Rotten Row they all must go
The whole hog or none.

73. Cf above, p. 27. The tickle, or continuous stroking with the spur point "so as to keep the animal in a continued state of irritation", was a technique of continental écuyères d'école (circus riders) taken for granted by even the humane Mrs. Alice Hayes (*Horsewoman*, p. 111).

The sexual symbolism here, and the formal analogy between spurring and coital techniques, becomes inescapable in a passage dating supposedly from the 1880s, and cited in *London Life:* "There are four methods (of spurring) used by the French. *Piqûre* consists of a very slight but continuous pricking. *Saccade* (or staccato) consists of a succession of light staccato thrusts in the same spot. *Attaque* is the most severe of all, consisting of a sudden and violent application of the spur by means of a sharp kick. It is used as a punishment, or in order to make a leap, or in order to provoke a spirited écart. The fourth method is *Pression*, which involves the insertion of the points and holding them in, so that even the quietest animal appears fiery. This is often used when the rider draws rein for a flirtatious conversation in the Bois, the horse appearing to fuss and to be impatient to be off, while the lady innocently caresses his neck with a daintily gloved hand."

74. It struck the French as an English peculiarity. Cf. "La Promenade en Bokei", a print of 1816 forming part of a series on English customs, showing the horse on so short a fixed rein that his long neck is vertical ("Caricatures historiques sur les Anglais" B.N. Tf. 60, p. 69). The analogy with the dandy cravat was made in 1818: (The dandy) "With head bridled up, like a four-in-hand leader, / And stays—devil's in them—too tight for a feeder . . ." (Brown, p. 24).

75. The *Queen*, 24 Oct. 1874.

76. Flower, 1875.

77. *The Animal World*, 1 March 1873, p. 37. *Life* magazine in 1892 used four times over the drawing of a bearing-rein on a man, "an ingenious device invented by the horse for adding to the comfort and beauty of man while exercising" (e.g. vol. 19, p. 5).

78. 26 July 1890.

CHAPTER SEVEN

Unfashionable Fetishism: The "Fetishist Family" of London Life 1923–1940

The major body of 20th century fetishist correspondence, and the last of its kind to be printed in a magazine of mass distribution, is that of *London Life*, and spans the better part of the inter-war period. The generation 1900 to 1930 witnessed a more radical transformation of women's fashion than had ever occurred in history within so short a period of time. The World War dealt a mortal blow not only to the old corset, but also to trailing skirts, a quantity of superfluous underclothing, outsize hats, and a host of other fashionable inconveniences. The flapper style of the '20s was loose and waistless; skirts rose to the knee, hair was bobbed to the ears, and girls jitterbugged their way to "freedom".

The new age certainly did offer the young middle-class woman a broad range of opportunities she had never enjoyed before, in education, employment, sport, and sexual relations. The new physical freedom and the new sexual permissiveness were, however, accompanied by new forms of psycho-social constraint. Feminism became dormant, or regressive after the First World War. It is true that sexology and psychoanalysis helped lift the taboo on discussion of all kinds of sexual matters, among the upper classes at any rate. But it also created a new spectrum and rigid parameters of sexual behavior which was stigmatized then as pathological and deviant, although today it is better termed merely "variant". The new sexual psychology induced in many people—fetishists and others—who would otherwise not have questioned their mental health, the fear that in fact they were psychosexually sick, and in need of medical treatment.

The Victorian tight-lacers had to defend themselves in the first instance against the accusation of courting physical disease; later

256

fetishists had to deal with the imputation that they were manifesting a sexual psychosis. They had to defend not just their fetishism, but their whole personality structure of which, as the new psychology taught them, their fetishism was an integral part. The hostility of the Victorian physicians had been overt, specific and (often enough) limited to the symptom itself. The repressive doctrine of the physician of the Freudian era was both more broad and more subtle. It demanded not just the elimination of a bad habit, but a reorientation of the personality, lumped fetishism together with severe psychoses, and treated the most extreme, pathological and even criminal cases as typical of the fetishist syndrome.

One should not be surprised to find in the fetishist correspondence virtually no reference to psychoanalysis and psychoanalytic concepts (even the word fetishism is avoided, "fads" and "kinks" being preferred), although the fetishists can hardly have been unaware of their existence. It is, one feels, in unconscious rejection of them, that a nurse who was also a starched linen fetishist, turned psychoanalysis upside down, by suggesting that her fetish was not a disease, but a cure.[1] The fetishists of a more sexually aware age could not take refuge in the rationalizations of the Victorians, that their addiction was solely motivated by concern for health and aesthetics. And while psychoanalysis and sexology left them in no doubt as to the sexual basis for their fetishism, this realization brought them into conflict with the taboos still prevailing in the mass media.

So the fetishists suffered from a threefold inhibition: that of fashion, psychoanalysis, and the mass media taboo. Not surprisingly, they retreated heavily into fantasy. Ensconced in a magazine which they virtually controlled, freed from editorial hostility, with a strong sense of group identity, they turned their fantasies into an autonomous cult. Fantasy was both escape from and affirmation of their fetishism. It manifests itself now as a literary alternative or equivalent to fetishist practice. In the correspondence columns it is admitted as a legitimate alternative to the real-life reports; and in the editorial section of the magazine, it becomes an "alternate reality" in itself, with some pretence at a literary genre. And, in the manner of any established literary genre, it assumes the right of blurring the distinction between its (purported) infrastructure, the real-life experience, and the imaginative superstructure. Since the cultural (fashionable) sanction for most kinds of fetishism had become tenuous, and in the case of tight-lacing, non-existent or negative, fetishist fantasy tended to withdraw from the here and now, and to locate in distant, "bizarre," non-Western cultures, and past ages. It was stimulated by popular anthropology, motifs and locales from which it incorporated.

When set in the mainstream culture, it acquired another kind of timelessness, that of the recent but imprecise and idealized past.

Reportage of real-life (or purportedly real-life) fetishist experience, denied reference point in contemporary fashion, seeks to connect with other, truly popular cultural forms: sport, dance, circus, and show business in general, all of which constitute the "normal" side of the magazine. The connection is fundamental, and deserves more exploration than we can undertake here. Fetishism is interpreted and practiced as a physical activity, unlike fashion, which is perceived as static and passively received. Fetishism is something you *do*, or play at, with someone else, is associated with all kinds of physical activity, some of them not obviously related. Fashion is merely something you *wear*, on your own, something which happens to you, rather than something which you make happen. Certain key concepts, already inherent in earlier correspondence, are emphasized in such a way as to reinforce the connection between fetishism on the one hand, and sport and physical spectacles on the other: training, competition, and "performance" in the sense of presenting oneself in a special role to a critical and (potentially) hostile or indifferent public. The idea of dress imposing extreme physical performance skills acted out in the everyday was incorporated into Baudelaire's philosophy of the dandy: "Discipline of impeccable toilet at every hour of the day and the night as of the most perilous feats of the sporting field, [is] no more than a system of gymnastics designed to fortify the will and discipline the soul."[2]

It is evident that London Lifers *worked* at their fetishism, and there is a sense in which fetishist practices, especially those involving corsets and high heels, constitute a sexually sublimated form of work. Despite its evident visual anti-work symbolism, tight-lacing was practiced, in its own bizarre way, as a form of labor: subjecting the body to physical stresses, usually endured for limited and socially specific periods, and demanding generally a strong constitution (contrary to the mythology, the constitutionally fragile did not—could not—tight-lace). It was a passive-aggressive, sexually exhibitionistic equivalent to the commoner form of work-sublimation, in sport. Even the tiresome mania for waist measurements irrespective of other qualifying dimensions, has its counterpart in the measurement of work which, in capitalist economics, is quantified rather than qualified. Fetishist, economic and sporting achievement is measured in statistical figures.

The extreme and deliberate unreality which clothes the fantasy writing conceals (or releases from) the greater tensions engendered by a higher consciousness of its sexual purpose. But there are also tensions of a political kind. The escapist and vicarious role of *London Life* becomes especially valued in the later '30s by readers complaining that the press at large is obsessed with fascism and the threat of war. The fetishist fantasy is certainly escapist; how far it represents vicarious experience for the writer as well as the reader, is another matter. The assumption that the degree of fantasy is inversely proportionate to that of the first-hand experience of the writer is untenable. But it is probable that as the primary literary vehicle for fetishism of the age, *London Life* often acted as a substitute for real-life experience, and the fetishist scenario often substituted for or predominated over real-life sexual interactions. It is surely significant that Will Granger, "arch fetishist" practitioner who was very active in the '30s, never once wrote to *London Life*, although he read it occasionally.

The very act of exchange between writer and reader became erotically charged, and writers sometimes tried to close the gap between the experience itself, and the writing about it: "As I write these words, I am being laced to an unbearable/exquisite degree . . ." Confident of a sympathetic audience, fantasists make visible the process of projecting their fantasy-self, or conjuring up from their readership the fantasy-other.

A happy marriage between fantasy and reportage appears to be lacking. One basic fetishist epistolary style, typical of males, is highly concrete and technical. It is designed to facilitate exchange of practical information, and belabors the mechanical minutiae and physical problems of fetishist practices. The constant rehash of information around the mechanical problems of easy fitting and release of a nose-stud tends to swamp occasional forays into the psychology of piercing. There is, generally speaking, a lack of overt humor, such as one might expect from a magazine with *Fun* among its fetishist forbears. Among the more successful light-hearted fictional applications of fetishism for the general audience, published by Herbert Jenkins who specialized in popular fiction (that of P.G. Wodehouse among others), are two novelettes, called *Wasp-waisted Arabella*, and *High-heeled Yvonne*, by John Bagley, which were also available through the Boots lending library. Here, fantasy blends pleasantly with a relaxed form of humor. Too much *London Life* fetishist fiction suffers from the usual repetitive patterns and adjectival reflexes of popular sentimental fiction, which are due, one suspects, to a lack not so much of literary ingenuity, as of basis in real-life experience. It is seldom (as far as I can judge) that the concrete experience is elevated by a truly imaginative impulse; or that the fantasy gains vivacity and credibility from the infusion of concrete experience. But it may also be that the fantasy, once imagined and publicized in the magazine, was later concretized in real life, as if acceptance of a letter for publication both gave permission to put it into practice, and guaranteed its feasibility.

The original *London Life* formula, which survived into the fetishist period in a diminished form, was that of a new major phenomenon of the mass culture: a cheaply priced, lavishly illustrated magazine composed of serialized fiction, show business gossip, cartoons, sport, women's fashion and some mild erotica (reproductions of art nudes, photographs of bathing beauties). In the advertising sections there was a preponderance of medical and sex-aid articles and literature, and birth-control devices. At the moment in 1923 when the fetishist penetration began, the magazine was priced at twopence and ran to sixteen pages. Three years later, when the fetishism had secured its hold through the absorption of other magazines and their editorial staff[3] it had grown to twice the size and three times the price. Throughout the '30s, when fetishism was completely dominant, the pages varied between thirty-two and fifty-four in number, and the price stayed at one shilling. In other words, fetishism and size were directly related.

With a weekly dosage of between three and six large quarto pages of four-column finely printed fetishist correspondence, with numerous articles of like tenor, and with the seasonal supplements and annuals, some of which were devoted exclusively to fetishist topics, all this continuing for about fifteen years—we have a volume of primary source material which may be estimated very roughly at over ten million words. It is likely that *London Life* was the only continuing openly available vehicle of its kind during the interwar period. The circulation figure in 1913 stood at 55,756, and later it must have risen much higher: in 1928 advertisements for *London Life* were placed on 1,000 cinema screens throughout Britain; a Bombay reader stated that he had never missed a copy, due to the fact that it was available on most railway bookstalls in India; in 1941, when the offices were bombed, 10,000 pounds worth of machinery—and all the files—were destroyed (at which one reader feigned not to be surprised, since "you are a military target of the first order, with your cheerfulness which does so much to overcome the discomforts of war.") The bombing, together with paper rationing, caused a sudden physical shrinkage of the magazine. Fetishism was excluded from what was left of it, and was not readmitted when it picked up again, presumably under new management, after the war. Never again was fetishism available in so pure and concentrated a form in a mass medium.

Fetishist infiltration began in the summer months of 1923, when increasing amounts of space were being devoted to ladies sports such as riding, swimming, gymnastics and dance. The discussion in which fetishism germinated makes the assumptions of a new age: that the fair sex is a sportswoman, physically active, and the competitor, in many areas, of man.

For a month or so heel heights are at issue; in November the first tight-lacing reminiscences appear ("Miseries of a Mannequin"). In the course of 1924 all the major and many minor (new) fetishes are introduced, and the correspondence section attains editorial autonomy. Within three years editor and reader have merged roles. Features written by readers "promoted" from the correspondence columns begin to proliferate, under such titles as "Recollections of a Corsetière", "Tales from the Barber's Chair", "Sins and Silk Stockings", "Love and Lingerie", "Rings for Authority", "Girl Ponies of Penang by a Malayan Rubber-Planter", "Seventeen Years of Love for Long Hair", "Globe-Trotter in Search of the Smallest Waist in the World", etc. Many or most of these are undisguised fiction. Meanwhile, the letters spilled over from the correspondence section at the back into just about any and every page. The fashion column called "Fashion Fads and Fancies" picked up the novel and bizarre tidbits from the regular fashion magazines, mixing public fashion with private fetishism, and casting the latter in the role of prophet without honor in its own time.

The pseudonyms which were required by editorial policy, and which conceal an incalculable number of participants, are sufficiently descriptive of the fetish spectrum: Barbarian, Bas de Soie, Bien Ganté, Bien Serré, Born Too Late, Busc Devant, Capeadora, Cap Cape, Buttonitis, Chinese Apple Blossom, Corsetiano por te Gusto, Creak-Lover, Diana, Hairpin, Happy One-Heel, Horsey Typist, Goggles, Glovely, Lady Godiva, Louis Quinze, Little White Wasp, Lens-Lover, Korduroy Kid, Human Eel, Modern Victorian, Much Bored, Maimed Merry and Married, Muddled about Mud, Macallure, Macamour, Pantalon Echancrure, Patent-Leather Kid, Rainbow, Rubberta, Stesroc, Taut Boy, Tommy Tight-lace, and Would-Be Eleven (inches).

These, and many others, see themselves as a family with diverse interests, united against the outside world which (in letters printed in their own magazine) angrily regarded them as "spineless puerile perverts" and "sex-starved fools". The fetishists treasured the vehicle which gave them an opportunity to air matters seldom discussed elsewhere. They treasure each other and their community. They admire, tease, caress, cajole, exhort. They are also critical, and watch out for impositions, technical errors, inconsistencies, and signs of intolerance. Like old friends or lovers, they complain of each other's silences, and excuse their own. They are nakedly contradictory, both fanatical and open-minded, solitary and sharing. They grow with and upon each other.

Their awareness that their particular fetishes are not those of all, and that theirs may be initially repugnant to others just as those of others may be initially repugnant to themselves, serves to expand psychological horizons. Without yielding an inch on the validity of their own rituals, they are at pains to learn about those of other sects. The bizarrest kink ever receives a sympathetic ear, although there is constant anxiety on the part of the smaller minorities that their voice is being drowned out by the majorities. The only major interest groups to suffer explicit editorial discrimination were the extreme sado-masochists, the flagellants, the bondage-and-torture addicts, and especially the paedo-fetishists (those who advocated the forcible discipline of children through corsets etc).

London Lifers, as they called themselves, ran a club open to anyone with an open mind. The discovery of *London Life* by the lonely fetishist could be highly therapeutic, and the cure for that "dread disease, mackintosh fever" (the phrase is couched half humorously, half fearfully) lay not with the psychiatrist, but in contact with a fellow-addict, preferably of the opposite sex. (Whether or not *London Life* ever facilitated personal introductions as well is not clear; the editors could hardly declare a policy of doing so). The magazine was the premises of a unique form of group therapy-by-correspondence, a means of self-revelation through the experience and advice of others; it offered a process of integration. Other popular magazines held up stars of sport and screen as models for the readers; *London Life* was more democratic, holding up as models to the readers, the readers themselves. Discovering that his abnormality was not unique, encouraged to manifest his fetish socially, the fetishist found release. The following is a typical sequence of self-discovery: "I shall always be grateful to London Life for my wife. It was through London Life that I first learned to love long hair [meaning, surely, to legitimate a pre-existent love]. I fell in love first with Madeline's long hair, and later I fell in love with her." And when an indifferent partner was the problem, *London Life* helped convert her. The magazine was both therapist and marriage counsellor.

London Life helped catalyze a dual release against two prohibitions: the deeply and unconsciously rooted prohibition against sex per se, which gave rise to the fetishism, and then the more consciously experienced prohibition against manifesting the fetishism. By helping raise the latter barrier, *London Life* paved the way for a raising of the first.

The magazine also became a fetish in itself, the object of a collection cult. By early 1939 a reader claimed to have amassed 8,500 column inches (or nearly 24 yards, or about half a million words) of correspondence on his favorite fetishes, methodically clipped and filed away in 34 Woolworth sixpenny looseleaf binders. Such files, and runs of the magazine are now extraordinarily valued.

Permissive as it was, editorial policy did not endorse all forms of public exhibitionism. For many years the only photographs to be printed were of high heel and boot wearers viewed from the back (thus hiding the face, but exposing the heel). Until 1934 the only snapshots were those taken in the home; later, the preferred locale was the busy urban street, in order to prove that the extreme heel height was indeed being worn in public. Photographs of tight-laced persons were extremely rare; so much so that the publication in 1940 of a full-page, full-length front view of a lady who came to be known as Magnificent Marianne, was hailed with delirious enthusiasm, as if an ancient and unnecessary taboo had at last been broken.

The editors cautioned generally against extreme public display, but to many such display was of the essence. There were disguises and compromises. The timid concealed a wasp-waist under a loose dress, or by wearing hip-pads to hide the indentation. Some hid in the street what they displayed in the dance-hall. One, afraid to expose her high heeled boots to the public gaze, attended dances wearing them under a long evening skirt "out of mischief". She would be amused by the innocent observation of her partner that she danced a little stiffly, and would drop a handkerchief in order to allow him to glimpse the boots as he stooped to pick it up. For one typist the secret of her tight-lacing came out when she was surprised by her boss resting her hand on her hip; another required a reputation for prudery because she was afraid of anyone touching her about the middle. The experts made it a point of honor to detect the symptoms of tight-lacing through the disguise. And those who, disqualified by age, poor looks or lack of motor coordination, brought the fetish into disrepute, were called to order.

The fetishist awaited his or her public début with a mixture of fear and pleasurable anticipation; its accomplishment provided a satisfaction both physical and moral. The girl who testified, "I felt so conspicuous when, for a wager, I first wore in public the 5¼-inch heels I normally wear only in private, walking in them in broad daylight from Marble Arch to Tottenham Court Road" regarded her feat as a "severe test of moral as well as physical courage." Fear of public ridicule was intense—and sometimes discovered to be unfounded, as it turned to a mixture of relief and disappointment when the public proved indifferent: "At first I suffered great agonies, so conscious was I of the white column of my neck; but I need not have worried; no one so much as looked twice at me." In this case, the "agonies" are part of the writer's own ambivalence towards the fetish object, for he continues: "At home, I trampled it (the collar) underfoot—before taking another tormentor from the drawer".

But to most, whatever the public reaction, the first exposure represented a triumph over self-consciousness, a new-found immunity from social censure in a wider sense. This was felt to be a major psychological function of fetishistic exhibitionism.

Anxious to escape from the idea of fetishism as a private obsession, and ever-conscious of its loss of social (fashionable) sanction, London Lifers sought to frame it within larger social groups. It was absurd to pretend that tight-lacing was still practiced in schools, so that tales of this kind are usually set in the pre-war period. But they are often elaborated into complex "tribal" rituals, involving many people. Fact here shades off into fiction, and one would be tempted to dismiss these tales as pure fantasy, but for their resemblance to better-documented contemporary sado-masochistic scenarios simulating "tribal" and "scholastic" rituals. A typical, if extreme, story from *London Life* recreates a kind of "rite of passage" or "coming-out" ceremony, at which the débutante would pass within a circle of senior girls, mistresses, governesses, and other interested parties (but not parents), it being the task and privilege of each person present to tighten the screw or lace by one fraction, until the desired limit was reached. This limit was defined either by the closure of the corset or belt, or the fainting away of the subject—unless her "seconds" could revive her quickly enough to allow her to resume. It was considered a social solecism to scream before passing out. Not a game, one hopes, which was enacted in reality.

Other rituals were modelled on sporting competition, complete with prizes and honors for the winner. One girl won a four mile walk in extreme heels with a time of one hour, forty minutes, including a fifteen minute rest at half-way point; another walked from the bottom to the top of Beachy Head in 6-inch heels which permitted 11-inch strides, and tight-laced as well ("plenty of climbers looked at me in astonishment"). Then there were contests organized like fairground sack-races, with gradual heightening and tightening, and a variety of shackles and hobbles.

In an increasingly technological age, *London Life* unfolds a panoply of mechanical aids, which, however, stop short of the regular bondage machinery and callisthenic tortures characteristic of the mid-century bondage magazines (cf. p. 291 below). As noted, editorial policy frowned on the more cruel and dangerous-sounding proposals. The ancient lacing bar, placed so that the corsettee could hang with her hands while her toes just touched the floor, was a commonplace; its utility in stretching the body and facilitating the lacing process is attested by fetishists today. A more drastic form of suspension was that from the laces themselves, fastened to the ceiling, with assistants holding the body horizontally, and allowing gravity, controlled, to do the work. (I have seen a modern fetishist raise a girl kneeling on all fours bodily from the floor by the laces; he assured me it was the most efficient means of extreme contraction).

London Life fetishists developed a concept of "training" akin to that of sport or circus, the acrobatic and horse-dressage elements from which were a constant feature of the magazine. Here lies another aspect of fetishist ritualism: the secret and arduous training for the public spectacle, in which the "art is to hide the art." Chaining the knees together taught the "hobble-skirt" walk (with and without high heels); severe constriction of the torso, shackling devices and the specially weighted "training shoes" (analogous to the placing of weights on horses' hooves to teach them to step high) caused when removed "amazing changes from great restraint to great freedom", "ethereal erectness of the body" and a "high-stepping tread almost that of the ballet-dancer on tip-toe, as light as thistledown." Fetishists turned to their own purposes the mechanical devices of stage dance schools, where pulleys were used to hoist the leg, and suspension from piano-wire was used to teach tip-toe work. The erotic appeal of acrobatic dance, female gymnastics and contortionism is evident in almost every issue of the magazine. Many readers practiced these arts as a hobby, combining them with their fetishes, and convincing themselves that an excessively tight belt facilitated the splits, and that corsetry boning was an advantage, rather than otherwise, to abdominal stretching exercises.

Walking was made into an acrobatic feat. High heel addicts pared down the base of the heel (the "standard" was a half-inch diameter, or half the narrowest available in the shops); they added deep rubber tips to increase the height and give a springy and insecure motion to the walk. Difficulties of balance were further enhanced by pitching the heel forwards, Louis Quinze style. Some even suggested fitting a dome-shaped tip to the heel-base, and/or a skate-like blade with a quarter-inch projection into the sole. The fetishist imagination was stimulated by certain circus and music-hall acts, such as those in which a girl walked a tightrope in six-inch pencil heels, or danced on a typewriter keyboard with an elongated and sharpened pointe, or (as Lola Menzeli did at the London Coliseum in 1926) performed new kinds of ballet turns in point shoes fitted with a foot-long heel.

The challenge of keeping the high heel stable induced a curious proprioceptive pleasure in imagining oneself viewed from the back: "Every time my foot touches the ground I think of my tall shining heels and poise myself to keep them always perfectly erect, perfectly in line with the seam of my stockings." (The straight stocking seam is almost a fetish in itself). Sometimes the sole arch behind the heel was polished mirror-smooth, so that it acted as a reflector.

A major development in footwear fetishism was the boot. This was, however, very expensive and had to be made to measure. The ready-to-wear fashion boots of the period, the so-called Russian and galosh boots, were despised for their looseness of fit at the ankle. The laced Vienna boot was better in this respect, but rarely rose to any height, either at the top or in the heel. Extreme fetish footwear was being made for London Lifers by the mid-twenties, but it was not until 1930 (26 April) that the first photograph appears—Swedish Lady (who was to become very popular) in crotch-length high-heeled lace-up boots.

The controversy raged: buttons or lacing. Some yearned for the old-fashioned button boot, but real compression could only be obtained by lacing, which tended to create problems of fit as the flesh was squeezed upwards. It seemed impossible to allow for this correctly when measuring. The lacing ritual could be enhanced and prolonged by close-placing and multiplying of the lace-holes. One reader announced that she had 58 holes on each side of a knee-high boot.

The high starched collar is a fetish oddly missing from the correspondence of the period when it was fashionable wear for men and women (1890s). It had passed its peak as an article of fashionable attire well before the First World War, and was worn only by a few conservative males in the 1930's. It may have been triggered as a topic of correspondence by the introduction of starched linen (notably cuffs) into haute couture by Elsa Schiaparelli in 1934. (She also precipitated zipper fetishism in the U.S. from 1937, but zippers were too little known in England to be become fetishized there at this time). Among the males who wrote on high collars, the two most prolific were also rubber mackintosh fetishists, and clearly homosexual. Various women, some of them nurses, wrote unusually extensive and authentic sounding accounts of their addiction, which was apparently developed and sustained independently of male interest. One nurse inherited from her mother, a matron, the fetish (which extended to starched table- and bed-linen), and a set of deep gauntlet cuffs with a three inch, custom-curved collar specially autographed by the Princess of Wales (Queen Alexandra), on the occasion when she came to open a new wing of the hospital and congratulated the matron on her appearance. It was a woman, Nurse Starched, who sings the loudest hymns of praise, under the heading "Renaissance of Starch": "Starch signifies re-birth; starched linen in reborn linen. Every time it is laundered it springs fresh to life. That is why linen substitutes like celluloid have little charm. It is the washing, starching and ironing that makes the appeal . . ." Petticoats without starch were not petticoats at all, and unstarchable silk or satin lingerie, although pleasant to the touch, could not compare with the starchable fine linen, muslin and batiste of old. (The fetishism of lingerie and "frillies" as such, was catered to in the agency photographs of actresses.)

A curious component of starch fetishism (shared also by rubber machintosh addiction) is aural sensitivity: to the cracking and creaking of starched linen, the rattling of links in shirt-cuffs, the tapping of earrings against a high stiff collar. The very sound of the words "stiff and starched" was thrilling. This is stated openly, as if to justify the ritual repetitions of the words.

London Life was and remains unique. What "popular" magazine was ever so perverse as to publish a "Coronation Souvenir Number" which did not contain a single picture of royalty? If it is a souvenir you want, go get yourself a Coronation Souvenir Tattoo.

Although privatized, and part-relegated to a fantasy world, "unfashionable fetishism" underwent a kind of anthropological and literary metamorphosis. It became broader in its scope, more intense in feeling, and at once more flamboyant and more vulnerable. Insofar as it validated impossible fantasies and offered channels for escapism, it worked like the new film medium. Film became the new vehicle for fashions in clothes, and in the mid-century era began to incorporate many of the fetishisms which had been pushed underground.

Notes

1. Thus wrote Nurse Starched to *London Life* (1935): "The matron of a nursing home told me that the stiffness of the nurses gives a new lease of life to the patients. Her form of psychotherapy for nervous breakdowns consisted, in part, in the perpetual presence of nurses encased in the stiffest and highest of collars, the broadest of waistbands and the deepest of cuffs."

2. *Painter of Modern Life* p. 28.

3. A rather complex bibliographical lineage of *London Life* fetishism may, on behalf of further research, be summarized as follows: fetishist correspondence, which disappeared from *Photobits* in the Spring of 1912 (cf above) in the course of 1911-12 gained a firm foothold in a similar magazine, under the same proprietorship, called *New Photo Fun*, under the rubric "Confidential Correspondence." Tight-lacing is here one of many other fetish and sado-masochistic interests. This and its successors carried advertisements for contraceptive and abortion devices as *London Life* was to do. The humorous purpose indicated in the titles of these magazines, the many cartoons and various frivolities, also affects the fetishist content.

In 1912 *New Photo Fun* became the slightly larger *New Fun*; by the following year tight-lacing had become prominent, and a New Fun Club, based on this fetish, was formed. In 1914 the fetishist correspondence, suddenly suspended 28 Feb. to 4 April, revived over excitement engendered by La Guêpe Humaine, an English girl exhibited at the Paris Fair, with an incredible waist-measure sustained for fifteen minute seánces, and a photograph of Mlle. Irma Goldenberg, "one of the tiniest-waisted (14 inches) music hall stars in Europe." The Confidential Correspondence continued despite the war and the consequent physical shrinkage of the magazine. It was sometimes printed on the back of large pull-out military maps. Transvestism (both ways) in particular flourished, although the "effeminate men" took heavy beatings from the editors and some readers. Medico wrote from the front to announce in disgust that a soldier had been killed by a bullet which would otherwise has passed clear through his body, but was deflected from a steel stay into his lung. This authentic-sounding letter (*Illustrated Bits* 1 July 1916), also comments on the "misery" of the many conspicuously tight-laced Belgian girls. There are several poignant letters from men unable to continue tight-lacing in the trenches, and others defending the "manliness" of their fetish against the typical response of "mingled amusement and disgust."

In 1916 *New Fun* shrank further in size, and in name, to *Fun*. Fetishists at this time develop an acute sense of the precariousness of their privilege in getting letters printed at all, as Confidential Correspondence is progressively cut back because of paper and staff shortages. In March 1917 *Fun* amalgamated with "two of our joyous contemporaries" *Photobits* and *Illustrated Bits* to form *Bits of Fun* (*Illustrated Bits* had also been a major vehicle of fetishism since 1914, and in 1916 became virtually a reprint of *Fun*). At this time a new fetish appears, related to the latest development in fashion technology: "cobwebby" silk stockings. The illustrations are perfectly schizophrenic in relation to fashion: either fetishistically wasp-waisted, or fashionably waistless, flapper-style. In the stress of the war, corsetting of men becomes as important as that of women. Serial fiction on fetishist subjects abounds. A short-lived personal advertisement column and forwarding service allowed one man, at least, to find a wife.

In 1919 *Bits of Fun* became the smaller *Little Bits of Fun,* and absorbed *Photo Bits* and the "granddad" of cheap illustrateds, *Ally Sloper's Half Holiday.* Monopede fetishism appears, presumably in connection with the return of limbless soldiers from the war. It is to flourish grotesquely in *London Life.* In 1920 a fetishist (mainly tight-lacers) club called the Xites was formed, all 171 members being employed in one or another branch of a large insurance company; they often wrote collectively. The term "kinky" (used since about 1916) is established ("fetish" does not become acceptable until after the Second World War).

A special Summer, 1920 number of *Fashion Fads and Fancies,* a new feature-title substituting for the old "Confidential Correspondence" and become the code-term for fetishism added to the masthead 19 June, failed to draw subscribers in advance as expected, apparently because readers were afraid to send their real names and addresses. Yet in terms of space, almost half the magazine was now fetishist. The terror of discovery was, in a sense, justified by the venomous eloquence of such a letter as that from a doctor and military surgeon (June 26), who blamed the rise in sexual debauchery, prostitution, divorce and unchristian marriage, on the fetishism displayed in a copy of the magazine he had chanced upon, which aroused in him more "amazement, contempt and disgust" than any publication he had ever seen or could imagine. This kind of response was considered by many other readers as the only sane one; and the editors were not inclined to disavow it.

On 30 October *Bits of Fun* dropped its subtitle *Fashion, Fads and Fancies,* and the correspondence. The coup, which was certainly due to a change in editorship and/or proprietorship, was accompanied by yet another change of name, back to *Fun,* which, now sanitized invited letters only of "moderate length and *general* interest," on such suggested topics as "the Ideal Husband" or "The Ideal Wife." The new editors registered that the response was nil. In 1921 they were still fighting the fetishist virus, which meanwhile tried to infect the mass daily press, with occasional but never lasting success. In 1923 *Fun* incorporated with *Photo Bits and Cinema Star,* and was merged into *London Life.*

CHAPTER EIGHT

Postwar Fashion and Media Exploitation of Fetishism

In the post-war era the press, advertising and fashion industries systematized and perfected methods for the commercial exploitation of all manner of sexual repression, including fetishism and fetishist fantasies. They did so under economic conditions in which middle-class women, who had been pressed into the labor force during the war, were now being pressed back into the home to assume the passive role of consumer, sex-object and servant to man as he set about his global conquests in science and industrialization. The alternative to unpaid menial service in the home was low-paid menial service in the office. There were fewer women with advanced university degrees and in high professional and managerial positions in 1960 than in 1930. The emancipation movement peaked before the First World War, atrophied after woman got the vote, and did not revive until the late '60s.

The fashion of the '50s, managed by male-dominated media, played a significant role in presenting to woman a more "feminine" self-image; but it had also to come to terms with certain contradictions, with vague aspirations for freedom—the new cult word of an anti-communist age. So the "new femininity" of fashion was accompanied by a "new masculinity"—women were simultaneously offered, along with waspies, stiletto heels and petticoats, simple practical styles of shirts, trousers, flat shoes, etc. The emphasis was upon choice and change, multiplicity of styles, to suit the individual personality and the particular occasion. Advertising copy promised sex appeal, psychological security and self-fulfillment, but the motivation behind the fashion industry was the same as behind every other consumer industry: to sell, to keep people buying, craving novelties. Corsetry was merely one among a host of devices designed to reshape the body and make women look and feel "different" (denied an autonomous personality, she had always to look different since she must never be satisfied with herself, she must always look "better"): exercise programs, slimming cures, diets, thigh reducers, bust developers, and the expensive paraphernalia and services of beauty and figure salons—all these were vigorously peddled in the women's magazines.

Of all these, however, only the corset carried a historical dimension and was thus able to play a dual role, embody some of the purpose associated with the stays of old—sexualization—and at the same time offer freedom from their erstwhile rigor. The new euphemism for corset, a word which was now felt to sound harsh and to be associated with too harsh a garment, was "girdle", an ancient term for any light, external waist-belt; the generic category (including the brassière) was called "foundation garments." The latter term was adopted for its broad associations with concepts of necessity, fundamental need, and basis for good appearance. The French, for similar reasons, changed from "corset" to "gaine" (sheath). The new foundation garments were indeed much lighter and more permissive of movement than their ancestors. This fact allowed advertisers to promise freedom (and repressed woman was assumed always to be seeking freedom) at the same time as they promised escape from the sordid work-reality of the present through associations with an age of elegance, leisure, and sexual privilege.

After the war (and after a false start in 1939), there was a gradual progressive revival of the mildly tight-laced effect, and of garments bearing some of the function and appearance of Victorian stays (waisted, boned, sometimes even laced). This revival was achieved despite the association, left over from the interwar period, of steels and laces with obese matrons and orthopedic garments. The industry plugged the style, which included full, petticoated skirts and stiletto heels, as a necessary complement to the more practical and prosaic styles of home and office wear, evening romance after daytime drudgery. Copywriters gushed, promising harmony, ecstasy, freedom, heaven on earth.

The purchase of the new girdle or shoe, however, did not mean it was necessarily worn much. There was always heavy competition in the overflowing wardrobe of the "affluent society." Manufacturers, moreover, exploited the commercial advantage of encouraging women to buy articles impractical in more than one sense: the tight but lightly constructed girdle and the pointed heel shoe wore out very quickly. This might not matter much to a woman with the money, but, pressured to replace one thing with the same, a similar or different thing, women generally found themselves trapped into a buying habit, and into acquiescence with the constant round of rapidly changing styles. (The commercial motive to encourage tight-lacing in corsets which thereby wore out more quickly, and the wearing of shoes with high, narrow and therefore quickly abraded heels may be assumed to have existed already in the late 19th century).

The 1939 Corset Revival

After the tubular 1920s, the waistline from the mid-1930s onwards settled in its natural place, and became gradually more emphatic to the accompaniment of fuller and longer skirts. By 1938 there were intermittent signs of a revival of back-laced and boned girdles, shorter on the hips than hitherto. The new corset was finally launched, with tremendous publicity fanfare, in the spring and summer of the following year, under the name "scissors-silhouette", and "spindle", "wafer", "champagne-glass", "hour-glass", etc., waist. A version featured in *Life* (12 June) was reputed to require ten yards of lacing to get in and out of; at the Paris Fall Fashion shows held in early August, Mainbocher stole the thunder with a backlaced version incorporating a new element—the bra-cup, which rated next to "Germany un-masking her heavy artillery to cow the Poles" as an Event of the Week in the 28 August issue of *Life* magazine.

The new corset gave a tremendous fillip to sales; corset advertising in August 1939 increased 22 percent over the same month the previous year. "The much heralded corset" was "the only cheerful head-line in papers black with forboding."[1] Nostalgia was rife, and the period associations were exploited to the full. Advertisements and window displays used old illustrations and actual period models for purposes of comparison. Altman's window in New York had "four tiny wasp-waisted corsets in plaster forms, equipped with mercury wings, the lacers drawn to the edge of a window where four pair of hands gracefully held them and almost created the illusion of a chariot."[2] The window of Franklin Simon on Fifth Avenue literally stopped traffic and created queues for a glimpse of some Gay Nineties Lily of France corsets. Advertisements and window-displays showed men literally with goggle eyes popping, and gnomes climbing up ladders to pull in the laces; advertisement-cartoons had the husband delightedly lacing in his wife as she hung onto the bedrail and saying, "You say it doesn't PINCH? It doesn't pinch me either (i.e., finan-cially) since you bought it at Macy's." A similar cartoon had the husband with the lace in one hand and the phone in the other, asking his grandfather advice on how to proceed. Manufacturers aimed at teenagers who had never before worn anything resembling a girdle but who now sought "the thrill of getting into these amusing little waspies" for that special occasion.

Talk of the physical danger and fainting added spice to the sales pitch. Twentieth century comfort was, of course, the guaranteed corollary of the new nineteenth century fragility. Altman's, claiming to be "one of the most famous names in really serious, lacing corsets (offered) corsets *that you can wear comfortably!* For all this talk about fainting . . . not being able to bend . . . forbidden to sit down . . . Our hand has acquired a great deal more skill since the days of the iron cage. We can make you a corset you won't faint in." Some advertisements suggestively invited "Milady to lace as tight as she desires;" but fitters in stores were warned not to pull the laces tight on the customer, unless specifically requested to do so, since it was expected that she might want to leave the back wide open. A two-inch reduction was considered both safe and sufficient, although Warner's offered to slenderize "several inches" for the "waist of a wasp without its sting." Most confident of all were Francette who, oddly, put their feasible reduction at the precise figure of 3½ inches (occasionally extended to "3½-5" inches) which disappeared "with one smooth easy pull" (the sizes, however, ranged from 23-28).

The "correct" waist size at this time was considered to be 26 inches (it had been around 28 in the '20s), and some manufacturers such as Poirette who were opposed to the new corset advised against turning that graceful 26 into a pinched 24. Others, such as the prestigious Maidenform Bra and Bien Jolie Companies—irked, one suspects, that they had been caught napping—hinted darkly at grave threats to health and the risk to the public image of the industry. The general feeling on all sides of the trade was that the fad would not last.

But for the war, it might well have done so. In the United States, it survived well into 1940, but cut off from the war-struck European centers of fashion, the American corset industry could hardly sustain so novel a mode on its own; and there were, moreover, sinister references to the corsetting of the Statue of Liberty, and "freedom being sacrificed to the führers of fashion." "That tempting tininess of waist, which makes brave men fear you will break in two" was hardly apposite at a time when, in Europe, women were being broken in reality—by bombs.

Postwar Return of the Waist

Even before the end of the war, soon after the liberation of Paris, rumors began to circulate of a wasp-waist revival. It was then necessarily associated with austerity, "purification"[3] (and even penance?). The verbally explicit character of this association could not be sustained when the ethic of austerity gave way to that of consumerism, but it is possible that the semi-restrictive corsetry of the "affluent Fifties" sought to compensate for the new physical and therefore "guilty" freedom offered by labor-saving devices and domestic leisure.

With the famous New Look of 1947, Christian Dior swept away the last vestiges of wartime utilitarianism, and brought back flowing lines, long, full skirts, fitted bodices and accentuated waists. The foundation for the new silhouette was laid by Marcel Rochas the previous year, with his "guêpière", a lighter, briefer (at first only four inches deep), laced or hooked version of Mainbocher's 1939 corset. The press suggested fashion was thrusting its hand into a guépier (wasp's or hornet's nest). But medical opposition was weak—less than what the trade itself would have considered useful publicity.

The press tried to cook up a little controversy in early 1948 out of the animadversions of the Academy of Medicine and Irene Popard, the creator of a rhythmic gymnastics system for women, who claimed to have helped Poiret kill the corset in 1912. The cover illustration and editorial of a popular medical journal called *Votre Santé* (Jan. 1948), comparing the anatomy of the corsetted and natural woman, might almost have been taken straight out of a Victorian journal. In the United States Dr. Andrew Lang, Vice President of the University of Illinois, aroused some attention in the press (Oct. 1947) for a $5,000 project to put corsets on forty apes and watch their progress over a period of two years. By May the following year his research had progressed sufficiently for him to announce that American women should be forbidden by law to wear such corsets (one ape had already died). This declaration prompted a class of recently qualified Parisian lawyers to a mock-debate on the question: "Can the inventor of the 'waspie' sue the American scientists?" The motion carried overwhelmingly. One patriotic lawyer exclaimed of the ape that died "the heart which beat beneath that waspie was not that of a French-woman!"

Last gasps of medical stricture were never quite the last: as late as 1964, when the waspie was virtually dead anyway, we find a Dr. John Parr in an English national daily vituperating in grand 19th century style about the stagnation of the lung base, restriction of vital capacity and even prolapsed wombs.

The moral authority of medical science had, in this matter, been superseded by a new and more permissive "science", that of advertising. The Madison Avenue psychologists played relentlessly on female narcissism, insecurity and sexual frustration. The corset be-

came openly eroticized in the lush language of its commercial promoters. We are dismally familiar with the sexual sales pitch whereby
a car, a cigarette, a beer becomes at once agency and object of love.
Consumerism has fetishized our culture in the broadest sense, turning objects into repositories of emotion. Underwear, being an en-
velope of the body, easily and obviously lends itself to the role of
lover-and love-substitute: "Gently (or tenderly) but firmly", "discreetly persuasive"—like the perfect lover, whose "powernet and
sheer nylon hands enfold you lightly in a caressing, curving embrace"
(Enhance Torso-bra, 1955); or, in a crypto-sexual crescendo: "lifting,
supporting, holding and molding, *separating* you beautifully" (Lady
Marlene bra, 1956). Advertising and editorial copy abounds in the
archetypal sexual and dream imagery of movement and suspension
in air and water which was in no way impeded by the presence of
light boning: flotation, ethereality, and sensuous oblivion in the
breezes of bouffant skirts and cascades of ruffled tulle.

Moral imperatives became part of a language both slick and brash.
When U.S. *Vogue* finally accepted the European waisted look after
some years of vacillation, it ordered: "IN YOU GO. Very much in."
So in went American and then European women, into Warner's
lace-up girdle, which was a longer, more complete (including bra)
and altogether more persuasive article than Rochas' guêpière. Under
the brand name "Merry Widow" (taken from the 1952 MGM movie of
that title) it gave the silhouette of the '50s, with swelling skirts and
rising heels. Historical associations were pressed: "Thanks to feather-
weight stays and gentle laces, you'll ease in those unfashionable
two inches quicker than you can say 'Come help me, Prissy.' So drop
those smelling salts, Scarlett (O'Hara, of *Gone with the Wind*) and lure
yourself a polka partner! You're a cinch to lead the ball in a cinch!"
The back-lacing was emphasized by means of a mirror and the heady
promise of a "two-to-three-inch intake" (Pl. 80) although the
frontside hook or zip-up model was generally found more convenient. Widely imitated, the original Merry Widow was selling six
million annually in the mid-'50s as the advertising shifted from
nostalgia to show-girl naughtiness ("How can you look so naughty
and feel so nice . . . it's simply *wicked* what it does for you" cry the
masked members of "the famous supporting cast").[4]

Neither Dior's new flattened bust line nor the "sack" line which
followed it disturbed Warner's sales or the basic silhouette of fashion.
In October 1958, Warner's pronounced the "waistline waspier (more
wicked than even before it disappeared into a sack)." 1960 marks the
turning point, and the shift to the new pitch for girdles which "fit like
wallpaper" and "smooth on like Body-Creme", metaphors which
eliminate altogether the idea of any degree of sculptural modification.

The popular magazines were full of enthusiasm for waistinches, "waist whittlers", "smoothies", etc. "Steel hand in the velvet glove . . . strikes a blow in the Battle for the Waist" is a typical header for the newspaper fashion page.[5] Small, crudely illustrated and worded display advertisements for popular lines of waist cinches strike an incongruous note when placed, as they so often were, in the august pages of *Vogue*. Wilco offered to create for a mere $2.98 a "Wisp of a Waist for that French Hourglass Figure . . . No longer do you have to suffer the tortures of a girdle." Fredericks of Hollywood commanded women to "STOP creeping waistline! Slice three inches from your waistline in a cincher that gives you a wedding-ring waist that's the merest handspan."

By 1960-61 the high-fashion editorials were in reverse gear, stressing the "unpinched" and "more clung to than constricted look", before performing another about-face and portentously announcing 1962 as the "Year the Waist Came Back". This, like all the other mini-revivals which succeeded each other at about two year intervals through the 1960s and into the 1970s, failed to catch on and may have been intended (like so many other fashion ideas of the whole era) more as a psychological stimulus than a practical proposal.

Dresses, coats, and even swimsuits in the 1950s made the most of the waist-cinching. One of the most prolific advertisers in *Vogue* and *Harper's Bazaar*, Lilli Ann Designs, invariably stressed the tight waist either by selecting particularly slender or well-corsetted human models, and/or by touching out the contour on the photograph ("The 'Ring-waist Suit'—with a waist no bigger than a wedding ring"— 1951). Boning and lacing became prominent features on dresses: Balmain showed balldresses with a boned back-lacing bodice, and popularized skirts with wide, boned back-lacing waistbands. Norell even tried putting into his short, tailored jackets pieces of boning which he called significantly, "a substitute for willpower," and which editors happily hailed as a revival of the Gibson Girl silhouette: "more a figure than a fashion—starchy in outline, with a tiny waist, a bustled skirt . . . a handspan waist."[6]

The idea did not catch on either then or two years later, when the prestigious Jacques Fath based his collection upon boned suit-jackets and dresses worn over "Victorian" lace-up waist cinchers. In the media, his success was with the popular press rather than the high fashion magazines (cf. below).

Since the Edwardian era with its frilled and ruffled dresses, periodic attempts had been made to turn underwear or underwear effects into outerwear. The distinction now vanished. Swimsuits, having little more to offer in the way of nudity, imitated lingerie and corsetry. Considerable ingenuity went into the development of new fabrics, often elasticized for close fit, and printed with lacy, tattoo-like patterns. Swimsuit designers created the "hour-glass maillot, which has the taking ways, and the stays, of an Edwardian evening dress . . . elasticized, boned"; and just to prove how comfortable the model is in such a swimsuit, she is shown asleep in the sun or running by the shore (Plate 83). Probably not many boned swimsuits were sold, and fewer still worn; the Cole version featured in *Vogue* (Jan. '55) complete with a stiffened cummerbund laced over studs down a 6-inch high front is clearly intended purely for visual effect. Later swimsuit designs made much play with erotic cutouts, see-through mesh, huge brass eyelets, and massive decorative lacing.

The waisted effect was further enhanced (or created, when no girdle and an unfitted dress was worn) by broad belts, introduced in 1952. The earlier elastic version went under such names as "waist-garter" and the "elastic rib-cage" and there was a variety of "fabulous fascias" using leather and metal which summoned up associations with the middle ages and veiled allusion to chastity belts. The magazines were always announcing "belt revivals", notably in 1957 with some extraordinarily fetishistic, solid brass "low-fashion" variants (cf. Pl. 82), and again in 1959, this time characterized by sheer expanse of rigid leather. Brightly colored leather belts up to six and seven inches tall were put over soft fabrics, evening dresses and coats as well, but they were not intended to indent, only to "glamorize" the waist. In the '60s belts acquired aggressive brass features, with huge buckles, studs and multiple rows of large eyelets, in accord with the "bondage" look. But they were worn loose, and eventually began to slip downwards, until they were worn slung about the hips to accentuate the "Gothic" swelling of the abdomen.

Rise of the Stiletto Heel

Dior's New Look shoes still resembled war-time footwear—high but thick heels, ankle straps, blunt or open toes, platform soles. In 1952, the year the waist went in, manufacturers came up with a decidedly thinner heel reinforced with a steel core, and began to use a last with a more pointed toe. Fashion was catching up with fetishism. The July 1952 *Vogue* used the term "stiletto heel" (known to London Lifers) which became the most commonly accepted, although it was soon joined by others, "flute", "match-stick", "hatpin", and the more aggressive (once "stiletto" became blunted through overuse) "saber", "rapier", "spike", and "needle". All these terms were also applied to the toe, which gradually sharpened from the equilateral triangle of 1952 to the very acute-angled triangle of 1957. (Rapier-Toe and Spire Toe were registered brand names). The words "toe" and especially "point" inspired a multitude of puns: "pointing with pride at the tiny look of your feet in Diminuentoes," heels and toes "pointing to the importance of the spectator," "pointing . . . from the dazzling height of a rapier-thrust heel, for the most elegant line between two points." They were endowed with a "piercing Castillian elegance." Arrows figured, too: "Beau 'n Arrow", "Toe 'n Arrow". The Eiffel Tower was pressed into service. Never was fashion copy more strenuously witty, as shoes became "as pointed as a Perelman riposte". The stiletto heel also offered advertising designers a wide variety of curious graphic permutations, often incorporating erotic symbolism (cf. Pl. 55). Just before their rather sudden detumescence, around 1960, the vaulting ambition of advertising copy o'er leapt itself and sent heels "soaring skyhigh" and created the "most-pointed pointed toe yet— reminiscent of the winkle-picker"—at the very moment when "true" winkle-pickers were launched at a lower social level by the London mods, who thereby gave it the kiss of death.

The interest of many trades connected with the fashion industry was to prolong the stiletto style as long as possible. The stiletto heel, with its extremely narrow base (down to one quarter inch diameter in the late 1950s) broke easily and wore out fast.[7] The slightest angular abrasion rendered balance even more precarious. The "stiletto heel wobble" was as much due to this abrasion as to the narrowness of the heel base in itself. Attempts to introduce heel tips in really durable materials, or to make them easily removable and replaceable, or to fit screw-in replaceable "lifts" (the steel or nylon stem which formed the backbone of the heel) were always frustrated. Shoe repair shops did a roaring trade, continuing to replace heel tips with minute scraps of leather and a nail.

The fashion shoe was less immune than the corset from medical stricture, although podiatric business did not demonstrably increase. The popular press revelled in and fomented the "controversy". Miss M. Marshall of Bexhill wrote artlessly to a mass daily: "Men are attracted by high heels. I know that when I wear a pair of 5-inch stiletto heels a man is not only attracted, he is fascinated. Can you wonder that smart women wear the highest, slenderest heels they can obtain?" Professional of Kent replied in these terms: "I wonder if those men who proclaim their admiration for women in high heels would be prepared to subject themselves to such torture, and furthermore, risk the danger of injuring themselves for life? If girls (and the men, too) could walk through one of our foot hospitals when operating was in progress, they would soon form a different opinion of incorrect footwear."

Serious papers sounded the alarm in articles headed "Where the Shoe Pinches" and "Murder Underfoot". Physicians estimated that fifty percent of girls under twenty years were suffering from corns, callouses and bunions: "Were animals treated to the same degree of inhumanity to which women are now prepared to submit their feet . . . there would be an outcry from all the humanitarian societies in the country." Educational administrators were, of course, in a better position to stem the scourge of high heel and pointed toe. The headmaster of Sturry Secondary School near Canterbury, under the headline "HIGH HEELS CAN CAUSE THE DOWNWARD PATH," warned that "high heels and winkle-pickers can lead to delinquency if worn at school." The press was tipped off by rebellious pupils and took the opportunity to support the recurrent press campaigns to brighten and feminize schoolgirls' uniforms. Even the family doctor was drafted: under a headline "FIFTH FORMER DEFIES STILETTO BAN" is the story of how a 15-year-old defeated a school principal by bringing a medical certificate testifying to her need to wear high heels.[8]

In the early years of the fashion the press liked to enlarge upon its more amusing inconveniences. An English family weekly demonstrated in a cinematic succession of photographs, under the headline HOW A MAN-HOLE BECOMES A WOMAN-TRAP, what happens to a tight-skirted woman who gets her stiletto heel caught in a man-hole cover. One civic administration, at least, protected itself (it could hardly protect the woman) against accidents provoked by the stiletto heel. According to an AP dispatch headed MOBILE PUTS ITS FOOT DOWN ON HIGH HEELS, the Alabama city had declared shoes with heels more than one-inch high and less than one-inch thick illegal. "No arrests are expected, but the City will not be responsible for accidents in streets, when women fall over gratings, cement joints, etc., in the street, causing broken arms, skinned noses, twisted legs, and loss of dignity."

Other authorities, with other interests, joined the opposition. Appalled by the denting of their beautiful floors, many museums, galleries and country-houses banned visitors from wearing sharp heels, adding thereby to the international vocabulary of highway signs, a new symbol of prohibition: the cancelled stiletto shoe. Many a house-proud hostess, surveying the pock-marked wreck of a newly polished floor, would have done the same. The more enterprising flooring manufacturers, meanwhile, saw the stiletto as a challenge. An architect told me that this fashion was the best thing to happen in years to the flooring industry; without it, certain synthetics marketed in the '60s might never have become generally available. Vinyl, for instance, unlike the old linoleum it replaced, does not dent, but springs back under sharp pressure, is chip and scratch resistant, and even when marked by a severe glancing blow, can be polished smooth. In 1962 the National Coal Board announced the END OF STILETTO VENDETTA, with an advertisement promoting Armour-tile flooring's capacity to resist the "trail of destruction left in the fashionable wake of woman. One ton of femininity—the average im-pact of the stiletto heel—is the lacerating, splintering, tearing scourge that confronts the floorcovering industry."

"One ton" is no exaggeration, as was corroborated by certain in-terested newspaper readers. One found that while the surface area of the average stiletto heel tip measured one-twentieth of an inch, the pressure a 140 pound woman exerts on the floor, assuming she puts her weight on one heel, is well above one ton per square inch—considerably more than that exerted by an outsize elephant. And this is a purely static pressure. If she rolls back on one heel—as in a tango—or if she skips, the pressure on the floor would greatly increase. If she pirouettes, the effect would be comparable with that of a heavy power drill of the type used in mining or quarrying.

Rise of the Boot

The new footwear of the 1960s was not a shoe, but a boot. Once a functional object used for bad weather, it now became a fashion article in its own right, rising in height until it could literally go no further ("boot-tights"), chasing the miniskirt to crotch-length. The high stiletto heel had kept the skirt down and concentrated attention on the foot and ankle; the boot sent the skirt up, and turned the leg into a single visual unit. By the fall of 1963 the close-fitting, laced, thigh length boot had emerged. Well publicized attempts in London, leader in the boot fashion, to add a three-inch spike heel foundered against the opposition of haute couture. But Pop Art, from its London base, embraced the boot cult, and helped to introduce the word "kinky" and "fetish" to the vocabulary of fashion writers, and later, to that of advertising copy itself. *Vogue* promoted the boot idea in a major editorial (15 Aug. '64), enshrining it in a broad, heroic-fetishistic-fantastic pop-cult. Pop Artists produced plastic moulded boot multiples, and drew inspiration from the boot illustrations of the little fetish magazines (Allen Jones). Shiny red colored boots, gladiator sandals with things criss-crossing onto the thigh, and golden lingerie, were boosted by association with the sex-and-sadism of James Bond movies, as the sale of black leather outfits was helped by their exploitation in the *Avenger* television series.

Two trends in bootery may be distinguished, each with its own fetishistic appeal: the ultra-smooth, shiny, light and tight look, and the heavier, aggressively decorated look, with chains, tassles, straps and lacings reminiscent of the ceremonial military or riding boot. All boots tended (like the shoes at this time) to develop wide, square or round, never pointed toes;[9] and wide, stacked heels, which rose and broadened further in the early 1970s. By 1973 deep orthopedic-fetishistic platform soles were common, sometimes rising to an extraordinary height. A cartoon showed a girl in such platforms saying to a policeman: "If you try to arrest me, I'll jump." The sadomasochistic appeal of the new boot was incarnated in the "Kinky Boot Beast" which, in the animated film *The Yellow Submarine*, went around gleefully stomping on people's toes.

"Bind" of the Sixties

The soft and fragile look of the politically passive '50s yielded to the hard and brash look of the politically restive and more openly fetishistic '60s. Fashion absorbed another range of fetishes, new only in their broader cultural manifestation, for they had been intensively nurtured a generation before in *London Life*. Glossy effects formerly limited to accessories invaded the whole arena of dress. The "wet-look" once restricted to aquatic sports clothing, with shiny leather, rubberized, P.V.C. and vinyl materials became fashionable day and evening wear. Face make-up became theatrical in the extreme. Colors turned fluorescent and metallic, designs geometric and streamlined. Clothes no longer cinched the body, but threw a stiff mask around it. They were worn like accessories with little direct relationship to the natural human shape.

Fashion went unisex, intersex and nonsex; primitive, minimal and anarchic. Hemlines fluctuated wildly; women wore flowing floor-length dresses for daytime shopping, and mini-skirts for formal evening parties. In a kind of ethnocentrifugal spasm, and in an attempt, perhaps, to deal with contradictions which were breaking out into the most serious social domestic and global unrest, fashion embraced all kinds of Third World cultural symbols, and poverty-styles associated with hippies and protest marchers, mixing symbols of oppression with symbols of liberation: neo-primitive decoration (Indian beads, African feathers), worn-out and patched proletarian overalls, faded denim guerrilla outfits, army surplus uniforms. Haute Couture absorbed "hippie" counter-fashion, just as the mass media tried to absorb the anti-war movement and the counter-culture. At the same time it paid homage to technology, in kinky-looking neo-medieval chainmail suits and astronautical, flashy vinyl catsuits. Homage, too, to the new police state, in chains and cartridge belts and other Free World symbols and toys.

Fashion seemed, for a moment, to be entering a new iron age and played with metal clasps, hinges, studs, spikes, catches, buckles, straps and chains. The heavier apparatus of fetishist bondage was evoked with slave-bracelets, slave-rings, handcuffs, leg-shackles, huge iron collars and sculptured gorgets. The effort of fashion to absorb social contradiction is perhaps nowhere better epitomized than in the launching of the all-steel brassière, at the same time as "hippie" nudity and feminine bralessness.

Décolletage, overplayed by show business and the media, ceded to other foci. The throat was eroticized, collars became important. Women were severely enjoined to "keep your head pulled up—way up. The length of the neck is crucially, cruelly important . . ." The neck must be lengthened "by inches" in seconds through improved posture; throats were shown alternately in voluptuous extension and nakedness, and expensively confined. Nureyev's Michelangelesque throat, over a full page, was offered as the very throb of sexuality, and the long-necked, tremendously beringed neck of the African Samburu tribeswoman was presented as the acme of elegance.

Fashion indulged in highly refined, symbolic (and realisable?) fantasies of neck-restriction. There were iridescent photographs of chokers composed of conjoined necklaces and solid articulated plaques, rigidly clasping the full length of a model's swan-throat. Over the ecstatically extended neck of the "femme-bijoux" any movement of the head threatens to scrape the soft underjaw against a rigid pearl-topped rail (Pl. 75). Another choker terminates under the chin in a row of tiny upturned turquoise bells, scalloped to a sharp edge.[10] The Victorian holly-branch had nothing on this. But then the *Vogue* model had to hold the pose only as long as it took to make the photograph.

The whole head, meanwhile, was masked and stifled in astro-medieval-fetishist helmets. It was almost as if the luxurious world of haute couture were deliberately blinding its vision, cutting off its senses, to a world of which it could no longer make sense. And yet most of all this was conceived as only a game. The industry knew that the vast majority of women would never have contemplated buying such a helmet, choker, steel bra, or manacles. These were essentially upper-class toys for middle-class fantasy to conjure with, in shop-windows and magazines. If we have been concerned, in past chapters, with lower-to-middle class women adopting what they thought of as upper-class insignia, we are now dealing with insignia available in reality *only* to the rich, and enjoyed vicariously or envied by the less-than-rich. The 1950s waspie was, relatively, still democratic; and the broad (and cheap) elastic cinch belts were worn characteristically by young working-class girls.

We have also shifted our attention to the U.S., the economic and cultural pace-setter of the capitalist world. The American economy has become accustomed to peddling luxuries as if they were universal necessities; the American culture has embraced the disparity it deems irreconcilable, between symbol and reality, dream and need, froth and substance, and treated the former as the latter. So much so, that it defies analysis to say exactly which fashion or fetish of the moment corresponds to which or whose reality.

Lacing and Tight-Lacing in the Period Film, and the Measurement Mania

The stage and the screen (cinema and television) have done perhaps more than any medium to formulate the fantasies of the 20th century. Actors and actresses have replaced the aristocracy as social models and vehicles of social dreams. The ideas of the fashion designers, first promulgated in the press, imprint the mass imagination when they are translated onto the screen. Haute couture has blent with theatre, as the couturiers have hitched their wagons to the stars by designing clothes for them, and as the luxury fashion magazines have filled with exotic theatrical fantasies. It is also the film, perhaps even more than the fashion magazine, which has served to validate the otherwise private fantasies of fetishists.

As the media have grown more sexually explicit, the social prevalence of various forms of fetishism has grown more apparent. Recently a number of general distribution films have played out the fetishes of the '60s, especially leather and rubber. In the '50s the mild and residual cultural fetish for small waists and tight-lacing may be deduced from the movies, and the obsession of the press for actresses' body-measurements has made a numerical, fetishistic reduction of what was already a fetishist reduction. For a time it seemed as if the latest concept in ideal female form was compressible into a triad of hyphenated double digits, and that the "measurement mania" of the Victorian fetish correspondence had become a cultural phenomenon. "Vital statistics," as the triad of bust-waist-hip measurements were called, clung like some bureaucratic-age Homeric epithet to the names of many actresses, whether they were noted for their physique or not. It was the social security number against which reputation income was entered, and a label of recognition: newspapers even ran quizzes requiring one to fit names to measurements. In *Breakfast of Champions* Kurt Vonnegut establishes a satirical litany of female "vital statistics" alternating with penis measurements: could the former be a sublimation of a taboo obsession with the latter?

We may start with the premature "waspie renaissance" of 1939 precipitated in the popular imagination by the film *Gone With the Wind* of that year. Both film and novel of 1936 by Margaret Mitchell upon which the film was based (two million copies sold by 1939) were instant popular successes, and have become "classics." The powerful figure of Scarlett O'Hara (played by Vivien Leigh, thus launched into fame) offered a fantasy of the emancipated, socially competitive and sexually aggressive woman, who used the archetypal femininity of a wasp-waist and petticoats as weapons in the socio-sexual struggle. Egotistic and passionate, putting her lust for sexual conquest before the interests of family, Scarlett resolves to have no more children rather than risk losing her figure. To many millions of readers and film-goers, the famous tight-lacing scene, described in the novel with exceptional period detail and sufficiently emphasized in the film and musical versions, incarnates an era, a way of life, and a social type, that of the "Southern Belle." Studio and press put it about that Vivien Leigh acquired Scarlett's textual 16-inch waist for the role, although the connoisseur's eye estimates it at much more.

In the postwar era, fashion and film industries in close alliance, promoted new standards of ideal proportions. Film promoters fostered the cult of the maximum bust, fashion promoters that of the minimum waist, which even Dior at one time insisted be no more than 17 inches ("even if the wearer faints").[11] The trade magazine *Le Corset de France* (1948) settled the ideal less unreasonably at 20 inches, which was the measurement of two out of the four top French mannequins (the other two had waists of 19 inches, or 10 inches less than the average of a mannequin in 1922. These waistlines were between 33 or 34 hip and bust measurements, on women between 5 foot 5 and 5 foot 7 inches tall; window display dummies were given these proportions with a waist smaller yet).

In 1947–8 two prestigious personalities of the French stage, Madeleine Renaud and Edwige Feuillère, launched the period figure. Their "Belle Epoque" bearing was enhanced by the couturiers (notably Balmain) who dressed them offstage, and onstage by Rose-Marie Lebigot, who also made Rochas' waspies (15,000 sold from her shop alone within a year). She and her associate Gloriane provided film studios, night clubs, cabarets and dance revues with the necessary erotic period underwear. Lebigot, like Madame Billard before her, was publicized as anatomist and sculptress (she did actually exhibit some real sculpture). The success of the Feydeau farce *Occupe-toi d'Amélie* was due not least to the appearance of Madeleine Renaud in period stays and high black laced boots; her waist was stated to rival that of Vivien Leigh in *Gone With The Wind*. For her role in *Caroline Chérie* (1948) Martine Carol was supposedly laced down from her normal 22 to 19 inches and in the title role of *Nana*, was booted and corsetted with full fetishistic period flavor.

For most films with "period" (i.e. pre-1914) settings, an undressing and preferably a lacing scene was indispensable. Such scenes were also favored for pre-release publicity photographs, like the number from *Oklahoma!* (1955), featuring a panorama of multicolored corsets, which was double-spread across popular magazines. When a lacing scene was not actually written into the script, publicity photographs showed the actress being laced in by a co-star, director or husband— and even all in succession. Contemporary woman, who takes it for granted that she should be able to get in and out of her clothes unaided within minutes (or even seconds), was invited into a not-so-distant world where to get dressed at all required much time, servants and/or lovers. Lacking which, she relied on her own mechanical ingenuity; an actress straining away solo from a lace tied to a bedpost, is an "eloquent demonstration that an *elegante* can do without help when it comes to lacing a rebellious corset, and she has no friendly *soupirant* available."[12]

The stereotypical straining-away posture, although not functional, seemed the best way to express the required combination of erotic tension and physical sexual discipline. It conjured up also a kind of sexual aggressivity which was otherwise hard to represent on the movie screen. One magazine affected to doubt whether such a lacing-up scene, showing a fully dressed man heaving with his knee against the lady's rump, might not be censored as indecent.[13]

The period corset and silhouette invaded the contemporary setting in the most anachronistic and unrealistic way. Gina Lollobrigida was very visibly corsetted for her roles as a poor peasant or a modern acrobat. Only in 1962, when it was becoming unfashionable, was she at last persuaded by directors to abandon the "waspie" and 19-inch waist which had formed part of her public image. And as an example of the period corset worn purely as a publicity stunt, and with no connection to any film, we may cite Marilyn Monroe, whose photograph appeared over the invitation SQUEEZE ME full page on the back of a popular magazine (Plate 79).[14]

Some actresses enjoyed period costume so much that they proclaimed an ambition to launch a fashion for it; such was Geneviève Cluny, for whom it was doubly pleasurable—in the wearing and in the taking off. Jane Powell, when not corsetted for period films, liked to appear in cabaret in a combination of contemporary evening dress and Victorian stays; one such outfit, made in French lace, ostrich feathers and fourteen carat gold thread, was reported to have cost $50,000. Stage and film dancers such as Vera-Ellen and Renée Saint Cyr seemed to find a costume with boned-in waist no impediment to their acrobatics.

In reaction against the busty American actress of the immediate postwar years, European consensus by the mid '50s was that the bust should not exceed the hips; Gina Lollobrigida and Brigitte Bardot were small on top compared with their transatlantic counterparts. La Lollo herself announced in 1956 that she was fed up with the bosom focus and, with genial perversity, had herself photographed being laced into a period corset, over the caption: "Bust-up over bosom pals—Gina is more strait-laced these days." Bardot, on the other hand, posed in a conventional uncinched hook-up corselette for a photograph published life-size by means of five double pages folded in, a technical break-through "equal to that of the Americans and Soviets in rocketry." From the perfectly symmetrical ratio of 35–21–35, one could compute the curve of her trajectory into fame.[15] Bardot's antipathy to the period foundation was noted by reporters during the filming of *Viva Maria*, where her completely uncorsetted appearance and Saint Tropez lope appeared anachronistic compared with the correct "springy, swaying tarty" steps which her co-star Jeanne Moreau attributed to her stays.[16] Starlets promoted as "rivals" to BB tended to be more aggressively built, like Maguy Martini with her 37-inch bust and 19-inch waist; but the delicate, "natural" Bardot figure was the ideal which survived the 1960s.

Combining film bust with fashion waist, actresses in the late 1950s flaunted the most extraordinary disproportion. The best known in England was Sabrina, with a 42-inch bust (supposedly insured at a rate of £2,500 per inch under 41 at a premium of £10 per week) over a 19-inch waist. According to a news article entitled WOTTAWAIST, the latter measurement was challenged by a belt-maker of Plymouth called Zygfryd Szmidt, who made her a 19-inch belt. "She took a deep breath, and two husky he-men tugged and tugged until the buckle closed. 'Is it on?' she asked. 'I can't see it.'" Tenuously hinged in an all-steel belt, insectoid, Sabrina demonstrated her athletic prowess at a charity cricket match (Plate 82). Jayne Mansfield, first released to the world under the code 40 (or 42)–18–35 was judged to be in the film *The Girl Can't Help It* "the most extraordinary caricature of the female figure . . . a burlesque of all curvacious blondes from Mae West to Marilyn Monroe."[17] Her physical peculiarity was enhanced, it would seem, more by her very athletic posture, with chest hyper-inflated for photographs, than by corsetry.

Some actresses and mannequins—not as a rule the better-reputed—used drastic waist-reducing devices partly, at least, because an aura of martyrdom was good publicity. The mannequin who would be expected to preserve her figure through diet or exercise, found her use of a "waist-melter" belt blazoned forth in a mass daily under a banner headline "IS BEAUTY WORTH TORTURE?"—complete with a horrified medical reaction. Linda Darnell in 1951 was complaining that after a year of period parts, she was a mass of blisters and bruises that it would take her masseuse six months to eliminate. The French TV actress Marie Mansart (1967) blamed a twenty minute delay in arriving for a live performance on a period corset "which three persons couldn't close." She was on edge throughout the piece and only saved from fainting immediately afterwards by swift surgery on the stay-lace.

Such stories were part of the performance. One would-be starlet dramatized her martyrdom in front of the camera after the stage performance. In the central feature of a mass daily, a photograph showing her in her stage costume, conspicuously constricted in corset and wide steel belt, was given the heavy-type caption which played humorously on a blatant contradiction: "FLAT OUT—SO KEEN TO SMOOTHE HER CURVES THAT SHE FAINTED 10 SECONDS AFTER THIS PICTURE. Rochelle Lofting has a 42–20–36 figure that most girls in show business would envy. But she thinks her curves get in the way of her ambition to be a straight actress. Now . . . she is trying to flatten things out with a steel belt . . . Says Rochelle: 'The belt makes me feel so ill.' "[18]

The publicity and martyrological value of the waspie outlasted its fashionability. In 1965 Natalie Wood filled the cover of a popular magazine in a period corset which Hollywood was allegedly using to kill her. "Her directors apparently regard her as prime wasp-waist fodder only. Having reduced her to a 19-inch waist, the producers and publicity boys now call for a 17-inch one. 'I take a beating every time I step into one of these dresses.' "[19]

An excessively small waist, period-corsetted or not, was a proven means for the would-be starlet to seize the public eye. It also served the press to stimulate reader participation by appeals for emulation, as, for instance, of a minor horror film actress called Vampira, 38–17–36. A sixteen-year-old reader came forward to demonstrate how she could belt her natural 17 inches into 14, "a waisted talent that's not waisted" *(Reveille)*. [20] *Reveille*, a popular cheesecake but also a family magazine, showed something of a mania for featuring lacing on all kinds of garments, and for punning ad nauseam on such words as "lacing," "boning," "waist" and their cognates. The build-up to the launching of arch-fetishist Mrs. Ethel Granger (cf. appendix p. 336) used the tactic of summoning readers to compete for the smallest waist title. Mrs. Granger was to win easily (at 13 inches), and later to enter the 24 million copies (by 1974) of the *Guinness Book of Records* as the World's Smallest Waist. All this is a peculiar and almost parodistic manifestation of the familiar commercial media exploitation of human bodies: of women in sexual competition, as of men in sporting competition, the wasp-waist mania partaking of both kinds.

As in sport, there was cheating: precautions were taken to prevent contenders for beauty titles from improving their contour by means of waspies worn beneath the swimsuit, and yet Margit Nünke, Miss Germany of 1955, was known to do just this in aid of her 19 inch waist (diagrammed in the press by means of a plain circle 19 inches in circumference).

The well-known corset-cum-swimsuit of one of the primary sex symbols of the postwar age, the Playboy Bunny, was determined, in part, by the waspie of fashion, which has thereby left a cultural mark much longer lasting than the fashion itself. We have stressed that many of the fetishistic and sado-masochistic elements in the fashion of the Sixties seemed very ephemeral; they had little immediate popular impact. The Playboy Bunny, in her curious costume, preserves the connection between the ideas of underwear and outerwear, the inaccessible and the accessible, the service of sex and the sexuality of service.

There are complex social contradictions at work here. One of the most curious—and ephemeral—instances of haute couture trying to introduce the structure of underwear into outerwear, was the January 1954 show of Jacques Fath, briefly noted above. We mention it again because its success was with the popular media, and not at all with the high fashion magazines, where it received scant attention. The media embrace was intense and ambivalent. Fath's corset-suit and corset-dress were massively headlined in all the popular newspapers. Rumors were circulated that the master's mannequins had been mercilessly starved despite the freezing weather and that the loveliest of them had fainted away altogether. At the presentation one could hear them gasping for air while being prepared in the wings, before they stalked out before the spectators in haughty disdain of the sensation caused by their 18-inch waists. One Doubting Thomas, unable to believe in the reality of this fashionable resurrection, actually had to poke her finger into the solid side of a model as she passed.

The popular press complained at "whalebone straitjackets," the "suffering" and even fainting spells Fath was inflicting,[21] but was soon giving instructions on how to put boning into dresses, once the initial shock and the hostility (which was only superficial) wore off. Fath died soon after, and his idea with him, to be resurrected at odd times by the media. The famous socialite Gloria Vanderbilt, for instance (prompted, she said, by a particular taste of her husband's) appeared in cinched and boned gowns of period flavor, which elicited at least one (printed) traditional fetishist letter telling of matrimonial bliss through tight-lacing.[22]

In most period films the lacing is intended merely to spice a little incidental private strip-tease. There are, however, a number of exceptions, much cherished by fetishists, which relate tight-lacing to plot and/or characterization, and tap into some central symbolic and mythological structures. In the MGM film *Two Weeks With Love* (1950) the corset assumes a leading narrative role and functions as an instrument of punishment for vanity or sexual ambition, rather in the manner of a Freudian medieval fairy tale. A younger sister, envious of her elders' success with men which she attributes to their being allowed to wear an adult corset, determines to buy one on her own account. In her guilty haste and ignorance, she acquires from a sinister-looking Mephistophelean salesman, a corset which is (unknown to her) orthopedic in intent, although of no normal orthopedic use (it is really a "magic" corset): it locks when the back is arched at a certain angle. This happens suddenly when the heroine, proudly displaying her new figure in a fantasy sequence in which she dances ecstatically through marble halls, throws herself into a climactic, acrobatic pose. In great pain, fear and humiliation, she has to be carried off and cut free, well-punished for having striven for a form of sexual ecstasy by the very instrument of that striving.

The young girl's error here, perhaps, was to have undertaken so audacious an adventure all on her own. The corset is essentially a shared ritual. This emerges, in two complementary ways, in the period film *Waltz of the Toreadors* (1962). The heroine is shown in the bedroom wrestling desperately with her staylace, in mute but pathetic appeal for physical help and sexual relief from her elderly and evasive beau, who is meanwhile (in an intercut sequence) being boozed up for the nuptial night by dissolute hunting companions below. Here, the corset symbolizes love unrequited, hindered; but earlier in the same film it acted as the auxiliary of erotic pleasure. After she has been hooked out of a river where she was attempting suicide, she undergoes artificial respiration at the hands of a young fisherman. Far from taking the obvious precaution of unlacing her to ease her breath, and the equally obvious pretext for getting her naked, he presses through the steels over her belly, further enhancing the already corset-enhanced panting, which reaches semi-conscious ecstasy.

The period corset also asserted itself in films with contemporary settings. Sophia Loren, as the *Millionairess* (1960) chasing a poor Indian doctor (Peter Sellers), pays him a surprise visit in his office, and takes advantage of his back being turned and his call to the next patient to enter and undress. She quickly and dramatically sheds an elegant loose-fitting Balmain creation, to reveal herself in a black period corset of a solidity and shape exceeding the standards of even the most period-inspired theatrical corsetry of the day, with the lacing running in an unusual wide V from shoulders to waist. (The scene was also used on all the film posters and was the subject of a special feature in a popular magazine).[23] Her underwear is as incongruous to her outer dress as her action is to the situation; and the sudden revelation of her dark sexual purpose symbolized by the bizarre black corset, throws the object of her desire into a comic state of panic.

The effectiveness of such a scene was increased by the fact that the waisted silhouette was by this date out of fashion. It now became possible to use the fetishistic period detail with a kind of historical objectivity, rather than as a sexy and/or farcical adjunct to a strip-tease interlude. *La Viaccia* (about 1961) captures a chronologically and sociologically localized period atmosphere: that of a Florentine brothel around 1880. It sets out to be non-sexy and breathes a new kind of sleazy eroticism consonant with the mood of sexual disillusion of the 1960s. Costumier Pietro Tosi said he aimed to recapture a faded sub-demi-monde existence for which he found visual inspiration in an old art and pornographic photographs; he wished to reveal the second-rate provincial appearance of prostitutes, in their stiffly langourous poses, in their worn-out stuffs, and dress demonstrating the sartorial errors and tricks of the poor. The underwear, which is constantly on view, is redolent of tarnished sex and soiled luxury, rather than conventional eroticism.[24]

The leading actress, Claudia Cardinale, had never before played a period part or a prostitute and was doubly scared until corsetted and dressed. Tosi gave her an hour-glass, pouter-pigeon silhouette which somehow managed to have nothing to do with Hollywood glamour and everything to do with contemporary illustrations to *La Vie Parisienne*. Her alternately languorous and jerky movements seemed an emanation of her richly curved but very constricted corset shape. Never naked and hardly ever fully dressed, the ever-present heroine was confined to, as well as in, an unchanging corset, made of a once-white color, authentic in construction down to the last stitch, and worn more tightly laced than in any period film hitherto; so much so that, during the shooting the director Bolognini felt obliged constantly to monitor his leading lady's state of mind and body. Being the star of the brothel where most of the film is situated, she was also more obviously constricted than any of her colleagues, whose corsetry is the subject of comedy rather than pathos. This, then, was her uniform, whether for receiving clients below, or satisfying them above. It was the equipment of the professional who cannot afford to waste time in preliminary love-play or dressing and undressing between clients; the mark of an oppressed class which is never free to enjoy real love and real erotic pleasure. The symbolism of oppression extends to her naturally luxuriant hair, which is always piled in ungainly knots and straggling wisps on top of her head.

The implicit symbolic equation of her tight-laced state with her psychological and social oppression becomes explicit towards the end in a dramatic crux. She is at last obliged to leave her lover and return to her only paying job. "Come upstairs," she says dully to a grey, unappetizing Everyman, adding in a gloomy undertone, "I must get this corset off, it's killing me."

Tosi's hand also appears a little later in the costumes of Visconti's *Leopard*, during the filming of which the extras (drawn from the local Sicilian aristocracy) were said to have fainted away in droves, while lead-actress Claudia Cardinale was "skinned alive." The situation became so alarming that air-conditioning had finally to be installed in the palace of Palermo where most of the film was shot. The famous English television series *The Forsyte Saga* was also reported to have sent the actresses to the studio windows gasping for air.

Here, as in the publicity of the '50s exploiting the concepts of sacrifice and martyrdom, we are dealing less with individual responses, than with media tactics. Fainting and gasping at studio-windows may or may not have been real-life reactions to actual costumes; but such stories, formulaic in nature, served the mythology of Suffering in the Cause of Art. There is an obvious advantage in exaggerating this mythology, but the reality, where there are no publicity, commercial or professional stakes, can be rather different. This was brought home to me by an occasional theatrical director with many years experience at the Renaissance Pleasure Faire which is held annually in California. As an amateur using amateurs for his troupe, and from his observation of other amateurs (students, mostly) appearing on the various stages and wandering around the Faire site, he was struck by the readiness of young women to endure the most uncomfortable-looking, bulky, tight and occlusive costumes, all day long and in the blazing heat of a Southern California May. Girls who normally wore nothing more restrictive than the elastic waistband of their panty-hose, appeared actively to enjoy and said they enjoyed the unusual sensations of very waist- and breast-compressive renaissance/baroque stays, which some chose to wear, quite recklessly, next-to-skin.

In recent years the trend in period films has been away from the 19th century to the Renaissance, the flat-chested and high or un-waisted costumes of which are attuned to the fashion of the '60s. The torso of Geneviève Bujold as Ann Boleyn in *Anne of the Thousand Days* (1969) presented a rigidly smooth conical shape straight out of a

Holbein portrait, in contrast to the flagrant anachronism of Elizabeth Taylor's obstinately hourglass figure in the *Taming of the Shrew* (Zeffirelli, c. 1967), a film which was otherwise tastefully costumed in the early Venetian Renaissance style.

There is not enough to Renaissance underwear to exercise much erotic fascination; and the fetishism of corsets and frillies may well be on the way out. It is perhaps no accident that the Soviet Union, which is exempt from Western conventions in the matter of Victorian strip-tease, has produced a film which exploits in the most startling and imaginative way an object of so bizarre an appearance and of so obscure a history that no Western film costumier has thought or dared to use it: the iron stays of the late Renaissance, discussed above.

In Grigori Kozintsev's *Hamlet* (1963) a brief but distinct and chillingly silent episode is given to Ophelia just before the famous mad-scene, when she is dressed in mourning for her father by three hideous hags veiled in black. Iron stays exactly modelled on those surviving in Western museums are snapped into place around her stiff, entranced form with a sharp clang like the shutting of a prison door. Rejected by Hamlet, rejected by the court, she is thus incarcerated into her insanity. In a film which brings out like no other Hamlet production the oppressiveness of court life, and visualizes with such sinister profundity Hamlet's own metaphor of Denmark as a rotting dungeon, this use of corset-as-prison could not be more telling.

In both the Russian *Hamlet* and the Italian *Viaccia*, an authentically reconstructed historic corset assumes in an open, serious and expressive way, the symbolic role which the media has tended to mask in amused nostalgia: that of social and erotic oppression, in which the aura of self-imposed martyrdom is submerged.

Postwar Fetishist Literature

The mass media of print and film have necessarily presented fetishism in a very fragmentary and adulterated form. The concentrated distillations of fetishism are to be found in certain cultural fringe magazines, some more amateurish, some more professional looking, previously sold in seedy pornographic bookstores, and now in the less depressed and repressed-looking "Sex Shops" proliferating in the larger Western cities.[25] With names which stress their private, escapist function, they appear to have reached their high point of popularity or visibility in the later '50s and '60s, at which time a comparable, culturally significant phenomenon emerged: the steel-and-leather bondage magazines published by Nutrix.[26] These very sophisticated, torturously sado-machochistic, machinoid-bondage nightmares were eventually suppressed by law, but not before they had caught the imagination of some Pop artists, notably Allen Jones.

In tandem to such magazines, which were directed in part at least towards realizable fantasies, there sprang up, especially in California (ever a breeding-ground of the bizarre), a number of small manufacturers, operating out of their own homes on small or non-existent profit-margins, and publishing "Theatrical Corset" catalogues.[27] Certain big-city shoe stores specialized in extreme heel heights: in Paris, Ernest on the Boulevard de Clichy became known through regular "editorial advertisements" in the highly respectable *Elle* magazine; in London, there was the much bigger operation of Regent Shoes, with regular advertisements in *The Stage* "for High Heels up to 8 inches for stage and street" and a big, regularly updated catalogue. Regent Shoes, on its Wardour Street site, could trace its fetish-shoe lineage back to the 19th century; recently bought out and "conventionalized" by the giant Raoul shoe chain, an historic fetishist institution has been wiped out by the mass market. In the U.S. the best known blend of sexy fashion and fetishism is, of course, the Frederick's of Hollywood chain.

Among the most prominent and characteristic small fetishist manufacturers of the '60s was the Natural Rubber Company in London, which advertised by means of small advertisements in the "quality" magazines, and specialized in occlusive, more or less restrictive rubber and leather garments. This flourished from about 1960 to 1967, around which time the proprietor was convicted of "conspiring to debauch and debase," condemned to heavy punishment, and left personally and professionally wrecked. Such was the fate of one who liked to call himself a "maker of toys for adults." Still thriving, on the other hand, is Atomage, founded in 1963 by John Sutcliffe, whose three-to-four person firm makes elaborately tricked out, more or less restrictive vinyl and leatherwear for a hundred or so private clients, and occasionally for film, television and fashion companies.

In London there are two well-known specialists in "traditional" tight-lacing corsets: Mme. Medeq, who no longer needs to advertise, shuns publicity, refuses mail orders, and enjoys a reputation as high as her prices among her élite clientele (60 percent men, 40 percent women). Less wealthy fetishists go to Arthur Gardner and Son, founded 1899, and run by a direct descendant who also caters, with the help of much advertising in the popular press, to "conventional" old-fashioned taste (as does—or did—Voller's of Portsmouth).

These and other more ephemeral personal enterprises, testimony to the taste and activism of one sexual minority among many others, have in their small and indeterminable way both reflected and affected developments in fashion and the popular media (including the comic book, omitted here altogether). Fashion and the media have found common denominators among the various larger sexual minority tastes, have tapped all kinds of sexual vulnerability, and will no doubt continue to do so as long as we let them.

Notes

1. *Harper's Bazaar* 15 Sep., p. 51.
2. This, the following quotations and most of the information contained in this section are taken from the trade journals *Corset and Underwear Review* (Haire Publications, New York) and *Corsets and Brassières—The Foundation Garment Review* (Bowman Publications).
3. *Harper's Bazaar*, Dec. 1944, headline "Paris Purified."
4. "In You Go": *Vogue*, Aug. 1951. Prissy: *Harper's Bazaar*, Aug. 1951.
5. London *Sketch*, 4 Aug. 1954.
6. Balmain: *Vogue*, 1 Nov. 1951 and Oct. 1952. Norell: *HB* Feb. 1952.
7. The technology of the stiletto heel is a saga of materials science development in itself. As summarized for me by Dr. Michael Clarke, a Professor of Metallurgy at the City of London Polytechnic, in a private communication: "the heel went through several structural changes. At first it was made with the bottom half in aluminum screwing into a wooden top half. This was found unsatisfactory for several reasons, one of which was that the leather covering tended to come off; and, which was worse, with wear the one-eighth inch rivet screwed into the heel-tip began to stand out, and to wreak even greater havoc on wooden flooring. Experiments with copper plating failed, and the problem was not really solved until the whole heel was moulded in polystyrene."
8. Miss Marshall: *Star*, 21 April 1961. "Shoe Pinches": *Times*, 3 June 1957. "Murder Underfoot": *Observer*, 22 Oct. 1961. Downward path: *Evening News and Star*, 18 Oct. 1961. For an orthodox medical attack, see Dr. John Parr in *Daily Mail*, 8 Sep. 1964; the medical press itself was roused to a lengthy and hostile correspondence (*British Medical Journal*, 1957; for a lonely letter in defense of high heels, see McDonagh, ibid., 10 Aug., p. 353).
9. Which did not prevent the Dean of the California Podiatry Hospital and College in San Francisco from accusing them, Victorian-style, of causing everything from eye-strain to leg-muscle aches, arthritis, and displacement of the spine and neck (*National Enquirer*, 23 Apr. 1972).
10. Head up: *Vogue*, 1 Nov. 1966. Nureyev: Dec. 1967. Samburne: *H.B.* Feb. 1964. Turquoise bell choker: *Vogue*, 1 Nov. 1967, cover.
11. *Daily Mail*, 5 Nov. 1948.
12. Her mechanical ingenuity here is gratuitous; contemporary tight-lacers know that manual self-lacing is not hard, and that the method shown stereotypically by film, publicity and "girlie" photograph, of the lacer pulling the lace diametrically backwards while the lacee holds on to some point of support, is visually rather than functionally effective. Fetishists know that the easiest and most efficient way of lacing is to draw the laces, crossed over, parallel with the lacee's body and the corset edge, thus minimizing the angle of incidence, preserving the lacee's balance, and obviating the need for her to hold on to any furniture.
13. *Women's Sunday Mirror*, 29 Sep. 1957, "but the director of Naked Earth expects no trouble, for (they) are playing a married couple."
14. *Reveille*, 14 Feb. 1954. Cf. also an equally "gratuitous" photograph of Dawn Addams, by Philippe Halsman, no less, centerspread in the sober family magazine *Picture Post* 16 Oct. 1954.
15. *Reveille*, 31 Oct. 1957.

16. *Sunday Times* Magazine, 11 Apr. 1965.

17. *Evening News*, Feb. 1957. The 18-inch measurement was not, as far as I know, verified, but it was accepted—even by the reader who wrote enthusiastically to say his neck measured more than the actress' waist.

18. "Is Beauty Worth Torture": *Daily Sketch*, 2 Sep. 1957. Lofting: *Daily Sketch*, 25 May 1957.

19. *Tidbits*, 18 Dec. 1965.

20. *Reveille*, 5 April 1957.

21. E.g. *Daily Mail*, 26 Jan. and 4 March 1954.

22. *San Francisco Chronicle*, 18 Dec. 1968, p. 2W. Even more recently, cf. *Los Angeles Times*, 15 Aug. 1976, V, 12a.

23. Cover and inside story in *Today*, 6 Aug. 1960.

24. Cf. the view of Alain Robbe-Grillet (*Evergreen Review*, October 1966, p. 90), for whom the actress in this film represented "The most complete embodiment of modern eroticism . . . imposing (this panoply of eroticism) on her was a kind of rape."

25. These successors of *London Life*, small, expensive and inaccessible relative to their forbear, went under such names as *Bizarre* (published, drawn and written by ex-*London Life* contributor John Coutts ("Willie"), starting 1946, and reaching no. 26 around 1959; *Exotique* (or *Exotica*), Burmel Publishing Company, started in 1954, and reaching no. 38 around 1960; *Bizarre Life* (Gene Bilbrew, principal illustrator, later 1960s); *Fantasia; Extatique;* and *Manique.* In the early '60s the most accessible and perhaps successful type of fetish literature was the larger, glossier magazines called *Satana, Masque, High Heels,* and the intelligently sexological *Erotica* (1963 ff.). An English fetishist magazine, small, cheaply produced and obviously linked to *London Life,* was called *Fads and Fancies* (fl. 1950s, Plate 60).

John Coutts' *Sweet Gwendoline,* a fetishist classic, has recently been lavishly reprinted by Belier Press and gained recognition among comic book fans.

26. The emergence of Nutrix magazines may be connected with suppression of the horror comics, indicted in a famous book by Frederick Wertham (*Seduction of the Innocent,* 1954). The bondage elements in these comics went underground and acquired an intensified, fetishistic form in Nutrix. Cf. Freeman, ch. 9, "Our Fettered Friends" for a tongue-in-cheek, but more positive approach than Wertham's.

27. They advertised quite heavily in "girlie" magazines under such names as Finecraft, H. G. Specialty Co., Barry's Bazaar, and Renée Fashion Co., all of California.

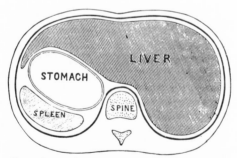

Fig. 6.—Section of the Body with a natural waist, showing the space available for the viscera and their natural position.

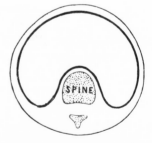

Fig. 7.—Section of a Body with a deformed waist, showing the altered outline and the greatly diminished space available for the viscera.

CONCLUSION

Civilized and Primitive Body-Sculpture

The rapidly advancing anthropology of the later 19th century offered new perspectives for the understanding of a "barbaric" European practice. The rigid Christian ethnocentricity of the reformers had to contend against a growing appreciation of the primitive, the sexual and the magical, derived from the study of non-European cultures. These cultures, although widely considered inferior, were also affecting vanguard developments in the visual arts generally. The flamboyant display of sartorial barbarisms apart from tight-lacing—gaudy, fake jewelry, clashing colors, "crippling" footwear, "naked" jersey and cuirasse styles, "tattooed" stockings, not to speak of unspeakable "secret" fetishes such as real tattooing and nipple-piercing, were early harbingers of a wave of cultural primitivism not established in art until the advent of Expressionism and Cubism in the early years of the century.

Chinese footbinding was a lesson to all. This ancient custom, practiced by an intelligent and cultivated people, was culturally ingrained and seemingly impossible to extirpate. Its resistance to criticism, both Chinese and European, underlined the futility of the campaign against a European primitivism considered as ancient in origin and even more dangerous.[1] One could no more reason with a European woman about her tight-lacing than with a Chinese lady about her footbinding.

However much Christian imperialism in China, Africa, or Oceania strove to uproot them, the native customs resisted. Their strength and significance were recognized by some as superior, in their way, to that of irrationally oscillating European fashions. They constituted a permanent feature of apparently unchanging societies which managed in the face of great odds to preserve their cultural identity. The knowledge that the body decoration and mutilation of primitive

295

peoples served to preserve tribal identities, raised the dread suspicion, fleetingly countenanced by popular German anthropology, that tight-lacing was unconsciously practised in order to enhance the supposedly "European racial characteristic" of a slender waist, in much the same way as the Chinese, with their "racial characteristic" of small feet and thick waists, bound the foot and left the waist free.[2] Theories along these lines were sought in pre-Darwinian writers such as Schopenhauer and Alexander von Humboldt (they are adumbrated as early as Bulwer), and seemed confirmed by Darwin's own theory of natural selection, although Darwin never mentioned tight-lacing as such. Since one of the purposes of comparative anthropology and ethnography in Germany was to demonstrate the physical-aesthetic superiority of the white "European race," the idea that tight-lacing represented an attempt to enhance a primary indicator of that racial aesthetic superiority, was exceedingly disquieting.

Critics of the corset had moreover to overcome a fairly widespread feeling that it represented an emblem of technological superiority, of civilization itself. The story was circulated that as soon as the female slaves were freed in Brazil, they rushed out to buy and wear corsets.[3] A reformer lamented that the "first thing a heathen convert desires is, not a Bible, but a corset."[4] In his satirical allegory *Penguin Island,* Anatole France imagines the very moment of transition from animal to human consciousness as signalled by the young female penguins binding themselves beneath the breast in order to attract male attention. And yet tight-lacers, in their disregard for progeny, placed themselves lower than the animals themselves.

Some writers regarded the corset less as an instrument of barbaric regression, than as an example of mechanical ingenuity and advanced technology applied to costume. Many 18th and 19th century corsets are indeed of very complex construction, and there must have been far more patents taken out relating to corset construction than any other article of clothing. The great Paris exhibition of 1867 was symbolized on a magazine cover of the time, as a fashionable lady on whose corset and chignon labourers haul, with cables and cranes, raising in her a mighty industrial-age structure, while the clamor of machinery and pleasure resounds about her.[5]

Against the recognition of the corset as an emblem of technological civilization, the historic association of tight-lacing with the animal, notably the ape, seems simply comic, although it was intended seriously. Time and again we have seen tight-laced women compared with apes and even literally treated as such in laboratory experiments repeated as late as the mid-20th century. The ape's amusing ability to imitate human activity, while remaining as "mindless" as any other wild animal, made it a favorite emblem of folly, while at the same time it served as a symbol of unbridled sexuality. This then was the tight-lacer: an anthropomorphic creature governed by animal instincts. From the later 18th century onwards, degrading comparisons reached further down the evolutionary scale, to the wasp of course (favored particularly because of its supposed viciousness) but also spider and ant, whose low, dangerous character, as well as shape, these women shared.[6]

Tight-lacing was not merely an embarrassing primitivism in the context of a great civilization dedicated to wiping savagery off the face of the globe, it was in the view of some actually *worse* than the barbarisms which the Europeans hoped to abolish. It had been since the late 18th century a commonplace of the reformers to find primitive mutilations less dangerous than tight-lacing and high heels, and primitive races generally in better health than Europeans. The argument was however complicated by the discovery of late 19th century anthropology that mutilations did not cause or reflect noticeable physical degeneration among primitives. Indeed, the very opposite might be the case. Sir William Flower, respected anthropologist, Director of the Natural History Museum and opponent of tight-lacing, was fain to accept the empirical explanations of the Peruvian Indians who claimed that head-flattening promoted health, strength and courage, and the conclusions of experts working among another group of head-flatteners, the Indians of Vancouver Island, that the practice did not have a visibly deleterious effect on the brain; on the contrary. Indeed, "some tribes appear to be more intelligent than their neighbors not practicing deformation."[7] In his polemic against tight-lacing, Flower is blind to the contradiction in his position, which held that while deformation among primitives may be harmless or even beneficial, deformation among the civilized must always be harmful. Characteristically, he understood more of the purpose of the custom practiced in a very remote part of the world than that which he saw around him in London. Or, sensing the sexual purpose of the latter, he was unable to deal with it.

Paradoxically it was certain "inferior" (if not primitive) cultures whose influence on fashion was making the task of the reformers easier—if not preempting it altogether. The looser, less form-fitting styles, as well as many materials and ornamental patterns tended to come from the East, especially the Muslim and (East) Indian cultures. Muslim harem and Indian dance-costume (notably that of the Bayadère so popular in European Ballet) was held to represent an ideal, natural and perhaps the nearest surviving classical form of attire.[8] But there were striking paradoxes in this area too: the Circassian slave-dancer (another favorite heroine of European ballet), widely praised for her sensuous dance and the "natural" and "classical" slenderness of her body, but seldom seen in her native habitat, was in reality encased from childhood in a tightly swathed bark or leather corset. This succeeded in inhibiting the growth of the whole of the upper torso and breasts much more drastically than the European corset.[9] Turkish upper-class ladies who in the early 18th century could only explain European stays as a bizarre form of body-prison imposed by the jealous husband,[10] by the middle of the 19th century were taking to those stays, as part of Western dress, in a gesture of emancipation. Mongéri, a French physician living in Constantinople where he admired Circassian dancers as the quintessence of the ancient Greek ideal, was shocked that the "Gothic shackles" of European stays should "threaten to invade the Orient in a manner as complete as it would be disastrous."

Africanists have noted that body decoration and sculpture is more important to nomadic than sedentary tribes, because it is the only way for those lacking in material possessions and a permanent base to express status and tribal identity. It is as if such identity is in constant need of affirmation and must be borne continuously, inseparably and permanently upon the body. It might further be argued that deformations and mutilations tend to become exaggerated in response to some continuous threat to cultural identity and survival, such as that posed by a neighboring tribe, the white slave-trader or alien rule. Such may be the case in China, where a traditional but mild degree of footbinding was possibly intensified under the alien, warlike (and large-footed) Manchu dynasty, and perhaps exaggerated even further when Europeans invaded in the 19th century.[11] As with tight-lacing, the period of the most severe footbinding may have coincided with the period when it was most heavily under attack and threatened altogether with extinction (which in fact followed soon afterwards). This period also represents, East and West, a major historical crisis.

The Christian West has undergone a series of crises ever since the later middle ages, precipitated in part by external invasion, notably that of Islam, whose "loose" costume and mores seemed in many ways diametrically opposed to those of "tight" Christianity. Since the 17th century there was no longer any fear of Islamic invasion, but the internal contradictions of feudal-Christian culture in conflict with expanding capitalism and capitalism in conflict with itself and early socialism, delivered seismic shocks to the European social system which threatened the identity not so much of "tribal" (national) as of socio-economic groups.

Modern Europe has been in an acute and continuous state of class struggle, the pattern of which might be traced (if only we knew how) rather precisely in the costume of the various periods and places, as it has been observed in war, religion, politics, etc. It is my contention that the more provocative and controversial fashions—among which tight-lacing is of course in the first rank—have been adopted by the socially mobile or, to pick up a distinction made earlier, the socially nomadic classes: those striving upwards, those resisting repression downwards, those feeling disenfranchised. We have adduced evidence that tight-lacing was practised primarily and typically by lower classes: by bourgeois aspiring to aristocratic rank (although here, in the pre-19th century period, the evidence is rather sparse) and more certainly by lower-middle and working-class elements aspiring to the symbols of bourgeois leisure; by women, always the disenfranchised vis-à-vis men, aspiring to social power by manipulating a sexuality which the patriarchy found threatening. Even when practised by people of more respectable classes, tight-lacing could be credibly stigmatized as the "very badge of vulgarity," as the habit of social primitives. The tight-lacers themselves never pointed to the social models among the upper classes—and there were virtually none.

One might construct from within these lower classes an individual psychological "tight-lacing type" who chafed individually under a special sense of social impotence and/or sexual frustration. This sense may have been tied to a particular period in life—often late adolescence and early maturity—when a sexualized form of self-constraint presented a means to protest social and parental constraint generally, and the model of the ever-breeding, child-centered mother particularly. The male tight-lacer was also protesting a dominant social stereotype, that of the asexual, work- and family-oriented man.

While the medical claims of the damage caused by tight-lacing were often wildly exaggerated, in some instances at least one cannot doubt that profoundly unhappy women and girls deliberately courted severe injury and even death, as happens today with anorexia, a disease peculiar to (and increasing among) young women. Tight-lacing comes out of pain—the individual pain, and particularly the woman's pain. It was always potentially and often actually a painful form of social resistance—against the unwanted pregnancy, which tight-lacing was used to abort, against the imposed maternal role, which tight-lacing more-than-symbolically protested. The pain was not only that of the relatively few who manifested the fetish publicly in this particular, exaggerated form, but part of the wider distress suffered by women generally at a time when sex-roles were for the first time being seriously challenged. The "morning nip" of the tight-lacer was likened to that of the drunkard; it was seriously, and correctly, likened to drugs like opium (which was also largely used by women); like opium it numbed pain, or else overlaid psychological stress with a physical stress and discipline easier to bear and better rewarded.

The capacity to transmute that physical pain into pleasure is a mystery that neither physiology nor psychology may ever solve. But a historical analysis such as this can show that it is tied to certain unique historical moments in the struggle for social and sexual liberation, a struggle which will never again manifest itself in quite the same form, but which nevertheless continues.

Notes

1. The Chinese themselves retaliated by pointing to the worse dangers of tight-lacing. Among them were the Minister Wu in his American lectures, and the Empress Dowager before Europeans visiting or residing in China, and Europeanized Chinese (Headland p. 291).

2. Cf. the widely read Stratz, *Racial Beauty of Women*, p. 39.

3. According to Witkowski p. 336, half a million corsets were sold in Brazil in three days. Cf Th. Z. in *Der Floh*, 23 June 1889.

4. Ecob, p. 114.

5. *Journal Amusant*, 13 April 1867.

6. The connection is made explicit by Fischer-Dunkel, p. 132f.

7. *Fashion in Deformity*, p. 336. Cranial deformation intrigued anthropologists because it was of ancient origin (it had been deplored by Greek physicians), was of world-wide distribution, and had survived in certain parts of 20th century Europe, notably outlying parts of France in the North and in the South around Toulouse (whence the name "déformation toulousaine"). French physicians were worried because a large proportion of the inmates of mental hospitals had apparently been subjected to the deformation in infancy. See Gosse, 1855, for a contemporary objective analysis of existing, highly contradictory opinion on the effects of cranial deformation as practiced in and outside Europe. For a more modern work, cf. Dembo, 1938.

8. The wasp-waist, while it was never the aim of Indian dress, was of course the ideal posited in famous Indian sculptures and the national epic: "Your magnificent breasts, fat and round . . . that waist which I can encircle with my fingers" (cited by Mode p. 40).

9. As any reader of Pallas' famous *Travels* (1793–4) I, p. 398f., must have known. Pallas' account was enlarged by Taitbout de Marigny in 1837 (p. 35) and picked up by other writers. According to Pallas, the men, reputed a fierce warrior race and fine dancers (they were models for the Russian cossacks), deliberately compressed their feet in shoes in which they danced almost on the pointe. "Circassian corsets" were marketed during the neo-classical period; advertisements in Gillham, No. 28 (cf. Laver, *Clothes*, p. 127, and Mundt p. 12 for the "natural" body of Circassian dancers).

10. Lady Mary Wortley Montague, *Letters*, 1717, p. 286

11. This is speculation. Howard Levy's book on Chinese footbinding, the only comprehensive treatment available in English, does not raise the question.

Appendix

A. Rituals

From the *Queen* 18 July 1862

Is it true that small waists are again coming into fashion generally? I am aware
that they cannot be said to have gone out of fashion altogether, for one often
sees very slender figures; but I think during the last few years they have been
less thought of than formerly. I have heard, however, from several sources,
and by the public prints, that they are again to be *La Mode*. Now I fortunately
possess a figure which will, I hope satisfy the demand of fashion in this
respect. What is the smallest-sized waist that one can have? Mine is sixteen-
and-a-half inches, and, I have heard, is considered small. I do not believe
what is said against the corset, though I admit that if a girl is an invalid, or has
a very tender constitution, too sudden a reduction of the waist may be
injurious. With a waist which is, I believe, considered small, I can truly say I
have good health. If all that was said against the corset were true, how is it so
many ladies live to an advanced age? A friend of mine has lately died at the
age of eighty-six, who has frequently told me anecdotes of how in her young
days she was laced cruelly tight and at the age of seventeen had a waist
fifteen inches. Yet she was eighty-six when she died. I know that it has been
so long the habit of public journals to take their example from medical men
(who, I contend, are not the best judges in the matter) in running down the
corset, and the very legitimate, and, if properly employed, harmless mode of
giving a graceful slenderness to the figure, that I can hardly expect that at
present you will have the courage to take the part of the ladies . . .

yours etc. Constance

From the *Queen*, 25 July 1863

In reply to her (Constance's) first question, there is little doubt, I think, that
slender and long waists will ere long be *la mode*. Ladies of fashion here who
are fortunate enough to possess such enviable and graceful attractions, take
most especial care by the arrangement of their toilets to show them off to the
very best advantage. A waist of sixteen and a-half inches would, I am of
opinion, be considered, for a lady of fair average size and stature, small
enough to satisfy even the most exacting of Fashion's votaries. The question
as to how small one's waist can be is rather hard to answer, and I am not
aware that any standard has yet been laid down on the subject, but an
application to any of our fashion corset-makers for the waist measurement of
the smallest sizes made would go far to clear the point up. Many of the

301

corsets worn at our late brilliant assemblies were about the size of your correspondent's, and some few, I have been informed, even less. I beg to testify most fully to the truth of the remarks made by Constance as to the absurdly-exaggerated statements (evidently made by persons utterly ignorant of the whole matter) touching the dreadfully injurious effects of the corset on the female constitution. My own, and a wide range of other experiences, leads me to a totally different conclusion, and I fully believe that, except in cases of confirmed disease or bad constitution, a well-made and nicely-fitting corset inflicts no more injury than a tight pair of gloves.

Up to the age of fifteen I was educated at a small provincial school, was suffered to run as nearly wild as could well be, and grew stout, indifferent and careless as to personal appearance, dress, manners, or any of their belongings. Family circumstances and change of fortune at this time led my relatives to the conclusion that my education required a continental finish . . .

. . . I was packed off to a highly-genteel and fashionable establishment for young ladies, situated in the suburbs of Paris. The morning after my arrival I was aroused by the clang of the "morning bell." I was in the act of commencing a hurried and by no means an elaborate toilet, when the under-governess, accompanied by a brisk, trim little woman, the bearer of a long cardboard case, made their appearance; corsets of various patterns, as well as silk laces of môst portentous length, were at once produced, and . . . my experiences in the art and mystery of tightlacing . . . commenced. My dresses were all removed, in order that the waists should be taken in and the make altered; a frock was borrowed for me for the day, and from that hour I was subjected to the strict and rigid system of lacing in force through the whole establishment, no relaxation of its discipline being allowed during the day on any pretence whatever. For the period (nearly three years) I remained as a pupil, I may say that my health was excellent, as was that of the great majority of my young companions in 'bondage,' and on taking my departure I had grown from a clumsy girl to a very smart young lady, and my waist was exactly seven inches less than on the day of my arrival.

From Paris I proceeded at once to join my relatives in the island of Mauritius, and on my arrival in the isle sacred to the memories of Paul and Virginia, I found the reign of "Queen Corset" most arbitrary and absolute, but without in any way that I could discover interfering with either the health or vivacity of her exceedingly attractive and pretty subjects . . .

Fanny

From the *Englishwoman's Domestic Magazine,* July and August 1868.

Perseverance writes—I had the good fortune recently to come across a work called *The Corset and The Crinoline,* which contained abundant extracts from an interesting correspondence which had appeared in your column on the merits and demerits of Tight-lacing. This discussion was new to me, and I confess I read with the greatest pleasure the testimony of so many votaries of the corset boldly speaking out the truth as to the advantages and comfort which are to be derived from its use, and proving that the health of the wearer does not suffer, even when the lacing has been most rigidly inflicted or unflinchingly self-imposed. I can corroborate them on all these points, as I am able to speak both from my own personal experience, and from the peculiar opportunities I have had of observing others who have been tight-lacers like myself . . .

. . . The small round taper waist . . . is so great and enhancing a charm in woman, and exercises, I do not hesitate to say, a most potent attraction on the majority of men. First then, I think that many neglected young ladies wishing to improve their figures will, on taking up their yard measure and finding their waists 23 or 24 inches or upwards round (sizes only too common), be discouraged by the high standard of perfection, 15 inches, to which many say they have reduced their figures, and who seem to write as if they were in the daily habit of wearing their corset thus closely confined. One lady alone I knew who could perform that feat, and she never exhibited her waist laced so small. I should be inclined to place the wearable limit at 17 inches, and should say that any girl may be proud of a waist 18 inches round, and that even 19 and 20 inches seem very neat and small on the English lady of average size and stature. When 15 inches and still smaller dimensions are mentioned, I cannot help thinking some mistake has been made—that the size has been taken from the corset when first sent home by the maker, perhaps only from her assertion meant to flatter and impose, and that it has not been fairly taken with the tape from the waist itself, even when most laced in for discipline or display. It is astonishing what mistaken notions many ladies, who are not in the habit of using the test of the measure, entertain, and, entertaining, assert in perfect good faith as to the dimensions of their figure. And it may be equally surprising to many to learn how much even the strongest and best made corset will stretch, if daily worn strictly and tightly laced. For example, I have mine made by one of our best artists, of silk or satin, stoutly lined, and when sent home they measure exactly 15 inches round, yet these will give an inch or more in a few days, after which they retain their size. Now I can, if disposed, lace into 16 inches, and always do so when fresh fitted, till the corset and I are one. But I confess I rarely ever lace into less than 17 inches, though I am very strict with myself never to allow my waist to exceed 18 inches; and, accordingly, I every morning, and whenever else opportunity serves, apply the measure—an article which I consider the indispensable handmaid of every tight-lacer who wishes to improve or keep her figure— and if I detect any excess I immediately reduce it. And now, though, with my dress on, 19 inches is about my size, still, if the voices of my friends and my own eyes do not deceive me, I display as small a figure as any of my countrywomen . . .

I must plead guilty to a touch of self-conceit in my last, but it will be perhaps explained when I confess that, though born a gentlewoman, and restored to that by marriage, I was once a lady's maid. Hence my experience. My first mistress (the smallness of whose figure—15 inches—I never saw surpassed) was, I fancy, attracted into engaging me on account of the trimness of mine. A lady who laces appreciates a sympathetic maid. And I have found that, where in girlhood it has been forgotten, in after life the maid can do much in promoting the use of the tight-fitting corset in the improve-ment of a neglected figure. As a missionary in the cause of tight-lacing, I can boast to have worked some marvellous conversions. My lady was an en-thusiast that way, and had her wardrobe filled with works of the best artistes of London and Paris. She soon placed me in possession of a tight little corset, and with its aid, and following her practice and example, I quickly managed, with ease and comfort to myself, to taper off my waist. Her simple practice was to have her corset first laced firmly, not too tightly, on from the top downwards; then securing the lace at bottom, and commencing there and lacing upwards, the stays were drawn in tightly round the small of the waist; some nine or ten eyelet-holes almost touching one another enabled this to be done effectually, and the pressure to be regulated to a nicety at the required spot. For under those circumstances the plaited lace will be found not to slip, however loose the lacing be elsewhere. The confinement of the waist causing the chest to expand, the slack of the lace was employed in easing the corset above, so as to leave the chest quite free and unconfined. The width of three fingers would have covered the restricted portion of the figure. Thus she, myself, and others, whom I have initiated in the same practice, have attained great tenuity where slimness is desirable without any ill effects, as far as I have ever perceived, on the health; besides winning that comfort and pleasurable sensation which, as several of your correspondents have mentioned, the support and pressure of the tightly-laced corset affording to the wearer, it is truly a reward and luxury to enjoy. I might tell an amusing story how, when from being a pupil I became a teacher in the art, I for some time educated the figure of an ambitious but shy young lady under the cover of a loose-fitting jacket; and how I was at last obliged to have recourse to a coup d'état to oblige her to exhibit the improvement made, and how she got an immediate reward for her pains in a present from an admiring brother of a riding-habit to show off her dainty little form; and how I am afraid this habit cost the little waist another inch to be taken off. But the details would be too long. However, it is an example of the fact which all who are the happy owners of little waists cannot but be aware of—that men will be found to admire them. My husband often laughingly tells me I caught him with my waist. I believe it first attracted his attention to me, though I flatter myself I won and held him by better qualities. Yet if he ever regrets the choice he made—and I believe not—I am sure I never regret that I was once, and still am, able to gratify his artistic taste by displaying in my figure that curved line of swelling wave and sinking hollow which Hogarth styled the Line of Beauty, and which the tight-laced corset alone so well produces, as is so well exhibited in the well-known engraving of that great painter, where he exemplifies its varied and graceful curves by as many sketches of the stays of his period. It is quite contrary to the fact, as some assert, that the tight-laced corset renders the figure stiff and ungainly; and if any one doubts me, I challenge them to ride behind some tight-laced beauty in Rotten-row, and compare the graceful undulations of her slightly-swaying figure with those of some companion untrammelled and unconfined by stays, and I feel certain of a verdict in favour of the corset and its effects.

Perseverance

From the *Englishwoman's Domestic Magazine*, September 1868.

I am also a widower, with two adopted nieces, and although I do not carry my admiration of tight-lacing to the point of wearing stays myself (rather a disgusting idea), I agree with the Widower who writes in your June number in his admiration of tight-lacing in young ladies. I will even go so far as to say that if a young lady has a pretty face and figure, there is no excess of tight-lacing in which she may please herself to indulge that is not an increase to her beauty. My nieces are respectively sixteen and seventeen years old, and as they are both very pretty and have lovely figures, I am anxious that they should make the best they can of them, and therefore join with the Widower in asking M. C. for her opinion in the matter of Viennese and French corsets. My nieces have a governess who is very severe with them in the matter of tight-lacing, and insists, through my orders, on the utmost amount of compression that they can bring when I wish them to look their prettiest. And here I must mention a point on which I quite disagree with M. C. No one would like a pretty girl to look slovenly at any time, but I cannot help thinking that coquetry is the gainer when a young lady, after having been seen in a trim morning dress, with its neatly-fitting belt of say 18 or 19 inches, appears at a picnic or a croquet party in an elegant dress, tightly fitting over a corset, in which, as M. C. says, "the potent lace" is made to do its work, and the utmost extremity of tight-lacing is employed to reduce the figure to its smallest dimensions. I tried this plan with my nieces quite lately, on the occasion of a picnic they went to. The elder came home delighted with the day, and avowed that she had never enjoyed herself so completely; indeed, she is always anxious to help her maid and governess in their efforts with the staylace, and delights in the half-pleasure, half-pain, of the intense pressure. But the younger was very much inclined to rebel at a corset much tighter than anything she had yet endured, but was forced to submit (by what process I know not, but the coercion was effectual), and could not but admit on her return that she was pleased with the amount of admiration she caused. She is a coquette by nature, but not old enough to know the value of the motto, "Il faut souffrir pour être belle." Now I want to know of M. C. what is the very best corset for compressing the figure that she knows of. Although not many will admit it, I am certain that half the charm in a small waist comes, not in spite of, but on account of, its being tight-laced, and that the uneasiness caused by the excessive pressure of a perfect corset gives an additional grace to the walk and movements of a graceful girl. Of course, the square-waisted and flat-breasted ladies who resemble raw schoolboys rather than anything female, cannot be expected to join in this view, and I suspect that it is to them that are due the letters that appear from time to time in your paper contrary to the run of the general opinion expressed. May I add that the occasional tight-lacing I describe cannot possibly be as harmful as the permanent alteration of the figure advocated by M. C.? If found to be too painful, which I doubt, it can be discontinued, or the pressure lessened on such important occasions as I speak of. For ordinary wear, no girl with any pretence to a good figure will find from 17 to 19 inches too small for comfort. I will not mention the size of the corset my elder niece wore on the above occasion, or I should not be believed, but her figure was a delight to the eye.

La Gêne

"My first corset" by a Parisienne, La Vie Parisienne *11 June, 1870, pp. 464–5, abridged.*

The first of my dreams when I evoke distant but undying memories, was to wear a corset, the dream of every Parisienne over twelve years old, I imagine—formerly, at least—for today they accept it as natural that they should come into the world with false hips, false calves and false hair. We were less spoiled in my childhood, which is not all that long ago, and artifice was limited to the bouffant petticoat which, together with a little bodice innocent of boning, comprised our underwear. We were very comfortable, supple, agile, but modelled about as much as a piece of board, and the coquettes suffered a great deal . . .

I will always remember a torture of my childhood. At dinner they made me show my décolletage, that is a little pair of rather red shoulders, with jutting collar-bone and shoulder blades; how I envied the round bust of mother and the other ladies! I observed that several of them had deceptive corsages, to judge by their hands, neck and face. . . One of my class-friends revealed the mystery to me. Until then, I had seen her as a tom-boy, badly built, frumpish. One day she arrived transformed: 48 cms (19 inches) around the waist, and such contours!!! "What's happened to you, for heaven's sake?" I asked her. "Nothing", she replied, "I have a corset on." That explained it all! But everyone at home said I was too young for one.

There is nothing like a good old ruse. My ambition, a few months before, had been to get a lorgnette which represented, in my view, the summit of coquetry, impertinence and audacity. I pretended to be short-sighted; but they gave me spectacles instead! So, the following day, I was to be found more short-sighted than ever, crouching over my desk, head bowed, body twisted, and I obstinately refused to abandon this uncomfortable position despite the cries of my entourage, the threat of those horrid spectacles, the prophesy of a hunched back and a certain pink ribbon by which Miss Penn, who was proficient in tortures, tied me to the back of my chair. On the point of suffocation, I did not yield. The vision of a corset, surrounded by an aureole of rewards, sustained my efforts, lent me the necessary heroism. Finally I wore down the opposition, with the complicity of my maid, Mlle Julie, who would repeat every morning, "Mademoiselle *is turning*. And to take one's first communion without a corset . . . well!"

I was measured for a corset. I shall never forget that ceremony. Curious to say, it was a man who came to certify that the time had come to prevent me from becoming hunch-backed and who noted minutely the proportions of my little person. He asked for a week to create his masterpiece, a week during which I thought I would die of joy. We all die of joy while we wait.

The disappointment, the corset I mean, arrived alas only too quickly! A horrible absolutely straight sheath, of which only the back was boned and which pulled my arms backwards, with no other busk moreover than an elastic, which looked horribly like rubber. I, who have never been able to think of rubber without nausea!

Hardly had I entered this prison, than I would have given everything in the world to be out of it. This has been the fate, you see, of all the dreams realised in my life. It was called *ceinture de grâce*, no doubt because it rendered me ungraceful, and that was proper, they said, for my age. My complaints, my tears, were in vain. I had wanted a corset . . . *that was it!*

Little by little, as I developed, the instrument of torture was modified and became progressively a fairly gentle mentor, then a support, almost a comrade with which I lived on the best of terms. At that point it should have been elegant and beautiful: I wanted it in white satin, and over a long interval of time, this corset successively coveted, cursed, tolerated and forgotten for other fancies, became once more my idée fixe: in white satin, stitched in cherry silk along the edge, swansdown trimming on the hips, silver fastenings, the whole tiny enough to fit in a fan-box.

"When you get married," said my mother.

Thus it was that I began to dream of marriage, because in my head marriage was indissolubly bound up with a satin corset. Even today the most precise memory I have of that morning which decided my future, was the gentle crackling of the silk which Mlle Julie was lacing respectfully, I should say piously; and the harmonious silhouette of that frail iridescent cuirasse which bowed to and trembled at my slightest movement. The veil, the orange-flowers, the lace dress, those were my right; but this was the satisfaction of a caprice!

And to think that I profited from my marriage in order to leave them off altogether!

"Memoirs of a Corset" by Jacques Redelsperger, L'Art de la Mode *1880, p. 33, abridged.*

I am no ordinary corset. I am made of white satin bordered with Valenciennes lace, my clasps and my eyelets are of silver, my silk lace, at least three centimetres wide (sic), is what one might call an absolutely remarkable lace, and my (breast) gussets in the most supple of rubber can without exaggeration boast of having contained more treasures than most gussets on this earth. I was born after a long interview, and six persons worked for two days to bring me into the world—and I was perfect! Imagine my disappointment when I learned that I had been cancelled because of a pregnancy. The next day when I saw the future little mother arrive, my busk clenched with anguish: heavens, how pretty she was! And built to perfection! So I reflected angrily that another than myself was about to enlace that delicious form.

I was placed in the window, on a wax-model, and soon bought by an equally pretty woman. I watched her undress, my gusset beating with impatience. When she put me on, my gusset swelled with pride. Listening to her breasts, I was able to empathise with all her emotions. I was so sad when she took me off at night and became so jealous of her husband, that I kept my eyelets wide-open all night. Then suddenly the whole house was thrown into disorder. The great ceremony was in my honour. Ah, I was going to see something! Monsieur, my lady's maid, the nurse, and the footman were all called in. And all four began to pull on my lace with all their force, to pull as on a boat returning to harbour, while my lady clung with both her hands at the chimney-piece.

"Come on," she said, "you are not pulling!" You are not pulling! And she said it seriously! Was I unhappy! With all the will in the world, I couldn't hold out any longer; my eyelets began to gape and my lace grew visibly thinner. But my fury reached its height when the husband placed his knee against his wife's back in order to give the final heave. I was within a hair of giving way on all seams. That's when it hurt us, her and me! Her even more than me! The poor sweet creature was violet; she breathed some salts, tried in vain to recover her breath, and smiled wanly as one must have done in the olden days during torture.

And thereupon we left for the ball! That's when I expected it, in the middle of the 45 degree heat! Well; she didn't flinch, and as her face remained impassive, I heard her poor little heart going toc toc toc, fit to burst. I was positively sorry for her. But it was much worse when she began to waltz; as each partner arrived nonchalantly and clasped her waist, in vain did I buttress her with my boning in order to preserve her, they seemed to be vying with each other in audacity. I was indignant! And the husband who saw nothing! Ah; if only I could have slipped him a few words about all I was witnessing! But no, he was playing whist, this husband, while I was bracing myself in order to preserve his wife; it was really too kind of me.

You will see just how far I pushed my magnanimity; towards three o'clock in the morning, a partner slipped a billet-doux into her hand, which she transferred immediately to her breast. I was in a position to recognize it as a stupid declaration of love, and determined to frustrate it. My mistress' heart began to beat wildly, I took my courage in both hands, and with a supreme effort I crushed her so powerfully on all sides that she lost consciousness, having just managed to swallow the note beforehand.

On returning home, she prayed ardently, calmed down, and since then I have been host to no more billets-doux. Her character, from that time, is charming; she is always gay, and do you know why? Because she no longer tight-laces furiously, which leads me to coin the phrase: A woman who laces has a bad character (La femme qui se serre / A mauvais caractère)!

B. Statistics

The Corset Trade in the Later 19th Century

The controversy surrounding corsets intensified in the later 19th century in part, at least, because of their increasing economic importance. The publicity accruing to tight-lacing was both stimulating and threatening to the trade. Around mid-century the corset became "democratised"; once a relative luxury, it now was available to the new urban masses. Improved methods of manufacture, and particularly the invention of the sewing-machine, made the price of the mass-produced article fall within reach of the working and rural classes.

England, France and Germany competed against each other, and for the lucrative Amerian market. Tons of metal eyelets were exported from Birmingham and Sheffield all over the world. Around 1860 there were already 3,772 corsetières working in Paris; the number must have risen considerably thereafter. In the London area 10,000 persons were employed in the manufacture of stays; provincial English firms used another 25,000 hands, mostly female. The industry was recognized at the time as particularly exploitative; wages were described as "excessively unremunerative," and profits for the owners were colossal. In Germany, many firms operated for the American market alone; one in Württemburg, where the industry was concentrated, was exporting 630,000 corsets annually in the early 1880s. By the end of the decade, however, local industrial development in the U.S. was ruining many of these firms. (Larousse 1869, Plummer, La Santé, and Heszky).

The medical campaign against the corset, and the introduction at the end of the century of the new "straight-fronted" and more "hygienic" versions seems to have acted as a spur to the trade, at least in France, where between 1889 and 1901 no less than 678 tradenames for new inventions in corsetry hardware (busks, springs, boning and lacing-systems), and 433 new tradesnames for the corset as a whole were registered, and often under the most peculiar names (*Les Dessous Elégants,* passim). New lacing devices included horizontal hinges, side-springs and conic ribbons; busk-clasps used cams, levers and mobile hooks; a combination of clasp and lacing "united in parallel conjunction" permitted instant donning and removal, tightening and loosening. There was a "compensatory corset" of porous asbestos and bisanté whalebone, and another (by the famous Léoty) "à construction spiraloïdale." Exotic sounding materials like fibre agate and something called itzle were used for boning; and in their attempts to simplify the putting on and off of the garment, inventors resorted to systems of ever increasing complexity, the drawings for which are those of the mechanical engineer. An invention of almost diabolical ingenuity was the Ligne corset of Abadie-Léotard (*Etude*, 1904) which was deliberately so constructed as to become extremely painful if any attempt was made to lace it too tight.

In 1900 the French wholesale industry sold 50–55 million francs worth of goods, rising in 1902 to 85 millions. Of this sum, 12–14 millions were from export sales, which were literally worldwide. In Germany, meanwhile, where the Reform Movement was most tangibly successful, the corset trade actually declined by 18 percent during the decade 1897–1907.

Until the 1860s, the primary means of luring customers was by the placing of corsetry on dummies in shopwindows, a practice at which Daumier and Dickens expressed amused shock. In the 1870s, magazine advertising became highly competitive, especially after 1877, when illustrated display advertisements were introduced in English magazines. This was also the peak of the cuirasse period, and the cuirasse corset proved a boon to the industry, since it involved a kind of steel busk (sometimes called the spoonbill) which not only rendered all previous corsets outmoded, but also discouraged the making of corsets at home, being exceedingly hard for private persons to obtain, and impossible to make without special rivetting tools. By the 1880s and '90s, in France and the U.S., the corset was literally part of the cityscape, being advertised on huge billboards.

Statistics of waist measurements

According to the dress reform literature, the "natural waist" of woman was that of the Venus de Milo, which varied, according to source, between 26 and 30 inches. The consensus was that in the "average fashionable waist" this figure was reduced by about 6 inches. Critics tended to regard any reduction beyond 3 inches as dangerous; the greatest recorded in the dress reform literature was 15 inches (Dr. Dio Lewis quoted in *Knowledge* 29 December 1882).

In 1866 typical reformist opinion found "most" women lacing down to 24, "tens of thousands" down to 22, and "many" down to "21 and even 20" (Cooley, p. 351–6). By 1882 the "ideal fashionable waist size" was set, by a moderate reformer, at that of an athletic man's neck (Treves p. 13f). The physicians very rarely cite individual examples.

Data from paper patterns, advertisements and dress stands

The principal German fashion magazine, *Der Bazar*, gave paper patterns for corsets in sizes ranging from 50 to 60 cm. (19½–23½), with 54 (21¼) and 56 (22) the commonest dimensions. In 1884 there appeared patterns for drill and satin corsets with waists of 46 (18); thick laces are recommended. By the mid-90's, however, the average minimum measurement had increased from 21 to 23 inches. Mass-produced corsets were available from size 48 (19) upwards; German women seldom bought smaller sizes, although Russians frequently demanded sizes 42–46 (16½–18).

In France, mass-produced corsets were generally available from size 46 (18)

(A La Ménagère corsets at 44 (17) were exceptional). In the U.S., Warner's sold "great quantities" in sizes 18, 19 and 20 (*Always Starting Things*, published by Warner's in 1954). Sears Roebuck sold from their mail-order catalogues sizes starting at 18 inches. Paper patterns in *La Mode Illustrée* tended to have larger waist sizes in children's corsets (between 20½ and 23½) than in adult corsets (19 to 23); in 1884 a pattern was offered for a deluxe corset in satin, with a 46 cm (18) waist. Continental dress stands advertised during the early 90s started at 19 inches; a proper bust-waist differential was 15 inches (in 1960 it was 10 inches). English dress stands started at 20 inches. Worth human models supposedly possessed waists varying between 18 and 21 inches (Flinn, p. 19).

The increase in tight-lacing encouraged advertisers in the 80s and 90s in England to emphasize unbreakability and pliability as much as hygiene and comfort. At the same time, the tendency of busks to break was cited (in 1890) "as approaching calamitous proportions." Steel increasingly replaced whalebone, as the whale was hunted almost to extinction, and other, non-rusting, pliable, and unbreakable substitues were sought. Platinum was claimed to be so flexible that it could be tied in knots. The French invented a corset made from the hair of the Russian boar which was "absolutely unbreakable."

Izod's were the first firm to direct conspicuous illustrated display advertisements specifically towards tight-lacers. They also used "action-vignettes" showing the wearer picking fruit, dancing, playing tennis, etc. In 1879, they announced their "patent steam-moulded corsets," designed according to Hogarth's Line of Beauty, which "fit so accurately and comfortably that a very small size can be worn without the slightest injury to the figure" (*Judy's Album*). Other advertisements recommended the corsets as "suitable for all ladies, whether votaries of tight-lacing or not." Oddly, sizes are not given, but a *Family Doctor* reader wrote to say (22 December 1882) that she was wearing Izod Sylphs of 14 and 15 inches. Dermathistic was, after Izod's, the second most prominent brand catering to tight-lacers. One model by Dermathistic was described (by Seeker, a fetishist writer) as containing forty leather-covered bones placed so close around a waist so small that they actually touched, forming a solid belt. This was, moreover, cheap by French standards, one quarter of the equivalent French article. Dermathistic corsets were advertised as impossible to wear out, with bones, busk and steels protected by leather, and came in a mouth-watering array of colors; cardinal, tabac, gold-ruby, terracotta, apricot, dove and khaki.

Other brands were touted as producing the effects of tight-lacing without its reputed ill-effects (Pingat's "make the waist small without undue pressure"), and reducing the figure in such a way that tight-lacing became "unnecessary." The Invigorator was not injurious "even when tight-laced" (*Queen*, 5 Sep. 1885—these words were often capitalized), and recommended by ten physicians. It was available in all sizes, including boys' and girls' 5–10 years. Those ladies who wanted an "exceptionally long and small waist" were summoned to try Giraud's Beauty and Smallwaist Corset for "ordinary figures," in sizes 18–27, and for "exceptionally small figures," retaining a "full" cut in hips and bust, in sizes 15–22. The high-class department store Dickens and Jones sold "Spécialité Guinea" corsets in sizes 17–24. The phrase "a much smaller size can be worn without injury to the figure" was singled out by Mrs. Haweis, one of the many dress reformers particularly outraged by this kind of advertising pitch, who gave special lectures attacking it.

Waist measurements: *The Family Doctor* surveys of the 1880s

The most reliable and complete statistical data for the prevalence of tight-lacing comes from the sales figures given by the made-to-measure and ready-to-wear trades. Most if not all the major London corsetières specializing in custom-made tight-lacing corsets were interviewed for the *Family Doctor* by comparatively objective, if reform-minded reporters, notably a woman calling herself Hygeia. During the late 1880s she made repeated visits to corsetières, corset wholesalers and dress stores; she talked to any tight-lacer she encountered. She reported not only to the *Family Doctor,* but also to the Rational Dress Society, confirming the latter's worst fears, and contributing much to the general opinion that tight-lacing was indeed on the increase quantitatively and qualitatively.

From her first series of interviews with specialist corsetières (5 March 1887) Hygeia found that "several" 14 inch corsets were sold (all for pupils at the same school), 16 inches was "fashionable"; one 15 incher came to an untimely end. Six months later (3 September 1887), Hygeia repeated her enquiries among other corsetières, both French and English. A Regent Street store (Walsh and Mirza?) which displayed a 13 inch corset in the window "identical with the one made for the 20 year-old Comtesse de V." reported that "we seldom make a pair now for young ladies above 20 inches . . . These here are all 15 inches, these 14, these 13; these two pairs of 12 inch ones are just finished, made for 13 year-old ladies at a fashionable Brighton school. I doubt whether they will be able to wear them . . . Their waists are nearly 15 inches now. I have known only one or two who have worn 12 inch corsets out of doors and their figures are simply superb. I know, however, several ladies who lace into 12 inches when in their boudoirs. But their maids say they seldom bear it for more than an hour at a time." While travelling in the north of England, Hygeia saw a sale poster advertising "5000 pairs of corsets, sizes 17 to 26 inches. Special line 16 inches." 300 pairs size 17, over 300 size 18 and 80–90 size 16 had been sold. Hygeia was also able, through a corsetière, to transcribe a school "tight-lacing register" which tabulated the degrees of reduction expected of various pupils.

Hygeia was soon improving on her results with some really precise sets of figures (28 January 1888). Insisting particularly on their accuracy, she concluded that the extent of "tight-lacing which emerges is, if anything, underrated." Her inquiries now covered both the ready-to-wear and custom trade. According to the figures supplied by twenty of the leading ready-to-wear firms, 52,432 corsets were sold in the year 1886. The average waist measure was 23 inches, which gave a compression total (taking the number of corset wearers in England at 3,543,000, and their natural waist measure at 27–28 inches) of 134 miles. The annual mortality rate resulting from this compression stood, according to a "competent authority," at 15,000.

The size breakdown was as follows: 16 inch—237; 17 inch—362; 17½ inch—189; 18 inch—543; 19 inch—602; 20 inch—1073; 21 inch—3451; 22 inch—6689; 23 inch—12,023; 24 inch—19,807; etc., down to 28 inch (maximum size).

For the same year, twenty of the best custom corsetières gave figures totaling as follows: 14 inch—76; 15 inch—127; 16 inch—103; 17 inch—208; 18 inch—527; 19 inch—437; 20 inch—609; 21 inch—347. Significantly, it was estimated that 30% of the corsets in the smaller sizes (14–18) were made for girls under 16 years of age.

A Lover of Health made her own enquiries (2 April 1887) with a French corsetière apparently omitted by Hygeia, for she came up with several sub-14 sizes: 12½ inch—3; 13 inch—9; 13½ inch—2; 14 inch—13; 15 inch—7; 16 inch—13; 17 inch—11; 18 inch—23; and a large number at 19 and 20 inches. The interviewer personally knew or had known "several" young ladies "admitting" to a 13-inch waist, all of whom had started at 14–15 years, and one person possessed of a 12-inch waist.

O. H. interviewed another noted French corsetière, and published her findings in a cover-story entitled "Does tight-lacing exist?" (2 November 1889). Although this corsetière disapproved of sub-18-inch waists, she had made twenty to thirty corsets of 15 or 16 inches and several of 13 and 14 inches, which she considered harmful and possible only with bodies trained from the age of ten or twelve years. The smallest waist she knew was the 13 inches of an Austrian countess. "At four other places I visited," concludes O. H., "it was the same story . . . The Rational Dress Society has much to accomplish." Roughly the same estimates are provided in a letter written by a corsetière's fitter-on (15 May 1886).

A few individuals wrote to claim possession of 11, 12 and 13 inch waists, but very few readers, whether for or against tight-lacing, had ever seen such a thing. Men who had practised extremes of waist-reduction on themselves tended to be less incredulous of the possibility, but many men generally sympathetic to the practice, and especially those themselves possessing 17 or 18 inch waists, categorically refused to believe that it was physically possible to lace to the low or sub-teens. The very notion was "preposterous, absurd, utterly impossible" (Civis, 22 Dec. 1888). To descend thither from the upper teens was to pass from the sublime to the ridiculous, dangerous and ugly. The consensus was that a "happy medium" lay between 16 and 19, depending on the person's build. Incredibility decreases when the corsettee admits that extremes are attempted and attained only on special occasions and for very limited periods of time, as a test of endurance, to be sustained privately rather than for public exhibition. One girl (19 June 1886), married in a 13 inch corset, at thirty years of age settled for 16 inches, a measurement which permitted her to enjoy all the outdoor sport she needed. A 21 year-old (12 June 1886) boasted of a 13½ inch waist, in which she could comfortably stand and walk, but not sit. All those (about a dozen in all) who claimed to have reduced to 14 inches started to train in their early teens, managed an immediate reduction of from 4 to 6 inches, and reached their limit at the rate of about one inch per year, around five years later. None maintained the extreme permanently; the 14 inches displayed at a twenty-first birthday party had expanded to 17 inches four years later (25 December 1886) or, in another instance, to 19 at the age of thirty-seven. The 14 inches possible at home became 16 on the tennis court. No-one claimed to be able to dance or play tennis in a waist under 15 inches.

Other Evidence

The best evidence of 13 inches as a permanent acquisition comes from a very different kind of source: the memoirs of the distinguished military authority General Sir Ian Hamilton (pp. 191 and 204; the date referred to is 1870): ". . . There were the Alexander Dennistouns at Roselea, a pretty place (where) many roses grew—including a bunch of pretty daughters: Edith, Augusta, Katty, and Beryl, all tall and fit and supple although they had the smallest waists in Scotland, Katty's being 14 inches and the others' 15 inches.

The sun-basking damsels of today may raise those streaks of pencil they call eyebrows, but not only was I told this over and over again, but I have squared these circles myself and should know. 'Come along, Katerina' I cried, one lovely afternoon at Armadale, to the lovely Katty Dennistoun as she stood—a dream of beauty under a laburnum tree, croquet mallet in hand, her far-famed fourteen inch waist, her masses of glistening hair twisted into a royal coronet of curls—'do come along and go snags in the waterproof bath and mosquito net.'"

From a letter written to the late Sir Basil Liddell-Hart by the author of the above, dated from 1 Hyde Park Gardens, W.2., 7 June 1939: "A line about two of your queries. The first concerned the 14 inch waist of my dear friend Kattie Dennistoun whose photograph I enclose. The fact is still known and can be vouched for by many that her waist was 14 inches and her sisters' 15 inches. She married Sir Marteine Lloyd (who may be found in) *Who's Who* . . . Send me back Kattie's photograph without fail." From another letter to Liddell-Hart, dated 7 October 1939 (enclosing a later photograph, to keep, of Kattie taken in the '90s): "Here is one taken after bearing three children. You can still see the remains of the 14 inch waist."

An unusually authentic-sounding letter to *New Fun* (30 January 1915, p. 14) was written by Medicus, a seventy-year-old doctor with professional experience coinciding with the whole peak period of tight-lacing, to which he was sympathetic. He testified that he had known a few extreme tight-lacers, notably the patient of a colleague who had died of tight-lacing, and had worn an 11½ inch corset. "I have had numbers of patients with 16 inch waists, and 17 and 18 was common enough." The extremest cases tended to be found among Irish girls. An Austrian countess set a record, at height 67 inches, bust 35½ inches, hips 38¼, and waist 18¾ uncorseted, and 12½ corseted. Medicus also remembered certain West End shops encouraging salesgirls to tight-lace (cf. below).

The situation as regards claims made of and credence given to low measurements remains roughly the same in the correspondence of the interwar era. Most corsetières and shop girls with experience dating from the pre-war period put the limit at around 15 inches. A long and credible letter from the corsetier Lawrence Lenton *(Bits of Fun,* 3 Jan 1920), who claimed to have had "thousands of clients, and to have made more wasp-waist corsets than anyone in the world," states that he had over the last ten years made less than a dozen size 13. The *London Life* correspondence, unlike that of previous eras, often brings up the 10 inch waist. This appears to have exercised a "magical" (cf. below) fascination with some readers, who invented obviously spurious bibliographical reference in support of its existence in the past, and autobiographical fantasies in favour of its present or recent existence. The more rational readers poured scorn upon it. From the Sales, Wants and Exchange column which flourished briefly in 1934, one may infer that few London Lifers actually laced much below 20 inches.

Correspondents in the Victorian era did not like to reveal bust and hip measurements. The small group of *Family Doctor* tight-lacers who did give such measurements, at around 34–35 inches both, were evidently of slender build. They had started with a roughly 8 inch bust hip and waist differential, and ended with one of about 18 inches. Height was included very rarely indeed, but tends to confirm the obvious: tight-lacers were of average height. Four Sisters (F.L.M., 23 February 1889) were all tall (around 66 inches), had bust/hips around 33–34, and waists trained since the age of twelve to 14–16 inches. Contrary to received opinion, women were not much shorter in the mid and later 19th century than today; the magazines inform inquiring readers that a "good" (i.e., tall) height was considered to be 65 inches, and that 63 was an average. This much is corroborated from surviving costumes by Doris Langley Moore. Reformist opinion put "ideal proportions" at 65 inches height, 31 inch bust, 26½ inch waist and 35 inch hips (Steele p. 72).

Most correspondents skirted the problem of "outside" as opposed to "inside" or corset-size measurements. If the measurement claimed is that of the corset size, the outside measurement could be between one and three or even four inches larger, depending on three factors: the arrangement of the underclothing, the amount the corset had stretched in wear, and the amount it was left open at the back. The latter factor carried the greatest margin of variability, but an excessive (over two inches) gap was inadvisable because it tended to cause chafing and distortion of the boning. The many who insisted on always being laced close presumably gave the most "truthful" measurements; others allowed themselves varying degrees of relaxation, according to occasion and mood, and presumably gave minimum and momentary measurements.

We have commented in the Introduction on the propensity of tight-lacers to reduce their underclothing. The difference between the over-the-corset and over-the-dress measure of tight-lacers was considerably less than the two inch minimum of the normal. One enthusiastic young wife, engaging in a crash lacing program, discovered that merely by discarding and rearranging her underclothing, she had reduced the bulk at her waist by two inches. Four extremist tight-lacers gave, on various occasions, both measurements, over-corset and over-dress; the difference was exactly one inch.

In sum: there were in the late 1880s, in London alone, by a conservative calculation, a few thousand women who laced below 20 inches; hundreds who laced below 18; dozens who laced below 15. These few thousands, these hundreds and dozens are admittedly not many in a youthful female population of a million or so. The visibility and notoriety they attained towards the end of the century was due to the publicity as much as the personal example.

Shop-Girls: letter to Modern Society, 14 January 1893, pp. 276–7

From 1875–1890, I was in charge of the figures of the girls [working in] a large West End establishment, and where tight-lacing was and still is 'encouraged.' Natural emulation played a great part, but 'premiums' also helped very considerably. I noticed that what was 'tight-lacing' to one girl was not to another. The pressure necessary to reduce one girl of twenty-four inches to our standard of 19 inches was sometimes four times as much as in another case.

Again, two other things are scarcely even taken into account, but which played a very important part in the practice—viz, the angle made at the waist by the lines drawn from the armpits to the waistband, a broad-shouldered girl being very tight in nineteen-inch corsets, while a narrow-shouldered girl would not be. Do I make myself plain? Second, a girl with a fully developed bust had often enormous difficulty to contend with, while a girl of identical dimensions except the bust would have none.

Would you like the figures taken from my note-book? I have the names and full particulars of over 1,500 girls. Out of every hundred, I found three could not lace at all; six could with difficulty; eight eventually gave up; ten endured the bondage; seventy really enjoyed it, and three laced excessively.

At admission we found out of one hundred, three had 24-inch waists; six only had 23-inch; eighteen had 22-inch; forty-five had 21-inch; twenty-five had 20-inch; and two had 19-inch. At the end of three months by judicious lacing the figures were these (omitting the three, who could not lace), 24 [through] 21-inch, four; 20-inch, eight; 19-inch, seventy-two; 18-inch, fourteen; less, two. In six months (our limit of allowance) we had 20-inch [and over, eight]; 19-inch, seventy-five; 18-inch, eleven; 17-inch, four; 16½-inch, two. The first eight were discharged, relentlessly, and this though they may have endured, as some did, sheer martyrdom to attain the desired slenderness.

The most devoted girls I ever saw came from the South of England, and used to lace to even less than I have quoted, for the above figures only relate to the first six months of their stay with us. There was a tall slender girl from Wales who took to lacing magnificently. The tighter she was laced the better she worked, and the happier she looked. I looked upon her as a good 'subject,' as the doctors say, and offered her a high premium, if she would lace as tightly as ever she could, to show me how small a waist she could attain. She asked for a year to do it, and by the aid of myself and another assistant, we gradually laced her in to the incredibly small size of eleven inches. Of course, many of our girls broke down, due, I think, mainly to injudicious, not tight, lacing.

The Gentlewoman Survey.

The following survey is transcribed here in an abridged form from the typescript given me by the distinguished military historian, the late Sir Basil Liddell-Hart, who believed it to be authentic. It is stated to be derived from The Gentlewoman, *a luxurious weekly which started in 1890. This magazine is, alas, far too bulky for me to have verified the exact date, but the language in which the survey is couched, and particularly the surprizing exclusion at the end of the upper classes from the practice of tight-lacing, speak for its authenticity.*

Factual Inquiry into Tight Corset Wearing [1890s?]

In addition to interviews with several leading *corsetières,* I have been able to elicit a large amount of interesting and valuable information by means of forms of enquiry, which have been sent to many of the best known *artistes en corsets* in London and elsewhere.

There seems to be but little doubt that tight-lacing is considerably more in favour than it was some years ago. As Madame— observed, "women will have waists," and during centuries they have vacillated, at the bidding of Dame Fashion, between the excruciating torture and comparative unstayed freedom.

It was with the object of satisfying myself, and gaining information for the benefit of my lady readers in particular, that one day some time ago I called on Madame—, whose extensive *clientèle* and long business experience makes her opinion of great value.

"Madame— will see you in a few minutes," was the message an extremely slender-waisted young lady assistant brought back, when she had taken my card.

Madame— disposes of her "confections", principally corsets and underclothing, in a semi-private manner at a private house in the West End; and her goods bear the *cachet* which patronage of Royalty and the aristocracy gives.

The young lady who brought me the message had been instructed to give me any information and to show me anything she could, and so I inspected the stock, which was displayed with charming effect on the various chairs and pegs in the two spacious showrooms, which had evidently once been a double drawing-room.

"An artiste in corsets such as Madame really is," exclaimed my instructress, "never fails to fit each type of figure. Madame does not really care to supply ready-made articles at all, but she keeps a certain stock, in about eighteen or twenty types of figures, so as to oblige her clients in case of emergency. Oh, yes! There are special corsets for the stout and thin, and for rowing, tennis, riding, and even bathing. Lady X—, for example, will never wear anything but cardinal satin, fan-stitched with black silk, and trimmed with a particular pattern lace. Then young Miss— has a fancy for cerise; the Hon. Mrs.— for pale blue, trimmed with white lace. But here comes Madame herself".

"No, I do not mind telling you anything in reason," said Madame—, "provided, of course, that you do not let my name slip out. If you were to, I should perhaps lose some of my customers. If you want to mention names, I must tell you very little."

I satisfied Madame that I should not divulge her identity.

"Most certainly the average waist is smaller, and in my opinion, it is going to be still smaller, than even two or three years back. Many of my customers lace exceedingly tight, although I never approve of the practice nor encourage them to do so. I am not a dressmaker, you see, and therefore I do not want to persuade them to have a hard, wooden figure, so that it might be easier for me to fit bodices. Very few, however, seem to be much the worse for doing so," Madame admitted after a pause. "But of course they must be. Moderate lacing does not in my opinion, cause injury, but it is the tight lacing which is so dangerous.

"What makes women lace?" continued Madame, repeating my question. "That I can hardly say. Probably, principally, vanity and the spirit of rivalry. Some few, no doubt, because the sensations of very tight-lacing, *when one has got over the pain,* are to many women not unpleasant. If you had been, as I was in my early days in Paris, very tightly laced, you would understand better. You see these?" taking up a pair of white coutil stays, laced with a pale blue silk lace, off a show case, "well, I made them only ten days ago, and now Miss de L— has sent them back to be repaired. They are 17 inches, and she has split them slightly trying to get into them. The reason is her younger sister is just home from a fashionable French school in Brussels with a 16 inch waist, and Miss de L—, though she isn't of nearly so slight a build, wants to rival her."

"Is there much tight-lacing in schools?" we asked.

"Well," replied Madame—, "not, of course, in *most* schools, but I know of one—two—three—four—five, yes five, what are called 'finishing' schools, where the young ladies are encouraged to tight-lace to an extreme extent; and two, at least, where the pupils are laced in small, as a matter of course. Oh, I can't tell you the names of these schools, it would never do, but two are in London, and all, except one, of the rest, within a hundred miles."

"What are the largest and smallest waisted corsets I have ever made? I can't tell you right off from memory for certain, but I believe the largest are thirty-nine inches, and the smallest thirteen inches. I think that I have a pair of the latter size finished for a customer abroad. Miss G—, are the Countess of M—'s corsets packed?"

"No, Madame; they are here".

They were brought by Miss G—, and Madame— handed them to me. They were of pale blue satin, beautifully finished, and looking almost too delicate to be touched.

"Does the Countess really wear them?" I asked incredulously.

"Oh dear yes," exclaimed Madame; "and has what—from a fashionable standpoint—I always say is the best figure I have ever seen."

"Though my *clientèle* is so large a one, of course, very few tight-lacers go to such extremes as the Countess; but two young ladies, the daughters of a North country cotton spinner, do; and fully a dozen more of my customers would tape *well* under sixteen inches. Tight-lacing to such an extent as I have mentioned is mostly indulged in by the ultra-fashionable members of the aristocracy, the *nouveau riche* class, and the lower middle class."

"Are children corseted earlier than formerly?" I asked.

"Most decidedly. Many young girls wear regular corsets at thirteen, and are well laced in from fourteen to fifteen . . .

Some women seem able to bear almost any amount of lacing in, whilst I have known others to go off in a dead faint when only drawn in moderately tight. Oh yes, I have seen some queer things and still queerer devices for getting slim and getting on corsets two or three sizes too small, laced close. You know some of my clients wear scarcely any underclothing in anything like mild weather. You would hardly credit what some of them risk and go through to get or retain a slim waist".

(At the next establishment I visited, that of Mrs.—):

There were two other young lady assistants in the shop, which was a large one, and the younger of the two had a waist which it was almost impossible to keep one's eyes off, it was so abnormally slender. I found myself in what might be fittingly be described as "a ladies paradise". Dainty and extravagantly befrilled, belaced and beribboned undergarments of all shapes and materials, from silk to finest nainsook, were displayed or negligently thrown across chairs or settees; whilst in a sort of alcove or *sanctum sanctorum* at the end of the room, the lace curtains of which were still pinned up, we caught a glimpse of two life-size figures, on which were displayed the newest departure in underclothing.

Mrs.— was both courteous and communicative, and the information she gave quite bore out Madame—'s statements as to the increase of tight-lacing.

"I am reputed," she said, "to have the tightest-lacing customers in London; and I think that some of the waists my corsets encircle would be hard to beat. Do you know," she continued, "I think that some of my customers positively like the sensations produced by tight-lacing, or they would never take all the pains they do to get thin, such as dieting and sleeping in corsets, as some of them do."

"Sleeping in corsets!" I exclaimed.

"Oh, yes, a good many, especially young ladies, do; an opera stay or riding one is a favourite made for the purpose. Let me think. Yes! The largest pair of corsets I have made had a waist measurement of thirty-five inches. The smallest—well, you won't believe me, perhaps, but twelve and a half inches was the size. No, I don't think she will be able to get them close. Every inch under fifteen with most ladies means a tremendous lot of lacing in. I've known a young lady break five or six silk laces, as strong ones as are made, in getting a pair of new stays close."

"How small is your pretty assistant's waist?" I asked.

"Miss—'s? Generally about fourteen to fourteen and a half inches."

"She scarcely seems to mind it at all," I remarked.

"Oh, no. She is used to it. I find it best for all my assistants to have trim figures; but she has tight-laced to that extent entirely of her own free will. Lots of my customers lace to seventeen, sixteen, and even fifteen inches. I suppose you haven't seen a smaller waist than Miss—'s?"

"No."

"Would you like to?"

"Yes," I replied if such a thing is practicable."

Mrs— rang a bell.

"Ask Miss— to come to me".

In a few minutes the young lady appeared, and Mrs.— and she went into the alcove. Another assistant was summoned, and then a whispered consulation took place. After a minute or two we heard Mrs.— ask, "Can you bear it?" and the answer, "Quite Madame."

Mrs.—'s voice again: "There, Miss—! I think that the laces are close; tie them tightly."

Two or three minutes later Mrs.— and Miss— came out from the alcove, the latter encased in a long-waisted black satin corset, which made her waist look scarcely larger than her throat. It seemed incredible that any girl—for she was little more—could breathe and move, let alone *move about*, without much apparent discomfort, when tight-laced to such an extent.

"I suppose," said Mrs.—, smiling at my look of astonishment, "that you will now believe what I told you before, namely, that a well-cut corset and strong arms will make a woman's waist almost any size she may wish. See!" she exclaimed, taking up a measuring tape off the chair, "Miss B—'s waist is just thirteen—thirteen and a quarter inches."

"How long could you bear being laced up like that?" I asked.

Miss— smiled. "Not very long—it is rather painful—half an hour; perhaps an hour."

Mrs.— said, just as we were leaving. "You know, I think tight-lacing becomes a positive mania with some women. There are two of my customers, for instance—theatrical people—who usually wear their waists about nineteen inches. Well, when at home they both screw themselves as tightly as their maids can do it."

I went to several other leading manufacturers, but the information on the whole was so similar that it does not necessitate detailing at length.

One celebrated *artiste en corsets* could not grant a personal interview, but promised to give any information on the subject in her power by letter. This suggested to my mind a novel and extended form of inquiry, a kind of symposium on the "corset question", the results of which I am able to place before you.

1. *In your experience, is tight-lacing increasing or decreasing?*

75 percent of the corsetières agreed that tight-lacing had increased during the last five years, many saying "most decidedly." Corsetière A, with twenty years experience, considered that during the last twelve years, and especially the last five, the practice had increased markedly.

2. *What is the size of the smallest waisted corset that you keep in stock?*

15 inches is the smallest, 16 inches common. Corsetière A said she kept no stock, but only made to measure.

3. *What is the smallest waisted corset you have made (a) recently; (b) ever made? Please give bust and hip measurements, if possible.*

Several makers have made, and now do make to order, as small as 13 inches, whilst 14 and 15 inches are far more usual than one would suppose. Corsetière A: "The smallest waisted corset I have made recently measured 40 inch bust, 14 inch waist and 38 inch hips. The bust was of course forced up, by the extreme lacing, out of all proportion. To my mind the lady (who was about twenty years of age) when laced into this corset, as she was in my presence, looked quite unnatural and ridiculous. The smallest I have made for a lady over thirty measured waist 16, bust 38, hips 37. Corsetière B: "Smallest waist: 13, with 37 bust and 38 hips, made for a young lady of twenty two years of age, one of the most inveterate tight-lacers I ever had for a customer. She wore these corsets, but was almost incapable of any movement or exertion when laced up in them. Am now making a pair of corsets for a young lady of about eighteen years of age, 16 inches waist, 36 inches bust, 37 inches hips.

4. *Are corsets worn by younger girls more than formerly? and at what age are real corsets commenced?*

More than 80 percent of the authorities consulted were of the opinion that girls are put into *real* corsets earlier than formerly, with the object of ensuring a slender waist. Corsetière B: "Real corsets are now frequently worn by girls of thirteen or fourteen, and I have always advised their adoption from about that age."

5. *Do any of your clientèle wear special, or specially arranged underclothing, so as to enable them to lace tightly with less discomfort?*

Nearly 70 percent declared that many of their customers who practiced extreme tight-lacing wore a minimum of underclothing—"quite insufficient" several wrote— or especially arranged garments. One well-known West End corsetière wrote "Five or six of my tightest-lacing customers wear what, if they were a little thinner, would be nothing more nor less than actresses' 'tights'." Corsetière A wrote "The majority of my customers wear woven, tight-fitting clothing to do away with the fulness of the old-fashioned underclothing, which I consider better and more comfortable, and certainly it enables them to lace more tightly." *Corsetière* B wrote: "The woven silk or wool combination now so much worn, skin-tight at the waist, is very popular with my customers, and is most comfortable underwear. It would never do for a lady who wishes to lace very tightly to wear the old-fashioned separate and cumbersome garments."

6. *Do you think (a) moderate lacing injurious; (b) very tight-lacing injurious?*

80 percent were opposed to extreme tight-lacing; as corsetière B put it, "it is injurious to both health and *figure;*" corsetière A: "it is most injurious, and cruel." But 90 percent considered moderate lacing not to be injurious, and "in some cases, essential."

7. *What in your opinion are the essentials of a good corset?*

Corsetière A: "Plenty of room in bust to allow the bosom to expand, especially when leaning or bending forward, and when sitting to be high and *tight* under the arms, shoulder blades to be well kept in, to slope well and *gradually* in to the waist, and to be long over both hips and abdomen."

Corsetière B: "Good materials of every kind; a good cut; giving the figure firm support without unduly compressing any vital part; plenty of room for the full and proper development of the bust."

8. *Do you know of any schools at which tight-lacing is encouraged, enforced, or much practised? Please give fullest details possible.*

Seven corsetières knew of fashionable schools where tight-lacing was either enforced or encouraged. Five had made many pairs of corsets for girls of sixteen and under (mostly residents at these schools) with waist measurements of 15 inches. According to corsetière A: "I know of one or two such schools, but am not allowed to mention their names. The system of tight-lacing carried on there is very rigorous. I might almost say—cruel." Corsetière B: "Yes, I know of two or three schools where tight-lacing is enforced; all of which, however, are abroad."

9. *Do any of your customers wear corsets at night?*

Corsetière B: "Yes, quite a few. Most ladies do so (they are nearly all quite young) wearing a riding or opera stay. I have, however, made stays especially for this purpose. A young lady customer who has a waist of 15 inches, told me the other day, that except during a short illness, for a change of linen, and the bath, she had worn corsets constantly for over three years. She showed me her bare figure, which was quite moulded to the shape of her corset."

10. *At what age (if a very slender figure is desired) should corset wearing be commenced?*

Corsetière A: "At fourteen to sixteen; not before in my opinion. And then tighter lacing should only be very carefully encouraged, and very gradually carried out." *Corsetière* B: "Twelve or thirteen years of age is quite early enough to begin, but many girls of ten or eleven are now-a-days laced up if a very slim waist is wished."

The conclusions I have arrived at by means of this special inquiry are: (1) that tight-lacing is decidedly on the increase, and that a revival of a rigorous nature is likely to recur; (2) that women, many of them will "lace", in spite of all warnings of dress reformers and medical men; (3) that the ultra-fashionable and the upper middle class are not given to the practice of waist compression; and (4) that the borderland of Kensington and Maida Vale [where courtesans lived] can show some of the smallest waists on record.

Tight-lacing, however, is not entirely confined to any one class, for only the other day, in Gray's Inn Road, we saw two factory girls with waists (probably not a whit over 15 inches) which would have been the envy of a fashionable belle.

C. Mythology

The Legend of Catherine de' Medici

This legend is broadcast in the literature, old and new, as known historical fact, with such astonishing frequency that it is worth considering its origins and significance in some detail. It would be tedious to enumerate all the modern costume histories which transmit it; suffice to say that it is endorsed by even the scholarly C. Willett Cunnington (1951, pp. 161–62), and has passed into the *Guinness Book of Records*, where it remains, despite a long letter I wrote to the publisher in 1977.

This legend, as legends generally do, accreted gradually. It appears to originate in France, although it receives its concrete numerical form at the hands of the statistically-minded English. Up to the early 19th century the corset literature makes no mention of Catherine de' Medici; rather, the corset is assumed to be non-French, of "Gothic" or Germanic origin. The French Queen makes her debut, to my knowledge, in an 1857 work on the hygiene of clothing (Debay, p. 160f) which tells us that the "corps baleiné" (whalebone bodice) was invented by Isabella of Bavaria (1370–1435), reputed a malevolent, Germanic political schemer, a lover of luxury, and inventor of brazen décolletage. This garment was then propagated through the direct influence of Catherine, to the point that "women could hardly breathe."

Bouvier, a more careful historian from the mid-century period, cites contemporary sources to prove the existence of tight-lacing under Catherine's regime, but without associating her personally with the practice. In 1863 we find Mongéri coupling the 16th century annalist Brantôme's description of the Queen ("she had a very fine and opulent figure . . . she always dressed very well . . . and grandly, and was always inventing novelties") with the curious gloss, that when she grew stout, she used the corset as a means of political control in a country racked by civil war. It then spread "like lightning." For Mongéri, the expansion of the Queen's own person paralleled that of her political repression. According to contemporaries, indeed, she was at her physical prime—slender and vigorous—in her thirties (i.e., in mid-century, before the outbreak of the civil wars and the consequent repression). By 1562 she is described as "already a stout woman" and she later became so fat she could scarcely walk—hardly a model for a tight-laced court (cf. Sichel).

According to the first English corset monograph (La Santé, 1865, p. 4), *"it is said* that Catherine fixed the standard waist-measurement at 13 inches (my stress). This supposition became declared fact and virtually "canonical" with the openly fetishist William Lord, who embroiders enthusiastically (p. 71): "at no period in the world's history were its (fashion's) laws more tremendously exacting, and the ladies of the court, as well as those in distinguished circles, were compelled to obey them. With her (Catherine) a thick waist was an abomination, and extraordinary tenuity was insisted upon, 13 inches being the standard of fashionable elegance." Lord links this "standard" with the old iron stays which survived in European museums (Plate 7), which he was apparently the first to notice and reproduce and which he describes minutely, evidently from first hand. They may indeed date from the later sixteenth century, but they measure much more than 13 inches around the waist, and neither Lord nor any of the innumerable authors who borrow from him, produce any contemporary evidence to corroborate the figure of 13 inches. (The figure may not be quite arbitrary; it was the lowest any of Lord's contemporaries could possibly have believed in.) The system he describes of "gradual determined constriction" necessary to arrive at this degree of attenuation is identical in spirit, of not in the physical means employed, to that being contemporaneously advocated in the *Englishwoman's Domestic Magazine,* the fetishist correspondence from which his book anthologizes.

It may be via Lord that the legend passes into the *Kostümkunde* of Hermann Weiss (pp. 226 and 582), an otherwise scholarly and one would suppose impartial writer who was apparently not, however, immune to a patriotic bias, and who accepts tight-lacing as having started in early 15th century France, to be revived and reinforced by Catherine. Weiss blames the rigorous French 17th century etiquette, formalized by the bigoted anti-Protestant (and therefore anti-German) Madame de Maintenon, for its perpetuation, down to the Revolution.

By the early twentieth century we find fantasy dialogues in which Queen Catherine expatiates on the marvelous transformations wrought by the corset, even as she callously watches her ladies-in-waiting actually dying under the torture (L'Heureux, p. 120f). In 1929, we learn from a professor of psychology at Columbia University (Hurlock, pp. 104 and 185f) that "every woman, no matter what her build might be, was expected to have a waist of 13 inch diameter (sic) if she wished to remain within the court circles (of Catherine)." This fact is deemed so crucial that it is repeated in the same form elsewhere in the same book; finally, we are assured that it was Queen Elizabeth who introduced the 13 inch waist into English fashion (the latter fiction is reproduced by Roach, 1965, p. 348). In a corset monograph of 1951 (Crawford, pp. 7 and 19f), we find the 13 inch figure cited as the model for both the period of Catherine and the year "1889."

Waist Size and Marriageable Age

"A great mass of contemporary evidence makes it clear that at the time of her marriage a young lady's waist should not exceed in inches the number of years of her age; and most hoped to marry before twenty" (Cunnington, 1941, pp. 161–52—my stress). This striking, much quoted, and entirely unsupported historical connection, made by the foremost authority on Victorian fashion, tempts one to seek another symbolic significance to the fetishist fixation on waist-size, which seems to be imbued with some numerological magic. Cunnington connects two Victorian concerns of a very different kind: tight-lacing and marriageable age. There can be little doubt that many young ladies hoped to get married before they were twenty, but they were not supposed to make this, the most critical choice of their life, until they had attained sufficient emotional and mental maturity, and gained sufficient experience of the world, to enable them to make it in a rational and balanced way. For complex economic reasons, middle-class girls were getting married much younger in mid-19th century than a century earlier. It was, above all, the tight marriage market and the fear of having a daughter remain on the shelf if any reasonable offer were refused, which forced anxious parents to countenance early marriage.

Magazine editors disapproved. To the question frequently fired at the editor of the *EDM*, "what is the correct age to get married," the answer was "not under twenty." To another often repeated question, "what is the correct waist measurement," the answer was the same. For normal purposes, twenty demarcated marriageable from non-marriageable age; acceptable lacing from tight-lacing. We may speculate whether the acquisition of a small waist by young teenagers did not serve, unconsciously, to advance their sense of nubility to an age when marriage was ill-advised; and whether the fetishist fantasies about 15 and 16 inch waists are not somehow grounded in fantasies (male of course as well as female) about 15 and 16 year-old brides. Both kinds of fantasy were, in a real sense, taboo. If, in respectable opinion, neither waists nor marriages should be contracted under 20, the fetishist imagination imbued the "natural" waist of nigh 30 inches with some of the dread of those for whom the approach of the third decade without a husband portended eternal spinsterhood.

To preserve the measure of one's waist was to preserve the measure of one's years; perhaps it still is. Lady Dolly in Ouida's popular novel *Moths* (1880, I, p. 5) is the stereotype of the frivolous, neurotic, depraved woman of fashion who, at 33, is still the Dresden statuette, the "eternal beauty," as pretty as when she was her 16 year-old daughter's age. Married at 17, she preserves a waist younger yet (15).

The categorical significance attached to the figure of twenty (years or inches) may be due, in part at least, to its decimality; and one wonders whether the same factor may not underlie the apparently arbitrary choice by the *Guinness Book of Records* of "close to ten inches" as the "theoretical limit" of the waist. The curious use of the word "theoretical" in this context reminds us of the extent to which "magical" numerological considerations may enter into tight-lacing fantasy and practice.

D. Case Histories

1. The Empress Elizabeth of Austria

The Empress was born in 1837 of the eccentric Bavarian Wittelsbach royal line, and married the young Emperor Francis Joseph of Austria-Hungary when she was sixteen. After the relative freedom of her Bavarian childhood, she found herself thrust into Europe's most ossified court. Her sense of personal dignity and independence as well as her very real democratic and humanitarian instincts continuously offended against the role into which she was cast.

Her first "political" duty was to breed. She had three children in quick succession, after which, despite her excellent health and natural fertility, she refused to have any more (although she was later to have a fourth child), and encouraged her husband to take a mistress and develop a ménage à trois rather than suffer his sexual attentions. This sexual rejection was all the more publicly scandalous and personally painful in that the Emperor was known to be (or have been) infatuated with his wife. The result was that the Empire, after the suicide of their only son, the Crown Prince Rudolph, was left without a male heir. In the oppressively rigid Habsburg court, and under the constant interference of her mother-in-law, the Archduchess Sophie, which prevented her from breast-feeding her children and developing a natural relationship with them, she became reputed sexually frigid (she had been virtually raped on her wedding-night), and unmaternal, as she herself confessed, "loath(ing) the whole business of child-bearing" (Haslip, p. 87; Paléologue, p. 17).

Her sexuality was sublimated in her attachment to her younger daughter Valerie, large animals (especially horses), and the cultivation of her own body. She was famous for her equestrianship—haute école, circus-style stunt riding, and hunting. At 44 years "she looked like an angel and rode like the devil" (Haslip p. 325). When she finally gave up riding in 1882, she devoted herself to marathon solitary hikes, swimming, gymnastics and fencing.

The Empress' fear of pregnancy, her mania for sport and violent exercise, her preoccupation with her physique, her peculiar diet, her attitude to dress—all had one common denominator: the preservation of a figure which was naturally very slender, small-boned and muscular. She was tall (five feet six inches), and never weighed over 50 kilos (120 pounds) all her adult life. Her legendary beauty and charm brought her oppressive adulation wherever she went in Europe. She preserved her youthful appearance in the face of what press and medical opinion viewed as bizarre, not to say improper, excesses in sport, diet and slimming. She hated to have to sit down to eat. She abominated banquets. For long periods she lived on a daily diet of raw steak and a glass of milk or orange-juice. She struck people as hyperactive, and astonishingly hardy. Her illnesses were all evidently psychosomatic, and her neurotic crises always cleared up when she was away from court, and was free to travel and ride, free of the gaze of courtiers and public, which she experienced as physically painful—as a visual rape.

Her diary, alas, was destroyed by the police after her death. But further study of archival material, of medical and newspaper reports, might reveal much more of the precise circumstances surrounding her youthful reputation for tight-lacing. It seems that around 1860–61 her waist measured no more than the 16 inches of the belt exhibited in London at the Great Exhibition (cf. pp. 220–21). Why was an object with such scandalous associations put on public display? With her horror of publicity, especially as regards details of her personal life, it seems inexplicable that the Empress would have encouraged gossip around so intimate a matter as a waist-measurement. If the numerous biographies remain silent on this curious episode, is it because domestically the matter was hushed up? After all, in order to protect the imperial dignity the police actively suppressed stories of her equine acrobatics, and destroyed photographs pertaining to it. If the 16 inch belt was displayed with her permission and knowledge (and it seems hard to conceive otherwise) or, worse, on her personal initiative, was it intended as a provocation? Was it the bizarre symbol of or satire upon the exhibitionism to which the most adulated woman in Europe was subject?

Her peak "tight-lacing" period seems to coincide with the prolonged and recurrent fits of paranoid depression which she suffered 1859–60, which have been attributed to her husband's political defeats, her three pregnancies, her sexual withdrawal, and quarrels with her mother-in-law over the rearing of her children. Immediately after each pregnancy, she dieted and exercised rigorously; the smallness of her waist, which she appeared to flaunt and exaggerate, angered the Archduchess, who wanted her to be continuously pregnant. There were frequent rumors of grave illnesses at this time; consumption was widely diagnosed, and she was even accused of killing herself with tight-lacing. Her health improved immediately after she left Vienna for extended travels, and was able to confront the physical hardships of nature and sport. On her return to Vienna in August 1862, a lady-in-waiting noted her improved sociability, and that "she looks splendidly, she eats properly, sleeps well, and does not tight-lace anymore" (Corti, p. 107). At this time her waist-measure had probably increased to 18 inches, its reputed extent (more or less) until her death (de Burgh, p. 198, put it at 20). (Cf. Pl. 86). Other costumes exhibited at the Museum of Modern Art had *external* measures of 18½ (bridal evening dress, 1854) and 19½ (two, including the bodice through which the Empress was stabbed to death, repr. Joseph Wechsbert). In 1882, she is described by the Prince of Hesse as "almost inhumanly slender." In 1887 she was "scarcely human in (her) fantastic attributes of hair and line" (Haslip, pp. 334 and 373). In 1890, she is still "graceful, but almost too slender" and "excessively slender, but still in terror of growing stout" (De Burgh, p. 58, Corti, p. 425). She was at this time having herself heavily massaged, and wrapped naked in wet sheets impregnated with seaweed. She transmitted her horror of fat women to her daughter Valerie, who was positively terrified when, as a little girl, she first met Queen Victoria.

Her body became a religious cult, but one of a highly ascetic and solitary nature. Clothing, as such, was excluded from the cult. She disliked the expensive accoutrements and the constant changes of outfit to which her role condemned her. She caused offence by the plainness, the preferred monochrome of her attire (De Burgh, p. 292). What mattered to her was perfect fit.

An essential and early constituent of her legend was that she was regularly sewn into her riding-habit. "It was common knowledge in the hunting-field that a tailor from Whitchurch went every day to the Abbey to sew the skirt of the Empress' habit onto her close-fitting bodice, so that there should not be the slightest crease or wrinkle around her 18 inch waist" (Haslip, p. 325). Her niece Countess Marie Larisch (p. 65) confirms this custom, and that "she wore high laced boots with tiny spurs." Her English hunting companions loved her for her warmth, modesty, ease of manner, for the fact that she was not (otherwise) at all "sewn-in," and for her anger at any instance of cruelty to horses which came to her attention (De Burgh, p. 289).

Some of her corsets were made in leather, like those of a Parisian courtesan. "Her many-coloured satin and moiré corsets were made in Paris, and she only wore them for a few weeks. They had no front-fastenings (i.e., no split busk, current since c. 1860), and Elizabeth was always laced into her corsets, a proceeding which sometimes took quite an hour (!-sic). She never wore petticoats . . . when she took her walks she slipped her unstockinged feet into her boots, and wore no underlinen of any description . . . she slept on an iron bedstead, with no pillows" (Larisch, p. 78).

Her hair was a glory, in texture very thick and wavy, a rich chestnut in colour, and hung down below her knees. Dressing it was the most important ritual of the toilette, which lasted up to two hours, during which she usually read, or studied languages. Many anecdotes testify how her self-imposed "enslavement" to her hair sublimated her sense of enslavement to the public role, how she used her capillary crown "in order to get rid of the other one" (the imperial crown). The hair was inviolable, mystical, almost literally sacred, a cult of which her spoiled and arrogant hairdresser was the high-priestess (Tschuppik, p. 114, De Burgh, p. 58, Corti, p. 112, etc.).

The biography of the Austrian Empress contains a whole psychology of fetishism, which emerges with peculiar intensity and pathos as a function of her struggle within her uniquely elevated social rank. The rituals around her riding, slimming cures, corsetting and hair were various channels of escape from and protest against her public role, attempts to recover an individual identity of which a pettifogging court, a devouring public, insatiable reporters and photographers constantly worked to deprive her.

2. Polaire

Polaire (1879–1939) was born in Algiers Emilie-Marie Bouchaud. As a girl she was naturally slender, endowed with the "sinewy, muscular body of a little Arab" and (as she expressed it herself) a "rib-cage like a Spanish bolero." Starting in music-hall, she was launched into fame as a straight actress by her friends Willy and Colette in their play *Claudine à Paris* (1902). It was they who promoted her as a young girl's ethereal sexual ideal, encouraged her to tight-lace and publicized her waist as "the envy of a fashionably corsetted bee," etc.

Her supposed ugliness—her large hands, large feet, thick mouth and long nose—were flaunted by her promoters. Publicity photographs compared her profile with that of her pet pig, which wore a jewelled collar. Like a pig, she wore a nose-ring, announced (for her U.S. tour of 1913) as a "protest against what the world calls refinement." She posed as an enemy of "civilisation," and cultivated, on stage, a sensually barbaric style. She was considered in her time a fine performer. "She fairly gloats over her perspiring passion—an untamed and untameable girl . . . as an actress more barbaric than tragic" (Archie Bell, "The Ugliest Actress," *The Green Book Magazine* (Chicago), May 1914, pp. 833–840). Her waspish waist is thus to be regarded not so much as a once-fashionable exaggeration but rather as a deliberately contrived barbarism.

For her first visit to the U.S. she was publicised as a kind of circus freak: "The ugliest woman in Paris with the smallest waist in the world." An immense fuss was made over her waist measure. "When she removed her black satin cloak last night, with a deliberate and tantalising delay appropriate to the revelation of such a famous physical peculiarity, the women present gasped sympathetically." Given away with the programme was a 14-inch rule marked with these words: "This is Polaire's waist measure. What's yours?" A song was written for her, starting "When I started in music-hall, my waist fitted into a man's collar ("Quand j'débutais au music-hall, / Ma taille tenait dans un faux-col."), a notion which inspired gallantries such as George Herriot's offer to buy her a diamond belt if she succeeded in demonstrating the claim with his collar. For her appearance at the London Coliseum in 1915, her publicity agent William Hammerstein put one of her 14 inch corsets on display in a show-case at the corner of the theater, and announced the waist to the press "as this gift of the gods."

She was 5-foot 3½ inches tall, with a bust 38 and hips 34. Her waist was, according to her autobiography *(Polaire par elle-même,* 1933), supposedly natural, and she explained the less waspy effects visible in the photographs taken before she became famous as the result of padding to "make her look more human." Her smallest publicised waist size in the early years (around 1902) was 41 and 42 cm (16¼–16½ inches); thereafter it varied, probably reflecting an actual physical increase, up to 48 cm (19 in., the figure noted in "an unretouched photograph" published in 1909). It is not clear how long she maintained the famous collar-size, and publicists evidently chose their own figure, with 14 the lowest. Her obituaries contain contradictory statements such as "the exact measure was never established" and "she was officially measured in 1910 at 14 inches."

The most evocative description of her performance is that of Jean Lorrain: "Polaire! The agitating and agitated Polaire! The tiny slip of a woman that you know, with the waist slender to the point of pain, of screaming out loud, of breaking in two, in a spasmically tight bodice, the prettiest slimness! And, under the aureole of an extravagant masher's hat, orange and plumed with iris leaves, the great voracious mouth [she put rouge on the gums and tongue], the immense black eyes, ringed, bruised, discoloured, the incandescence of her pupils, the bewildered nocturnal hair, the phosphorus, the sulphur, the red pepper of that ghoulish, Salome-like face, the agitating and agitated Polaire!

"What a devilish mimic, what a coffee-mill and what a belly-dancer! Yellow skirt tucked high, gloved in openwork stockings, Polaire skips, flutters, wriggles, arches from the hips, the back, the belly, mimes every kind of shock, twists, coils, rears, twirls . . . trembling like a stuck wasp, miaows, faints to what music and what words! The house, frozen with stupor, forgets to applaud . . ." (in Romi, *Petite Histoire des Cafés Concerts,* Ed. Chitry, 1950, p. 48).

3. Sir W. N. (1882–1968). Member of Parliament for fifty years, baronet, very distinguished figure in British public life (interviewed 1967).

His childhood was spent in an Irish village, with occasional trips to Dublin. Sir W.'s father was a fanatic for tight-lacing, and married a girl whose figure was already trained. He was an intellectual, very gentle by nature, and dominated by his wife who knew she held him by her figure. She kept her shape into her fifties, despite her seven children. The pregancy and birth in each case was easy; she was quickly bandaged back into shape after delivery, and had no difficulty in breast-feeding them all. There were four girls, all of whom were corset-trained from early childhood, but of whom only the eldest became, entirely of her own accord, a confirmed tight-lacer, determined to out-lace first her mother, and then her governess. At the age of seventeen, she could, on occasion, lace down to 13 and 14 inches. W.'s earliest erotic memories and his sexual apprenticeship consisted of helping to lace his sister, ten years his senior, who loved it. When he was a little older (about nine) she would place his head between her breasts and fondle him. By the time he was fourteen, he was having sex with her, with the lacing-in as the constant preliminary.

The governess was chosen partly, at least, on account of her waist, which with the encouragement of Sir W.'s father was reduced progressively while she stayed with them, reaching a limit of 11½ and 12 inches. "It was a miraculous thing." [At this point in our conversation, I registered incredulity. The octogenarian paused, as if doubting himself. Finally he rose, fetched a tape-measure, passed it about a tobacco-jar which was about eleven inches round. He gave a sigh of half-incredulous wonderment.] No, he had not measured his governess' waist himself; she always laced herself; he was sure about the figure 11½ and 12, for these are not details which one forgets; but he agreed that the figures may have represented the inside measure on the smallest corset she ever wore, when new and unstretched. She was very gay in temperament, and physically active, loving to romp with the children.

Corsets were regarded as functional not decorative objects. Each female member of the family had three of them at one time, the smallest in size being reserved for the evening. Tight-lacing was practised not only in the family, but also to a certain extent among their circle of friends. But the family lived a very isolated existence, which explained the lack of photographs, as well as the lack of social notoriety around the fetishism. Sir W. could remember only favourable comment, although there was the case of a cousin who refused to unlace during a pregnancy and died. The cause of death was mentioned at the funeral sermon, and caused some scandal.

W. chose his wife, whom he married when she was 26, for her figure "which appeared a natural 16 inches." He was not attracted to high heels until the 1950's. He now awaits the combination of mini-skirt (of which he heartily approves), high heels and tight waist.

W. himself has always been corsetted (in military, not wasp-waisted style), finding he always prepared and delivered a House of Commons speech better when thus supported. Three years ago he gave up corsets altogether, finding them no longer beneficial. He has always been very active (hetero-) sexually, and has tried "just about everything."

4. Letter from Aunt Helen to her sister, mother of interviewee S.S-H., undated but postmarked 1892, when the writer must have been about 17

Redgrave

Dearest Mooney,

. . . It's only a year now—or a bit less till I come out! I can stop lessons then, lovely! I'm much more interested in young men, and as you know in attracting them! Oh yes, I suppose I'm vain. Certainly I mean to have a really good figure with my tiny waist. There was a very nice friend of Eric's who came home with him from Harrow last holidays. He and Eric and I went for a walk towards Braiseworth one day, and after a time Eric who likes walking quickly said I was going too slowly, so John said he'd wait and come along with me while Eric went on. I was very glad this happened as I had a feeling he was attracted be me, and especially by my upright figure! But he was too shy to say anything until he had to help me over a stile. Then he happened to feel my waist, and said how small it was! Why didn't I show it more. Then I explained to him that Miss— (her governess) wouldn't let me do so until I came out with a really small waist. I then found that he was really interested and liked a very small tightly laced waist. He told me his mother had a beautiful figure and was beginning to do something about his two younger sisters who are 15 and 16½ but that they objected very much to being laced at all tightly. After that of course I had to tell him all about my training by Miss M— and told him I might be even smaller than 17 inches when I came out. He then said, "I believe my hands would go right around your waist, it's so small? I told him to try but they wouldn't quite get round. Anyway he then held me very tightly and kissed me!! It was lovely. I told him that if he liked I might be able to be even smaller in the evening if Miss— would let me wear the stays which she makes me wear when I have been rude to her or annoy her. All went well and that evening Miss— laced me into them. I can hardly move in them as they are only 16 inches in the waist and more heavily boned with wide side steels than my ordinary stays. John could not take his eyes off me! I told him I thought I was quite a lot smaller this evening and he said 'lovely'. I only wish he could have held me, but his admiration made up for the pain I was in by the end of the evening. I think my face must have given this away to John, as when we had a talk next day he said he had thought I was going to faint. Eric I'm sure is very proud of me though he's sorry I can't play tennis now.

While in London staying with the P—'s, Miss— took me to Madame [Dowding's?]. An inch smaller in the waist for everyday wear and made so as to lengthen my waist. I am wearing them today for the first time. The lengthening of the waist I find painful but Miss— insists that I must be laced right in to be really beautiful for my coming out dance. My ribs have been aching so much this last hour, but as Miss— is in a good temper today she is pleased that I have not complained before and I am going to bed. Dear Mooney, write to me when you have time.

Your affectionate sister
Helen

Letter to H. Y. from S. S-H. dated 15th September 1959, confirmed orally 1968

. . . what you say about the method of breathing when tightly-laced is so true. Most attractive as I remember from my aunt Helen. Of course she began her training as a girl of 14 or so in the Eighties, and progress in her case was steady and always supervised by her governess who slept next door to her. (Her mother had died when she was three.) My aunt used to tell me the whole story of her figure training, which until she came out was looked after by the governess. In my aunt's case too, she told me the first few months were irksome and painful. She was fortunate in being fairly slight, but from the beginning she always had night stays. I remember her telling me how for her first stays she was taken by her governess to a place in Bath, and how grown up she felt at the idea! But that when the first stays came she was rather rebellious after wearing them for a short time, as she was unable to play about so much in them and could only walk slowly and very uprightly, being encased tightly from below her hips to her armpits, and with shoulder braces to prevent or cure a slight stoop. But after a few months vanity took control, though she did not always look forward to new stays which meant further reduction and pain. When she grew up, the two or three men with whom she lived successively, saw to it that she was always very tightly laced. When I first remember her she cannot have been more than 16 inches in the waist, and I can still picture her much later on in a black close-fitting evening dress when she told me that her waist was only 14½ inches over the dress. She told me to hold it, and I did so easily with two hands. A very hard, unyielding middle . . . I was occasionally allowed to help lace her in myself, when her lover was expected. Seeing I was interested and admired her figure, she was always telling me of incidents when she was in her teens and the governess in charge. She told me how much she wanted to wear clothes which showed off her tightly laced figure, but until she was sixteen years old she was made to wear clothes which concealed her figure. . . She said that at times when she was doing lessons with the governess her stays hurt her very much (because of the seated posture). Her most anxious time, she said, was when she had to wear new stays for a week or so before her coming out dance. Smaller than she had ever worn before, making her waist 17 inches measured over her dress. It took her governess and maid about half an hour to lace her into them. During the week she fainted once or twice, but on the important night all went well, and there was no lack of partners . . .

5. Professor G. Vandermaas (not real name), artist and teacher of some distinction, born 1895 in S. Africa (letters of Feb. 1968)

I have always thought of my relationship with my grandmother as slightly abnormal. My own mother (a hospital matron, normally corsetted, not on very good terms with her mother-in-law) was busy at that time helping my father, and I was left with grandmother most of the time. My earliest recollection (I was about three at the time) is of her dandling me on her knee, or rather on her very plump lap and I derived great comfort and satisfaction from feeling the tight silk of her dresses stretched over the soft flesh. She rather encouraged me to pummell and push at her large breasts, which projected like a porch roof from above her tiny waist-line. I think my fingers discovered the top edge of the corset on one such occasion and I asked her what it was and she said she'd show me. I also was interested in the roll of flesh which protruded from beneath the corset when she sat down. My hands explored the round, hard shape of her waist and I finally was throwing my arms around it and hugging it. Trying to make it smaller! Grandmother quite evidently enjoyed all this and encouraged me in it, rewarding me with sweets and cookies.

So on the day that I discovered the corset edge, when grandmother was dressing for the evening, I was allowed to sit in the corner watching the operation of lacing her up, which took the utmost effort of two coloured maids. At the end grandmother lay on her face on the floor for the final tightening. When she staggered to her feet with the aid of the maids she invited me to examine the results with my hands which I did with great satisfaction to both of us.

Grandmother had a sister and some friends who came to take coffee with her in the afternoon. They all had similar figures. I suppose I came to associate the wasp-waist with femininity. They also all wore the spool-type high heels of the day. By present standards they were all fat women, but they laced to the limit and often their talk turned to methods of reducing the waist. If there was an evening party they often had their waistlines further reduced before they came down to the dinner table. I know, because I peeped into the dressing room!

Grandma corsetted her maids as well—the ones who appeared in the front of the house—and as tightly as they could stand without fainting at work, and if she caught them loosening the laces, as they would sometimes, she herself would see to it that they were laced tighter than ever, for punishment. She often inspected them to see if their figures were "neat."

The two maids in question, Sophie and Gladys, were more or less in personal attendance on grandma and were within call wherever she was. There was no longer slavery as such, but the negro servants hardly knew any difference and the attitude of the older Dutch people had changed very little either. Absolute dependence upon employer and absolute obedience was the rule. Sophie and Gladys were sort of personal extensions of grandma . . . Sophie was tall and inclined to be slender, while Gladys was shorter and quite plump. After they had helped grandma dress in the morning they were themselves inspected for appearance. Starched aprons and caps must be just so, and their corsets must be properly laced. Sophie seemed rather to enjoy being pulled in, if grandmother took a notion that she wasn't small enough. This would be done by Gladys, with grandma directing the process. But when it came Gladys turn she was invariably unhappy about it. She was the one Grandma bedevilled the most, for she was always surreptitiously loosening her laces, though Grandma saw to it that they were tied in such a way it was difficult for her to get at them.

These coloured maids, in common with most of their particular race, had rather unusual gluteal development and deeply arched backs, so that in corsets they presented an exaggerated effect. Even without lacing they walked with a pronounced sway of the hips from side to side and with lacing this undulating walk became much exaggerated, particularly if they were carrying a tray of tea things or something like that. Sophie was more graceful and achieved a kind of swivelling glide, but the rear view of Gladys, scuttling on some errand and carrying some light load, was truly amazing. It seemed to me there was more rotating of buttocks and jerk of narrow waist from side to side than there was movement forward.

Actually it was only a more pronounced form of the movement in walking which I came to think of as the normal feminine gait. I now know it to be almost entirely due to more or less tight-lacing. It was the walk of all of grandmother's friends, who came often to drink coffee in the afternoon. I saw very few women who did not walk this way and so I assume all of them were more or less laced. Only my mother and one or two others seemed to walk without this peculiar rotating sway of the hips and so I came to think of them as a little odd!

Shortly after this we came to America and I forgot all about my grandmother for years. In fact never saw her again. But I found myself preferring plump women and being stirred in a puzzling way by the sight of a tight waist and high heels. This had apparently persisted to this day, when I am 73 years of age.

For myself, I regard my interest in tight-lacing as a sort of introversion—an attempt of dammed-up sexual impulses to find *some* expression. I find that when these pressures are released by the more usually acceptable paths I lose all interest in any form of fetishism. I was happily married for years. At first I rather hoped for tight-lacing on the part of my wife, but since we were so happy without any such additional stimulus I soon forgot it. (When I once expressed this preference to her, she rejected it so vigorously I never brought it up again. Neither did she wish to encourage my weakness for high heels.) She was the "sensible" type and felt that her own womanhood should be enough, without the trimmings I hankered for. This proved to be the case. For some thirty-six happy years I was only occasionally reminded that once I had had a fetishistic interest in corsets and high-heels.

About a year after my wife died (quite suddenly and tragically) I saw, in the newspaper, a picture of Mrs. Granger, of Peterborough, England. I was suddenly moved to write him of my admiration for his wife's figure, and I did. I received an answer and a copy of his little book (cf. p. xii). For a short time it appeared that my interest in this particular fetish was reviving. But as soon as I found myself engaged in a very satisfying affair with a lady (which still continues, I may say), all such interests dropped away. Apparently (when I can get it) my sex-satisfactions are better served by a normally proportioned woman. But when I can't find much satisfaction, I find myself enamored of huge bosoms, small waists and high heels!

I have just returned from a 6000 mile tour of South Africa, where there is a huge tribe of Vandermaas. There are some 180 in the Johannesburg region alone! I inevitably was treated to some tid-bits of family history of which I had not been previously aware. A visit to a cousin, "well-preserved", vigorous, but of my own advanced years, brought forth some interesting information. She had been a successful career violinist in her day (Salzburg Music Festival and all that!). In S. Africa it is the custom for relatives to embrace warmly and when I put my arm around my cousin I discovered that her loose blouse concealed a very small and tightly laced waist!

I suppose my surprise and interest showed in my face, for she immediately smiled knowingly and said: "You are a true Vandermaas! You *like* small waists, don't you!" She announced to the visitors who had accompanied me that we were going into another room to look at some old pictures she had. So I followed her, somewhat bewildered.

She showed me a small engraving of a lady of the time of Louis XIII. "This is Mme Du Plessis, a close relative of Cardinal Richelieu. She is our ancestor. There are many interesting things to be said about her, but the chief one for us is that she transferred her strong-minded tastes to the whole family. At the time of the Revocation of the Edict of Nantes and the consequent persecution of the Huguenots (1685–6), she eloped to South Africa with a certain François Vandermaas, a court musician and painter, who was of northern Dutch blood. You'll see the house they finally built in Kimberley. But even as pioneer here, she continued dressing in the manner of the French court. She had a fantastically small waist for a woman of her vigor and size. This has become almost a trademark amongst Vandermaas women and a taste that shows itself in the preferences of the men. They marry small-waisted wives, as you'll see when you meet them in various places here! I am no exception. I enjoy the sensation of being tight-laced. This may surprise you, but the *process* of being tight-laced by a man who likes the hour-glass figure and corsets is even yet very satisfying to me!"

I found myself quite excited by all this from a cousin, who was nevertheless practically unknown to me until this meeting. I didn't quite know how to react to her confidence. But she made "no bones" about what she considered a shared taste!

"Don't be shocked, because I know you are going to like my corsets when you see them. Don't feel guilty. You are an artist, and art is always an improvement on nature! I'm going to show you my laced figure because I can tell you are thrilled by it. Maybe you'd even like to pull me a little . . ."

She shed the somewhat voluminous blouse and stood in front of a long mirror, so that I got the front-and-back image at the same time. Now this was a lady of nearly seventy, I think. But I found myself responding in a quite "uncousinly" way! I was really uncertain as to how to act in all this. She took the positive side.

"I feel a little slack. The laces always stretch. I use new ones once a week, but they still stretch. Wouldn't you pull them back together until they almost meet? I'm skinny around the middle, but there's a little fat on my back that presses thru the laces and is uncomfortable . . . and chafes . . . unless I'm really laced up."

So I drew her in.

My feelings were sort of mixed. (Guilty? Sexual? I don't really know!) I completed my task and she slipped her blouse on again and smiled at me. "You are a Vandermaas, all right! Do you notice how my corset improves my breasts?"

I admitted I did.

"Well, I'm a *kissing* cousin, you know! Am I so old and repulsive that you don't want to kiss me?"

She wasn't and I did.

Then with perfect aplomb she lead the way to the living room where a mixed crowd of relatives was gathered around and said: "We've just checked up on some old pictures! We *are* truly first cousins! Isn't it fun? . . . here are some other "kissing cousins" . . . see if they aren't true descendants of Mme Du Plessis too!"

I met many "kissing cousins", some of them quite discouragingly young and beautiful. (I say discouraging, because it bothers me when age tries to become too familiar with young beauty!) I thought perhaps my cousin of a similar age was carrying on a tradition that had been forgotten, so it had sort of passed from my mind when I met other young, feminine relatives. But on the Vaal River, on a picnic, I discovered otherwise!

How we happened to be in a speed-boat together and me sitting beside her while she piloted the water-borne "bomb" I'll not describe. Suffice to say a huge, sensual type identified himself as a "relative" and proceeded to wine and dine us in the vicinity of Johannesburg. *She* was his daughter.

"I'm only a *second*-cousin" she said, smiling, "But . . ."

So we kissed. The results were harmless and pleasant. I was her particular "beau" during the various family gatherings.

She shall be nameless for obvious reasons, but she is the reason an old (72 *year old!*) man might think of going back to S. Africa! But, I'll be wise, and stay here!

All that concerns us here is that she laced and delighted to be laced to a point I considered almost excruciating. When I demurred, she'd say: "Why this is they way *all* Vandermaas women like it! Don't you remember grandmother . . .?"

So I found myself in bed with the fulfillment of my wildest sexual dreams! A beautiful lady, in very tight corsets, wanting to be affectionate!

When I commented, she said "Well, I enjoy pulling in, although it isn't the fashion right now. I think it somehow focusses and concentrates the *libido*. It's a well-known Vandermaas *thing*, you know . . . At least for *us*, it's the normal thing! What fun to meet someone, from across the sea, who likes *me!*"

I said I hardly knew her and that I was going 15,000 miles away soon.

"Well, we've had a good time—I won't say 'come again'. But really, you know Vandermaas have always loved each other and proved it by intermarrying! I'm being naughty. I'm thinking of pinning you down . . . and keeping you for myself! But, I think you'll always respond to tight corsets in general rather than to women in particular! That seems to be the Vandermaas way . . . I want to be in particular . . . but, in spite of difference of years and so forth, haven't we had just a wonderful time? . . . OK, all this bed-gymnastic has loosened up my corsets. Pull them in a little and I'll say goodbye . . . And I *mean* GOODBYE! We'll never see each other again. Tho it hurts a little!"

That evening I took the long plane ride to London and via the North Pole, home. I'm here now trying to pick up the pieces and start what is called normal life.

I have been unusually frank because I recognize the necessity of scientific detachment. We fetishists are so apt to mistake fancy for reality. I'm trying to be objective in recounting all this.

6. *Mrs Cayne*, "How I acquired and maintained a 14 inch waist" Summary of a polytyped booklet available to the customers of Mrs. Cayne, a corsetière who placed advertisements in the *Illustrated Sporting and Dramatic News* etc. 1933–1940. She does not give her age, but appears to have been born in the late 19th century. Cf. Pl. 8.

There is nothing injurious to the health in tight-lacing; my own health has benefitted from the practice. What is injurious is the attempt to reduce rapidly; time and patience is of the essence.

At the age of twelve I was introduced to a fmily of tight-lacers and wore my first tight-lacing corset, with a waist of 18 inches, to a fancy-dress ball. At first I felt I was in the grip of a vice, but at the end I was sorry to have to take it off. During my teens I wore my waist permanently at 20 inches, but often suffered from backache. High heels alleviated the problem, and eliminated certain twinges of pain from the thighs and hip-bones. Many years of experience have taught me that high heel wearing is essential to any tight-lacing program.

Then I met a man who confessed himself particularly attracted by my slender waist and small, high-perched feet. He encouraged me to reduce further. I always tightened one inch between morning and afternoon, and after six months was down to 18 in the morning and 17 in the afternoon. My backaches were gone, I loved the compression and experienced a sense of well-being as never before. I could not sleep unless tight-laced. I bathed in rubber corsets. Within a few more months I was comfortable at 15 inches, and I never walked except on very high heeled shoes and boots. I well remember being driven in a car to Salisbury. We toured the Cathedral, I in my 15 inch corset and 5 inch heels. Within a year of my marriage I could manage 14 inches in the afternoons, after sleeping in short 15 inch corsets with a steel bolt to flatten the waist at the sides. 13 inches was my absolute limit, which I could bear for an evening at most—the theatre or a dinner—and I was only too glad to resume 14 inches. Posture is all important, and perfect balance on high heels helps to prevent body pains. Above all, it is the undying attentions of a husband which have sustained me in the practice of tight-lacing, and made it seem relatively easy.

7. Christa R., Bad Friedrichshall, corsetière, 32 years old at time of letter (1968). I make no attempt to reproduce the racy German style.

My interest started when I first worked eighteen years ago in a corset and dress shop which acquired period corsets for window-display. I would try them on secretly, and then began to imitate them myself, in the finest materials. Whenever I see a beautiful material, I imagine it as a corset, not a dress. About seven years ago I met Mr. G—, who was very enthusiastic about tight-lacing, and brought me down "with gentle violence" *(mit sanfter Gewalt)* to 50 cm (20 in.). This was the Taming of the Shrew. I reduced a further 5 cm on my own. Although I could hardly admit it, I loved these corsets passionately. With them I felt for the first time what it really means to be a woman. This peculiar, tingling, exciting feeling during the lacing. An indescribable feeling, one approached fainting point, down to 48 cm it is O.K., but tighter than that, it can become damned uncomfortable. Then desires are aroused, desires that reason can simply not suppress. Desires for caresses. But one must have the right partner, otherwise it is all purposeless.

Women tend to have a very hostile reaction; my family thinks I am simply crazy. The Lords of Creation are wild about this figure of 94—45—86 (37—17½—34; height 5 ft. 6 in.), but appearing thus in the streets is no easy matter. Don't ask about all the unpleasant comments and approaches I have had to put up with. It is simply horrible to be treated like a prostitute. And the fact that I usually wear high stiletto heels makes my appearance all the more provocative. I adopt an icy cold manner, but sometimes I have difficulty in restraining myself from rewarding some impertinence with a box on the ear. I often hide the wasp-waist in public.

People think I am an impossible revolutionary person, merely because I am different from others and do not allow myself to be pressed into a single mould.

8. The Californian Ibitoe, S. N., born 1936, advertising executive (letter and conversations 1967–69). (See Plates 71 and 72)

I was fifteen when I first discovered about the itaburi (the belt in beaten bark-hide, or boned snakeskin worn by the males of the Ibitoe tribe of New Guinea). At that time I read how a French naturalist had forcibly removed an itaburi from a grown Ibitoe, which was found to measure 20 inches on the inside over a depth of four inches. When I first saw the photograph of the boy-about-to-fall-in-two, my pulse jumped: that solid black four inch belt! I immediately emulated him, and after a few months I was quite accustomed to my home-made itaburi. It is much less comfortable than a corset, for the edges are not padded or conical. Even when well powdered or greased, these edges soon feel like two hot wires, one running round your pouting chest, the other around your hips. I eventually got into 16 inches, and gradually developed a tough, calloused skin, without experiencing any more cutting and burning; but the belt left permanently embossed marks on me, where its notches and slits were.

"When I entered the army, my natural 22½ inch waist (I am 5 foot 9 inches tall) amazed and confounded officials; when I was released, having been unable to continue with the belt, I was a miserable 32 around the middle. I soon got back to 24 however, and made a collection of belts varying in width between 2 and 7 inches, some wrapping round, some fastening with straps, and some like vises with built-in screws.

"I then began to practise other rites which I read about. I tried some East Indian "Kavandi bearing": a steel framework with fifty to a hundred and fifty spears resting on the breast and shoulders, piercing the skin. I added weights on the spears, a thing which the Indians do not do. Sometimes I seemed to be leaving my body, and experienced for a while afterwards a peculiar elation. I also pierced my nose and nipples, and practised the Sun Dance of the Dakota Sioux. This consists of fasting, inserting thongs (in my case, piano wire) through the breast, attaching the thongs to a post, and dancing against their jerk and pull, for hours on end, staring all the while at the sun. I believe that this custom, which was outlawed in the nineteenth century, was last performed by American Indians, illegally, around 1930; I may be the only living man who has attempted it. The first two times I did it without supervision; the other two times, with." (The ritual is enacted in the film *Return of a Man called Horse*.)

S. N. showed me a film of his hanging suspended from piano wires passed through the quarter inch thick rings in his nipples, and being spun around. He subjected himself to this (always under supervision) for fifteen minutes at a time, and often blacked out in the process. The total suspension and spinning he derives from another American Indian (Mandan) custom, called the O-Kee-pa, the first account of which was published in an obscure little work by George Catlin (London 1867) and was universally disbelieved at the time.

For two and half years S. N. was engaged full-time in the manufacture of custom-made tight-lacing corsetry; then his interest turned to tattooing and, increasingly, to Sadhu Yoga (he is master of fairly advanced positions). His back is covered by a design most unusual for its homogeneity, coherence and abstract-totemistic quality. For the past few years he has not engaged in the more dangerous rites, but continues from time to time to put on little shows at private parties and fairs—such as lying on beds of nails, or splitting a potato placed on his wife's neck with a machete.

9. From Anne Fogarty, *Wife Dressing* (New York, 1959, pp. 11, 33, 66 and 154)

The author, a dress-designer known as the "Queen of the full skirt," was possessed of a narrow rib-cage and a much publicised 18 inch waistline. Her figure in wax wearing the dress in which she received a fashion award is (or was) in the Philadelphia Museum.

If I had to boil down my thinking about clothes into one word, that word would be Discipline of the mind, of the body, of the emotions. When feeling drab or upset, a tight belt or firm foundation will make you feel alert. Don't wear a tight dress to a buffet party, where you will end up sitting on the floor, your body awkwardly rigid because of the constricting lines which looked so great standing up. As for slim, tight, skirts, I think there should be a federal law against wearing them girdleless. There is no situation in which a girdle can be dispensed with—even with shorts.

The feeling of after-five wear should be one of *constraint* rather than comfort . . . Elegance and queenly bearing go hand in hand with constraint. You're not meant to suffer, but you are supposed to be "aware" . . . People ask me "How do you keep your slim figure?" Most of my adult life I've been lucky enough to have an 18 inch waistline, which I'm convinced is because of the cinch or wide, tight belts I've always worn. The theory is very much akin to the old Japanese (sic) tradition of binding feet to keep them small. When the loose, beltless look came in, I got lazy and stopped wearing a cinch. In no time my measurement jumped to 19½. At this writing, I'm trying to work it back to normal. To maintain your figure at its flattering best, depend on foundation garments to control and distribute, a cinch or tight belt to restrain.

10. Archfetishists: The Grangers.

In 1957, with fashion at a peak of high heel and waist-consciousness, and with the media manically tallying body-measurements, an extreme case of privately practised tight-lacing fetishism received the full glare of publicity in the popular weeklies. Mr. William Granger, of Peterborough, England, an amateur astronomer of some distinction, was asked to appear on television in order to show and comment upon his photograph of a comet. He was accompanied to the studios by his wife Ethel, the size of whose waist immediately became the subject of animated conversation and substantial bets among studio hands. It also came to the attention of a woman producer who had recently done a programme with the fashion historian and costume expert Doris Langley Moore, known for her heretical rejection of the historic 18-inch waist as a physical impossibility. This producer tipped off Marjorie Proops, the enterprising fashion reporter for *Woman's Sunday Mirror* (the same who four years earlier had expressed her dismay at the Jacques Fath boned suit). Proops prepared the ground by printing, over a full page (12 May), the results of an extensive enquiry headed "CAN A GIRL HAVE A 17 INCH WAIST?" The panel of experts consulted on this question included a fashion designer, a clothes manufacturer, a fashion photographer, a physician, two historians and the head of a model agency. The consensus of opinion was that today a 17 waist would be both physically abnormal and a professional disadvantage. The actress Sabrina (cf. pl. 82) was dismissed as a freak. The historians on the panel (Laver and Moore) denied that such a waist had ever existed, always excepting Polaire, also a freak. The head of the model agency attested that the only girl on their books approaching this exiguity of waist, Pamela Styche at 35-18-35, had difficulty finding work (which seems astonishing in view of the fact that she conformed almost exactly to the dimensions of the standard window-display dummy.) It was paradoxically the spokesman for the British Medical Association who seemed disposed both to believe in the common existence of the 18-inch waist in the past and (stranger still) in its viability from the health point of view. The last word went to Doris Langley Moore: "if you can produce the girl who, breathing freely, has a 17 inch waist, I should like to meet her."

On 16 June, Marjorie Proops more than kept her part of the bargain under the headline "IS THIS THE SMALLEST WAIST IN THE WORLD? The waist of Mrs. Ethel Granger is only 14 inches." An accompanying photograph showed her holding the tape-measure around herself to prove it (pl. 67). The owner of the waist accounted for its size with the evasion that whereas thirty years ago, when she was twenty-three years old, it had measured 23 inches, it had since shrunk and seemed to be shrinking all the time. "I wonder how much smaller it will get" she added, rather as if it were some uncontrollable phenomenon, like a star gradually diminishing on the lens of her husband's telescope. "Just before the war it went down to 13 inches, but I don't know if I want it to be as small as that again. People stare enough as it is." With the *Woman's Sunday Mirror* another mass weekly, the *Empire News and Sunday Chronicle* also carried the story on the same day (a Sunday), under the headline "SHE'S 52 AND OH! WHAT A WONDERFUL WAISTLINE ETHEL HAS!" (Other mass papers, such as the *Daily Sketch* and *Sunday Graphic* also featured Mrs. Granger, as did an Australian paper. (On 26 February 1957, the Communist *Daily Worker* had printed a photograph of Will (who is a party member) with Ethel in his observatory, to accompany an article on his observation of the comet; but the Left readership did not react to the very evident wasp-waist.)

Mrs. Granger returned to public view two years later (June 18, 1959) over a full page in yet a third popular weekly, *Reveille*. This time the headline went exactly one better: "13 INCH WAIST—HOUSEWIFE ACHIEVES AMBITION. 'I've been knocking off inches for years, and I'll get it to 12 inches within a year.' " Mrs. Granger now publicly admitted that the waist was neither a natural phenomenon nor the result of dieting or exercise, but the product of systematic tight-lacing, undertaken to please her husband. She was granted a place beside the famous wasp-waisted women of history—Catherine de' Medici, Polaire and the women of the Victorian and Edwardian eras who (the article darkly adds) "thereby reduced their life-expectancy to 35."

By now the Grangers were nationally and even internationally known, and correspondence was coming into their tiny Peterborough home from all over the world. There was further publicity in the later 60's with television and radio appearances; on 6 January, 1968, the Associated Press International wire service carried the story around the globe, with a photograph oddly captioned "while most women are envious of the fellow female who can display 13 inch calves, Mrs. Ethel Granger shows off her 13 inch waist." A French popular weekly (*Noir et Blanc*, 23 November 1968) also carried a feature, which unlike the more reticent English journals, made free use of the words "fetishist" and "fetishism". An entry in a specially created category in the *Guinness Book of Records* placed the achievement on permanent historical record (with Polaire's; there were no living rivals), which emboldened the proud husband to have the words "world's smallest waist" entered under the rubric "special peculiarities" in his wife's passport. Letters expressing interest and admiration poured in afresh from all over the world, some bearing the simple address, "Mrs. Ethel Granger, 13 inch waist, Peterborough, England." Men in whom the fetish had lain dormant for almost a lifetime found themselves stirred to put pen to paper on this subject.

Ethel had been a familiar curiosity in her home town even before the publicity, since the time shortly after the Second World War when she first began to display her figure in public. She had learned to adjust to the minor traffic disturbances she caused as she rode her motorcycle down Peterborough High Street; she grew accustomed to people following her as she walked with her husband (never alone) in the centre of London; she adapted to really ebullient reactions such as those of Parisians when they visited France, where their passage caused a tremendous squealing of brakes and hanging out of windows.

Their lifelong common endeavour to materialise a never-fading dream has been recounted by the husband William simply, factually and soberly in a 34 page pamphlet privately printed in California in 1961 (now deposited in public libraries; cf. p. xii. A typescript recounting the latter part of his life also exists). The authenticity of the personal and technical detail is unimpeachable; against a lightly sketched social-historical background, he describes his gradual, tender-cruel wearing down of a very real if spasmodic opposition; the ambivalence of Ethel's. feelings throughout the continuing operations; their mutual vacillation between the instinct to keep their fetishes secret and the desire to display them in public, thus risking even more social disapproval than they were already suffering from friends and relatives. Will does not gloss over health problems, but these turn out to have been relatively minor. He details the setbacks occasioned by war, pregnancy, or a bungling corsetière. Through it all the author never expresses a moment's doubt that all the tightening and piercing, barbaric as it may appear, is in a worthy cause, and that it constitutes the most solid emotional and physical bond in a marriage which has never faltered. Indeed it may be said to have strengthened over the years, and Will finds that both his and his wife's sexuality have improved with age, especially since the publicity of the last decade.

At 13 inches, the waistline is reckoned to have reached its limit, as has the ear, with its 13 piercings, and the nose, perforated in both nostrils and in the septum. The breast-rings are a relatively recent adjunct, and there are plans for piercings elsewhere. William Granger himself is a large, genial, untidy, bear-like man, with a waist which gets bigger as his wife's gets smaller ("I've tried corsets meself, but it didn't do much good"). He can pass his wife's shoe-heel through a hole in his septum. His address book contains the names of about a hundred fellow-fetishists with many of whom he maintains regular correspondence. He is in every sense the hub of the fetishist world.

Until his retirement, Granger taught crafts in a secondary school in Peterborough. He is a member and on the Council of the Royal Astronomical Society, and was an active official in the National Union of Teachers. Other hobbies include market-gardening and bee-keeping, in which his wife helps; she is also good at masonry concrete work. (*Private Eye,* p. 9, on 12 Feb. 1971, picked up the following snippet from the London press: "Participating in a discussion about the value of women as labourers, Mr. W. A. Granger of Peterborough cited his wife as an example: while building his observatory she shovelled well over six tons of wet cement; she features in the *Guinness Book of Records* as having the world's smallest waist (13 inches); and she—like her husband—is an old age pensioner.") In manner, Ethel is shy and delicate, and still seems rather bewildered by it all. Although totally dependent on her corsets, which she removes only to bathe, she is obviously in good health, eats more than the average for her weight and age, and is actually far more supple than most women of her years, being capable of touching her toes with straight legs, sitting for an hour squeezed up like a ball in the back of her husband's stationwagon, and generally fending for herself on their annual camping holidays. Her breasts are still firm, and the only permanent visible side-effects are a certain discolouration and roughness of the flesh at the waist. Her feet are also well-shaped; she now wears flat shoes in the home, but can still walk for hours in her size three shoes with their five inch stiletto heels.

Recently, and since the above was written, Will Granger died.

Bibliography

Abadie Léotard, *Etude sur la Théorie et l'Application d'un bon corset. Le Corset "Ligne,"* Paris 1904

Abraham, Karl, "Bemerkungen zur Psychoanalyse eines Falles von Fuss und Korsettfetischismus," in *Jahrbuch für Psychoanalytische und Psychopathologische Forschungen,* 1912, p. 557

Adburgham, Alison, *A Punch History of Manners and Modes,* London 1961

Aigremont, *Fuss—und Schuhsymbolik und—erotik in folkloristischen und sexualwissenschaftlichen Untersuchungen,* Leipzig, Aktiengesellschaft, 1909

Aincourt, Marguerite d', *Etudes sur le Costume Féminin,* Paris 1883

Andry, M., *Orthopedia, or, the art of correcting and preventing deformities in children,* London 1743, I, pp. 88–89

Animal World, The, 1 March 1873, p. 37 (A.J.R., "The bearing-rein and its evils").

Antal, Frederick, *Hogarth and his Place in European Art,* London 1962

Anthony, Katherine, *Feminism in Germany and Scandinavia,* New York 1915

Arringer, Rudolf, *Der Weibliche Körper und seine Verunstaltungen durch die Mode,* 5. Auflage, Berlin 1906

Arringer, Rudolf, Else Rasch, and A. M. Karlin, *Der Weibliche Körper und seine Beeinflussung durch Mode und Sport,* 7. Auflage, Berlin-Leipzig 1931

Art of Beauty, or, the best methods of improving and preserving the shape, carriage and complexion. Together with, the Theory of Beauty, London, Knight and Lacey 1825

Art of Beauty, The. A Book for Women and Girls, by A Toilet Specialist (edited by 'Isobel' of *Home Notes),* Isobel Handbooks No. 7, C. Arthur Pearson Ltd, 1899

Audry, C., "Cicatrices exubérantes consécutives au corset," *Journal des maladies cutanées et syphilitiques,* Paris, v. 12, June 1900, pp. 346–347.

Aunt Fanny's Album, Perry Colourprint, n.d.

B. M. Sat. see George, Mary Dorothy, *Catalogue of Political and Personal Satires preserved in the Department of Prints and Drawings of the British Museum,* 11v. London 1935–54

B. N. Est., = Bibliothèque Nationale, Paris, Département des Estampes

Bächthold-Stäubli, Hanns (herausg.), *Handwörterbuch des Deutschen Aberglaubens,* Berlin and Leipzig 1932/33

Bagley, John, *High-Heeled Yvonne,* London 1943

Bagley, John, *Wasp-Waisted Arabella,* London 1936

Bagshawe, Thomas W, "Souvenirs of Tight-Lacing. Stay busks carved for the Lass who loved a Sailor", *Antique Collector* v. 8, 1937 p. 322

Balzac, Honoré de, *La Cousine Bette* (1846), Pléiade ed. 1950

Balzac, Honoré de, *La Vieille Fille* (1836), Pléiade ed. pp. 301–304.

Bampfield, R. W., *An Essay on Curvatures and Diseases of the Spine,* London 1824.

Banks, J. A. and Olive, *Feminism and Family Planning in Victorian England,* New York 1964

Barnett, Edith A., *Common Sense Clothing,* London, Ward, Lock (1882).

Baudelaire, Charles, *Art in Paris,* ed. Jonathan Mayne, London 1965.

Baudelaire, Charles, *Oeuvres Complètes,* ed. Crépet, Paris 1925, v. 3, p. 25.

Baudelaire, Charles, *The Painter of Modern Life,* ed. Jonathan Mayne, London 1964.

Baus, Gabriel, *Etude sur le Corset,* thèse, Université de Bordeaux, Faculté de Médecine et de Pharmacie, 1909–10, no. 26, Bordeaux 1910.

Becker, Lydia E., "On Stays and Dress Reform", *The Sanitary Record* 15 Oct. 1888, pp. 149–151.

Bergler, Edmund, *Fashion and the Unconscious,* New York 1953.

Bertelli, Ferdinando, *Omnium Fere Gentium nostrae Aetatis,* Venice 1563.

Bigg, Henry Heather, *Orthopraxy; the Mechanical Treatment of Deformities, Debilities and Deficiencies of the Human Frame* (1865), 2nd ed. London 1869, p. 58.

Binet, Alfred, *Le Fétichisme dans l'amour,* Paris 1891.

Birdwhistell, Ray L., *Kinesics and Context, Essays on Body Motion Communication,* Philadelphia, 1970.

Blaisdell, Thomas, and Peter Selz, *The American Presidency in Political Cartoons 1776–1976,* University Art Museum, Berkeley 1976.

Blason des Basquines et Vertugalles . . . Lyon, par Benoist Rigaud 1563 (facsimile, A. Pinard, Paris, 1833), opposite p. A iv.

[Boileau, l'Abbé J.], *De l'Abus des Nudités de la Gorge* (1675) Paris 1858. English edition: *A Just and Seasonable Reprehension of Nakes Breasts and Shoulders* . . . translated by Edward Cooke, preface by Richard Baxter, London, Jonathan Edwin 1677, pp. 33–34.

Blanc, Charles, *Art and Ornament in Dress* (1875), New York 1877.

Bonnaud, *Dégradation de l'espèce humaine par l'usage des corps à baleines, ouvrage dans lequel on démontre que c'est aller contre les lois de la nature, augmenter la dépopulation et abâtardir pour ainsi dire l'homme que de le mettre à la torture dès les premiers moments de son existence, sous prétexte de le former.* Paris, chez Hérissaut, 1770. The only copy known to me is in the University Library, Vienna, which also lists a German translation (this was not on the shelf when I applied in 1979): *Abhandlung von der schädlichen Wirkung der Schnürbrüste,* Leipzig, Jacobäer 1773.

Bouchot, Henri, *Femmes de Brantôme,* Paris 1890.

Bouvier S—H—V, "Recherches sur l'usage des corsets", *Bulletin de l'Académie Royale/ Impériale de Médecine,* sér. 1, v. 18, 1853 pp. 355–386.

Bouvier, S—H—V., "Rapport sur un busc inventé par Mesdames Brasseur Cordelois et Becquet", *Bulletin de l'Académie Royale/Impériale de Médecine,* Paris, v. 20, 1854–55, pp. 1106–1110.

Bouvier and Bouland, "corset", *Dictionnaire Encyclopédique des Sciences Médicales,* Paris, v. 20, 1877, pp. 745–761.

Braddon, Mary Elizabeth, *Asphodel,* London 1881.

Bray, John, *All About Dress. Being the Story of the Dress and Textile Trades,* London 1913.

Brooke, Iris, *A History of English Footwear,* London 1949.

Brown, Thomas, the Younger (i.e. Thomas Moore), *The Fudge Family in Paris,* London, 3rd ed. 1818.

Browne, Lennox, and Emil Behnke, *Voice, Song, and Speech. A Practical Guide for Singers and Speakers* (1883), 12th ed. 1890.

Brummell, George Bryan, *Male and Female Costume,* edited and with an introduction by Eleanor Parker, New York 1932.

Buchan, William, *Domestic Medecine,* and *Advice to Mothers,* editions cited.

Buffon, Comte de, *Histoire Naturelle Générale et Particulière,* v. II, 1749.

Bulwer, John, *Anthropometamorphosis,* London 1650

Busch, Wilhelm, *Werke,* ed. Friedrich Bohne, Hamburg 1959

Butin, Fernand, *Considérations hygiéniques sur le corset, thèse,* Paris 1900

Cabanès, Dr, "L'Antiquité du Corset," *Journal de la Santé,* v. 19, 28 Dec. 1902, pp. 505–507.

Camper, Petrus, *Dissertation sur la meilleure forme des souliers,* The Hague, 1781

Cannaday, Charles G., "The relation of tight-lacing to uterine development, abdominal and pelvic disease," *American Gynaecological and Obstetrical Journal,* New York, v. 5, 1894, pp. 632–640.

Cantlie, James, *Physical Efficiency,* London and New York 1906

Caplin, Madame Roxey A., *Health and Beauty or, Corsets and Clothing constructed in accordance with the physiological laws of the human body,* London (1850).

Carter, T. W., "The morbid effects of tight lacing," *The Southern Medical and Surgical Journal*, Augusta, vol. n.s. ii, 1846, pp. 405–9

Castelot, André, *Queen of France*, New York 1957

Castelot, André, *Napoléon*, Paris 1968

A Cavalry Officer, *The Whole Art of Dress or the Road to Elegance and Fashion*, London 1830

Cavendish, Georgiana, *The Sylph* (1779), 3rd ed. London, 1783

Ceyssens, E., "Epilepsie par des habits trop serrés", *Annales Médicales de la Flandre Occidentale*, Roulers, v. 9, 1857, pp. 365–370

Chapotot, Eugène, "*L'Estomac et le Corset, Déviations, dislocations, troubles fonctionnels provoqués par le corset*," thèse no. 59, Faculté de Médecine et de Pharmacie, Lyon 1891

Childs, G. B., *On the Improvement and Preservation of the Female Figure*, London 1840

Celnart, Mme, *Manuel des Dames ou l'Art de la Toilette*, Paris 1827

Clough, James, *The First Masochist. A Biography of Leopold von Sacher-Masoch*, New York 1967

Cobbe, Frances Power, *Life, By Herself*, Boston 1894

Cobbe, Frances Power, "The Little Health of Ladies," *The Contemporary Review*, Jan. 1878, pp. 276–296

Cocteau, Jean, *Paris Album* (i.e. *Portraits-Souvenirs*). transl. by Margaret Crosland, London 1956

Cole, Herbert M., *African Arts of Transformation*. An Exhibition Catalogue, Art Gallery, University of California at Santa Barbara, 1970

Colette, *My Apprenticeships*, transl. by Helen Beauclerk, London 1957.

Colette, *The Gentle Libertine*, transl. by R. C. B., London 1931

Colette, "La Dame du Photographe", *Oeuvres Complètes de Colette* v. XIII, Paris 1950 pp. 93–129

Collineau, "corset", *La Grande Encyclopédie, Inventaire Raisonné des Sciences des Lettres et des Arts*, Paris (c. 1880).

Combe, Andrew, *The Principles of Physiology applied to the preservation of health . . .* (1834), 15th ed., edited and adapted by James Coxe, Edinburgh and London 1860.

Comfort, Alex, *The Anxiety Makers*, London 1967.

Congreve, William, *Complete Works*, v. IV, London 1923, p. 150 (Aurelia figures in the poem "Of Pleasing; an Epistle to Sir Richard Temple").

Conring, Franz, *Das Deutsche Militär in der Karikatur*, Stuttgart (1907).

Conrad, Joseph, "The Heart of Darkness", *Blackwood's Edinburgh Magazine*, v. 165, Feb. 1899, p. 207.

Corbin, Eus., "Des Effets produits par les corsets sur les organes de l'abdomen, et en particulier sur le foie," *Gazette Médicale de Paris, Journal de Médecine et des Sciences Accessoires*, Paris, v. 1, 1830, pp. 151–153.

Cooley, Arnold J., *The Toilet and Cosmetic Arts in Ancient and Modern Times*, London 1866.

Corti, Count Egon, *Elizabeth Empress of Austria*, trans. by Catherine Alison Philips, New Haven 1936.

Cortes, Robert, *The Unmentionables*, New York 1933.

Cotgrave, Randle, *Dictionarie of French and English*, 1611.

Cox, Marian Rolfe, *Cinderella, 345 Variants*, London 1893.

Cravatiana, ou Traité Général des Cravates, Paris 1823.

Crawford, M.D.C. and Elizabeth A. Guernsey, *The History of Corsets in Pictures*, Fairchild, New York 1951

Crépet, Jacques, *Dessins de Baudelaire*, Paris 1927.

Creve, Carl C., *Medizinischer Versuch einer Modernen Kleidung, die Brüste betreffend . . .*, Wien 1794, p. 49.

Crewe, Quentin, *The Frontiers of Privilege. A Century of social conflict as reflected in the Queen*, London 1961.

Crossick, Geoffrey (ed.), *The Lower Middle Class in Britain*, London 1977.

Crowley, Robert, *The Select Works*, ed. by J. M. Cooper, Early English Text Society, Extra Series 15, 1872.

Crown, Pat., *Edward E. Burney, an historical study in English Romantic art*, PhD dissertation, University of California, Los Angeles, 1977.

Crutchfield, E. L., "Some ill effects of the corset", *Gaillard's Medical Journal,* New York, lxviii, 1897, pp.1–11.

Curiosa Theologica vel diversa diversorum de modernis quibusdam tam clericorum quam laicorum moribus corruptis . . . collecta et edita per D.H.M. Wedel, apud Heinricum Wernerum, 1690 (copy in Lipperheide Library, Berlin).

Cunnington, C. Willett, *English Women's Clothing in the 19th Century,* London 1937.

Cunnington, C. Willett, *Feminine Attitudes in the 19th Century,* London 1935.

Cunnington, C. Willett, and Phyllis, *The History of Underclothes,* London 1951.

Cunnington, C. Willett, *Why Women Wear Clothes,* London 1941.

D., Charles, *Boutade contre l'usage du corset. Récit qui s'addresse à tout le monde, mais plus particulièrement au beau sexe, aux Lions civils ou autres* (Paris 1855).

The Dandies' Ball, or, High Life in the City. Embellished with Sixteen coloured Engravings (by Robert Cruikshank), London, John Marshall 1819.

The Dandies' Perambulations. Embellished with Sixteen Coloured Engravings, London, Carvalho, n.d. (c. 1819).

Davies, Martin, *The British School,* National Gallery Catalogues, London 1959.

Debay, A., *Hygiène Vestimentaire. Les Modes et les Parures chez les Français depuis l'établissement de la monarchie jusqu'à nos jours,* Paris 1857.

De Burgh, A. de, *Elizabeth, Empress of Austria. A Memoir,* London, 1899.

Delorme, Marion, *Allerlei Fetische,* Leipziger Verlag, Leipzig 1908.

Delteil, Loys, *Honoré Daumier,* 11 v., Paris 1925–30.

Dembo, Adolfo and Imbelloni, J., *Deformaciones Intencionales del cuerpo humano de carácter etnico,* Humanior, Biblioteca del Americanista Moderno, Secciòn A, tomo III, Buenos Aires (1938).

Dickens, Charles, *Bleak House,* 1853.

Dickens, Charles, *Martin Chuzzlewit,* 1844.

Dickens, Charles, *Pickwick Papers,* 1837.

Dickinson, R. L., "The corset; questions of pressure and displacement", *The New York Medical Journal,* v. 46, 1887, pp. 507–516.

Diffloth, Paul, *La Beauté s'en va. Des Méthodes propres à la Rénovation de la Beauté Féminine,* Paris (1905).

Dinesen, Isak, *Seven Gothic Tales,* introd. by Dorothy Canfield, New York 1934.

Dods, Andrew, *Pathological Observations on the Rotated or Contorted Spine,* London 1824, pp. 135–143.

Doffémont, Sieur, Maître Tailleur pour femmes, *Avis très important au Public . . . pour remédier extérieurement aux différentes difformités de conformation,* Paris 1754.

Doffémont, *Avis Très Important au Public sur différentes espèces de Corps et de Bottines d'une nouvelle Invention,* Paris 1758.

Domingo, Xavier, *Erotique de l'Espagne,* Pauvert 1967.

Douglass, Mrs., *The Gentlewoman's Book of Dress,* London n.d. (only copy known to me in Lipperheide Library, Berlin).

Dolorosa (i.e. Frau Maria von Eichorn), *Korsettgeschichten,* Leipziger Verlag, Leipzig 1907.

Downman, Hugh, *Infancy, or the Management of Children, a Didactic Poem in Six Books,* 6th ed., Exeter 1803, pp. 102–3.

Drouineau, Dr. Gustave, *L'Hygiène et la Mode,* La Rochelle 1886.

Dubois, Capt. Charles, *Considérations sur cinq Fléaux. L'Abus du Corset, L'Usage du Tabac, La Passion du Jeu, L'Abus des liqueurs fortes et L'Agiotage,* Paris 1857.

Duckworth, D., "On Tight Lacing", *The Practitioner. A Monthly Journal of Therapeutics,* London, v. 24, 1880, pp. 11–15.

Duffin, Edward W., *An Inquiry into the Nature and Causes of Lateral Deformity of the Spine,* 2nd. ed., London 1835.

Eberhard, Dr. E.F.W., *Die Frauenemanzipation und ihre erotischen Grundlagen,* Wilhelm Braumüller, Wien and Leipzig, 1924.

Ecob, Helen Gilbert, *The Well-Dressed Woman. A Study in the Practical Application to Dress of the Laws of Health, Art and Morals,* New York 1893.

Eisenbart, Liselotte Constanze, *Kleiderordnungen der deutschen Städte zwischen 1350 und 1700,* Göttingen 1962.

Ellis, Havelock, *Man and Woman. A Study of Human Secondary Sexual Characters* (1914), 6th ed. 1926.

Ellis, Havelock, *Studies in the Psychology of Sex* (1910), Random House ed., n.d.

Ellis, Havelock, *Studies in the Psychology of Sex*, Vol III, *Analysis of the Sexual Impulse . . .*, 2nd ed., Philadelphia 1926.

Ellis, John, M.D., *The Great Evil of the Age. A Medical Warning* (189–?)

Encyclopedia of Sexual Behavior, ed. by Albert Ellis and Albert Abarbanel, New York 1961 p. 435 f.

England's Vanity or the Voice of God Against the Monstrous Sin of Pride in Dress and Apparel, by a Compassionate Conformist, London 1683.

Espagne, Adelphe, "Observation d'état chlorotique ancien compliqué de phthisie pulmonaire, necropsie, désordres . . . produits par l'usage du corset," *Annales Cliniques de Montpellier*, v. 3, 1855–56, p. 310

Estienne, Henri, *Apologie pour Hérodote* (1566), ed. par P. Ristelhuber, Paris, Liseux 1879, t. I.

Estienne, Henri, *Deux Dialogues du Nouveau Langage François Italianizé* (1578), Paris, Liseux 1883.

European Magazine, July 1785, pp. 23–27.

Evans, Arthur, *The Palace of Minos. A comparative account of the successive stages of the early Cretan civilisation as illustrated by the discoveries at Knossos*, London 1921.

Evelyn, John, *Tyrannus or the Mode* (1661), Oxford 1951

Every Woman's Encyclopedia, [London. c. 1900], p. 1830, Mary Howarth, "The Art of Wearing the Corset."

Fairholt, F. W. *Costume in England*, London 1846

Fairholt, F. W., *Satirical Songs and Poems on Costume from the 13th to the 19th Century*, London 1849

Fanton, "Aperçu historique et hygiénique sur le vêtement; le corset," *Marseille Médical*, Marseille, 1879–80, v. 16 pp. 708–713 and v. 17 pp. 48–59,

Farrar, Joseph, "Lung capacity and tight-lacing," *Good Words* v. 21, March 1880, p. 202

F. B., *How to train the figure and attain perfection of form*, London, Central Publishing Co., 1896.

Figure Training; or, art the handmaid of nature, by E.D.M., London, Ward, Lock and Tyler [1871]

Filippo da Siena, Frate, *Novelle ed Esempi Morali* (1397), Bologna 1862

Fischer-Duckelmann, Dr Med. Anna, *Die Frau als Hausärztin* (1908), München und Wien 1917.

Flinn, D. Edgar, *Our Dress and Our Food in Relation to Health*, Dublin 1886

Flower, Sir William, *Fashion in Deformity, as illustrated in the customs of barbarous and civilised races*, London 1881. (Also in his *Essays on Museums and other Subjects . . .* 1898, pp. 315–353).

Flower, Edward Fordham, *Bits and Bearing-Reins*, London 1875

Flower, Edward Fordham, *Horses and Harness*, London 1876

Flügel, J. C., *The Psychology of Clothes* (1930), London 1950.

Fogarty, Anne, *Wife Dressing*, New York 1959

Folklore Fellows Communications, Helsinki, vol. 90 [1929–1931] no. 453 p. 63

Fox-Genovese, Elizabeth, "Yves Saint-Laurent's Peasant Revolution," *Marxist Perspectives*, v. 1, no 2, summer 1978, pp. 58–92

Forbes, John, *The Cyclopedia of Practical Medecine*, v. I, London 1833, pp. 694–6

Forster, John, *Life of Charles Dickens*, London 1911

Fournier, Dr, *Dictionnaire des Sciences Médicales*, Paris 1813, p. 117, "corset."

Fowler, Orson Squire, *Intemperance and Tight Lacing. Founded on the laws of life as developed by Phrenology and Physiology*, Manchester 1898.

Frampton, Mary, *The Journal of Mary Frampton from the Year 1779 until the year 1846*, ed. by Harriott Mundy, 2nd ed. 1885

France, Anatole, *Penguin Island* (1909), with an Introduction by H. R. Steevens, New York 1960, pp. 34–40.

Franckenau, Franck de, *Satyrae Medicae XX*, Lipsiae, apud Georg Weidmann, 1722 pp. 213–220

Frank, Johann Peter, *A System of Complete Medical Police* (1786), ed. Erna Lasky, Johns Hopkins, 1975

Frederick's of Hollywood 1947–1973. 26 Years of Mail Order Seduction, Strawberry Hill, Drake, New York 1970

Freeman, Gillian, *The Undergrowth of Literature,* London 1967

Freud, Michael, *Alamode-Teuffel, Oder, Gewissens-fragen von der heutigen Tracht und Kleider-Pracht,* Hamburg 1682

Friday, Nancy, *My Secret Garden,* New York 1973

Fuchs, Eduard, *Illustrierte Sittengeschichte,* Ergänzungsband III, München 1912.

Gâches-Sarraute, Mme Dr., *Le Corset. Etude Physiologique et pratique,* Paris 1900.

Gänssbauer, Hans, *Statistische Untersuchung über die Häufigkeit der Schnürleber und den Einfluss des Schnürens auf die Entstehung des Ulcus Ventriculi. Nach den Befunden des pathologichen Instituts zu Erlangen aus den Jahren 1895–1910,* Inaugural Dissertation, 1913, Nürnberg 1914.

Galen, *Claudii Galini Medicorum,* ed. Carolus Gottlobus Kuhn, Vol VII, Leipzig, 1824, pp. 26–34.

Gallichen, Walter M., *A Textbook of Sex Education,* London 1918.

Garnier, Paul, *Les Fétichistes. Pervertis et Invertis Sexuels,* Paris 1896.

Garsault, Fr.-A.de, *Art du tailleur contenant le tailleur d'habits d'hommes, les culottes de peau, le tailleur de corps de femmes et enfans,* Paris 1769.

Garson, J. G., "The Effects produced by wearing corsets or stays," *Illustrated Medical News,* London, v. 1, 1888–89, pp. 78–79, 103–105 and 133–134.

Gassaud, Dr. Prosper, *Considérations médicales sur les corsets,* Paris 1821, pp. 11 and 16.

Gautier, Théophile, *Militona (The Work of Théophile Gautier,* transl. by F-C de Sumichrast, Jenson Society, 1907, vol. 21 p. 64).

Gec (Enrico Gianeri), *La Donna, La Moda, L'Amore in tre secoli di caricatura,* Milan 1942.

Genlis, Madame de, *Mémoires inédits de Madame la Comtesse de Genlis sur le 18me siècle et la Révolution française depuis 1756 jusqu'á nos jours.* Paris, L'Advocat, 1825. An English translation was published the same year.

Genlis, Madame de, "corps Baleinés", *Dictionnaire critique et raisonné des étiquettes de la cour, des moeurs, et des usages du monde.* (Added at end of volume 10 of the above).

Gernsheim, Alison, *Fashion and Reality 1840–1914,* London 1963.

Gesunde Frau, Die, Zeitschrift zur Verbreitung gesundheitlicher Anschauungen in der Frauenwelt. Mitteilungen des Allgemeinen Vereins fur Verbesserung der Frauenkleidung (started under latter title, *Mitteilungen . . .*)

Gibson, Charles Dana, *The Gibson Girl. Drawings of Charles Dana Gibson,* ed. by Steven Warshaw, Berkeley, 1968

Gillham, F., *Excerpts on fashion and fashion accessories 1705–1915,* section VII: "Corsets and Tight Lacing" (a volume of clippings in the Victoria and Albert Museum Library).

Gillray, *Works,* ed. by Thomas Wright and R. H. Evans, Benjamin Blom Inc., 1968

Glotz, Gustave, *The Aegean Civilisation,* London 1925

Godman, John D, "Injurious Effects of Tight Lacing upon the Organs and Functions of Respiration, Digestion, Circulation etc.," *Addresses delivered on various public occasions,* Philadelphia, 1829, pp. 107–194.

Golish, Vitold de; *Au Pays des Femmes Girafes,* Arthaud [1958].

Gosse, Dr L-A, "Essai sur les déformations artificielles du crâne," *Annales d'Hygiène Publique et de Médecine Légale,* 2me série, v. 3, Jan. 1855 p. 317ff. and v. 4, July 1855 pp. 5–83

Gosson, Stephen, *Pleasant Quippes for Upstart Newfangled Gentlewomen* (1595), Totham, Charles Clark, 1847, pp. IV–V.

Gottlieb, Ernest, *Gedoppelte Blas-Balg Der Üppigen Wollust Nemlich Die Erhöhete Fontange und Die Blosse Brüst Mit welchen das alamodische und die Eitelkeit liebende Frauenzimmer . . .* 1689

Graber, E-Paul, *Le Corset de Fer du Fascisme 1919–34,* La Chaux-de-Fonds, 1935

Grand-Carteret, John, *Le Décolleté et le Retroussé,* Paris 1887

Grand-Carteret, John, *Les Moeurs et la Caricature en France,* Paris 1888.

Grand-Carteret, John, *Zola en Images,* Paris 1908

Grant, Vernon W., "A Problem in Sex-Pathology", *American Journal of Psychiatry*, v. 110, no. 8, Feb. 1954, p. 589

Greer, Germaine, *The Female Eunuch*, New York 1971

Grose, Francis, *Lexicon Balatronicum. A Dictionary of Buckish slang* (1785), London 1811

Günther, Dr G. B., *Ueber den Bau des menschlichen Fusses und dessen zweckmässigste Bekleidung*, Leipzig und Heidelberg, 1863.

Habits of Good Society, A Handbook of Etiquette for Ladies and Gentlemen, London [1859]

Hackmann, Karl, *Schnürwirkungen*, Inaugural-Dissertation der medizinischen Fakultät Kiel, Kiel 1894

Haldane, Mary Elizabeth, *A Record of a Hundred Years 1825–1925*, London 1925, p. 45

Haller, John S. and Robin M., *The Physician and Sexuality in Victorian America*, Urbana etc. 1974

Hamilton, General Sir Ian, *When I was a boy*, London 1939

Hamilton, Gerald, *Mr Norris and I, an Autobiographical sketch*, London 1956.

Hardy, Henri-Joseph, de Cambrai, *Dissertation sur l'Influence des Corsets et l'opération du cancer de la mamelle*, thèse, Paris 1824.

Harsanyi, Zsolt, *Mit den Augen einer Frau*, Hamburg 1950 (English translation 1941)

Haslip, Joan, *The Lonely Empress. A Biography of Elizabeth of Austria*, Cleveland and New York, 1965

Haughton, Edward, letter to *Sanitary Record* 15 Dec. 1888 pp. 292–3.

Haweis, Mrs. H. R., in *Dress, Health and Beauty. A book for ladies* London [1878]

Haweis, Mrs H. R., *Art of Beauty*, London 1878

Haweis, Mrs H. R., *Art of Dress*, London 1879

Hayes, Mrs Alice, *The Horsewoman*, London 1893

Hawkes, Jacquetta, *Dawn of the Gods*, New York 1968

Headland, Isaac Taylor, *Home Life in China*, London 1914 p. 291

Held, Anna, *Mémoires. Une Etoile Française au ciel de l'Amérique*, La Nef de Paris, n.d.

Hemmings, F.W.J., *Culture and Society in France 1848–1898, Dissidents and Philistines*, London 1971

Hérédia, José Maria de, *Les Trophées*, Paris 1893

Hermit in London, or, Sketches of English Manners, London, Colburn 1819, 5 vols.

Heszky, Max, *Die Kulturgeschichte des Korsetts von ihren Uranfängen in den Römerzeiten bis zum Ende des 19ten Jahrhunderts*, Berlin [1901].

Hirschfeld, Felix, and Loewy, A., "Korsett und Lungenspitzenatmung," *Berliner Klinische Wochenschrift*, Berlin, v. 49, 1912, pp. 1702–04

Hiscock, W. G., *John Evelyn and his Family Circle*, London 1955

Hogg, Thomas Jefferson, *Life of Percy Bysshe Shelley* (1855), London 1933 v. II, pp. 18–19

Hollander, Anne, *Seeing Through Clothes*, Viking 1978

Holmes, Oliver Wendell, *Poems*, New York 1836

Hurlock, Elizabeth B, *The Psychology of Dress*, New York 1929

Hyde, Hartford Montgomery, *Mr and Mrs Beeton*, London 1951

Ivière, R., "Du Corset," *Revue de littérature médicale*, Paris, v. 1, 1876 pp. 5–7

John Bull beim Erziehen. Aus dem Family Doctor übersetzt von E. Neumann. Eine Sammlung Briefe von Anhängern und Gegnern der körperlichen Züchtigung und der Korsett-Disziplin im Englischen Erziehungswesen

Johnson, Edgar, *Dickens and his Readers. An Introduction to his Novels*, New York 1969

Juvernay, Pierre, *Discours particulier contre les femmes desbraillées de ce temps* (Paris 1637), Geneva 1867, p. 35.

Kany, Charles E., *Life and Manners in Madrid 1750–1800*, Berkeley 1932.

Kellogg, J. H., *Ladies Guide in Health and Disease*, Des Moines 1884.

Kellogg, J. H., *Plain Facts for Old and Young, embracing the natural History and Hygiene of Organic Life*, Burlington, Iowa 1888 (Arno Press reprint 1974).

Kenealy, Arabella, "The Curse of Corsets", *Nineteenth Century*, v. 55, 1904, pp. 131–137.

Key, Ellen, *The Century of the Child* (1903), New York 1972.

Kilner, Dorothy, *The Holiday Present*, New York 1803.

King, Mrs. E. M., *Rational Dress;–or, the Dress of Women and Savages*, London 1882.

Kinsey, Alfred, *Sexual Behavior in the Human Female*, Philadelphia, 1953 p. 678.

Kositski, Carolus Ernestus, of Dansk, *Noxas Fasciarum, Gestationis et thoracum*, Dissertation, Göttingen, J. C. Dieterich 1775.

Kositski's der Arzneiwissenschaft Doctors Abhandlungen von dem Schaden des Einwickelns und des Tragens der Kinder, wie auch der Schnürbrüste. Frei übersetzt und mit Anmerkungen vermehrt von Peter Gottfried Joerdens d. A. W. K., Erlangen, bei Wolfgang Walther 1788. My text reference is to pp. 94–103, a part presumably by Joerdens, who says he wrote it before seeing Kositski's Latin dissertation.

Krafft-Ebing, Richard, *Psychopathia Sexualis*, transl. from the 12th German ed. and with an Introduction by Franklin S. Klaf, New York 1965.

Kraditor, Aileen S. (ed. and introd.) *Up from the Pedestal. Selected Writings in the history of American feminism*, Chicago 1968.

Kronhausen, Eberhard and Phyllis, *The Sexually Responsive Woman*, New York 1964.

Kuhnow, Anna, *Die Frauenkleidung vom Standpunkt der Hygiene*, Vortrag für Frauen gehalten zu Leipzig am 14. Feb. 1893, Leipzig.

Kunzle, David, "The Corset as Erotic Alchemy: from rococo galanterie to Montaut's Physiologies in La Vie Parisienne", in *Woman as Sex-Object*, ed. Thomas Hess and Linda Nochlin, New York, Art News Annual v. 38, 1972, pp. 90–165.

Kunzle, David, "Dress Reform as Antifeminism: A Response to Helene E. Roberts's 'The Exquisite Slave . . .,' " *Signs, Journal of Women in Culture and Society* v. 2, no. 3, 1977 pp. 554–569.

Lacroix, Mme. and M. F., *Le Corset de Toilette au point de vue esthèthique et physiologique et son histoire*, Paris (1904).

Lacroix, Paul, *Recueil de Pièces Originales rares ou inédites . . . Costumes Historiques de la France*, Paris (1852) v. 3.

Lane, W. A., "Civilisation in relation to the abdominal viscera; with remarks on the corset", *The Lancet*, 13 Nov. 1909, pp. 1416–18.

Langley (Langley Moore), Doris, *The Woman in Fashion*, London 1949.

Langner, Lawrence, *The Importance of Wearing Clothes*, New York 1959.

Larisch, Rudolf von, *Der Schönheitsfehler der Frau. Eine anthropometrische-ästhetische Studie*, München 1896.

Larisch von Moennich, Countess Marie, *My Past*, New York 1913

Larousse, "corset", *Grand Dictionnaire Universel du 19e siècle*, 1869.

La Santé, Madame de, *The Corset Defended*, London, Carter, 1865 (a 2nd ed. appeared 1871 under the title *Health, Beauty and Fashion*).

Latour-Landry, *The Book of the Knight of La Tour-Landry* (1371–72), translated and edited by Thomas Wright, London 1906.

Laver, James, *Clothes*, London 1952.

Laver, James, *Modesty in Dress*, Boston 1969.

Laver, James, *Museum Piece, or the Education of an Iconographer*, Boston 1964.

Laver, James, *Taste and Fashion from the French Revolution to the Present Day* (1937), London 1945.

Layet, M-A, *Dangers de l'usage des corsets et des buscs*, Dissertation, Faculté de Médecine de Paris, Paris 1827

Leathem, Harvey T., with Hugh Jones, *The Anatomy of the Fetish*, Venice Books 1967

Le Blanc, H., *The Art of Tying the Cravat Demonstrated in Sixteen Lessons*, New York 1829

Lelièvre, Jean, *Pathologie du Pied* (1952) Paris 1971.

Lemoisne, P-A, *Gavarni*, Paris 1928

Léoty, Ernest, *Le Corset à travers les Ages*, Paris 1893

Leroy, Alphonse, *Recherches sur les Habillemens des femmes et des enfants*, Paris 1772

Lethève, Jacques, *La Caricature et la Presse sous la IIIe République*, Paris 1961

Levy, Howard, *Chinese Footbinding*, New York 1966

Lewin, Philip, *The Foot and Ankle*, Philadelphia 1940

L'Heureux, Mme Marie-Anne, *Pour bien s'habiller*, Paris 1911

Libron, Fernand and Henri Clouzot, *Le Corset dans l'Art et les Moeurs du XIIIe au XXe siècle*, Paris 1933

Lichtenberg, Geroge Christoph, *The World of Hogarth, Lichtenberg's Commentaries on Hogarth's Engravings*, translated from the German and with an introduction by Innes and Gustav Herdan, Boston 1966

Lieb, Anton, *Unter den Pantoffeln der Mode. Schuhgeschichtliche Betrachtungen eines Arztes.* Privatdruck, 1951

Limner, Luke (i.e. John Leighton), *Madre Natura versus the Moloch of Fashion,* London 1870

Livermore, Mary, *The Story of my Life,* Hartford, 1899, p. 122

Locke, John, *Some Thoughts concerning Education* (1693), ed. Peter Gay, New York 1964

Lord, William Barry, *The Corset and the Crinoline. A Book of Modes and Costumes from remote periods to the present time,* by W. B. L., London 1868.

Mant, Catherine, *Caroline Lismore, or the Error of Fashion,* London 1815.

Marcus, Steven, *The Other Victorians,* New York 1964

Marcuse, Max (ed.), *Handwörterbuch der Sexualwissenschaften. Enzyklopädie der natur- und kulturwissenschaftlichen Sexualkunde des Menschen,* 2nd ed., Bonn 1926

Marie de Saint-Ursin, P. J., *L'Ami des Femmes ou Lettres d'un Médecin* . . . Paris 1804, p. 54.

Martin, Peter, *Wasp Waists. A study of tight-lacing in the Victorian era,* privately printed, 1979

Maupassant, Guy de, *Short Stories,* Dunne, 1903

McCormick, Malcolm, "Notes on the design of the costumes," *Baroque Dance 1675–1725,* a film made under the sponsorship of the Department of Dance, University of California at Los Angeles, 1977.

McMurtrie, Douglas C., "Figure characteristics in the female as factors in sexual allurements: the influence of the corset," *Lancet-Clinic,* Cincinnati, v. 110, 1913, pp. 171–174

Meinert, E., *Modetorheiten,* Leipzig 1890

Mercer, General Cavalié, *Journal of the Waterloo Campaign kept throughout the campaign of 1815,* Edinburgh and London, 2 vols 1870.

Mereau (Maître de Danse), *Réflexions sur le Maintien et sur les moyens d'en corriger les défauts,* Gotha 1760 p. 116f.

Merrifield, Mrs, *Dress as a Fine Art,* Boston 1854

Merritt, Mrs M. Angeline, *Dress Reform practically and physiologically considered,* Buffalo 1852

Mespoulet, Marguerite, *Images et Romans,* Paris 1939

Meyer, Dr G. Hermann, *Die Richtige Gestalt der Schuhe,* Zurich 1858

Milizia, Francesco, "Moda," *Dizionario delle Belle Arti del Disegno,* Bassano 1797, pp. 75–76.

Mill, John Stuart, *The Subjection of Women,* London 1869

Mitton, F. *Les Dessous féminins et leurs transformations,* Paris 1911 (extrait de *Paris-Galant* 1911).

Mode, Heinz, *The Woman in Indian Art,* New York 1970

Moers, Ellen, *The Dandy,* London 1960

Mohr, James, *Abortion in America,* Oxford 1978.

Mongéri, "Le Corset et ses Dangers," *Gazette Médicale d'Orient* Constantinople, v. 7, July 1863 pp. 49–54.

Montagu, Lady Mary Wortley, *The Letters and Works,* I, London 1895

Montez, Lola, *The Arts of Beauty,* London 1858

Montherlant, Henri de, *Pitié pour les Femmes,* Paris 1936.

Mundt, Ernestus Edmundus, *De Thoracum Abusu Noxio.* Dissertatio Inauguralis Medico-Diatetica . . . Berlin 1828.

Murger, Henry, *Le Pays Latin* (1851), Paris 1856.

M'Whinnie, A.M., "Displacement of an enlarged liver from tight-lacing", *Lancet,* 5 Jan. 1861, p. 5.

Naecke, P., "Uber Kleiderfetischismus", *Archiv fur Kriminologie,* Leipzig, v. 37, 1910 pp. 160–175.

Nashe, Thomas, "Christ's Tears over Jerusalem" (1593), in *Works,* ed. by Ronald McKerrow, London 1910, vol. II.

Neuburg, Victor, *Popular Literature. A History and Guide,* Penguin 1977.

Neustätter, Dr. Med. Otto, *Die Reform der Frauenkleidung auf gesundheitlicher Grundlage,* München (1903).

New Lady's Magazine, April 1786 pp. 131–13: "On the Inconveniences and Disorders arising from *Strait-Lacing* in *Stays*" by a Physician (R.B.)

Newton, Stella Mary, *Health, Art and Reason. Dress Reformers of the 19th century,* London 1974.

Noah, M. M., *Gleanings from a Gathered Harvest* (1845), New York 1847.

Nørgaard, Erik, *When Ladies Acquired Legs,* London 1967.

Norris, Frank, *Blix,* New York 1890.

North, Maurice (Morris), *The Outer Fringe of Sex, a Study in Fetishism,* London 1971.

Nottingham, J., "Compression of the female Waist by stays", *Provincial Medical and Surgical Journal,* London, Worcester, v. 3, 1841 p. 110.

Noverre, Jean-Georges, *Lettres sur la Danse,* Paris 1760

Oelssner, Gottlieb, *Philosophisch- Moralisch- und Medicinische Betrachtung Ueber mancherley Zur Hoffart und Schönheit hervorgesuchte, schädliche Zwang-mittel, junger und erwachsener Leute, beyderley Geschlechtes, Nebst dem schädlichen Missbrauche der Schnüurbrüste und Planchette oder sogenannte Blanckscheite der Frauenzimmer,* Bey ruhigen Abend-stunden wohlmeinend entworfen von G.O., Bresslau und Leipzig, Daniel Pietsch (copy in Lipperheide Library, Berlin).

O'Followell, Dr. Ludovic, *Le Corset, Histoire, Médecine, Hygiène, Etude historique,* Paris 1905

O'Followell, Dr Ludovic, *Le Corset, Histoire, Médecine, Hygiène, Etude médicale,* Paris 1908

Packard, Vance, *The Wastemakers,* New York 1960

Panizza, Oskar, *Das Liebeskonzil und andere Schriften,* ed. by Hans Prescher, Neuwied am Rhein und Berlin-West, 1964, pp. 34–52

Padover, Saul, *The Revolutionary Emperor: Joseph II of Austria,* London 1967

Paléologue, Georges Maurice, *Tragic Empress. The Story of Elizabeth of Austria* (1939), translated and annotated by H. J. Stenning, London n.d.

Pallas, Paul, *Travels through the Southern Provinces of the Russian Empire in the years 1793 and 1794.* Translated from the German, London 1802.

Paré, Ambroise, *Oeuvres Complètes,* ed. Malgaigne, Paris 1840

Paré, Ambroise, *Collected Works,* transl. out of the Latin by Thomas Johnson (1634), facsimile, Milford House Inc., New York 1968

Parr, Dr John, "For Every Woman who has a bottom like a hot cross bun. . . ," *Daily Mail,* London, 31 Aug. 1964 p. 6

Parr, Dr John, "No wonder your feet are killing you!" *Daily Mail,* 8 Sep. 1964

Paston Letters, A Selection in Modern Spelling, ed. by Norman Davis, London 1963. (My citation is modernized).

Paulin Paris, M., *Les Manuscrits Français de la Bibliothèque du Roi,* v. II, Paris 1838, p. 156

Paull, Dr Med. Hermann, *Die Frau. Ein gemeinverständliches Gesundheitsbuch für die Moderne Frau,* 3rd ed., Vienna and Leipzig 1908

Paulson, Ronald, *Hogarth: His Life, Art, and Times,* Yale 1971

Pearsall, Ronald, *The Worm in the Bud. The World of Victorian Sexuality,* MacMillan 1969

Pearse, T. Frederick, *Modern Dress and Clothing in its Relation to Health and Disease,* London, 1882

Pendlebury, J. D. S., *The Archeology of Crete,* London 1939

Penny Cyclopedia of the Society for the Diffusion of Useful Knowledge, 1837, s.v. "Corset"

Pestalozzi, J. H., *Leonard and Gertrude* (1781–87), transl. and abridged by Eva Channing, Boston 1889

Petit, Isabelle, *De L'Utilité du Corset pour Préserver des Difformités et Maladies et pour donner de la prestance et conserver la souplesse,* 1851

Phelps, Elizabeth Stuart, *What to Wear?* Boston 1873

Pierquin de Gembloux, Dr Claude Charles, *Des Corsets sous le rapport de l'hygiène et de la Cosmétique,* Bourges [c. 1841/45]

Pike, E. Royston, *Human Documents of the Victorian Golden Age,* London 1967.

Planche, James Robinson, *Cyclopedia of Costume,* London 1876.

Plummer, John, "Commercial Importance of Corsets," *Once A Week.* 12 April 1862 p. 445.

Polaire, clippings in Lincoln Center Library, New York. Cf. particularly Archie Bell, "The Ugliest Actress", in *The Green Book*, May 1914.

Polman, Jean, *Le Chancre ou Couvre-sein féminin ensemble le Voile ou Couvre-Chef Féminin* (Douay, 1635), Geneva 1868.

Potter, Cora Brown, *The Secrets of Beauty and Mysteries of Health*, London (1908).

Pour la Beauté Naturelle de la femme contre la mutilation de la taille par le corset, préface de Ed. Haraucourt, Ligue des Mères de Famille, 1909.

Rachewiltz, Boris de, *Black Eros. Sexual Customs of Africa from Prehistory to the present day*, New York 1964.

Reade, Charles, *A Simpleton* (1873), Grolier Society, Paris and Boston, n.d.

Registrar-General, *Second Annual Report of the Registrar General of Births, Death and Marriages in England*, 1840 p. 73; *Nineteenth Annual Report*, 1858 pp. 194–5.

Reik, Theodor, *Masochism in Sex and Society* (1941), New York 1962.

Reinhard, D. Christian Tobias Ephraim, *Satyrische Abhandlung von den Krankheiten der Frauenspersonen welche sich durch ihren Putz und Anzug zuziehen*, Glogau and Leipzig, bey Christian Friedrich Günthern, 1757. (Copy in Lipperheide Library, Berlin. Longer passage cited, p. 30).

Reisser, M. l'aîné, *Avis Important au Sexe ou Essai sur les corps baleinés pour former et conserver la taille aux jeunes personnes*, Lyon 1770.

Relotius, Everhard, *De abusu Thoracum balenaceorum*, Dissertatio Medica Inauguralis. Groningen 1783 (Copy in National Library of Medecine, Bethesda, Md).

Renoir, Jean, *Renoir, My Father*, transl. by Randolph and Dorothy Weaver, Boston and Toronto 1958

Restif de la Bretonne, *Monsieur Nicholas or the Human Heart Laid Bare*, transl., ed., and introd. by Robert Baldick, New York 1966

Réveillé Parise, "Hygiène du Corset," *Gazette Médicale de Paris; Journal de Médecine et des Sciences Accessoires*, Paris, v. 9, 1841, pp. 785–792, v. 10, 1842, pp. 49–52 and 145–153

Reynolds, Sir Joshua, *Discourses on Art*, ed. by Robert Wark, Collier, 1966.

Rhead, G. Woolliscroft, *Chats on Costume*, London 1906

Richardson, Benjamin Wood, "Dress in Relation to Health" (lecture delivered at the London Institution, March 1, 1880), *The Gentleman's Magazine* 1880, pp. 469–488

Riegl, Robert E., "Women's Clothes and Women's Rights," *American Quarterly* v. 15, Fall 1963, no 3, pp. 390–401

Roach, Mary and Joanne Eiches (ed.), *Dress, Adornment and the Social Order*, New York 1965.

Roberts, Helene, "The Exquisite Slave: The Role of Clothes in the Making of the Victorian Woman," *Signs: Journal of Woman in Culture and Society*, v. 2, no. 3 1977 pp. 554–579.

Rondeau, Peter, *Nouveau Dictionnaire François-Allemand* (1711), Leipzig et Francfort, 1739

Rosenblum, Robert, "Caritas Romana; some Romantic Lactations," *Woman as Sex Object*, ed. Thomas Hess and Linda Nochlin, Art News Annual 1972

Rossi, William A., *The Sex Life of the Foot and Shoe*, New York 1976.

Roth, Bernard, *Dress: Its Sanitary Aspect* (paper read before the Brighton Social Union, January 30 1880), London and Brighton 1880.

Rougemont, Josephus Claudius, *Etwas über Kleidertracht in wie Ferne sie einen nachteiligen Einfluss auf die Gesundheit hat*, bei J. F. Abshoven (Bonn, ca. 1787/88).

Rousseau, Jean-Jacques, *Oeuvres*, Dufour, Paris and Amsterdam, tome 12, 1796, pp. 179–180.

Rousseau, Jean-Jacques, *Emile, ou l'Education*, Amsterdam 1762.

Rousseau, Jean-Jacques, "Sophie, ou la Femme", *La Nouvelle Héloïse (Oeuvres Complètes*, Pléiade ed. v. II, p. 265).

Roux, Charles, *Contre le Corset. Souvenir d'une leçon de M. Serres au Museum d'Histoire Naturelle*, extrait de la *Presse Littéraire*, Paris 1855.

Roy, C. S. and J. G. Adami, "The Physiological Bearing of Waistbelts and Stays", *National Review*, 1888, pp. 341–349.

Rudofsky, Bernard, *Are Clothes Modern?* Chicago 1947.

Rudofsky, Bernard, *The Unfashionable Human Body*, New York 1971.
Russell, Lilian, clippings on, in Lincoln Center Library, New York. cf. New York *Telegraph* for 3 June 1898.
S....., Madame, de Lyon, *Physiologie du Corset*, Montpellier 1847 pp. 75–76.
Sackville-West, Victoria, *The Edwardians*, London 1930.
Sagarra, Eda, *Tradition and Revolution in German Literature and Society 1830–1980*, London 1971.
Sancta Clara, Abraham à, *Judas der Ertz-Schelm*, vol. 4, Saltzburg 1695, p. 514–5.
Saint-Laurent, Cécile, *L'Histoire imprévue des Dessous Féminins*, Paris 1966.
Sandford, Mrs. Elizabeth, *Woman in her Social and Domestic Character* (1831), 6th ed. London 1839.
Sangiovanni, Robert, *The Abolition of the Corset and Dietetic Experiments of Immunized lean raw meat and its derivatives upon consumptives*, New York 1910.
Sargent, D. A., "The Physical Development of Women", *Scribner's Magazine*, Feb. 1889, pp. 180–2.
Saturday Review, *Modern Women and What is said of them*. A reprint of a series of articles in the *Saturday Review* with an Introduction by Mrs. Calhourn, New York 1868.
Schachermeyr, Fritz, *Die Minoische Kultur des alten Kreta*, Stuttgart 1964.
Schneider, Dr. (of Fulda), "Corsette und Blanchette, eine unsern Schönen bei der gegenwärtigen Modeeinrichtung . . .", *Adolph Henki's Zeitschrift fur die Staatsarzneikunde*, Erlangen, v. 7, 1824, pp. 341–60.
Schopenhauer, Johanna, *My Youthful Life and Pictures of Travel* (1837), London 1847, I, p. 238.
Schosulan, Dr. Johann Michael, *Abhandlung uber die Schädlichkeit der Schnürbrüste (Mieder)*, Wien, Johann Thomas Edlen von Trattern, 1783.
Schultze-Naumburg, Paul, *Die Kultur des Weiblichen Korpers als Grundlage der Frauenkleidung* (1901), Leipzig 1903.
Schweninger, Prof., "Korsett und Frauenzukunft", *Hygieia*, Stuttgart v. 6, 1893, pp. 193–9.
Sears Roebuck, Montgomery Ward, *Catalogue* No. 71, 1902/03.
Seeker, Miss, *Monographie du Corset*, Louvain 1887.
Sello, Gottfried (ed.), *Grandville, das gesamte Werk*, München 1969.
Shoemaker, John V., *Heredity, Health and Personal Beauty*, Philadelphia and London, 1890.
Sichel, Edith, *Catherine de' Medici and the French Revolution*, London 1905
Siebert, Friedrich, *Ein Buch fur Eltern. I: "Den Müttern heranreifender Töchter"*, 3rd ed. München 1903.
Sigogne, Sieur de, *Les Oeuvres Satiriques*. Première édition complète . . . par Fernand Fleuret et Louis Perceau, Paris 1920.
Silber, Kate, *Pestalozzi, the Man and his Work*, New York 1973.
Smith, Hugh, M.D., *Letters to Married Ladies, to which is added, a Letter on Corsets* (by the American editor, pp. 199–226), 3rd ed. Boston and New York 1832.
Smith, W. Wilberforce, "Corset-Wearing and its Pathology", *Sanitary Record* 15 Nov. 1888, p. 201–3.
Soemmerring, Samuel, *Ueber die Schädlichkeit der Schnürbrüste*. Zwey Preisschriften durch eine von der Erziehungsanstalt zu Schnepfenthal aufgegebene Preisfrage veranlasst, Leipzig, bey Siegfried Lebrecht Crusius, 1788. The first essay presumably by Soemmerring, the second (pp. 117–192) by a writer who remains anonymous. (The description of masturbation is on p. 182).
Soemmerring, Samuel, *Ueber die Wirkungen der Schnürbrüste*, Berlin 1793.
Somerville, Martha, *Personal Recollections from early life to old age, with Selections from her Correspondence*, London 1874.
South, John Flint, *Household Surgery or, Hints on Emergencies* (1847), London 1852.
Southgate, Henry, *Things a lady would like to know*, London 1875
Spain, Nancy, *Mrs. Beeton and her Husband*, London 1948.
Sronkova, Olga, *Gothic Woman's Fashions*, Prague 1954.
Staniland, Kay, in *Costume, the Journal of the Costume Society* no. 3, 1969, p. 10.

Steele, Frances Mary, and Elizabeth Livingston Adams, *Beauty of Form and Grace of Vesture,* London 1892.

Steinberg, Leo, "Metaphors of Love and Birth in Michelangelo's Pietàs", *Studies in Erotic Art,* Theodore Bowie and Corneliá V. Christensen eds., Basic Books, New York 1970, pp. 231–335.

Steinbrucker, Charlotte, *Daniel Chodowiecki. Briefwechsel Zwischen ihm und seinen Zeitgenossen,* Berlin 1919.

Stekel, Wilhelm, *Sexual Aberrations. The Phenomena of Fetishism in relation to Sex* (1923), New York 1964.

Sterne, Laurence, *Tristram Shandy* (1767), 1843 p. 108

Stone, Lawrence, *Family, Sex and Marriage in England 1500–1800,* Harper and Row, 1977

Stratz, Dr C. H., *Rassenschönheit des Weibes,* 4th ed. Stuttgart 1903.

Stratz, Dr C. H., *Die Schönheit des weiblichen Körpers* (1898), 42nd ed. (!) 1936

Stringer, Mabel E., *Golfing Reminiscences,* London 1924

Strutt, Joseph, *A Compleat View of the Dress and Habits of the People of England* (1799), new ed. by J. R. Planché, London 1842.

Sylvia's Book of the Toilet. A Lady's Guide to Dress and Beauty, Ward, Lock and Co. [after 1878]

Synge, M. B., *A Short History of Social Life in England,* London 1906

Taitbout de Marigny, Chev., *Three Voyages in the Black Sea to the Coast of Circassia,* London 1837

Taliaferro, V. H., "The Corset in its relations to uterine diseases," *Atlanta Medical and Surgical Journal,* Atlanta, v. 10, 1872–3, pp. 683–693

Tallemant des Réaux, *Les Historiettes,* 3rd ed., Paris, 1862

Thackeray, William Makepeace, "Continental Snobbery," in *Book of Snobs* (1852).

Thiersch, Justus, "Experimentelle Untersuchungen über Corsetdruck", *Deutsches Archiv fur klinische Medizin,* Leipzig, v. 67, 1900, pp. 559–73.

Thompson, Stith, *Motif-Index of Folk-literature,* Bloomington, Ind. 1955.

Tillotson, Mary E., *History of the first Thirty-Five Years of the Science Costume Movement . . .* Vineland, N.J. 1885.

Tillotson, Mary E., *Progress versus Fashion. An Essay on the Sanitary and Social Influences of Women's Dress,* Vineland, N.J. 1873/4.

Tilt, E.J., *Elements of Health and Principles of Female Hygiene,* Philadelphia 1853.

Tissot, S. A., *Abhandlung über die Nerven und deren Krankheiten,* II, Leipzig 1781. pp. 19–20.

Tissot, S. A., *Three Essays: First, on the disorders of people of fashion . . . Third, on Onanism, or a Treatise upon the disorders produced by Masturbation: or, the effects of secret and excessive venery,* Dublin 1772.

Tode, D. Johannes Clemens, *Der Unterhaltende Arzt,* Copenhagen and Leipzig, III, 1786 pp. 39–54.

Töpffer, Rodolphe, *Réflexions et Menus Propos d'un Peintre Genevois,* Paris 1858.

Tommaseo, M. Niccolo, *Relations des Ambassadeurs Vénitiens sur les Affaires de France au XVIe siècle,* recueillies et traduites par N.M.T., t. II, Paris 1838.

Treich, Léon, "Le Corset à travers les siècles", *C'est Paris,* December 1950, numéro spécial, "Les Corsets".

Treves, Sir Frederick, *The Dress of the Period in its Relations to Health* (Lecture on behalf of the National Health Society), London 1882.

Treves, Sir Frederick, *The Influence of Clothing on Health,* London (1886).

Troll-Borostanyi, Irma von, *Das Weib und seine Kleidung,* Leipzig 1897 p. 4.

Tschudi, Clara, *Elizabeth Empress of Austria and Queen of Hungary,* transl. by E.M. Cope, London 1901.

Tylicka, Madame, née Budzinska, *Du Corset. Ses Méfaits au point de vue Hygiénique et Pathologique,* thèse, Paris 1898.

Vallotton, Henry, *Elizabeth, l'Impératrice Tragique,* Paris 1947.

Vanier, Henriette, *La Mode et ses Métiers, Frivolités et Luttes des Classes,* Paris 1960.

Vaughan, Walter, M.D., *An Essay Philosophical and Medical concerning Modern Clothing,* Rochester and London 1792.

Veblen, Theodore, *Theory of the Leisure Class*, New York 1899.

Vecellio, Cesare, *Habiti Antichi et Moderni di Tutto il Mondo* (1590), Paris 1859.

Veriphantor, Dr, *Der Fetischismus, Ein Beitrag zur Sittengeschichte unserer Zeit*, Berlin, Lilienthal, 1903 (copy in Kinsey Institute library)

Vernünftige und bewährte Mittel zur Erlangung und Erhaltung einer schönen Gorge. Ein diätetisch Büchlein für Mädchen und Mutter, Berlin 1795.

Vicinas, Martha (ed.), *Suffer and Be Still*, Indiana University Press, 1972.

Vieth, Gerhard Ulich Anton, *Versuch einer Encyclopädie der Leibesübungen*, Berlin 1795.

Vigny, Alfred de, *Stello, A Session with Doctor Noir* (1832), transl. by Irving Massey, Montreal 1963.

Vischer, Friedrich Theodor, *Mode und Cynismus* (1878), Stuttgart 1888, pp. 9–10.

Vogel, Lisa, review of *Woman as Sex Object* in *Feminist Studies*, v. 2, no. 1, 1974.

Voiart, Mme. Elise, *Lettres sur la Toilette des Dames*, Paris 1822.

Voilà, Paris 1940, contains fetishist correspondence.

Vonnegut, Kurt, *The Breakfast of Champions*, New York 1973, pp. 144–45.

Wachtel, Joachim, *A la Mode, 600 Jahre europäische Mode in Zeitgenössischen Dokumenten*, München 1963.

Walker, Donald, *Exercises for Ladies calculated to preserve and improve beauty . . .* London 1836.

Walshe, W. H., "On the breathing-movements in the two sexes, and on the alleged influence of stays in producing pulmonary consumption," *The Medical Times and Gazette*, London, v. 6, 1853, pp. 366–8.

Ward and Co, E., of Bradford, *The Dress Reform Problem*, 1886

Warner's, *Always Starting Things. Through 80 Eventful Years*, 1954.

Warner, William, *Albion's England*, 3rd ed. 1586, Bk. 7, ch. XXXVI.

Watts, George Frederic, "On Taste in Dress" (1883), *Annals of an Artist's Life*, III, pp. 202–227.

Waugh, Norah, *Corsets and Crinolines*, London 1954.

Webb, Wilfred Mark, *The Heritage of Dress* (1907), London 1912.

Wechsbert, Joseph etc., *The Imperial Style. Fashions of the Hapsburg Era*, Rizzoli 1980.

Weiss, Hermann, *Kostümkunde*, Stuttgart 1872.

Weitenkampf, Frank, *Social History of the United States in Caricature. How the Comic Artists saw us*, 1953 (typescript deposited with New York Public Library).

Welch, Margaret, "Corsets Past and Present," *Harper's Bazaar*, v. 35, Sept. 1901, pp. 450–1.

Wendel, Friedrich, *Die Mode in der Karikatur*, Dresden 1928.

Wertham, Frederic, *Seduction of the Innocent*, New York 1954.

West, Charlotte C., M.D., "The Use and Abuse of the Corset," *Delineator*, v. 74, Sept. 1909, p. 220.

Wettstein-Adelt, Minna, *Macht euch Frei. Ein Wort an die deutschen Frauen*, Berlin 1893

Williams, W. Matthieu, *The Philosophy of Clothing*, London 1890.

Willie, John, (i.e. John Coutts) *The Adventures of Sweet Gwendoline, being an Anthology of the Drawings and Photographs of J.W.*, Bélier Press, 1978.

Winslow, Dr., "Reflexions Anatomiques sur les incommodités, infirmités etc. qui arrivent au Corps à l'occasion de certaines attitudes et de certains habillements," *Mémoires de l'Académie Royale des Sciences*, 1740 (published Paris 1742), p. 59 ff.

Winslow, Dr., "Sur les mauvais effets de l'usage des corps à baleines," *Mémoires de l'Académie Royale des Sciences*, 1741, pp. 172–184.

Witkowski, Dr. G-J., *Anecdotes historiques et religieuses sur les seins et l'allaitement comprenant l'histoire du décolletage et du corset*, Paris 1898.

[Wolcott, John G.] *The Gift of the Noble Corset*, by Nicholas de Mandeville, 1962 (privately duplicated fetishist document, deposited with New York Public Library).

The Woman at Home (Annie S. Swan's Magazine), 1894, pp. 236–7.

Woolson, Abba Goold (ed.), *Dress Reform. A Series of Lectures delivered in Boston, on dress as it affects the health of women*, Boston 1874.

Worthington, Marjorie, *The Strange World of Willie Seabrook*, New York 1966.

Wraxall, Sir Nathaniel William, *Historical and posthumous memoirs 1772–1784*, ed. Henry Wheatley, vol. V, 1884

Zedler, Johann Heinrich, "Schnürbrust," *Grosses vollständiges Universal-lexicon,* Leipzig und Halle, v. 35, 1743, c. 592–600.

Zell's Popular Encyclopedia, Philadelphia 1871.

Ziegler, Philip, *The Black Death,* Penguin, 1970.

Zola, Emile, *Au Bonheur des Dames* (1883), 1895, pp. 430–1.

Zola, Emile, *Fécondité,* 1899.

Zola, Emile, *Pot-Bouille,* Paris 1882.

Zola Emile, *Le Ventre de Paris* (1873), Pléiade ed. 1960.

Index